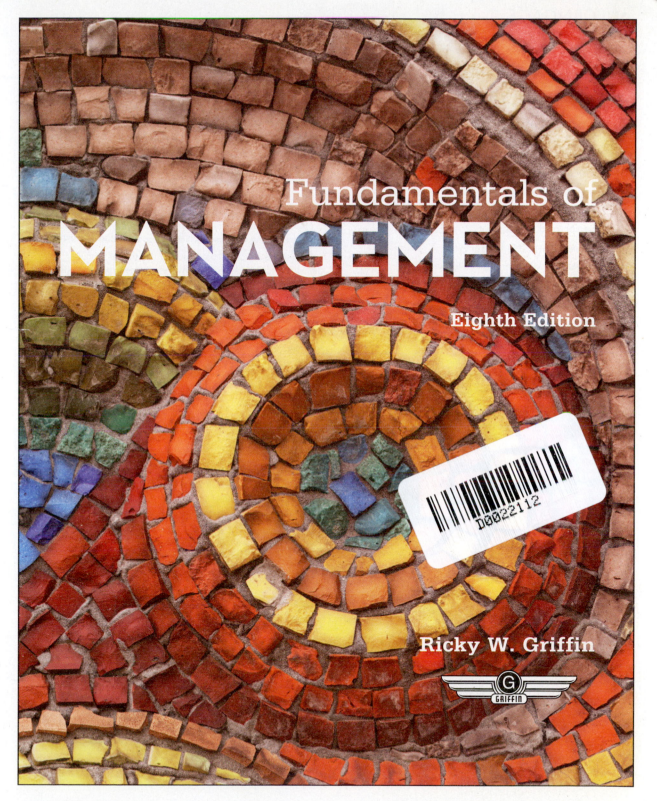

Fundamentals of
MANAGEMENT

Eighth Edition

Ricky W. Griffin

CENGAGE Learning

Australia • Brazil • Japan • Korea • Mexico • Singapore • Spain • United Kingdom • United States

Fundamentals of Management, Eighth Edition
Ricky W. Griffin

Vice President, General Manager, Social Science & Qualitative Business: Erin Joyner

Product Director: Michael Schenk

Senior Product Manager: Scott Person

Senior Content Developer: Julia Chase

Senior Product Assistant: Brian Pierce

Brand Manager: Robin LeFevre

Marketing Manager: Emily Horowitz

Marketing Director: Kristen Hurd

Marketing Coordinator: Christopher Walz

Media Developer: Sally Neiman

Manufacturing Planner: Ron Montgomery

Art and Cover Direction, Production Management, and Composition: Integra Software Services Pvt. Ltd.

Cover Image: Sergii Tsololo/Photos.com

Design elements: © iStockphoto.com/ BrianAJackson; © iStockphoto.com/ bo1982; © iStockphoto.com/adventtr and © iStockphoto.com/trullyinspired

Intellectual Property
Analyst: Diane Garrity
Project Manager: Sarah Shainwald

For product information and technology assistance, contact us at
Cengage Learning Customer & Sales Support, 1-800-354-9706

For permission to use material from this text or product,
submit all requests online at **www.cengage.com/permissions**
Further permissions questions can be emailed to
permissionrequest@cengage.com

Library of Congress Control Number: 2014937601

ISBN: 978-1-285-84904-1

Cengage Learning
20 Channel Center Street
Boston, MA 02210
USA

Cengage Learning is a leading provider of customized learning solutions with office locations around the globe, including Singapore, the United Kingdom, Australia, Mexico, Brazil, and Japan. Locate your local office at: **www.cengage.com/global**

Cengage Learning products are represented in Canada by Nelson Education, Ltd.

To learn more about Cengage Learning Solutions, visit **www.cengage.com**.

Purchase any of our products at your local college store or at our preferred online store **www.cengagebrain.com**

Printed in Canada
Print Number: 01   Print Year: 2015

For Matt and Lura—Thank you for what you add to our family.

Brief Contents

Contents

PART 2   Planning

PART 3   Organizing

PART 4 Leading

CHAPTER 9

PART 5   Controlling

Preface

Literally hundreds of books have been written for introductory management courses. As the body of material comprising the theory, research, and practice of management has grown and expanded, textbook authors have continued to mirror this expansion of material in their books. Writers have understood the importance of adding new material about traditional topics, such as planning and organizing, while simultaneously adding coverage of emerging newer topics, such as sustainability, ethics, and social media. As a by-product of this trend, our general survey textbooks have grown longer and longer, making it increasingly difficult to cover all the material in one course.

Another trend in management education is a focus on teaching in a broader context—that is, introductory management courses are increasingly being taught with less emphasis on theory alone and more emphasis on application of concepts. Teaching students how to apply management concepts successfully often involves focusing more on skills development and the human side of the organization. This trend requires that textbooks cover theoretical concepts within a flexible framework that enables instructors to make use of interactive tools such as case studies, exercises, and projects. It also dictates that a text be as relevant to students as possible. Hence, while this book draws examples and cases from older large firms like Ford, IBM, and Nissan, it also makes extensive use of newer firms such as Google, Netflix, Facebook, Starbucks, Urban Outfitters, and others.

This textbook represents a synthesis of these trends toward a more manageable and practical approach. By combining concise text discussion, standard pedagogical tools, lively and current content, an emphasis on organizational behavior, and exciting skills development material, *Fundamentals of Management* answers the need for a new approach to management education. This book provides almost limitless flexibility, a solid foundation of knowledge-based material, and an action-oriented learning dimension unique in the field. Indeed, over half a million students were introduced to the field of management using the first seven editions of this book. This eighth edition builds solidly on the successes of the earlier editions.

ORGANIZATION OF THE BOOK

Most management instructors today organize their course around the traditional management functions of planning, organizing, leading, and controlling. *Fundamentals of Management* uses these functions as its organizing framework. The book consists of five parts, with fifteen chapters.

Part One introduces management through two chapters. Chapter 1 provides a basic overview of the management process in organizations, and Chapter 2 introduces students to the environment of management. Part Two covers the first basic management function, planning. Chapter 3 introduces the fundamental concepts of planning and discusses strategic management. Managerial decision making is the topic of Chapter 4. Finally, Chapter 5 covers entrepreneurship and the management of new ventures.

The second basic management function, organizing, is the subject of Part Three. In Chapter 6, the fundamental concepts of organization structure and design are introduced and discussed. Chapter 7 explores organization change and organizational innovation. Chapter 8 is devoted to the management of human resources.

Many instructors and managers believe that the third basic management function, leading, is especially important in contemporary organizations. Thus, Part Four consists of five chapters devoted to this management function. Basic concepts and processes associated with individual behavior are introduced and discussed in Chapter 9. Employee motivation is the subject of Chapter 10. Chapter 11 examines leadership and influence processes in organizations. Communication in organizations is the topic of Chapter 12. The management of groups and teams is covered in Chapter 13.

The fourth management function, controlling, is the subject of Part Five. Chapter 14 introduces the fundamental concepts and issues associated with management of the control process. A special area of control today, managing for total quality, is discussed in Chapter 15.

SKILLS-FOCUSED PEDAGOGICAL FEATURES

Both the overarching framework and streamlined topical coverage make it possible to address new dimensions of management education without creating a book so long that it is unwieldy. Specifically, each chapter is followed by an exciting set of skills-based exercises and related activities. These resources have been created to bring an active and a behavioral orientation to management education by requiring students to solve problems, make decisions, respond to situations, and work in groups. In short, these materials simulate many of the day-to-day challenges and opportunities that real managers face.

Among these skills-based exercises are two different *Building Effective Skills* features organized around the set of basic management skills introduced in Chapter 1. The *Skills Self-Assessment Instrument* exercise helps readers learn something about their own approach to management. Feedback for the *Self-Assessment Instruments* can be found in the Appendix. Finally, an *Experiential Exercise* provides additional action-oriented learning opportunities, usually in a group setting.

New to the eighth edition, each chapter also contains interesting boxed features, two per chapter, centered around **sustainability, leadership**, the **service sector**, and **managing during tough times**. These features depart briefly from the flow of the chapter to highlight or extend especially interesting or emerging points and issues related to boxed feature titles.

In addition to the end-of-chapter exercises, every chapter includes important standard pedagogy: learning objectives, a chapter outline, an opening incident, key terms, a summary of key points, questions for review, questions for analysis, and an end-of-chapter case with questions.

CHANGES TO THE EIGHTH EDITION

The eighth edition of *Fundamentals of Management* retains the same basic structure and format as the previous edition. However, within that framework the content of the book has been thoroughly revised and updated. The following changes are illustrative of the new material:

(1) New topical coverage related to both domestic and global economic conditions is included. The book also places greater emphasis on the services sector of the economy. Coverage of the economic impact of unrest in the Middle East and Hurricane Sandy has also been added. Moreover, all data regarding international business

activity, entrepreneurship and small businesses, and workforce diversity have been updated to the most current figures available.

(2)   Several new management techniques are also included in this edition. Examples include the tiered workforce and evidence-based management. These and other new techniques are discussed in several places in the book.

(3)   The latest research findings regarding globalization, strategic management, organizing, motivation, leadership, and control have been incorporated into the text and referenced at the end of the book. Over 150 new articles and books are cited.

(4)   Virtually all of the cases and boxed inserts are new to this edition of *Fundamentals of Management*, while the few retained from earlier editions have been updated as needed. They reflect a wide variety of organizations and illustrate both successful and less successful practices and decisions.

(5)   As noted earlier, this book features a rich and diverse array of end-of-chapter materials to facilitate both learning and skill development. For this edition, a substantial portion of this material has been replaced or substantially revised.

SUPPLEMENTS

Instructor Supplements

Instructor's **Resource Companion Website.** Find all of the helpful, time-saving teaching resources you need to create a dynamic, interactive management course. The Instructor's Website includes the Instructor's Manual (IM) files, Testing files, PowerPoint slides, and a DVD Guide to help you most effectively use this edition's accompanying video cases. Updated content throughout the IM and PowerPoint slides reflects the latest edition of the text. Almost one-third of the Test Bank questions are new. ***New to this edition, we are now providing our Test Bank in Cognero.*** Cengage Learning Testing Powered by Cognero is a flexible, online system that allows you to:

- author, edit, and manage test bank content
- create multiple test versions in an instant
- deliver tests from your LMS, your classroom, or wherever you want

Cengage Learning Testing Powered by Cognero works on any operating system or browser.

- No special installs or downloads are needed.
- Create tests from school, home, the coffee shop—anywhere with Internet access.

What will you find?

- Simplicity at every step. A desktop-inspired interface features drop-down menus and familiar, intuitive tools that take you through content creation and management with ease.
- Full-featured test generator. Create ideal assessments with your choice of question types. Searchable metadata helps ensure your tests are complete and compliant.
- Cross-compatible capability. Import and export content into other systems.

Video Case DVD. Put management in action with this edition's new video package. All new "On the Job" videos illustrate management concepts at work within familiar companies, large and small, giving students an insider's perspective.

Student Supplements
MindTap™

Students who purchase the MindTap product will enjoy a number of innovative features designed to enhance their learning experience. The e-book has been enriched with interactive figures and animated videos that increase comprehension of the most challenging topics, and the insightful video cases are embedded directly into the end-of-chapter materials. At the beginning of each chapter, students will be asked to take a self-assessment questionnaire that introduces an important topic and shows how it relates to students' current experience. Students will also have ready access to the assignments chosen by the instructor, which may include test-prep quizzes, homework questions, Write Experience essay-writing practice, and experiential exercises (role-play activities and group project activities).

New to this edition, the role-play activities give students opportunities to practice their managerial and communication skills in an online, real-time environment, while the group project activities encourage them to take a modern approach to applying key concepts using a digital collaborative workspace. By giving them opportunities to collaborate online, apply course concepts, and create solutions to realistic management problems, all of these learning activities are designed to enable students to Engage, Connect, Perform, and Lead—in short, to learn to "Think and Act Like Managers," with demonstrable skills in critical thinking, analysis, and much more.

Augmenting the entire MindTap experience, robust diagnostic tools powered by Knewton provide students with feedback and personalized study plans based on actual assigned coursework rather than a separate set of quizzes. Using recommendations provided by Knewton, students can focus their efforts on the most important concepts they need to learn at that moment in time, as well as more effectively prepare for exams. Furthermore, Knewton gives instructors the ability to focus class time on the most relevant material and effectively assist struggling students. Using the MindTap Progress App, instructors can track student proficiency, which will allow them to quickly react to where students are in their learning and make the best use of class time. This creates even more opportunities to train students to "Think and Act Like Managers.

Acknowledgments

I would like to acknowledge the many contributions that others have made to this book. My faculty colleagues at Texas A&M University have contributed enormously both to this book and to my thinking about management education. The fine team of professionals at Cengage Learning has also been instrumental in the success of this book. Erin Joyner, Mike Schenk, Scott Person, Julia Chase, Jennifer Ziegler, Sarah Shainwald, and the team at Integra Software Services were instrumental in the creation of this edition.

Many reviewers have played a critical role in the continuous evolution and improvement of this project. They examined my work in detail and with a critical eye. I would like to tip my hat to the following reviewers, whose imprint can be found throughout this text:

Joseph Adamo (Cazenovia College), Sally Alkazin (Linfield College), Robert Ash (Santiago Canyon College), Sherryl Berg-Ridenour (DeVry College–Pomona), Alain Broder (Touro College), Murray Brunton (Central Ohio Tech), Sam Chapman (Diablo Valley College), Elizabeth Anne Christo-Baker (Terra Community College), Gary Corona (Florida State College–Jacksonville), Dr. Anne Cowden (California State University), Suzanne Crampton (Grand Valley State University), Thomas DeLaughter (University of Florida), Anita Dickson (Northampton Community College), Joe Dobson (Western Illinois University), Michael Dutch (University of Houston), Dale Eesley (University of Nebraska–Omaha), Norb Elbert (Eastern Kentucky University), Teri Elkins (University of Houston), Jan Feldbauer (Schoolcraft College), Tamela D. Ferguson (University of Louisiana at Lafayette), Anne Fiedler (Barry University), Eugene Garaventa (College of Staten Island), Phillip Gonsher (Johnson Community College), Patricia Green (Nassau Community College), John Guess (Delgado Community College), Joseph S. Hooker, Jr. (North Greenville College), David Hudson (Spalding University), George W. Jacobs (Middle Tennessee State University), Tim McCabe (Tompkins Cortland Community College), Garry McDaniel (Franklin University), Lauryn Migenes (University of Central Florida), Christopher Neck (Arizona State University), Judy Nixon (University of Tennessee–Chattanooga), Ranjna Patel (Bethune-Cookman College), Lisa Reed (University of Portland), Virginia Rich (Caldwell College), Dr. Joan Rivera (Angelo State University), Roberta B. Slater (Pennsylvania College of Technology), Bob Smoot (Hazard Community College), Howard Stanger (Canisius College), Sheryl A. Stanley (Newman University), Roy Strickland (Ozarks Technical Community College), Mike L. Stutzman (Mt. Mercy College and Kirkwood College), Abe Tawil (Baruch University), Lynn Turner (California Polytech University–Pomona), Barry Van Hook (Arizona State University), Ruth Weatherly (Simpson College), and Mary Williams (Community College of Nevada).

My wife, Glenda, and our children, Dustin, Ashley, Matt, and Lura, are of course due the greatest thanks. Their love, care, interest, and enthusiasm help sustain me in all that I do. And my granddaughter, Griffin, brings joy to my life and a smile to my face every time I think about her.

I enthusiastically invite your feedback on this book. If you have any questions, suggestions, or issues to discuss, please feel free to contact me. The most efficient way to reach me is through e-mail. My address is rgriffin@tamu.edu.

R.W.G.

CHAPTER 1

Understanding the Manager's Job

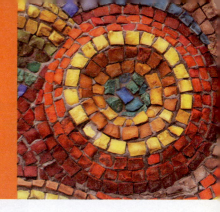

Sergii Tsololo/Photos.com

Learning Outcomes

After studying this chapter, you should be able to:

1 Define management, describe the kinds of managers found in organizations, identify and explain the four basic management functions, describe the fundamental management skills, and comment on management as a science and art.

2 Justify the importance of history and theory to managers, and explain the evolution of management thought through the classical, behavioral, and quantitative perspectives.

3 Identify and discuss key contemporary management perspectives represented by the systems and contingency perspectives, and identify the major challenges and opportunities faced by managers today.

Management in Action

Reed Hastings Doesn't Like Standing Still

"Don't be afraid to change the model."

—Netflix CEO Reed Hastings

Several years ago, Reed Hastings, a California entrepreneur between start-up ventures, incurred a $40 late fee at Blockbuster. "It was six weeks late," he admits. "I had misplaced the cassette [and] I didn't want to tell my wife.... I was embarrassed about it." The next day he dropped off the VHS cassette and paid the late fee on his way to the gym. As it turns out, his itinerary for the day was quite opportune: In the middle of his workout, he recalls, "I realized [the gym] had a much better business model. You could pay $30 or $40 a month and work out as little or as much as you wanted."

Thus was born the idea for Netflix. But Hastings knew he needed to start slowly. So, when Netflix was launched in 1997, its only innovations involved the convenience of ordering movies over the Internet and receiving and returning them by mail; Netflix merely rented movies for $4 apiece plus $2 for postage (and, yes, it charged late fees). Basically, the customer base consisted of people who wanted to watch movies without having to leave the house. But Hastings and co-founder Marc Randolph then quickly decided to test a subscription-based model, unlimited rentals by mail for a flat fee and, perhaps most important, no due dates (and thus no late fees). Current customers were first offered the opportunity to shift from their pay-per-rental plans to subscription plans on a free, trial basis and then given the chance to renew the subscription plan on a paid basis. "We knew it wouldn't be terrible," says Hastings, "but we didn't

Reed Hastings has used a variety of management techniques to build Netflix into an entertainment powerhouse.

know if it would be great." In the first month, however, 80 percent of Netflix users who'd tried the no-cost subscription plan had renewed on a paid basis.

"Having unlimited due dates and no late fees," said Hastings back in 2003, "has worked in a powerful way and now seems obvious, but at that time, we had no idea if customers would even build and use an online queue." The "queue," as any Netflix user will tell you, is the list of movies that the customer wants to watch. Netflix maintains your queue, follows your online directions in keeping it up to date, and automatically sends you the next movie you want each time you send one back.

The essence of queuing—and of the Netflix business model—is clearly convenience. Although the ability to enhance customer convenience, even when combined with cost savings, often gives a company a competitive advantage in its industry, it doesn't always have the industry-wide effect that it's had in the case of Netflix. Not only did the Netflix subscriber model improve the service provided by the industry in an unexpected way, but ultimately it also weakened the competitive positions of companies already doing business in the industry— notably, Blockbuster. In late 2012, the onetime industry leader's market capitalization, which had peaked at $5 billion in 2002, was languishing at $35 million. At the same time, Netflix's market cap stood at nearly $10 billion and would top $15 billion by 2013.

How had Hastings's upstart company managed to put itself in such an enviable position? For one thing, it got off to a fast start. In 1997, when DVDs were just being test-marketed in the United States, Hastings and Randolph gambled that the new medium would eventually overtake videocassettes as the format of choice for both the home-movie industry and the home-movie renter. They were right, of course—by 2002, one in four U.S. households owned a DVD player, but the number today is close to nine in ten. (In any case, it would have cost about $4 to mail a videocassette both ways, compared to the $0.78 that it costs to ship a DVD back and forth.)

More important, as the first company to rent movies by mail, Netflix was the first to establish a rental-by-mail customer base. At first, says Hastings, "people thought the idea was crazy. But it was precisely because it was a contrarian idea that [it] enabled us to get ahead of our competitors." As Netflix has continued to expand and nurture its subscriber base, it's also generated both brand recognition and brand loyalty. "Netflix has customer loyalty. It's a passion brand," explains Hastings, who hastens to add that keeping customers happy is crucial "because the more someone uses Netflix, the more likely they are to stay with us."

Netflix also puts a premium on hiring the very best people. Hastings hires bright people, pays them above-market wages, and provides innovative and interesting benefits. For instance, Netflix employees can take as much vacation time as they want so long as they perform their jobs at a high level. But at the same time, the firm has very high performance standards and employees sometimes complain about too much pressure. As Hastings says, "We treat our top performers very well. We provide average employees with reasonable severance package[s]."

Today Netflix continues to be at the forefront of innovation and has established a strong position in the emerging video-on-demand market. In 2013, the company obtained exclusive rights to distribute the original series *The House of Cards, Hemlock Grove, Orange Is the New Black,* and the revival of *Arrested Development.* And each proved to be a big smash. All told, Netflix's 36 million subscribers watch about 4 billion hours of programs every quarter on more than 1,000 different devices—indeed, on a normal evening Netflix accounts for over a third of all Internet usage in North America!

Never one to stand still, Reed Hastings continues to look for the "next big thing." Unlike most traditional managers, Hastings doesn't have an office. He simply wanders around headquarters, talking to people about their work and their ideas, and occasionally grabbing an empty chair or desk to check his e-mail. When he needs solitude to think and ponder major decisions, he retreats to a rooftop "cube" with four glass walls overlooking the Santa Cruz mountains. And from that cube Hastings will continue to make the right moves.[1]

This book is about managers like Reed Hastings and the work they do. In this chapter, we examine the general nature of management, its dimensions, and its challenges. We explain the basic concepts of management and managers, discuss the management process, and summarize the origins of contemporary management thought. We conclude this chapter by introducing critical challenges and issues that managers are facing now and will continue to encounter in the future.

organization
A group of people working together in a structured and coordinated fashion to achieve a set of goals

AN INTRODUCTION TO MANAGEMENT

An **organization** is a group of people working together in a structured and coordinated fashion to achieve a set of goals, which may include profit (Netflix or Starbucks), the discovery of knowledge (the University of Nebraska or the National Science Foundation), national defense (the U.S. Navy or Marines), the coordination of various local charities (the United Way of America), or social satisfaction (a fraternity or sorority).

Managers are responsible for using the organization's resources to help achieve its goals. More precisely, **management** can be defined as a set of activities (including planning and decision making, organizing, leading, and controlling) directed at an organization's resources (human, financial, physical, and information), with the aim of achieving organizational goals in an efficient and effective manner. A **manager**, then, is someone whose primary responsibility is to carry out the management process. By **efficient**, we mean using resources wisely, in a cost-effective way. By **effective**, we mean making the right decisions and successfully implementing them. In general, successful organizations are both efficient and effective.[2]

Today's managers face various interesting and challenging situations. The average executive works 60 hours a week; has enormous demands placed on his or her time; and faces increased complexities posed by globalization, domestic competition, government regulation, shareholder pressure, emerging technologies, the rise of social media, and other Internet-related uncertainties. Their job is complicated even more by rapid changes, unexpected disruptions, and both minor and major crises. The manager's job is unpredictable and fraught with challenges, but it is also filled with opportunities to make a difference. Good managers can propel an organization into unprecedented realms of success, whereas poor managers can devastate even the strongest of organizations.[3]

Kinds of Managers

Many different kinds of managers work in organizations today. Figure 1.1 shows how various kinds of managers within an organization can be differentiated by level and by area.

Levels of Management   One way to classify managers is in terms of their level in the organization. *Top managers* make up the relatively small group of executives who manage the overall organization. Titles found in this group include president, vice president, and chief executive officer (CEO). Top managers create the organization's goals, overall strategy, and operating policies. They also officially represent the organization to the external environment by meeting with government officials, executives of other organizations, and so forth.

Howard Schultz, CEO of Starbucks, is a top manager, as are Paula Boggs and Peter Gibbons, two of the firm's executive vice presidents. Likewise, Reed Hastings, Sergey Brin and Larry Page (Google's founders and top executives), Marissa Mayer (CEO of Yahoo!), Richard Hayne (CEO of Urban Outfitters), and Mary Barra (CEO of General Motors) are also top managers. The job of a top manager is likely to be complex and varied. Top managers make decisions about activities such as acquiring other companies, investing in research and development (R&D), entering or abandoning various markets, and building new plants and office facilities. They often work long hours and spend much of their time in meetings or on the telephone. In most cases, top managers are also very well paid. In fact, the elite top managers of very large firms sometimes make several million dollars a year in salary, bonuses, and stock.[4] In 2012, Ford paid Alan Mulally $1,400,000 in salary for his work as CEO. He was also awarded a bonus of $9,450,000 and around $15,000,000 in stock and option awards.[5]

Middle management is probably the largest group of managers in most organizations. Common middle-management titles include plant manager, operations manager, and division head. *Middle managers* are primarily responsible for implementing the policies and plans developed by top managers and for supervising and coordinating the activities

management
A set of activities (including planning and decision making, organizing, leading, and controlling) directed at an organization's resources (human, financial, physical, and information), with the aim of achieving organizational goals in an efficient and effective manner

manager
Someone whose primary responsibility is to carry out the management process

efficient
Using resources wisely in a cost-effective way

effective
Making the right decisions and successfully implementing them

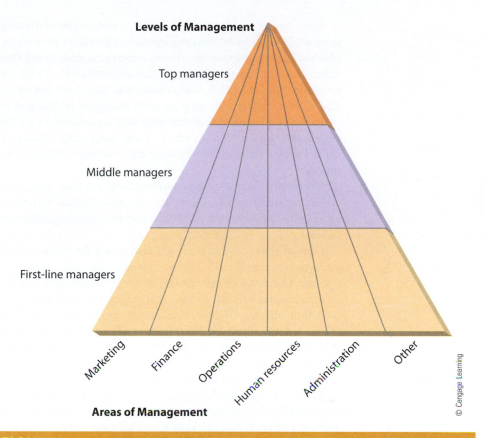

Levels of Management

Top managers

Middle managers

First-line managers

Marketing   Finance   Operations   Human resources   Administration   Other

Areas of Management

© Cengage Learning

FIGURE 1.1

Kinds of Managers by Level and Area

Organizations generally have three levels of management, represented by top managers, middle managers, and first-line managers. Regardless of level, managers are also usually associated with a specific area within the organization, such as marketing, finance, operations, human resources, administration, or some other area.

---

of lower-level managers.[6] Jason Hernandez, a regional manager at Starbucks responsible for the firm's operations in three eastern states, is a middle manager.

First-line managers supervise and coordinate the activities of operating employees. Common titles for first-line managers are supervisor, coordinator, and office manager. Positions like these are often the first held by employees who enter management from the ranks of operating personnel. Wayne Maxwell and Jenny Wagner, managers of Starbucks coffee shops in Texas, are first-line managers. They oversee the day-to-day operations of their respective stores, hire operating employees to staff them, and handle other routine administrative duties required of them by the parent corporation. In contrast to top and middle managers, first-line managers typically spend a large proportion of their time supervising the work of their subordinates.

Managing in Different Areas of the Organization   Regardless of their level, managers may work in various areas within an organization. In any given firm, for example, these areas may include marketing, financial, operations, human resources, administrative, and others.

Marketing managers work in areas related to the marketing function—getting consumers and clients to buy the organization's products or services (be they Samsung smartphones, Toyota automobiles, *Vogue* magazines, Associated Press news reports, streaming video rentals from Netflix, or lattes at Starbucks). These areas include new product development, promotion, and distribution. Given the importance of marketing for virtually all organizations, developing good managers in this area is critical.

Financial managers deal primarily with an organization's financial resources. They are responsible for activities such as accounting, cash management, and investments. In some businesses, especially banking and insurance, financial managers are found in large numbers.

Operations managers are concerned with creating and managing the systems that create an organization's products and services. Typical responsibilities of operations managers include production control, inventory control, quality control, plant layout, and site selection.

Human resources managers are responsible for hiring and developing employees. They are typically involved in human resource planning, recruiting and selecting employees, training and development, designing compensation and benefit systems, formulating performance appraisal systems, and discharging low-performing and problem employees.

Administrative, or general, managers are not associated with any particular management specialty. Probably the best example of an administrative management position is that of a hospital or clinic administrator. Administrative managers tend to be generalists; they have some basic familiarity with all functional areas of management rather than specialized training in any one area.[7]

Many organizations have specialized management positions in addition to those already described. Public relations managers, for example, deal with the public and media for firms such as Facebook and the Dow Chemical Company to protect and enhance the image of their organizations. R&D managers coordinate the activities of scientists and engineers working on scientific projects in organizations such as Google, Shell Oil, and NASA. Internal consultants are used in organizations such as Prudential Insurance to provide specialized expert advice to operating managers. International operations are often coordinated by specialized managers in organizations like Walmart and Halliburton. The number, nature, and importance of these specialized managers vary tremendously from one organization to another. As contemporary organizations continue to grow in complexity and size, the number and importance of such managers are also likely to increase.

Basic Management Functions

Regardless of level or area, management involves the four basic functions of planning and decision making, organizing, leading, and controlling. This book is organized around these basic functions, as shown in Figure 1.2.

Planning and Decision Making In its simplest form, **planning** means setting an organization's goals and deciding how best to achieve them. **Decision making**, a part of the planning process, involves selecting a course of action from a set of alternatives. Planning and decision making help managers maintain their effectiveness by serving as guides for their future activities. In other words, the organization's goals and plans clearly help managers know how to allocate their time and resources. Part 1 of this book is devoted to planning and decision-making activities and concepts.

Organizing Once a manager has set goals and developed a workable plan, his or her next management function is to organize people and the other resources necessary to carry out the plan. Specifically, **organizing** involves determining how activities and

planning
Setting an organization's goals and deciding how best to achieve them

decision making
Part of the planning process that involves selecting a course of action from a set of alternatives

organizing
Determining how activities and resources are to be grouped

© Cengage Learning

FIGURE 1.2

The Management Process

Management involves four basic activities—planning and decision making, organizing, leading, and controlling. Although there is a basic logic for describing these activities in this sequence (as indicated by the solid arrows), most managers engage in more than one activity at a time and often move back and forth between the activities in unpredictable ways (as shown by the dotted arrows).

resources are to be grouped. Although some people equate this function with the creation of an organization chart, we will see in Part 3 that it is actually much more.

Leading   The third basic managerial function is leading. Some people consider leading to be both the most important and the most challenging of all managerial activities. **Leading** is the set of processes used to get members of the organization to work together to further the interests of the organization. We cover the leading function in detail in Part 4.

Controlling   The final phase of the management process is **controlling**, or monitoring the organization's progress toward its goals. As the organization moves toward its goals, managers must monitor progress to ensure that it is performing in such a way as to arrive at its "destination" at the appointed time. Part 5 explores the control function. The "Sustainability Matters" feature also illustrates how control can be applied to waste management.

Fundamental Management Skills

To carry out these management functions most effectively, managers rely on a number of different fundamental management skills, of which the most important are technical, interpersonal, conceptual, diagnostic, communication, decision-making, and time management skills.[8]

leading
The set of processes used to get members of the organization to work together to further the interests of the organization

controlling
Monitoring organizational progress toward goal attainment

SUSTAINABILITY MATTERS

Toward Zero Waste

DuPont was once a major generator of trash, routinely dumping thousands of tons of waste materials in landfills each year. But a few years ago, the firm announced its intentions to dramatically reduce the waste it was sending to landfills, with a goal of achieving total recycling wherever possible. To initiate this effort, the firm first set a standard for each of its business units and facilities. Next, it developed procedures for monitoring progress toward those standards.

Take DuPont's Building Innovations unit, for example, which makes products like kitchen countertops and Tyvek building wrap. In 2008, the business was sending 81 million pounds of waste to landfills each year. But by January 2013, it was not sending anything to landfills! Among the new practices leading to this milestone are the following:

- Composting cafeteria waste and using it in landscaping
- Repairing shipping pallets to extend their use life, and shredding those not repairable for use as animal bedding
- Recycling countertop waste into landscape stone

A new term has even been coined to reflect this accomplishment: *zero-landfill status.* DuPont isn't alone, of course. GM recently reported that 81 of its North American manufacturing plants have achieved zero-landfill status. Moreover, GM also says that it recycles 92 percent of all waste generated by its facilities worldwide. Honda reports that 10 of its 14 North American factories have achieved zero-landfill status. And Toyota claims that its North American operations are at "near zero" landfill status.

Outside the auto industry, Boeing says that a renovated Chinook helicopter plant is at zero landfill status. And PepsiCo's Frito-Lay facilities are, in the words of the company, approaching zero landfill status at some of its facilities. For now, though, a few roadblocks and challenges are still being faced by businesses trying to improve their environmental footprint through control procedures. For one thing, some waste products are simply difficult to recycle. For example, DuPont noted that reducing waste by 80 percent was surprisingly easy, but that last 20 percent posed real challenges. There is also no independent resource for verifying zero-landfill status. Regardless, though, critics agree that even if a firm takes small liberties in reporting waste reductions, they are still making progress.

References: "Companies Air for Zero Success in Waste Recycling," *USA Today,* January 30, 2013, p. 3B; "Ford to Accelerate Waste Reduction Effort," greenbiz.com/news, March 4, 2013; "Waste Reduction," www.gm.com/vision/waste_reduction_.html, March 5, 2013.

---

technical skills
The skills necessary to accomplish or understand the specific kind of work done in an organization

Technical Skills   Technical skills are necessary to accomplish or understand the specific kind of work done in an organization. Technical skills are especially important for first-line managers. These managers spend much of their time training their subordinates and answering questions about work-related problems. If they are to be effective managers, they must know how to perform the tasks assigned to those they supervise. While Reed Hastings now spends most of his time dealing with strategic and management issues, he also keeps abreast of new and emerging technologies and trends that may affect Netflix.

interpersonal skills
The ability to communicate with, understand, and motivate both individuals and groups

Interpersonal Skills   Managers spend considerable time interacting with people both inside and outside the organization. For obvious reasons, then, they also need interpersonal skills—the ability to communicate with, understand, and motivate both individuals and groups. As a manager climbs the organizational ladder, he or she must be able to get along with subordinates, peers, and those at higher levels of the organization. Because of the multitude of roles that managers must fulfill, a manager must also be able to work with suppliers, customers, investors, and others outside the organization.

conceptual skills
The manager's ability to think in the abstract

Conceptual Skills   Conceptual skills depend on the manager's ability to think in the abstract. Managers need the mental capacity to understand the overall workings of the organization and its environment, to grasp how all the parts of the organization fit together, and to view the organization in a holistic manner. This ability allows them to think strategically, to see the "big picture," and to make broad-based decisions that serve the overall organization. Reed Hastings's idea to extend the payment model used by health clubs to the video rental market came from his strong conceptual skills.

diagnostic skills
The manager's ability to visualize the most appropriate response to a situation

Diagnostic Skills Successful managers also possess **diagnostic skills**—skills that enable them to visualize the most appropriate response to a situation. A physician diagnoses a patient's illness by analyzing symptoms and determining their probable cause. Similarly, a manager can diagnose and analyze a problem in the organization by studying its symptoms and then developing a solution.[9]

communication skills
The manager's abilities both to effectively convey ideas and information to others and to effectively receive ideas and information from others

Communication Skills **Communication skills** refer to the manager's abilities to both effectively convey ideas and information to others and effectively receive ideas and information from others. These skills enable a manager to transmit ideas to subordinates so that they know what is expected, to coordinate work with peers and colleagues so that they work well together, and to keep higher-level managers informed about what is going on. In addition, communication skills help the manager listen to what others say and understand the real meaning behind e-mails, letters, reports, and other written communication.

decision-making skills
The manager's ability to correctly recognize and define problems and opportunities and to then select an appropriate course of action to solve problems and capitalize on opportunities

Decision-Making Skills Effective managers also have good decision-making skills. **Decision-making skills** refer to the manager's ability to correctly recognize and define problems and opportunities and to then select an appropriate course of action to solve problems and capitalize on opportunities. No manager makes the right decision all the time. However, effective managers make good decisions most of the time. And, when they do make a bad decision, they usually recognize their mistake quickly and then make good decisions to recover with as little cost or damage to their organization as possible. Managers at Netflix made a poor decision when they decided to split their services into two businesses, but they quickly reversed themselves before things got too bad.

time management skills
The manager's ability to prioritize work, to work efficiently, and to delegate appropriately

Time Management Skills Finally, effective managers usually have good time management skills. **Time management skills** refer to the manager's ability to prioritize work, to work efficiently, and to delegate work appropriately. As already noted, managers face many different pressures and challenges. It is too easy for a manager to get bogged down doing work that can easily be postponed or delegated to others.[10] When this happens, unfortunately, more pressing and higher-priority work may get neglected.[11]

The Science and the Art of Management

Given the complexity inherent in the manager's job, a reasonable question relates to whether management is a science or an art. In fact, effective management is a blend of both science and art. Successful executives recognize the importance of combining both the science and art of management as they practice their craft.[12]

The Science of Management Many management problems and issues can be approached in ways that are rational, logical, objective, and systematic. Managers can gather data, facts, and objective information. They can use quantitative models and decision-making techniques to arrive at "correct" decisions. And they need to take such a scientific approach to solving problems whenever possible, especially when they are dealing with relatively routine and straightforward issues. When Starbucks considers entering a new market, its managers look closely at a wide variety of objective details as they formulate their plans. Technical, diagnostic, and decision-making skills are especially important when approaching a management task or problem from a scientific perspective.

© Elena Kharichkina/Shutterstock.com

Most successful managers have strong time management skills. This allows them to stay on top of their work, meet deadlines, achieve their goals, and avoid unnecessary stress. Poor time management skills, however, often lead to falling behind on work, not meeting goals, being late on projects, and excessive stress.

The Art of Management   Even though managers may try to be scientific as often as possible, they must frequently make decisions and solve problems on the basis of intuition, experience, instinct, and personal insights. Relying heavily on conceptual, communication, interpersonal, and time management skills, for example, a manager may have to decide among multiple courses of action that look equally attractive. And even "objective facts" may prove to be wrong. When Starbucks was planning its first store in New York City, market research clearly showed that New Yorkers preferred drip coffee to more exotic espresso-style coffees. After first installing more drip coffee makers and fewer espresso makers than in their other stores, managers had to backtrack when New Yorkers lined up clamoring for espresso. Starbucks now introduces a standard menu and layout in all its stores, regardless of presumed market differences, and then makes necessary adjustments later.[13] Thus, managers must blend an element of intuition and personal insight with hard data and objective facts.[14]

THE EVOLUTION OF MANAGEMENT

Most managers today recognize the importance of history and theory in their work. For instance, knowing the origins of their organization and the kinds of practices that have led to success—or failure—can be an indispensable tool in managing the contemporary organization. Thus, in our next section, we briefly trace the history of management thought. Then we move forward to the present day by introducing contemporary management issues and challenges.

The Importance of Theory and History

Some people question the value of history and theory. Their arguments are usually based on the assumptions that history is not relevant to contemporary society and that theory is abstract and of no practical use. In reality, however, both theory and history are important to all managers today.

theory

A conceptual framework for organizing knowledge and providing a blueprint for action

Why Theory?   A **theory** is simply a conceptual framework for organizing knowledge and providing a blueprint for action.[15] Although some theories seem abstract and irrelevant, others appear very simple and practical. Management theories, which are used to build organizations and guide them toward their goals, are grounded in reality.[16] Practically any organization that uses assembly lines (such as Nissan and Samsung) is drawing on what we describe later in this chapter as *scientific management*. Many organizations, including Nucor Steel and Google, use the behavioral perspective (also introduced later in this chapter) to improve employee satisfaction and motivation. And naming a large company that does not use one or more techniques from the quantitative management perspective would be difficult. For example, retailers such as Best Buy and Target routinely use operations management to determine how many checkout lines they need to have open at any given time. In addition, most managers develop and refine their own theories of how they should run their organizations and manage the behavior of their employees. James Sinegal, founder and CEO of Costco Wholesale, believes that paying his employees well while keeping prices as low as possible are the key ingredients in success for his business. This belief is based essentially on his personal theory of competition in the warehouse retailing industry.

Why History?   Awareness and understanding of important historical developments are also important to contemporary managers.[17] Understanding the historical context of management provides a sense of heritage and can help managers avoid the mistakes of others. Most courses in U.S. history devote time to business and economic developments in this country, including the Industrial Revolution, the early labor movement, and the Great Depression, and to captains of U.S. industry such as Cornelius Vanderbilt (railroads), John D. Rockefeller (oil), and Andrew Carnegie (steel). The contributions of those and other industrialists left a profound imprint on contemporary culture.[18]

Many managers are also realizing that they can benefit from a greater understanding of history in general. For example, Ian M. Ross of AT&T's Bell Laboratories cites *The Second World War* by Winston Churchill as a major influence on his approach to leadership. Other books often mentioned by managers for their relevance to today's business problems include such classics as Plato's *Republic*, Homer's *Iliad*, Sun Tzu's *The Art of War*, and Machiavelli's *The Prince*.[19] And new business history books have also been directed at women managers and the lessons they can learn from the past.[20]

Managers at Wells Fargo clearly recognize the value of history. For example, the company maintains an extensive archival library of its old banking documents and records, and even employs a full-time corporate historian. As part of their orientation and training, new managers at Wells Fargo take courses to become acquainted with the bank's history.[21] Similarly, Shell Oil, Levi Strauss, Walmart, Lloyd's of London, Disney, Honda, and Unilever all maintain significant archives about their pasts and frequently evoke images from those pasts in their orientation and training programs, advertising campaigns, and other public relations activities.

The Historical Context of Management

The practice of management can be traced back thousands of years. The Egyptians used the management functions of planning, organizing, and controlling when they constructed the pyramids. Alexander the Great employed a staff organization to coordinate

classical management perspective
Consists of two distinct branches—scientific management and administrative management

scientific management
Concerned with improving the performance of individual workers

soldiering
Employees deliberately working at a slow pace

activities during his military campaigns. The Roman Empire developed a well-defined organizational structure that greatly facilitated communication and control. Socrates discussed management practices and concepts in 400 BC, Plato described job specialization in 350 BC, and the Persian scientist and philosopher al-Farabi listed several leadership traits in AD 900.[22]

In spite of this history, the serious study of management did not begin until the nineteenth century. Two of its pioneers were Robert Owen and Charles Babbage. Owen (1771–1858), a British industrialist and reformer, was one of the first managers to recognize the importance of an organization's human resources and to express concern for the personal welfare of his workers. Babbage (1792–1871), an English mathematician, focused his attention on efficiencies of production. He placed great faith in the division of labor and advocated the application of mathematics to such problems as the efficient use of facilities and materials.

The Classical Management Perspective

Early in the twentieth century, the preliminary ideas and writings of these and other managers and theorists converged with the emergence and evolution of large-scale businesses and management practices. This created interest and focused attention on how businesses should be operated. The first important ideas to emerge are now called the **classical management perspective**, which actually includes two different viewpoints: scientific management and administrative management.

Scientific Management   Productivity emerged as a serious business problem during the early years of the twentieth century. Business was expanding and capital was readily available, but labor was in short supply. Hence, managers began to search for ways to use existing labor more efficiently. In response to this need, experts began to focus on ways to improve the performance of individual workers. Their work led to the development of **scientific management**. Some of the earliest advocates of scientific management included Frederick W. Taylor (1856–1915), Frank Gilbreth (1868–1924), and Lillian Gilbreth (1878–1972).[23] Taylor played the dominant role.

One of Taylor's first jobs was as a foreman at the Midvale Steel Company in Philadelphia. There he observed what he called **soldiering**—employees deliberately working at a pace slower than their capabilities. Taylor studied and timed each element of the steelworkers' jobs. He determined what each worker should be producing, and then he designed the most efficient way of doing each part of the overall task. Next, he implemented a piecework pay system. Rather than paying all employees the same wage, he began increasing the pay of each worker who met and exceeded the target level of output set for his or her job.

After Taylor left Midvale, he worked as a consultant for several companies, including Simonds Rolling Machine Company and Bethlehem Steel. At Simonds he studied and redesigned jobs, introduced rest periods to reduce fatigue, and implemented a piecework pay system. The results were higher quality and quantity of output, and improved morale. At Bethlehem Steel, Taylor studied efficient ways of loading and unloading railcars and applied his conclusions with equally impressive results. During these experiences, he formulated the basic ideas that he called *scientific management*.

Bettmann/CORBIS

Frederick W. Taylor was one of the first management consultants and helped create scientific management. Time-and-motion studies and performance-based pay systems were among the innovations Taylor and his associates introduced. Mass-production assembly line technologies also benefited from Taylor's ideas and insights.

1	2	3	4
Develop a science for each element of the job to replace old rule-of-thumb methods	Scientifically select employees and then train them to do the job as described in step 1	Supervise employees to make sure they follow the prescribed methods for performing their jobs	Continue to plan the work, but use workers to get the work done

© Cengage Learning

FIGURE 1.3

Steps in Scientific Management

Frederick Taylor developed this system of scientific management, which he believed would lead to a more efficient and productive workforce. Bethlehem Steel was among the first organizations to profit from scientific management and still practices some parts of it today.

Figure 1.3 illustrates the basic steps Taylor suggested. He believed that managers who followed his guidelines would improve the efficiency of their workers.[24]

Taylor's work had a major impact on U.S. industry. By applying his principles, many organizations achieved major gains in efficiency. Taylor was not without his detractors, however. Labor argued that scientific management was just a device to get more work from each employee and to reduce the total number of workers needed by a firm. There was a congressional investigation into Taylor's ideas, and evidence suggests that he falsified some of his findings.[25] Nevertheless, Taylor's work left a lasting imprint on business.[26]

Frank and Lillian Gilbreth, contemporaries of Taylor, were a husband-and-wife team of industrial engineers. One of Frank Gilbreth's most interesting contributions was to the craft of bricklaying. After studying bricklayers at work, he developed several procedures for doing the job more efficiently. For example, he specified standard materials and techniques, including the positioning of the bricklayer, the bricks, and the mortar at different levels. The results of these changes were a reduction from 18 separate physical movements to 5 and an increase in the output of about 200 percent. Lillian Gilbreth made equally important contributions to several different areas of work, helped shape the field of industrial psychology, and made substantive contributions to the field of personnel management. Working individually and together, the Gilbreths developed numerous techniques and strategies for eliminating inefficiency. They applied many of their ideas to their family and documented their experiences raising 12 children in the book and original 1950 movie *Cheaper by the Dozen*.

administrative management

Focuses on managing the total organization

Administrative Management   Whereas scientific management deals with the jobs of individual employees, **administrative management** focuses on managing the total organization. The primary contributors to administrative management were Henri Fayol (1841–1925), Lyndall Urwick (1891–1983), and Max Weber (1864–1920).

Henri Fayol was administrative management's most articulate spokesperson. A French industrialist, Fayol was unknown to U.S. managers and scholars until his most important work, *General and Industrial Management*, was translated into English in 1930.[27] Drawing on his own managerial experience, he attempted to systematize management practice to provide guidance and direction to other managers. Fayol was also the first to identify the specific managerial functions of planning, organizing, leading, and controlling. He believed that these functions accurately reflect the core of the management process. Most contemporary management books (including this one) still use this framework, and practicing managers agree that these functions are critical parts of their jobs.

After a career as a British army officer, Lyndall Urwick became a noted management theorist and consultant. He integrated scientific management with the work of Fayol and other administrative management theorists. He also advanced modern thinking about the functions of planning, organizing, and controlling. Like Fayol, he developed a list of guidelines for improving managerial effectiveness. Urwick is noted not so much for his own contributions as for his synthesis and integration of the work of others.

Although Max Weber lived and worked at the same time as Fayol and Taylor, his contributions were not recognized until some years had passed. Weber was a German sociologist, and his most important work was not translated into English until 1947.[28] Weber's work on bureaucracy laid the foundation for contemporary organization theory, which is discussed in detail in Chapter 6. The concept of bureaucracy, as we discuss later in this book, is based on a rational set of guidelines for structuring organizations in the most efficient manner.

The Classical Management Perspective Today The classical management perspective provides many management techniques and approaches that are still relevant today. For example, many of the job specialization techniques and scientific methods espoused by Taylor and his contemporaries are still reflected in how several industrial jobs are designed today.[29] Moreover, many contemporary organizations still use some of the bureaucratic procedures suggested by Weber. Also, these early theorists were the first to focus attention on management as a meaningful field of study. Several aspects of the classical perspective are also relevant to our later discussions of planning, organizing, and controlling. And recent advances in areas such as business-to-business (B2B) digital commerce and supply chain management also have efficiency as their primary goal. On the other hand, the classical perspective focused on stable, simple organizations; many organizations today, in contrast, are changing and complex. They also proposed universal guidelines that we now recognize do not fit every organization. A third limitation of the classical management perspective is that it slighted the role of the individual in organizations. This role was much more fully developed by advocates of the behavioral management perspective.

The Behavioral Management Perspective

Early advocates of the classical management perspective viewed organizations and jobs from an essentially mechanistic point of view; that is, they sought to conceptualize organizations as machines and workers as cogs within those machines. Even though many early writers recognized the role of individuals, their focus tended to be on how managers could control and standardize the behavior of their employees. In contrast, the **behavioral management perspective** placed much more emphasis on individual attitudes, behaviors, and group processes and recognized the importance of behavioral processes in the workplace.

The behavioral management perspective was stimulated by many writers and theoretical movements. One of those movements was industrial psychology, the practice of applying psychological concepts to industrial settings. Hugo Munsterberg (1863–1916), a noted German psychologist, is recognized as the father of industrial psychology. He established a psychological laboratory at Harvard University in 1892, and his pioneering book, *Psychology and Industrial Efficiency*, was translated into English in 1913.[30] Munsterberg suggested that psychologists could make valuable contributions to managers in the areas of employee selection and motivation. Industrial psychology is still a major course of study at many colleges and universities. Another early advocate of the behavioral approach to management was Mary Parker Follett (1868–1933).[31] Follett worked during the scientific management era but quickly came to recognize the human element in the workplace. Indeed, her work clearly anticipated the behavioral management perspective, and she appreciated the need to understand the role of human behavior in organizations.

behavioral management perspective
Emphasizes individual attitudes and behaviors and group processes

The Hawthorne Studies   Although Munsterberg and Follett made major contributions to the development of the behavioral approach to management, its primary catalyst was a series of studies conducted near Chicago at Western Electric's Hawthorne plant between 1927 and 1932. The research, originally sponsored by General Electric, was conducted by Elton Mayo and his associates.[32] Mayo was a faculty member and consultant at Harvard. The first study involved manipulating illumination for one group of workers and comparing their subsequent productivity with the productivity of another group whose illumination was not changed. Surprisingly, when illumination was increased for the experimental group, productivity went up in both groups. Productivity continued to increase in both groups, even when the lighting for the experimental group was decreased. Not until the lighting was reduced to the level of moonlight did productivity begin to decline (and General Electric withdrew its sponsorship).

Another experiment established a piecework incentive pay plan for a group of nine men assembling terminal banks for telephone exchanges. Scientific management would have predicted that each man would try to maximize his pay by producing as many units as possible. Mayo and his associates, however, found that the group itself informally established an acceptable level of output for its members. Workers who overproduced were branded *rate busters*, and underproducers were labeled *chiselers*. To be accepted by the group, workers produced at the accepted level. As they approached this acceptable level of output, workers slacked off to avoid overproducing.

Other studies, including an interview program involving several thousand workers, led Mayo and his associates to conclude that human behavior was much more important in

The Hawthorne studies were a series of early experiments that focused on behavior in the workplace. In one experiment involving this group of workers, for example, researchers monitored how productivity changed as a result of changes in working conditions. The Hawthorne studies and subsequent experiments led scientists to the conclusion that the human element is very important in the workplace.

Courtesy of AT&T Archives and History Center

human relations movement
Argued that workers respond primarily to the social context of the workplace

Theory X
A pessimistic and negative view of workers consistent with the views of scientific management

Theory Y
A positive view of workers; it represents the assumptions that human relations advocates make

Douglas McGregor developed Theory X and Theory Y. He argued that Theory X best represented the views of scientific management and Theory Y represented the human relations approach. McGregor believed that Theory Y was the best philosophy for all managers.

the workplace than had been previously believed. In the lighting experiment, for example, the results were attributed to the fact that both groups received special attention and sympathetic supervision for perhaps the first time. The incentive pay plans did not work because wage incentives were less important to the individual workers than was social acceptance in determining output. In short, individual and social processes played major roles in shaping worker attitudes and behavior.

The Human Relations Movement   The **human relations movement**, which grew from the Hawthorne studies and was a popular approach to management for many years, proposed that workers respond primarily to the social context of the workplace, including social conditioning, group norms, and interpersonal dynamics. A basic assumption of the human relations movement was that the manager's concern for workers would lead to increased satisfaction, which would in turn result in improved performance. Two writers who helped advance the human relations movement were Abraham Maslow (1908–1970) and Douglas McGregor (1906–1964).

In 1943, Maslow advanced a theory suggesting that people are motivated by a hierarchy of needs, including monetary incentives and social acceptance.[33] Maslow's hierarchy, perhaps the best-known human relations theory, is described in detail in Chapter 10. Meanwhile, Douglas McGregor's Theory X and Theory Y model best represents the essence of the human relations movement (see Table 1.1).[34] According to McGregor, Theory X and Theory Y reflect two extreme belief sets that different managers have about their workers. **Theory X** is a relatively pessimistic and negative view of workers and is consistent with the views of scientific management. **Theory Y** is more positive and represents the assumptions made by human relations advocates. In McGregor's

Table 1.1	Theory X and Theory Y
Theory X Assumptions	1. People do not like work and try to avoid it.
	2. People do not like work, so managers have to control, direct, coerce, and threaten employees to get them to work toward organizational goals.
	3. People prefer to be directed, to avoid responsibility, and to want security; they have little ambition.
Theory Y Assumptions	1. People do not naturally dislike work; work is a natural part of their lives.
	2. People are internally motivated to reach objectives to which they are committed.
	3. People are committed to goals to the degree that they receive personal rewards when they reach their objectives.
	4. People will both seek and accept responsibility under favorable conditions.
	5. People have the capacity to be innovative in solving organizational problems.
	6. People are bright, but under most organizational conditions, their potential is underutilized.

Source: D. McGregor and W. Bennis, *The Human Side Enterprise: 25th Anniversary Printing*, 1960, Copyright © 1960 The McGraw-Hill Companies, Inc. Reprinted with permission.

view, Theory Y was a more appropriate philosophy for managers to adhere to. Both Maslow and McGregor notably influenced the thinking of many practicing managers.

Contemporary Behavioral Science in Management Munsterberg, Mayo, Maslow, McGregor, and others have made valuable contributions to management. Contemporary theorists, however, have noted that many of the human relationists' assertions were simplistic and provided inadequate descriptions of work behavior. Current behavioral perspectives on management, known as **organizational behavior**, acknowledge that human behavior in organizations is much more complex than the human relationists realized. The field of organizational behavior draws from a broad, interdisciplinary base of psychology, sociology, anthropology, economics, and medicine. Organizational behavior takes a holistic view of behavior and addresses individual, group, and organization processes. These processes are major elements in contemporary management theory.[35] Important topics in this field include job satisfaction, stress, motivation, leadership, group dynamics, organizational politics, interpersonal conflict, and the structure and design of organizations.[36] A contingency orientation also characterizes the field (discussed more fully later in this chapter). Our discussions of organizing (Chapters 6–8) and leading (Chapters 9–13) are heavily influenced by organizational behavior. And, finally, managers need a solid understanding of human behavior as they address diversity-related issues such as ethnicity and religion in the workplace. Indeed, all these topics are useful to help managers better deal with the consequences of layoffs and job cuts and to motivate today's workers.

> **organizational behavior**
> Contemporary field focusing on behavioral perspectives on management

The Behavioral Management Perspective Today The primary contributions of this approach relate to how it has changed managerial thinking. Managers are now more likely to recognize the importance of behavioral processes and to view employees as valuable resources instead of mere tools. However, organizational behavior is still relatively imprecise in its ability to predict behavior, especially the behavior of a specific individual. It is not always accepted or understood by practicing managers. Hence the contributions of the behavioral school are just beginning to be fully realized.

The Quantitative Management Perspective

The third major school of management thought began to emerge during World War II. During the war, government officials and scientists in England and the United States worked to help the military deploy its resources more efficiently and effectively. These groups took some of the mathematical approaches to management developed decades earlier by Taylor and Gantt and applied these approaches to logistical problems during the war.[37] They learned that problems regarding troop, equipment, and submarine deployment, for example, could all be solved through mathematical analysis. After the war, companies such as DuPont and General Electric began to use the same techniques for deploying employees, choosing plant locations, and planning warehouses. Basically, then, this perspective is concerned with applying quantitative techniques to management. More specifically, the **quantitative management perspective** focuses on decision making, cost-effectiveness, mathematical models, and the use of computers. The two branches of the quantitative approach are management science and operations management.

> **quantitative management perspective**
> Applies quantitative techniques to management

Management Science Unfortunately, the term *management science* appears to be related to scientific management, the approach developed by Taylor and others early in the twentieth century. But the two have little in common and should not be confused. **Management science** focuses specifically on the development of mathematical models. A mathematical model is a simplified representation of a system, process, or relationship.

> **management science**
> Focuses specifically on the development of mathematical models

At its most basic level, management science focuses on models, equations, and similar representations of reality. For example, managers at Detroit Edison use mathematical models to determine how best to route repair crews during blackouts. Citizens Bank of New England uses models to figure out how many tellers need to be on duty at each location at various times throughout the day. In recent years, paralleling the advent of the personal computer, management science techniques have become increasingly sophisticated. For example, automobile manufacturers Daimler AG and General Motors use realistic computer simulations to study collision damage to cars. These simulations help them lower costs by crashing actual test cars only after multiple simulations.

operations management

Concerned with helping the organization more efficiently produce its products or services

Operations Management   Operations management is somewhat less mathematical and statistically sophisticated than management science, and it can be applied more directly to managerial situations. Indeed, we can think of **operations management** as a form of applied management science. Operations management techniques are generally concerned with helping the organization produce its products or services more efficiently and can be applied to a wide range of problems.

For example, Unilever and Home Depot each use operations management techniques to manage their inventories. (Inventory management is concerned with specific inventory problems, such as balancing carrying costs and ordering costs, and determining the optimal order quantity.) Linear programming (which involves computing simultaneous solutions to a set of linear equations) helps United Airlines plan its flight schedules, Consolidated Freightways develop its shipping routes, and General Instrument Corporation plan what instruments to produce at various times. Other operations management techniques include queuing theory, break-even analysis, and simulation. All these techniques and procedures apply directly to operations, but they are also helpful in areas such as finance, marketing, and human resource management.[38]

The quantitative management perspective is important to a variety of management situations today. Computer simulations, mathematical modeling, and statistical analyses are all commonly used in many different organizations.

© tmcphotos/Shutterstock.com

The Quantitative Management Perspective Today   Like the other management perspectives, the quantitative management perspective has made important contributions and has certain limitations. It has provided managers with an abundance of decision-making tools and techniques and has increased understanding of overall organizational processes. This perspective has been particularly useful in the areas of planning and controlling. Relatively new management concepts such as supply chain management and new techniques such as enterprise resource planning, both discussed later in this book, also evolved from the quantitative management perspective. Even more recently, mathematicians are using tools and techniques from the quantitative perspective to develop models that might be helpful in the war against terrorism.[39] However, mathematical models cannot fully account for individual behaviors and attitudes. Some believe that the time needed to develop competence in quantitative techniques retards the development of other managerial skills. Finally, mathematical models typically require a set of assumptions that may not be realistic.

CONTEMPORARY MANAGEMENT PERSPECTIVES

It is important to recognize that the classical, behavioral, and quantitative approaches to management are not necessarily contradictory or mutually exclusive. Even though each of the three perspectives makes very different assumptions and predictions, each can also complement the others. Indeed, a complete understanding of management requires an appreciation of all three perspectives. The systems and contingency perspectives can help us integrate these earlier approaches and enlarge our understanding of all three.

The Systems Perspective

system
An interrelated set of elements functioning as a whole

The systems perspective is one important contemporary management perspective. A **system** is an interrelated set of elements functioning as a whole.[40] As shown in Figure 1.4, by viewing an organization as a system, we can identify four basic elements: inputs, transformation processes, outputs, and feedback. First, inputs are the material, human, financial, and information resources that an organization gets from its environment. Next, through technological and managerial processes, inputs are transformed into outputs. Outputs include products, services, or both (tangible and intangible); profits, losses, or both (even

FIGURE 1.4

The Systems Perspective of Organizations

By viewing organizations as systems, managers can better understand the importance of their environment and the level of interdependence among their organization's subsystems. Managers must also understand how their decisions affect and are affected by the organization's other subsystems.

open systems
A system that interacts with its environment

closed systems
A system that does not interact with its environment

subsystems
A system within another system

synergy
Two or more subsystems working together to produce more than the total of what they might produce working alone

entropy
A normal process leading to system decline

universal perspectives
An attempt to identify the one best way to do something

contingency perspective
Suggests that appropriate managerial behavior in a given situation depends on, or is contingent on, unique elements in a given situation

not-for-profit organizations must operate within their budgets); employee behaviors; and information. Finally, the environment reacts to these outputs and provides feedback to the system.

Thinking of organizations as systems provides us with a variety of important viewpoints on organizations, such as the concepts of open systems, subsystems, synergy, and entropy. **Open systems** are systems that interact with their environment, whereas **closed systems** do not interact with their environment. Although organizations are open systems, some make the mistake of ignoring their environment and behaving as though it is not important.

The systems perspective also stresses the importance of **subsystems**—systems within a broader system. For example, the marketing, production, and finance functions within Mattel are systems in their own right but are also subsystems within the overall organization. Because they are interdependent, a change in one subsystem can affect other subsystems as well. If the production department at Mattel lowers the quality of the toys being made (by buying lower-quality materials, for example), the effects are felt in finance (improved cash flow in the short run owing to lower costs) and marketing (decreased sales in the long run because of customer dissatisfaction). Managers must therefore remember that although organizational subsystems can be managed with some degree of autonomy, their interdependence should not be overlooked. For instance, recent research has underscored the interdependence of strategy and operations in businesses.[41]

Synergy suggests that organizational units (or subsystems) may often be more successful working together than working alone. The Walt Disney Company, for example, benefits greatly from synergy. The company's movies, theme parks, television programs, and merchandise-licensing programs all benefit one another. Children who enjoy Disney movies such as *Monsters University* and *Frozen* want to go to Disney World to see the attractions and shows based on the movies and their favorite characters; and when they shop at Target, they see and want to buy stuffed toys and action figures of the same characters. Music from the films generates additional revenues for the firm, as do computer games and other licensing arrangements for lunchboxes, clothing, and so forth. Synergy was also the major objective of Procter & Gamble's acquisition of Gillette; the firm decided it could use its own retailing presence and international distribution networks to substantially increase Gillette's sales. And Gillette's products are natural complements to P&G's existing line of grooming products.[42] Synergy is an important concept for managers because it emphasizes the importance of working together in a cooperative and coordinated fashion.[43]

Finally, **entropy** is a normal process that leads to system decline. When an organization does not monitor feedback from its environment and make appropriate adjustments, it may fail. For example, witness the problems and eventual demise of Studebaker (an automobile manufacturer) and Circuit City (a major retailer). Each of these organizations went bankrupt because it failed to revitalize itself and keep pace with changes in its environment. A primary objective of management, from a systems perspective, is to continually reenergize the organization to avoid entropy.

The Contingency Perspective

Another noteworthy recent addition to management thinking is the contingency perspective. The classical, behavioral, and quantitative approaches are considered **universal perspectives** because they try to identify the "one best way" to manage organizations. The **contingency perspective**, in contrast, suggests that universal theories cannot be applied to organizations because each organization is unique. Instead, the contingency perspective suggests that appropriate managerial behavior in a given situation depends on, or is contingent on, unique elements in that situation.[44]

Stated differently, effective managerial behavior in one situation cannot always be generalized to other situations. Recall, for example, that Frederick Taylor assumed that all workers would generate the highest possible level of output to maximize their own personal economic gain. We can imagine some people being motivated primarily by money—but we can just as easily imagine other people being motivated by the desire for leisure time, status, social acceptance, or any combination of these (as Mayo found at the Hawthorne plant). In 2000, Cisco Systems had the largest market cap in the world and was growing at a rate of 50 percent per year. A recession and the terrorist attacks in September 2001, however, caused the technology sector to crash, and Cisco's stock dropped in value by 86 percent. Cisco's CEO, John Chambers, had to downsize the company through layoffs and divestitures and transform it into a smaller company. As he went through this process, he also changed his management style. He had previously been an autocratic manager and led Cisco using a command-and-control hierarchy. As a result of the transformation at Cisco, however, Chambers decided he needed to change his own management style as well. So, he began to adopt a much more democratic approach and run Cisco using a more democratic organizational structure.[45]

Contemporary Management Issues and Challenges

Interest in management theory and practice has heightened in recent years as new issues and challenges have emerged. No new paradigm has been formulated that replaces the traditional views, but managers continue to strive toward a better understanding of how they can better compete and lead their organizations toward improved effectiveness.

Contemporary Applied Perspectives   Several applied authors have significant influence on modern management theory and practice. Among the most popular applied authors today are Peter Senge, Stephen Covey, Tom Peters, Jim Collins, Michael Porter, John Kotter, and Gary Hamel.[46] Their books highlight the management practices of successful firms such as Shell Oil, Ford, and IBM, or they outline conceptual or theoretical models or frameworks to guide managers as they formulate strategies or motivate their employees. Malcolm Gladwell's books *The Tipping Point, Blink*, and *Outliers* have all caught the attention of many contemporary managers. Scott Adams, creator of the popular comic strip *Dilbert*, also remains popular today. Adams is a former communications industry worker who developed his strip to illustrate some of the absurdities that occasionally afflict contemporary organizational life. The daily strip is routinely e-mailed and posted outside office doors, above copy machines, and beside water coolers in hundreds of offices.

Contemporary Management Challenges   Managers today also face an imposing set of challenges as they guide and direct the fortunes of their companies. Coverage of each of these challenges is thoroughly integrated throughout this book. In addition, many of them are highlighted or given focused coverage in one or more special ways.

One significant challenge (and opportunity) is globalization. Managing in a global economy poses many different challenges and opportunities. For example, at a macro level, property ownership arrangements vary widely. So does the availability of natural resources and infrastructure components, as well as government's role in business. Moreover, behavioral processes vary widely across cultural and national boundaries. For example, values, symbols, and beliefs differ sharply among cultures. Different work norms and the role that work plays in a person's life, for example, influence patterns of both work-related behavior and attitudes toward work. They also affect the nature of supervisory relationships, decision-making styles and processes, and organizational configurations. Group and intergroup processes, responses to stress, and the nature of political behaviors also differ from culture to culture.

Another management challenge that has taken on renewed importance is ethics and social responsibility and their relationship to corporate governance. Unfortunately, business scandals involving unethical conduct have become almost commonplace today. For example, the effects of Allen Stanford's alleged $7 billion Ponzi scheme ruined the financial futures of thousands of people. From a social responsibility perspective, increasing attention has been focused on pollution and business's obligation to help clean up our environment, business contributions to social causes, and so forth. The proper framework for corporate governance is often at the center of these debates and discussions.[47]

Quality also continues to pose an important management challenge today. Quality is an important issue for several reasons. First, more and more organizations are using quality as a basis for competition. Lexus, for example, stresses its high rankings in the J. D. Power survey of customer satisfaction in its print advertising. Second, improving quality tends to increase productivity because making higher-quality products generally results in less waste and rework. Third, enhancing quality lowers costs. Managers at Whistler Corporation once realized that the firm was using 100 of its 250 employees to repair defective radar detectors that had been built incorrectly in the first place.

The shift toward a service economy also continues to be important. Traditionally, most U.S. businesses were manufacturers—using tangible resources like raw materials and machinery to create tangible products like automobiles and steel. And manufacturing is indeed still important in the U.S. economy. In the last few decades, however, the service sector of the economy has become much more important. This is documented more fully in the "At Your Service" feature. Although there are obviously many similarities between managing in a manufacturing and a service organization, there are also many fundamental differences.

The economic recession of 2008–2010 and slow recovery in 2011–2014 have also created myriad challenges, as well as some opportunities, for managers. Most businesses struggled, and some failed to survive. But some managers also used this period as a framework for reducing their costs, streamlining their operating systems and procedures, and fine-tuning their business strategies. As the economy slowly began to rebound in 2013, firms like Ford, Target, and Delia seemed to be well positioned for new growth and cautiously began hiring new employees.

A related challenge for managers is the rapidly changing workplace.[48] Indeed, this new workplace is accompanied by both dramatic challenges and amazing opportunities. Among other things, workplace changes relate in part to both workforce reductions and expansion. For example, many firms hired large numbers of new workers during the economic expansion that was taking place between 2002 and early 2008. But as the recession of 2008–2010 took hold, many of those same firms had to reduce their workforces, while others cut hours and pay and suspended all hiring until conditions showed signs of improvement. But even more central to the idea of workplace change are developments such as workforce diversity and the characteristics of new workers themselves.

The management of diversity continues to be an important organizational opportunity—and challenge—today. The term *diversity* refers to differences among people. Diversity may be reflected along numerous dimensions, but most managers tend to focus on age, gender, ethnicity, and physical abilities and disabilities.[49] For example, the average age of workers in the United States is gradually increasing. An increasing number of women have also entered the U.S. workforce. Fifty years ago, only about one-third of U.S. women worked outside their homes; today, 60 percent of women aged 16 and older are in the workforce. The ethnic composition of the workplace is also changing.

Aside from its demographic composition, the workforce today is changing in other ways. During the 1980s, many people entering the workforce came to be called yuppies, slang for *young urban professionals*. These individuals were highly motivated by career prospects, sought employment with big corporations, and often were willing to make

AT YOUR SERVICE

The Rise of the Service Sector

Manufacturing is a form of business that combines and transforms resources into tangible outcomes that are then sold to others. Goodyear is a manufacturer because it combines rubber and chemical compounds and uses blending equipment and molding machines to create tires. Broyhill is a manufacturer because it buys wood and metal components, pads, and fabric and then combines them into furniture. And Apple is a manufacturer because it uses electronic, metal, plastic, and composite components to build smartphones, computers, and other digital products.

Manufacturing was once the dominant technology in the United States. During the 1970s, though, manufacturing entered a long period of decline, primarily because of foreign competition. U.S. firms had grown lax and sluggish, and new foreign competitors came onto the scene with better equipment and much higher levels of efficiency. For example, steel companies in Asia were able to produce high-quality steel for much lower prices than large U.S. steel companies such as Bethlehem Steel and U.S. Steel. Faced with a battle for survival, some companies disappeared, but many others underwent a long and difficult period of change by eliminating waste and transforming themselves into leaner, more efficient, and responsive entities. They reduced their workforces dramatically, closed antiquated or unnecessary plants, and modernized their remaining plants. Over the last decade or so, however, their efforts have started to pay dividends and U.S. manufacturing has regained a competitive position in many different industries. While low wages continue to center a great deal of global manufacturing in Asia, once-strong manufacturers are again thriving in the United States.

During the decline of the manufacturing sector, a tremendous growth in the service sector, often fueled by visionary entrepreneurs, kept the overall U.S. economy from declining at the same rate. A service organization is one that transforms resources into an intangible output and creates time or place utility for its customers. For example, Netflix provides video rentals through mail order and online delivery options. Facebook offers its members a venue for networking and interacting with others. And your local hairdresser cuts your hair. In 1947, the service sector was responsible for less than half of the U.S. gross national product (GNP). By 1975, however, this figure reached 65 percent, and by 2010 had surpassed 80 percent. The service sector has been responsible for almost 90 percent of all new jobs created in the United States since 1990. Moreover, according to the U.S. Bureau of Labor Statistics, employment in service occupations is expected to grow 26.8 percent between 2010 and 2020.

Managers have come to see that many of the tools, techniques, and methods that are used in a factory are also useful to a service firm. For example, managers of automobile plants and hair salons each have to decide how to design their facility, identify the best location for it, determine optimal capacity, make decisions about inventory storage, set procedures for purchasing raw materials, and set standards for productivity and quality. At the same time, though, service-based firms must hire and train employees based on a skill set that is different from that required by most manufacturers. For instance, consumers seldom come into contact with the Toyota employee who installs the seats in their car, so that person can be hired based on technical skills. But Toyota must also recruit people for sales and customer service jobs who not only know how to do a job but who can also effectively interface with a variety of consumers.

work their highest priority. Thus, they put in long hours and could be expected to remain loyal to the company, regardless of what happened.

But younger people entering the workforce over the past 20 to 30 years are frequently quite different from their parents and other older workers. Generation X, Generation Y, and the Millennials, as these groups are called, tend to be less devoted to long-term career prospects and less willing to adapt to a corporate mindset that stresses conformity and uniformity. Instead, they often seek work in smaller, more entrepreneurial firms that allow flexibility and individuality. They also place a premium on lifestyle preferences, often putting location high on their list of priorities when selecting an employer.

Thus, managers are increasingly faced with the challenge of, first, creating an environment that will be attractive to today's worker; and, second, addressing the challenge of providing new and different incentives to keep people motivated and interested in their work. They must build enough flexibility into the organization to accommodate an ever-changing set of lifestyles and preferences. And, of course, as these generations eventually move into top spots of major corporations, there may even be entirely new paradigms for managing that cannot be foreseen today.[50]

Managers must also be prepared to address organization change.[51] This has always been a concern, but the rapid, constant environmental change faced by businesses today has made change management even more critical. Simply put, an organization that fails to monitor its environment and to change to keep pace with that environment is doomed to failure. But more and more managers are seeing change as an opportunity, not a cause for alarm. Indeed, some managers think that if things get too calm in an organization and people start to become complacent, they should shake things up to get everyone energized.

New technology, especially as it relates to information, also poses an increasingly important challenge for managers. Communications advances such as smartphones and other wireless communication networks have made it easier than ever for managers to communicate with one another. Social media has also quickly established itself as a major force in all walks of contemporary life. At the same time, these innovations have increased the work pace for managers, cut into their time for thoughtful contemplation of decisions, and increased the amount of information they must process. Issues associated with employee privacy have also emerged. For instance, controversies have arisen when businesses take action against people for things they do in their personal lives—posting negative comments about their employer on Facebook, for example.

SUMMARY OF LEARNING OUTCOMES AND KEY POINTS

1. Define management, describe the kinds of managers found in organizations, identify and explain the four basic management functions, describe the fundamental management skills, and comment on management as a science and art.

   - Management is a set of activities (planning and decision making, organizing, leading, and controlling) directed at using an organization's resources (human, financial, physical, and information) to achieve organizational goals in an efficient and effective manner.
   - A manager is someone whose primary responsibility is to carry out the management process within an organization.
   - Managers can be classified by level: top managers, middle managers, and first-line managers.
   - Managers can also be classified by area: marketing, finances, operations, human resources, administration, and specialized.
   - The basic activities of the management process include planning and decision making (determining courses of action), organizing

   (coordinating activities and resources), leading (motivating and managing people), and controlling (monitoring and evaluating activities).
   - Effective managers also tend to have the following skills: technical, interpersonal, conceptual, diagnostic, communication, decision making, and time management.
   - The effective practice of management requires a synthesis of science and art: a blend of rational objectivity and intuitive insight.

2. Justify the importance of history and theory to managers, and explain the evolution of management thought through the classical, behavioral, and quantitative perspectives.

   - Understanding the historical context and precursors of management and organizations provides a sense of heritage and can also help managers avoid repeating the mistakes of others.
   - The classical management perspective, which paid little attention to the role of workers, had two major branches: scientific management

(concerned with improving efficiency and work methods for individual workers) and administrative management (concerned with how organizations themselves should be structured and arranged for efficient operations).

- The behavioral management perspective, characterized by a concern for individual and group behavior, emerged primarily as a result of the Hawthorne studies. The human relations movement recognized the importance and potential of behavioral processes in organizations but made many overly simplistic assumptions about those processes. Organizational behavior, a more realistic outgrowth of the behavioral perspective, is of interest to many contemporary managers.

- The quantitative management perspective, which attempts to apply quantitative techniques to decision making and problem solving, has two components: management science and operations management. These areas are also of con-

siderable importance to contemporary managers. Their contributions have been facilitated by the tremendous increase in the use of personal computers and integrated information networks.

3. Identify and discuss key contemporary management perspectives represented by the systems and contingency perspectives, and identify the major challenges and opportunities faced by managers today.

- Two relatively recent additions to management theory that can serve as frameworks for integrating the other perspectives are the systems perspective and the contingency perspective.

- The important issues and challenges that contemporary managers face include globalization, ethics and social responsibility, product and service quality, the service economy, the economic recession of 2008–2010, the new workplace, workforce diversity, organization change, and technology.

DISCUSSION QUESTIONS

Questions for Review

1. What three basic levels of management can be identified in most organizations? How precise are the lines differentiating these levels? In which of the basic areas do managers work?
2. What four basic functions make up the management process? How are they related to one another?
3. Identify several of the important skills that help managers succeed. Give an example of each. How might the importance of different skills vary by level and area within an organization?
4. Briefly describe the principles of scientific management and administrative management. What assumptions do these perspectives make about workers? To what extent are these assumptions still valid today?
5. Describe the systems perspective. Why is a business organization considered an open system?

Questions for Analysis

1. Recall a recent group project or task in which you have participated. Explain how members of the group displayed each of the managerial skills.

2. The text notes that management is both a science and an art. Recall an interaction you have had with someone at a higher level in an organization (manager, teacher, group leader, or the like). In that interaction, how did the individual use science? If he or she did not use science, what could have been done to use science? In that interaction, how did the individual use art? If she or he did not use art, what could have been done to use art?
3. Watch a movie that involves an organization of some type. *Harry Potter, Avatar, The Avengers, Flight,* and *Up in the Air* would all be good choices. Identify as many management activities and skills as you can.
4. Young, innovative, or high-tech firms often adopt the strategy of ignoring history or attempting to do something radically new. In what ways might this strategy help them? In what ways might this strategy hinder their efforts?
5. Can a manager use tools and techniques from several different perspectives at the same time? For example, can a manager use both classical and behavioral perspectives? Give an example of a time when a manager did this, and explain how it enabled him or her to be effective.

BUILDING EFFECTIVE TIME MANAGEMENT SKILLS

Exercise Overview

Time management skills refer to the ability to prioritize tasks, to work efficiently, and to delegate appropriately. This exercise allows you to assess your own current time management skills and to gather some suggestions for how you can improve in this area.

Exercise Background

As we saw in this chapter, effective managers must be prepared to switch back and forth among the four basic activities in the management process. They must also be able to fulfill a number of different roles in their organizations, and they must exercise various managerial skills in doing so. On top of everything else, their schedules are busy and full of tasks—personal and job-related activities that require them to "switch gears" frequently throughout the workday.

Stephen Covey, a management consultant and the author of *The 7 Habits of Highly Effective People*, has developed a system for prioritizing tasks. First, he divides them into two categories—urgent and critical. *Urgent* tasks, such as those with approaching deadlines, must be performed right away. *Critical* tasks are tasks of high importance—say, those that will affect significant areas of one's life or work. Next, Covey plots both types of tasks on a grid with four quadrants: A task may be *urgent*, *critical*, *urgent and critical*, or *not urgent and not critical.*

Most managers, says Covey, spend too much time on tasks that are *urgent* when in fact they should be focused on tasks that are *critical.* He observes, for example, that managers who concentrate on urgent tasks meet their deadlines but tend to neglect critical areas such as long-term planning. (Unfortunately, the same people are also prone to neglect critical areas of their personal lives.) In short, effective managers must learn to balance the demands of urgent tasks with those of critical tasks by redistributing the amount of time devoted to each type.

Exercise Task

1. Visit one of the websites of Franklin Covey (the firm cofounded by Stephen Covey) and locate a time management survey. If you cannot locate one associated with Franklin Covey, many others are available through a quick Internet search. Complete a survey that will provide you with a time management score.

2. Now spend some time interpreting your score, examine the assessment of your current use of time and the suggestions for how you can improve your time management. In what ways do you agree and disagree with your personal assessment? Explain your reasons for agreeing or disagreeing.

3. Think of a task that you regularly perform and that, if you were being perfectly honest, you could label *not urgent and not critical.* How much time do you spend on this task? What might be a more appropriate amount of time? To what other tasks could you give some of the time that you spend on this *not urgent and not critical* task?

4. What one thing can you do today to make better use of your time? Try it to see if your time management improves.

BUILDING EFFECTIVE DECISION-MAKING SKILLS

Exercise Overview

Decision-making skills include the ability to recognize and define problems or opportunities and then select the appropriate course of action. This exercise will help you develop your own decision-making skills while also underscoring the importance of subsystem interdependencies in organizations.

Exercise Background

You're the vice president of a large company that makes outdoor furniture for decks, patios, and pools. Each product line and the firm itself have grown substantially in recent years. Unfortunately, your success has attracted the attention of competitors, and several have entered the market in the last two years. Your CEO wants you to determine how to cut costs by 10 percent so that prices can be cut by the same amount. She's convinced that the move is necessary to retain market share in the face of new competition.

You've examined the situation and decided that you have three options for cutting costs:

• Begin buying slightly lower-grade materials, including hardwood, aluminum, vinyl, and nylon.

- Lay off a portion of your workforce and then try to motivate everyone who's left to work harder; this option also means selecting future hires from a lower-skill labor pool and paying lower wages.
- Replace existing equipment with newer, more efficient equipment; although this option entails substantial up-front investment, you're sure that you can more than make up the difference in lower production costs.

Exercise Task

With this background in mind, respond to the following questions:

1. Carefully examine each of your three options. In what ways might each option affect other parts of the organization?
2. Which is the most costly option in terms of impact on other parts of the organization, not in terms of absolute dollars? Which is the least costly?
3. What are the primary obstacles that you might face in trying to implement each of your three options?
4. Are there any other options for accomplishing your goal of reducing costs?

SKILLS SELF-ASSESSMENT INSTRUMENT

How Do I Rate as a Manager?*

This self-assessment will help you with your current understanding of the practice of management and your own approach to management. This assessment outlines four important functions of management: planning, organizing, leading, and controlling. You should respond to this in one of three ways:

(a) Respond based on your own managerial experience if you have any.
(b) Respond about effective (or ineffective) managers you have observed in your work experience.
(c) Respond in terms of how you think an ideal manager should behave.

Instructions: Recall a situation in which you were a member of a group or team that had a specific task or project to complete. This may have been at work, in a class, or in a church, club, or civic organization. Now assess your behavior in each of the functions. For each question, rate yourself according to the following scale:

Rating Scale

Insert your score from one of the following five options for each of the statements that follow.

- *5 Definitely true of me*
- *4 Probably true of me*
- *3 Neither true nor not true, or undecided*
- *2 Probably not true of me*
- *1 Definitely not true of me*

I. Planning

_____ 1. I prepare an agenda for meetings.

_____ 2. I try to anticipate what will happen in the future as a result of my current actions and decisions.

_____ 3. I establish clear goals for myself and others.

_____ 4. I carefully analyze the pros and cons involved in situations before reaching decisions.

_____ 5. I am quite willing to try new things, to experiment.

_____ 6. I have a clear vision for accomplishing the task at hand.

_____ 7. I put plans in writing so that others can know exactly what they are.

_____ 8. I try to remain flexible so that I can adapt to changing conditions.

_____ 9. I try to anticipate barriers to goal accomplishment and how to overcome them.

_____ 10. I discuss plans and involve others in arriving at those plans.

_____ **Section I Total**

II. Organizing

_____ 1. I try to follow the plan while working on the task.

_____ 2. I try to develop any understanding of the different steps or parts needed to accomplish the task at hand.

_____ 3. I evaluate different ways of working on the task before deciding on which course of action to follow.

_____ 4. I have a clear sense of the priorities necessary to accomplish the task.

_____ 5. I arrange for others to be informed about the degree of progress in accomplishing the task.

_____ 6. I am open to alternative, even novel, ways of working on the task.

_____ 7. I adapt the sequence of activities involved if circumstances change.

_____ 8. I have a clear sense of how the steps involved in accomplishing the task should be structured.

_____ 9. I lead or follow where appropriate to see to it that progress is made toward accomplishing the task.

_____ 10. I coordinate with others to assure steady progress on the task.

_____ **Section II Total**

III. Leading

_____ 1. I set an example for others to follow.

_____ 2. I am effective at motivating others.

_____ 3. I try to keep a balance between getting the work done and keeping a spirit of teamwork.

_____ 4. I try to handle conflict in nonthreatening, constructive ways.

_____ 5. I help others in the group and provide them with guidance and training to better perform their roles.

_____ 6. I am open to suggestions from others.

_____ 7. I keep everyone informed about the group's activities and progress.

_____ 8. I show a genuine interest in the work of others.

_____ 9. I am considerate when providing constructive suggestions to others.

_____ 10. I understand the needs of others and encourage their initiative in meeting those needs.

_____ **Section III Total**

IV. Controlling

_____ 1. I regularly assess the quantity and quality of progress on the task at hand.

_____ 2. I try to assure that the information I have is timely, accurate, complete, and relevant.

_____ 3. I routinely share information with others to help them accomplish their tasks.

_____ 4. I compare progress with plans and take corrective action as warranted.

_____ 5. I manage my time and help others to manage theirs.

_____ 6. I have good sources of information or methods for obtaining information.

_____ 7. I use technology (computers, tablets, smartphones, etc.) to aid in monitoring progress and communicating with others.

_____ 8. I anticipate possible negative reactions and take action to minimize them.

_____ 9. I recognize that fixing problems *before* they occur is better than fixing problems *after* they occur.

_____ 10. I try to balance my attention on the many different steps needed to accomplish the task at hand.

_____ **Section IV Total**

Source: Adapted from Van Fleet, D. D., Van Fleet, E. W., and Seperich, G. J. 2013. *Principles of Management for Agribusiness.* Clifton Park, NY: Delmar/Cengage Learning; Griffin, R. W. 2011. *Management.* Mason, OH: South-Western Cengage Learning; and Van Fleet, D. D. 1991. *Behavior in Organizations.* Boston: Houghton Mifflin, in collaboration with G. Moorhead and R. W. Griffin.

EXPERIENTIAL EXERCISE

Johari Window

Purpose: This exercise has two purposes: to encourage you to analyze yourself more accurately and to start you working on small-group cohesiveness. This exercise encourages you to share data about yourself and then to assimilate and process feedback. Small groups are typically more trusting and work better together, as you will be able to see after this exercise has been completed. The Johari Window is a particularly good model for understanding the perceptual process in interpersonal relationships.

My Own Perceptions

	Things I Know About Myself	Things I Do Not Know About Myself

Quadrant 1

"The Open Self"

Characteristics apparent to me and to others

_____

_____

_____

Quadrant 2

"The Blind Self"

Characteristics not apparent to me

_____

_____

_____

Quadrant 3

"The Concealed Self"

Characteristics known to me but kept hidden from others

_____

_____

_____

Quadrant 4

"The Unknown Self"

The Blind Area

Things Others Know About Me

Things Others Do Not Know About Me

Other Persons' Perceptions

© Cengage Learning

This skill builder focuses on the human resources model and will help you develop your mentor role. One of the skills of a mentor is self-awareness.

Introduction: Each individual has four sets of personality characteristics. One set, which includes such characteristics as working hard, is well known to the individual and to others. A second set is unknown to the individual but obvious to others. For example, in a working situation, a peer group might observe that your jumping in to move the group off dead center is appropriate. At other times, you jump in when the group is not really finished, and you seem to interrupt. A third set of personality characteristics is known to the individual but not to others. These are situations that you have elected not to share, perhaps because of a lack of trust. Finally, there is a fourth set, which is not known to the individual or to others, such as why you are uncomfortable at office parties.

Instructions: Look at the Johari Window. In quadrant 1, list three things that you know about yourself and that you think others know. List three things in quadrant 3 that others do not know about you. Finally, in quadrant 2, list three things that you did not know about yourself last semester that you learned from others.

*****Source:** Adapted from Joseph Luft, *Group Processes: An Introduction to Group Dynamics* (Palo Alto, CA: Mayfield, 1970), pp. 10–11; and William C. Morris and Marshall Sashkin, *Organizational Behavior in Action* (St. Paul, MN: West, 1976), p. 56.

MANAGEMENT AT WORK

Some Keys to Making a Steinway

Everybody knows what a grand piano looks like, although it's hard to describe its contour as anything other than "piano shaped." From a bird's-eye view, you might recognize something like a great big holster. The *case*—the curved lateral surface that runs around the whole instrument—appears to be a single continuous piece of wood, but it isn't really. If you look carefully at the case of a piano built by Steinway & Sons, you'll see that you're actually looking at a remarkable composite of raw material, craftsmanship, and technology. The process by which this component is made—like most of the processes for making a Steinway grand—is a prime example of a *technical*, or *task, subsystem* at work in a highly specialized factory.

The *case* starts out as a *rim*, which is constructed out of separate slats of wood, mostly maple (eastern rock maple, to be precise). Once raw boards have been cut and planed, they're glued along their lengthwise edges to the width of 12¹/₂ inches. These composite pieces are then jointed and glued end-to-end to form slats 22 feet long—the measure of the piano's perimeter. Next, a total of 18 separate slats—14 layers of maple and 4 layers of other types of wood—are glued and stacked together to form a *book*—one (seemingly) continuous "board" 3¹/₄ inches thick. Then comes the process that's a favorite of visitors on the Steinway factory tour—bending this rim into the shape of a piano. Steinway does it pretty much the same way that it has for more than a century—by hand and all at once. Because the special glue is in the process of drying, a crew of six has just 20 minutes to wrestle the book, with block and tackle and wooden levers and mallets, into a *rim-bending press*—"a giant piano-shaped vise," as Steinway describes it—which will force the wood to "forget" its natural inclination to be straight and assume the familiar contour of a grand piano.

Visitors report the sound of splintering wood, but Steinway artisans assure them that the specially cured wood isn't likely to break or the specially mixed glue to lose its grip. It's a good thing, too, both because the wood is expensive and because the precision Steinway process can't afford much wasted effort. The company needs 12 months, 12,000 parts, 450 craftspeople, and countless hours of skilled labor to produce a grand piano. Today, the New York factory turns out about 10 pianos in a day or 2,500 a year. (A mass producer might build 2,000 pianos a week.) The result of this painstaking task system, according to one business journalist with a good ear, is "both impossibly perfect instruments and a scarcity," and that's why Steinways are so expensive—currently, somewhere between $45,000 and $110,000.

But Steinway pianos, the company reminds potential buyers, have always been "built to a standard, not to a price." "It's a product," says company executive Leo F. Spellman, "that in some sense speaks to people and will have a legacy long after we're gone. What [Steinway] craftsmen work on today will be here for another 50 or 100 years." Approximately 90 percent of all concert

pianists prefer the sound of a Steinway, and the company's attention to manufacturing detail reflects the fact that when a piano is being played, the entire instrument vibrates—and thus affects its sound. In other words—and not surprisingly—the better the raw materials, design, and construction, the better the sound.

That's one of the reasons Steinway craftsmen put so much care into the construction of the piano's case: It's a major factor in the way the body of the instrument resonates. The maple wood for the case, for example, arrives at the factory with water content of 80 percent. It's then dried, both in the open air and in kilns, until the water content is reduced to about 10 percent —suitable for both strength and pliability. To ensure that strength and pliability remain stable, the slats must be cut so that they're horizontally grained and arranged, with the "inside" of one slat—the side that grew toward the center of the tree—facing the "outside" of the next one in the book. The case is removed from the press after one day and then stored for ten weeks in a humidity-controlled *rim-bending room*. Afterward, it's ready to be sawed, planed, and sanded to specification—a process called *frazing*. A black lacquer finish is added, and only then is the case ready to be installed as a component of a grand piano in progress.

The Steinway process also puts a premium on skilled workers. Steinway has always been an employer of immigrant labor, beginning with the German craftsmen and laborers hired by founder Henry Steinway in the 1860s and 1870s. Today, Steinway employees come from much different places—Haitians and Dominicans in the 1980s, exiles from war-torn Yugoslavia in the 1990s—and it still takes time to train them. It takes about a year, for instance, to train a case maker, and "when you lose one of them for a long period of time," says Gino Romano, a senior supervisor hired in 1964, "it has a serious effect on our output." Romano recalls one year in mid-June when a case maker was injured in a car accident and was out for several weeks. His department fell behind schedule, and it was September before Romano could find a suitable replacement (an experienced case maker in Florida who happened to be a relative of another Steinway worker).

The company's employees don't necessarily share Spellman's sense of the company's legacy, but many of them are well aware of the brand recognition commanded by the products they craft, according to Romano:

"The payback is not in [the factory]. The payback is outside, when you get the celebrity treatment for

building a Steinway, when you meet somebody for the first time and they ooh and ahh: 'You build Steinways? Wow.' You're automatically put on a higher level, and you go, 'I didn't realize I was that notable.'"

Case Questions

1. Explain the process by which a Steinway grand piano is constructed as a *subsystem* of a larger *system*. From what the text tells you, give some examples of how the production subsystem is affected by the management, financial, and marketing subsystems.

2. Discuss the Steinway process in terms of the *systems perspective* of organizations summarized in Figure 1.4. Explain the role of each of the three elements highlighted by the figure—*inputs from the environment*, the *transformation process*, and *outputs into the environment*.

3. Discuss some of the ways the principles of *behavioral management* and *operations management* can throw light on the Steinway process. How about the *contingency perspective*? In what ways does the Steinway process reflect a *universal perspective*, and in what ways does it reflect a *contingency perspective*?

Case References

Steinway & Sons, "The Steinway Restoration Center," www.steinway.com, accessed on July 27, 2013; Steinway & Sons, "Online Factory Tour," http://www.steinway.com, accessed on July 27, 2013; WGBH (Boston), "Note by Note: The Making of Steinway L1037," www.wgbh.org, accessed on July 27, 2013; Maya Roney, "Steinway: Worth Much More Than a Song," *BusinessWeek*, www.businessweek.com, accessed on July 27, 2013; James Barron, "88 Keys, Many Languages, One Proud Name," *New York Times*, www.nytimes.com, accessed on July 27, 2013; Michael Lenehen, "K 2571: The Making of a Steinway Grand," *Atlantic Monthly*, August 1982, www.sherwinbeach.com, accessed on July 27, 2013; and Rick Rogers, "Steinway Builds a Legacy with Distinctive Pianos," *Daily Oklahoman* (Oklahoma City), www.richardhuggins.com, accessed on July 27, 2013.

You Make the Call

Reed Hastings Doesn't Like Standing Still

1. You're a Netflix employee, and Reed Hastings has just stopped by your desk. "I'd like to know," he says, "what you like most and least about working here." How do you think you might respond?

2. You're a major Netflix stockholder attending the firm's annual board meeting. When you bump into Reed Hastings at a reception, he asks you, "How do you think we're doing with this company?" How would you respond?

3. You're the founder and owner of a small media company, and Netflix has indicated an interest in buying your business. In addition to price, what other factors (if any) are important to you?

4. You've been contacted by a marketing research company doing work for Netflix. The researcher asks if you use Netflix and, if not, why? If you do use Netflix, the researcher asks what you like and dislike most about it. What would you say?

ENDNOTES

1 "How Netflix Got Started," *CNNMoney.com*, January 28, 2009, http://money.cnn.com on July 25, 2013; Reed Hastings, "How I Did It: Reed Hastings, Netflix," *Inc.com*, December 1, 2005, www.inc.com on July 25, 2013; Sally Aaron, "Netflix Script Spells Disruption," *Harvard Business School Working Knowledge*, March 22, 2004, http://hbswk.hbs.edu on July 25, 2013; John M. Caddell, "Frontiers of Innovation—Netflix Demolishes Its Own Business Model," *PennLive.com*, February 11, 2009, http://blog.pennlive.com on July 25, 2013; "Netflix Subscriber Loss Triggers Panic Selling," *CBSNews.com*, October 24, 2011, www.cbsnews.com on July 25, 2013; Andrew Goldman, "Reed

Hastings Knows He Messed Up," *New York Times*, October 20, 2011, www.nytimes.com on July 25, 2013; "The Man Who Ate the Internet," *Bloomberg BusinessWeek*, May 13, 2013–May 19, 2013, pp. 56–62.

2 Fred Luthans, "Successful vs. Effective Real Managers," *Academy of Management Executive*, May 1988, Vol. 2, No. 2, pp. 127–132. See also "The Best Performers," *BusinessWeek*, Special Issue, Spring 2012, pp. 38–49.

3 See "The Best (& Worst) Managers of the Year," *Bloomberg Businessweek*, January 10, 2013, pp. 68–74; see also "Two Days

With a Tech Titan on a Mission," *USA Today*, January 10, 2013, pp. 1B, 2B.

4 See "Executive Compensation for 50 of the Largest U.S. Companies," *USA Today*, March 28, 2013, p. 2B. See also Jim Collins, "The Ten Greatest CEOs of All Times," *Fortune*, July 21, 2003, pp. 54–68.

5 "Executive Compensation for 50 of the Largest U.S. Companies," *USA Today*, March 28, 2013, p. 2B.

6 Rosabeth Moss Kanter, "The Middle Manager as Innovator," *Harvard Business Review*, July–August 2004, pp. 150–161; and Bill Woolridge, Torsten Schmid, and Steven W. Floyd, "The Middle Management Perspective on Strategy Process: Contributions, Synthesis, and Future Research," *Journal of Management*, 2008, Vol. 34, No. 6, pp. 1190–1221.

7 John P. Kotter, "What Effective General Managers Really Do," *Harvard Business Review*, March–April 1999, pp. 145–155. See also Peter Drucker, "What Makes an Effective Executive," *Harvard Business Review*, June 2004, pp. 58–68.

8 For a classic discussion of several of these skills, see Robert L. Katz, "The Skills of an Effective Administrator," *Harvard Business Review*, September–October 1974, pp. 90–102. For a recent perspective, see J. Brian Atwater, Vijay R. Kannan, and Alan A. Stephens, "Cultivating Systemic Thinking in the Next Generation of Business Leaders," *Academy of Management Learning & Education*, 2008, Vol. 7, No. 1, pp. 9–25. See also Ricky W. Griffin and David D. Van Fleet, *Building Management Skills* (Mason, OH: Cengage, 2013).

9 For an interesting application, see Mark Gottfredson, Steve Schaubert, and Hernan Saenz, "The New Leader's Guide to Diagnosing the Business," *Harvard Business Review*, February 2008, pp. 63–72.

10 See "The Real Reasons You're Working So Hard … and What You Can Do about It," *BusinessWeek*, October 3, 2005, pp. 60–68; and "I'm Late, I'm Late, I'm Late," *USA Today*, November 26, 2002, pp. 1B, 2B.

11 For a thorough discussion of the importance of time management skills, see David Barry, Catherine Durnell Cramton, and Stephen J. Carroll, "Navigating the Garbage Can: How Agendas Help Managers Cope with Job Realities," *Academy of Management Executive*, May 1997, pp. 26–42.

12 Gary Hamel and C. K. Prahalad, "Competing for the Future," *Harvard Business Review*, July–August 1994, pp. 122–128; see also Joseph M. Hall and M. Eric Johnson, "When Should a Process Be Art, Not Science?" *Harvard Business Review*, March 2009, pp. 58–65.

13 "Starbucks' Big Mug," *Time*, June 25, 2012, pp. 53–54; "Starbucks CEO Reinvents The Spiel," *USA Today*, April 25, 2013, p. 3B.

14 "Grounds Zero," *Bloomberg BusinessWeek*, February 9, 2012, pp. 69–71.

15 Terence Mitchell and Lawrence James, "Building Better Theory: Time and the Specification of When Things Happen," *Academy of Management Review*, 2001, Vol. 26, No. 4, pp. 530–547.

16 Peter F. Drucker, "The Theory of the Business," *Harvard Business Review*, September–October 1994, pp. 95–104.

17 "Why Business History?" *Audacity*, Fall 1992, pp. 7–15. See also Alan L. Wilkins and Nigel J. Bristow, "For Successful Organization Culture, Honor Your Past," *Academy of Management Executive*, August 1987, Vol. 1, No. 3, pp. 221–227.

18 Daniel Wren, *The Evolution of Management Thought*, 5th ed. (New York: Wiley, 2005); and Page Smith, *The Rise of Industrial America* (New York: McGraw-Hill, 1984).

19 Martha I. Finney, "Books That Changed Careers," *HR Magazine*, June 1997, pp. 141–145. See also "Leadership in Literature," *Harvard Business Review*, March 2006, pp. 47–55.

20 See Harriet Rubin, *The Princessa: Machiavelli for Women* (New York: Doubleday/Currency, 1997). See also Nanette Fondas, "Feminization Unveiled: Management Qualities in Contemporary Writings," *Academy of Management Review*, January 1997, Vol. 22, No. 1, pp. 257–282.

21 Alan M. Kantrow, ed., "Why History Matters to Managers," *Harvard Business Review*, January–February 1986, pp. 81–88.

22 Wren, *The Evolution of Management Thought*.

23 Wren, *The Evolution of Management Thought*.

24 Frederick W. Taylor, *Principles of Scientific Management* (New York: Harper and Brothers, 1911).

25 Charles D. Wrege and Amedeo G. Perroni, "Taylor's Pig-Tale: A Historical Analysis of Frederick W. Taylor's Pig-Iron Experiment," *Academy of Management Journal*, March 1974, Vol. 17, No. 1, pp. 6–27; and Charles D. Wrege and Ann Marie Stoka, "Cooke Creates a Classic: The Story behind F.W. Taylor's Principles of Scientific Management," *Academy of Management Review*, October 1978, Vol. 3, No. 4, pp. 736–749.

26 Robert Kanigel, *The One Best Way* (New York: Viking, 1997); Oliver E. Allen, "'This Great Mental Revolution,'" *Audacity*, Summer 1996, pp. 52–61; and Jill Hough and Margaret White, "Using Stories to Create Change: The Object Lesson of Frederick Taylor's 'Pig-Tale,'" *Journal of Management*, 2001, Vol. 27, pp. 585–601.

27 Henri Fayol, *General and Industrial Management*, trans. J. A. Coubrough (Geneva: International Management Institute, 1930).

28 Max Weber, *Theory of Social and Economic Organizations*, trans. T. Parsons (New York: Free Press, 1947); and Richard M. Weis, "Weber on Bureaucracy: Management Consultant or Political Theorist?" *Academy of Management Review*, April 1983, Vol. 8, No. 2, pp. 242–248.

29 "The Line Starts Here," *Wall Street Journal*, January 11, 1999, pp. R1, R25.

30 Hugo Munsterberg, *Psychology and Industrial Efficiency* (Boston: Houghton Mifflin, 1913).

31 Wren, *The Evolution of Management Thought*, pp. 255–264.

32 Elton Mayo, *The Human Problems of an Industrial Civilization* (New York: Macmillan, 1933); and Fritz J. Roethlisberger and William J. Dickson, *Management and the Worker* (Cambridge, MA: Harvard University Press, 1939).

33 Abraham Maslow, "A Theory of Human Motivation," *Psychological Review*, July 1943, pp. 370–396.

34 Douglas McGregor, *The Human Side of Enterprise* (New York: McGraw-Hill, 1960).

35 Sara L. Rynes and Christine Quinn Trank, "Behavioral Science in the Business School Curriculum: Teaching in a Changing Institutional Environment," *Academy of Management Review*, 1999, Vol. 24, No. 4, pp. 808–824.

36 See Ricky W. Griffin and Gregory Moorhead, *Organizational Behavior*, 11th ed. (Cincinnati, OH: Cengage, 2013), for a recent review of current developments in the field of organizational behavior.

[37] Wren, *The Evolution of Management Thought*, pp. 255–264.

[38] "Math Will Rock Your World," *BusinessWeek*, January 23, 2006, pp. 54–61.

[39] "Quantitative Analysis Offers Tools to Predict Likely Terrorist Moves," *Wall Street Journal*, February 17, 2006, p. B1.

[40] For more information on systems theory in general, see Ludwig von Bertalanffy, C. G. Hempel, R. E. Bass, and H. Jonas, "General Systems Theory: A New Approach to Unity of Science," I–VI *Human Biology*, 1951, Vol. 23, pp. 302–361. For systems theory as applied to organizations, see Fremont E. Kast and James E. Rosenzweig, "General Systems Theory: Applications for Organizations and Management," *Academy of Management Journal*, December 1972, pp. 447–465. For a recent update, see Donde P. Ashmos and George P. Huber, "The Systems Paradigm in Organization Theory: Correcting the Record and Suggesting the Future," *Academy of Management Review*, October 1987, pp. 607–621.

[41] See Robert S. Kaplan and David P. Norton, "Mastering the Management System," *Harvard Business Review*, January 2008, pp. 63–72.

[42] "Gillette's New Edge," *BusinessWeek*, February 6, 2006, p. 44.

[43] Kathleen M. Eisenhardt and D. Charles Galunic, "Coevolving—At Last, a Way to Make Synergies Work," *Harvard Business Review*, January–February 2000, pp. 91–103.

[44] Fremont E. Kastand James E. Rosenzweig, *Contingency Views of Organization and Management* (Chicago: Science Research Associates, 1973).

[45] "There Is No More Normal," *BusinessWeek*, March 23–30, 2009, pp. 30–34.

[46] "The BusinessWeek Best-Seller List," *BusinessWeek*, November 4, 2002, p. 26.

[47] See Phanish Puranam and Bart S. Vanneste, "Trust and Governance: Untangling a Tangled Web," *Academy of Management Review*, January 2009, Vol. 34, No. 1, pp. 11–31.

[48] "The Way We'll Work," *Time*, May 25, 2009, pp. 39–51.

[49] Patricia L. Nemetz and Sandra L. Christensen, "The Challenge of Cultural Diversity: Harnessing a Diversity of Views to Understand Multiculturalism," *Academy of Management Review*, 1996, Vol. 21, No. 2, pp. 434–462; and Frances J. Milliken and Luis L. Martins, "Searching for Common Threads: Understanding the Multiple Effects of Diversity in Organizational Groups," *Academy of Management Review*, 1996, Vol. 21, No. 2, pp. 402–433.

[50] "When Gen X Runs the Show," *Time*, May 25, 2009, p. 48.

[51] Craig L. Pearce and Charles P. Osmond, "Metaphors for Change: The ALPS Model of Change Management," *Organizational Dynamics*, Winter 1996, pp. 23–35.

CHAPTER 2

The Environments of Organizations and Managers

Sergii Tsololo/Photos.com

Learning Outcomes

After studying this chapter, you should be able to:

1. Discuss the nature of an organization's environments and identify the components of its general, task, and internal environments.

2. Describe the ethical and social environment of management, including individual ethics, the concept of social responsibility, and how organizations can manage social responsibility.

3. Discuss the international environment of management, including trends in international business, levels of international business activities, and the context of international business.

4. Describe the importance and determinants of an organization's culture, as well as how organizational culture can be managed.

Social Entrepreneurship at Its Finest

"We function much as venture capitalists do in the private sector. You could say we're social VCs."

—Neal Keny-Guyer, CEO of Mercy Corps

In the aftermath of the devastating earthquake that struck the island nation of Haiti in January 2010, Oregon-based Mercy Corps arrived with a team of emergency-response experts from around the world. Focusing on immediate humanitarian needs, the team delivered food to overwhelmed hospitals and set up services to provide clean water. Mercy Corps also initiated a work-for-cash program that paid survivors to aid in clearing debris and restoring buildings, thus providing them with a little dignity along with the means to purchase supplies for their families and jumpstart the local economy. In addition, the organization set up trauma centers for children, using counseling methods that it had helped to develop in the wake of the 9/11 terrorist attacks in New York City eight years earlier. Similarly, following the devastating earthquake and tsunami that struck Japan in March 2011, Mercy Corps delivered emergency supplies and set up such programs as Comfort for Kids to help children deal with the emotional effects of a large-scale disaster.

Obviously, Mercy Corps isn't a newcomer to the enterprise of providing humanitarian aid. Founded in 1979 as the Save the Refugees Fund, a task force to help victims of famine and genocide in Cambodia, it expanded in 1982, becoming Mercy Corps International to reflect its broader mission. Since its

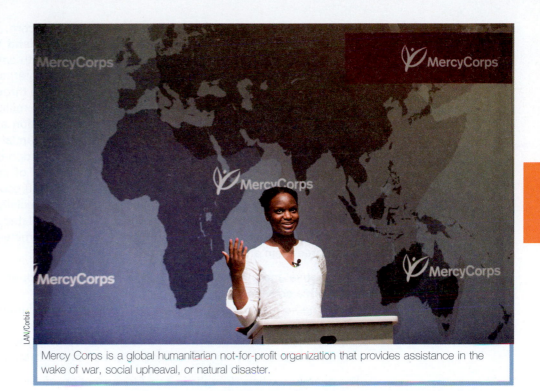

Mercy Corps is a global humanitarian not-for-profit organization that provides assistance in the wake of war, social upheaval, or natural disaster.

founding, the nonprofit organization has provided $2.2 billion in humanitarian aid and development assistance to people in 114 countries and annually reaches nearly 19 million people in 36 nations.

Mercy Corps' approach to on-the-ground assistance also involves more than immediate-response and emergency-relief services, as noted in its mission statement:

> Mercy Corps has learned that communities recovering from war or social upheaval must be the agents of their own transformation for change to endure. It's only when communities set their own agendas, raise their own resources, and implement programs themselves that the first successes result in the renewed hope, confidence, and skills to continue their development independently.

Mercy Corps thus works to foster "sustainable community development that integrates agriculture, health, housing and infrastructure, economic development, education, and environment and local management," as well as launching "initiatives that promote citizen participation, accountability, conflict management, and the rule of law." In India, for example, Mercy Corps has taught small-scale tea farmers sustainable ways to grow organic teas and get fair prices for them. On plantations owned by big tea companies, it's helped not only to improve living and economic conditions in worker villages but also to form self-governing Community Initiative Groups to manage ongoing community needs in education, infrastructure, and employment. In southern Sudan, which has been torn by Africa's longest civil war, Mercy Corps has built networks of local organizations to provide such essential services as adult literacy, orphan care, and HIV/AIDS counseling; other programs have helped to build roads and community centers and to electrify villages.

In Indonesia, where sanitation is a major area of concern, Mercy Corps has launched a long-term Hygiene Promotion Program. On Hand Washing Day, for instance, community representatives take to the streets with colorful buckets and teach children how to wash their hands with soap and water; similarly equipped hand-washing stations have been set up in neighborhoods throughout the capital of Djakarta. (Dirty hands can cause diarrhea, which kills 2 million children under the age of 5 every year.) Other programs focus on education and equipment for harvesting rainwater and removing solid waste from residential neighborhoods.

In addition to the devastating effects of war, social upheaval, and natural disaster, Mercy Corps is also concerned with the effects of climate change on developing communities. Thus, it works to provide "viable economic options as communities adapt to new environmental realities," especially in helping poor communities cope with "the rising incidence of climate-related disasters such as flooding and drought." According to Mercy Corps, its climate-related programs fall into three main areas:

1. *Alternative energy:* promoting energy sources that support sustainable economic activities
2. *Sustainable resource management:* supporting a community's ability to provide its own environmental and ecological services
3. *Advocacy, outreach, and models that work:* inspiring governments and communities to rely on proven environment- and climate-friendly programs

For example, when drought in the African nation of Niger threatened nearly 8 million people with malnutrition and starvation, Mercy Corps not only mobilized efforts to provide food commodities but also helped local farmers deal with chronic debt arising from inefficient methods and prior crop failures. A year later, Mercy Corps responded when Timor-Leste, an island nation northwest of Australia, faced just the opposite in climate-related crises: Because seasonal rains continued throughout the dry season, when farmers planted and harvested the country's food supply, drainage systems failed and crops could not be delivered over impassable roads. In addition to providing immediate relief, Mercy Corps trained local blacksmiths to make portable silos for storing rice and corn, the country's main staples.[1]

Organizations exist for a variety of reasons. Some, like Netflix, pursue profits, while others, like Mercy Corps, promote the general social welfare. Regardless of its purpose or mission, though, any organization must be properly aligned with its environment if it is to be effective. But there are disparate views on how this alignment should be achieved and how an organization can legitimately pursue and then use revenues or profits. Some companies aggressively seek to maximize their profits, grow at any cost, and focus on nothing but what is best for the company. Others take a much different approach to business and actively work for the betterment of society, even when it means less profit for the owners. Clearly, then, the environmental context of business today is changing in unprecedented ways.

THE ORGANIZATION'S ENVIRONMENTS

The **external environment** is everything outside an organization's boundaries that might affect it. There are two separate external environments: the **general environment** and the **task environment**. An organization's **internal environment** consists of conditions and forces within the organization.

The General Environment

Each of the following dimensions embodies conditions and events that have the potential to influence the organization in significant ways.

The Economic Dimension   The **economic dimension** of an organization's general environment is the overall health and vitality of the economic system in which the organization operates.[2] Particularly important economic factors for business are general economic growth, inflation, interest rates, and unemployment. After several strong years of growth, the U.S. economy fell into a recession during 2008 and only began to recover from it in 2012. During this period, energy and related prices jumped, business and economic growth slowed dramatically, and unemployment mushroomed as one struggling business after another made workforce cuts.

As one specific example, in 2014, McDonald's U.S. operation was functioning in an economy characterized by weak growth, moderate unemployment, and low inflation. These conditions produce paradoxical problems. Moderate unemployment means that fewer people can eat out, but those who do are looking for inexpensive options—like McDonald's. McDonald's can also pay lower wages to attract new employees, since many people are looking for work and fewer opportunities are available than was the case a few years earlier. Similarly, low inflation means that the prices McDonald's must pay for its supplies remain relatively constant, but it also is somewhat constrained from increasing the prices it charges consumers for a hamburger or milkshake. The economic dimension is also important to nonbusiness organizations. For example, during weak economic conditions, funding for state universities may drop, and charitable organizations such as the Salvation Army are asked to provide greater assistance at the same time that their incoming contributions dwindle. Similarly, hospitals are affected by the availability of government grants and the number of low-income patients they must treat free of charge. The economic dimension of the general environment is discussed more fully in the "Tough Times, Tough Choices" feature.

The Technological Dimension   The **technological dimension** of the general environment is made up of the methods available for converting resources into products or services. Although technology is applied within the organization, the forms and availability of that technology come from the general environment. Computer-assisted manufacturing and design techniques, for example, allowed Boeing to simulate the more than three miles of hydraulic tubing that runs through its 787 aircraft. The results include decreased warehouse needs, higher-quality tube fittings, lower labor costs, and major time savings. Although some people associate technology with manufacturing firms, it is also relevant in the service sector. For example, just as an automobile follows a predetermined path along an assembly line as it is built, a hamburger at McDonald's follows a predefined path as the meat is cooked, the burger assembled, and the finished product wrapped and bagged for a customer. The rapid infusion of the Internet and web-based technologies into all areas of business also reflects the technological dimension. Another recent advancement is the rapid growth of integrated business software systems. New modes of communication, ranging from social network sites like Facebook

external environment
Everything outside an organization's boundaries that might affect it

general environment
The set of broad dimensions and forces in an organization's surroundings that determines its overall context

task environment
Specific organizations or groups that affect the organization

internal environment
The conditions and forces within an organization

economic dimension
The overall health and vitality of the economic system in which the organization operates

technological dimension
The methods available for converting resources into products or services

TOUGH TIMES, TOUGH CHOICES

What Goes Around ...

It seems like just yesterday. In 2005, the global economy was booming. In the United States, for example, business profits were soaring, jobs were plentiful, and home ownership was at an all-time high. The stock market reached unprecedented highs, pension plans were burgeoning, and new business opportunities were plentiful.

Fast-forward just five short years to 2010, and things looked a lot different. Business profits were down, hundreds of thousands of jobs had been lost, unemployment claims soared, and mortgage foreclosures were the order of the day. The stock market plummeted, pension plans went broke, and it seemed like no one wanted to start a new business (and even those who did had a hard time getting financing).

What happened in this short period of time? Economists call it the *business cycle*. Historically, our economy has followed long periods of growth and prosperity with periods of cutbacks and retreats. And that's what started in 2008. During extended periods of prosperity, people sometimes start to act as though good times will last forever. They continue to bid up stock prices, for instance, far beyond rational value. They also take on too much debt, save too little money, and spend beyond their means. Businesses, too, start taking more risks,

carrying larger inventories, expanding too quickly, and hiring too many people. But things have a way of correcting themselves, and that's what happened when our economy went into recession beginning in 2008.

So what does the future hold? Well, while no one has a real crystal ball, most experts agree that the bad times have likely run their course and things will start looking up again. Indeed, by mid-2011, the stock market was inching back up, continued to slowly recover throughout 2012, and hit an all-time high in early 2013. By 2014, many firms were hiring again, interest rates began to inch up, and profits started to grow again. The housing market continues to improve, and unemployment is gradually declining, with many businesses cautiously hiring again. It may take a while longer for growth to really take off again, but one day profits will again start to surge, businesses will embark on even more ambitious hiring plans, the stock market will continue to soar, and business opportunities will again be plentiful. Until then, though, managers have to focus on following core business principles and do their best to steer their organizations through today's turbulence. And they should try to remember, of course, that even when the good times are rolling again, another correction will occur somewhere down the road.

and Twitter to hardware like smartphones and the iPad, are also influencing businesses in many different ways.

political–legal dimension

The government regulation of business and the relationship between business and government

The Political–Legal Dimension   The **political–legal dimension** of the general environment consists of government regulation of business and the relationship between business and government. This dimension is important for three basic reasons. First, the legal system partially defines what an organization can and cannot do. Although the United States is basically a free-market economy, major regulation of business activity still exits. McDonald's, for example, is subject to a variety of political and legal forces, including food preparation standards and local zoning requirements.

Second, pro- or anti-business sentiment in government influences business activity. For example, during periods of pro-business sentiment, firms find it easier to compete and have fewer concerns about antitrust issues. On the other hand, during a period of anti-business sentiment, firms may find their competitive strategies more restricted and have fewer opportunities for mergers and acquisitions because of antitrust concerns. During the prolonged period of economic growth that ended in 2008, the U.S. government adopted a very "hands-off" approach to business, letting market forces determine business successes and failures. However, as the economy ground to a halt in 2008, and first one and then another industry began to stumble, critics began to point to lack of regulation and oversight as contributing factors. As a result, lawmakers began to take a much more pronounced interest in adopting new and stricter regulations for business.[3]

Finally, political stability has ramifications for planning. No business wants to set up shop in another country unless trade relationships with that country are relatively well defined and stable. Hence, U.S. firms are more likely to do business in England, Mexico, and Canada than in Syria and Afghanistan. Similar issues are relevant to assessments of local and state governments. A new mayor or governor can affect many organizations, especially small firms that do business in only one location and are susceptible to deed and zoning restrictions, property and school taxes, and the like.

The Task Environment

competitor
An organization that competes with other organizations for resources

Because the general environment's impact is often vague, imprecise, and long term, most organizations tend to focus attention on their task environment, which includes competitors, customers, suppliers, strategic partners, and regulators. Although the task environment is also quite complex, it provides useful information more readily than the general environment because the manager can identify environmental factors of specific interest to the organization, rather than deal with the more abstract dimensions of the general environment.[4] Figure 2.1 depicts the task environment of McDonald's.

customer
Whoever pays money to acquire an organization's products or services

Competitors   An organization's **competitors** are other organizations that compete with it for resources. The most obvious resources that competitors vie for are customer dollars. Under Armour, Adidas, and Nike are competitors, as are Albertson's, Safeway, and Kroger. McDonald's competes with other fast-food operations, such as Burger King, Wendy's, Subway, and Dairy Queen; it's also taken on Starbucks with its McCafe line of premium coffee products. But competition also occurs among substitute products. Thus, Ford competes with Yamaha (motorcycles), Schwinn (bicycles), and various public transportation systems for your transportation dollars; and Walt Disney World, Carnival Cruise Lines, and the National Park System compete for your vacation dollars. Nor is competition limited to business firms. Universities compete with trade schools, the military, other universities, and the external labor market to attract good students; and art galleries compete with one another to attract the best collections and exhibits.

supplier
An organization that provides resources for other organizations

J.P. MOCZULSKI/AFP/Newscom

Organizations can serve a variety of different kinds of customers. For example, customers can be individuals, the government, or other businesses. This pizza deliveryman, for example, is dropping off pizzas for the staff of a hospital emergency room.

Customers   A second dimension of the task environment is **customers**, or whoever pays money to acquire an organization's products or services. Most McDonald's customers are individuals who buy food. But customers need not be individuals. Schools, hospitals, government agencies, wholesalers, retailers, and manufacturers are just a few of the many kinds of organizations that may be major customers of other organizations. Some institutional customers, such as schools, prisons, and hospitals, also buy food in bulk from restaurants such as McDonald's.

Supplier   **Suppliers** are organizations that provide resources for other organizations. McDonald's buys soft-drink products from Coca-Cola; individually packaged servings of ketchup, salt, and pepper from various wholesalers; Big Mac ingredients from wholesale food processors; and napkins, sacks, and wrappers from packaging manufacturers. Besides material resources such as these, businesses also rely on suppliers for information (such as economic statistics), labor (in the form of employment agencies), and capital (from lenders such as banks). Some businesses strive to avoid depending exclusively on particular suppliers. Others, however, find it beneficial to create strong relationships with single suppliers.

regulator
A body that has the potential to control, legislate, or otherwise influence the organization's policies and practices

Regulators   **Regulators** are elements of the task environment that have the potential to control, legislate, or otherwise influence an organization's policies and practices. There are two important kinds of regulators. **Regulatory agencies** are created by the government to protect the public from certain business practices or to protect organizations from one another. Powerful federal regulatory agencies include the Environmental Protection Agency (EPA), the Securities and Exchange Commission (SEC), the Food and Drug Administration (FDA), and the Equal Employment Opportunity Commission (EEOC). Many of these agencies play important roles in protecting the rights of individuals. The FDA, for example, helps ensure that food is free from contaminants; thus, it is an important regulator for McDonald's and Starbucks. Numerous state, regional, and local regulatory agencies also affect businesses. Perhaps it is no surprise that some managers complain that there is too much government regulation. Most large companies must dedicate thousands of labor hours and hundreds of thousands of dollars a year to complying with government regulations. To complicate managers' lives even more, different regulatory agencies sometimes provide inconsistent—and even contradictory—mandates.

regulatory agency
An agency created by the government to regulate business activities

interest group
A group organized by its members to attempt to influence organizations

The other basic form of regulator is the **interest group**. Prominent interest groups include the National Organization for Women (NOW), Mothers Against Drunk Driving (MADD), the National Rifle Association (NRA), the League of Women Voters, the Sierra Club, Ralph Nader's Center for the Study of Responsive Law, Consumers Union, and industry self-regulation groups such as the Council of Better Business Bureaus. Although interest groups lack the official power of government agencies, they can exert considerable influence by using the media to call attention to their positions. MADD, for example, puts considerable pressure on alcoholic-beverage producers (to put warning labels on their products), automobile companies (to make it more difficult for intoxicated people to start their cars), local governments (to stiffen drinking ordinances), and bars and restaurants (to refuse to sell alcohol to people who are drinking too much).

strategic partners (also called strategic ally)
An organization working together with one or more other organizations in a joint venture or similar arrangement

Strategic Partners   Another dimension of the task environment is **strategic partners** (also called *strategic allies*)—two or more companies that work together in joint ventures or other partnerships.[5] As shown in Figure 2.1, McDonald's has several strategic partners. For example, it has one arrangement with Walmart whereby small McDonald's restaurants are built in many Walmart stores. The firm also has a long-term deal with Disney: McDonald's promotes Disney movies in its stores, and Disney has allowed McDonald's to open restaurants near its resorts. And many of the firm's foreign stores are built in collaboration with local investors. Strategic partnerships help companies get the expertise they lack from other companies. The partnerships also help spread risk and open new market opportunities. Indeed, most strategic partnerships are among international firms. For example, Ford has strategic partnerships with Volkswagen (sharing a distribution and service center in South America) and Nissan (building minivans in the United States). Even bitter rivals Ford and General Motors are working together as strategic partners designing a new 10-speed transmission.[6]

© Cengage Learning

■ Internal environment

■ Task environment

McDonald's Task Environment

An organization's task environment includes its competitors, customers, suppliers, strategic partners, and regulators. This figure clearly highlights how managers at McDonald's can use this framework to identify and understand their key constituents.

The Internal Environment

Organizations also have an internal environment that consists of their owners, board of directors, employees, and physical work environment. (Another especially important part of the internal environment is the organization's culture, discussed separately later in this chapter.)

owners
Whoever can claim property rights to an organization

Owners   The **owners** of a business are, of course, the people who have legal property rights to that business. Owners can be a single individual who establishes and runs a small business, partners who jointly own the business, individual investors who buy stock in a corporation, or other organizations. McDonald's has 1.02 billion shares of stock, each of which represents one unit of ownership in the firm. The family of McDonald's founder Ray Kroc stills owns a large block of this stock, as do several large institutional investors. In addition, thousands of individuals own just a few shares each. McDonald's, in turn, owns other businesses. For example, it owns several large regional bakeries that supply its restaurants with buns. Each of these is incorporated as a separate legal entity and managed as a wholly owned subsidiary by the parent company. McDonald's is also a partner in some Russian farms that grow potatoes to supply regional restaurants with french fries.

board of directors
Governing body that is elected by a corporation's stockholders and charged with overseeing the general management of the firm to ensure that it is being run in a way that best serves the stockholders' interests

Board of Directors   A corporate **board of directors** is a governing body that is elected by the stockholders and charged with overseeing a firm's general management to ensure that it is run to best serve the stockholders' interests. Some boards are relatively passive: They perform a general oversight function but seldom get actively involved in how the company is really run. But this trend is changing as more and more boards carefully scrutinize the firms they oversee and exert more influence over how they are being managed. This trend has been accelerated by numerous recent business scandals. In some cases, board members have been accused of wrongdoing. In other cases, boards have been found negligent for failing to monitor the actions of the firm's executives.[7] At issue is the concept of corporate governance—who is responsible for governing the actions of a business? McDonald's has a board of directors composed of 14 members. This board includes 4 inside members (full-time executives of the firm) and 10 outside members (individuals who do not work directly for the firm). This presumably allows decisions to be made in ways that protect the interests of diverse stakeholders.

Employees   An organization's employees are also a major element of its internal environment. Of particular interest to managers today is the changing nature of the workforce, which is becoming increasingly more diverse in terms of gender, ethnicity, age, and other dimensions. Workers are also calling for more job ownership—either partial ownership in the company or at least more say in how they perform their jobs.[8] Another trend in many firms is increased reliance on temporary workers—individuals hired for short periods of time with no expectation of permanent employment. Employers often prefer to use "temps" because they provide greater flexibility, earn lower wages, and often do not participate in benefits programs. But these managers also have to deal with what often amounts to a two-class workforce and with a growing number of employees who have no loyalty to the organization where they work because they may be working for a different one tomorrow.[9]

Physical Work Environment   A final part of the internal environment is the organization's actual physical environment and the work that people do. Some firms have their facilities in downtown skyscrapers, usually spread across several floors. Others locate in suburban or rural settings and may have facilities more closely resembling a college campus. Some facilities have long halls lined with traditional offices. Others have modular cubicles with partial walls and no doors. Pitney Bowes Credit Corporation re-created its offices to resemble something like an indoor theme park with cobblestone look-alike carpet, a town square clock, a café, and a diner. Increasingly, newer facilities have an even more open arrangement, where people work in large rooms, moving among different tables to interact with different people on different projects. Freestanding computer workstations are available for those who need them, and a few small rooms might be off to the side for private business.[10]

Employee safety and health regulations have caused many organizations to pay more attention to their internal environment. This concern, in turn, has also fostered new business opportunities. Rebecca Boenigk, founder and CEO of Neutral Posture, turned a small operation in her garage into an international company selling neutral body posture chairs designed by her father, Dr. Jerome Congleton.

THE ETHICAL AND SOCIAL ENVIRONMENT OF MANAGEMENT

The ethical and social environment has become an especially important area for managers in the last few years. In this section, we first explore the concept of individual ethics and then describe social responsibility.

Individual Ethics in Organizations

ethics
An individual's personal beliefs about whether a behavior, action, or decision is right or wrong

We define **ethics** as an individual's personal beliefs about whether a behavior, action, or decision is right or wrong.[11] Note that we define ethics in the context of the individual— people have ethics, whereas organizations do not. Likewise, what constitutes ethical behavior varies from one person to another. For example, one person who finds a $20 bill on the floor of an empty room may believe that it is okay to keep it, whereas another may feel compelled to turn it in to the lost-and-found department. Further, although **ethical behavior** is in the eye of the beholder, the term usually refers to behavior that conforms to generally accepted social norms. **Unethical behavior**, then, is behavior that does not conform to generally accepted social norms.

ethical behavior
Behavior that conforms to generally accepted social norms

Managerial Ethics   **Managerial ethics** consists of the standards of behavior that guide individual managers in their work.[12] One important area of managerial ethics is the treatment of employees by the organization. It includes, for example, hiring and firing, wages and working conditions, and employee privacy and respect. An example of how different managers might approach this area involves minimum wages. While the U.S. government sets a minimum hourly wage, this amount is often not enough to live above the poverty level in high-cost areas such as New York and San Francisco. Some

unethical behavior
Behavior that does not conform to generally accepted social norms

managerial ethics
Standards of behavior that guide individual managers in their work

James Lauritz/Digital Vision/Getty Images

Unethical behavior refers to behavior that does not conform to generally accepted social norms. Bribery is one form of behavior that is both illegal and unethical. This individual, for example, might be paying off a building inspector to get a favorable inspection or a customer to get a big order.

managers might say that paying only the legal minimum is the right business practice, while others might be inclined to pay a wage more attuned to local conditions (sometimes called a *living wage*).

Numerous ethical issues stem from how employees treat the organization, especially in regard to conflicts of interest, secrecy and confidentiality, and honesty. A *conflict of interest* occurs when an employee's decision potentially benefits the individual to the possible detriment of the organization. To guard against such practices, most companies have policies that forbid their buyers from accepting gifts from suppliers. Divulging company secrets is also clearly unethical. Employees who work for businesses in highly competitive industries—electronics, software, and fashion apparel, for example—might be tempted to sell information about their companies' plans to competitors. A third area of concern is honesty in general. Relatively common problems in this area include activities such as using a business telephone to make personal long-distance calls, visiting and updating personal Facebook sites during work hours, stealing supplies, and padding expense accounts. Although most employees are inherently honest, organizations must nevertheless be vigilant to avoid problems with such behaviors.

Managerial ethics also comes into play in the relationship between the firm and its employees with other economic agents. The primary agents of interest include customers, competitors, stockholders, suppliers, dealers, and unions. The behaviors between the organization and these agents that may be subject to ethical ambiguity include advertising and promotions, financial disclosures, ordering and purchasing, shipping and solicitations, bargaining and negotiation, and other business relationships.

For example, state pharmacy boards are charged with overseeing prescription drug safety in the United States. All told, almost 300 pharmacists serve on such boards. It was recently reported that 72 of these pharmacists were employees of major drugstore chains and supermarket pharmacies. These arrangements, while legal, could create the potential for conflicts of interest because they might give the pharmacists' employers influence over the regulatory system designed to monitor their own business practices.[13]

Another recent area of concern involves financial reporting by various e-commerce firms. Because of the complexities inherent in valuing the assets and revenues of these firms, some of them have been very aggressive in presenting their financial position in a highly positive light. And at least a few firms have substantially overstated their earnings projections to entice more investment. Moreover, some of today's accounting scandals in traditional firms have stemmed from similarly questionable practices. For example, Diamond Foods, a distributor of nuts and popcorn snacks, has had to restate its earnings twice in the last two years after announcing it had improperly accounted for $80 million in payments to almond growers.[14]

Hilton Hotels hired two senior executives away from rival Starwood Hotels. It was later found that the executives took eight boxes of electronic and paper documents; much of the material in the boxes related to plans and details related to how Starwood had started its popular chain of W hotels. When Hilton announced plans to launch such a brand itself, to be called Denizen Hotels, officials at Starwood became suspicious and investigated. When they learned about the theft of confidential materials, which Hilton subsequently returned, Starwood filed a lawsuit against Hilton.[15]

Managing Ethical Behavior Spurred partially by increased awareness of ethics scandals in business and partially by a sense of enhanced corporate consciousness about the distinction between ethical and unethical behaviors, many organizations have reemphasized ethical behavior on the part of employees. This emphasis takes many forms, but any effort to enhance ethical behavior must begin with top management. It is top managers, for example, who establish the organization's culture and define what will and what will not be acceptable behavior. Some companies have also started offering employees training in how to cope with ethical dilemmas. At Boeing, for example, line managers lead training sessions for other employees, and the company has an ethics committee that reports directly to the board of directors. The training sessions involve discussions of different ethical dilemmas that employees might face and how managers might handle those dilemmas. Chemical Bank, Halliburton, and Xerox also have ethics training programs for their managers. Still, issues continue to arise. For instance, one recent study found an increase in the number of employees who called in sick when they were not, in fact, ill but just wanted to have a day off.[16]

Organizations are also making greater efforts to formalize their ethical standards. Some, such as General Mills and Johnson & Johnson, have prepared guidelines that detail how employees are to treat suppliers, customers, competitors, and other constituents. Others, such as Whirlpool, Texas Instruments, and Hewlett-Packard, have developed formal **codes of ethics**—written statements of the values and ethical standards that guide the firms' actions. Of course, firms must adhere to such codes if they are to be of value. In one now-infamous case, Enron's board of directors voted to set aside the firm's code of ethics to implement a business plan that was in violation of that code.[17]

Of course, no code, guideline, or training program can truly substitute for the quality of an individual's personal judgment about what is right behavior and what is wrong behavior in a particular situation. Such devices may prescribe what people should do, but they often fail to help people understand and live with the consequences of their choices. Making ethical choices may lead to very unpleasant outcomes—firing, rejection by colleagues, and the forfeiture of monetary gain, to name a few. Thus, managers must be prepared to confront their own conscience and weigh the options available when making difficult ethical decisions.

codes of ethics
A formal, written statement of the values and ethical standards that guide a firm's action

Emerging Ethical Issues

Ethical scandals have become almost commonplace in today's world. Ranging from business and sports to politics and the entertainment industry, these scandals have rocked stakeholder confidence and called into question the moral integrity of our society. At the same time, most women and men today conduct themselves and their affairs in accordance with high ethical standards. Hence, as we summarize several emerging ethical issues in organizations, it is important to remember that one cannot judge everyone by the transgressions of a few.

Justin Sullivan/Getty Images

Ethical leadership has taken on increased importance in recent years. One recent high-profile example involved an executive named Mark Hurd. Hurd was appointed CEO of Hewlett-Packard but was subsequently forced to resign following allegations of sexual harassment.

Ethical Leadership   In recent years, the media have been rife with stories about unscrupulous corporate leaders. For every unethical senior manager, of course, there are many highly ethical ones. But the actions of such high-profile deposed executives as Mark Hurd (Hewlett Packard), Dennis Kozlowski (Tyco), Kenneth Lay (Enron), and Allen Stanford (Stanford Financial Group) have substantially increased the scrutiny directed at all executives. As a direct result, executives everywhere are expected to exhibit nothing but the strongest ethical conduct. This leadership, in turn, is expected to help set the tone for the rest of the organization and to establish both norms and a culture that reinforce the importance of ethical behavior.

The basic premise behind ethical leadership is that because leaders serve as role models for others, their every action is subject to scrutiny. If a senior executive exercises questionable judgment, this sends a signal to others that such actions are acceptable. This signal may, in turn, be remembered by others when they face similar situations. As a result, CEOs such as American Express's Kenneth Chenault and Costco's James Sinegal are now being held up as the standard against which others are being measured. The basic premise is that CEOs must set their company's moral tone by being honest and straightforward and by taking responsibility for any shortcomings that are identified. To support this view, Congress passed the **Sarbanes–Oxley Act of 2002**, requiring CEOs and CFOs to vouch personally for the truthfulness and fairness of their firms' financial disclosures. The law also imposes tough new measures to deter and punish corporate and accounting fraud and corruption.

Sarbanes–Oxley Act of 2002
A law that requires CEOs and CFOs to vouch personally for the truthfulness and fairness of their firms' financial disclosures and imposes tough new measures to deter and punish corporate and accounting fraud and corruption

Corporate Governance   A related area of emerging concern is ethical issues in corporate governance. As discussed earlier in this chapter, the board of directors of a public corporation is expected to ensure that the business is being properly managed and that the decisions made by its senior management are in the best interests of shareholders and other stakeholders. But many of the recent ethical scandals discussed here actually started with a breakdown in the corporate governance structure. For instance, World-Com's board once approved a personal loan to the firm's then-CEO, Bernard Ebbers, for $366 million, even though there was little evidence that he could repay it. And Tyco's board approved a $20 million bonus for one of its own members for helping with the acquisition of another firm. Boards of directors are also criticized when they are seen as not being sufficiently independent from senior management.[18] Only 4 of the 14 directors at McDonald's are also members of the firm's top management team.

Ethics and Information Technology   A final set of issues that has emerged in recent times involves information technology. Among the specific focal points in this area are individual rights to privacy and individuals' potential abuse of information technology. Indeed, online privacy has become a hot topic as companies sort out the related ethical and management issues. Both Facebook and Google have come under fire in recent years when it was discovered that these firms were looking into ways to track people's movement as individuals logged into the sites.

One way management can address these concerns is to post a privacy policy on the company website. The policy should explain exactly what data the company collects and who gets to see the data. It should also allow people a choice about having their information shared with others and indicate how people can opt out of data collection. Disney, IBM, and other companies support this position by refusing to advertise on websites that have no posted privacy policies.

In addition, companies can offer web surfers the opportunity to review and correct information that has been collected, especially medical and financial data. In the offline world, consumers are legally allowed to inspect their own credit and medical records. In the online world, this kind of access can be costly and cumbersome because data are often spread across several computer systems. Despite the technical difficulties, government agencies are already working on Internet privacy guidelines, which means that companies will need internal guidelines, training, and leadership to ensure that they are in compliance.

Social Responsibility in Organizations

As we have seen in this chapter, ethics are associated with individuals and their decisions and behaviors. Organizations themselves do not have ethics, but they relate to their environments in ways that often involve ethical dilemmas and decisions. These situations are generally referred to within the context of the organization's **social responsibility**. Specifically, social responsibility is the set of obligations an organization has to protect and enhance the societal context in which it functions. Some of the more salient arguments on both sides of this contemporary debate are summarized in Figure 2.2 and are further explained in the following sections.

social responsibility
The set of obligations that an organization has to protect and enhance the societal context in which it functions

Arguments for Social Responsibility   People who argue in favor of social responsibility claim that—because organizations create many of the problems that need to be addressed, such as air and water pollution and resource depletion—organizations should play a major role in solving them. The Sustainability Matters feature discusses one such example. They also argue that, because corporations are legally defined entities with most of the same privileges as private citizens, businesses should not try to avoid their obligations as citizens. Advocates of social responsibility point out that, whereas governmental organizations have stretched their budgets to the limit, many large businesses often have surplus revenues that could be used to help solve social problems. For example, Dell donates surplus computers to schools, and many restaurants give leftover food to homeless shelters.

Arguments Against Social Responsibility   Some people, however, including the famous economist Milton Friedman, argue that widening the interpretation of social responsibility will undermine the U.S. economy by detracting from the basic mission of

Arguments for Social Responsibility

1. Business creates problems and should therefore help solve them.

2. Corporations are citizens in our society.

3. Business often has the resources necessary to solve problems.

4. Business is a partner in our society, along with the government and the general population.

Social Responsibility

Arguments against Social Responsibility

1. The purpose of business in U.S. society is to generate profit for owners.

2. Involvement in social programs gives business too much power.

3. There is potential for conflicts of interest.

4. Business lacks the expertise to manage social programs.

© Cengage Learning

FIGURE 2.2

Arguments for and Against Social Responsibility

Although many people want everyone to see social responsibility as a desirable aim, in fact, several strong arguments can be advanced both for and against social responsibility. Hence, organizations and their managers should carefully assess their own values, beliefs, and priorities when deciding which stance and approach to take regarding social responsibility.

business: to earn profits for owners. For example, money that Chevron or General Electric contributes to social causes or charities is money that could otherwise be distributed to owners in the form of dividends. Shareholders of Ben & Jerry's Homemade Holdings once expressed outrage when the firm refused to accept a lucrative exporting deal to Japan simply because the Japanese distributor did not have a strong social agenda.[19]

Another objection to increasing the social responsibility of businesses reflects the position that corporations already wield enormous power and that involvement in social programs gives them even more power. Still another argument against social responsibility focuses on the potential for conflicts of interest. Suppose, for example, that one manager is in charge of deciding which local social program or charity will receive a large grant from her business. The local civic opera company (a not-for-profit organization that relies on contributions for its existence) might offer her front-row tickets for the upcoming season in exchange for her support. If opera is her favorite form of music, she may be tempted to direct the money toward the local company when it might be needed more in other areas.[20]

Finally, critics argue that organizations lack the expertise to understand how to assess and make decisions about worthy social programs. How can a company truly know, they ask, which cause or program is most deserving of its support or how money might best be spent?

Managing Social Responsibility

The demands for social responsibility placed on contemporary organizations by an increasingly sophisticated and educated public are probably stronger than ever. As we have seen, there are pitfalls for managers who fail to adhere to high ethical standards and for companies that try to circumvent their legal obligations. Organizations, therefore, need to fashion an approach to social responsibility in the same way that they develop any other business strategy. In other words, they should view social responsibility as a major challenge that requires careful planning, decision making, consideration, and evaluation. They may accomplish this through both formal and informal dimensions of managing social responsibility.

Formal Organizational Dimensions   Some dimensions of managing social responsibility are formal and planned activities on the part of the organization. The formal organizational dimensions through which businesses can manage social responsibility include legal compliance, ethical compliance, and philanthropic giving.

legal compliance
The extent to which an organization complies with local, state, federal, and international laws

Legal compliance is the extent to which the organization conforms to local, state, federal, and international laws. The task of managing legal compliance is generally assigned to the appropriate functional managers. For example, the organization's top human resource executive is responsible for ensuring compliance with regulations concerning hiring, pay, and workplace safety and health. Likewise, the top finance executive generally oversees compliance with securities and banking regulations. The organization's legal department is likely to contribute to this effort by providing general oversight and answering queries from managers about the appropriate interpretation of laws and regulations. Unfortunately, though, legal compliance may not be enough—in some cases, for instance, perfectly legal accounting practices have still resulted in deception and other problems.[21]

ethical compliance
The extent to which an organization and its members follow basic ethical standards of behavior

Ethical compliance is the extent to which the organization's members follow basic ethical (and legal) standards of behavior. We noted earlier that organizations have increased their efforts in this area—providing training in ethics and developing guidelines and codes of conduct, for example. These activities serve as vehicles for

SUSTAINABILITY MATTERS

Greening the Business Environment: HP Keeps Itself in the Recycling Loop

Hewlett-Packard (HP), which offers a comprehensive product line of computer hardware, software, and services, was one of the first companies to recycle computer software and hardware products and components. The project became a matter of sustained companywide policy with the inception of HP Planet Partners in 1991, and today HP proudly proclaims that it's "committed to providing customers with inventive, high-quality products and services that are environmentally sound and to conduct[ing] our operations in an environmentally responsible manner." As "one of [the] guiding principles ... deeply ingrained in our values," that commitment, says HP, has become a legitimate reflection of the firm's overall culture.

How does Planet Partners work? First of all, HP takes back discarded hardware and cartridges from individual and business users. Cartridge recycling has always been free, and since 2009, HP has offered free recycling for any brand of computer equipment (up to five items per customer). HP has also expanded the Planet Partners print cartridge return and recycling program under which users can return HP ink and LaserJet toner cartridges directly to HP or (using special postage-paid envelopes or boxes) to authorized retail and recycling locations such as Staples, the world's largest office products retailer.

Once they're returned, cartridges enter the HP Closed Loop System for Plastics Recycling—so-called because plastic from discarded cartridges goes right back into new cartridges. At facilities in Nashville and Germany, the plastic (about 80 percent of an ink-jet cartridge) is separated from electrical circuits, foam, metal, and residual ink and shipped to a plant run by the Lavergne Group, which makes plastic resins from recycled material, in Montreal, Canada. There, it's mixed with other materials (including a lot of plastic-bottle waste), and when the process is complete, the new compound is ready to be used in the manufacture of new cartridges. Since launching the closed-loop system in 2005, HP has produced more than 500 million new cartridges, and at present the company's entire cartridge product line contains 60 percent recycled materials.

It is no surprise that making cartridges is cheaper with recycled materials than with virgin materials, but its closed-loop recycling operations haven't yet had any positive effect on HP's bottom line. In fact, the Nashville facility operates as a *cost center*—it costs money to run it but it doesn't directly contribute to profits. At the same time, of course, saving the environment is not what HP does for a living, and few people, either outside or inside HP, would argue that its culture is inherently altruistic. HP has been investing money in its recycling infrastructure for decades, and that investment has paid off handsomely in lower production costs and a competitive advantage in the secondary market for computer equipment. HP has even turned "asset management"—the process of protecting the data left on discarded equipment—into a profitable customer service operation.

References: Hewlett-Packard, "HP Planet Partners Recycling," "United States—Computer Hardware Recycling," "Product Reuse and Recycling," "Environmental, Health and Safety Policy," www.hp.com, accessed on July 30, 2013; Sarah Meyer, "How HP Does Green: Recycling Facility Tour," *PrinterComparison.com*, www.printercomparison.com, accessed on July 30, 2013; Cora Nucci, "Inside HP's Ink Jet Cartridge Recycling Process," *InformationWeek*, www.informationweek.com, accessed on July 30, 2013; Keith Kmetz, *HP Shows Off Another Phase of Its "Closed Loop" Inkjet Cartridge Recycling Process with a Tour of the Lavergne Group Facility* (Framingham, MA: IDC, April 2010), www.hp.com, accessed on July 30, 2013; and Jim Motavalli, "See How Printer Cartridges Are Recycled," *The Daily Green*, http://www.goodhousekeeping.com/home/green-living/the-daily-green, accessed on July 30, 2013.

enhancing ethical compliance. Many organizations also establish formal ethics committees, which may be asked to review proposals for new projects, to help evaluate new hiring strategies, or to assess a new environmental protection plan. They might also serve as a peer review panel to evaluate alleged ethical misconduct by an employee.[22]

philanthropic giving
Awarding funds or gifts to charities or other worthy causes

Finally, **philanthropic giving** is the awarding of funds or gifts to charities or other worthy causes. Target routinely gives a share of pretax income to charity and social programs. Omaha Steaks gives more than $100,000 per year to support the arts.[23] Giving across national boundaries is also becoming more common. For example, Alcoa gave $112,000 to a small town in Brazil to build a sewage treatment plant. And Japanese firms such as Sony and Mitsubishi make contributions to many social programs in the United States. However, in the current climate of cutbacks, many corporations have also had to limit their charitable gifts over the past several years as they continue to trim their own budgets.[24] And many firms that continue to make contributions are increasingly targeting them to programs or areas where the firm will get something in return. For example, firms today are more likely than they were a few years ago to give money to job-training programs rather than to the arts. The logic is that they get a more direct payoff from the former type of contribution—in this instance, a better-trained workforce from which to hire new employees.[25] And, indeed, corporate donations to arts programs declined 5 percent between 2003 and 2008, declined further during the recession, and have generally remained flat since the economic recovery started in 2012.

Informal Organizational Dimensions   In addition to these formal dimensions of managing social responsibility, there are also informal ones. Leadership, organizational culture, and how the organization responds to whistle-blowers all help shape and define people's perceptions of the organization's stance on social responsibility.

Leadership practices and organizational culture can go a long way toward defining the social responsibility stance an organization and its members will adopt.[26] As described earlier in this chapter, ethical leadership often sets the tone for the entire organization. For example, Johnson & Johnson executives for years provided a consistent message to employees that customers, employees, communities where the company did business, and shareholders were all important—and primarily in that order. Thus, when packages of poisoned Tylenol showed up on store shelves, Johnson & Johnson employees did not need to wait for orders from headquarters to know what to do: They immediately pulled all the packages from shelves before any other customers could buy them.[27] From a different perspective, Walmart has recently been charged with bribing officials in other countries in order to sidestep local regulations and expedite building permits for new stores. Investigators allege that top managers, including then-CEO H. Lee Scott, knew about these practices but did nothing to stop them.[28]

whistle-blowing
The disclosure, by an employee, of illegal or unethical conduct on the part of others within the organization

Whistle-blowing is an employee's disclosure of illegal or unethical conduct by others within the organization.[29] How an organization responds to this practice often indicates its values as they relate to social responsibility. Whistle-blowers may have to proceed through a number of channels to be heard, and they may even get fired for their efforts.[30] Many organizations, however, welcome their contributions. A person who observes questionable behavior typically first reports the incident to his or her boss. If nothing is done, the whistle-blower may then inform higher-level managers or an ethics committee, if one exists. Eventually, the person may have to go to a regulatory agency or even the media to be heard. Harry Markopolos, a portfolio manager at Rampart Investments, spent nine years trying to convince the Securities and Exchange Commission (SEC) that a money management firm run by Bernard Madoff was falsifying the results it was reporting to investors. Only when the U.S. economy went into recession in 2008 did the truth about Madoff come out.[31] In response, the SEC announced plans to overhaul its whistle-blowing system.[32] More recently, Bradley Birkenfeld provided evidence proving that Swiss banking giant UBS was evading corporate taxes. UBS eventually was fined $780 million for its transgressions.[33]

THE INTERNATIONAL ENVIRONMENT OF MANAGEMENT

Another important competitive issue for managers today is the international environment. After describing recent trends in international business, we examine levels of internationalization and the international context of business.

Trends in International Business

The stage for today's international business environment was set at the end of World War II. Businesses in war-torn countries such as Germany and Japan had no choice but to rebuild from scratch. Consequently, they had to rethink every facet of their operations, including technology, production, finance, and marketing. Although these countries took many years to recover, they eventually did so, and their economic systems were subsequently poised for growth. During the same era, many U.S. companies grew somewhat complacent. Their customer base was growing rapidly. Increased population, spurred by the baby boom, and increased affluence resulting from the postwar economic boom greatly raised the average person's standard of living and expectations. The U.S. public continually wanted new and better products and services. Many U.S. companies profited greatly from this pattern, but most were also guilty of taking it for granted.

U.S. firms are no longer isolated from global competition or the global market. A few simple numbers help tell the full story of international trade and industry. First of all, the volume of international trade increased more than 1300 percent between 1960 and 2013. Further, although 184 of the world's largest corporations are headquartered in the United States, there are also 34 in Japan, 24 in France, 23 in China, and 36 in Britain.[34] Within certain industries, the preeminence of non-U.S. firms is even more striking. For example, only three of the world's ten largest banks and one of the largest electronics companies are based in the United States. Only two of the ten largest chemical companies are U.S. firms. On the other hand, U.S. firms comprise seven of the nine largest aerospace companies, three of the seven largest airlines, four of the ten largest information technology companies, six of the seven largest diversified financial companies, and six of the ten largest retailers.[35]

U.S. firms are also finding that international operations are an increasingly important element of their sales and profits. For example, in 2012, ExxonMobil realized 67 percent of its revenues and 61 percent of its profits abroad. For Avon, these percentages were 73 percent and 68 percent, respectively.[36] Hollywood is also getting in on the act. *The Life of Pi* grossed a healthy $124 million in the United States but then raked in another $484 million abroad. Overseas markets are even more important when a film bombs domestically. For example, *Battleship* cost $200 million to make and then earned a paltry $65 million at the domestic box office. But $238 million in foreign sales pushed the movie into the black.[37] From any perspective, then, it is clear that we live in a truly global economy. Virtually all businesses today must be concerned with the competitive situations they face in lands far from home and with how companies from distant lands are competing in their homelands.

Levels of International Business Activity

Firms can choose various levels of international business activity as they seek to gain a competitive advantage in other countries. The general levels are exporting and importing, licensing, strategic alliances, and direct investment. Table 2.1 summarizes the advantages and disadvantages of each approach.

When organizations decide to increase their level of internationalization, they can adopt several strategies. Each strategy is a matter of degree, as opposed to being a discrete and mutually exclusive category. And each has unique advantages that must be considered.

Table 2.1	Advantages and Disadvantages of Different Approaches to Internationalization	
Approach to Internationalization	**Advantages**	**Disadvantages**
Importing or exporting	1. Small cash outlay 2. Little risk 3. No adaptation necessary	1. Tariffs and taxes 2. High transportation costs 3. Government restrictions
Licensing	1. Increased profitability 2. Extended profitability	1. Inflexibility 2. Competition
Strategic alliances or joint ventures	1. Quick market entry 2. Access to materials and technology	1. Shared ownership (limits control and profits)
Direct Investment	1. Enhanced control 2. Existing infrastructure	1. Complexity 2. Greater economic and political risk 3. Greater uncertainty

© Cengage Learning

exporting
Making a product in the firm's domestic marketplace and selling it in another country

importing
Bringing a good, service, or capital into the home country from abroad

licensing
An arrangement whereby one company allows another company to use its brand name, trademark, technology, patent, copyright, or other assets in exchange for a royalty based on sales

Exporting and Importing   Importing or exporting (or both) is usually the first type of international business in which a firm gets involved. **Exporting**, or making a product in the firm's domestic marketplace and selling it in another country, can involve both merchandise and services. **Importing** is bringing a good, service, or capital into the home country from abroad. For example, automobiles (Mazda, Ford, Volkswagen, Mercedes-Benz, and Ferrari) and stereo equipment (Sony, Bang & Olufsen, and Sanyo) are routinely exported by their manufacturers to other countries. Likewise, many wine distributors buy products from vineyards in France, Italy, or the United States and import them into their own country for resale. U.S. sports brands, such as team jerseys and logo caps, have become one of the latest hot exports.[38]

When organizations decide to increase their level of internationalization, they can adopt several strategies. Each strategy is a matter of degree, as opposed to being a discrete and mutually exclusive category. And each has unique advantages that must be considered.

Licensing   A company may prefer to arrange for a foreign company to manufacture or market its products under a licensing agreement. Factors leading to this decision may include excessive transportation costs, government regulations, and home production costs. **Licensing** is an arrangement whereby a firm allows another company to use its brand name, trademark, technology, patent, copyright, or other assets. In return, the licensee pays a royalty, usually based on sales. Franchising, a special form of licensing, is also widely used in international business. Kirin Brewery, Japan's largest producer of beer, wanted to expand its international operations but feared that the time involved in shipping it from Japan would cause the beer to lose its freshness. Thus, it has entered into a number of licensing arrangements with breweries in other markets. These brewers make beer according to strict guidelines provided by the Japanese firm and then package and market it as Kirin Beer. They pay a royalty to Kirin for each case sold. Molson produces Kirin in Canada under such an agreement, and the Charles Wells Brewery does the same in England.[39]

strategic alliance
A cooperative arrangement between two or more firms for mutual gain

joint venture
A special type of strategic alliance in which the partners share in the ownership of an operation on an equity basis

direct investment
When a firm builds or purchases operating facilities or subsidiaries in a different country from the one where it has its headquarters

maquiladoras
Light assembly plants that are built in Northern Mexico close to the U.S. border and are given special tax breaks by the Mexican government

Strategic Alliances　In a **strategic alliance**, two or more firms jointly cooperate for mutual gain.[40] For example, Unisys and Oracle have a strategic alliance that provides customers with the service and technology of Unisys and the enterprise software of Oracle. A **joint venture** is special type of strategic alliance in which the partners actually share ownership of a new enterprise. Strategic alliances have enjoyed a tremendous upsurge in the past few years.

Direct Investment　Another level of commitment to internationalization is direct investment. **Direct investment** occurs when a firm headquartered in one country builds or purchases operating facilities or subsidiaries in a foreign country. The foreign operations then become wholly owned subsidiaries of the firm. Examples include British Petroleum's acquisition of Amoco, Dell Computer's massive factory in China, and the newest Disney theme park in Hong Kong. Coca-Cola recently invested $150 million to build a new bottling and distribution network in India. Similarly, PepsiCo paid $4.2 billion for a Russian yogurt company.[41] Many U.S. firms use maquiladoras for the same purpose. **Maquiladoras** are light assembly plants built in Northern Mexico close to the U.S. border. The plants are given special tax breaks by the Mexican government, and the area is populated with workers willing to work for low wages.

The Context of International Business

Managers involved in international business should also be aware of the cultural environment, controls on international trade, the importance of economic communities, and the role of the GATT and WTO.

The Cultural Environment　One significant contextual challenge for the international manager is the cultural environment and how it affects business. A country's culture includes all the values, symbols, beliefs, and language that guide behavior. Cultural values and beliefs are often unspoken; they may even be taken for granted by those who live in a particular country. Cultural factors do not necessarily cause problems for managers when the cultures of two countries are similar. Difficulties can arise, however, when there is little overlap between a manager's home culture and the culture of the country in which business is to be conducted. For example, most U.S. managers find the culture and traditions of England relatively familiar. The people of both countries speak the same language and share strong historical roots, and there is a history of strong commerce between the two countries. When U.S. managers begin operations in Vietnam, the People's Republic of China, or the Middle East, however, many of those commonalities disappear.

Cultural differences between countries can have a direct impact on business practice. For example, the religion of Islam teaches that people should not make a living by exploiting the misfortune of others; as a result, charging interest is seen as immoral. This means that in Saudi Arabia, few businesses provide towing services to transport stalled cars to a repair shop (because doing so would be capitalizing on misfortune), and in the Sudan, banks cannot pay or charge interest. Given these cultural and religious constraints, those two businesses—automobile towing and banking—seem to hold little promise for international managers in those particular countries!

Some cultural differences between countries can be even more subtle and yet have a major impact on business activities. For example, in the United States, most managers clearly agree about the value of time. Most U.S. managers schedule their activities very tightly and then try hard to adhere to their schedules. Other cultures do not put such a premium on time. In the Middle East, managers do not like to set appointments, and they rarely keep appointments set too far into the future. U.S. managers interacting with managers from the Middle East might misinterpret the late arrival of a potential business partner as a negotiation ploy or an insult, when it is merely a simple reflection of different views of time and its value.[42]

Language itself can be an important factor. Beyond the obvious and clear barriers posed when people speak different languages, subtle differences in meaning can also play a major role. For example, Imperial Oil of Canada markets gasoline under the brand name Esso. When the firm tried to sell its gasoline in Japan, it learned that *esso* means "stalled car" in Japanese. Likewise, when Chevrolet first introduced a U.S. model called the Nova in Latin America, General Motors executives could not understand why the car sold poorly. They eventually learned, though, that, in Spanish, *no va* means, "It doesn't go." The color green is used extensively in Muslim countries, but it signifies death in some other lands. The color associated with femininity in the United States is pink, but in many other countries yellow is the most feminine color. And when Disney was initially promoting its new theme park in Hong Kong, its print ads featured a family consisting of two parents and two children, failing to consider that the Chinese government limits most families to a single child. As a result, people who saw the ad were confused until Disney relaunched the campaign to show parents and a single child visiting the park.[43]

Controls on International Trade   Another element of the international context that managers need to consider is the extent to which there are controls on international trade. These controls include tariffs, quotas, export restraint agreements, and "buy national" laws. A **tariff** is a tax collected on goods shipped across national boundaries. Tariffs can be collected by the exporting country, by countries through which goods pass, or by the importing country. Import tariffs, which are the most common, can be levied to protect domestic companies by increasing the cost of foreign goods. Japan charges U.S. tobacco producers a tariff on cigarettes imported into Japan as a way to keep their prices higher than the prices charged by domestic firms. Tariffs can also be levied, usually by less developed countries, to raise money for the government.

Quotas are the most common form of trade restriction. A **quota** is a limit on the number or value of goods that can be traded. The quota amount is typically designed to ensure that domestic competitors will be able to maintain a certain market share. Honda is allowed to import 425,000 autos each year into the United States. This quota is one reason Honda opened manufacturing facilities here. The quota applies to cars imported into the United States, but the company can produce as many other cars within U.S. borders as it wants; such cars are not considered imports. **Export restraint agreements** are designed to convince other governments to limit voluntarily the volume or value of goods exported to or imported from a particular country. They are, in effect, export quotas. Japanese steel producers voluntarily limit the amount of steel they send to the United States each year.

"Buy national" legislation gives preference to domestic producers through content or price restrictions. Several countries have this type of legislation. Brazil requires that Brazilian companies purchase only Brazilian-made computers. The United States requires that the Department of Defense purchase military uniforms manufactured only in the

tariff
A tax collected on goods shipped across national boundaries

quota
A limit on the number or value of goods that can be traded

export restraint agreements
Accords reached by governments in which countries voluntarily limit the volume or value of goods they export to or import from one another

Greg Smith/Corbis

Most countries impose controls on international trade. These U.S. Customs Inspectors in El Paso, Texas, are verifying that proper tariffs were paid on merchandise being exported from Mexico into the United States.

economic community

A set of countries that agree to markedly reduce or eliminate trade barriers among member nations (a formalized market system)

European Union (EU)

The first and most important international market system

United States, even though the price of foreign uniforms would be only half as much. Mexico requires that 50 percent of the parts of cars sold in Mexico be manufactured inside its own borders.

Economic Communities   Just as government policies can either increase or decrease the political risk that international managers face, trade relations between countries can either help or hinder international business. Relations dictated by quotas, tariffs, and so forth can hurt international trade. There is currently a strong movement around the world to reduce many of these barriers. This movement takes its most obvious form in international economic communities.

An international **economic community** is a set of countries that agree to markedly reduce or eliminate trade barriers among member nations. The first (and in many ways still the most important) of these economic communities is the European Union. The **European Union** (or **EU**, as it is often called) can be traced to 1957 when Belgium, France, Luxembourg, Germany, Italy, and the Netherlands signed the Treaty of Rome to promote economic integration. Between 1973 and 1986, these countries were joined by Denmark, Ireland, the United Kingdom, Greece, Spain, and Portugal, and the group became known first as the European Committee and then as the European Union. Austria, Finland, and Sweden joined the EU in 1995; 12 additional countries (mostly from the formerly communist-controlled Eastern European region) joined between 2004 and 2007, bringing the EU's membership to 27 countries. For years, these countries have followed a basic plan that led to the systematic elimination of most trade barriers. The new market system achieved significantly more potential when most of the EU members eliminated their home currencies (such as French francs and Italian lira) beginning on January 1, 2002, and adopted a new common currency called the *euro*.

Another important economic community encompasses the United States, Canada, and Mexico. These countries have long been major trading partners with one another; more than 80 percent of Mexico's exports go to the United States, and more than 65 percent of Mexico's imports come from the United States. During the last several years, these countries have negotiated a variety of agreements to make trade even easier. The most important of these, the **North American Free Trade Agreement (NAFTA)**, eliminates many of the trade barriers—such as quotas and tariffs—that existed previously.[44]

The Role of the GATT and WTO   The context of international business is also increasingly being influenced by the **General Agreement on Tariffs and Trade (GATT)** and the World Trade Organization (WTO). The GATT was first negotiated following World War II in an effort to avoid trade wars that would benefit rich nations and harm poorer ones. Essentially, the GATT is a trade agreement intended to promote international trade by reducing trade barriers and making it easier for all nations to compete in international markets. The GATT was a major stimulus to international trade after it was first ratified in 1948 by 23 countries; by 1994, a total of 117 countries had signed the agreement.

One key component of the GATT was the identification of the so-called *most favored nation* (MFN) principle. This provision stipulates that if a country extends preferential treatment to any other nation that has signed the agreement, then that preferential treatment must be extended to all signatories to the agreement. Members can extend such treatment to nonsignatories as well, but they are not required to do so.

The **World Trade Organization (WTO)** came into existence on January 1, 1995. The WTO replaced the GATT and absorbed its mission. The WTO is headquartered in Geneva, Switzerland, and currently includes 140 member nations and 32 observer countries. Members are required to open their markets to international trade and to follow WTO rules. The WTO has three basic goals:

1. To promote trade flows by encouraging nations to adopt nondiscriminatory and predictable trade policies
2. To reduce remaining trade barriers through multilateral negotiations
3. To establish impartial procedures for resolving trade disputes among its members

The WTO is certain to continue to play a major role in the evolution of the global economy. At the same time, it has also become a lightning rod for protesters and other activists, who argue that the WTO focuses too narrowly on globalization issues to the detriment of human rights and the environment.

THE ORGANIZATION'S CULTURE

As we noted earlier in this chapter, an especially important part of an organization's internal environment is its culture. **Organizational culture** is the set of values, beliefs, behaviors, customs, and attitudes that helps the organization's members understand what it stands for, how it does things, and what it considers important.[45]

The Importance of Organizational Culture

Culture determines the organization's "feel." A strong and clear culture can play an important role in the competitiveness of a business. At the same time, though, there is no universal culture that will help all organizations. The stereotypic image of Microsoft, for example, is that of a workplace where people dress very casually and work very long hours. In contrast, the image of Bank of America for some observers is that of a formal setting with rigid work rules and people dressed in conservative business attire. And Texas Instruments likes to talk about its "shirtsleeve" culture, in which ties are avoided and few managers even wear jackets. Southwest Airlines maintains a culture that stresses fun and excitement.

Of course, the same culture is not necessarily found throughout an entire organization. For example, the sales and marketing department may have a culture quite different from that of the operations and manufacturing department. Regardless of its nature, however, culture is a powerful force in organizations, one that can shape the firm's overall effectiveness and long-term success. Companies that can develop and maintain a strong culture, such as Starbucks and Procter & Gamble, tend to be more effective than companies that have trouble developing and maintaining a strong culture, such as Kmart.[46]

Determinants of Organizational Culture

Where does an organization's culture come from? Typically, it develops and blossoms over a long period of time. Its starting point is often the organization's founder. For example, James Cash Penney believed in treating employees and customers with respect and dignity. Employees at J. C. Penney are still called *associates* rather than *employees* (to reflect partnership), and customer satisfaction is of paramount importance. The impact of Sam Walton, Ross Perot, and Walt Disney is still felt in the organizations they founded.[47] As an organization grows, its culture is modified, shaped, and refined by symbols, stories, heroes, slogans, and ceremonies. Many decisions at Walt Disney Company today are still framed by asking, "What would Walt have done?"

Corporate success and shared experiences also shape culture. For example, Hallmark Cards has a strong culture derived from its years of success in the greeting card industry. Employees speak of "the Hallmark family" and care deeply about the company; many have worked there for years. At Kmart, in contrast, the culture is quite weak, the management team changes rapidly, and few people sense any direction or purpose in the company. The differences in culture at Hallmark and Kmart are in part attributable to past successes and shared experiences.

Managing Organizational Culture

How can managers deal with culture, given its clear importance but intangible nature? Essentially, the manager must understand the current culture and then decide whether it should be maintained or changed. By understanding the organization's current culture, managers can take appropriate actions. Culture can also be maintained by rewarding and promoting people whose behaviors are consistent with the existing culture and by articulating the culture through slogans, ceremonies, and so forth.

Managers must walk a fine line, however, between maintaining a culture that still works effectively and changing a culture that has become dysfunctional. For example, many of the firms already noted, as well as numerous others, take pride in perpetuating their culture. Shell Oil, for example, has an elaborate display in the lobby of its Houston headquarters that tells the story of the firm's past. But other companies may face situations in which their culture is no longer a strength. For example, some critics feel that General Motors' culture places too much emphasis on product development and internal competition among divisions, and not enough on marketing and competition with other firms. They even argue that this culture was a major contributing factor in the business crisis that GM faced in 2009.

Culture problems sometimes arise from mergers or the growth of rival factions within an organization. For example, Delta recently merged with Northwest Airlines. Combining the two companies led to numerous cases of conflict and operational difficulties because the cultures of the two firms were so different.[48] To change culture, managers must have a clear idea of what they want to create. When United and Continental Airlines merged, top managers stressed that they wanted the new firm to personify Continental's employee-friendly culture and avoid the old United culture that was fraught with hostility and mistrust between management and labor.[49]

SUMMARY OF LEARNING OUTCOMES AND KEY POINTS

1. Discuss the nature of an organization's environments, and identify and describe the components of its general, task, and internal environments.

   • Managers need to have a thorough understanding of the environment in which they operate and compete. The general environment consists of the economy, technology, and the political–legal climate. The task environment consists of competitors, customers, suppliers, strategic partners, and regulators.

   • The internal environment consists of the organization's owners, board of directors, employees, physical environment, and culture. Owners are those who have claims on the property rights of the organization. The board of directors, elected by stockholders, is responsible for overseeing a firm's top managers. Individual employees are other important parts of the internal environment. The physical environment, yet another part of the internal environment, varies greatly across organizations.

2. Describe the ethical and social environment of management, including individual ethics, the concept of social responsibility, and how organizations can manage social responsibility.

   • The ethical and social environment of management is also quite important. Understanding the differences between ethical and unethical behavior, as well as appreciating the special nature of managerial ethics, can help guide effective decision making. Understanding the meaning of and arguments for and against

social responsibility can help a manager effectively address both the formal and informal dimensions of social responsibility.

3. Discuss the international environment of management, including trends in international business, levels of international business activities, and the context of international business.

   • The international environment of management can be a crucial one. Current trends have resulted in the increasing globalization of markets, industries, and businesses. Organizations seeking to become more international can rely on importing, exporting, licensing (including franchising), strategic alliances, and direct investment to do so. National culture, controls on international trade, economic communities, and the WTO combine to determine the context of international business.

4. Describe the importance and determinants of an organization's culture, as well as how organizational culture can be managed.

   • Organizational culture is the set of values, beliefs, behaviors, customs, and attitudes that helps the organization's members understand what it stands for, how it does things, and what it considers important. Organizational culture is an important environmental concern for managers. Managers must understand that culture is a key determinant of how well their organization will perform. Culture can be assessed and managed in a number of different ways.

DISCUSSION QUESTIONS

Questions for Review

1. Identify and discuss each major dimension of the general environment and the task environment.
2. Do organizations have ethics? Why or why not?

3. What are the arguments for and against social responsibility on the part of businesses? In your opinion, which set of arguments is more compelling?

4. Describe the basic levels of international business involvement. Why might a firm use more than one level at the same time?

5. Describe various barriers to international trade. Why do such barriers exist?

Questions for Analysis

1. Can you think of dimensions of the task environment that are not discussed in this chapter? Indicate their linkages to those that are discussed.

2. What is the relationship between the law and ethical behavior? Can a behavior be ethical but illegal at the same time?

3. What is your opinion of whistle-blowing? If you were aware of criminal activity in your organization but knew that reporting it would probably cost you your job, what would you do?

4. What industries do you think will feel the greatest impact of international business in the future? Will some industries remain relatively unaffected by globalization? If so, which ones? If not, explain why not.

5. What is the culture of your college, university, or place of employment? How clear is it? What are its most positive and its most negative characteristics?

BUILDING EFFECTIVE INTERPERSONAL SKILLS

Exercise Overview

Interpersonal skills reflect the manager's ability to communicate with, understand, and motivate individuals and groups. Managers in international organizations must understand how cultural manners and norms affect communication with people in different parts of the world. Similarly, as organizations become more diverse, it is also important to understand the roles that various forms of diversity play in the development of interpersonal skills.

Exercise Background

Managers spend a lot of their time working with others. These other individuals may be supervisors, subordinates, team members, or peers and colleagues. They may also be as close as the next office or on the other side of the planet. To interact with such a diverse set of people effectively, you must first develop an awareness of and sensitivity to people from other parts of the world and to people different from yourself.

Exercise Task

A list of five scenarios involving people communicating with others on work-related matters follows. Your first task, working alone, is to rank these scenarios in order of the likelihood of interaction difficulties. Rank the scenario that seems to have the lowest likelihood of difficulty as number 1 (for example, all else equal, interactions between two white males from the same home town and of the same age and similar interests will not likely be difficult). Rank the scenario with the highest likelihood of difficulty as number 5 (for example, an employee with racial prejudices interacting with someone of a different race might have a higher likelihood of interpersonal difficulty).

_____ Young U.S. female manager meeting with older female manager from Mexico

_____ German and French colleagues exchanging e-mails about a new project

_____ Skype call involving a male Jordanian manager, a female Australian manager, and a male Israeli manager

_____ Telephone conference call between a young Indian male manager and an older Chinese male manager

_____ A face-to-face committee meeting with five people of the same gender from Indonesia, Russia, Canada, Pakistan, and Israel

After you have finished your ranking, form small groups of three to five people and compare your rankings. Discuss the similarities and differences. Try to identify the relative impact of global differences, other differences, and technology.

BUILDING EFFECTIVE COMMUNICATION SKILLS

Exercise Overview

Communication skills consist of a manager's ability to effectively receive information and ideas from others and to effectively convey information and ideas to others. This exercise will help you develop your communication skills while also helping you understand the importance of knowing the customer segments in an organization's task environment.

Exercise Background

Assume that you are a newly hired middle manager in the marketing department of a large food manufacturer. You have just completed your formal study of management and are excited about the opportunity to apply some of those theories to the real-life problems of your firm. One problem in particular intrigues you. Your boss, the marketing vice president, recently developed a consumer survey to solicit feedback about products from customers. The feedback the firm has received varies considerably, ranging from 2 to 5 on a scale from 1 to 5, which gives your firm no helpful data. In addition, sales of your company's products have been slowly but steadily declining over time, and the marketing department is under some pressure from upper management to determine why.

You have an idea that the survey is not an accurate reflection of consumer preferences, so you make a suggestion to your boss: "Why don't we gather some information about our customers, in order to under- stand their needs better? For example, our products are purchased by individual consumers, schools, restaurants, and other organizations. Maybe each type of consumer wants something different from our product." Your boss's response is to stare at you, perplexed, and say, "No. We're not changing anything about the survey." When you ask, "Why?" the boss responds that the product has been a bestseller for years, that "good quality is good quality," and thus that all customers must want the same thing. He then says, "I'll spare you the embarrassment of failure by refusing your request."

Exercise Task

1. With this background in mind, compose a written proposal for your boss, outlining your position. Be sure to emphasize your fundamental concern— that the marketing department must understand the needs of each customer segment better in order to provide products that meet those needs. Consider ways to persuade your boss to change his mind. (*Hint:* Telling him bluntly that he is wrong is unlikely to be effective.)

2. On the basis of what you wrote in response to Exercise Task 1, do you think your boss will change his mind? If yes, exactly what will persuade him to change his mind? If no, what other actions could you take in a further effort to have your ideas adopted by the firm?

SKILLS SELF-ASSESSMENT INSTRUMENT

Global Awareness

Introduction: As we have noted, the environment of business is becoming more global. The following assessment is designed to help you determine your readiness to respond to managing in a global context.

Instructions: You will agree with some of the following statements and disagree with others. In some cases, you may find it difficult to make a decision, but you should force yourself to make a choice. Record your answers next to each statement according to the following scale:

4 Strongly agree

3 Somewhat agree

2 Somewhat disagree

1 Strongly disagree

_____   1. Some areas of Switzerland are very much like Italy.

_____   2. Although aspects of behavior such as motivation and attitudes within organizational settings remain quite diverse across cultures, organizations themselves appear to be increasingly similar in terms of design and technology.

_____   3. Spain, France, Japan, Singapore, Mexico, Brazil, and Indonesia have cultures with a strong orientation toward authority.

_____ 4. Japan and Austria define male and female roles more rigidly and value qualities such as forcefulness and achievement more than do Norway, Sweden, Denmark, and Finland.

_____ 5. Some areas of Switzerland are very much like France.

_____ 6. Australia, Great Britain, the Netherlands, Canada, and New Zealand have cultures that view people first as individuals and place a high priority on their own interests and values, whereas Colombia, Pakistan, Taiwan, Peru, Singapore, Mexico, Greece, and Hong Kong have cultures in which the good of the group or of society is considered of greatest importance.

_____ 7. The United States, Israel, Austria, Denmark, Ireland, Norway, Germany, and New Zealand have cultures with a low orientation toward authority.

_____ 8. The same manager may behave differently in different cultural settings.

_____ 9. Denmark, Canada, Norway, Singapore, Hong Kong, and Australia have cultures in which employees tolerate a great deal of uncertainty, but such high levels of uncertainty are not well tolerated in Israel, Austria, Japan, Italy, Argentina, Peru, France, and Belgium.

_____ 10. Some areas of Switzerland are very much like Germany.

EXPERIENTIAL EXERCISE

Assessing Organizational Culture

Purpose: While organizational culture is intangible, it is not difficult to observe. This activity will help you improve your skills in observing and interpreting organizational culture, which can help make you a more effective participant and leader in organizations.

Introduction: Clues to organizational culture may be found by observing details that relate to member behavior, traditions or customs, stories, attitudes, values, communication patterns, organizational structure, employee dress and appearance, and even office space arrangements. Do members address each other by first names? Are office doors left open or closed? What do members wear? How are achievements recognized? Does the workplace feel energized or laid-back? Do members smile and laugh often? Does seniority or expertise earn more respect?

Instructions: First, observe clues to organizational behavior at your school, college, or university. To the extent possible, observe a diversity of members, including students, teaching faculty, and nonteaching staff. Write down specific examples. For example, students typically wear blue jeans, while instructors usually wear suits. In the cafeteria, freshmen sit mainly with other freshmen. A professor may be referred to as "Doctor" by staff, while she may refer to staff by their first names.

Second, interpret the facts. Use your observations to describe the organization's core values. What does it value most? How did you come to that conclusion?

Third, with the class or in small groups, discuss your facts and interpretations. Focus especially on areas of disagreement. Where individuals disagree about the culture, try to understand why the disagreement occurs. If the facts differ, perhaps the individuals observed two different groups. For example, students majoring in business may be different from students in engineering or education. Or perhaps the organizational culture tolerates or encourages lots of differences. If there is agreement on facts but interpretations differ, then perhaps the individuals making the interpretations can explore their differing perceptions.

MANAGEMENT AT WORK

Is Fair Trade a Fair Trade-Off?

Do you know where chocolate comes from? It comes from cocoa, which is produced by roasting and grinding the almond-sized beans that grow on cacao trees.

More than 40 percent of the world's cacao-bean supply comes from small farms scattered throughout the West African nation of Ivory Coast, which may ship as much as 47,000 tons per month to the United States.

According to reports issued at the end of the 1990s by the United Nations Children's Fund and the U.S. State Department, much of the labor involved in Ivory Coast cocoa production is performed by children, chiefly boys ranging in age from 12 to 16. Most of them have been tricked or sold into forced labor—slavery—many by destitute parents unable to feed them.

How did enslaving children become business as usual in the Ivory Coast cocoa industry? Because fully one-third of the country's economy is based on cocoa exports, Ivory Coast is heavily dependent on world market prices for cocoa. Unfortunately, cocoa is an extremely unstable commodity—global prices fluctuate significantly. Profitability in the industry, therefore, depends on prices over which farmers have no control. This problem is compounded by unpredictable natural conditions, such as drought, over which they also have no control. To improve their chances of making a profit, they look for ways to cut costs, and the use of slave labor is the most effective money-saving measure.

This is where the idea of "fair trade" comes in. *Fair trade* refers to programs designed to ensure that export-dependent farmers in developing countries receive fair prices for their crops. Several such programs are sponsored by Fairtrade Labelling Organizations International (FLO), a global nonprofit network of fair-trade groups headquartered in Germany. Here's how it works: FLO partners with cooperatives representing cocoa producers in Africa and Latin America to establish certain standards, not only for the producers' products but also for their operations and socially relevant policies (such as enforcing anti–child labor laws and providing education and healthcare services). In return, FLO guarantees producers a "Fairtrade Minimum Price" for their products. Since 2007, FLO has guaranteed cocoa farmers a price of $1,750 per ton. If the market price falls below that level, FLO guarantees the difference. If the market price tops $1,750, FLO pays producers a premium of $150 per ton.

Where does the money come from? The cost is borne by the importers, manufacturers, and distributors who buy and sell cocoa from FLO-certified producers. These companies are in turn monitored by a network of FLO-owned organizations called TransFair, which ensures that FLO criteria are met and that FLO-certified producers receive the fair prices guaranteed by FLO.

What incentive encourages importers, manufacturers, and distributors not only to adopt FLO-TransFair standards but also to bear the costs of subsidizing overseas producers? They get the right to promote their chocolate products not only as "fair-trade" but also, often, as "organic" products—both of these categories typically command premium retail prices. In fact, organic fair-trade chocolate products are priced in the same range as luxury chocolates, but consumers appear to be willing to pay the relatively high asking prices—not only for organic products but also for all kinds of chocolate products bearing the "Fair Trade Certified™" label. TransFair USA Chief Executive Paul Rice explains that when consumers know they're supporting programs to empower farmers in developing countries, sellers and resellers can charge "dramatically higher prices, often two to three times higher." Consumers, he says, "put their money where their mouth is and pay a little more."

A 3.5-ounce candy bar labeled "organic fair trade" may sell for $3.49, compared to about $1.50 for one that's not. Why so much? Because the fair-trade candy bar, says TransFair USA spokesperson Nicole Chettero, still occupies a niche market. She predicts, however, that, "as the demand and volume of Fair Trade–certified products increase, the market will work itself out… . [R]etailers will naturally start to drop prices to remain competitive." Ultimately, she concludes, "there is no reason why fair-trade [products] should cost astronomically more than traditional products."

Some critics of fair-trade practices and prices agree in principle but contend that consumers don't need to be paying such excessive prices even under *current* market conditions. They point out that, according to TransFair's own data, cocoa farmers get only 3 cents of the $3.49 that a socially conscious consumer pays for a Fair Trade–certified candy bar. "Farmers often receive very little," reports consumer researcher Lawrence Solomon. "Often fair trade is sold at a premium," he charges, "but the entire premium goes to the middlemen."

Critics like Solomon suggest that sellers of fair-trade products are taking advantage of consumers who are socially but not particularly price conscious. They point out that if sellers priced that $3.49 candy bar at $2.49, farmers would still be entitled to 3 cents. The price, they allege, is inflated to $3.49 simply because there's a small segment of the market willing pay it (while farmers still get only 3 cents). Fair-trade programs, advises English economist Tim Harford, "make a promise that the producers will get a good deal. They do not promise that the consumer will get a good deal. That's up to you as a savvy shopper."

Case Questions

1. How does the environment affect fair trade?
2. What are the trade-offs in the fair-trade process? Do you think that fair trade promotes fair trade-offs? Why or why not?
3. Do you pay attention to fair-trade products in your own purchasing behavior? For what kind of products might you be willing to pay premium prices?
4. Under what circumstances might fair trade actually cause harm? To whom? At what point would fair-trade trade-offs no longer be acceptable?

Case References

"Enjoy Those Chocolate Hearts While You Can," *Bloomberg Businessweek*, February 11–February 17, 2013, p. 19; Rodney North, "VDay's Dark Side," Equal Exchange, February 2010, www.equalexchange.coop, accessed on July 30, 2013; "Cocoa's Bitter Child Labour Ties," *BBC News*, February 24, 2010, http://newsvote.bbc.co.uk, accessed on July 30, 2013; Bill Baue, "Abolishing Child Labor on West African Cocoa Farms," *Social Funds*, April 24, 2008, www.socialfunds.com, accessed on July 30, 2013; Fairtrade International, "Our Vision," "Aims of Fairtrade Standards," "Cocoa," 2010, www.fairtrade.net, accessed on July 30, 2013; TransFair USA, "What Is Fair Trade?" "Cocoa," 2010, fairtradeusa.org, accessed on July 30, 2013; Leslie Josephs, "Selling Candy with a Conscience," *Wall Street Journal*, December 24, 2010, http://online.wsj.com, accessed on July 30, 2013; and Jennifer Alsever, "Fair Prices for Farmers: Simple Idea, Complex Reality," *New York Times*, March 19, 2006, www.nytimes.com, accessed on July 30, 2013.

You Make the Call

Social Entrepreneurship at Its Finest

1. What environmental events and forces have led to the existence of organizations such as Mercy Corps?
2. In what ways does Mercy Corps interact with its environment in order to fulfill its mission?
3. Discuss how the economic, global, and ethical environments interact with respect to an organization like Mercy Corps.
4. If you were asked to critique Mercy Corps in terms of effectiveness, what factors would you focus on?

ENDNOTES

1 Mercy Corps, "What We're Doing in Haiti," January 23, 2010, www.mercycorps.org accessed on July 30, 2013; Mercy Corps, "Our History," 2012, www.mercycorps.org accessed on July 30, 2013; Roger Burks, "Change Brewing in the Tea Lands," Mercy Corps, April 9, 2008, www.mercycorps.org accessed on July 30, 2013; Mercy Corps, "Sudan," 2012, www.mercycorps.org accessed on July 30, 2013; Mercy Corps Indonesia, 2012, http://www.mercycorps.org/indonesia accessed on July 30, 2013; Roger Burks, "Responding to Niger's Latest Hunger Crisis," Mercy Corps, July 23, 2010, www.mercycorps.org accessed on July 30, 2013; USAID, "USAID Helps Drought-Affected Niger with First Award under the Emergency Food Security Program," press release, June 17, 2010, www.usaid.gov accessed on July 30, 2013; Wahyu Nugroho, "Farmers in Timor-Leste Store Up for a Better Future," Mercy Corps, March 22, 2011, www.mercycorps.org accessed on July 30, 2013.

2 See Jay B. Barney and William G. Ouchi, eds., *Organizational Economics* (San Francisco: Jossey-Bass, 1986), for a detailed analysis of linkages between economics and organizations.

3 See, for example, "Political Pendulum Swings toward Stricter Regulation," *Wall Street Journal*, March 24, 2008, pp. A1, A11; see also "Changing Safety Rules Perplex and Polarize," *USA Today*, February 5, 2009, pp. 1B, 2B; and Nina Easton and Telis Demos, "The Business Guide to Congress," *Fortune*, May 11, 2009, pp. 72–75.

4 For example, see Susanne G. Scott and Vicki R. Lane, "A Stakeholder Approach to Organizational Identity," *Academy of Management Review*, 2000, Vol. 25, No. 1, pp. 43–62.

5 Richard N. Osborn and John Hagedoorn, "The Institutionalization and Evolutionary Dynamics of Interorganizational Alliances and Networks," *Academy of Management Journal*, April 1997, pp. 261–278. See also "More Companies Cut Risk by Collaborating with Their 'Enemies,'" *Wall Street Journal*, January 31, 2000, pp. A1, A10.

6 "GM, Ford Team to Develop 10-Speed Transmission," *USA Today*, April 16, 2013, p. 2B.

7 The Best & Worst Boards," *BusinessWeek*, October 7, 2002, pp. 104–114. See also Amy Hillman and Thomas Dalziel, "Boards

of Directors and Firm Performance: Integrating Agency and Resource Dependence Perspectives," *Academy of Management Review*, 2003, Vol. 23, No. 3, pp. 383–396.

8 "The Wild New Workforce," *BusinessWeek*, December 6, 1999, pp. 38–44.

9 "Temporary Workers Getting Short Shrift," *USA Today*, April 11, 1997, pp. 1B, 2B.

10 "Curves Ahead," *Wall Street Journal*, March 10, 1999, pp. B1, B10.

11 See Norman Barry, *Business Ethics* (West Lafayette, IN: Purdue University Press, 1999).

12 Thomas Donaldson and Thomas W. Dunfee, "Toward a Unified Conception of Business Ethics: An Integrative Social Contracts Theory," *Academy of Management Review*, Vol. 19, No. 2, 1994, pp. 252–284.

13 "Chains' Ties Run Deep on Pharmacy Boards," *USA Today*, December 31, 2008, pp. 1B, 2B.

14 "Diamond Foods Restating Profits after an Audit," *Bloomberg Businessweek*, February 13–19, 2012, p. 28.

15 "U.S. Probes Hilton over Theft Claims," *Wall Street Journal*, April 22, 2009, pp. B1, B4.

16 "The Lies We Tell at Work," *Bloomberg Businessweek*, February 4–February 10, 2013, pp. 71–73.

17 William Dill, "Beyond Codes and Courses," *Selections*, Fall 2002, pp. 21–23.

18 "How to Fix Corporate Governance," *BusinessWeek*, May 6, 2002, pp. 68–78. See also Catherine Daily, Dan Dalton, and Albert Cannella, "Corporate Governance: Decades of Dialogue and Data," *Academy of Management Review*, 2003, Vol. 28, No. 3, pp. 371–382.

19 "Is It Rainforest Crunch Time?" *BusinessWeek*, July 15, 1996, pp. 70–71; and "Yo, Ben! Yo, Jerry! It's Just Ice Cream," *Fortune*, April 28, 1997, p. 374.

20 Andrew Singer, "Can a Company Be Too Ethical?" *Across the Board*, April 1993, pp. 17–22.

21 "Legal but Lousy," *Fortune*, September 2, 2002, p. 192.

22 Lynn Sharp Paine, "Managing for Organizational Integrity," *Harvard Business Review*, March–April 1994, pp. 106–115.

23 "To Give, or Not to Give," *Time*, May 11, 2009, p. 10.

24 "Battling 'Donor Dropsy,'" *Wall Street Journal*, July 19, 2002, pp. B1, B4.

25 "A New Way of Giving," *Time*, July 24, 2000, pp. 48–51. See also Michael Porter and Mark Kramwe, "The Competitive Advantage of Corporate Philanthropy," *Harvard Business Review*, December 2002, pp. 57–66.

26 David M. Messick and Max H. Bazerman, "Ethical Leadership and the Psychology of Decision Making," *Sloan Management Review*, Winter 1996, pp. 9–22.

27 "Ethics in Action: Getting It Right," *Selections*, Fall 2002, pp. 24–27.

28 "Walmart's Discounted Ethics," *Time*, May 7, 2012, p. 19.

29 For a recent review of the literature on whistle-blowing, see Janet P. Near and Marcia P. Miceli, "Whistle-Blowing: Myth and Reality," *Journal of Management*, 1996, Vol. 22, No. 3, pp. 507–526. See also Michael Gundlach, Scott Douglas, and Mark Martinko, "The Decision to Blow the Whistle: A Social Information Processing Framework," *Academy of Management Review*, 2003, Vol. 28, No. 1, pp. 107–123.

30 For instance, see "The Complex Goals and Unseen Costs of Whistle-Blowing," *Wall Street Journal*, November 25, 2002, pp. A1, A10.

31 "He Blew a Whistle for 9 Years," *USA Today*, February 13, 2009, pp. 1B, 2B.

32 "SEC Announces a Whistle-Blower Overhaul Plan," *USA Today*, March 6, 2009, p. 1B.

33 "IRS Pays UBS Whistle-Blower $104 Million," *USA Today*, September 12, 2012, p. 2B.

34 "The Fortune Global 500—World's Largest Corporations," *Fortune*, June 20, 2013, pp. 74–120.

35 "The Fortune Global 500 Ranked within Industries," *Fortune*, June 23, 2013, pp. 74–80.

36 *Hoover's Handbook of American Business* 2013, pp. 119–120, 322–323.

37 "Our Films Are Poppin' With Overseas Audiences," *USA Today*, April 15, 2013, p. 1D.

38 See "Spanning the Globe," *USA Today*, April 30, 2002, pp. 1C, 2C.

39 "Creating a Worldwide Yen for Japanese Beer," *Financial Times*, October 7, 1994, p. 20.

40 Kenichi Ohmae, "The Global Logic of Strategic Alliances," *Harvard Business Review*, March–April 1989, pp. 143–154.

41 "PepsiCo Prepares for a Snack War in Russia," *Bloomberg Businessweek*, March 4–March 10, 2013, pp. 21–22.

42 "What If There Weren't Any Clocks to Watch?" *Newsweek*, June 30, 1997, p. 14.

43 "Main Street, H.K.—Disney Localizes Mickey to Boost Its Hong Kong Theme Park," *Wall Street Journal*, January 23, 2008, pp. B1, B2.

44 For an excellent discussion of the effects of NAFTA, see "In the Wake of NAFTA, a Family Firm Sees Business Go South," *Wall Street Journal*, February 23, 1999, pp. A1, A10.

45 Terrence E. Deal and Allan A. Kennedy, *Corporate Cultures: The Rights and Rituals of Corporate Life* (Reading, MA: Addison-Wesley, 1982).

46 Jay B. Barney, "Organizational Culture: Can It Be a Source of Sustained Competitive Advantage?" *Academy of Management Review*, July 1986, pp. 656–665.

47 For example, see Carol J. Loomis, "Sam Would Be Proud," *Fortune*, April 17, 2000, pp. 131–144.

48 *Hoover's Handbook of American Business* 2013 (Austin, TX: Hoover's Business Press, 2013), pp. 268–269.

49 "Marriage at 30,000 Feet," *Bloomberg Businessweek*, February 6–12, 2012, pp. 58–63.

CHAPTER 3

Planning and Strategic Management

Learning Outcomes

After studying this chapter, you should be able to:

1 Summarize the planning process and describe organizational goals.

2 Discuss the components of strategy and the types of strategic alternatives.

3 Describe how to use SWOT analysis in formulating strategy.

4 Identify and describe various alternative approaches to business-level strategy formulation.

5 Identify and describe various alternative approaches to corporate-level strategy formulation.

6 Discuss how tactical plans are developed and implemented.

7 Describe the basic types of operational plans used by organizations.

Management in Action

Google's Strategy for Dominance

"We don't talk about our strategy ... because it's strategic. I would rather have people think we're confused than let our competitors know what we're going to do."

—Larry Page, Google Co-founder

Sergey Brin and Larry Page met at Stanford University in 1995 when both were graduate students in computer science. At the time, Page was working on a software-development project designed to create an index of websites by scouring sites for key words and other linkages. Brin joined him on the project, and when they were satisfied that they'd developed something with commercial value, they tried to license the technology to other search companies. As luck would have it, they couldn't find a buyer and settled instead for procuring enough investment capital to keep refining and testing their product.

In 2000, Brin and Page ran across a discussion of a business model based on the concept of selling advertising in the form of sponsored links and search-specific ads. They adapted it to their own concept and went into business for themselves. They named their new venture Google and, as you probably know, it has grown to become the world's largest search engine. Google generally processes more than 11,300 million searches a month by a user base of 380 million people in 181 different countries and using 146

65

Rob Kim/Landov

Sergey Brin and Larry Page, founders of Google, spend much of their time planning and developing new strategies. When they bought YouTube, they made the announcement in a YouTube video.

languages. Following an IPO in 2004, the company's market capitalization rose steadily; it stood at more than $243.65 billion by 2012, when Google controlled 66.7 percent of the U.S. search market (compared to Yahoo!'s 12.1 percent and Microsoft's 16.3 percent).

Google, however, is much more than a mere search engine. Services include searches for news, shopping, local businesses, interactive maps, and discussion groups, as well as blogs, web-based e-mail and voice mail, and a digital photo-management system. You can access the results of any Google search from the Google website, from your own user's toolbar, from your Windows taskbar, and from wireless devices such as smartphones and tablets. Amazingly, Google estimates that 15 percent of searches conducted each day are new—never having been searched before.

How did two young computer scientists build this astoundingly successful company, and where will they take it in the future? Brin and Page remain in the forefront of Google's search for technological innovations. They believe in the power of mathematics and have developed unique algorithms for just about every form of activity in the firm. One of the most successful is an algorithm for auctioning advertising placements that ensures the highest possible prices. Brin and Page have also been remarkably successful in attracting talented and creative employees and providing them with a work environment and culture that foster the kind of productivity and innovation for which they were hired.

Finally, although the founders avoid formal strategic planning, they've managed to diversify extensively through acquisitions and key alliances. Typically, Google absorbs an acquired firm and then improves on its technology, thereby adding variety to its own online offerings. Recent acquisitions include YouTube, a leader in online video sharing, Postini, a leader in communications-security products, and Double Click, a leader in online advertising services. Strategic alliances include those with foreign online service providers that offer Google searches on their sites.

For the immediate future, at least, Google plans on following its basic proven recipe for success, competing head to head with financial-service providers for stock information and with iTunes for music and videos. Also committed to the in-house development of new features and services, Google spent $2.8 billion on R&D in 2012 (up from $1.2 billion in 2006) and another $1 billion to acquire new IT assets. Innovations in the works include an automated universal language translator for translating documents in any language into any other language and personalized home pages that will allow users to design automatic searches and display the results in personal "newspapers."

Nobody knows for sure what else is on the drawing board. In fact, outsiders—notably potential investors—often criticize Google for being a "black box" when they want a few more details on Google's long-range strategy. "We don't talk about our strategy," explains Page, "... because it's strategic. I would rather have people think we're confused than let our competitors know what we're going to do."[1]

Strategic thinking is at the heart of effective management in any business, including old-line industrial giants like Ford and General Electric to newer web-based businesses such as Google and Yahoo!. This chapter discusses how organizations manage strategy and how managers engage in strategic planning. As we note in Chapter 1, planning and decision making comprise the first managerial functions that organizations must address. This chapter is the first of three that explore planning and decision making.

PLANNING AND ORGANIZATIONAL GOALS

The planning process itself can best be thought of as a generic activity. All organizations engage in planning activities, but no two organizations plan in exactly the same fashion. Figure 3.1 is a general representation of the planning process that many organizations attempt to follow. But although most firms follow this general framework, each also has its own nuances and variations.[2]

As Figure 3.1 shows, all planning occurs within an environmental context. If managers do not understand this context, they are unable to develop effective plans. Thus, understanding the environment is essentially the first step in planning. Chapter 2 covered many of the basic environmental issues that affect organizations and how they plan. With this understanding as a foundation, managers must then establish the organization's mission. The mission outlines the organization's purpose, premises, values, and directions. Flowing from the mission are parallel streams of goals and plans. Directly following the mission are strategic goals. These goals and the mission help determine strategic plans. Strategic goals and plans are primary inputs for developing tactical goals. Tactical goals and the original strategic plans help shape tactical plans. Tactical plans, in turn, combine with the tactical goals to shape operational goals. These goals and the appropriate tactical plans determine operational plans. Finally, goals and plans at each level can also be used as inputs for future activities at all levels.

© Cengage Learning

FIGURE 3.1

The Planning Process

The planning process takes place within an environmental context. Managers must develop a complete and thorough understanding of this context to determine the organization's mission and to develop its strategic, tactical, and operational goals and plans.

Organizational Goals

Goals are critical to organizational effectiveness, and they serve a number of purposes. Organizations can also have several different kinds of goals, all of which must be appropriately managed. And a number of different kinds of managers must be involved in setting goals.

Purposes of Goals Goals serve four important purposes.[3] First, they provide guidance and a unified direction for people in the organization. Goals can help everyone understand where the organization is going and why getting there is important.[4] Mark Pincus, founder and CEO of the social-gaming company Zynga, recently noted that "it's important to know what your goal is, because if you don't know what your goal is, you will … never achieve it."[5] IBM announced a goal to achieve earnings per share of $20 (up from $11.52 in 2010) by 2015. The company also plans to reach $100 billion in cash flow and return 70 percent to shareholders by that same year.[6] Top managers at General Electric (GE) have a long-standing goal that every business owned by the firm will be either number one or number two in its industry. This goal helps set the tone for decisions made by GE managers as it competes with other firms such as Whirlpool and Electrolux.[7]

Second, goal-setting practices strongly affect other aspects of planning. Effective goal setting promotes good planning, and good planning facilitates future goal setting. For example, IBM's financial goals demonstrate how setting goals and developing plans to reach them should be seen as complementary activities. Specifically, the firm will need to work aggressively to boost both profits and cash flow to meet its goals.

Third, goals can serve as a source of motivation for an organization's employees. Goals that are specific and moderately difficult can motivate people to work harder, especially if attaining the goal is likely to result in rewards.[8] The Italian furniture manufacturer Industrie Natuzzi SpA uses goals to motivate its workers. Each craftsperson has a goal for how long it should take to perform his or her job, such as sewing leather sheets together to make a sofa cushion or building wooden frames for chair arms. At the completion of assigned tasks, workers enter their ID numbers and job numbers into the firm's computer system. If they get a job done faster than their goal, a bonus is automatically added to their paycheck.[9]

Finally, goals provide an effective mechanism for evaluation and control. This means that performance can be assessed in the future in terms of how successfully today's goals are accomplished. For example, suppose that officials of the United Way of America set a goal of collecting $250,000 from a particular small community. If, midway through the campaign, they have raised only $50,000, they know that they need to change or intensify their efforts. If they raise only $100,000 by the end of their drive, they will carefully study why they did not reach their goal and what they need to do differently next year. On the other hand, if they succeed in raising $250,000 or more, evaluations of their efforts will take on an entirely different character.

mission
A statement of an organization's fundamental purpose

Kinds of Goals   Goals are set for and by different levels within an organization. An organization's **mission** is a statement of its "fundamental, unique purpose that sets a business apart from other firms of its type and identifies the scope of the business's operations in product and market terms."[10] For instance, Starbucks' mission statement is to be "the premier purveyor of the finest coffee in the world while maintaining our uncompromising principles while we grow." The principles to which the mission refers help managers at Starbucks make decisions and direct resources in clear and specific ways.

strategic goal
A goal set by and for an organization's top management

Strategic goals are set by and for an organization's top management. They focus on broad, general issues. For example, Starbucks has a strategic goal of increasing the profitability of each of its coffee stores by 25 percent over the next five years. **Tactical goals** are set by and for middle managers. Their focus is on how to operationalize actions necessary to achieve the strategic goals. To achieve Starbucks' goal of increasing its per-store profitability, managers are working on tactical goals related to company-owned versus licensed stores and the global distribution of stores in different countries. **Operational goals** are set by and for lower-level managers. Their concern is with shorter-term issues associated with the tactical goals. An operational goal for Starbucks might be to boost the profitability of a certain number of stores in each of the next five years. (Some managers use the words *objective* and *goal* interchangeably. When they are differentiated, however, the term *objective* is usually used instead of *operational goal*.)

tactical goal
A goal set by and for an organization's middle managers

operational goal
A goal set by and for an organization's lower-level managers

Kinds of Organizational Plans

Organizations establish many different kinds of plans. At a general level, these include strategic, tactical, and operational plans.

strategic plan
A general plan outlining decisions about the resource allocation, priorities, and action steps necessary to reach strategic goals

Strategic Plans   Strategic plans are developed to achieve strategic goals. More precisely, a **strategic plan** is a general plan outlining decisions about resource allocation, priorities, and action steps necessary to reach strategic goals. These plans are set by the board of directors and top management, generally have an extended time horizon, and address questions of scope, resource deployment, competitive advantage, and synergy. We discuss strategic planning further in the next major section of this chapter.

Tactical Plans   A tactical plan, aimed at achieving tactical goals, is developed to implement specific parts of a strategic plan. Tactical plans typically involve upper and middle management and, compared with strategic plans, have a somewhat shorter time horizon and a more specific and concrete focus. Thus, tactical plans are concerned more

LEADING THE WAY

Setting a New Direction for General Motors

General Motors is over a hundred years old, and for much of that time was the world's dominant automobile manufacturer. But rising employee health care costs, an onslaught of new foreign competitors, and high wage contracts with its major unions severely weakened GM in the early years of the twenty-first century, Perhaps it is no surprise, then, that GM was knocked to the mat when the global economy plunged into recession a few years ago.

The auto giant lost $38 billion in 2007, another $32 billion in 2008, and was forced to declare Chapter 11 bankruptcy. Using Chapter 11 protection, GM cancelled several joint ventures, renegotiated some of its labor contracts, shed brands like Pontiac and Saturn, lowered its operating costs, and reduced its debt. And when it emerged from bankruptcy in 2010, the firm was ready to compete in new and different ways.

To the surprise of many observers, Daniel Akerson was appointed CEO of the new GM and charged with leading the company back to profitability. His appointment was unexpected because he had no automobile industry experience—he is an electrical engineer by training, spent several years as a Naval officer, and had worked in the telecommunications, technology, and private investments industries. To the naysayers, he "wasn't a car guy." And to some, that doomed him to failure.

One thing he did have, though, was a long history of effective leadership. Akerson had been successful at every stop along the way, and was consistently hailed as both a strong leader and an astute manager. In his words, a CEO's role is "to articulate [the] vision, and a strategy, what you want to accomplish." And virtually everyone who ever worked for Akerson agreed that he played that role with integrity and effectiveness.

While his detractors expected him to fail, those who knew him expected just the opposite. And as things developed, they were right. Following Akerson's appointment and GM's emergence from

Chapter 11 in 2010, the firm has been on a consistent upward trajectory, regaining lost market share, launching successful new products, and posting record profits—$25 billion in 2012. His supporters attributed his success to a consistent message of product quality, innovation, and openness to change (traits apparently not found at GM for a long time). Akerson also spent a lot of time out in GM factories talking to the people who build the cars and in GM dealerships talking to the people who buy cars.

What happened next was even more amazing. In late 2013, Akerson was just starting to think about his replacement when his wife was diagnosed with cancer and he decided to step down sooner than anticipated. Akerson informed the board that he thought the best candidate to replace him was Mary Barra, the firm's executive vice president of global product development, purchasing, and supply chain. The board quickly decided that Akerson was right and appointed Barra to the position of CEO in January 2014. This marked the first time a woman has ever led a major U.S. auto company. So, what does the future hold for Barra and GM? On the one hand, she will likely have to deal with sexism from some quarters and still faces stiff competition from both domestic and foreign rivals. A major product recall and allegations about a cover-up of defects leading to that recall will also pose challenges. But others believe that GM has been successfully transformed from a staid, old car company into an innovative and flexible company that will remain competitive for a long time.

References: "GM CEO: 'Good Enough' Isn't," *USA Today*, August 5, 2013, p. 1B; *Hoover's Handbook of American Business 2013* (Austin: Mergent, 2013), pp. 381–383; "Mary Barra Named GM CEO, Automaker's First Female Chief," *Forbes*, December 10, 2013, pp. 23–24; "GM CEO Mary Barra Admired by Fellow Auto Executives, Competitors," http://www.mlive.com/auto/, accessed on February 16, 2014.

operational plan
A plan that focuses on carrying out tactical plans to achieve operational goals

with actually getting things done than with deciding what to do. Tactical planning is covered in detail later in this chapter.

Operational Plans   An **operational plan** focuses on carrying out tactical plans to achieve operational goals. Developed by middle- and lower-level managers, operational plans have a short-term focus and are relatively narrow in scope. Each one deals with a fairly small set of activities. We also cover operational planning in more detail later in this chapter.

THE NATURE OF STRATEGIC MANAGEMENT

strategy

A comprehensive plan for accomplishing an organization's goals

A **strategy** is a comprehensive plan for accomplishing an organization's goals. **Strategic management**, in turn, is a way of approaching business opportunities and challenges—it is a comprehensive and ongoing management process aimed at formulating and implementing effective strategies. Finally, **effective strategies** are those that promote a superior alignment between the organization and its environment and the achievement of strategic goals.[11]

strategic management

A comprehensive and ongoing management process aimed at formulating and implementing effective strategies; a way of approaching business opportunities and challenges

The Components of Strategy

In general, a well-conceived strategy addresses three areas: distinctive competence, scope, and resource deployment. A **distinctive competence** is something the organization does exceptionally well. A distinctive competence of Abercrombie & Fitch is its speed in moving inventory. It tracks consumer preferences daily with point-of-sale computers, electronically transmits orders to suppliers in Hong Kong, charters 747 cargo planes to fly new products to the United States, and has those products in stores 48 hours later. Because other retailers take weeks or sometimes months to accomplish the same things, Abercrombie & Fitch uses this distinctive competence to remain competitive.[12]

effective strategy

A strategy that promotes a superior alignment between the organization and its environment and the achievement of strategic goals

The **scope** of a strategy specifies the range of markets in which an organization will compete. Hershey Foods has essentially restricted its scope to the confectionery business,

distinctive competence

An organizational strength possessed by only a small number of competing firms

scope

When applied to strategy, it specifies the range of markets in which an organization will compete

Resource deployment is an important part of strategic management. General Electric, for example, has often used profits from its U.S. operations to invest in new business opportunities abroad. In 2013, for example, the firm broke ground on a new energy business in Berlin. Much of the start-up costs for the new business were funded from other GE operations.

resource deployment
How an organization distributes its resources across the areas in which it competes

business-level strategy
The set of strategic alternatives from which an organization chooses as it conducts business in a particular industry or market

corporate-level strategy
The set of strategic alternatives from which an organization chooses as it manages its operations simultaneously across several industries and several markets

strategy formulation
The set of processes involved in creating or determining an organization's strategies; it focuses on the content of strategies

strategy implementation
The methods by which strategies are operationalized or executed within the organization; it focuses on the processes through which strategies are achieved

with a few related activities in other food-processing areas. In contrast, its biggest competitor, Mars, has adopted a broader scope by competing in the pet food business and the electronics industry, among others. Some organizations, called *conglomerates*, compete in dozens or even hundreds of markets.

A strategy should also include an outline of the organization's projected **resource deployment**—how it will distribute its resources across the areas in which it competes. General Electric, for example, has been using profits from its highly successful U.S. operations to invest heavily in new businesses in Europe and Asia. Alternatively, the firm might have chosen to invest in different industries in its domestic market or to invest more heavily in Latin America. The choices it makes as to where and how much to invest reflect issues of resource deployment.

Types of Strategic Alternatives

Most businesses today develop strategies at two distinct levels: the business level and corporate level. These levels provide a rich combination of strategic alternatives for organizations. **Business-level strategy** is the set of strategic alternatives from which an organization chooses as it conducts business in a particular industry or market. Such alternatives help the organization focus its competitive efforts for each industry or market in a targeted and focused manner.

Corporate-level strategy is the set of strategic alternatives from which an organization chooses as it manages its operations simultaneously across several industries and several markets. As we discuss later in this chapter, most large companies today compete in various industries and markets. Thus, although they develop business-level strategies for each industry or market, they also develop an overall strategy that helps define the mix of industries and markets that are of interest to the firm.

Drawing a distinction between strategy formulation and strategy implementation is also instructive. **Strategy formulation** is the set of processes involved in creating or determining the organization's strategies, whereas **strategy implementation** is the methods by which those strategies are operationalized or executed. The primary distinction is along the lines of content versus process: The formulation stage determines what the strategy is, and the implementation stage focuses on how the strategy is achieved.

USING SWOT ANALYSIS TO FORMULATE STRATEGY

The starting point in formulating strategy is usually **SWOT** (strengths, weaknesses, opportunities, and threats) analysis. As shown in Figure 3.2, SWOT analysis is a careful evaluation of an organization's internal strengths and weaknesses as well as its environmental opportunities and threats. In SWOT analysis, the best strategies accomplish an organization's mission by (1) exploiting an organization's opportunities and strengths while (2) neutralizing its threats and (3) avoiding (or correcting) its weaknesses.

Evaluating an Organization's Strengths

Organizational strengths are skills and capabilities that enable an organization to create and implement its strategies. Strengths may include things like a deep pool of managerial talent, surplus capital, a unique reputation and/or brand name, and well-established

Mission
An organization's fundamental purpose

↓

SWOT Analysis
To formulate strategies that support the mission

Internal Analysis
Strengths (distinctive competencies)

Weaknesses

External Analysis
Opportunities

Threats

↓

Good Strategies
Those that support the mission and
• exploit opportunities and strengths
• neutralize threats
• avoid weaknesses

© Cengage Learning

FIGURE 3.2

SWOT Analysis

SWOT analysis is one of the most important steps in formulating strategy. Using the organization's mission as a context, managers assess internal strengths (distinctive competencies) and weaknesses as well as external opportunities and threats. The goal is then to develop good strategies that exploit opportunities and strengths, neutralize threats, and avoid weaknesses.

SWOT

An acronym that stands for strengths, weaknesses, opportunities, and threats

organizational strength

A skill or capability that enables an organization to create and implement its strategies

distribution channels.[13] Sears, for example, has a nationwide network of trained service employees who repair its appliances. Jane Thompson, a Sears executive, created a plan to consolidate repair and home improvement services nationwide under the well-known Sears brand name and to promote them as a general repair operation for all appliances, not just those purchased from Sears. Thus, the firm capitalized on existing capabilities and the strength of its name to launch a new operation.

A *distinctive competence*, introduced earlier in this chapter, is a strength possessed by only a small number of competing firms. Distinctive competencies are rare among a set of competitors. When George Lucas founded Industrial Light & Magic (ILM), for example, the new venture brought the cinematic art of special effects to new heights. Some of ILM's special effects can be produced by no other organization; these rare special effects are thus ILM's distinctive competencies. Indeed, ILM (now owned by Disney) had no real competitor until Peter Jackson formed Weta Digital Effects to help bring *The Lord of the Rings* to the screen. But even so, although ILM and Weta have some of the same competences, each also has proprietary technology that gives it certain unique advantages. Organizations that exploit their distinctive competencies often obtain a competitive advantage and attain above-normal economic performance.[14] Indeed, a main purpose of SWOT analysis is to discover an organization's distinctive competencies so that the organization can choose and implement strategies that exploit its unique organizational strengths.

Evaluating an Organization's Weaknesses

Organizational weaknesses are skills and capabilities that do not enable an organization to choose and implement strategies that support its mission. An organization has essentially two ways of addressing weaknesses. First, it may need to make investments to obtain the strengths required to implement strategies that support its mission. Second, it may need to modify its mission so that it can be accomplished with the skills and capabilities that the organization already possesses.

In practice, organizations have a difficult time focusing on weaknesses, in part because organization members are often reluctant to admit that they do not possess all the skills and capabilities needed. Evaluating weaknesses also calls into question the judgment of managers who chose the organization's mission in the first place and who failed to invest in the skills and capabilities needed to accomplish it.

American Airlines sought bankruptcy protection in 2012–13 in order to restructure itself. Poor labor relations, a reputation for indifferent customer service, insufficient cash reserves, and an aging jet fleet were all organizational weaknesses that led to the firm's problems.

Evaluating an Organization's Opportunities and Threats

Whereas evaluating strengths and weaknesses focuses attention on the internal workings of an organization, evaluating opportunities and threats requires analyzing an organization's environment. **Organizational opportunities** are areas that may generate higher performance. **Organizational threats** are areas that increase the difficulty of an organization performing at a high level.

FORMULATING BUSINESS-LEVEL STRATEGIES

A number of frameworks have been developed for identifying the major strategic alternatives that organizations should consider when choosing their business-level strategies. Two of the most important ones are Porter's generic strategies and strategies based on the product life cycle.

Porter's Generic Strategies

According to Michael Porter, organizations may pursue a differentiation, overall cost leadership, or focus strategy at the business level.[15] An organization that pursues a **differentiation strategy** seeks to distinguish itself from competitors through the quality (broadly defined) of its products or services. Firms that successfully implement a differentiation strategy are able to charge more than competitors because customers are willing to pay more to obtain the extra value they perceive.[16] Rolex pursues a differentiation strategy. Rolex watches are handmade of stainless steel and precious metals such as gold or platinum, and they are subjected to strenuous tests of quality and reliability. The firm's reputation enables it to charge thousands of dollars for its watches. Coca-Cola and Pepsi compete in the market for bottled water on the basis of differentiation. Coke touts its Dasani brand on the basis of its fresh taste, whereas Pepsi promotes its Aquafina brand on the basis of its purity.[17] Other firms that use differentiation strategies are Lexus, Godiva, Nikon, Mont Blanc, Apple, and Ralph Lauren. During the recent

organizational weakness
A skill or capability that does not enable an organization to choose and implement strategies that support its mission

organizational opportunity
An area in the environment that, if exploited, may generate higher performance

organizational threat
An area that increases the difficulty of an organization performing at a high level

differentiation strategy
A strategy in which an organization seeks to distinguish itself from competitors through the quality of its products or services

economic recession, most youth-oriented retailers such as American Eagle Outfitters, Quiksilver, and Aéropostale slashed prices to generate sales. But Abercrombie & Fitch decided to hold firm to standard pricing in an attempt to maintain a differentiated image for its products.[18] Similarly, other firms tried to provide strong differentiation on the basis of outstanding customer service.[19]

overall cost leadership strategy

A strategy in which an organization attempts to gain a competitive advantage by reducing its costs below the costs of competing firms

An organization implementing an **overall cost leadership strategy** attempts to gain a competitive advantage by reducing its costs below the costs of competing firms. By keeping costs low, the organization is able to sell its products at low prices and still make a profit. Timex uses an overall cost leadership strategy. For decades, this firm has specialized in manufacturing relatively simple, low-cost watches for the mass market. The price of Timex watches, starting around $39.95, is low because of the company's efficient high-volume manufacturing capacity. Poland Springs and Crystal Geyser bottled waters are promoted on the basis of their low cost. Other firms that implement overall cost leadership strategies are Hyundai, BIC, Old Navy, and Hershey. When the 2008 economic recession hit, Hershey actually experienced a jump in sales—during hard times, consumers started cutting back on high-end chocolate products from Godiva but weren't willing to forgo chocolate altogether.[20] Likewise, other low-cost producers also benefited as consumers avoided higher-priced brand-name products (i.e., those with a differentiation strategy) in favor of lower-priced goods. For instance, both P&G and Colgate saw sales of products such as Tide, Pampers, and Colgate toothpaste decline, whereas sales of lower-priced private-label products jumped.[21]

focus strategy

A strategy in which an organization concentrates on a specific regional market, product line, or group of buyers

A firm pursuing a **focus strategy** concentrates on a specific regional market, product line, or group of buyers. This strategy may have either a differentiation focus, whereby the firm differentiates its products in the focus market, or an overall cost leadership focus, whereby the firm manufactures and sells its products at low cost in the focus market. In the watch industry, Tag Heuer follows a focus differentiation strategy by selling only rugged waterproof watches to active consumers. Tata Motors follows a focus cost leadership strategy by selling its inexpensive automobiles only in India. Alfa Romeo uses focus differentiation to sell its high-performance cars only in markets where customers can pay over a hundred thousand dollars for a car. Fisher-Price uses focus differentiation to sell electronic calculators with large, brightly colored buttons to the parents of preschoolers; stockbroker Edward Jones focuses on small-town settings. General Mills focuses one part of its new-product development on consumers who eat meals while driving—its watchword is "Can we make it 'one-handed'?" so that drivers can safely eat or drink it. Two investors realized that most Las Vegas casinos were targeting either high-end big spenders or the young hip market. So, they bought the venerable old Tropicana casino, renovated it, and began marketing it to so-called Middle America—middle-aged or older gamblers who aren't into big dollar wagering. Their occupancy rates have soared, as have their profits.[22]

product life cycle

A model that portrays how sales volume for products changes over the life of products

©iStockphoto.com/evemilia

Hershey uses an overall cost leadership strategy to promote its candy bars. By keeping its costs as low as possible, the firm can provide good-quality snacks at competitive prices. This strategy benefited the firm during the recent recession as customers cut back on higher-priced candy, allowing Hershey to gain new market share.

Strategies Based on the Product Life Cycle

The **product life cycle** is a model that shows how sales volume changes over the life of products. Understanding the four stages in the product life cycle helps managers recognize that strategies need to evolve

High
Sales volume
Low

Stages

Introduction   Growth   Maturity   Decline

Time

© Cengage Learning

The Product Life Cycle

Managers can use the framework of the product life cycle—introduction, growth, maturity, and decline—to plot strategy. For example, management may decide on a differentiation strategy for a product in the introduction stage and a prospector approach for a product in the growth stage. By understanding this cycle and where a particular product falls within it, managers can develop more effective strategies for extending product life.

over time. As Figure 3.3 shows, the cycle begins when a new product or technology is first introduced. In this introduction stage, demand may be very high and sometimes outpaces the firm's ability to supply the product. At this stage, managers need to focus their efforts on "getting product out the door" without sacrificing quality. Managing growth by hiring new employees and managing inventories and cash flow are also concerns during this stage.

During the growth stage, more firms begin producing the product, and sales continue to grow. Important management issues include ensuring quality and delivery and beginning to differentiate an organization's product from competitors' products. Entry into the industry during the growth stage may threaten an organization's competitive advantage; thus, strategies to slow the entry of competitors are important.

After a period of growth, products enter a third phase. During this maturity stage, overall demand growth for a product begins to slow down, and the number of new firms producing the product begins to decline. The number of established firms producing the product may also begin to decline. This period of maturity is essential if an organization is going to survive in the long run. Product differentiation concerns are still important during this stage, but keeping costs low and beginning the search for new products or services are also important strategic considerations.

In the *decline stage*, demand for the product or technology decreases, the number of organizations producing the product drops, and total sales drop. Demand often declines because all those who were interested in purchasing a particular product have already done so. Organizations that fail to anticipate the decline stage in earlier stages of the life cycle may go out of business. Those that differentiate their product, keep their costs low, or develop new products or services may do well during this stage.

FORMULATING CORPORATE-LEVEL STRATEGIES

Most large organizations are engaged in several businesses, industries, and markets. Each business or set of businesses within such an organization is frequently referred to as a *strategic business unit* (SBU). An organization such as GE operates hundreds of different businesses, making and selling products as diverse as jet engines, nuclear power plants, and lightbulbs. GE organizes these businesses into approximately 20 SBUs. Even organizations that sell only one product may operate in several distinct markets.

Decisions about which businesses, industries, and markets an organization will enter, and how to manage these different businesses, are based on an organization's corporate strategy. The most important strategic issue at the corporate level concerns the extent and nature of organizational diversification. **Diversification** describes the number of different businesses that an organization is engaged in and the extent to which these businesses are related to one another. There are three types of diversification strategies: single-product strategy, related diversification, and unrelated diversification.[23]

diversification
The number of different businesses that an organization is engaged in and the extent to which these businesses are related to one another

Single-Product Strategy

An organization that pursues a **single-product strategy** manufactures just one product or service and sells it in a single geographic market. The WD-40 Company, for example, basically manufactures one product, WD-40 spray lubricant, and for years sold it just in North America. WD-40 has started selling its lubricant in Europe and Asia, but it continues to center all manufacturing, sales, and marketing efforts on one product. Similarly, Michelin has remained faithful to the cause of strictly manufacturing quality tires.

The single-product strategy has one major strength and one major weakness. By concentrating its efforts so completely on one product and market, a firm is likely to be very successful in manufacturing and marketing the product. Because it has staked its survival on a single product, the organization works very hard to make sure that the product is a success. Of course, if the product is not accepted by the market or is replaced by a new one, the firm will suffer. This happened to slide-rule manufacturers when electronic calculators became widely available and to companies that manufactured only black-and-white televisions when low-priced color televisions were first mass-marketed. Similarly, Wrigley long practiced what amounted to a single-product strategy with its line of chewing gums. But, because younger consumers are buying less gum than earlier generations, Wrigley experienced declining revenues and lower profits. As a result, the Wrigley family eventually sold their business to Mars.[24]

single-product strategy
A strategy in which an organization manufactures just one product or service and sells it in a single geographic market

Related Diversification

Given the disadvantage of the single-product strategy, most large businesses today operate in several different businesses, industries, or markets.[25] If the businesses are somehow linked, that organization is implementing a strategy of **related diversification**. Virtually all larger businesses in the United States use related diversification.

Pursuing a strategy of related diversification has three primary advantages. First, it reduces an organization's dependence on any one of its business activities and thus reduces economic risk. Even if one or two of a firm's businesses lose money, the organization as a whole may still survive because the healthy businesses will generate enough cash to support the others.[26] At Disney, a decline in theme park attendance may be offset by an increase in box office and DVD sales of Disney movies and vice versa. When the firm lost millions on the poorly conceived movies *John Carter* in 2012 and

related diversification
A strategy in which an organization operates in several businesses that are somehow linked with one another

AP Images/Disney-Pixar

Disney has successfully used related diversification strategies for years. For instance, an annual slate of both animated and live-action movies complements its attractions at theme parks and retail outlets and then feeds directly into DVD and streaming video operations. Recent smash hits *Monsters University* (shown here), *Frozen*, and *Iron Man 3*, for instance, will help fuel Disney profits for years.

The Lone Ranger in 2013, Disney was still profitable due to strong theme park revenues and other hit movies like *The Avengers* in 2012 and *Iron Man 3*, *Monsters University*, and *Frozen* in 2013.

Second, by managing several businesses at the same time, an organization can reduce the overhead costs associated with managing any one business. In other words, if the normal administrative costs required to operate any business, such as legal services and accounting, can be spread over a large number of businesses, then the overhead costs per business will be lower than they would be if each business had to absorb all costs itself. Thus the overhead costs of businesses in a firm that pursues related diversification are usually lower than those of similar businesses that are not part of a larger corporation.[27]

Third, related diversification allows an organization to exploit its strengths and capabilities in more than one business. When organizations do this successfully, they capitalize on synergies, which are complementary effects that exist among their businesses. Synergy exists among a set of businesses when the businesses' economic value together is greater than their economic value separately. McDonald's is using synergy as it diversifies into other restaurant and food businesses. For example, both its McCafe premium coffee stands in some McDonald's restaurants and its investments in Pret A Manger, a European chain of sandwich shops, allow the firm to create new revenue opportunities while using the firm's existing strengths in food-product purchasing and distribution. "Tough Times, Tough Choices" discusses how diversification can also occasionally create ethical challenges.

Unrelated Diversification

unrelated diversification

A strategy in which an organization operates multiple businesses that are not logically associated with one another

Firms that implement a strategy of **unrelated diversification** operate multiple businesses that are not logically associated with one another. At one time, for example, Quaker Oats owned clothing chains, toy companies, and a restaurant business. Unrelated diversification was a very popular strategy several years ago. During that time, several conglomerates such as ITT and Transamerica grew by acquiring literally hundreds of other organizations and then running these numerous businesses as independent entities. Even if there are important potential synergies among their different businesses, organizations implementing a strategy of unrelated diversification do not attempt to exploit them.

In theory, unrelated diversification has two advantages. First, a business that uses this strategy should be able to achieve stable performance over time. During any given period, some businesses owned by the organization are in a cycle of decline, whereas others may be in a cycle of growth. Second, unrelated diversification is also thought to have resource allocation advantages. Every year, when a corporation allocates capital, people, and other resources among its various businesses, it must evaluate information about the future of those businesses so that it can place its resources where they have the highest potential for return. Given that it owns the businesses in question and thus has full access to information about the future of those businesses, a firm implementing unrelated diversification should be able to allocate capital to maximize corporate performance.

Despite these presumed advantages, research suggests that unrelated diversification usually does not lead to high performance. First, corporate-level managers in such a company usually do not know enough about the unrelated businesses to provide helpful strategic guidance or to allocate capital appropriately. To make strategic decisions, managers must have complete and subtle understanding of a business and its environment. Because corporate managers often have difficulty fully evaluating the economic importance of investments for all the businesses under their wing, they tend to concentrate only on a business's current performance. This narrow attention at the expense of broader planning eventually hobbles the entire organization.

Second, because organizations that implement unrelated diversification fail to exploit important synergies, they are at a competitive disadvantage compared to organizations that use related diversification. Universal Studios has been at a competitive disadvantage relative to Disney because its theme parks, movie studios, and licensing divisions are less integrated and therefore achieve less synergy.

For these reasons, almost all organizations have abandoned unrelated diversification as a corporate-level strategy. Transamerica, for instance, sold off numerous unrelated businesses and now concentrates on a core set of related businesses and markets. Large corporations that have not concentrated on a core set of businesses have eventually been acquired by other companies and then broken up. Research suggests that these organizations are actually worth more when broken up into smaller pieces than when joined.[28]

Managing Diversification   However an organization implements diversification—whether through internal development, vertical integration, or mergers and acquisitions—it must monitor and manage its strategy. **Portfolio management techniques** are methods that diversified organizations use to determine in which businesses to engage and how to manage these businesses to maximize corporate performance. Two important portfolio management techniques are the BCG matrix and the GE Business Screen.

BCG Matrix   The **BCG (Boston Consulting Group) matrix** provides a framework for evaluating the relative performance of businesses in which a diversified organization operates. It also prescribes the preferred distribution of cash and other resources among these businesses.[29] The BCG matrix uses two factors to evaluate an organization's set of businesses: the growth rate of a particular market and the organization's share of that market.

portfolio management techniques
Methods that diversified organizations use to determine in which businesses to engage and how to manage these businesses to maximize corporate performance

BCG (Boston Consulting Group) matrix
A framework for evaluating businesses relative to the growth rate of their market and the organization's share of the market

TOUGH TIMES, TOUGH CHOICES

The Little-White-Lie Strategy

It may surprise you to learn that The Coca-Cola Company does not make Coca-Cola. Coke and the other beverage brands owned by The Coca-Cola Company are actually manufactured by what the company calls *bottling partners*—more than 300 franchises worldwide that both make and distribute final Coke products to grocery stores, restaurants, and other places where consumers can purchase them. Up until 2010, the largest of these franchises had been Coca-Cola Enterprises (CCE), which held the franchise for most of North America and much of Europe.

According to Coke CEO Muhtar Kent, "the franchise model is the best way to win in the marketplace," and in November 2009, he extolled the Coke franchise system for fostering a "magnificent fusion of scalable, global brands." Three months later, however, Coke announced plans to purchase CCE's North American operations in a "substantially cashless" deal that would make CCE a European-oriented bottler and give Coke 90 percent control of its own bottling operations in North America. The deal was finalized in February 2010.

Coke admitted that negotiations with CCE had been in the works for about 18 months and that a confidentiality agreement between the two firms had been in effect since November 2008, long before Kent and other Coke executives had gone on record to support the company's franchise-bottling system. Had they been saying one thing in public while doing another behind boardroom doors? "There's no question," says Wall Street analyst Phil Gorham, that the CCE deal "flies in the face of what they've done in the past. This acquisition is absolutely an about-face." Does Gorham believe that Kent and other Coke leaders damaged the company's credibility? "I think so," he says. "I think investors will think twice from now on when they're told something from Coke."

Many corporate governance experts, however, observe that Kent was not legally obligated to explain the fine distinction between his simultaneous support of Coke's franchise system and his intention to take over its largest franchise. Legally speaking, executives cannot deny outright that they're engaged in negotiations, but they're also barred from mentioning negotiations in public: Such statements would amount to leaking inside information and might affect stock prices—in which case, investors who lost money when the market reacted to an executive's statement could sue the company.

"Part of this is the artful use of words," suggests Paul Lapides, director of the Corporate Governance Center at Kennesaw State University, who does not feel that Coke CEO Kent was misleading his investors. "Shareholders would really like to know everything that management is thinking about," says Lapides, "but that's just bad business." In this case, for example, hints of an imminent deal could have driven up the price that Coke ultimately paid for CCE. According to John Sicher, a former corporate lawyer who's now editor of *Beverage Digest*, Kent had skillfully walked a thin legal and ethical line. "He couldn't say too little or too much. His 'committed to the franchise system' message was accurate and an appropriate communication."

On the point that Kent saved money for Coke investors, even Gorham tends to agree: "If it involves telling a little white lie for a few months while negotiations are going on," he admits, "that's probably the best way to go about it."

References: Michael J. de la Merced, "Coke Confirms Purchase of a Bottling Unit," *New York Times*, February 26, 2010, www.nytimes.com, accessed on September 1, 2013; Jeremiah McWilliams, "Coca-Cola's Mixed Message Draws Critics," *Atlanta Journal-Constitution*, March 13, 2010, www.ajc.com, accessed on September 1, 2013; The Coca-Cola Co., "The Coca-Cola Company and Coca-Cola Enterprises Strategically Advance and Strengthen Their Partnership," press release, February 25, 2010, www.coca-colacompany.com, accessed on September 1, 2013; and "Coca-Cola Acquires CCE North America Business, Closes Sale of Norway and Swedish Bottling Operations to CCE," *DBR*, October 2, 2010, http://soft drinks.drinks-business-review.com, accessed on September 1, 2013.

The matrix suggests that fast-growing markets in which an organization has the highest market share are more attractive business opportunities than slow-growing markets in which an organization has small market share. Dividing market growth and market share into two categories (low and high) creates the simple matrix shown in Figure 3.4.

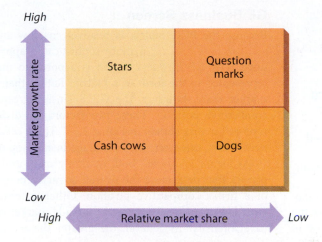

FIGURE 3.4

The BCG Matrix

The BCG matrix helps managers develop a better understanding of how different strategic business units contribute to the overall organization. By assessing each SBU on the basis of its market growth rate and relative market share, managers can make decisions about whether to commit further financial resources to the SBU or to sell or liquidate it.

Source: *Perspectives*, No. 66, "The Product Portfolio." Adapted by permission from The Boston Consulting Group, Inc., 1970.

The matrix classifies the types of businesses in which a diversified organization can engage as dogs, cash cows, question marks, and stars. Dogs are businesses that have a very small share of a market that is not expected to grow. Because these businesses do not hold much economic promise, the BCG matrix suggests that organizations either should not invest in them or should consider selling them as soon as possible. Cash cows are businesses that have a large share of a market that is not expected to grow substantially. These businesses characteristically generate high profits that the organization should use to support question marks and stars. (Cash cows are "milked" for cash to support businesses in markets that have greater growth potential.) Question marks are businesses that have only a small share of a quickly growing market. The future performance of these businesses is uncertain. A question mark that is able to capture increasing amounts of this growing market may be very profitable. On the other hand, a question mark unable to keep up with market growth is likely to have low profits. The BCG matrix suggests that organizations should invest carefully in question marks. If their performance does not live up to expectations, question marks should be reclassified as dogs and divested. Stars are businesses that have the largest share of a rapidly growing market. Cash generated by cash cows should be invested in stars to ensure their preeminent position. For example, BMW bought Rover a few years ago, thinking that its products would help the German automaker reach new consumers. But the company was not able to capitalize on this opportunity, so it ended up selling Rover's car business to a British firm and Land Rover to Ford. Ford couldn't get leverage out of Rover either and ended up selling it (along with Jaguar) to India's Tata Motors.

GE Business Screen

Because the BCG matrix is relatively narrow and overly simplistic, GE developed the **GE Business Screen**, a more sophisticated approach to managing diversified business units. The GE Business Screen is a portfolio management technique that can also be represented in the form of a matrix. Rather than focusing solely on market growth and market share, however, the GE Business Screen considers industry attractiveness and competitive position. These two factors are divided into three categories to make the nine-cell matrix shown in Figure 3.5.[30] These cells, in turn, classify business units as winners, losers, question marks, average businesses, or profit producers.

As Figure 3.5 shows, both market growth and market share appear in a broad list of factors that determine the overall attractiveness of an industry and the overall quality of a firm's competitive position. Other determinants of an industry's attractiveness (in addition to market growth) include market size, capital requirements, and competitive intensity. In general, the greater the market growth, the larger the market, the

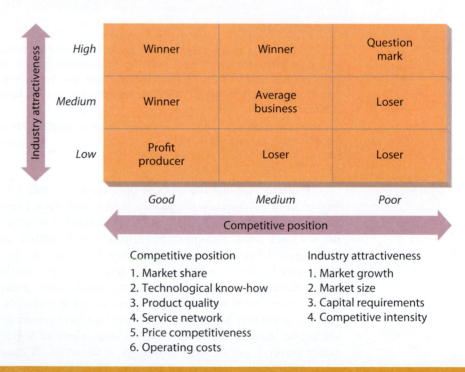

Competitive position
1. Market share
2. Technological know-how
3. Product quality
4. Service network
5. Price competitiveness
6. Operating costs

Industry attractiveness
1. Market growth
2. Market size
3. Capital requirements
4. Competitive intensity

FIGURE 3.5

The GE Business Screen

The GE Business Screen is a more sophisticated approach to portfolio management than the BCG matrix. As shown here, several factors combine to determine a business's competitive position and the attractiveness of its industry. These two dimensions, in turn, can be used to classify businesses as winners, question marks, average businesses, losers, or profit producers. Such a classification enables managers to allocate the organization's resources more effectively across various business opportunities.

Source: From *Strategy Formulation: Analytical Concepts*, 1st edition, by Charles W. Hofer and Dan Schendel. Copyright © 1978. Reprinted with permission of South-Western, a division of Thomson Learning: www.cengagelearning.com.

smaller the capital requirements, and the less the competitive intensity, the more attractive an industry will be. Other determinants of an organization's competitive position in an industry (besides market share) include technological know-how, product quality, service network, price competitiveness, and operating costs. In general, businesses with large market share, technological know-how, high product quality, a quality service network, competitive prices, and low operating costs are in a favorable competitive position.

Think of the GE Business Screen as a way of applying SWOT analysis to the implementation and management of a diversification strategy. The determinants of industry attractiveness are similar to the environmental opportunities and threats in SWOT analysis, and the determinants of competitive position are similar to organizational strengths and weaknesses. By conducting this type of SWOT analysis across several businesses, a diversified organization can decide how to invest its resources to maximize corporate performance. In general, organizations should invest in winners and question marks (where industry attractiveness and competitive position are both favorable), should maintain the market position of average businesses and profit producers (where industry attractiveness and competitive position are average), and should sell losers. For example, Unilever recently assessed its business portfolio using a similar framework and, as a result, decided to sell off several specialty chemical units that were not contributing to the firm's profitability as much as other businesses. The firm then used the revenues from these divestitures and bought more related businesses such as Ben & Jerry's Home-made and Slim-Fast.[31] During the recent economic recession, many diversified businesses took an especially aggressive approach to selling or closing underperforming businesses. For instance, Japan's Pioneer electronics business sold its television business, Home Depot shut down its Expo home-design stores, and Textron closed a business unit that financed real estate deals.[32]

TACTICAL PLANNING

As we noted earlier, tactical plans are developed to implement specific parts of a strategic plan. You have probably heard the saying about winning the battle but losing the war. **Tactical plans** are to battles what strategy is to a war: an organized sequence of steps designed to execute strategic plans. Strategy focuses on resources, environment, and mission, whereas tactics focus primarily on people and action.[33]

Developing Tactical Plans

Although effective tactical planning depends on many factors, which vary from one situation to another, we can identify some basic guidelines. First, the manager needs to recognize that tactical planning must address a number of tactical goals derived from a broader strategic goal.[34] An occasional situation may call for a stand-alone tactical plan, but most of the time tactical plans flow from and must be consistent with a strategic plan.

For example, top managers at Coca-Cola developed a strategic plan for cementing the firm's dominance of the soft-drink industry. As part of developing the plan, they identified a critical environmental threat—considerable unrest and uncertainty among the independent bottlers that packaged and distributed Coca-Cola's products. To simultaneously counter this threat and strengthen the company's position, Coca-Cola bought several large independent bottlers and combined them into one new organization called Coca-Cola Enterprises. Selling half of the new company's stock reaped millions in profits while effectively keeping control of the enterprise in Coca-Cola's hands. Thus, the

tactical plans
A plan aimed at achieving tactical goals and developed to implement parts of a strategic plan; an organized sequence of steps designed to execute strategic plans

creation of the new business was a tactical plan developed to contribute to the achievement of an overarching strategic goal.[35] More recently, as discussed earlier in this chapter in "Tough Times, Tough Choices," the firm eventually reacquired its largest franchised bottling operation.

Second, although strategies are often stated in general terms, tactics must specify resources and time frames. A strategy can call for being number one in a particular market or industry, but a tactical plan must specify precisely what activities will be undertaken to achieve that goal. Consider the Coca-Cola example again. Another element of its strategic plan involves increased worldwide market share. To facilitate additional sales in Europe, managers developed tactical plans for building a new plant in the south of France to make soft-drink concentrate and for building another canning plant in Dunkirk. The firm has also invested heavily in India.[36] Building these plants represents a concrete action involving measurable resources (funds to build the plants) and a clear time horizon (a target date for completion).

Finally, tactical planning requires the use of human resources. Managers involved in tactical planning spend a great deal of time working with other people. They must be in a position to receive information from others within and outside the organization, process that information most effectively, and then pass it on to others who might use it. Coca-Cola executives have been intensively involved in planning the new plants, setting up the new bottling venture noted earlier in this chapter, and exploring a joint venture with Cadbury Schweppes in the United Kingdom. Each activity has required considerable time and effort from dozens of managers. One manager, for example, crossed the Atlantic 12 times while negotiating the Cadbury deal.

Executing Tactical Plans

Regardless of how well a tactical plan is formulated, its ultimate success depends on the way it is carried out. Successful implementation, in turn, depends on the astute use of resources, effective decision making, and insightful steps to ensure that the right things are done at the right times and in the right ways. A manager can see an absolutely brilliant idea fail because of improper execution.

Proper execution depends on a number of important factors. First, the manager needs to evaluate every possible course of action in light of the goal it is intended to reach. Next, he or she needs to make sure that each decision maker has the information and resources necessary to get the job done. Vertical and horizontal communication and integration of activities must be present to minimize conflict and inconsistent activities. And, finally, the manager must monitor ongoing activities derived from the plan to make sure they are achieving the desired results. This monitoring typically takes place within the context of the organization's ongoing control systems.

OPERATIONAL PLANNING

Another critical element in effective organizational planning is the development and implementation of operational plans. Operational plans are derived from tactical plans and are aimed at achieving operational goals. Thus, operational plans tend to be narrowly focused, have relatively short time horizons, and involve lower-level managers. The two most basic forms of operational plans and specific types of each are summarized in Table 3.1.

Table 3.1	Types of Operational Plans
Plan	**Description**
Single-use plan	Developed to carry out a course of action not likely to be repeated in the future
Program	Single-use plan for a large set of activities
Project	Single-use plan of less scope and complexity than a program
Standing plan	Developed for activities that recur regularly over a period of time
Policy	Standing plan specifying the organization's general response to a designated problem or situation
Standard operating procedure	Standing plan outlining steps to be followed in particular circumstances
Rules and regulations	Standing plans describing exactly how specific activities are to be carried out

© Cengage Learning

Organizations develop various operational plans to help achieve operational goals. In general, there are two types of single-use plans and three types of standing plans.

Single-Use Plans

single-use plan
Developed to carry out a course of action that is not likely to be repeated in the future

A **single-use plan** is developed to carry out a course of action that is not likely to be repeated in the future. As Disney planned its newest theme park in Hong Kong, it developed numerous single-use plans for individual rides, attractions, and hotels. The two most common forms of single-use plans are programs and projects.

program
A single-use plan for a large set of activities

Programs A **program** is a single-use plan for a large set of activities. It might consist of identifying procedures for introducing a new product line, opening a new facility, or changing the organization's mission. When United and Continental Airlines merged, a program was needed to integrate every facet of the two firms' operations. The overall program required the integration of 1,400 technology systems (600 at Continental and 800 at United) and took three years to complete.[37]

project
A single-use plan of less scope and complexity than a program

Projects A **project** is similar to a program but is generally of less scope and complexity. A project may be a part of a broader program, or it may be a self-contained single-use plan. During the United–Continental merger, one project that was handled by the beverage committee involved deciding what coffee to use on the new airline. What might seem like a simple decision required thousands of taste tests and changes in both coffee suppliers and coffee-making equipment, and took over a year. Projects are also used to introduce a new product within an existing product line or to add a new benefit option to an existing salary package.

Standing Plans

standing plan
Developed for activities that recur regularly over a period of time

Whereas single-use plans are developed for nonrecurring situations, a **standing plan** is used for activities that recur regularly over a period of time. Standing plans can greatly enhance efficiency by making decision making routine. Policies, standard operating procedures (SOPs), and rules and regulations are three kinds of standing plans.

policy
A standing plan that specifies the organization's general response to a designated problem or situation

Policies   As a general guide for action, a **policy** is the most general form of standing plan that specifies the organization's general response to a designated problem or situation. For example, McDonald's has a policy that it will not grant a franchise to an individual who already owns another fast-food restaurant. Similarly, Starbucks has a policy that it will not franchise to individuals at all, instead retaining ownership of all Starbucks coffee shops. Likewise, a university admissions office might establish a policy that admission will be granted only to applicants with a minimum SAT score of 1,200 and a ranking in the top quarter of their high school class. Admissions officers may routinely deny admission to applicants who fail to reach these minimums. A policy is also likely to describe how exceptions are to be handled. The university's policy statement, for example, might create an admissions appeals committee to evaluate applicants who do not meet minimum requirements but may warrant special consideration.

SOP
A standard plan that outlines the steps to be followed in particular circumstances

Standard Operating Procedures   Another type of standing plan is the **SOP**. An SOP is more specific than a policy, in that it outlines the steps to be followed in particular circumstances. The admissions clerk at the university, for example, might be told that, when an application is received, he or she should (1) set up an electronic file for the applicant; (2) merge test score records, transcripts, and letters of reference to the electronic file as they are received; and (3) forward the electronic file to the appropriate admissions director when it is complete. Gallo Vineyards in California has a 300-page manual of SOPs. This planning manual is credited with making Gallo one of the most efficient wine-making operations in the United States. McDonald's has SOPs explaining exactly how Big Macs are to be cooked, how long they can stay in the warming rack, and so forth.

rules and regulations
Describe exactly how specific activities are to be carried out

Rules and Regulations   The narrowest of the standing plans, **rules and regulations** describe exactly how specific activities are to be carried out. Rather than guiding decision making, rules and regulations actually take the place of decision making in various situations. Each McDonald's restaurant has a rule prohibiting customers from using its telephones, for example. The university admissions office might have a rule stipulating that if an applicant's file is not complete two months before the beginning of a semester, the student cannot be admitted until the next semester. Of course, in most organizations a manager at a higher level can suspend or bend the rules. If the high school transcript of the child of a prominent university alumnus and donor arrives a few days late, the director of admissions might waive the two-month rule. Indeed, rules and regulations can become problematic if they are excessive or enforced too rigidly.

contingency planning
The determination of alternative courses of action to be taken if an intended plan is unexpectedly disrupted or rendered inappropriate

Rules and regulations and SOPs are similar in many ways. They are both relatively narrow in scope, and each can serve as a substitute for decision making. An SOP typically describes a sequence of activities, whereas rules and regulations focus on one activity. Recall our examples: The admissions SOP consisted of three activities, whereas the two-month rule related to only one activity. In an industrial setting, the SOP for orienting a new employee could involve enrolling the person in various benefit options, introducing him or her to coworkers and supervisors, and providing a tour of the facilities. A pertinent rule for the new employee might involve when to come to work each day.

Contingency Planning and Crisis Management

crisis management
The set of procedures the organization uses in the event of a disaster or other unexpected calamity

Another important type of planning is **contingency planning**, or the determination of alternative courses of action to be taken if an intended plan of action is unexpectedly disrupted or rendered inappropriate.[38] **Crisis management**, a related concept, is the set of procedures the organization uses in the event of a disaster or other unexpected calamity. Some elements of crisis management may be orderly and systematic, whereas others may be more ad hoc and develop as events unfold.

Dana White/PhotoEdit

Rules and regulations are standing plans describing how activities are to be carried out. This workplace, for example, has posted a set of safety rules to be followed by all employees near the time clock where they register their hours of work.

A classic example of widespread contingency planning occurred during the late 1990s in anticipation of what was popularly known as the *Y2K bug*. Concerns about the impact of technical glitches in computers stemming from their internal clocks' changing from 1999 to 2000 resulted in contingency planning for most organizations. Many banks and hospitals, for example, had extra staff available; some organizations created backup computer systems; and some even stockpiled inventory in case they could not purchase new products or materials.[39]

The devastating hurricanes—Katrina and Rita—that hit the Gulf Coast in 2005 dramatically underscored the importance of effective crisis management. For example, inadequate and ineffective responses by the Federal Emergency Management Agency (FEMA) illustrated to many people that organization's weaknesses in coping with crisis situations. On the other hand, some organizations responded much more effectively. Walmart began ramping up its emergency preparedness on the same day Katrina was upgraded from a tropical depression to a tropical storm. In the days before the storm struck, Walmart stores in the region were supplied with powerful generators and large supplies of dry ice so they could reopen as quickly as possible after the storm had passed. In neighboring states, the firm also had scores of trucks standing by crammed with both emergency-related inventory for its stores and emergency supplies it was prepared to donate—bottled water, medical supplies, and so forth. And Walmart often beat FEMA by several days in getting those supplies delivered.[40]

Seeing the consequences of poor crisis management after the terrorist attacks of September 11, 2001, and the 2005 hurricanes, many firms today are actively working to create new and better crisis management plans and procedures. For example, both

Reliant Energy and Duke Energy rely on computer trading centers where trading managers actively buy and sell energy-related commodities. If a terrorist attack or a natural disaster such as a hurricane were to strike their trading centers, they would essentially be out of business. Prior to September 11, each firm had relatively vague and superficial crisis plans. But now they and most other companies have much more detailed and comprehensive plans in the event of another crisis. Both Reliant and Duke, for example, have created secondary trading centers at other locations. In the event of a shutdown at their main trading centers, these firms can quickly transfer virtually all their core trading activities to their secondary centers within 30 minutes or less.[41] More recently, many businesses have developed contingency plans for dealing with a potential pandemic such as the H1N1 virus.

Unfortunately, however, because it is impossible to forecast the future precisely, no organization can ever be perfectly prepared for all crises. For example, due to 2011's disastrous earthquake and tsunami in Japan, many U.S. companies faced shortages of goods and materials imported from that country. General Motors was the first automaker forced to temporarily shut down one of its truck plants because it could not get enough Japanese-made parts. Two months after the disaster, Toyota's facilities in the United States were operating at less than 30 percent of capacity and did not return to full production until several months later.[42]

The mechanics of contingency planning are shown in Figure 3.6. In relation to an organization's other plans, contingency planning comes into play at four action points. At action point 1, management develops the organization's basic plans. These may include strategic, tactical, and operational plans. As part of this development process, managers usually consider various contingency events. Some management groups even assign someone the role of devil's advocate, who asks, "But what if … ?" about each course of action. A variety of contingencies is usually considered.

At action point 2, the plan that management chooses is put into effect. The most important contingency events are also defined. Only the events that are likely to occur and whose effects will have a substantial impact on the organization are used in the contingency-planning process. Next, at action point 3, the company specifies certain

© Cengage Learning

FIGURE 3.6

Contingency Planning

Most organizations develop contingency plans. These plans specify alternative courses of action to be taken if an intended plan is unexpectedly disrupted or rendered inappropriate.

indicators or signs that suggest a contingency event is about to take place. A bank might decide that a 2 percent drop in interest rates should be considered a contingency event. An indicator might be two consecutive months with a drop of 0.5 percent in each month. As indicators of contingency events are being defined, the contingency plans themselves should also be developed. Examples of contingency plans for various situations are delaying plant construction, developing a new manufacturing process, and cutting prices.

After this stage, the organization's managers monitor the indicators identified at action point 3. If the situation dictates, a contingency plan is implemented. Otherwise, the primary plan of action continues in force. Finally, action point 4 marks the successful completion of either the original or a contingency plan.

Contingency planning is becoming increasingly important for most organizations, especially for those operating in particularly complex or dynamic environments. Few managers have such an accurate view of the future that they can anticipate and plan for everything. Contingency planning is a useful technique for helping managers cope with uncertainty and change. However, crisis management, by its very nature, is more difficult to anticipate. But organizations that have a strong culture, strong leadership, and a capacity to deal with the unexpected stand a better chance of successfully weathering a crisis than other organizations.[43]

SUMMARY OF LEARNING OUTCOMES AND KEY POINTS

1. Summarize the planning process, and describe organizational goals.

   - The planning process includes understanding the environment, formulating a mission, and creating goals and plans.
   - Goals serve four basic purposes: They provide guidance and direction, facilitate planning, inspire motivation and commitment, and promote evaluation and control.
   - With an understanding of the environmental context, managers develop a number of different types of goals and plans, including strategic, tactical, and operational plans.

2. Discuss the components of strategy and types of strategic alternatives.

   - A strategy is a comprehensive plan for accomplishing the organization's goals.
   - Effective strategies address three organizational issues: distinctive competence, scope, and resource deployment.

3. Describe how to use SWOT analysis in formulating strategy.

   - SWOT analysis considers an organization's strengths, weaknesses, opportunities, and threats.

   - Using SWOT analysis, an organization chooses strategies that support its mission, exploit its opportunities and strengths, neutralize its threats, and avoid its weaknesses.

4. Identify and describe various alternative approaches to business-level strategy formulation.

   - A business-level strategy is the plan an organization uses to conduct business in a particular industry or market.
   - Porter suggests that businesses may formulate a differentiation strategy, an overall cost leadership strategy, or a focus strategy.
   - Business-level strategies may also take into account the stages in its products' life cycles.

5. Identify and describe various alternative approaches to corporate-level strategy formulation.

   - A corporate-level strategy is the plan an organization uses to manage its operations across several businesses.
   - A firm that does not diversify is implementing a single-product strategy.
   - An organization pursues a strategy of related diversification when it operates a set of businesses that are somehow linked.

- An organization pursues a strategy of unrelated diversification when it operates a set of businesses that are not logically associated with one another.
- Organizations manage diversification through the organization structure that they adopt and through portfolio management techniques. The BCG matrix classifies an organization's diversified businesses as dogs, cash cows, question marks, or stars according to market share and market growth rate. The GE Business Screen classifies businesses as winners, losers, question marks, average businesses, or profit producers according to industry attractiveness and competitive position.

6. Discuss how tactical plans are developed and executed.

- Tactical plans are at the middle of the organization, have an intermediate time horizon, and are moderate in scope.
- Tactical plans are developed to implement specific parts of a strategic plan.

- Tactical plans must flow from strategy, specify resource and time issues, and commit human resources.

7. Describe the basic types of operational plans used by organizations.

- Operational plans are at the lower level of the organization, have a shorter time horizon, and are narrower in scope. They are derived from a tactical plan and are aimed at achieving one or more operational goals.
- Two major types of operational plans are single-use and standing plans. Single-use plans are designed to carry out a course of action that is not likely to be repeated in the future. Programs and projects are examples of single-use plans. Standing plans are designed to carry out a course of action that is likely to be repeated several times. Policies, SOPs, and rules and regulations are all standing plans.
- Contingency planning and crisis management are also emerging as very important forms of operational planning.

DISCUSSION QUESTIONS

Questions for Review

1. Describe the nature of organizational goals. Be certain to include both the purposes and the kinds of goals.
2. Identify and describe Porter's generic strategies.
3. What are the basic differences among a single-product strategy, a strategy based on related diversification, and one based on unrelated diversification?
4. What is tactical planning? What is operational planning? What are the similarities and differences between them?
5. What is contingency planning? How is it similar to and different from crisis management?

Questions for Analysis

1. Managers are sometimes criticized for focusing too much attention on the achievement of short-term goals. In your opinion, how much attention should be given to long-term versus short-term goals? In the event of a conflict, which should be given priority? Explain your answers.

2. Which strategy—business or corporate level—should a firm develop first? Describe the relationship between a firm's business- and corporate-level strategies.
3. Volkswagen sold its original Beetle automobile in the United States until the 1970s. The original Beetle was made of inexpensive materials, was built using an efficient mass-production technology, and offered few options. Then, in the 1990s, Volkswagen introduced its new Beetle, which has a distinctive style, provides more optional features, and is priced for upscale buyers. What was Volkswagen's strategy with the original Beetle—product differentiation, low cost, or focus? Which strategy did Volkswagen implement with its new Beetle? Explain your answers.
4. What kind of plan—tactical or operational—should be developed first? Why? Does the order really matter? Why or why not?
5. Cite examples of operational plans that you use or encounter (now or in the past) at work, at school, or in your personal life.

BUILDING EFFECTIVE DECISION-MAKING SKILLS

Exercise Overview

Decision-making skills refer to the ability to recognize and define problems and opportunities correctly and then to select an appropriate course of action for solving problems or capitalizing on opportunities. As we noted in this chapter, many organizations use SWOT analysis as part of the strategy formulation process. This exercise will help you better understand both how managers obtain the information they need to perform such an analysis and how they use it as a framework for making decisions.

Exercise Background

The idea behind SWOT is that a good strategy exploits an organization's opportunities and strengths while neutralizing threats and avoiding or correcting weaknesses.

You've just been hired to run a medium-sized company that manufactures electric motors, circuit breakers, and similar electronic components for industrial use. In recent years, the firm's financial performance has gradually eroded, and your job is to turn things around.

At one time, the firm was successful in part because it was able to charge premium prices for top-quality products. In recent years, however, management has tried cutting costs as a means of bringing prices in line with those of new competitors in the market. Unfortunately, the strategy hasn't worked very well, with the effect of cost cutting being primarily a fall-off in product quality. Convinced that a new strategy is called for, you've decided to begin with a SWOT analysis.

Exercise Task

Reviewing the situation, you take the following steps:

1. List the sources that you'll use to gather information about the firm's strengths, weaknesses, opportunities, and threats.
2. Then ask yourself: For what types of information are data readily available on the Internet? What categories of data are difficult or impossible to find on the Internet? (*Note*: When using the Internet, be sure to provide specific websites or URLs.)
3. Next, rate each source that you consult in terms of probable reliability.
4. Finally, ask yourself how confident you would be in basing decisions on the information that you've obtained.

BUILDING EFFECTIVE COMMUNICATION AND INTERPERSONAL SKILLS

Exercise Overview

Interpersonal skills refer to the manager's ability to communicate with, understand, and motivate individuals and groups. Communication skills are used both to convey information to others effectively and to receive ideas and information effectively from others. Communicating and interacting effectively with many different types of individuals are essential planning skills. This exercise allows you to think through communication and interaction issues as they relate to an actual planning situation.

Exercise Background

Larger and more complex organizations require greater planning complexity to achieve their goals. NASA is responsible for the very complex task of managing U.S. space exploration and therefore has very complex planning needs.

In April 1970, NASA launched the Apollo 13 manned space mission, which was charged with exploration of the lunar surface. On its way to the moon, the ship developed a malfunction that could have resulted in the death of all the crew members. The crew members worked with scientists in Houston to develop a solution to the problem. The capsule was successful in returning to Earth, and no lives were lost.

Exercise Task

1. Watch and listen to the short clip from *Apollo 13*. (This movie was made by Universal Studios in 1995 and was directed by Ron Howard. The script was based on a memoir by astronaut and Apollo 13 Mission Captain Jim Lovell.) Describe the various types of planning and decision-making activities taking place at NASA during the unfolding of the disaster.

2. The biggest obstacles to effective planning in the first few minutes of this crisis were the rapid and unexpected changes occurring in a dynamic and complex environment. List elements of the situation that contributed to dynamism (elements that were rapidly changing). List elements that contributed to complexity. What kinds of actions did NASA's planning staff take to overcome the obstacles presented by the dynamic and complex environment? Suggest any other useful actions the staff could have taken.

3. NASA managers and astronauts did not use a formal planning process in their approach to this situation. Why not? Is there any part of the formal planning process that could have been helpful? What does this example suggest to you about the advantages and limitations of the formal planning process?

SKILLS SELF-ASSESSMENT INSTRUMENT

Goal-Setting Questionnaire

This exercise will help you understand how to conceptualize the elements of goal setting and your own goal-setting tendencies.

Instructions: Indicate your concepts of your goal-setting behaviors and feelings by circling the appropriate number on the scale for each statement.

Statements	Strongly Agree	Slightly Agree	Not Sure	Slightly Disagree	Strongly Disagree
1. Rewards should be allocated based on goal achievement.	5	4	3	2	1
2. I set goals for all key results areas.	5	4	3	2	1
3. Goals should have clear deadlines.	5	4	3	2	1
4. I work hard to give others feedback on how they're doing.	5	4	3	2	1
5. I tend to set goals that I can't quite achieve to force me to try harder.	1	2	3	4	5
6. Sometimes when I think maybe I'm not doing so well, I don't want feedback from others.	1	2	3	4	5
7. My goals are always clearly stated.	1	2	3	4	5
8. My goals are stated in quantifiable terms.	5	4	3	2	1
9. Achieving goals is the way to promotion and success.	5	4	3	2	1
10. My boss (parent, etc.) will not get on my case if I don't achieve my goals.	1	2	3	4	5
11. My boss (parent, etc.) usually sets my goals.	1	2	3	4	5
12. I don't always know what the key result areas are.	1	2	3	4	5
13. I work better without specific deadlines.	1	2	3	4	5
14. Others allow me to take part in setting my goals.	5	4	3	2	1
15. The more challenging my goals, the better I work.	5	4	3	2	1
16. If I'm not on target to achieve my goals, my boss (parent, etc.) should get on my case.	5	4	3	2	1

(continued)

Statements	Strongly Agree	Slightly Agree	Not Sure	Slightly Disagree	Strongly Disagree
17. When I'm working on my goals, my boss (parent, etc.) doesn't always give me the support I need.	1	2	3	4	5
18. Specific goals make me nervous, so I prefer general goals.	1	2	3	4	5
19. My goals state exactly what results I plan to achieve.	5	4	3	2	1
20. I challenge myself by setting goals that are just out of my reach.	1	2	3	4	5

Scoring: Sum all of your responses on the questionnaire and place your total score here: _____

Scores can range from 20 to 100. The higher your score, the closer you are to effective goal-setting behaviors.

Source: From Burton, *Exercises in Management*, 3E. © 1990 Cengage Learning.

EXPERIENTIAL EXERCISE

The SWOT Analysis

Purpose: The SWOT analysis provides the manager with a cognitive model of the organization and its environmental forces. By developing the ability to conduct such an analysis, the manager builds both process knowledge and a conceptual skill. This skill builder focuses on the *administrative management model*. It will help you develop the *coordinator role* of the administrative management model. One of the skills of the coordinator is the ability to plan.

Introduction: This exercise helps you understand the complex interrelationships between environmental opportunities and threats and organizational strengths and weaknesses. Strategy formulation is facilitated by a SWOT analysis. First, the organization should study its internal operations to identify its strengths and weaknesses. Next, the organization should scan the environment to identify existing and future opportunities and threats. Then, the organization should identify the relationships that exist among these strengths, weaknesses, opportunities, and threats. Finally, major business strategies usually result from matching an organization's strengths with appropriate opportunities or from matching the threats it faces with weaknesses that have been identified.

Instructions: First, read the short narrative of the Trek Bicycle Corporation's external and internal environments, found next in this chapter.

Second, divide into small groups and conduct a SWOT analysis for Trek based on the short narrative. You may also use your general knowledge and any information you have about Trek or the bicycle-manufacturing industry. Then prepare a group response to the discussion questions.

Third, as a class, discuss both the SWOT analysis and the groups' responses to the discussion questions.

Discussion Questions

1. What was the most difficult part of the SWOT analysis?
2. Why do most firms not develop major strategies for matches between threats and strengths?
3. Under what conditions might a firm develop a major strategy around a match between an opportunity and a weakness?

Trek's External and Internal Environments

Today in the United States, inflation, cost of materials, and unemployment are all relatively stable. Emerging economies are growing more rapidly than the U.S. economy in general. Foreign trade is relatively open, so manufacturers face intense international and local competition, with pressure to keep prices low and opportunities to utilize low-cost labor and raw materials from around the world. New manufacturing technologies, futuristic materials, and e-commerce are becoming more prevalent and affordable. The political–legal climate is favorable to business in the United States and most developing nations, whereas regulation is higher in the European Union. The standard of living is stable, the population is aging, and ethnic diversity is increasing.

Today in the bicycle-manufacturing industry, manufacturers must invest very heavily in research and development (R&D) to compete effectively on a global scale. Domestically, the bicycle-manufacturing industry is fragmented, with the largest firm, Trek, controlling just 24 percent of sales. The industry's customers are primarily local, independent bike retailers, a very fragmented group. The Internet, and eBay in particular, provides alternate channels for new and used bike sales. Bike riders, the ultimate purchasers, are interested in style, comfort, and high-tech features, as well as environmental and health issues. Suppliers of many bike components are small, local manufacturers located in developing countries. However, a few suppliers are more powerful, such as Shimano, an internationally known maker of bicycle components and cycling gear. Regulators are not a significant force for bicycle manufacturers, but Trek and others have numerous joint ventures. In one example, Trek teamed with AMD, Nike, and other companies to produce the high-performance cycle used by Lance Armstrong and other leading cyclists in the Tour de France and other races.

Trek has excellent R&D capability and effectively utilizes low-cost manufacturers in producing the more affordable products in its broad line of bikes. However, its Wisconsin factory produces its high-end lines and can customize a bike to a customer's exact specifications. Trek is beginning to push to improve the customer bike-buying experience. The company will limit the number of retailers it uses and require retailers to stock a higher percentage of Trek products. In return, it will provide training and funds to improve in-store marketing and increase customer loyalty.

MANAGEMENT AT WORK

Acting on a Strategic Vision

Established as Amazin' Software in 1982 by an ex-Apple marketing executive named Trip Hawkins, Electronic Arts (EA) was a pioneer in the home computer game industry. From the outset, EA published games created by outside developers—a strategy that offered higher profit margins and forced the new company to stay in close contact with its market. By 1984, having built the largest sales force in the industry, EA had generated revenue of $18 million. Crediting its developers as "software artists," EA regularly gave game creators photo credits on packaging and advertising spreads and, what's more important, developed a generous profit-sharing policy that helped it to attract some of the industry's best development talent.

By 1986, the company had become the country's largest supplier of entertainment software. It went public in 1989, and net revenue took off in the early 1990s, climbing from $113 million in 1991 to $298 million in 1993. In the next 13 years, the company continued to grow by developing two key strategies:

- Acquiring independent game makers (at the rate of 1.2 studios per year between 1995 and 2006)
- Rolling out products in series, such as *John Madden Football*, *Harry Potter*, and *Need for Speed*

Activision's path to success in the industry wasn't quite as smooth as EA's. Activision was founded in 1979 as a haven for game developers unhappy with prevailing industry policy. At the time, systems providers like Atari hired developers to create games only for their own systems; in-house developers were paid straight salaries and denied credit for individual contributions, and there was no channel at all for would-be independents. Positioning itself as the industry's first third-party developer, Activision began promoting creators as well as games. The company went public in 1983 and successfully rode the crest of a booming market until the mid-1980s. Between 1986 and 1990, however, Activision's growth strategies—acquisitions and commitment to a broader product line—fizzled, and it had become, as *Forbes* magazine put it, "a company with a sorry balance sheet but a storied history."

Enter Robert Kotick, a serial entrepreneur with no particular passion for video games, who bought one-fourth of the firm in December 1990 and became CEO two months later. Kotick looked immediately to Electronic Arts for a survey of best practices in the industry. What he discovered was a company whose culture was disrupted by internal conflict—namely, between managers motivated by productivity and profit and developers driven by independence and imagination. It seems that EA's strategy for acquiring and managing a burgeoning portfolio of studios had slipped into a counterproductive pattern: Identify an extremely popular game, buy the developer, delegate the original creative team to churn out sequels until either the team burned out or the franchise fizzled, and then close down or absorb what was left.

On the other hand, EA still sold a lot of video games, and to Kotick, the basic tension in EA culture wasn't entirely surprising: Clearly the business of making and marketing video games succeeded when the creative side of the enterprise was supported by financing and distribution muscle, but it was equally true that a steady stream of successful games came from the company's creative people. The key to getting Activision back in the game, Kotick decided, was managing this complex of essential resources better than his competition did.

So the next year Kotick moved the company to Los Angeles and began to recruit the people who could furnish the resources that he needed most—creative expertise and a connection with the passion that its customers brought to the video-game industry. Activision, he promised prospective developers, would not manage its human resources the way that EA did: EA, he argued, "has commoditized development. We won't absorb you into a big Death Star culture."

Between 1997 and 2003, Kotick proceeded to buy no fewer than nine studios, but his concept of a video-game studio system was quite different from that of EA, which was determined to make production more efficient by centralizing groups of designers and programmers into regional offices. Kotick allows his studios to keep their own names, often lets them stay where they are, and further encourages autonomy by providing seed money for Activision alumni who want to launch out on their own. Each studio draws up its own financial statements and draws on its own bonus pool, and the paychecks of studio heads reflect companywide profits and losses.

The strategy paid off big time. For calendar year 2007, the company, now known as Activision Blizzard, estimated compiled revenues of $3.8 billion—just enough to squeeze past EA's $3.7 billion and sneak into the top spot as the bestselling video game publisher in the world not affiliated with a maker of game consoles (such as Nintendo and Microsoft).

Revenues for calendar year 2012 were $4.6 billion, up more than 22 percent over 2009, making Activision Blizzard the number one video game publisher in North America and Europe. Today, its market capitalization of $14.5 billion is twice that of EA.

Kotick attributes the firm's success to a "focus on a select number of proven franchises and genres where we have proven development expertise.... We look for ways to broaden the footprints of our franchises, and where appropriate, we develop innovative business models like subscription-based online gaming."

Case Questions

1. How might a *SWOT analysis* have helped Electronic Arts assess its slippage in the video game market?
2. How might *Porter's generic strategies* theory help to explain why Electronic Arts lost its leadership in the video game market to Activision Blizzard?
3. Is the concept of product life cycle relevant to the video game market? Why or why not?
4. If you ran a small video game start-up, what would be your strategy for competing with EA and Activision Blizzard?
5. If you're a video game player, what aspects of Activision's strategy have led to your playing more (or fewer) of its games? If you're not a video game player, what aspects of Activision Blizzard's strategy might induce you to try a few of its games?

Case References

Eric-Jon Rossel Waugh, "A Short History of Electronic Arts," *BusinessWeek*, www.businessweek.com, on September 1, 2013; Peter C. Beller, "Activision's Unlikely Hero," *Forbes*, www.forbes.com, accessed on September 1, 2013; "Activision Beats EA as Top Third Party Publisher in U.S.," *Gamasutra*, www.gamasutra.com, accessed on September 1, 2013; "Activision Posts 92% Revenue Increase in Record Year," *Gamasutra*, www.gamasutra.com, accessed on September 1, 2013; and "Activision Blizzard Reports December Quarter and Calendar Year 2011 Financial Results," *PRNewswire*, http://investor.activision.com, accessed on September 1, 2013.

Google's Strategy for Dominance

1. Explain how each of its strategic *components—distinctive competence, scope*, and *resource deployment*—plays a role in Google's success.
2. In what ways is Google prepared to respond to both *organizational opportunities* and *organizational threats* in the U.S. market?

3. How can *Porter's generic strategies* approach help to explain Google's U.S. strategy?
4. Identify situations in which Google might use tactical, operational, and contingency planning.

ENDNOTES

1 Google, "Corporate Information," April 11, 2013, at http://www.google.com, accessed on September 1, 2013; "The Secret to Google's Success," *BusinessWeek*, March 6, 2008, http://www.businessweek.com, accessed on September 1, 2013; "In Search of the Real Google," *Time*, February 20, 2007, http://time.com/, accessed on September 1, 2013; www.google.com, accessed on September 1, 2013.

2 See Peter J. Brews and Michelle R. Hunt, "Learning to Plan and Planning to Learn: Resolving the Planning School/Learning School Debate," *Strategic Management Journal*, 1999, Vol. 20, pp. 889–913.

3 Max D. Richards, *Setting Strategic Goals and Objectives*, 2nd ed. (St. Paul, MN: West, 1986).

4 Jim Collins, "Turning Goals into Results: The Power of Catalytic Mechanisms," *Harvard Business Review*, July–August 1999, pp. 71–81.

5 "Set a Goal First, Says CEO of Zynga," *USA Today*, April 23, 2012, pp. 1B, 2B.

6 "IBM Execs Tout Success of Roadmap, Reiterate 2015 Targets," *Wall Street Journal*, March 8, 2011.

7 *Hoover's Handbook of American Business 2013* (Austin, TX: Mergent, 2013), pp. 232–233; and "GE, No. 2 in Appliances, Is Agitating to Grab Share from Whirlpool," *Wall Street Journal*, July 2, 1997, pp. A1, A6. See also "A Talk with Jeff Immelt," *BusinessWeek*, January 28, 2002, pp. 102–104.

8 Kenneth R. Thompson, Wayne A. Hochwarter, and Nicholas J. Mathys, "Stretch Targets: What Makes Them Effective?" *Academy of Management Executive*, August 1997, pp. 48–58.

9 "A Methodical Man," *Forbes*, August 11, 1997, pp. 70–72.

10 John A. Pearce II and Fred David, "Corporate Mission Statements: The Bottom Line," *Academy of Management Executive*, May 1987, p. 109.

11 For early discussions of strategic management, see Kenneth Andrews, *The Concept of Corporate Strategy*, rev. ed. (Homewood, IL: Dow Jones–Irwin, 1980); and Igor Ansoff, *Corporate Strategy* (New York: McGraw-Hill, 1965). For more recent perspectives, see Michael E. Porter, "What Is Strategy?" *Harvard Business Review*, November–December 1996, pp. 61–78; Kathleen M. Eisenhardt, "Strategy as Strategic Decision Making," *Sloan Management Review*, Spring 1999, pp. 65–74; and Sarah Kaplan and Eric Beinhocker, "The Real Value of Strategic Planning," *Sloan Management Review*, Winter 2003, pp. 71–80.

12 *Hoover's Handbook of American Business 2013*, pp. 28–29.

13 T. R. Holcomb, R. M. Holmes Jr., and B. L. Connelly, "Making the Most of What You Have: Managerial Ability as a Source of Resource Value Creation," *Strategic Management Journal*, 2009, Vol. 30, No. 5, pp. 457–486.

14 Jay Barney, "Firm Resources and Sustained Competitive Advantage," *Journal of Management*, June 1991, pp. 99–120. See also T. Russell Crook, David J. Ketchen Jr., James G. Combs, and Samuel Y. Todd, "Strategic Resources and Performance: A Meta-Analysis," *Strategic Management Journal*, 2008, Vol. 29, pp. 1141–1154.

15 Michael Porter, *Competitive Strategy* (New York: Free Press, 1980). See also Colin Campbell-Hunt, "What Have We Learned about Generic Competitive Strategy? A Meta-Analysis," *Strategic Management Journal*, 2000, Vol. 21, pp. 127–154. See also Michael E. Porter, "The Five Competitive Forces That Shape Strategy," *Harvard Business Review*, January 2008, pp. 79–90, for a recent update.

16 Ian C. MacMillan and Rita Gunther McGrath, "Discovering New Points of Differentiation," *Harvard Business Review*, July–August 1997, pp. 133–136.

17 "In a Water Fight, Coke and Pepsi Try Opposite Tacks," *Wall Street Journal*, April 18, 2002, pp. A1, A8.

18 "Abercrombie Fights Discount Tide," *Wall Street Journal*, December 8, 2008, p. B1.

19 "When Service Means Survival," *BusinessWeek*, March 2, 2009, pp. 26–40.

20 "Recession Puts Hershey in Sweet Spot," *Wall Street Journal*, January 28, 2009, p. B1.

21 "P&G, Colgate Hit by Consumer Thrift," *Wall Street Journal*, May 1, 2009, pp. B1, B8.

22 "It Ain't the Bellagio …" *BusinessWeek*, June 20–26, 2011, pp. 84–85.

23 Alfred Chandler, *Strategy and Structure: Chapters in the History of the American Industrial Enterprise* (Cambridge, MA: MIT Press, 1962); Richard Rumelt, *Strategy, Structure, and Economic Performance* (Cambridge, MA: Division of Research, Graduate School of Business Administration, Harvard University, 1974); and Oliver Williamson, *Markets and Hierarchies* (New York: Free Press, 1975).

24 "Mars's Takeover of Wrigley Creates a Global Powerhouse," *Wall Street Journal*, April 29, 2009, p. 1A.

25 K. L. Stimpert and Irene M. Duhaime, "Seeing the Big Picture: The Influence of Industry, Diversification, and Business Strategy on Performance," *Academy of Management Journal*, 1997, Vol. 40, No. 3, pp. 560–583.

26 See Chandler, *Strategy and Structure*; and Yakov Amihud and Baruch Lev, "Risk Reduction as a Managerial Motive for Conglomerate Mergers," *Bell Journal of Economics*, 1981, pp. 605–617.

27 Chandler, *Strategy and Structure*; and Williamson, *Markets and Hierarchies.*

28 For a discussion of the limitations of unrelated diversification, see Jay Barney and William G. Ouchi, *Organizational Economics* (San Francisco: Jossey-Bass, 1986).

29 See Barry Hedley, "A Fundamental Approach to Strategy Development," *Long Range Planning*, December 1976, pp. 2–11; and Bruce Henderson, "The Experience Curve-Reviewed: IV. The Growth Share Matrix of the Product Portfolio," *Perspectives*, 1973, No. 135, pp. 1–18.

30 Michael G. Allen, "Diagramming G.E.'s Planning for What's WATT," in Robert J. Allio and Malcolm W. Pennington (eds.), *Corporate Planning: Techniques and Applications* (New York: AMACOM, 1979). Limits of this approach are discussed in R. A. Bettis and W. K. Hall, "The Business Portfolio Approach: Where It Falls Down in Practice," *Long Range Planning*, March 1983, pp. 95–105.

31 "Unilever to Sell Specialty-Chemical Unit to ICI of the U.K. for About $8 Billion," *Wall Street Journal*, May 7, 1997, pp. A3, A12; and "For Unilever, It's Sweetness and Light," *Wall Street Journal*, April 13, 2000, pp. B1, B4.

32 "Unprofitable Businesses Getting Axed More Often," *Wall Street Journal*, February 17, 2009, pp. B1, B2.

33 James Brian Quinn, Henry Mintzberg, and Robert M. James, *The Strategy Process* (Englewood Cliffs, NJ: Prentice Hall, 1988).

34 Vasudevan Ramanujam and N. Venkatraman, "Planning System Characteristics and Planning Effectiveness," *Strategic Management Journal*, 1987, Vol. 8, No. 2, pp. 453–468.

35 "Coca-Cola May Need to Slash Its Growth Targets," *Wall Street Journal*, January 28, 2000, p. B2. See also "Pepsi and Coke Roll Out Flavors to Boost Sales," *Wall Street Journal*, May 7, 2002, pp. B1, B4.

36 "Finally, Coke Gets It Right," *BusinessWeek*, February 10, 2003, p. 47.

37 "Marriage at 30,000 Feet," *Bloomberg BusinessWeek*, February 6–12, 2012, pp. 58–64.

38 K. A. Froot, D. S. Scharfstein, and J. C. Stein, "A Framework for Risk Management," *Harvard Business Review*, November–December 1994, pp. 91–102.

39 "How the Fixers Fended Off Big Disasters," *Wall Street Journal*, December 23, 1999, pp. B1, B4.

40 "At Wal-Mart, Emergence Plan Has Big Payoff," *Wall Street Journal*, September 12, 2005, pp. B1, B3.

41 "Next Time," *USA Today*, October 4, 2005, pp. 1B, 2B. See also Judith A. Clair and Ronald L. Dufresne, "How Companies Can Experience Positive Transformation from a Crisis," *Organizational Dynamics*, 2007, Vol. 36, No. 1, pp. 63–77.

42 "Lacking Parts, G. M. Will Close Plant," *New York Times*, March 17, 2011.

43 Michael Watkins and Max Bazerman, "Predictable Surprises: The Disasters You Should Have Seen Coming," *Harvard Business Review*, March 2003, pp. 72–81.

CHAPTER 4

Managing Decision Making

Learning Outcomes

After studying this chapter, you should be able to:

1 Define decision making and discuss types of decisions and decision-making conditions.

2 Discuss rational perspectives on decision making, including the steps involved.

3 Describe the behavioral aspects of decision making.

4 Discuss group and team decision making, including its advantages and disadvantages and how it can be more effectively managed.

Paul Katzeff is the founder of Thanksgiving Coffee Co. Katzeff would like to see the U.S. government drop its decades-long embargo on Cuban coffee, arguing that it has not been effective and that it hurts the Cuban people more than the Cuban government.

Management in Action

The Embargo Grinds On

"I'm not going to risk everything I've worked for [for] over 30 years by violating U.S. law."

—**Paul Katzeff, founder of Thanksgiving Coffee Co.**

Because they love certain types of coffee, some American coffee enthusiasts only buy coffee that's labeled "Cuban." As it turns out, though, such brands as Nescafé Café con Leche and Pilon Café Cubano aren't actually made from Cuban coffee beans: Because of a U.S. embargo against Cuban products, the so-called "Cuban coffee" available in this country comes from beans grown in such countries as Nicaragua, Mexico, or Guatemala, basically anywhere but Cuba. Indeed, Americans cannot legally buy any products from Cuba—coffee, cigars, alcohol, or anything else. So coffee distributors in the United States are limited in the products they can offer and must be careful in how they promote those coffees they do sell. In short, they face risk and uncertainty in every decision they make.

Consider the Canadian firm Merchants of Green Coffee. Its mission "is to deliver the best-tasting coffee experience to discerning consumers through a supply chain with integrity and a unique commitment to quality." The company buys only the finest beans from small growers in Africa, Latin America, and Cuba and stocks premium products like Cuba Turquino. This premium coffee is made from beans grown under shade-tree canopies at elevations above 3,000 feet. As the name indicates, Cuba Turquino is made from Cuban coffee beans, and for that reason, again, American coffee connoisseurs can't buy it.

Now, coffee beans from other Latin American nations are also of high quality, and they're often certified organic. They're just not *Cuban* coffee beans, and to some people in the coffee business, it's the principle that matters. Paul Katzeff, founder of Thanksgiving Coffee Co., a California producer of specialty coffees, regards the U.S. embargo as impractical (on the grounds that it hasn't achieved its goals) and immoral (on the grounds that it punishes the Cuban people rather than their government). These two reasons are why his company has been marketing a line of beans called "End the Embargo Coffee" for over a decade. The coffee actually comes from Nicaragua, but the packaging, emblazoned with the image of Cuban revolutionary Che Guevara, gets the point across. Katzeff hastens to point out that he's not going "to risk everything I've worked for [for] over 30 years" by violating U.S. law, but in addition to selling distinctive, high-quality coffee, he's determined "to bring awareness to U.S. consumers on Cuba issues." Explains Johanna Schulz, director of Thanksgiving's social and environmental policy: "Since we can't import Cuban coffee directly, we're using [End the Embargo] as an awareness tool to educate customers about the embargo on Cuba." For the past eight years, Thanksgiving has also donated 15 cents from every package sold to the U.S.-Cuba Sister Cities Association, a nonprofit that works to establish relationships between similar-sized cities in the two countries.

The U.S. embargo, which was first imposed in 1962 in response to the revolutionary communist government's appropriation of American land holdings in the country, prevents "U.S. persons" and entities "owned or controlled" by "U.S. persons" from engaging in any transactions in which Cuba has an "interest of any nature whatsoever, direct or indirect." Cuba, therefore, has no access to the American market, does without U.S. imports, and amasses substantial debts to other trading partners. But, says a Canadian businessman with investments in Cuba, "anyone who thinks there will be a 'for sale' sign [put] up by a bankrupt Cuban government is wrong." Why? Basically because the embargo doesn't really have much effect on Cuba or its people.

Cubans now buy ice cream and soft drinks from Swiss-based Nestlé, soap and shampoo from Anglo-Dutch Unilever, and cigarettes from Brazil's Souza Cruz. The fact that the United States is the world's largest market for rum did not deter French-owned Pernod-Ricard from building a new distillery in Cuba, and Britain's Imperial Tobacco expects to double sales when Americans can once again purchase premium hand-rolled Cuban cigars. Most of the directors of Canada's Sherritt International are barred from the United States by provisions of the embargo, but they apparently regard the ban as a small price to pay for future returns on a $1.5 billion investment in Cuba's nickel and oil and gas industries. Cuba has also lifted restrictions on many products once unavailable to Cuban consumers, such as computers, DVDs, and smartphones, and sales of all these products will be a boon to Telecom Italia, which holds a 27 percent stake in the country's state-owned telecom operations.

Katzeff is thinking the same thing that a lot of American businesspeople are undoubtedly thinking: "When the embargo is over," he says, "I want to be there." As he sees it, Cuban coffee has a promising post-embargo future: Its potential, he points out, "is phenomenal. The climate hasn't changed. The soil hasn't changed." And while Katzeff's geopolitics may rankle some people, his business sense seems sound. At present, of course, he can't actually do business with Cuban coffee growers, but he has figured out a way to lay the groundwork. He has already established working relationships with coffee cooperatives, groups of individual growers who pool their crops to enter the export market and secure higher prices, in Latin America and Africa. "Right now," he says, "my objective is to show those cooperatives that I'm willing to risk something on their behalf," but a longer-term goal is to invest the same capital and acquired know-how in relationships with Cuban growers.

The director of Thanksgiving's Cuba project, Nick Hoskins, has already developed contacts in Cuba's coffee-growing regions, and Katzeff hopes to establish a *twinning agreement*, an exchange of people-to-people programs, with cooperatives in the coffee-growing province of Santiago de Cuba. "We're trying to create models that other companies can use and benefit from," explains Katzeff, who is meanwhile willing to settle for a public relations program of transactions—monetary and otherwise—with American coffee drinkers.[1]

Managers make decisions every day. Some have immediate consequences. Others, like those made in the context of the Cuban embargo, are much more long-term in nature. Making effective decisions, as well as recognizing when a bad decision has been made and quickly responding to it, is a key ingredient in organizational effectiveness. Indeed, some experts believe that decision making is the most basic and fundamental of all managerial activities.[2] Thus, we discuss it here, in the context of the first management function, planning. Keep in mind, however, that although decision making is perhaps most closely linked to the planning function, it is also part of organizing, leading, and controlling.

We begin our discussion by exploring the nature of decision making. We then describe rational perspectives on decision making. Behavioral aspects of decision making are then introduced and described. We conclude with a discussion of group and team decision making.

THE NATURE OF DECISION MAKING

Managers at Disney recently made the decision to buy all of George Lucas's properties, including the characters and stories in the *Star Wars* mythology. At about the same time, the general manager of the Ford dealership in Bryan, Texas, made a decision to sponsor a local youth soccer team for $200. Each of these examples reflects a decision, but the decisions differ in many ways. Thus, as a starting point in understanding decision making, we must first explore the meaning of decision making as well as types of decisions and the conditions under which decisions are made.[3]

Decision Making Defined

Decision making can refer to either a specific act or a general process. **Decision making** is the act of choosing one alternative from among a set of alternatives. The decision-making process, however, is much more than this. One step of the process, for example, is that the person making the decision must both recognize that a decision is necessary and identify the set of feasible alternatives before selecting one. Hence, the **decision-making process** includes recognizing and defining the nature of a decision situation, identifying alternatives, choosing the "best" alternative, and putting it into practice.[4]

decision making
The act of choosing one alternative from among a set of alternatives

decision-making process
Recognizing and defining the nature of a decision situation, identifying alternatives, choosing the best alternative, and putting it into practice

The word *best*, of course, implies effectiveness. Effective decision making requires that the decision maker understands the situation driving the decision. Most people would consider an effective decision to be one that optimizes some set of factors, such as profits, sales, employee welfare, and market share. In some situations, though, an effective decision may be one that minimizes loss, expense, or employee turnover. It may even mean selecting the best method for going out of business, laying off employees, or terminating a strategic alliance.

We should also note that managers make decisions about both problems and opportunities. For example, making decisions about how to cut costs by 10 percent reflects a problem—an undesirable situation that requires a solution. But decisions are also necessary in situations of opportunity. Learning that the firm is earning higher-than-projected profits, for example, requires a subsequent decision. Should the extra funds be used to increase shareholder dividends, reinvest in current operations, or expand into new markets?[5]

Of course, it may take a long time before a manager can know if the right decision was made. For example, in late 2008 and early 2009, government leaders made the decision to invest billions of dollars in failing financial institutions and other businesses. It will be years—or perhaps decades—before economists and other experts will know if those were sound decisions or if the United States would have been better off by allowing those businesses to fail.

Types of Decisions

Managers must make many different types of decisions. In general, however, most decisions fall into one of two categories: programmed and nonprogrammed.[6]

Programmed decisions are relatively structured or recur with some frequency (or both). Starbucks uses programmed decisions to purchase new supplies of coffee

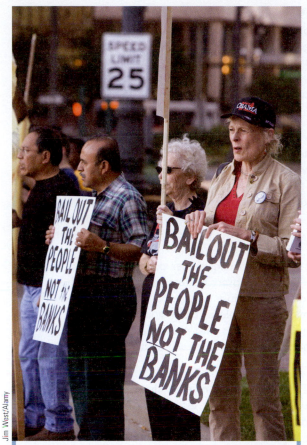

Jim West/Alamy

Decision making plays a major role in all organizations, both public and private. For example, poor decision making at major financial institutions led to the financial crisis that swept the United States in 2008 and 2009. And then the U.S. government made several controversial decisions to help pull the economy out of recession. These protesters were among the critics who thought decisions to support the bailouts were inappropriate.

programmed decision

A decision that is relatively structured or recurs with some frequency (or both)

nonprogrammed decision

A decision that is relatively unstructured and occurs much less often than a programmed decision

beans, cups, and napkins, and its employees are trained in exact procedures for brewing coffee. Likewise, the Bryan Ford dealer made a decision that he will sponsor a youth soccer team each year. Thus, when the soccer club president calls, the dealer already knows what he will do. Many decisions regarding basic operating systems and procedures and standard organizational transactions are of this variety and can therefore be programmed.[7]

Nonprogrammed decisions, on the other hand, are relatively unstructured and occur much less often than programmed decisions. Disney's decision to buy George Lucas's assets was a nonprogrammed decision. Managers faced with such decisions must treat each one as unique, investing enormous amounts of time, energy, and resources into exploring the situation from all perspectives. Intuition and experience are major factors in nonprogrammed decisions. Most of the decisions made by top managers involving strategy (including mergers, acquisitions, and takeovers) and organization design are nonprogrammed. So are decisions about new facilities, new products, labor contracts, and legal issues.

Decision-Making Conditions

Just as there are different kinds of decisions, there are also different conditions under which decisions are made. Managers sometimes have an almost perfect understanding of the conditions surrounding a decision, but at other times they have few clues about those conditions. In general, as shown in Figure 4.1, the circumstances that exist for the decision maker are conditions of certainty, risk, or uncertainty.[8]

state of certainty
A condition in which the decision maker knows with reasonable certainty what the alternatives are and what conditions are associated with each alternative

Decision Making Under Certainty   When the decision maker knows with reasonable certainty what the alternatives are and what conditions are associated with each alternative, a **state of certainty** exists. Suppose, for example, that managers at Singapore Airlines make a decision to buy five new jumbo jets. Their next decision would be from whom to buy them. Because only two companies in the world make jumbo jets, Boeing and Airbus, Singapore Airlines knows its options exactly. Each has proven products and will guarantee prices and delivery dates. The airline thus knows the alternative conditions associated with each. There is little ambiguity and relatively little chance of making a bad decision.

Few organizational decisions, however, are made under conditions of true certainty. The complexity and turbulence of the contemporary business world make such situations rare. Even the airplane purchase decision we just considered has less certainty than it appears. The aircraft companies may not be able to really guarantee delivery dates, so they may write cost increase or inflation clauses into contracts. Thus, the airline may be only partially certain of the conditions surrounding each alternative.

state of risk
A condition in which the availability of each alternative and its potential payoffs and costs are all associated with probability estimates

Decision Making Under Risk   A more common decision-making condition is a state of risk. Under a **state of risk**, the availability of each alternative and its potential payoffs and costs are all associated with probability estimates.[9] Suppose, for example, that a labor contract negotiator for a company receives a "final" offer from the union right before a strike deadline. The negotiator will have two alternatives: to accept or to reject the offer. The risk centers on whether the union representatives are bluffing. If the

© Cengage Learning

FIGURE 4.1

Decision-Making Conditions

Most major organizational decisions today are made under a state of uncertainty. Managers making decisions in these circumstances must be sure to learn as much as possible about the situation and approach the decision from a logical and rational perspective.

company negotiator accepts the offer, she avoids a strike but commits to a relatively costly labor contract. If she rejects the contract, she may get a more favorable contract if the union is bluffing, but she may provoke a strike if it is not.

On the basis of past experiences, relevant information, the advice of others, and her own judgment, she may conclude that there is about a 75 percent chance that union representatives are bluffing and about a 25 percent chance that they will back up their threats. Thus, she can base a calculated decision on the two alternatives (accept or reject the contract demands) and the probable consequences of each. When making decisions under a state of risk, managers must reasonably estimate the probabilities associated with each alternative. For example, if the union negotiators are committed to a strike if their demands are not met, and the company negotiator rejects their demands because she guesses they will not strike, her miscalculation will prove costly.

As indicated in Figure 4.1, decision making under conditions of risk is accompanied by moderate ambiguity and the chances of a bad decision. Managers at Ford Motor Company often face risky decisions. For instance, like many other automobile companies, Ford laid off thousands of workers during 2008. But shortly thereafter, Ford executives noted that as fuel prices were dropping, demand for its new F-150 pickup was increasing in spite of the recession. So, the firm rehired 1,000 of its former workers to help build more pickups. The risk was that if gas prices had surged unexpectedly and/or demand for the F-150 had cooled, Ford would have been in the embarrassing position of recalling workers and then once again terminating them. But the upside was that Ford's assessment that it would generate new revenues and more profits was correct.[10]

More recently, Ford launched the newest version of the F-150 in early 2014. The risk? Truck makers have historically used steel for most of their product's exterior sheet metal, but the new F-150 uses aluminum. Aluminum construction reduces the weight of the trucks by several hundred pounds, promising much better fuel economy. If pickup buyers accept aluminum construction and embrace better fuel economy, Ford will have gained a competitive advantage. But if buyers resist the idea of aluminum, then the F-150 may see a drop in market share. The "Tough Times, Tough Choices" box explores risk managers face due to increased globalization.

state of uncertainty
A condition in which the decision maker does not know all the alternatives, the risks associated with each, or the likely consequences of each alternative

Decision Making Under Uncertainty   Most of the major decision making in contemporary organizations is done under a state of uncertainty, where the decision maker does not know all the alternatives, the risks associated with each, or the likely consequences of each alternative. This uncertainty stems from the complexity and dynamism of contemporary organizations and their environments. For example, airlines continually face uncertainty stemming from fluctuations in fuel costs. In large part to reduce this uncertainty, Delta Air Lines recently took the unusual step of buying its own oil refinery.[11] The emergence of new technology and social media as significant forces in today's competitive environment has served to increase both revenue potential and uncertainty for most managers.

To make effective decisions in these circumstances, managers must acquire as much relevant information as possible and approach the situation from a logical and rational perspective. Intuition, judgment, and experience always play major roles in the decision-making process under conditions of uncertainty. Even so, uncertainty is the most ambiguous condition for managers and the one in which they are most prone to error.[12] Indeed, many of the problems associated with the downfall of Arthur Andersen resulted from the firm's apparent difficulties in responding to ambiguous and uncertain decision parameters regarding the firm's moral, ethical, and legal responsibilities.[13]

TOUGH TIMES, TOUGH CHOICES

The Wide World of Risk

Decision making under a condition of risk is becoming an increasingly common challenge for all managers today. One reason for the increased risk is the fact that globalization has become such a factor in everyday business life. The general impact of the global economy and the expanded reach and power of multinational companies are the basic causes of increased risk stemming from globalization. Many large corporations have actually become engines for innovation as well as growth, adapting to new markets and new economic circumstances. In a highly interconnected world, however, it's often hard to figure out the complex ownership and organizational structures of many global corporations. Sometimes, for example, their branding strategies and management structures lead people to think that they're local companies when, in fact, the real source of corporate power may lie thousands of miles away on another continent. For example, there are several hundred Aldi supermarkets in the United States, but

Aldi itself is a German firm. One thing's for sure, if you're going to be dealing with a company overseas, you'd better have a good idea of where and how decisions are made, and who has the real power to make them.

Remember, too, that different cultures have different attitudes when it comes to risk, especially as it relates to entrepreneurship. In some countries and cultures, like that of the United States, there's a lively entrepreneurial spirit. Businesspeople are open to taking risks, and if they fail, they tend to pick themselves up and move on to something else. In some Asian countries, though, the entrepreneurial spirit is often tempered by the need for consensus and getting everyone on board. This approach requires a lot of patience and the ability to compromise. Knowing the economic cultural forces that shape both a business organization and people's attitudes toward risk, success, and failure is an increasingly important component of the manager's job today.

RATIONAL PERSPECTIVES ON DECISION MAKING

Most managers like to think of themselves as rational decision makers. And, indeed, many experts argue that managers should try to be as rational as possible in making decisions.[14] This section highlights the fundamental and rational perspectives on decision making.

The Classical Model of Decision Making

classical decision model

A prescriptive approach to decision making that tells managers how they should make decisions; it assumes that managers are logical and rational and that their decisions will be in the organization's best interests

The **classical decision model** is a prescriptive approach that tells managers how they should make decisions. It rests on the assumptions that managers are logical and rational and that they make decisions that are in the organization's best interests. Figure 4.2 shows how the classical model views the decision-making process:

1. Decision makers have complete information about the decision situation and possible alternatives.
2. They can effectively eliminate uncertainty to achieve a decision condition of certainty.
3. They evaluate all aspects of the decision situation logically and rationally.

As we see later, these conditions rarely, if ever, actually exist.

FIGURE 4.2 The Classical Model of Decision Making

Steps in Rational Decision Making

steps in rational decision making
Recognize and define the decision situation; identify appropriate alternatives; evaluate each alternative in terms of its feasibility, satisfactoriness, and consequences; select the best alternative; implement the chosen alternative; and follow up and evaluate the results of the chosen alternative

A manager who really wants to approach a decision rationally and logically should try to follow the **steps in rational decision making** listed in Table 4.1. These steps in rational decision making help keep the decision maker focused on facts and logic and help guard against inappropriate assumptions and pitfalls.

Although the presumptions of the classical decision model rarely exist, managers can still approach decision making with rationality. By following the steps of rational decision making, managers ensure that they are learning as much as possible about the decision situation and its alternatives.

Recognizing and Defining the Decision Situation The first step in rational decision making is recognizing that a decision is necessary—that is, there must be some stimulus or spark to initiate the process. For many decisions and problem situations, the stimulus may occur without any prior warning. When equipment malfunctions, the manager must decide whether to repair or replace it. Or, when a major crisis erupts, as described in Chapter 3, the manager must quickly decide how to deal with it. As we already noted, the stimulus for a decision may be either positive or negative. A manager who must decide how to invest surplus funds, for example, faces a positive decision situation. A negative financial stimulus could involve having to trim budgets because of cost overruns.

Inherent in problem recognition is the need to define precisely what the problem is. The manager must develop a complete understanding of the problem, its causes, and its relationship to other factors. This understanding comes from careful analysis and thoughtful consideration of the situation. Consider the situation currently being faced in the international air travel industry. Because of the growth of international travel related to business, education, and tourism, global carriers such as Singapore Airlines, KLM, JAL, British Airways, and American Airlines need to increase their capacity for international travel. Because most major international airports are already operating at or near capacity, adding a significant number of new flights to existing schedules is not feasible. As a result, the most logical alternative is to increase capacity on existing flights. Thus, Boeing and Airbus, the world's only manufacturers of large commercial aircraft, recognized an important opportunity and defined their decision situation as how to best respond to the need for increased global travel capacity.[15]

Identifying Alternatives Once the decision situation has been recognized and defined, the second step is to identify alternative courses of effective action. Developing both obvious, standard alternatives and creative, innovative alternatives is generally useful.[16] In general, the more important the decision, the more attention is directed to developing alternatives.[17] If the decision involves a multimillion-dollar relocation, a great deal of time and expertise will be devoted to identifying the best

Although the presumptions of the classical decision model rarely exist, managers can still approach decision making with rationality. By following the steps of rational decision making, managers ensure that they are learning as much as possible about the decision situation and its alternatives.

Table 4.1	Steps in the Rational Decision-Making Process	
Step	**Detail**	**Example**
1. Recognizing and defining the decision situation	Some stimulus indicates that a decision must be made. The stimulus may be positive or negative.	A plant manager sees that employee turnover has increased by 5 percent.
2. Identifying alternatives	Both obvious and creative alternatives are desired. In general, the more important the decision, the more alternatives should be generated.	The plant manager can increase wages, increase benefits, or change hiring standards.
3. Evaluating alternatives	Each alternative is evaluated to determine its feasibility, its satisfactoriness, and its consequences.	Increasing benefits may not be feasible. Increasing wages and changing hiring standards may satisfy all conditions.
4. Selecting the best alternative	Consider all situational factors, and choose the alternative that best fits the manager's situation.	Changing hiring standards will take an extended period of time to cut turnover, so increase wages.
5. Implementing the chosen alternative	The chosen alternative is implemented into the organizational system.	The plant manager may need permission from corporate headquarters. The human resources department establishes a new wage structure.
6. Following up and evaluating the results	At some time in the future, the manager should ascertain the extent to which the alternative chosen in Step 4 and implemented in Step 5 has worked.	The plant manager notes that, six months later, turnover dropped to its previous level.

© Cengage Learning

locations. AT&T spent over a year searching before selecting the Dallas–Fort Worth area for its new corporate headquarters. If the problem is to choose a color for the company softball team's uniforms, less time and expertise will be brought to bear.

Although managers should seek creative solutions, they must also recognize that various constraints often limit their alternatives. Common constraints include legal restrictions, moral and ethical norms, authority constraints, available technology, economic considerations, and unofficial social norms. Boeing and Airbus identified three different alternatives to address the decision situation of increasing international airline travel capacity: They could independently develop new large planes, they could collaborate in a joint venture to create a single new large plane, or they could modify their largest existing planes to increase their capacity.

Evaluating Alternatives   The third step in the decision-making process is evaluating each of the alternatives. Figure 4.3 presents a decision tree that can be used to judge different alternatives. The figure suggests that each alternative be evaluated in terms of its feasibility, satisfactoriness, and consequences. The first question to ask is whether an alternative is feasible. Is it within the realm of probability and practicality? For a small, struggling firm, an alternative requiring a huge financial outlay is probably out of the question. Other alternatives may not be feasible because of legal barriers. And limited human, material, and information resources may make other alternatives impractical.

When an alternative has passed the test of feasibility, it must next be examined to see how well it satisfies the conditions of the decision situation. For example, a manager searching for ways to double production capacity might initially consider purchasing an existing plant from another company. If more detailed analysis reveals that the new plant would increase production capacity by only 35 percent, this alternative may not be satisfactory. Finally, when an alternative has proven both feasible and satisfactory, its probable consequences must still be assessed. To what extent will a particular alternative influence other parts of the organization? What financial and nonfinancial costs will be associated with such influences? For example, a plan to boost sales by cutting prices may disrupt cash flows, require a new advertising program, and alter the behavior of sales representatives because it requires a different commission structure. The manager, then, must put "price tags" on the consequences of each alternative. Even an alternative that is both feasible and satisfactory must be eliminated if its consequences are too expensive for the total system. Airbus felt it would be at a disadvantage if it tried to simply enlarge its existing planes because the Boeing 747 was already the largest aircraft being made and could readily be expanded to remain the largest. Boeing, meanwhile, was seriously concerned about the risk inherent in building a new and even larger plane, even if it shared the risk with Airbus as a joint venture.

FIGURE 4.3

Evaluating Alternatives in the Decision-Making Process

Managers must thoroughly evaluate all the alternatives; this increases the chances that the alternative that is finally chosen will be successful. Failure to evaluate an alternative's feasibility, satisfactoriness, and consequences can lead to a wrong decision.

Selecting the Best Alternative   Even though many alternatives fail to pass the triple tests of feasibility, satisfactoriness, and affordable consequences, two or more alternatives may remain. Choosing the best of these is the real crux of decision making. One approach is to choose the alternative with the optimal combination of feasibility, satisfactoriness, and affordable consequences. Even though most situations do not lend themselves to objective, mathematical analysis, the manager can often develop subjective estimates and weights for choosing an alternative.

Optimization is also a frequent goal. Because a decision is likely to affect several individuals or units, any feasible alternative will probably not maximize all of the relevant goals. Suppose that the manager of the Kansas City Royals needs to select a new outfielder for the upcoming baseball season. Bill hits .350 but sometimes has difficulty catching fly balls, Joe hits only .225 but is outstanding in the field, and Sam hits .290 and is a solid but not outstanding fielder. The manager would probably select Sam because of the optimal balance of hitting and fielding. Decision makers should also remember that finding multiple acceptable alternatives may be possible; selecting just one alternative and rejecting all the others might not be necessary. For example, the Royals' manager might decide that Sam will start each game, Bill will be retained as a pinch hitter, and Joe will be retained as a defensive substitute. In many hiring decisions, the candidates remaining after evaluation are ranked. If the top candidate rejects the offer, it may be automatically extended to the number-two candidate and, if necessary, to the remaining candidates in order. For the reasons noted earlier, Airbus proposed a joint venture with Boeing. Boeing, meanwhile, decided that its best course of action was to modify its existing 747 to increase its capacity. As a result, Airbus then decided to proceed on its own to develop and manufacture a new jumbo jet. Boeing, however, also decided that in addition to modifying its 747, it would develop a new plane to offer as an alternative, albeit one not as large as the 747 or the proposed Airbus plane.

Implementing the Chosen Alternative   After an alternative has been selected, the manager must put it into effect. In some decision situations, implementation is fairly easy; in others, it is more difficult. In the case of an acquisition, for example, managers must decide how to integrate all of the new business's activities, including purchasing, human resource practices, and distribution, into an ongoing organizational framework. For example, when Hewlett-Packard made the decision to buy Compaq Computer, managers estimated that it would take at least a year to integrate the two firms into a single one. Similarly, the decision made by executives at American Airlines and US Airways to merge into a single airline will take two or three years to implement. Operational plans, which we discussed in Chapter 3, are useful in implementing alternatives.

Managers must also consider people's resistance to change when implementing decisions. The reasons for such resistance include insecurity, inconvenience, and fear of the unknown. Managers should anticipate potential resistance at various stages of the implementation process. (Resistance to change is covered in Chapter 7.) Managers should also recognize that even when all alternatives have been evaluated as precisely as possible and the consequences of each alternative weighed, unanticipated consequences are still likely. Any number of factors—such as unexpected cost increases, a less-than-perfect fit with existing organizational subsystems, or unpredicted effects on cash flow or operating expenses—could develop after implementation has begun. Boeing set its engineers to work expanding the capacity of its 747 from 416 passengers to as many as 520 passengers by adding 30 feet to the plane's body. The company has also been developing its new plane intended for international travel, the Boeing 787 Dreamliner. Airbus engineers, meanwhile, spent years developing and constructing its new jumbo jet, the A380; it is equipped with

Boeing and Airbus used rational perspectives to arrive at different decisions about major investments in developing new airplanes. Airbus decided to build the A380, the world's largest passenger plane. Boeing, meanwhile, chose to develop a smaller but much more fuel efficient plane named the 787 Dreamliner.

escalators and elevators, and capable of carrying 655 passengers. Airbus's development costs alone are estimated to be more than $12 billion.

Following Up and Evaluating the Results   The final step in the decision-making process requires that managers evaluate the effectiveness of their decision—that is, they should make sure that the chosen alternative has served its original purpose. If an implemented alternative appears not to be working, the manager can respond in several ways. Another previously identified alternative (the original second or third choice, for instance) could be adopted. Or the manager might recognize that the situation was not correctly defined to begin with and start the process all over again. Finally, the manager might decide that the original alternative is in fact appropriate but has not yet had time to work or should be implemented in a different way.[18]

Failure to evaluate decision effectiveness may have serious consequences. The Pentagon once spent $1.8 billion and eight years developing the Sergeant York antiaircraft gun. From the beginning, tests revealed major problems with the weapon system, but not until it was in its final stages, when it was demonstrated to be completely ineffective, was the project scrapped.

At this point, both Boeing and Airbus are still learning about the consequences of their decisions. Airbus's A380 has been placed in commercial service. However, the plane has suffered numerous mechanical problems. Moreover, because the weakened economy has dealt a blow to large international airlines, some of them—such as Qantas Airways and Emirates Airlines—deferred or cancelled orders for the plane. Airbus estimated that it needs to sell 420 A380s before it starts making a profit. Current projections suggest that sales of the plane may not hit that target until at least 2020.[19] Meanwhile, it appeared for a while that Boeing's commitment to the new 787 might prove to be the best decision of all. A key element of the new plane is that it is much more fuel efficient than other international airplanes. Given the dramatic surge in fuel costs in recent years, a fuel-efficient option like the 787 is likely to be an enormous success. However, the 787 has suffered from numerous manufacturing problems and was not available for passenger service until 2012 (over 3 years late). The plane also experienced problems in 2013 and was grounded for several weeks. New problems surfaced in early 2014 as well. So, its real impact will not be known for a few more years.[20]

Evidence-Based Management

Rational perspectives on decision making have recently been reformulated under the concept of evidence-based management. Stanford University professors Jeffrey Pfeffer and Bob Sutton, authors of *Hard Facts, Dangerous Half-Truths, and Total Nonsense*, have put out a call for a renewed reliance on rationality in managerial decision making—an approach that they call *evidence-based management (EBM)*. "Management decisions," they argue, "[should] be based on the best evidence, managers [should] systematically learn from experience, and organizational practices [should] reflect sound principles of thought and analysis." They define *evidence-based management* as "a commitment to finding and using the best theory and data available at the time to make decisions," but their "Five Principles of Evidence-Based Management" make it clear that EBM means more than just sifting through data and crunching numbers. Here's what they recommend:

1. Face the hard facts and build a culture in which people are encouraged to tell the truth, even if it's unpleasant.
2. Be committed to "fact-based" decision making—which means being committed to getting the best evidence and using it to guide actions.
3. Treat your organization as an unfinished prototype—encourage experimentation and learning by doing.
4. Look for the risks and drawbacks in what people recommend (even the best medicine has side effects).
5. Avoid basing decisions on untested but strongly held beliefs, what you have done in the past, or uncritical "benchmarking" of what winners do.

Pfeffer and Sutton are particularly persuasive when they use EBM to question the outcomes of decisions based on "untested but strongly held beliefs" or on "uncritical 'benchmarking." Take, for instance, the popular policy of paying high performers significantly more than low performers. Pfeffer and Sutton's research shows that pay-for-performance policies get good results when employees work solo or independently. But it's another matter altogether when it comes to collaborative teams—the kind of teams that make so many organizational decisions today. Under these circumstances, the greater the gap between highest- and lowest-paid executives, the weaker the firm's financial performance. Why? According to Pfeffer and Sutton, wide disparities in pay often weaken both trust among team members and the social connectivity that contributes to strong team-based decision making.

Or consider another increasingly prevalent policy for evaluating and rewarding talent. Pioneered at General Electric by the legendary Jack Welch, the practice of "forced ranking" divides employees into three groups based on performance—the top 20 percent, middle 70 percent, and bottom 10 percent—and terminates those at the bottom. Pfeffer and Sutton found that, according to many HR managers, forced ranking impaired morale and collaboration and ultimately reduced productivity. They also concluded that automatically firing the bottom 10 percent resulted too often in the unnecessary disruption of otherwise effective teamwork. That's how they found out that 73 percent of the errors committed by commercial airline pilots occur on the first day that reconfigured crews work together.[21]

BEHAVIORAL ASPECTS OF DECISION MAKING

If all decision situations were approached as logically as described in the previous section, more decisions might prove to be successful. Yet decisions are often made with little consideration for logic and rationality. Some experts have estimated that U.S. companies use rational decision-making techniques less than 20 percent of the time.[22] And, even when organizations try to be logical, they sometimes fail. For example, when Starbucks opened its first coffee shop in New York, it relied on scientific marketing research, taste tests, and rational deliberation in making a decision to emphasize drip over espresso coffee. However, that decision still proved wrong, as New Yorkers strongly preferred the same espresso-style coffees that were Starbucks mainstays in the West. Hence, the firm had to hastily reconfigure its stores to better meet customer preferences.

On the other hand, sometimes when a decision is made with little regard for logic, it can still turn out to be correct.[23] An important ingredient in how these forces work is the behavioral aspect of decision making. The administrative model better reflects these subjective considerations. Other behavioral aspects include political forces, intuition and escalation of commitment, risk propensity, and ethics.

The Administrative Model

administrative model
A decision-making model that argues that decision makers (1) use incomplete and imperfect information, (2) are constrained by bounded rationality, and (3) tend to "satisfice" when making decisions

Herbert A. Simon was one of the first experts to recognize that decisions are not always made with rationality and logic.[24] Simon was subsequently awarded the Nobel Prize in Economics. Rather than prescribing how decisions should be made, his view of decision making, now called the **administrative model**, describes how decisions often actually are made. As illustrated in Figure 4.4, the model holds that decision makers (1) use incomplete and imperfect information, (2) are constrained by bounded rationality, and (3) tend to "satisfice" when making decisions.

bounded rationality
A concept suggesting that decision makers are limited by their values and unconscious reflexes, skills, and habits

Bounded rationality suggests that decision makers are limited by their values and unconscious reflexes, skills, and habits. They are also limited by less-than-complete information and knowledge. Bounded rationality partially explains how U.S. auto executives allowed Japanese automakers to get such a strong foothold in the U.S. domestic market. For years, executives at GM, Ford, and Chrysler compared their companies' performance only to one another's and essentially ignored foreign imports. The foreign "threat" was not acknowledged until the domestic auto market had been changed forever. If managers had gathered—and acknowledged—complete information from the beginning, they might have been better able to thwart foreign competitors. Essentially,

© Cengage Learning

| When faced with a decision situation managers *actually*… | → | • use incomplete and imperfect information
• are constrained by bounded rationality
• tend to satisfice | → | …and end up with a decision that may or may not serve the interests of the organization. |

FIGURE 4.4

The Administrative Model of Decision Making

The administrative model is based on behavioral processes that affect how managers make decisions. Rather than prescribing how decisions should be made, it focuses more on describing how they are made.

satisficing
The tendency to search for alternatives only until one is found that meets some minimum standard of sufficiency

then, the concept of bounded rationality suggests that although people try to be rational decision makers, their rationality has limits.

Another important part of the administrative model is **satisficing**, which suggests that rather than conducting an exhaustive search for the best possible alternative, decision makers tend to search only until they identify an alternative that meets some minimum standard of sufficiency. A manager looking for a new plant site, for example, may select the first site she finds that meets basic requirements for transportation, utilities, and price, even though further searching might yield a better location. People satisfice for a variety of reasons. Managers may simply be unwilling to ignore their own motives (such as reluctance to spend time making a decision) and therefore not be able to continue searching after a minimally acceptable alternative is identified. The decision maker may be unable to weigh and evaluate large numbers of alternatives and criteria. Also, subjective and personal considerations often intervene in decision situations.

Because of the inherent imperfection of information, bounded rationality, and satisficing, a manager's decisions may or may not actually be in the organization's best interests. A manager may choose a particular location for a new plant because it offers the lowest price and best availability of utilities and transportation. Or she may choose the location because it is located in a community where she wants to live.

In summary, then, the classical and administrative models paint quite different pictures of decision making. Which is more correct? Actually, each can be used to better understand how managers make decisions. The classical model is prescriptive: It explains how managers can at least attempt to be more rational and logical in their approaches to decisions. The administrative model can be used by managers to develop a better understanding of their inherent biases and limitations.[25] In the following sections, we describe more fully other behavioral forces that can influence decisions.

Political Forces in Decision Making

coalition
An informal alliance of individuals or groups formed to achieve a common goal

Political forces are another major element that contributes to the behavioral nature of decision making. Organizational politics is covered in Chapter 11, but one major element of politics, coalitions, is especially relevant to decision making. A **coalition** is an informal alliance of individuals or groups formed to achieve a common goal. This common goal is often a preferred decision alternative. For example, coalitions of stockholders frequently band together to force a board of directors to make a certain decision.

When General Motors (GM) decided to launch Saturn as a new automobile company several years ago, the idea had the full backing and support of its CEO, Roger Smith. Saturn was to have its own factories, design teams, and dealer networks and was to compete directly with high-quality foreign imports such as Toyota and Honda. Just as the first Saturn cars were being introduced, however, Smith retired. As it turned out, a coalition of senior GM executives had opposed the Saturn concept but had been unable to do anything about it because Smith was such a powerful product champion. When Smith left GM, though, the coalition managed to divert resources intended for Saturn to other GM brands. As a result, new Saturn products were delayed, the brand received weak marketing support, and it never lived up to expectations.[26]

The impact of coalitions can be either positive or negative. They can help astute managers get their organization on a path toward effectiveness and profitability, or they can strangle well-conceived strategies and decisions. Managers must recognize when to use coalitions, how to assess whether coalitions are acting in the organization's best interests, and how to constrain their dysfunctional effects.[27]

Intuition and Escalation of Commitment

Two other important decision processes that go beyond logic and rationality are intuition and escalation of commitment to a chosen course of action.

intuition
An innate belief about something, without conscious consideration

Intuition   **Intuition** is an innate belief about something without conscious consideration. Managers sometimes decide to do something because it "feels right" or they have a "hunch." This feeling usually is not arbitrary, however. Rather, it is based on years of experience and practice in making decisions in similar situations.[28] An inner sense may help managers make an occasional decision without going through a full-blown rational sequence of steps. For example, Kip Tindell, CEO of The Container Store, emphasizes the use of intuition throughout his company and urges employees to believe that it is critical in the workplace. He is quoted as saying, "Intuition is only the sum total of your life experiences. So why would you want to leave it at home when you come to work in the morning?"[29] Of course, all managers, but especially the inexperienced ones, should be careful not to rely too heavily on intuition. If rationality and logic are continually flouted for "what feels right," the odds are that disaster will strike one day. This situation is illustrated in the "At Your Service" feature.

escalation of commitment
When a decision maker stays with a decision even when it appears to be wrong

Escalation of Commitment   Another important behavioral process that influences decision making is **escalation of commitment** to a chosen course of action. In particular, decision makers sometimes make decisions and then become so committed to the courses of action suggested by those decisions that they stay with them, even when the decisions appear to have been wrong.[30] For example, when people buy stock in a company, they sometimes refuse to sell it even after repeated drops in price. They choose a course of action—buying the stock in anticipation of making a profit—and then stay with it even in the face of increasing losses. Moreover, after the value drops, they rationalize that they can't sell now because they will lose money.

For years, Pan American World Airways ruled the skies and used its profits to diversify into real estate and other businesses. But, with the advent of deregulation, Pan Am began to struggle and lose market share to other carriers. When Pan Am managers finally realized how ineffective their airline operations had become, experts today point out that the "rational" decision would have been to sell off the remaining airline operations and concentrate on the firm's more profitable businesses. But because they still saw the company as being first and foremost an airline, they instead began to slowly sell off the firm's profitable holdings to keep the airline flying. Eventually, the company was left with nothing but an ineffective and inefficient airline, and then it had to sell off its more profitable routes before being taken over by Delta. Had Pan Am managers made the more rational decision years earlier, chances are the firm could still be a profitable enterprise today, albeit one with no involvement in the airline industry.[31]

AT YOUR SERVICE

A Bad Decision at Wesabe

As far as U.S. small business was concerned, the first quarter of 2010 could have been worse: There was a net loss of only 96,000 companies with fewer than 100 employees. As a matter of fact, the first quarter of 2009 *was* worse—a *lot* worse: By the end of the quarter, there were 400,000 fewer small businesses than there had been at the beginning. And service businesses were especially hard hit.

One of the companies that shut down in 2010 was Wesabe, which had launched in 2006 as an online service provider to help people manage their money and make better financial decisions. It was one of the first companies to enter the financial sector of what's often referred to as *Web 2.0*—the world of web applications that allow users to interact and collaborate on content that they create themselves. The idea was to let customers access data from several financial institutions and then compare their own money management practices to those of online peers.

Wesabe actually got off to a reasonably good start. Within the first year, founders Marc Hedlund and Jason Knight secured venture capital totaling $4.7 million and attracted 150,000 members. The first signs of trouble appeared in the second year, just after a competitor called Mint.com came online. Nine months after its launch, Mint.com boasted $17 million in venture capital and 300,000 users. In 2009, Intuit, a creator of financial and tax-preparation software, purchased Mint.com for $170 million. Wesabe held on until mid-2010, when Hedlund and Knight announced that the company could no longer handle users' highly sensitive data "with shoestring operations and security staff."

So what went wrong? Naturally, there's no single reason for Wesabe's failure, but both Hedlund, who blogged a postmortem shortly after the shutdown, and independent observers point to one crucial business decision as a key factor. In the early stages of the startup process, Hedlund and Knight rejected a partnership with a firm called Yodlee, which had already developed a system for accessing transaction data from banks. But because the Yodlee process worked with users' passwords, Wesabe considered it too great a security risk and proceeded to work on its own process, which, though more secure, was also more cumbersome.

"Everyone—I mean 90-percent-plus of everybody," says Hedlund, "told me that they would never in a million years use a startup website that asked them for their bank passwords." When Mint came online in 2007, it was using Yodlee technology, password-access included, and Hedlund acknowledges that he'd made a poor decision by relying on his own informal market research: "We should have known," he admits, "that somebody would go with Yodlee, and we should have aimed at [Yodlee] as what we needed to achieve." By 2008, Wesabe, too, was accepting users' passwords in order to simplify the process of pulling bank data into its system. "We just didn't build it nearly fast enough," says Hedlund of Wesabe's own data-access system. "That one mistake—not using or replacing Yodlee before Mint had a chance to launch on Yodlee—was probably enough to kill Wesabe alone."

References: Eilene Zimmerman, "How Six Companies Failed to Survive 2010," *New York Times*, January 5, 2011, www.nytimes.com, accessed on September 5, 2013; Anthony Ha, "Personal Finance Startup Wesabe to Shut Down," *VentureBeat*, June 30, 2010, http://venturebeat.com, accessed on September 5, 2013; Marc Hedlund, "Why Wesabe Lost to Mint," *Marc Hedlund's Blog*, October 1, 2010, http://blog.precipice.org, accessed on September 5, 2013; "Some Lessons Learned from the Rise and Fall of Wesabe," *Credit Union Journal*, December 16, 2010, www.cunatechnologycouncil.org, accessed on September 5, 2013.

In contrast, a group of investors licensed the use of Hard Rock logos and trademarks for a large theme park—Hard Rock Park—to be built in South Carolina. After six years of planning and construction and an investment of over $400 million, the park in Myrtle Beach opened to dismal reviews and poor attendance. Rather than increasing their investment and trying to increase attendance, owners decided after only nine months to shut down the park and sell off its assets.[32]

Thus, decision makers must walk a fine line. On the one hand, they must guard against sticking too long with an incorrect decision. To do so can bring about financial decline. On the other hand, they should not bail out of a seemingly incorrect decision too soon, as Adidas once did. Adidas had dominated the market for professional athletic shoes. It subsequently entered the market for amateur sports shoes and did well there also. But managers interpreted a sales slowdown as a sign that the boom in athletic shoes was over. They thought that they had made the wrong decision and ordered drastic cutbacks. The market took off again with Nike at the head of the pack, and Adidas never recovered. Fortunately, a new management team has changed the way Adidas makes decisions, and the firm is again on its way to becoming a force in the athletic shoe and apparel markets.

Risk Propensity and Decision Making

risk propensity

The extent to which a decision maker is willing to gamble when making a decision

The behavioral element of **risk propensity** is the extent to which a decision maker is willing to gamble when making a decision. Some managers are cautious about every decision they make. They try to adhere to the rational model and are extremely conservative in what they do. Such managers are more likely to avoid mistakes, and they infrequently make decisions that lead to big losses. Other managers are extremely aggressive in making decisions and are willing to take risks.[33] They rely heavily on intuition, reach decisions quickly, and often risk big investments on their decisions. As in gambling, these managers are more likely than their conservative counterparts to achieve big successes with their decisions; they are also more likely to incur greater losses.[34] The organization's culture is a prime ingredient in fostering different levels of risk propensity.

Ethics and Decision Making

As we introduced in Chapter 2, individual ethics are personal beliefs about right and wrong behavior. Ethics are clearly related to decision making in a number of ways. For example, suppose that, after careful analysis, a manager realizes that his company could save money by closing his department and subcontracting with a supplier for the same services. But to recommend this course of action would result in the loss of several jobs,

De Meester Johan/Arterra Picture Library/Alamy

It is both unethical and illegal to make a decision to improperly dump trash and hazardous waste. Nevertheless, some people make this decision in order to save time and money. Of course, others incur additional costs in cleaning up dumping sites such as this one.

including his own. His own ethical standards will clearly shape how he proceeds.[35] Indeed, each component of managerial ethics (relationships of the firm to its employees, of employees to the firm, and of the firm to other economic agents) involves a wide variety of decisions, all of which are likely to have an ethical component. Thus, a manager must remember that, just as behavioral processes such as politics and risk propensity affect the decisions he makes, so, too, do his ethical beliefs.[36]

GROUP AND TEAM DECISION MAKING IN ORGANIZATIONS

In more and more organizations today, important decisions are made by groups and teams rather than by individuals. Examples include the executive committee of Abercrombie & Fitch, product design teams at Texas Instruments, and marketing planning groups at Red Lobster. Managers can typically choose whether to have individuals or groups and teams make a particular decision. Thus, knowing about forms of group and team decision making and their advantages and disadvantages is important.[37]

Forms of Group and Team Decision Making

The most common methods of group and team decision making are interacting groups, Delphi groups, and nominal groups. Increasingly, these methods of group decision making are being conducted online.[38]

interacting group or team
A decision-making group or team in which members openly discuss, argue about, and agree on the best alternative

Interacting Groups or Teams **Interacting groups or teams** are the most common decision-making group. The format is simple—either an existing or a newly designated group or team is asked to make a decision. Existing groups or teams might be functional departments, regular work teams, or standing committees. Newly designated groups or teams can be ad hoc committees, task forces, or newly constituted work teams. The group or team members talk among themselves, argue, agree, form internal coalitions, and so forth. Finally, after some period of deliberation, the group or team makes its decision. An advantage of this method is that the interaction among people often sparks new ideas and promotes understanding. A major disadvantage, though, is that political processes can play too big a role.

Delphi group
A form of group decision making in which a group arrives at a consensus of expert opinion

Delphi Groups A **Delphi group** is sometimes used to arrive at a consensus of expert opinion. Developed by the Rand Corporation, the Delphi procedure solicits input from a panel of experts who contribute individually. Their opinions are combined and, in effect, averaged. Assume, for example, that the problem is to establish an expected date for a major technological breakthrough in converting coal into usable energy. The first step in using the Delphi procedure is to obtain the cooperation of a panel of experts. For this situation, experts might include various research scientists, university researchers, and executives in a relevant energy industry. At first, the experts are asked to anonymously predict a time frame for the expected breakthrough. The persons coordinating the Delphi group collect the responses, average them, and ask the experts for another prediction. In this round, the experts who provided unusual or extreme predictions may be asked to justify them. These explanations may then be relayed to the other experts. When the predictions stabilize, the average prediction is taken to represent the decision of the group of experts. The time, expense, and logistics of the Delphi technique rule out its use for routine, everyday decisions, but it has been successfully used for forecasting technological breakthroughs at Boeing, market potential for new products at GM, research and development patterns at Eli Lilly, and future economic conditions by the U.S. government.[39] Moreover, although the Delphi method originally relied on paper-and-pencil responses obtained and shared through the mail, modern communication technologies such as e-mail and the Internet have enabled Delphi users to get answers much more quickly than in the past.

nominal group
A structured technique used to generate creative and innovative alternatives or ideas

Nominal Groups   Another useful group and team decision-making technique that is occasionally used is the **nominal group**. Unlike the Delphi method, in which group members do not see one another, nominal group members are brought together in a face-to-face setting. The members represent a group in name only, however; they do not talk to one another freely like the members of interacting groups. Nominal groups are used most often to generate creative and innovative alternatives or ideas. To begin, the manager assembles a group of knowledgeable experts and outlines the problem to them. The group members are then asked to individually write down as many alternatives as they can think of. The members then take turns stating their ideas, which are recorded on a flip chart or board at the front of the room. Discussion is limited to simple clarification. After all alternatives have been listed, more open discussion takes place. Group members then vote, usually by rank, ordering the various alternatives. The highest-ranking alternative represents the decision of the group. Of course, the manager in charge may retain the authority to accept or reject the group decision.[40]

To increase the chances that a group or team decision will be successful, managers must learn how to manage the process of group and team decision making. Federal Express and IBM are increasingly using groups and teams for decision making.

Advantages of Group and Team Decision Making

The advantages and disadvantages of group and team decision making relative to individual decision making are summarized in Table 4.2. One advantage is simply that more information is available in a group or team setting—as suggested by the old axiom, "Two heads are better than one." A group or team represents a variety of education, experience, and perspective. Partly as a result of this increased information, groups and teams typically can identify and evaluate more alternatives than can one person.[41] The people involved in a group or team decision understand the logic and rationale behind it, are more likely to accept it, and are equipped to communicate the decision to their work group or department.[42] Finally, research evidence suggests that groups may make better decisions than individuals.[43]

To increase the chances that a group or team decision will be successful, managers must learn how to manage the process of group and team decision making. Federal Express and IBM are increasingly using groups and teams for decision making.

Table 4.2	Advantages and Disadvantages of Group and Team Decision Making	
Advantages	**Disadvantages**	
More information and knowledge are available.	The process takes longer than individual decision making, so it is costlier.	
More alternatives are likely to be generated.	Compromise decisions resulting from indecisiveness may emerge.	
More acceptance of the final decision is likely.	One person may dominate the group.	
Enhanced communication of the decision may result.	Groupthink may occur.	
Better decisions generally emerge.		

© Cengage Learning

Disadvantages of Group and Team Decision Making

Perhaps the biggest drawback of group and team decision making is the additional time and hence the greater expense entailed. The increased time stems from interaction and discussion among group or team members. If a given manager's time is worth $50 an hour, and if the manager spends two hours making a decision, the decision "costs" the organization $100. For the same decision, a group of five managers might require three hours of time. At the same $50-an-hour rate, the decision "costs" the organization $750. Assuming the group or team decision is better, the additional expense may be justified, but the fact remains that group and team decision making is more costly.

Group or team decisions may also represent undesirable compromises.[44] For example, hiring a compromise top manager may be a bad decision in the long run because he or she may not be able to respond adequately to various subunits in the organization and not have everyone's complete support. Sometimes one individual dominates the group process to the point where others cannot make a full contribution. This dominance may stem from a desire for power or from a naturally dominant personality. The problem is that what appears to emerge as a group decision may actually be the decision of one person.

groupthink
A situation that occurs when a group or team's desire for consensus and cohesiveness overwhelms its desire to reach the best possible decision

Finally, a group or team may succumb to a phenomenon known as **groupthink**, which occurs when the desire for consensus and cohesiveness overwhelms the goal of reaching the best possible decision.[45] Under the influence of groupthink, the group may arrive at decisions that are made not in the best interests of either the group or the organization, but rather to avoid conflict among group members. One of the most clearly documented examples of groupthink involved the space shuttle Challenger disaster. As NASA was preparing to launch the shuttle, numerous problems and questions arose. At each step of the way, however, decision makers argued that there was no reason to delay and that everything would be fine. Shortly after its launch, the shuttle exploded, killing all seven crew members.

Managing Group and Team Decision-Making Processes

Managers can do several things to help promote the effectiveness of group and team decision making. One is simply being aware of the pros and cons of having a group or team make a decision to start with. Time and cost can be managed by setting a deadline by which the decision must be made final. Dominance can be at least partially avoided if a special group is formed just to make the decision. An astute manager, for example, should know who in the organization may try to dominate and can either avoid putting that person in the group or put several strong-willed people together.

To avoid groupthink, each member of the group or team should critically evaluate all alternatives. So that members present divergent viewpoints, the leader should not make his or her position known too early. At least one member of the group or team might be assigned the role of devil's advocate. And, after reaching a preliminary decision, the group or team should hold a follow-up meeting wherein divergent viewpoints can be raised again if any group members wish to do so.[46] Gould Paper Corporation used these methods by assigning managers to two different teams. The teams then spent an entire day in a structured debate presenting the pros and cons of each side of an issue to ensure the best possible decision.

SUMMARY OF LEARNING OUTCOMES AND KEY POINTS

1. Define decision making, and discuss types of decisions and decision-making conditions.

   - Decision making is the act of choosing one alternative from among a set of alternatives.
   - The decision-making process includes recognizing and defining the nature of a decision situation, identifying alternatives, choosing the "best" alternative, and putting it into practice.
   - Two common types of decisions are programmed and nonprogrammed.
   - Decisions may be made under states of certainty, risk, or uncertainty.

2. Discuss rational perspectives on decision making, including the steps involved.

   - Rational perspectives on decision making rest on the classical model.
   - This model assumes that managers have complete information and that they will behave rationally. The primary steps in rational decision making are the following:
     - Recognizing and defining the situation
     - Identifying alternatives
     - Evaluating alternatives
     - Selecting the best alternative
     - Implementing the chosen alternative
     - Following up and evaluating the effectiveness of the alternative after it is implemented

3. Describe the behavioral aspects of decision making.

   - Behavioral aspects of decision making rely on the administrative model.
   - This model recognizes that managers use incomplete information and do not always behave rationally.
   - The administrative model also recognizes the concepts of bounded rationality and satisficing.
   - Political activities by coalitions, managerial intuition, and the tendency to become increasingly committed to a chosen course of action are all important.
   - Risk propensity is also an important behavioral perspective on decision making.
   - Ethics also affect how managers make decisions.

4. Discuss group and team decision making, including its advantages and disadvantages and how it can be more effectively managed.

   - To help enhance decision-making effectiveness, managers often use interacting, Delphi, or nominal groups or teams.
   - Group and team decision making in general has several advantages and disadvantages relative to individual decision making.
   - Managers can adopt a number of strategies to help groups and teams make better decisions.

DISCUSSION QUESTIONS

Questions for Review

1. Describe the difference between programmed and nonprogrammed decisions. What are the implications of these differences for decision makers?
2. What are the different conditions under which decisions are made?
3. Describe the behavioral nature of decision making. Be certain to provide some detail about political forces, risk propensity, ethics, and commitment in your description.
4. What is meant by the term *escalation of commitment*? In your opinion, under what conditions is escalation of commitment likely to occur?
5. Explain the differences among three common methods of group decision making—interacting groups, Delphi groups, and nominal groups.

Questions for Analysis

1. Was your decision about what college or university to attend a rational decision? Did you go through each step in rational decision making? If not, why not?
2. Most business decisions are made under conditions of either risk or uncertainty. In your opinion, is it easier to make a decision under a condition of risk or a condition of uncertainty? Why?
3. Recall a decision that you recently made that had ethical implications. Did these implications make the decision easier or harder?

4. In what ways are escalation of commitment and decision making under conditions of risk related to one another?
5. Consider the following list of business decisions. Which decisions would be handled most effectively by group or team decision making? Which would be handled most effectively by individual decision making? Explain your answers.

- A decision about switching pencil suppliers
- A decision about hiring a new CEO
- A decision about firing an employee for stealing
- A decision about calling 911 to report a fire in the warehouse
- A decision about introducing a brand-new product

BUILDING EFFECTIVE CONCEPTUAL SKILLS

Exercise Overview

Conceptual skills refer to the manager's ability to think in the abstract. This exercise will aid you in understanding the effects that nonrational biases and risk propensity can have on decision making.

Exercise Background

Two psychologists, Amos Tversky and Daniel Kahneman, conducted much of the research that led to our knowledge of decision-making biases. Tversky and Kahneman found that they could understand individuals' real-life choices by presenting experimental subjects with simulated decisions in a laboratory setting. They developed a theory called *prospect theory*, which uses behavioral psychology to explain why individuals are nonrational when making economic decisions. Their work has contributed a great deal to the developing discipline of behavioral economics. In fact, Kahneman won the 2002 Nobel Prize in Economics for development of these concepts. (Tversky could not share in the award because the Nobel Prize cannot be given posthumously.)

Tversky and Kahneman's most important finding was that an individual's perception of gain or loss in a situation is more important than an objective measure of gain or loss. Thus, individuals are nonrational—that is, they do not make decisions based purely on rational criteria.

Related to this conclusion, Tversky and Kahneman found that humans think differently about gains and losses. This is called *framing*. Another finding is that people allow their perceptions to be skewed positively or negatively, depending on information they receive. Later, when new information becomes available, people have a hard time letting go of their initial perceptions, even if the new information contradicts their original impressions. This effect is referred to as *anchoring* and *adjustment*.

To answer the following questions, you must be able to calculate an expected value. To calculate an expected value, multiply each possible outcome value by the probability of its occurrence, and then sum all the results. Here is a simple example: You have a 50 percent chance of earning 80 points on an exam and a 50 percent chance of earning 70 points. The expected value can be calculated as $(.5 + 80) + (.5 \times 70)$, or a .5 chance of 80 points (equal to 40 points) plus a .5 chance of 70 points (equal to 35 points). Therefore, the expected value of your exam is 75 points.

Exercise Task

1. Answer the list of brief questions that your professor provides to you. No answer is correct or incorrect; simply choose your most likely response. Then, when the professor asks, share your answers with the class.
2. Discuss the answers given by the class. Why do students' answers differ?
3. What have you learned about decision-making biases and risk propensity from these experiments?

BUILDING EFFECTIVE TECHNICAL SKILLS

Exercise Overview

Technical skills are the skills necessary to accomplish or understand the specific kind of work being done in an organization. This exercise will enable you to practice your Internet skills to obtain information for making a decision.

Exercise Background

Assume that you are a business owner seeking a location for a new factory. Your company makes products that are relatively "clean"—that is, they do not pollute the environment, nor will they produce any dangerous waste products. Thus, most communities would welcome your plant.

You are seeking a place that has a stable and well-educated workforce, as well as ample affordable housing, access to quality health care, and a good educational system. You have narrowed your choice to the following towns:

1. Santa Cruz, California
2. Madison, Wisconsin
3. Manhattan, Kansas
4. College Station, Texas
5. Amherst, Massachusetts
6. Athens, Georgia

Exercise Task

With this background information as context, do the following:

1. Use the Internet to research each of these cities.
2. Rank-order the cities on the basis of the criteria noted.
3. Select the best city for your new factory.

SKILLS SELF-ASSESSMENT

Decision-Making Styles

Introduction: Decision making is clearly important. However, individuals differ in their decision-making style, or the way they approach decisions. The following assessment is designed to help you understand your decision-making style.

Instructions: Respond to the following statements by indicating the extent to which they describe you. Circle the response that best represents your self-evaluation.

1. Overall, I'm _____ to act.
   1. quick 2. moderately fast 3. slow
2. I spend _____ amount of time making important decisions as/than I do making less important ones.
   1. about the same 2. a greater 3. a much greater
3. When making decisions, I _____ go with my first thought.
   1. usually 2. occasionally 3. rarely
4. When making decisions, I'm _____ concerned about making errors.
   1. rarely 2. occasionally 3. often

5. When making decisions, I _____ check my work more than once.
   1. rarely 2. occasionally 3. usually
6. When making decisions, I gather _____ information.
   1. little 2. some 3. lots of
7. When making decisions, I consider _____ alternatives.
   1. few 2. some 3. lots of
8. I usually make decisions _____ before the deadline.
   1. way 2. somewhat 3. just
9. After making a decision, I _____ look for other alternatives, wishing I had waited.
   1. rarely 2. occasionally 3. usually
10. I _____ regret having made a decision.
   1. rarely 2. occasionally 3. often

Source: Adapted from Robert N. Lussier, *Supervision: A Skill-Building Approach*, 2nd ed., 1994, pp. 122–123, © 1994 by Richard D. Irwin, Inc. Reproduced with permission of The McGraw-Hill Companies.

EXPERIENTIAL EXERCISE

Decision Making with Journaling and Affinity Diagrams

Purpose: This exercise gives you practice in using both journaling and affinity diagrams, both of which are tools for effective decision making. These techniques can be used to help expand and improve your decision making in many areas of your life, both personal and professional.

Introduction: The chemist Linus Pauling, winner of Nobel Prizes in both Chemistry and Peace, said, "The

best way to have a good idea is to have a lot of ideas." Journaling is one technique to increase the quantity of ideas generated in response to a decision situation. Affinity diagrams can be used alone or in conjunction with journaling or other idea-generating techniques. Affinity diagrams help you to interpret and organize a quantity of diverse ideas. The diagrams are particularly useful in decision situations that involve lots of ideas, where the ideas are very different from each other and the relationships between the ideas are not well understood, and where the underlying questions seem overwhelming or too complex to analyze rationally.

Instructions:

1. Have on hand a number of index cards or sticky notes, at least 50. Or use several sheets of paper cut into at least 50 smaller slips. Set aside 30 minutes or so of quiet time. Assume that graduation day is approaching and you are faced with the decision about where to live. Assume that your options are broad and that the decision will be for at least five years but would not necessarily commit you for the rest of your life. You could choose to live in an urban, suburban, or rural community. You could choose a large or small community, various regions of the country or world, and many different types of social and economic settings.

2. Think about the qualities you desire for your future hometown. Briefly jot down qualities that you desire, putting one quality on each piece of paper. Relax and visualize your ideal community, and then commit the ideas to paper. For example, your ideas might include "ethnic diversity" or "upscale suburb." Or something quite different might be important to you. Allow the answers to just "come to" you. Don't try to force your thinking along any one path, and don't edit yourself or criticize your thoughts at this point in the process. It's okay to have some ideas that don't seem rational, that are duplicates, or even that seem meaningless.

    If you can, work quickly and without interruption. Try to generate at least 25 ideas. If that number comes easily to you, generate some more. Stop when you feel that you've exhausted your supply of ideas. This process is one way to use the technique known as *journaling*.

3. Lay out the slips of paper so you can see all of them, and then read them. Begin to move the slips of paper into groups of ideas that are similar to each other. Gradually, as you rearrange the slips, patterns of ideas will emerge. Again, don't try to be critical or rational at this point; simply consider the relationships among the ideas. Keep moving the slips into different combinations until you find a set of groups that "feels right."

    Then assign each of these groups a theme that identifies the common element. For example, you might group the ideas *green housing*, *good public transportation*, and *vegetarian restaurants* into a theme called *environmentally conscious*. Or you might group *good public transportation*, *short commute to work*, and *walk to restaurants and stores* into a theme called *convenience*. The finished project, a grouping of a diverse set of ideas into related themes, is called an *affinity diagram*.

Follow-Up Questions

1. Did the techniques of journaling and affinity diagramming help you generate more ideas and better see the connections between ideas? If so, explain how. If not, what technique(s) would have worked better?

2. Note that both techniques explicitly encourage the behavioral aspects of decision making, especially intuition. Do you think this is appropriate when making this type of decision? Or would a more rational approach be more effective?

3. How might a manager use these techniques at work? What situations would not be appropriate for the use of these techniques?

MANAGEMENT AT WORK

The Verdict on Groupthink

In the 1957 movie *Twelve Angry Men*, Henry Fonda plays a mild-mannered architect who's been selected to serve on a jury with 11 other white, middle-class, middle-aged men. Within the confines of the claustrophobic jury room, attitudes and preconceptions gradually begin to harden and the group's decision seems increasingly like a foregone conclusion—guilty in a case of capital murder. Fonda, however, has his doubts and starts to suggest alternative interpretations of the

case until, by movie's end, he has steered the group to a more cogently considered decision. "My favorite part of a trial," reports one Texas attorney, "is when the judge … tells the jurors that deliberations should involve discussions, the questioning of their beliefs, and a willingness to change their minds. I really want jurors to do that," he says, but "I don't think they do." Like many lawyers, he doubts very seriously if the kind of deliberative decision making extolled in *Twelve Angry Men* goes on in many real jury rooms.

David A. Mitchell and Daniel Eckstein, authors of "Jury Dynamics and Decision-Making: A Prescription for Groupthink," aren't so sure either. They characterize a jury as "a unique variety of an autonomous work group … one in which group members are chosen, essentially at random, to perform a function of great importance for which they generally have no direct training." It's a prescription, they suggest, for "group dynamics that are not conducive to quality decision making." The problem, they argue, is *groupthink*, and they agree with Irving Janis, who conducted early studies on the phenomenon, that it infects groups whose members let their "strivings for unanimity override their motivation to realistically appraise alternative courses of action."

Mitchell (a clinical psychologist) and Eckstein (a psychologist and consultant on leadership development) focus on Janis's seven "antecedent conditions" for group-think—factors that make groupthink more likely—in order to show how "the conditions under which juries operate" add up to "a substantial risk of jury decisions being tainted by groupthink":

- *Cohesiveness*. A number of factors combine to ensure that the jury is a cohesive group. From the moment that jurors are selected, for example, they're "treated as a unit [and] their individual identities become submerged in the group identity." They eat together and often spend a great deal of time together prior to deliberations, and because they're not supposed to discuss the case during the trial itself, they often talk about such topics as the shared experience of being on a jury.
- *Insulation*. Once it's impaneled, the jury is isolated from other individuals and groups; jurors are physically separated from other people in the courthouse and sometimes even kept under guard to ensure their isolation.
- *Lack of a tradition of impartial leadership*. The only leadership in the group comes from the foreperson, who typically has an opinion on the case and therefore can't really be impartial in relating to other members.
- *Lack of norms requiring methodical procedures*. Juries have no set rules for how to proceed in arriving at a decision. In fact, the only specific requirement—to reach a unanimous decision—increases the likelihood of faulty decision making.
- *Homogeneity of social background and ideology*. Juries are rarely valid cross sections of the community. Desirable jury members, for example, share certain qualities that lawyers look for, and because lawyers try to seat jurors who share qualities favorable to their cases, juries often tend toward homogeneity on those qualities.
- *High stress from external threats and low hope of a solution better than the leader's*. This factor basically underscores the fact that stress—and the desire to avoid it—contribute to groupthink, and it reflects two hypotheses: (1) Jurors find that having to choose among unpleasant or complicated alternatives increases stress, especially if the group leader is authoritarian or tends to promote a particular decision, and (2) jurors are more likely to agree with the leader's decision if they feel that opposing it will increase stress among group members.
- *Temporarily low self-esteem induced by situational factors*. The more difficult it becomes to sort out alternatives and reach a decision, the lower a juror's sense of *self-efficacy* may become (see Chapter 9); in other words, as jurors lose their confidence in their ability to perform the task at hand, they may try to alleviate the feeling by taking refuge in conformity and consensus.

Mitchell and Eckstein acknowledge that none of these seven conditions by itself "is sufficient to cause … groupthink," but they hasten to point out that "the greater the number of these conditions that exist, the greater the propensity toward" groupthink. They also admit that any group is susceptible to groupthink, but they emphasize that "the structure of the jury system places juries at particularly high risk… . Considering the regularity with which many of the preceding antecedent conditions occur in juries," they argue, "the structure of the jury system may not only be conducive but often helps create the occurrence of groupthink." Finally, they observe that different types of groups make different types of errors, but caution that groupthink "increases the risk that all types of decision-making errors will occur."

Case Questions

1. In your experience, have you found that decision-making groups tend toward *groupthink*? If so, what factors contributed to this tendency? If not, what factors helped to prevent it?

2. Review the steps in the *rational decision-making model* (especially Steps 1–4). This model, of course, applies to individuals and might be difficult to apply to group decision-making situations. If, however, you were a juror, how might

you apply these steps to your own deliberations? How might they give you some useful guidance? What adjustments would you have to make because of the context (a trial) and situation (a group process)?

3. In what ways might *bounded rationality* affect a juror's approach to a decision? How about *satisficing*? *Intuition*? *Ethics*?

4. A recent study found that racially mixed juries "deliberated longer, raised more facts, and conducted broader and more wide-ranging deliberations" than either all-white or all-black juries. Why do you think this was so? Do you think that "mixed" juries are more likely to avoid group-think than racially homogeneous juries? Explain your reasoning.

Case References

Twelve Angry Men (United Artists, 1957); David H. Mitchell and Daniel Eckstein, "Jury Dynamics and Decision-Making: A Prescription for Group-think," *International Journal of Academic Research*, Vol. 1 (September 2009), www.ijar.lit.az, accessed on May 1, 2012; Irving L. Janis, *Groupthink*, 2nd ed. (Boston: Houghton Mifflin, 1972); Michael P. Maslanka, "The Dirty Realities of Group-Think," *Texas Lawyer*, December 23, 2009, http://texaslawyer.typepad.com, accessed on May 1, 2012; and Samuel R. Sommers, "On Racial Diversity and Group Decision Making: Identifying Multiple Effects of Racial Composition on Jury Deliberations," *Journal of Personality and Social Psychology*, Vol. 90, No. 4 (2006), http://ase.tufts.edu, accessed on March 5, 2011.

You Make the Call

The Embargo Grinds On

1. Describe the original decision made by the U.S. government to impose a trade embargo on Cuba. What conditions existed at the time, and what behavioral forces may have come into play?

2. In your opinion, is Thanksgiving Coffee's Paul Katzeff doing the right thing in working against the U.S. embargo? Explain your opinion. If your answer is yes, can you think of any additional steps that Katzeff might take?

3. Speculate on behavioral forces that might affect Katzeff's decisions.

4. How might U.S. businesses best prepare themselves for a possible elimination of the embargo? What kinds of decisions do they need to be making?

ENDNOTES

[1] Merchants of Green Coffee, "About the Merchants," www.merchantsofgreencoffee.com, accessed on April 5, 2013; "Cuban Organic Shade-Grown Coffee from Merchants of Green Coffee," *TreeHugger.com*, accessed on May 19, 2005, www.treehugger.com, accessed on September 5, 2013; Thanksgiving Coffee Co., "End the Embargo on Cuba," www.endtheembargo.com, accessed on September 5, 2013; Larry Luxner, "Coffee with a Cause," *Tea & Coffee Trade Journal*, www.teaandcoffee.net, accessed on September 5, 2013; Carol J. Williams, "Some Cuban Exiles Hope Obama Can Help," *Los Angeles Times*, November 10, 2008, http://articles.latimes.com, accessed on September 5, 2013; Doug Palmer, "Business Urges Obama to Loosen Cuba Embargo," December 4, 2008, *Reuters*, www.reuters.com, accessed on September 5, 2013; "Cuba Embargo Benefits European, Canadian Firms," *Reuters*, March 20, 2008, www.reuters.com, accessed on September 5, 2013; Paul Katzeff, "Cooperatives," Thanksgiving Coffee Co., www.thanksgivingcoffee.com, accessed on September 5, 2013.

[2] Richard Priem, "Executive Judgment, Organizational Congruence, and Firm Performance," *Organization Science*, August 1994, pp. 421–432. See also R. Duane Ireland and C. Chet Miller, "Decision-Making and Firm Success," *Academy of Management Executive*, 2004, Vol. 18, No. 4, pp. 8–12.

[3] Paul Nutt, "The Formulation Processes and Tactics Used in Organizational Decision Making," *Organization Science*, May 1993, pp. 226–240.

[4] For a review of decision making, see E. Frank Harrison, *The Managerial Decision Making Process*, 5th ed. (Boston: Houghton Mifflin, 1999). See also Elke U. Weber and Eric J. Johnson, "Mindful Judgment and Decision Making," in Susan T. Fiske, Daniel L. Schacter, and Robert Sternberg (eds.), *Annual Review of Psychology 2009* (Palo Alto, CA: Annual Reviews, 2009), pp. 53–86.

[5] "Too Much Cash Is a Problem?" *USA Today*, February 12, 2013, p. 1B.

[6] George P. Huber, *Managerial Decision Making* (Glenview, IL: Scott, Foresman, 1980).

[7] For an example, see Paul D. Collins, Lori V. Ryan, and Sharon F. Matusik, "Programmable Automation and the Locus of Decision-Making Power," *Journal of Management*, 1999, Vol. 25, No.1, pp. 29–53.

8 George P. Huber, *Managerial Decision Making* (Glenview, IL: Scott, Foresman, 1980). See also David W. Miller and Martin K. Starr, *The Structure of Human Decisions* (Englewood Cliffs, NJ: Prentice Hall, 1976); and Alvar Elbing, *Behavioral Decisions in Organizations*, 2nd ed. (Glenview, IL: Scott, Foresman, 1978).

9 Rene M. Stulz, "Six Ways Companies Mismanage Risk," *Harvard Business Review*, March 2009, pp. 86–94; See also Robert Merton, "Innovation Risk: Make Smarter Decisions," *Harvard Business Review*, April 2013, pp. 48–56.

10 "Ford Lays Bet on New Truck by Rehiring 1,000 Workers," *Wall Street Journal*, October 31, 2008, pp. B1, B2.

11 "Delta Air Lines to Buy Oil Refinery," *USA Today*, May 1, 2012, p. 1B.

12 Gerard P. Hodgkinson, Nicola J. Bown, A. John Maule, Keith W. Glaister, and Alan D. Pearman, "Breaking the Frame: An Analysis of Strategic Cognition and Decision Making Under Uncertainty," *Strategic Management Journal*, 1999, Vol. 20, No. 10, pp. 977–985.

13 "Andersen's Fall from Grace Is a Tale of Greed and Miscues," *Wall Street Journal*, June 7, 2002, pp. A1, A6.

14 Glen Whyte, "Decision Failures: Why They Occur and How to Prevent Them," *Academy of Management Executive*, August 1991, pp. 23–31. See also Jerry Useem, "Decisions, Decisions," *Fortune*, June 27, 2005, pp. 55–154.

15 Jerry Useem, "Boeing vs. Boeing," *Fortune*, October 2, 2000, pp. 148–160; and "Airbus Prepares to 'Bet the Company' as It Builds a Huge New Jet," *Wall Street Journal*, November 3, 1999, pp. A1, A10.

16 Robert C. Litchfield, "Brainstorming Reconsidered: A Goal-Based View," *Academy of Management Review*, 2008, Vol. 33, No. 3, pp. 649–668.

17 Paul Nutt, "Expanding the Search for Alternatives During Strategic Decision-Making," *Academy of Management Executive*, 2004, Vol. 18, No. 4, pp. 13–22.

18 See Paul J. H. Schoemaker and Robert E. Gunther, "The Wisdom of Deliberate Mistakes," *Harvard Business Review*, June 2006, pp. 108–115.

19 "Airbus Clips Superjumbo Production," *Wall Street Journal*, May 7, 2009, p. B1.

20 "Accommodating the A380," *Wall Street Journal*, November 29, 2005, p. B1; "Boeing Roars Ahead," *BusinessWeek*, November 7, 2005, pp. 44–45; and "Boeing's New Tailwind," *Newsweek*, December 5, 2005, p. 45; "Flyers Losing Faith in Dreamliner," *USA Today*, January 17, 2013, pp. 1B, 2B; "Dreamliner Reliability in Doubt After Failures," *USA Today*, January 9, 2013, pp. 1A, 5A.

21 Jeffrey Pfeffer and Robert I. Sutton, *Hard Facts, Dangerous Half-Truths, and Total Nonsense: Profiting from Evidence-Based Management* (Cambridge, MA: Harvard Business School Press, 2006); Pfeffer and Sutton, *"Evidence-Based Management,"* 2010, www.evidence-basedmanagement.com, accessed on September 4, 2013; Donald W. McCormick, "Ethics and the 15 Minute Evidence-Based Manager," *Organization Management Journal*, Vol. 7 (2010), www.palgrave-journals.com, accessed on September 4, 2013.

22 "The Wisdom of Solomon," *Newsweek*, August 17, 1987, pp. 62–63.

23 "Making Decisions in Real Time," *Fortune*, June 26, 2000, pp. 332–334. See also Eugene Sadler-Smith and Erella Shefy, "The Intuitive Executive: Understanding and Applying 'Gut Feel' in Decision-Making," *Academy of Management Executive*, 2004, Vol. 18, No. 4, pp. 76–91; and Don A. Moore and Francis J. Flynn, "The Case of Behavioral Decision Research in Organizational Behavior," in James P. Walsh and Arthur P. Brief (eds.), *The Academy of Management Annals*, Vol. 2 (London: Routledge, 2008), pp. 399–432.

24 Herbert A. Simon, *Administrative Behavior* (New York: Free Press, 1945). Simon's ideas have been refined and updated in Herbert A. Simon, *Administrative Behavior*, 3rd ed. (New York: Free Press, 1976); and Herbert A. Simon, "Making Management Decisions: The Role of Intuition and Emotion," *Academy of Management Executive*, February 1987, pp. 57–63.

25 Patricia Corner, Angelo Kinicki, and Barbara Keats, "Integrating Organizational and Individual Information Processing Perspectives on Choice," *Organization Science*, August 1994, pp. 294–302.

26 "Lessons from Saturn's Fall," *BusinessWeek*, March 2, 2009, p. 25.

27 Kimberly D. Elsbach and Greg Elofson, "How the Packaging of Decision Explanations Affects Perceptions of Trustworthiness," *Academy of Management Journal*, 2000, Vol. 43, No. 1, pp. 80–89.

28 Kenneth Brousseau, Michael Driver, Gary Hourihan, and Rikard Larsson, "The Seasoned Executive's Decision-Making Style," *Harvard Business Review*, February 2006, pp. 111–112. See also Erik Dane and Michael G. Pratt, "Exploring Intuition and Its Role in Managerial Decision Making," *Academy of Management Review*, 2007, Vol. 32, No. 1, pp. 33–54.

29 "Three Good Hires? He'll Pay More for One Who's Great," *New York Times*, March 13, 2010.

30 Barry M. Staw and Jerry Ross, "Good Money after Bad," *Psychology Today*, February 1988, pp. 30–33; and D. Ramona Bobocel and John Meyer, "Escalating Commitment to a Failing Course of Action: Separating the Roles of Choice and Justification," *Journal of Applied Psychology*, 1994, Vol. 79, No. 3, pp. 360–363.

31 Mark Keil and Ramiro Montealegre, "Cutting Your Losses: Extricating Your Organization When a Big Project Goes Awry," *Sloan Management Review*, Spring 2000, pp. 55–64.

32 "Closing Time for a Rock Theme Park," *Wall Street Journal*, January 7, 2009, p. B1.

33 Gerry McNamara and Philip Bromiley, "Risk and Return in Organizational Decision Making," *Academy of Management Journal*, 1999, Vol. 42, No. 3, pp. 330–339.

34 For an example, see Brian O'Reilly, "What It Takes to Start a Startup," *Fortune*, June 7, 1999, pp. 135–140.

35 Martha I. Finney, "The Catbert Dilemma—the Human Side of Tough Decisions," *HRMagazine*, February 1997, pp. 70–78.

36 See Ann E. Tenbrunsel and Kristen Smith-Crowe, "Ethical Decision Making: Where We've Been and Where We're Going," in J. Walsh and A. P. Brief (eds.), *The Academy of Management Annals*, Taylor and Francis, Philadelphia Pennsylvania, 2010, pp. 545–607.

37 Edwin A. Locke, David M. Schweiger, and Gary P. Latham, "Participation in Decision Making: When Should It Be Used?"

Organizational Dynamics, Winter 1986, pp. 65–79; and Nicholas Baloff and Elizabeth M. Doherty, "Potential Pitfalls in Employee Participation," *Organizational Dynamics*, Winter 1989, pp. 51–62.

38 "The Art of Brainstorming," *BusinessWeek*, August 26, 2002, pp. 168–169.

39 Andre L. Delbecq, Andrew H. Van de Ven, and David H. Gustafson, *Group Techniques for Program Planning* (Glenview, IL: Scott, Foresman, 1975); and Michael J. Prietula and Herbert A. Simon, "The Experts in Your Midst," *Harvard Business Review*, January–February 1989, pp. 120–124.

40 For an extension of the nominal group method, see Kevin P. Coyne, Patricia Gorman Clifford, and Renee Dye, "Breakthrough Thinking from Inside the Box," *Harvard Business Review*, December 2007, pp. 71–80.

41 Norman P. R. Maier, "Assets and Liabilities in Group Problem Solving: The Need for an Integrative Function," in J. Richard Hackman, Edward E. Lawler III, and Lyman W. Porter (eds.),

Perspectives on Business in Organizations, 2nd ed. (New York: McGraw-Hill, 1983), pp. 385–392.

42 Anthony L. Iaquinto and James W. Fredrickson, "Top Management Team Agreement about the Strategic Decision Process: A Test of Some of Its Determinants and Consequences," *Strategic Management Journal*, 1997, Vol. 18, No. 1, pp. 63–75.

43 Tony Simons, Lisa Hope Pelled, and Ken A. Smith, "Making Use of Difference: Diversity, Debate, and Decision Comprehensiveness in Top Management Teams," *Academy of Management Journal*, 1999, Vol. 42, No. 6, pp. 662–673.

44 Richard A. Cosier and Charles R. Schwenk, "Agreement and Thinking Alike: Ingredients for Poor Decisions," *Academy of Management Executive*, February 1990, pp. 69–78.

45 Janis, *Groupthink.*

46 Janis, *Groupthink.*

CHAPTER 5

Entrepreneurship and New Venture Management

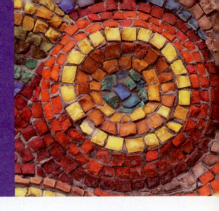

Sergii Tsololo/Photos.com

Learning Outcomes

After studying this chapter, you should be able to:

1 Discuss the nature of entrepreneurship.

2 Describe the role of entrepreneurship in society.

3 Understand the major issues involved in choosing strategies for small firms and the role of international management in entrepreneurship.

4 Discuss the structural challenges unique to entrepreneurial firms.

5 Understand the determinants of the performance of small firms.

Management in Action

Putting the Greek into Yogurt

"We had the right product. And we had it in the right place. And I think we used the right approach, which was making a delicious, nutritious, natural, and accessible product."

—Hamdi Ulukaya, founder of Chobani yogurt

Hamdi Ulukaya is the founder and CEO of Chobani yogurt. His entrepreneurial vision has transformed Chobani into a multibillion-dollar corporation.

Michael Okoniewski/Newscom

Hamdi Ulukaya was born and raised in Turkey. He helped work in the family dairy, and loved eating the thick, tangy yogurt that his mother prepared from an old family recipe. As he traveled through Europe as a young man, he found similar kinds of yogurt all along the way and became a real aficionado. He later learned that European yogurt has almost always been made using the so-called Greek process that removes the whey from the final product (water left after the milk has been cultured) resulting in a thick, creamy yogurt.

Ulukaya moved to the United States in 1994 to study English. While he loved his new country, he quickly grew to detest the yogurt varieties marketed in this country by Dannon, Yoplait, and other companies. These manufacturers produced yogurt using a different process that left the whey in the yogurt—harmless, but resulting in a thinner, less creamy product. He thought its taste was poor in comparison to the yogurt he grew up with. Meanwhile, Ulukaya started a small business called Euphrates that produced feta

127

cheese for restaurants. He built it into a successful operation and accumulated some savings.

One day in 2004, Ulukaya read an article about an old yogurt plant that Kraft Foods was closing. As he thought about the old yogurt factory being shuttered and his own disdain for local yogurt products, an idea began to take shape. The next day, he drove to upstate New York, inspected the plant, and quickly decided to buy it. He used a combination of personal savings and a loan from the U.S. Small Business Association to buy the plant at a bargain price (he declined to disclose the amount). He also hired four of the former Kraft employees who had worked at the plant plus a skilled yogurt maker he knew by reputation from Turkey.

Next, he needed to set up equipment and develop a production system. The old Kraft plant had all of the basic yogurt-making equipment he needed. However, because he wanted to extract the whey, he also needed some additional machinery. After a brief search he found a used machine called a separator in Wisconsin and bought it for $50,000. In addition, he bought a few other pieces of specialized equipment—mostly used—and was ready to start testing recipes and production processes.

He also wanted to create some unique packaging for his new line of yogurt. Ulukaya didn't feel that he could afford traditional advertising for his start-up operation but concluded that he could attract consumer attention. He created a model of his yogurt containers that was squatter and fatter than what other manufacturers were using. This would both attract attention and make the containers look a bit larger. In addition, he decided that he wanted the labels to be shrunken-on plastic sleeves instead of being printed directly on the yogurt containers—this would result in sharper and brighter colors, attracting further attention.

But these decisions resulted in some temporary roadblocks for Ulukaya. The first step in making the yogurt containers would be to create a mold. The lowest bid he could get from a U.S. supplier for this job was $250,000—half of his working capital. Eventually, though, he found a company in Colombia that would do the job for half that amount. So, now he had a plant, equipment, workers, and packing. But he still needed a product.

Finally, after a couple of years of trying and testing recipes and getting his business plan finalized, Ulukaya launched his new yogurt in 2007. He named it Chobani—Turkish for shepherd. To keep control over the product, as well as its pricing and placement, Ulukaya and his first marketing representative approached retailers directly rather than going through distributors. It was important to Ulukaya, for example, that his yogurt be sold with all of the other yogurts rather than in the organic section. Their first order was for 300 cases for a grocer on Long Island. A week later, the grocer called Ulukaya, told him the product was flying off the shelf, and ordered another 300 cases.

To say Chobani has been successful would be an understatement. For example, Ulukaya's business plan called for achieving a sell rate of 20,000 cases of Chobani a week within 36 months. If the new start-up could not reach that level, Ulukaya knew he would need to close the operation. As it turned out, his target was way too low—by a year and a zero. By mid-2009, 200,000 cases a week were going out the door. Now Ulukaya is a billionaire. Chobani has become a market leader and is also being made and sold in Europe and Australia.

It is no surprise, of course, that his bigger competitors have taken note of Ulukaya's success and attempted to thwart his efforts. Both Dannon and Yoplait have aggressively introduced their own versions of Greek yogurt and are gaining market share. But for the time being, at least, Chobani still hasn't found its ceiling. Indeed, the firm is now shipping 1.2 million cases a week, and sales are still growing. Not bad for a Turkish immigrant just looking to learn a foreign language![1]

Just like Hamdi Ulukaya, thousands of people all over the world start new businesses each year. Some of them succeed and many, unfortunately, fail. Some of the people who fail in a new business try again, and sometimes it takes two or more failures before a successful business gets under way. Henry Ford, for example, went bankrupt twice before succeeding with Ford Motor Company. On the other hand, of course, there are the Hamdi Ulukayas who succeed once (with Euphrates, in his case), try again, and succeed a second time.

This process of starting a new business or business venture, sometimes failing and sometimes succeeding, is part of what is called *entrepreneurship*, the subject of this chapter. We begin by exploring the nature of entrepreneurship. We then examine the role of entrepreneurship in the business world and discuss strategies for entrepreneurial organizations. We then describe the structure and performance of entrepreneurial organizations.

THE NATURE OF ENTREPRENEURSHIP

entrepreneurship
The process of planning, organizing, operating, and assuming the risks of a business venture

entrepreneur
Someone who engages in entrepreneurship

small business
A business that is privately owned by one individual or a small group of individuals and has sales and assets that are not large enough to meaningfully influence its environment

Entrepreneurship is the process of planning, organizing, operating, and assuming the risks of a business venture. An **entrepreneur**, in turn, is someone who engages in entrepreneurship. Hamdi Ulukaya, who's featured in our opening story, fits this description. He put his own resources on the line and took a personal stake in the success or failure of Chobani.[2] Business owners who hire professional managers to run their businesses and then turn their attention to other interests are not true entrepreneurs. Although they are assuming the risk of the venture, they are not actively involved in organizing or operating it. Likewise, professional managers whose job is running someone else's business are not entrepreneurs, for they assume less-than-total personal risk for the success or failure of the business.

Entrepreneurs start new businesses. We define a **small business** as one that is privately owned by one individual or a small group of individuals and has sales and assets that are not large enough to meaningfully influence its environment. A two-person software development company with annual sales of $100,000 would clearly be a small business, whereas Microsoft Corporation is just as clearly a large business. But the boundaries are not always this clear-cut. For example, a regional retail chain with 20 stores and annual revenues of $30 million may sound large but is really very small when compared to giants such as Walmart and Macy's.

THE ROLE OF ENTREPRENEURSHIP IN SOCIETY

The history of entrepreneurship and of the development of new businesses is in many ways the history of great wealth and of great failure. Some entrepreneurs have been very successful and have accumulated vast fortunes from their entrepreneurial efforts.

For example, when Microsoft Corporation first sold its stock to the public in 1986, Bill Gates, then just 30 years old, received $350 million for his share of Microsoft.[3] Today his holdings—valued at over $53 billion—make him the richest person in the United States and one of the richest in the world.[4] Many more entrepreneurs, however, have lost a great deal of money. Research suggests that the majority of new businesses fail within the first few years of founding.[5] Many that last longer do so only because the entrepreneurs themselves work long hours for very little income.

As Figure 5.1 shows, most U.S. businesses employ fewer than 100 people, and most U.S. workers are employed by small firms. For example, Figure 5.1(a) shows that approximately 86 percent of all U.S. businesses employ fewer than 20 people; another 11.7 percent employ between 20 and 99 people. In contrast, only about 2.1 percent employ between 100 and 499 workers, and another 0.2 percent employ 500 or more. Figure 5.1(b) shows that 24.5 percent of all U.S. workers are employed by firms with fewer than 20 people; another 29.6 percent work in firms that employ between 20 and 99 people. The vast majority of these companies are owner-operated.[6] Figure 5.1(b) also shows that

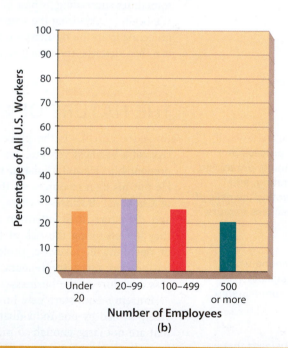

FIGURE 5.1

The Importance of Small Business in the United States

(a) Approximately 86 percent of all U.S. businesses employ fewer than 20 people; another 11.7 percent employ between 20 and 99 people. In contrast, only about 2.1 percent employ between 100 and 499 workers, and another 0.2 percent employ 500 or more.

(b) 24.5 percent of all U.S. workers are employed by firms with fewer than 20 people; another 29.6 percent work in firms that employ between 20 and 99 people. 25.5 percent of U.S. workers are employed by firms with 100–499 employees, and another 20.3 percent work for businesses that employ 500 or more total employees.

Source: U.S. Census Bureau, *Statistical Abstract of the United States*, 2010 (Washington, DC: Government Printing Office, 2011).

25.5 percent of U.S. workers are employed by firms with 100 to 499 employees, and another 20.3 percent work for businesses that employ 500 or more total employees.

On the basis of numbers alone, then, small business is a strong presence in the economy, which is also true in virtually all of the world's mature economies. In Germany, for example, companies with fewer than 500 employees produce two-thirds of the nation's gross national product, train nine of ten apprentices, and employ four of every five workers. Small businesses also play major roles in the economies of Italy, France, and Brazil. In addition, experts agree that small businesses will be quite important in the emerging economies of countries such as Russia and Vietnam. The contribution of small business can be measured in terms of its effects on key aspects of an economic system. In the United States, these aspects include job creation, innovation, and importance to big business.

Job Creation

In the early 1980s, a widely cited study suggested that small businesses are responsible for creating eight of every ten new jobs in the United States. This contention touched off considerable interest in the fostering of small business as a matter of public policy. As we will see, though, relative job growth among businesses of different sizes is not easy to determine. But it is clear that small business—especially in certain industries—is an important source of new (and often well-paid) jobs in the United States. According to the Small Business Administration (SBA), for example, seven of the ten industries that added the most new jobs in 2007 were in sectors dominated by small businesses. Moreover, small businesses currently account for over one-third of all jobs in high-technology sectors of the economy.[7]

Note that new jobs are also being created by small firms specializing in international business. For example, Bob Knosp operates a small business in Bellevue, Washington, that makes computerized sign-making systems. Knosp gets over half his sales from abroad and has dedicated almost 75 percent of his workforce to handling international sales. Indeed, according to the SBA, small businesses account for 33.5 percent of all U.S. exporters.[8]

It is important to note, though, that tracking job gains and losses is very complicated and somewhat imprecise. For instance, suppose a business eliminates one full-time job but later replaces it with two part-time jobs. Some statistics would count this as a loss of one job followed by a gain of two jobs. Similarly, the jobs within a company can fluctuate when it acquires or sells a business unit. For instance, a few years ago statistics showed that Halliburton had cut 53,000 jobs. But in reality, these "losses" actually came when the firm sold its largest subsidiary, KBR. Only a handful of jobs were actually eliminated; instead, over 50,000 jobs were simply moved to a new firm.

At least one message is clear: Entrepreneurial business success, more than business size, accounts for most new job creation. Whereas successful retailers such as Walmart and Starbucks have been growing and adding thousands of new jobs, struggling chains such as Kmart have been eliminating thousands. Hence, most firms, especially those in complex and dynamic environments, go through periods of growth when they add new jobs but also have periods when they cut jobs.

The reality, then, is that jobs are created by entrepreneurial companies of all sizes, all of which hire workers and all of which lay them off. Although small firms often hire at a faster rate than large ones, they are likely to eliminate jobs at a far higher rate. Small firms are also usually the first to hire in times of economic recovery, whereas large firms are generally the last. Conversely, however, big companies are also the last to lay off workers during economic downswings.

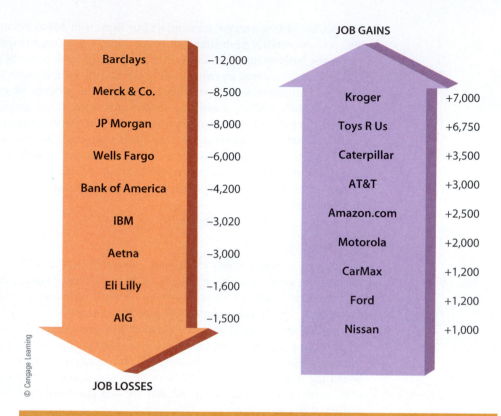

© Cengage Learning

JOB LOSSES		JOB GAINS	
Barclays	−12,000		
Merck & Co.	−8,500	Kroger	+7,000
JP Morgan	−8,000	Toys R Us	+6,750
Wells Fargo	−6,000	Caterpillar	+3,500
Bank of America	−4,200	AT&T	+3,000
IBM	−3,020	Amazon.com	+2,500
Aetna	−3,000	Motorola	+2,000
Eli Lilly	−1,600	CarMax	+1,200
AIG	−1,500	Ford	+1,200
		Nissan	+1,000

FIGURE 5.2

Representative Jobs Created and Lost in 2013

All businesses create and eliminate jobs. Because of their size, the magnitude of job creation and elimination is especially pronounced in bigger businesses. This figure provides several representative examples of job creation and elimination at several big U.S. businesses during 2013. For example, while Barclay's cut 12,000 jobs and Merck cut 8,500 jobs, Kroger added 7,000 jobs and Toys R Us added 6,750 jobs during this same period.

Innovation

History has shown that major innovations are as likely to come from small businesses (or individuals) as from big businesses. For example, small firms and individuals invented the personal computer, the stainless-steel razor blade, the transistor radio, the photocopying machine, the jet engine, and the self-developing photograph. They also gave us the helicopter and power steering, automatic transmissions and air conditioning, cellophane, and the disposable ballpoint pen. Today, says the SBA, small businesses consistently supply over half of all "innovations" introduced into the U.S. marketplace each year.[9]

It is no surprise that history is repeating itself with increasing rapidity in the age of computers and high-tech communication. For example, much of today's most innovative software is being written at relatively new start-up companies. Yahoo! and Netscape brought the Internet into the average U.S. living room, and online companies such as Amazon.com, eBay, and Google are using it to redefine our shopping habits. Facebook and Twitter have changed how we interact with one another.[10] Each of these firms started out as a small business.

Of course, not all successful new start-ups are leading-edge dot-com enterprises. Take Sacha White, for example. He moved to Oregon a few years ago and got a job as a bicycle messenger. He began to tinker with his bike and eventually built himself a custom one from scratch. Other riders took note and wanted him to build bikes for them as well. White eventually started his own business called Vanilla Bicycles. He hand-crafts each one and has a waiting list of four years. All told, he makes between 40 and 50 bikes per year; about 40 percent of these bikes are sold domestically, the rest to international customers. The average price of each of his custom bikes is around $7,000.[11] Entrepreneurs have also achieved success in diverse fields such as specialized dog training, handcrafted musical instruments, and delicate fly-fishing reels. And the popular television program *Duck Dynasty* features a family's successful business making duck calls.

Importance to Big Business

Most of the products made by big manufacturers are sold to consumers by small businesses. For example, the majority of dealerships selling Fords, Chevrolets, Toyotas, and Kias are independently owned and operated. Moreover, small businesses provide big businesses with many of the services, supplies, and raw materials they need. Likewise, Microsoft relies heavily on small businesses in the course of its routine business operations. For example, the software giant outsources much of its routine code-writing functions to hundreds of sole proprietorships and other small firms. It also outsources much of its packaging, delivery, and distribution to smaller companies. Dell Computer uses this same strategy, buying most of the parts and components used in its computers from small suppliers around the world.

STRATEGY FOR ENTREPRENEURIAL ORGANIZATIONS

One of the most basic challenges facing an entrepreneurial organization is choosing a strategy. The three strategic challenges facing small firms, in turn, are choosing an industry in which to compete, emphasizing distinctive competencies, and writing a business plan.[12]

Choosing an Industry

It also is no surprise that small businesses are more common in some industries than in others. The major industry groups that include successful new ventures and small businesses are services, retailing, construction, financial and insurance, wholesaling, transportation, and manufacturing. Obviously, each group differs in its requirements for employees, money, materials, and machines. In general, the more resources an industry requires, the harder it is to start a business and the less likely it is that the industry is dominated by small firms. Remember, too, that *small* is a relative term: The criteria (number of employees and total annual sales) differ from industry to industry and are often meaningful only when compared with businesses that are truly large. Figure 5.3 shows the distribution of all U.S. businesses employing fewer than 20 people across industry groups.

Services   Primarily because they require few resources, service businesses are the fastest-growing segment of small-business enterprise. In addition, no other industry group offers a higher return on time invested. Finally, services appeal to the talent for innovation typified by many small enterprises. As Figure 5.3 shows, 40.53 percent of all U.S. businesses with fewer than 20 employees are services.

FIGURE 5.3

Small Businesses (Businesses with Fewer than 20 Employees) by Industry

Small businesses are especially strong in certain industries, such as retailing and services. On the other hand, there are relatively fewer small businesses in industries such as transportation and manufacturing. The differences are primarily a result of factors such as the investment costs necessary to enter markets in these industries. For example, starting a new airline would require the purchase of large passenger aircraft and airport gates, and hiring an expensive set of employees.

Source: U.S. Census Bureau, *www.census.gov/econ/susb/*, accessed on March 2014.

Small-business services range from shoeshine parlors to car rental agencies, from marriage counseling to computer software, from accounting and management consulting to professional dog walking. In Dallas, for example, Jani-King has prospered by selling commercial cleaning services to local companies. In Virginia Beach, Virginia, Jackson Hewitt Tax Services has found a profitable niche in providing computerized tax preparation and electronic tax-filing services. Great Clips, Inc., is a fast-growing family-run chain of hair salons headquartered in Minneapolis.

Retailing   A retail business sells directly to consumers products manufactured by other firms. There are hundreds of different kinds of retailers, ranging from wig shops and frozen yogurt stands to automobile dealerships and department stores. Usually, however, people who start small businesses favor specialty shops—for example, big-men's clothing or gourmet coffees—which let them focus limited resources on narrow market segments. Retailing accounts for 11.71 percent of all U.S. businesses with fewer than 20 employees.

John Mackey, for example, launched Whole Foods out of his own frustration at being unable to find a full range of natural foods at other stores. He soon found, however, that he had tapped a lucrative market and started an ambitious expansion program. Today, with 310 outlets in North America and the United Kingdom, Whole Foods is the largest natural-foods retailer in the United States—three times larger than its biggest competitor.[13] Likewise, when Olga Tereshko found it difficult to locate just the right cloth diapers and breast-feeding supplies for her newborn son, she decided to start selling them herself. Instead of taking the conventional retailing route, however, Tereshko set up shop on the Internet. Her business, called Little Koala, has established a customer base of over 10,000 loyal customers. The "Sustainability Matters" feature highlights another successful business that has combined retailing and services.

SUSTAINABILITY MATTERS

A New Model for Going Green

Darin Budwig, a registered nurse in Glendale, California, wanted to do the green thing by going solar. Price, however, was a problem: "I wanted to do the right thing for the environment," says Budwig, "but I really had to ask whether it was worth taking on $30,000 in debt." According to Lyndon Rive, CEO of SolarCity, a provider of solar-energy systems located in Foster City, California, the average cost is actually closer to $20,000, but he understands Budwig's reservations. "Even those who really want to make an environmental change," admits Rive, "can't part with $20,000.... The solution is just too costly for them."

That's why Rive revamped his business model in order to make solar panels affordable for a much broader range of environmentally conscious consumers. He realized that he could put solar panels on people's roofs in much the same way that automakers put more expensive vehicles in their garages: by leasing them rather than selling them outright. So instead of borrowing $20,000, Darin Budwig only had to put

$1,000 down and agree to lease a SolarCity system for 15 years. At a cost of $73 a month, Budwig figured to save about $95 a month and recoup his $1,000 in less than a year. Too good to be true? "We hear that a lot," says Rive. "But we do save you money, and it doesn't cost you a cent to go solar." With leasing, he adds, "we can essentially make it so that everybody can now afford clean power."

At the same time, however, Rive understands that price isn't the only consideration for potential customers like Darin Budwig. "Widespread adoption," he admits, "will come if you can take away the complexity and hassle of installing solar." SolarCity thus made things easier for Budwig by lining up building permits, financing, and tax breaks. The company also streamlined costs by using innovative computer automation to custom-design Budwig's installation, which was based on satellite images of his rooftop. SolarCity even compiled utility-rate data to estimate Budwig's return on his solar investment.

© Elena Elisseeva/Shutterstock.com

Surging energy prices, increased consumer awareness, and the availability of new technologies have combined to lead many people to explore alternative energy sources, including solar power. Unfortunately, many of these individuals are often discouraged when they learn how much solar power equipment actually costs. SolarCity, though, has built a lucrative business by leasing solar panels to homeowners. This installer, for example, is putting leased solar panels on the roof of a home in California.

(continued)

SUSTAINABILITY MATTERS (Continued)

The company recently added another automated service to its innovative product line. With the acquisition of Building Solutions, a firm specializing in software-controlled home energy audits, SolarCity entered the market for home-efficiency upgrades. Company auditors now come into a house armed with duct blowers, infrared cameras, and combustion analyzers to check for leaks and test heaters. The data are then analyzed to determine what can be done at what cost and to calculate the homeowner's best return on his or her upgrade investment. COO Peter Rive (Lyndon's older brother) is especially optimistic about the company's ability to combine panel-installation services with such services as energy audits and building-envelope sealing (sealing leaks in walls, doors, and windows). "As of right now," he points out, "there aren't residential energy-efficiency providers with any serious scale. We're going to be able to bring serious economies of scale" to bear on the costs to both the provider and the customer.

Like Darin Budwig, Google engineer Michael Flaster leased a SolarCity system for his home in Menlo Park, California. He saves $100 a month on his energy bill and expects to save more than $16,000 over the 15 years of his lease. His employers at Google, a longtime supporter of clean-energy innovations, were impressed and recently announced a $280 million fund to help SolarCity finance solar installations across the country.

References: Pete Engardio and Adam Aston, "The Next Energy Innovators," *BusinessWeek*, July 16, 2009, *www.businessweek.com*, accessed on September 11, 2013; Julie Schmidt, "SolarCity Aims to Make Solar Power More Affordable," *USA Today*, November 10, 2009, *www.usatoday.com*, accessed on September 11, 2013; Eric Wesoff, "SolarCity Adds Energy Efficiency to Solar Finance, Design, and Monitoring," *Greentech Media*, October 14, 2010, *www.greentechmedia.com*, accessed on September 11, 2013; David A. Hill, "Solar City Takes Aim at Home Energy Audit Market," *Colorado Energy News*, May 14, 2010, *http://coloradoenergynews.com*, accessed on September 11, 2013; Rick Needham, "Helping Homeowners Harness the Sun," *The Official Google Blog*, June 14, 2011, *http://googleblog.blogspot.in/*, accessed on September 11, 2013.

Construction   About 11.73 percent of businesses with fewer than 20 employees are involved in construction. Because many construction jobs are relatively small, local projects, local construction firms are often ideally suited as contractors. Many such firms are begun by skilled craftspeople who start out working for someone else and subsequently decide to work for themselves. Common examples of small construction firms include home builders, wood finishers, roofers, painters, and plumbing, electrical, and roofing contractors.

For example, Marek Brothers Construction in College Station, Texas, was started by two brothers, Pat and Joe Marek. They originally worked for other contractors but started their own partnership in 1980. Their only employee is a receptionist. They manage various construction projects, including new-home construction and remodeling, subcontracting out the actual work to other businesses or to individual craftspeople. Marek Brothers has an annual gross income of about $5 million.

Finance and Insurance   Finance and insurance businesses comprise about 4.2 percent of all firms with fewer than 20 employees. In most cases, these businesses either are affiliates of or sell products provided by larger national firms. Although the deregulation of the banking industry has reduced the number of small local banks, other businesses in this sector are still doing quite well.

Typically, for example, local State Farm Mutual offices are small businesses. State Farm itself is a major insurance company, but its local offices are run by 16,500 independent agents. In turn, agents hire their own staff, run their own offices as independent businesses, and so forth. They sell various State Farm insurance products and earn commissions from the premiums paid by their clients. Some local savings-and-loan-operations, mortgage companies, and pawnshops also fall into this category.

Wholesaling Small-business owners often also do very well in wholesaling; about 5.2 percent of businesses with fewer than 20 employees are wholesalers. A wholesale business buys products from manufacturers or other producers and then sells them to retailers. Wholesalers usually buy goods in bulk and store them in quantity at locations that are convenient for retailers. For a given volume of business, therefore, they need fewer employees than manufacturers, retailers, or service providers.

They also serve fewer customers than other providers—usually those who repeatedly order large volumes of goods. Wholesalers in the grocery industry, for instance, buy packaged food in bulk from companies such as Del Monte and Campbell's and then sell it to both large grocery chains and smaller independent grocers. Luis Espinoza has found a promising niche for Inca Quality Foods, a Midwestern wholesaler that imports and distributes Latino foods for consumers from Mexico, the Caribbean, and Central America. Partnered with the large grocery store chain Kroger, Espinoza's firm continues to grow steadily.[14]

Transportation Some small firms—about 2.8 percent of all U.S. companies with fewer than 20 employees—do well in transportation and transportation-related businesses. Such firms include local taxi and limousine companies, charter airplane services, and tour operators. In addition, in many smaller markets, bus companies and regional airlines subcontract local equipment maintenance to small businesses.

Consider, for example, some of the transportation-related small businesses at a ski resort like Steamboat Springs, Colorado. Most visitors fly to the town of Hayden, about 15 miles from Steamboat Springs. Although some visitors rent vehicles, many others use the services of Alpine Taxi, a small local operation, to transport them to their destinations in Steamboat Springs. While on vacation, they also rely on the local bus service, which is subcontracted by the town to another small business, to get to and from the ski slopes each day. Other small businesses offer van tours of the region, hot-air balloon rides, and helicopter lifts to remote areas for extreme skiers. Still others provide maintenance support at Hayden for United and American aircraft that serve the area during ski season.

Manufacturing More than any other industry, manufacturing lends itself to big business—and for good reason. Because of the investment normally required in equipment, energy, and raw materials, a good deal of money is usually needed to start a manufacturing business. Automobile manufacturing, for example, calls for billions of dollars of investment and thousands of workers before the first automobile rolls off the assembly line. Obviously, such requirements shut out most individuals. Although Henry Ford began with $28,000, it has been a long time since anyone started a new U.S. car company from scratch.

Research has shown that manufacturing costs often fall as the number of units produced by an organization increases. This relationship between cost and production is called an *economy of scale*.[15] Small organizations usually cannot compete effectively on the basis of economies of scale. As depicted in Figure 5.4(a), organizations with higher levels of production have a major cost advantage over those with lower levels of production. Given the cost positions of small and large firms when there are strong economies of scale in manufacturing, it is not surprising that small manufacturing organizations generally do not do as well as large ones.

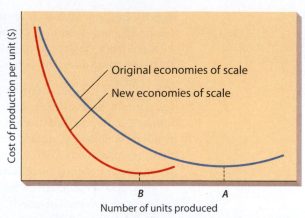

(a) Standard economies-of-scale curve

(b) Change in technology that shifts economies of scale and may make small-business manufacturing possible

© Cengage Learning

FIGURE 5.4

Economies of Scale in Small-Business Organizations

Small businesses sometimes find it difficult to compete in manufacturing-related industries because of the economies of scale associated with plants, equipment, and technology. As shown in (a), firms that produce a large number of units (that is, larger businesses) can do so at a lower per-unit cost. At the same time, however, new forms of technology occasionally cause the economies-of-scale curve to shift, as illustrated in (b). In this case, smaller firms may be able to compete more effectively with larger ones because of the drop in per-unit manufacturing cost.

It is interesting that when technology in an industry changes, it often shifts the economies-of-scale curve, thereby creating opportunities for smaller organizations. For example, steel manufacturing was historically dominated by a few large companies, which owned several huge facilities. With the development of mini-mill technology, however, extracting economies of scale at a much smaller level of production became possible. This type of shift is depicted in Figure 5.4(b). Point *A* in this panel is the low-cost point with the original economies of scale. Point *B* is the low-cost point with the economies of scale brought on by the new technology. Notice that the number of units needed for low costs is considerably lower for the new technology. This has allowed the entry of numerous smaller firms into the steel industry. Such entry would not have been possible with the older technology.

This is not to say that no small-business owners do well in manufacturing—about 3.78 percent of businesses with fewer than 20 employees are involved in some aspect of manufacturing. Indeed, it is not uncommon for small manufacturers to outperform big business in innovation-driven industries such as chemistry, electronics, toys, and computer software. Some small manufacturers prosper by locating profitable niches. For example, brothers Dave and Dan Hanlon and Dave's wife Jennie started a new motorcycle-manufacturing business called Excelsior-Henderson. (Excelsior and Henderson are actually names of classic motorcycles from the early years of the twentieth century; the Hanlons acquired the rights to these brand names because of the images they evoke among motorcycle enthusiasts.) The Hanlons started by building 4,000 bikes in 1999 and soon had annual production of 20,000 per year. Excelsior-Henderson motorcycles have been well received (the top-end Excelsior-Henderson Super X sells for about $18,000), and some Harley-Davidson dealers have started to sell them as a means of diversifying their product line.[16]

Emphasizing Distinctive Competencies

As we defined in Chapter 3, an organization's distinctive competencies are the aspects of business that the firm performs better than its competitors. The distinctive competencies of small business usually fall into three areas: the ability to identify new niches in established markets, the ability to identify new markets, and the ability to move quickly to take advantage of new opportunities.

Identifying Niches in Established Markets   An **established market** is one in which several large firms compete according to relatively well-defined criteria. For example, throughout the 1970s, several well-known computer-manufacturing companies, including IBM, Digital Equipment, and Hewlett-Packard, competed according to three product criteria: computing power, service, and price. Over the years, the computing power and quality of service delivered by these firms continued to improve, while prices (especially relative to computing power) continued to drop.

Enter Apple Computer and the personal computer. For Apple, user-friendliness, not computing power, service, or price, was to be the basis of competition. Apple targeted every manager, every student, and every home as the owner of a personal computer. Apple's major entrepreneurial act was not to invent a new technology (indeed, the first Apple computers used all standard parts taken from other computers), but to recognize a new kind of computer and a new way to compete in the computer industry.

Apple's approach to competition was to identify a new niche in an established market. A **niche** is simply a segment of a market that is not currently being exploited. In general, small entrepreneurial businesses are better at discovering these niches than are larger organizations. For example, David Tran launched a new hot sauce product, Sriracha Hot Chili Sauce, because he thought existing products were a bit too mild. From a modest beginning about 10 years ago, Tran now sells over 20 million bottles of Sriracha a year.[17] Another example is described in the "Leading the Way" feature. Large organizations usually have so many resources committed to older, established business practices that they may be unaware of new opportunities. Entrepreneurs can see these opportunities and move quickly to take advantage of them.

Dave Gilboa and Neil Blumenthal recently founded Warby Parker, a business that sells prescription eyewear through the mail. The entrepreneurs realized that most consumers disliked the experience of going to an optical shop to try on glasses and then were irritated at the price of those glasses. So, Warby Parker offers lower-priced glasses with hip designs and a money-back guarantee. Astute marketing then allowed them to get a quick start with their niche business, selling over 50,000 pairs of glasses and generating profits after only a single year of operation.[18]

Identifying New Markets   Successful entrepreneurs also excel at discovering whole new markets. Discovery can happen in at least two ways. First, an entrepreneur can transfer a product or service that is well established in one geographic market to a second market. This is what Marcel Bich did with ballpoint pens, which occupied a well-established market in Europe before Bich introduced them to the United States. Bich's company, Société Bic, eventually came to dominate the U.S. market.

Second, entrepreneurs can sometimes create entire industries. Entrepreneurial inventions of the dry paper-copying process and the semiconductor have created vast new industries. Not only have the first companies into these markets been very successful (Xerox and Texas Instruments, respectively), but their entrepreneurial activity also has spawned the development of hundreds of other companies and hundreds of thousands of jobs. Again, because entrepreneurs are not encumbered with a history of doing business in a particular way, they are usually better at discovering new markets than are larger, more mature organizations.

established market
A market in which several large firms compete according to relatively well-defined criteria

niche
A segment of a market not currently being exploited

LEADING THE WAY

Samuel Adams Makes Headway

James Koch used his own personal savings to launch Boston Beer, makers of Samuel Adams and other premium beers. Koch's success with Boston Beer has come in part from his business acumen and in part from his strong leadership skills.

In 1984, James Koch was a high-flying management consultant earning over $250,000 a year. To the surprise of his family and friends, however, he quit this job and invested his life's savings to start a business from scratch and go head-to-head with international competitors in a market that had not had a truly successful specialty product in decades. To everyone's even greater surprise, he succeeded. Part of his success as an entrepreneur is attributable to his business acumen and part to his leadership capabilities.

Koch's company is Boston Beer, and its flagship product is a premium beer called Samuel Adams. James set up shop in an old warehouse in Boston, bought some surplus equipment from a large brewery, and started operations. Because he used only the highest-quality ingredients, Koch had to price his product at about $1 more per case than such premium imports as Heineken. Most distributors, doubting consumers would pay $6 per six-pack for an American beer, refused to carry it. So Koch began selling directly to retailers and bars.

His big break came when Samuel Adams Lager won the consumer preference poll at the Great American Beer Festival. Koch quickly turned this victory into an advertising mantra, proclaiming Samuel Adams "The Best Beer in America." As sales took off, national distributors came calling; to meet surging demand, Koch contracted parts of his brewing operations to facilities in Pittsburgh and Cincinnati.

Annual sales of Samuel Adams products began to skyrocket and in 2012 exceeded $628 million. Demand grew to the point the point that Koch decided to purchase a large brewery outside Philadelphia. This increased the firm's brewing capacity by over 1.6 million barrels per year. Boston Beer even exports Samuel Adams to Germany, where it's become popular among finicky beer drinkers. Koch, who retains controlling interest in the business, still oversees day-to-day brewing operations. Indeed, he claims to have sampled at least one of the firm's products every day. In his words, "To best lead a business you have to lead on every front, and this includes sampling the merchandise!"

References: "Sam Adams Beer to Expand Cincinnati Brewery," *USA Today*, www.usa.com, accessed on September 11, 2013; Christopher Edmunds, "Bottom of the Barrel: Boston Beer's Winning Formula," realmoney. thestreet.com, accessed on September 11, 2013; "Boston Beer Company—Company Profile, Information, Business Description, History, Background Information on Boston Beer Company," at http://www.referenceforbusiness. com/history2/74/Boston-Beer-Company.html, accessed on September 11, 2013.

Boston Globe/Getty Images

first-mover advantage
Any advantage that comes to a firm because it exploits an opportunity before any other firm

First-Mover Advantages   A **first-mover advantage** is any advantage that comes to a firm because it exploits an opportunity before any other firm does. Sometimes large firms discover niches within existing markets or new markets at just about the same time as small entrepreneurial firms but are not able to move as quickly as small companies to take advantage of these opportunities.

This difference occurs for numerous reasons. For example, many large organizations make decisions slowly because each of their many layers of hierarchy must approve an action before it can be implemented. Also, large organizations may sometimes put a great deal of their assets at risk when they take advantage of new opportunities. Every time Boeing decides to build a new model of a commercial jet, it is making a decision that could literally bankrupt the company if it does not turn out well. The size of the risk may make large organizations cautious. The dollar value of the assets at risk in a small organization, in contrast, is quite small. Managers may be willing to "bet the company" when the value of the company is only $100,000. They might be unwilling to "bet the company" when the value of the company is $1 billion.

Writing a Business Plan

business plan
A document that summarizes the business strategy and structure

Once an entrepreneur has chosen an industry in which to compete and has determined which distinctive competencies to emphasize, these choices are usually included in a document called a business plan. In a **business plan**, the entrepreneur summarizes the business strategy and how that strategy is to be implemented. The very act of preparing a business plan forces prospective entrepreneurs to crystallize their thinking about what they must do to launch their business successfully and obliges them to develop their business on paper before investing time and money in it. The idea of a business plan is not new. What is new is the growing use of specialized business plans by entrepreneurs, mostly because creditors and investors demand them for use in deciding whether to help finance a small business.[19]

The plan should describe the match between the entrepreneur's abilities and the requirements for producing and marketing a particular product or service. It should define strategies for production and marketing, legal aspects and organization, and accounting and finance. In particular, it should answer three questions: (1) What are the entrepreneur's goals and objectives? (2) What strategies will the entrepreneur use to obtain these goals and objectives? (3) How will the entrepreneur implement these strategies?

Business plans should also account for the sequential nature of much strategic decision making in small businesses. For example, entrepreneurs cannot forecast sales revenues without first researching markets. The sales forecast itself is one of the most important elements in the business plan. Without such forecasts, it is all but impossible to estimate intelligently the size of a plant, store, or office, or to determine how much inventory to carry or how many employees to hire.

Another important component of the overall business plan is financial planning, which translates all other activities into dollars. Generally, the financial plan is made up of a cash budget, an income statement, balance sheets, and a breakeven chart. The most important of these statements is the cash budget because it tells entrepreneurs how much money they need before they open for business and how much money they need to keep the business operating.

Entrepreneurship and International Management

Although many people associate international management with big business, many smaller companies are finding expansion and growth opportunities in foreign countries.

For example, Fuci Metals, a small but growing enterprise, buys metal from remote locations in areas such as Siberia and Africa and then sells it to big automakers such as Ford and Toyota. Similarly, California-based Gold's Gym is expanding into foreign countries and has been especially successful in Russia. And Markel Corporation, a small Philadelphia-based firm that manufactures tubing and insulated wiring, derives 40 percent of its annual revenues (currently around $32 million) from international sales. Although such ventures are accompanied by considerable risks, they give entrepreneurs new opportunities and can be a real catalyst for success.

STRUCTURE OF ENTREPRENEURIAL ORGANIZATIONS

With a strategy in place and a business plan in hand, the entrepreneur can then proceed to devise a structure that turns the vision of the business plan into a reality. Many of the same concerns in structuring any business, which are described in the next five chapters of this book, are also relevant to small businesses. For example, entrepreneurs need to consider organization design and develop job descriptions, organization charts, and management control systems.

The Internet, of course, has virtually rewritten all the rules for starting and operating a small business. Getting into business is easier and faster than ever before, there are many more potential opportunities than at any other time in history, and the ability to gather and assimilate information is at an all-time high. And social media introduces new companies to larger potential markets than ever before.[20] For example, HardToFindPartySupplies.com has been successful marketing discontinued or hard-to-find supplies like Power Ranger paper plates, Lone Ranger napkins, and Snow White drinking cups. The firm relies solely on social media and its website.[21]

Even so, would-be entrepreneurs must still make the right decisions when they start. They must decide, for example, precisely how to get into business. Should they buy an existing business or build from the ground up? In addition, would-be entrepreneurs must find appropriate sources of financing and decide when and how to seek the advice of experts.

Starting the New Business

The first step in starting a new business is the individual's commitment to becoming a business owner. Next comes choosing the goods or services to be offered—a process that means investigating one's chosen industry and market. Making this choice also requires would-be entrepreneurs to assess not only industry trends but also their own skills. Like the managers of existing businesses, new business owners must also be sure that they understand the true nature of the enterprise in which they are engaged.

Buying an Existing Business   After choosing a product and making sure that the choice fits their own skills and interests, entrepreneurs must decide whether to buy an existing business or to start from scratch. Consultants often recommend the first approach. Quite simply, the odds are better: If successful, an existing business has already proved its ability to draw customers at a profit. It has also established working relationships with lenders, suppliers, and the community. Moreover, the track record of an existing business gives potential buyers a much clearer picture of what to expect than any estimate of a new business's prospects. Around 30 percent of the new businesses started in the past decade were bought from someone else. As another example, the McDonald's empire was started when Ray Kroc bought an existing hamburger business and then turned it into a global phenomenon. Likewise, Starbucks was a struggling mail-order business when Howard Schultz bought it and turned his attention to retail expansion.

Starting from Scratch   Some people, however, prefer the satisfaction that comes from planting an idea, nurturing it, and making it grow into a strong and sturdy business. There are also practical reasons to start a business from scratch. A new business does not suffer the ill effects of a prior owner's errors. The start-up owner is also free to choose lenders, equipment, inventories, locations, suppliers, and workers, unbound by a predecessor's commitments and policies. Of the new businesses begun in the past decade, 64 percent were started from scratch.

It is no surprise, though, that the risks of starting a business from scratch are greater than those of buying an existing firm. Founders of new businesses can make only predictions and projections about their prospects. Success or failure thus depends heavily on identifying a genuine business opportunity—a product for which many customers will pay well but which is currently unavailable to them. To find openings, entrepreneurs must study markets and answer the following questions: (1) Who are my customers? (2) Where are they? (3) At what price will they buy my product? (4) In what quantities will they buy? (5) Who are my competitors? (6) How will my product differ from those of my competitors?

Finding answers to these questions is a difficult task, even for large, well-established firms. Where can the new business owner get the necessary information? Other sources of assistance are discussed later in this chapter, but we briefly describe three of the most accessible here. First, the best way to gain knowledge about a market is to work in it before going into business in it. For example, if you once worked in a bookstore and now plan to open one of your own, you probably already have some idea about the kinds of books people request and buy. Second, a quick scan of the local Yellow Pages or an Internet search will reveal many potential competitors, as will advertisements in trade journals. Personal visits to these establishments and websites can give you insights into their strengths and weaknesses. And, third, studying magazines, books, and websites aimed specifically at small businesses can be of help, as can hiring professionals to survey the market for you.

Financing the New Business

Although the choice of how to start is obviously important, it is meaningless unless a new business owner can obtain the money to set up shop. Among the more common sources for funding are family and friends, personal savings, banks and similar lending institutions, investors, and government agencies. Lending institutions are more likely to help finance the purchase of an existing business than a new business because the risks are better understood. Individuals starting up new businesses, on the other hand, are more likely to have to rely on their personal resources.

Personal Resources   According to a study by the National Federation of Independent Business (NFIB), an owner's personal resources, not loans, are the most important source of money. Including money borrowed from friends and relatives, personal resources account for over two-thirds of all money invested in new small businesses and one-half of that invested in the purchase of existing businesses. John Mackey started Whole Foods with a $10,000 loan from his father. Fred Smith used $4 million he had inherited from his father to launch FedEx. And Rebecca Boenigk started Neutral Posture, an ergonomic chair company, with personal savings and loans from several family members.

AP Images/Paul Zoeller

Rebecca Boenigk is the founder and CEO of Neutral Posture. Neutral Posture makes a variety of ergonomic seating products. Beonigk's father, Dr. Jerome Congleton, developed the technology but did not have the expertise to commercialize it. Ms. Boenigk used personal savings and family loans to found what is now an international business.

venture capital companies

A group of small investors seeking to make profits on companies with rapid growth potential

Strategic Alliances   Strategic alliances are also becoming a popular method for financing business growth. When Steven and Andrew Grundy decided to launch an Internet CD-exchange business called Spun.com, they had very little capital and thus made extensive use of alliances with other firms. They partnered, for example, with wholesaler Alliance Entertainment Corporation as a CD supplier. Orders to Spun.com actually go to Alliance, which ships products to customers and bills Spun.com directly. This setup has allowed Spun.com to promote a vast inventory of labels without actually having to buy inventory. All told, the firm created an alliance network that has provided the equivalent of $40 million in capital.[22]

Lenders   Although banks, independent investors, and government loans all provide much smaller portions of start-up funds than the personal resources of owners, they are important in many cases. Getting money from these sources, however, requires some extra effort. Banks and private investors usually want to see formal business plans—detailed outlines of proposed businesses and markets, owners' backgrounds, and other sources of funding. Government loans have strict eligibility guidelines.

Venture Capital Companies   **Venture capital companies** are groups of small investors seeking to make profits on companies with rapid growth potential. Most of these firms do not lend money: They invest it, supplying capital in return for stock. The venture capital company may also demand a representative on the board of directors. In some cases, managers may even need approval from the venture capital company before making major decisions. Of all venture capital currently committed in the United States, around 25 percent comes from true venture capital firms.[23] In 2010, venture capital firms invested about $18 billion in new start-ups in the United States. SoftBank Capital is a venture capital firm that has provided funds to over 300 web companies, including Yahoo! and E*Trade.

As noted earlier, Fred Smith used his inheritance to launch FedEx. Once he got his business plan developed and started service, though, he needed an infusion of substantial additional capital. All told, he raised about $80 million in venture capital to buy his first small fleet of planes. Venture capital was also important in the launch of both Facebook and Twitter.

Small-Business Investment Companies   Taking a more balanced approach in their choices than venture capital companies, small-business investment companies (SBICs) seek profits by investing in companies with potential for rapid growth. Created by the Small Business Investment Act of 1958, SBICs are federally licensed to borrow money from the SBA and to invest it in or lend it to small businesses. They are themselves investments for their shareholders. Past beneficiaries of SBIC capital include Apple Computer, Intel, and Federal Express (now FedEx). In addition, the government has recently begun to sponsor minority enterprise small-business investment companies (MESBICs). As the name suggests, MESBICs specialize in financing businesses that are owned and operated by minorities.

SBA Financial Programs   Since its founding in 1953, the SBA has offered more than 20 financing programs to small businesses that meet standards of size and independence. Eligible firms must also be unable to get private financing at reasonable terms. Because of these and other restrictions, SBA loans have never been a major source of small-business financing. In addition, budget cutbacks at the SBA have reduced the number of firms benefiting from loans. Nevertheless, several SBA programs currently offer funds to qualified applicants.

For example, under the SBA's guaranteed loans program, small businesses can borrow from commercial lenders. The SBA guarantees to repay 75 to 85 percent of the loan amount, not to exceed $750,000. Under a related program, companies engaged in international trade can borrow up to $1.50 million. Such loans may be made for as long as 15 years. Most SBA lending activity flows through this program.

Sometimes, however, both desired bank and SBA-guaranteed loans are unavailable (perhaps because the business cannot meet stringent requirements). In such cases, the SBA may help finance the entrepreneur through its immediate participation loan program. Under this arrangement, the SBA and the bank each put up a share of the money, with the SBA's share not to exceed $150,000. Under the local development companies (LDCs) program, the SBA works with a corporation (either for-profit or nonprofit) founded by local citizens who want to boost the local economy. The SBA can lend up to $500,000 for each small business to be helped by an LDC.

Spurred in large part by the boom in Internet businesses, both venture capital and loans are in general becoming easier to get. Most small businesses, for example, report that it became increasingly easier to obtain loans between 1995 and 2005. And firms such as Facebook and Twitter are being offered so much venture capital that they are turning down part of it to keep from unnecessarily diluting their ownership. Unfortunately, the credit crunch that began in 2008 has made it harder for most entrepreneurs to obtain funds, but experts believe this is only a short-term problem.[24] But in response, some entrepreneurs have turned to other sources of funding such as microloans and cash-flow lenders.[25]

Sources of Management Advice

Financing is not the only area in which small businesses need help. Until World War II, for example, the business world involved few regulations, few taxes, few records, few big competitors, and no computers. Since then, simplicity has given way to complexity. Today, few entrepreneurs are equipped with all the business skills they need to survive. Small-business owners can no longer be their own troubleshooters, lawyers, bookkeepers, financiers, and tax experts. For these jobs, they rely on professional help. To survive and grow, however, small businesses also need advice regarding management. This advice is usually available from four sources: advisory boards, management consultants, the SBA, and networking.

Advisory Boards   All companies, even those that do not legally need boards of directors, can benefit from the problem-solving abilities of advisory boards. Thus, some small businesses create boards to provide advice and assistance. For example, an advisory board might help an entrepreneur determine the best way to finance a plant expansion or to start exporting products to foreign markets.

Management Consultants   Opinions vary widely about the value of management consultants—experts who charge fees to help managers solve problems. They often specialize in one area, such as international business, small business, or manufacturing. Thus, they can bring an objective and trained outlook to problems and provide logical recommendations. They can be quite expensive, however, as some consultants charge $1,000 or more for a day of assistance.

Like other professionals, management consultants should be chosen with care. They can be found through major corporations that have used their services and that can provide references and reports on their work. Not surprisingly, they are most effective when the client helps (for instance, by providing schedules and written proposals for the work to be done).

The Small Business Administration   Even more important than its financing role is the SBA's role in helping small-business owners improve their management skills. It is easy for entrepreneurs to spend money; SBA programs are designed to show them how to spend it wisely. The SBA offers small businesses four major management-counseling programs at virtually no cost.

A small-business owner who needs help in starting a new business can get it free through the Service Corps of Retired Executives (SCORE). All SCORE members are retired executives, and all are volunteers. Under this program, the SBA tries to match the expert to the need. For example, if a small-business owner needs help putting together a marketing plan, the SBA will send a SCORE counselor with marketing expertise.

Like SCORE, the Active Corps of Executives (ACE) program is designed to help small businesses that cannot afford consultants. The SBA recruits ACE volunteers from virtually every industry. All ACE volunteers are currently involved in successful activities,

Todd Bannor/Alamy

The U.S. Small Business Administration (SBA) was created in 1953 as a resource to help would-be business owners learn more about starting and managing a business, avenues for securing financing for new ventures, and techniques for effective management. Today the SBA uses a national network of headquarters offices, regional offices, district offices, and disaster officers to provide assistance to both potential and current small business owners.

mostly as small-business owners themselves. Together, SCORE and ACE have more than 12,000 counselors working out of 350 chapters throughout the United States. They provide assistance to some 140,000 small businesses each year.

The talents and skills of students and instructors at colleges and universities are fundamental to the Small Business Institute (SBI). Under the guidance of seasoned professors of business administration, students seeking advanced degrees work closely with small-business owners to help solve specific problems, such as sagging sales or rising costs. Students earn credit toward their degree, with their grades depending on how well they handle a client's problems. Several hundred colleges and universities counsel thousands of small-business owners through this program every year.

Finally, the newest of the SBA's management counseling projects is its Small Business Development Center (SBDC) program. Begun in 1976, SBDCs are designed to consolidate information from various disciplines and institutions, including technical and professional schools. Then they make this knowledge available to new and existing small businesses. In 1995, universities in 45 states took part in the program.

Networking   More and more, small-business owners are discovering the value of networking—meeting regularly with one another to discuss common problems and opportunities and, perhaps most important, to pool resources. Businesspeople have long joined organizations such as the local chamber of commerce and the NFIBs to make such contacts.

Today, organizations are springing up all over the United States to facilitate small-business networking. One such organization, the Council of Smaller Enterprises of Cleveland, boasts a total membership of more than 10,000 small-business owners, the largest number in the country. This organization offers its members not only networking possibilities but also educational programs and services tailored to their needs. In a typical year, its 85 educational programs draw more than 8,500 small-business owners.

In particular, women and minorities have found networking to be an effective problem-solving tool. The National Association of Women Business Owners (NAWBO), for example, provides a variety of networking forums. The NAWBO also has chapters in most major cities, where its members can meet regularly. Increasingly, women are relying more on other women to help locate venture capital, establish relationships with customers, and provide essential services such as accounting and legal advice. According to Patty Abramson of the Women's Growth Capital Fund, all these tasks have traditionally been harder for women because, until now, they have never had friends in the right places. "I wouldn't say this is about discrimination," adds Abramson. "It's about not having the relationships, and business is about relationships."

franchising agreements

A contract between an entrepreneur (the franchisee) and a parent company (the franchiser); the entrepreneur pays the parent company for the use of its trademarks, products, formulas, and business plans

Franchising

The next time you drive or walk around town, be on the alert for a McDonald's, Taco Bell, Subway, Denny's, or KFC restaurant; a 7-Eleven or Circle K convenience store; a RE/MAX or Coldwell Banker real estate office; a Super 8 or Ramada Inn motel; a Merry Maids cleaning service; a Sylvan Learning educational center; an Express Oil Change or Precision Auto Wash service center; or a Supercuts hair salon. What do these businesses have in common? In most cases, they are franchised operations, operating under licenses issued by parent companies to local entrepreneurs who own and manage them.

As many would-be businesspeople have discovered, **franchising agreements** are an accessible doorway to entrepreneurship. A franchise is an arrangement that permits the *franchisee* (buyer) to sell the product of the *franchiser* (seller, or parent company).

Franchisees can thus benefit from the selling corporation's experience and expertise. They can also consult the franchiser for managerial and financial help.

For example, the franchiser may supply financing. It may pick the store location, negotiate the lease, design the store, and purchase necessary equipment. It may train the first set of employees and managers and provide standardized policies and procedures. Once the business is open, the franchiser may offer franchisees savings by allowing them to purchase from a central location. Marketing strategy (especially advertising) may also be handled by the franchiser. Finally, franchisees may benefit from continued management counseling. In short, franchisees receive—that is, invest in—not only their own ready-made business but also expert help in running it.

Franchises offer many advantages to both sellers and buyers. For example, franchisers benefit from the ability to grow rapidly by using the investment money provided by franchisees. This strategy has enabled giant franchisers such as McDonald's and Subway to mushroom into billion-dollar concerns in a brief time.

For the franchisee, the arrangement combines the incentive of owning a business with the advantage of access to big-business management skills. Unlike the person who starts from scratch, the franchisee does not have to build a business step by step. Instead, the business is established virtually overnight. Moreover, because each franchise outlet is probably a carbon copy of every other outlet, the chances of failure are reduced. McDonald's, for example, is a model of consistency—Big Macs taste the same everywhere.

Of course, owning a franchise also involves certain disadvantages. Perhaps the most significant is the start-up cost. Franchise prices vary widely. Fantastic Sams hair salon franchise fees are $25,000 to $30,000. Extremely profitable or hard-to-get franchises are much more expensive, though. A McDonald's franchise costs a minimum of $500,000 plus the cost of building and outfitting a new restaurant (estimated to be between $1 million and $1.8 million), and a professional sports team can cost several hundred million dollars. Franchisees may also have continued obligations to contribute percentages of sales to the parent corporation.

Buying a franchise also entails less tangible costs. For one thing, the small-business owner sacrifices some independence. A McDonald's franchisee cannot change the way its hamburgers or milkshakes are made. Nor can franchisees create an individual identity in their community; for all practical purposes, the McDonald's owner is anonymous. In addition, many franchise agreements are difficult to terminate.

Finally, although franchises minimize risks, they do not guarantee success. Many franchisees have seen their investments—and their dreams—disappear because of poor location, rising costs, or lack of continued franchiser commitment. Moreover, figures on failure rates are artificially low because they do not include failing franchisees bought out by their franchising parent companies. An additional risk is that the chain itself could collapse. In any given year, dozens—sometimes hundreds—of franchisers close shop or stop selling franchises.

THE PERFORMANCE OF ENTREPRENEURIAL ORGANIZATIONS

The formulation and implementation of an effective strategy play major roles in determining the overall performance of an entrepreneurial organization. This section examines how entrepreneurial firms evolve over time and the attributes of these firms that enhance their chances of success. For every Henry Ford, Walt Disney, Mary Kay Ash, or Bill Gates—people who transformed small businesses into major corporations—there are many small-business owners and entrepreneurs who fail.

Exact numbers of start-ups and failures are surprisingly difficult to determine, however. For instance, a business may shut down because it is out of money (a failure) or simply because the owner decides to do something else; or the business may be sold to another business and cease to exist as an independent entity. Likewise, an ongoing sole proprietorship that becomes a partnership or corporation is not really a new business but may be counted as such in some statistics; similarly, a large corporation might launch a new enterprise as a new wholly owned but separately incorporated enterprise.

In general, though, experts believe that new business start-ups generally run between around 700,000 and 900,000 per year and that business failures generally run between 600,000 and 950,000 per year. Figure 5.5 illustrates trends in new business start-ups and failures through 2008 (the most current data available).

Trends in Small-Business Start-Ups

Thousands of new businesses are started in the United States every year. Several factors account for this trend, and in this section we focus on four of them.

Emergence of E-Commerce   Clearly, one of the most significant recent trends in small-business start-ups is the rapid emergence of electronic commerce. Because the Internet has provided fundamentally new ways of doing business, savvy entrepreneurs have been able to create and expand new businesses faster and more easily than ever before. Leading-edge firms such as Facebook, Google, and eBay, for example, owe their

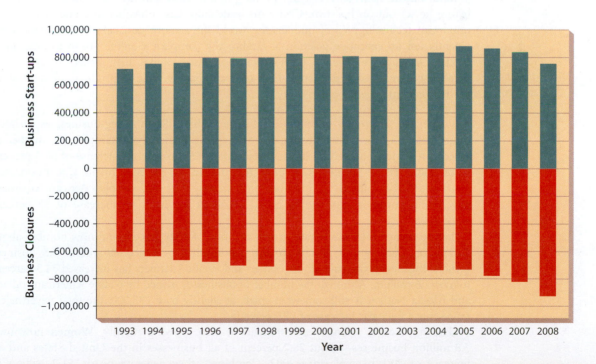

FIGURE 5.5

Business Start-Up Successes and Failures

Over the most recent ten-year period for which data are available, new business start-ups numbered between 700,000 and 900,000 per year. Business failures during this same period, meanwhile, ranged from about 600,000 to 950,000 per year.

Source: http://www.bls.gov/bdm/entrepreneurship/bdm_chart5.htm, accessed on March 2014.

very existence to the Internet. At the same time, however, many would-be Internet entrepreneurs have gone under in the last few years, as the so-called dot-com boom quickly faded. In 2010, online retail sales exceeded $142 billion, an increase of 3 percent from the previous year.

Indeed, it seems as if new ideas emerge virtually every day. Andrew Beebe, for example, is scoring big with Bigstep, a web business that essentially creates, hosts, and maintains websites for other small businesses. So far, Bigstep has signed up 75,000 small-business clients. Beebe actually provides his basic services for free but earns money by charging for the so-called premium services such as customer billing. Karl Jacob's Keen.com is a web business that matches people looking for advice with experts who have the answers. Keen got the idea when he and his father were struggling to fix a boat motor and did not know where to turn for help. Keen.com attracted 100,000 subscribers in just three months.[26]

Crossovers from Big Business

Crossovers from Big Business   It is interesting to note that increasingly more businesses are being started by people who have opted to leave big corporations and put their experience and know-how to work for themselves. In some cases, these individuals see great new ideas they want to develop. Often, they get burned out working for a big corporation. Sometimes they have lost their jobs, only to discover that working for themselves was a better idea anyway.

Cisco Systems CEO John Chambers is acknowledged as one of the best entrepreneurs around. But he spent several years working first at IBM and then at Wang Laboratories before he set out on his own. Under his leadership, Cisco has become one of the most important technology companies in the world. In a more unusual case, Gilman Louie recently left an executive position at Hasbro toy company's online group to head up a Central Intelligence Agency (CIA)–backed venture capital firm called In-Q-It. The firm's mission is to help nurture high-tech companies making products of interest to the nation's intelligence community.[27]

Opportunities for Minorities and Women

Opportunities for Minorities and Women   In addition to big-business expatriates, minorities and women are starting more small businesses. For example, the number of African-American–owned businesses totals about 1.9 million, an increase of 60.5 percent since 2002. These businesses account for around 7.1 percent of all U.S. businesses, generate $137.5 billion in revenue, and employ 921,032 people. African-American purchasing power is expected to hit $1.2 trillion by 2013, an increase of 35 percent since 2008.[28]

Latino-owned businesses have grown at a rate of 43.6 percent and now number about 2.3 million. Other ethnic groups are also making their presence felt among U.S. business owners. Business ownership among Asians and Pacific Islanders has increased 34.3 percent, to over 1.6 million. Although the number of businesses owned by Native American Indians and Alaska Natives is still somewhat small, at slightly over 235,000, the total nevertheless represents a five-year increase of 17.9 percent.

The number of women entrepreneurs is also growing rapidly. Women now own 7.8 million businesses—about 28.7 percent of all businesses in the United States and an increase of 20.1 percent since 2002. Combined, they generate nearly $1.2 trillion in revenue a year and employ 7.6 million people. Celeste Johnson, for example, left a management position at Pitney Bowes to launch Obex, Inc., which makes gardening and landscaping products from mixed recycled plastics. Katrina Garnett gave up a lucrative job at Oracle to start her own software company, Crossworlds Software. Laila Rubenstein closed her management-consulting practice to create Greeting Cards.com, Inc., an Internet-based business selling customizable electronic greetings.

Better Survival Rates   Finally, more people are encouraged to test their skills as entrepreneurs because the failure rate among small businesses has been declining in recent years. As of 2008, seven out of ten new businesses survived at least two years, whereas about 49 percent survived five years; 34 percent of businesses survived at least ten years, and 26 percent lasted 15 years or longer. For reasons discussed in the next section, small businesses suffer a higher mortality rate than larger concerns. Among those that manage to stay in business for six to ten years, however, the survival rate levels off.

Reasons for Failure

Why do some succeed and others fail? Although no set pattern has been established, four general factors contribute to new business failure. One factor is managerial incompetence or inexperience. Some would-be entrepreneurs assume that they can succeed through common sense, overestimate their own managerial acumen, or think that hard work alone will lead to success. But if managers do not know how to make basic business decisions or understand the basic concepts and principles of management, they are unlikely to be successful in the long run.

Second, neglect can also contribute to failure. Some entrepreneurs try either to launch their ventures in their spare time or to devote only a limited amount of time to a new business. But starting a new business requires an overwhelming time commitment. Entrepreneurs who are not willing to put in the time and effort that a business requires are unlikely to survive.

Third, weak control systems can lead to serious problems. Effective control systems are needed to keep a business on track and to help alert entrepreneurs to potential trouble. If control systems do not signal impending problems, managers may be in serious trouble before more visible difficulties alert them.

Finally, insufficient capital can contribute to new business failure. Some entrepreneurs are overly optimistic about how soon they will start earning profits. In most cases, however, it takes months or years before a business is likely to start turning a profit. Amazon.com, for example, has still not earned a profit. Most experts say that a new business should have enough capital to operate for at least six months without earning a profit; some recommend enough to last a year.[29]

Reasons for Success

Similarly, four basic factors are typically cited to explain new business success. One factor is the combination of hard work, drive, and dedication. New business owners must be committed to succeeding and be willing to put in the time and effort to make it happen. Having positive feelings and a good outlook on life may also play an important role.[30] Gladys Edmunds, a single teenaged mother in Pittsburgh, washed laundry, made chicken dinners to sell to cab drivers, and sold fire extinguishers and Bibles door to door to earn money to launch her own business. Today, Edmunds Travel Consultants employs eight people and earns about $6 million in annual revenues.[31]

Second, careful analysis of market conditions can help new business owners assess the probable reception of their products in the marketplace. This will provide insights about market demand for proposed products and services. Whereas attempts to expand local restaurants specializing in baked potatoes, muffins, and gelato have been largely unsuccessful, hamburger and pizza chains continue to have an easier time expanding into new markets.

Third, managerial competence also contributes to success. Successful new business owners may acquire competence through training or experience or by using the expertise of others. Few successful entrepreneurs succeed alone or straight out of college. Most spend time working in successful companies or partner with others to bring more expertise to a new business.

Finally, luck also plays a role in the success of some firms. For example, after Alan McKim started Clean Harbors, an environmental cleanup firm based in New England, he struggled to keep his business afloat. Then the U.S. government committed $1.6 billion to toxic waste cleanup—McKim's specialty. He was able to get several large government contracts and put his business on solid financial footing. Had the government fund not been created at just the right time, McKim may well have failed. Similarly, when retailers like Circuit City and Linens and Things close their doors, others firms that specialize in liquidating inventories of bankrupt companies step in.[32] Similarly, in the wake of such recent disasters—both natural and industrial—as Hurricane Sandy, the Japanese tsunami and nuclear plant disaster, and the BP Deepwater oil spill, new businesses have sprung up to help cope with the aftermath, including relocating people, waste clean-up, and so forth.[33]

SUMMARY OF LEARNING OUTCOMES AND KEY POINTS

1. Discuss the nature of entrepreneurship.

   - Entrepreneurship is the process of planning, organizing, operating, and assuming the risk of a business venture.
   - An entrepreneur is someone who engages in entrepreneurship. In general, entrepreneurs start small businesses.

2. Describe the role of entrepreneurship in society.

   - Small businesses are an important source of innovation.
   - Small businesses create numerous jobs.
   - Small businesses contribute to the success of large businesses.

3. Understand the major issues involved in choosing strategies for small firms and the role of international management in entrepreneurship.

   - In choosing strategies, entrepreneurs have to consider the characteristics of the industry in which they are going to conduct business.
   - Small businesses generally have several distinctive competencies that they should exploit in choosing their strategy. They are usually skilled at identifying niches in established markets, identifying new markets, and acting quickly to obtain first-mover advantages.
   - Small businesses are usually not skilled at exploiting economies of scale.

   - Once an entrepreneur has chosen a strategy, the strategy is normally written down in a business plan. Writing a business plan forces an entrepreneur to plan thoroughly and to anticipate problems that might occur.

4. Discuss the structural challenges unique to entrepreneurial firms.

   - With a strategy and business plan in place, entrepreneurs must choose a structure to implement them. All of the structural issues summarized in the next five chapters of this book are relevant to the entrepreneur.
   - In addition, the entrepreneur has some unique structural choices to make. For example, the entrepreneur can buy an existing business or start a new one.
   - In determining financial structure, an entrepreneur has to decide how much personal capital to invest in an organization, how much bank and government support to obtain, and whether to encourage venture capital firms to invest.
   - Entrepreneurs can also rely on various sources of advice.

5. Understand the determinants of the performance of small firms.

   - Several interesting trends characterize new business start-ups today.
   - There are several reasons some new businesses fail and others succeed.

DISCUSSION QUESTIONS

Questions for Review

1. Describe the similarities and differences between entrepreneurial firms and large firms in terms of their job creation and innovation.
2. What characteristics make an industry attractive to entrepreneurs? Based on these characteristics, which industries are most attractive to entrepreneurs?
3. Describe recent trends in new business start-ups.
4. What are the different sources of advice for entrepreneurs? What type of information would an entrepreneur be likely to get from each source? What are the drawbacks or limitations for each source?
5. What are the basic reasons small businesses succeed and what are the basic reasons they fail?

Questions for Analysis

1. Entrepreneurs and small businesses play a variety of important roles in society. If these roles are so important, do you think that the government should do more to encourage the development of small business? Why or why not?
2. Consider the four major reasons for new business failure. What actions can entrepreneurs take to minimize or avoid each cause of failure?
3. The U.S. automotive industry is well established, with several large and many small competitors. Describe the unexploited niches in the U.S. auto industry and tell how entrepreneurs could offer products that fill those niches.
4. List five entrepreneur-owned businesses in your community. In which industry does each business compete? Based on the industry, how do you rate each business's long-term chances for success? Explain your answers.
5. Using the information about managing a small business presented in this chapter, analyze whether you would like to work in a small business—either as an employee or as a founder. Given your personality, background, and experience, does working in or starting a new business appeal to you? What are the reasons for your opinion?

BUILDING EFFECTIVE DIAGNOSTIC SKILLS

Exercise Overview

Diagnostic skills enable a manager to visualize the most appropriate response to a situation. This exercise is designed to develop your diagnostic skills by asking you to think about your chances of becoming an entrepreneur.

Exercise Background

Scholars of entrepreneurship are naturally interested in the reasons some people choose to start new businesses while other people—indeed, most people—don't. Researchers have surveyed thousands of individuals, both entrepreneurs and nonentrepreneurs, in efforts to identify some of the factors that distinguish individuals in the two groups. Out of these hundreds of studies, some consensus has emerged. The results tell us that the following types of individuals are most likely to become entrepreneurs:

- Parents, children, spouses, or siblings of entrepreneurs
- Immigrants to the United States or the children of immigrants
- Members of the Jewish or Protestant faiths
- Professional degree holders in fields such as medicine, law, or engineering
- People who've recently experienced life-changing events, such as getting married, having a child, moving to a new city, or losing a job

Exercise Task

Considering the preceding information, do the following:

1. Choose one of the categories of individuals and explain why this type of person might be more likely to become a business owner.
2. Being sure to choose a category other than the one that you discussed for question 1, select one of these categories that applies to *you*. In your opinion, does that factor make it more likely that you'll become an entrepreneur? Why or why not? If none of the categories applies to you, discuss whether that fact itself makes it *less* likely that you'll become an entrepreneur.

BUILDING EFFECTIVE CONCEPTUAL SKILLS

Exercise Overview

Conceptual skills require you to think in the abstract. This exercise will help you apply your conceptual skills to an analysis of certain criteria for successful entrepreneurship.

Exercise Background

Now that you're about to graduate, you've decided to open a small business in the local community where you've been attending college. We won't ask where you got them, but we'll assume that you have enough funds to start a business without having to worry about finding investors.

Based solely on your personal interests, list five businesses that you might want to open and operate. For the moment, forget about technicalities such as market potential or profitability. If, for example, you like riding your bicycle, think about opening a shop that caters to cyclists.

Next, *without regard for any personal interest you might have in them*, list five businesses that you might want to open and operate. In this case, your only criteria are market opportunity and profitability. What types of businesses might be profitable in your chosen

community? Use the Internet to gather information on factors such as population, local economic conditions, local competition, and franchising opportunities.

Finally, evaluate the prospects for success of each of the ten businesses that you've listed, and jot down some notes to summarize your conclusions.

Exercise Task

Reviewing your lists, the information that you've gathered, and the conclusions that you've drawn, do the following:

1. Form a small group of four or five classmates, and discuss your respective lists. Look for instances in which the same type of business appears on either both of your lists or one of your lists and one of a classmate's lists. Also look for cases in which the same business appears on one or more than one list with either similar or dissimilar prospects for success.
2. At this point, how important do you regard personal interest as a factor in small-business success?
3. How important do you regard market potential as a factor in small-business success?

SKILLS SELF-ASSESSMENT INSTRUMENT

An Entrepreneurial Quiz

Introduction: Entrepreneurs are starting ventures all the time. These new businesses are vital to the economy. The following assessment is designed to help you understand your readiness to start your own business—to be an entrepreneur.

Instructions: Place a checkmark or an X in the box next to the response that best represents your self-evaluation.

1. Are you a self-starter?
   - ❑ I do things on my own. Nobody has to tell me to get going.
   - ❑ If someone gets me started, I keep going all right.
   - ❑ Easy does it. I don't push myself until I have to.
2. How do you feel about other people?
   - ❑ I like people. I can get along with just about anybody.

   - ❑ I have plenty of friends—I don't need anybody else.
   - ❑ Most people irritate me.
3. Can you lead others?
   - ❑ I can get most people to go along when I start something.
   - ❑ I can give orders if someone tells me what we should do.
   - ❑ I let someone else get things moving. Then I go along if I feel like it.
4. Can you take responsibility?
   - ❑ I like to take charge of things and see them through.
   - ❑ I'll take over if I have to, but I'd rather let someone else be responsible.
   - ❑ There are always eager beavers around wanting to show how smart they are. I let them.

5. How good an organizer are you?
   - ❏ I like to have a plan before I start. I'm usually the one to get things lined up when the group wants to do something.
   - ❏ I do all right unless things get too confused. Then I quit.
   - ❏ You get all set and then something comes along and presents too many problems. So I just take things as they come.

6. How good a worker are you?
   - ❏ I can keep going as long as I need to. I don't mind working hard for something I want.
   - ❏ I'll work hard for a while, but when I've had enough, that's it.
   - ❏ I can't see that hard work gets you anywhere.

7. Can you make decisions?
   - ❏ I can make up my mind in a hurry if I have to. It usually turns out OK, too.
   - ❏ I can if I have plenty of time. If I have to make up my mind fast, I think later I should have decided the other way.
   - ❏ I don't like to be the one who has to decide things.

8. Can people trust what you say?
   - ❏ You bet they can. I don't say things I don't mean.
   - ❏ I try to be on the level most of the time, but sometimes I just say what's easiest.
   - ❏ Why bother if the other person doesn't know the difference?

9. Can you stick with it?
   - ❏ If I make up my mind to do something, I don't let anything stop me.
   - ❏ I usually finish what I start—if it goes well.
   - ❏ If it doesn't go well right away, I quit. Why beat your brains out?

10. How good is your health?
    - ❏ I never run down!
    - ❏ I have enough energy for most things I want to do.
    - ❏ I run out of energy sooner than most of my friends.

Total the checks or Xs in each column here_____.

Source: Dible, Donald, *Business Startup Basics*, 1st Ed., © 1978, pp. 9–10. Reprinted by permission of Pearson Education, Inc., Upper Saddle River, NJ.

EXPERIENTIAL EXERCISE

Negotiating a Franchise Agreement

Step 1: Assume that you are the owner of a rapidly growing restaurant chain. To continue your current level of growth, you are considering the option of selling franchises for new restaurants. Working alone, outline the major points of most concern to you that you would want to have in a franchising agreement. Also note the characteristics you would look for in potential franchisees.

Step 2: Assume that you are an individual investor looking to buy a franchise in a rapidly growing restaurant chain. Again working alone, outline the major factors that might determine which franchise you elect to buy. Also note the characteristics you would look for in a potential franchiser.

Step 3: Now form small groups of four. Randomly select one member of the group to play the role of the franchiser; the other three members will play the roles of potential franchisees. Role-play a negotiation meeting. The franchiser should stick as closely as possible to the major points developed in Step 1. Similarly, the potential franchisees should try to adhere to the points they developed in Step 2.

Follow-Up Questions

1. Did doing both Step 1 and Step 2 in advance help or hinder your negotiations?
2. Can a franchising agreement be so one-sided as to damage the interests of both parties? How so?

MANAGEMENT AT WORK

The Creative Imprint of Bigfoot

Have you seen *Midnight Movie*? You wouldn't have caught it in a theater because it went straight to DVD, but that doesn't prevent hardcore horror-film fans from tracking it down—after all, it was selected as the Best Feature Film at the 10th Annual Chicago Horror Film Festival. It also found an audience outside the United States, with producer Bigfoot selling distribution rights in such countries as Germany, Greece, Thailand, and Japan. How about *3 Needles*, a Canadian-made movie about the worldwide AIDS crisis? It was no blockbuster, but it was endorsed by the United Nations and did well enough at international film festivals to find distributors in such countries as Australia, New Zealand, and Brazil. Bigfoot CEO Kacy Andrews was pleased with the film's reception: "The positive response from critics and audiences," she said, "… once again affirms our conviction to promote independent filmmakers."

Bigfoot Entertainment is responsible for a host of independently produced films, many of which follow similar distribution paths to venues and audiences around the world. The company, says Andrews, "is dedicated to the community of filmmakers who possess the vision and passion to create critically acclaimed independent films." It was founded in 2004 by a German serial entrepreneur named Michael Gleissner, who is in some ways a model for the sort of creative people that Bigfoot likes to back. He was certainly the model for the hero of *Hui Lu*, a 2007 Bigfoot film that Gleissner wrote and directed about a highly successful young entrepreneur who sells his company but finds himself pushed to the edge despite his millions. "What was I going to do," Gleissner replied when asked about his unusual career move, "buy more boats, buy more houses? I discovered there's a creative side in me."

Gleissner was an e-commerce pioneer in Germany, where he founded Telebook, Germany's number-one online bookstore, and WWW-Service GmbH, the country's first, and one of its most successful, web-hosting companies. In 1998, he sold Telebook to Amazon.com, where he served two years as a vice president before cashing in and, in 2001, moving to Asia to make it a base for a new round of entrepreneurial activities. When he bought Bigfoot, it was an e-mail management firm, but Gleissner quickly re-created it as an international entertainment company whose main business, according to its mission statement, is producing and financing "innovative entertainment content, including independent feature films, television series, and reality shows." As head of Bigfoot, Gleissner served as executive producer on *Midnight Movie* and *3 Needles*, as well as on *Irreversi*, his second effort at writing and directing, and on *Shanghai Kiss*, in which he also tried his hand at acting.

Bigfoot maintains offices in Los Angeles and a small production facility in Venice, California, but the centerpiece of its operations is Bigfoot Studios, which opened in 2004 on the island of Mactan, in Cebu, home to the second-largest city in the Philippines. The state-of-the-art facility features six large soundstages, fully equipped editing suites and sound-mixing studios,

and the latest in high-tech cameras and other equipment. In 2007, under the auspices of Bigfoot Properties, Gleissner expanded Bigfoot Studios as the first phase of Bigfoot Center, a complex that will eventually house not only film and TV production facilities but also Bigfoot Executive Hotel, an array of restaurants, boutiques, and sidewalk shops, and an 11-story office building (home to Bigfoot Outsourcing, which specializes in business-process services). The Bigfoot Center in the Philippines, by the way, should not be confused with the 26-story Bigfoot Centre in Hong Kong, where Bigfoot Properties is headquartered.

Gleissner's goal is to turn Cebu into a destination of choice for filmmakers who want to cut costs by shooting and finishing movies outside the United States, and when Bigfoot Entertainment finds a film suitable for financing and development, the deal usually requires the director to do some production work at the Cebu facility. By the time the studio opened in 2004, the Philippines were already an attractive location for animators looking for inexpensive post-production help, but the pool of talent available for work on live-action films was quite limited. Gleissner's solution? He founded the International Academy of Film and Television (IAFT), not only to staff Bigfoot Studios but also to train what executive director Keith Sensing calls "the next generation of global filmmakers." IAFT, says Sensing, looks for creative people who "have a desire for adventure" and "an education that will set them apart from people who have a strictly Hollywood background."

IAFT enrollment is currently 60 percent international and 40 percent Filipino, but "all of our students," says Sensing, "have the opportunity to participate in real projects going on at Bigfoot Studios … . Many IAFT graduates," he adds, "have gone on to write, produce, and direct their own films" and often follow in Bigfoot's steps by finding distribution for their independent features on the international festival circuit. Three recent graduates landed jobs on Gleissner's most recent project, a Philippines-set thriller revolving around a female diver. Gleissner not only cowrote and directed *Deep Gold* but also drew on his experience as an underwater photographer to shoot key scenes in Bigfoot's specially designed 170,000-gallon Underwater Studio.

In 2010, Bigfoot moved to expand into the areas of acquisition, distribution, and foreign sales with the purchase of Ascendant Pictures. Much like Bigfoot itself, Ascendant carved out its niche in the industry by integrating the budgeting sensibility of "indie" producers with the marketing skills of larger studios. "Our schools are profitable," explains Andrews, "but overall we're not profitable yet. We're hoping the distribution side will get us there in one or two years."

The new unit, called Bigfoot Ascendant Distribution, will buy four to six English-language movies annually—"genre films," says Andrews, "horror and action that will sell well internationally and play well theatrically, too." In order to bolster its ability to get its films into theaters (most of the company's features have gone straight to DVD or sold to cable TV), Bigfoot has also become the largest shareholder in Carmike Cinemas, the fourth-largest theater chain in the United States. In 2010, it also purchased the historic Majestic Crest Theater in Los Angeles. The acquisition, says Andrews, goes hand in hand with Bigfoot's purchase of Ascendant: "We wanted a great theater to showcase our films—not only ones we produce but also ones we plan to acquire. Everyone knows the Crest," she adds. "It gives us a lot of prestige."

Case Questions

1. In what ways is Bigfoot *innovative*? In what ways does it deal with *big business*? In what *industries* does it operate?
2. Which *niches* does Bigfoot serve in established markets? What *new markets* does it target? Can you think of any other niches or new markets that it should consider in the future?
3. Does Bigfoot have any *first-mover advantages*? If so, what are these advantages, and how important do you think they are now and will be in the future?

4. In what ways does Bigfoot rely on *distinctive competencies*? In what ways is experience in *international management* among these competencies? In what ways do you expect this particular competency to become even more important in the future?

Case References

Kellen Merrill, "The Big Imprint in the Film Industry," *inmag.com*, 2010, www.inmag.com, accessed on September 11, 2013; Stephanie N. Mehta, "Hollywood, South Pacific-Style," *CNNMoney.com*, accessed on June 8, 2006, http://money.cnn.com, accessed on September 11, 2013; Marlene Rodriguez, "Bigfoot Entertainment's International Academy of Film and Television in Mactan Island, Cebu," *NEDA Knowledge Emporium*, November 5, 2007, www.neda.gov.ph, accessed on September 11, 2013; Josh Elmets with Rebecca Pahle, "International Academy of Film and TV Flourishes in the Philippines," *MovieMaker*, January 29, 2010, www.moviemaker.com, accessed on September 11, 2013; Jonathan Landreth, "Bigfoot Entertainment Expands, Launches Distribution Company," *Hollywood Reporter*, November 2, 2010, www.hollywoodreporter.com, accessed on September 11, 2013; and Richard Verrier, "Indie Filmmaker Bigfoot Has an Insider Track to Theater," *Los Angeles Times*, October 6, 2010, http://articles.latimes.com, accessed on September 11, 2013.

Putting the Greek into Yogurt

1. What ingredients (no pun intended!) led to Hamdi Ulukaya's success with Chobani?
2. What are the distinctive competencies illustrated by Ulukaya?
3. Comment on the role that globalization has played in Chobani's success.
4. If Ulukaya were to ask you what strategy he should adopt going forward, what advice would you give him?

ENDNOTES

1 "How a Turkish Immigrant Made a Billion Dollars in Eight Years Selling … Yogurt, *Bloomberg Businessweek*, January 31, 2013, pp. 60–64; *Hoover's Handbook of World Business 2013* (Austin, Texas: Hoover's Business Press, 2013), pp. 450–451; "The World's 50 Most Innovative Companies in 2012," *Fast Company*, February 2013, p. 56; "A Conversation with the 'Steve Jobs of Yogurt'," *USA Today*, June 17, 2013, p. 3B.

2 See also John Byrne, "The 12 Greatest Entrepreneurs of Our Time—and What You Can Learn from Them," *Fortune*, April 9, 2012, pp. 68–86.

3 Bro Uttal, "Inside the Deal That Made Bill Gates $350,000,000," *Fortune*, July 21, 1986, pp. 23–33.

4 "The Richest People in America," *Forbes*, May 25, 2009.

[5] Murray B. Low and Ian MacMillan, "Entrepreneurship: Past Research and Future Challenges," *Journal of Management*, June 1988, pp. 139–159.

[6] U.S. Bureau of the Census, *Statistical Abstract of the United States, 2009* (Washington, DC: Government Printing Office, 2009).

[7] "Small Business 'Vital Statistics,'" http://www.sba.gov/category/navigation-structure/about-sba, accessed on July 17, 2012.

[8] "Small Business 'Vital Statistics,'" http://www.sba.gov/category/navigation-structure/about-sba, accessed on July 17, 2012.

[9] "Small Business 'Vital Statistics,'" http://www.sba.gov/category/navigation-structure/about-sba, accessed on July 17, 2012.

[10] "A World That's a-Twitter," *USA Today*, May 26, 2009, pp. 1B, 2B.

[11] "Heaven on Wheels," *Forbes*, April 13, 2009, pp. 74–75.

[12] Amar Bhide, "How Entrepreneurs Craft Strategies That Work," *Harvard Business Review*, March–April 1994, pp. 150–163.

[13] *Hoover's Handbook of American Business 2013* (Austin, TX: Hoover's Business Press, 2013), pp. 888–889; and "Peace, Love, and the Bottom Line," *BusinessWeek*, December 7, 1998, pp. 79–82.

[14] Nancy J. Lyons, "Moonlight over Indiana," *Inc.*, January 2000, pp. 71–74.

[15] F. M. Scherer, *Industrial Market Structure and Economic Performance*, 2nd ed. (Boston: Houghton Mifflin, 1980).

[16] "Three Biker-Entrepreneurs Take on Mighty Harley," *New York Times*, August 20, 1999, p. F1.

[17] "Burning Sensation," *Bloomberg Businessweek*, May 10, 2013, pp. 66–69.

[18] "A Startup's New Prescription for Eyewear," *Business Week*, July 4–10, 2011, pp. 49–51.

[19] D. Kirsch, B. Goldfarb, and A. Gera, "Form or Substance: The Role of Business Plans in Venture Capital Decision Making," *Strategic Management Journal*, Vol. 30, No. 5, 2009, pp. 487–516.

[20] "Online Rep Crucial for Small Companies," *USA Today*, October 30, 2012, p. 5B.

[21] "Doing Their Part for Your Perfect Party," *USA Today*, February 26, 2013, p. 4B.

[22] "Cheap Tricks," *Forbes*, February 21, 2000, p. 116.

[23] U.S. Bureau of the Census, *Statistical Abstract of the United States*, May 24, 2009 (Washington, DC: Government Printing Office, 2009). See also "Too Much Ventured, Nothing Gained," *Fortune*, November 25, 2002, pp. 135–144.

[24] "This Recession Isn't Being Kind to Entrepreneurs," *USA Today*, June 8, 2009, p. 1B.

[25] "Small Businesses Go Alternative for Loans," *USA Today*, November 14, 2012, p. 1B.

[26] "Up-and-Comers," *BusinessWeek*, May 15, 2000, pp. EB70–EB72.

[27] "High-Tech Advances Push CIA into New Company," *New York Times*, September 29, 1999, p. A14.

[28] "BET: African-Americans Grow in Numbers, Buying Power," *Multichannel News*, January 26, 2010.

[29] Norman M. Scarborough and Thomas W. Zimmerer, *Effective Small Business Management: An Entrepreneurial Approach*, 6th ed. (Upper Saddle River, N.J.: Prentice Hall, 2000), pp. 412–413.

[30] See Robert A. Baron, "The Role of Affect in the Entrepreneurial Process," *Academy of Management Review*, 2008, Vol. 33, No. 2, pp. 328–340. See also Keith M. Hmieleski and Robert A. Baron, "Entrepreneurs' Optimism and New Venture Performance: A Social Cognition Perspective," *Academy of Management Journal*, 2009, Vol. 52, No. 3, pp. 540–572.

[31] "Expert Entrepreneur Got Her Show on the Road at an Early Age," *USA Today*, May 24, 2000, p. 5B.

[32] "Flush Times for Liquidators," *Wall Street Journal*, January 20, 2009, p. B1.

[33] "Apocalypse 24/7," *Bloomberg Businessweek*, June 15, 2013, pp. 60–65.

CHAPTER 6

Organization Structure and Design

Learning Outcomes

After studying this chapter, you should be able to:

1 Identify the basic elements of organizations.

2 Describe the bureaucratic perspective on organization design.

3 Identify and explain key situational influences on organization design.

4 Describe the basic forms of organization design that characterize many organizations.

5 Identify and describe emerging issues in organization design.

Management in Action

Authority & Function at A&F

"Paying $90 for torn jeans isn't that cool anymore."

—Analyst on declining sales at Abercrombie & Fitch

Along with American Eagle and Aéropostale, Abercrombie & Fitch (A&F) is one of the "Three A's" of retailing for younger consumers, the three largest specialty retailers catering to young adults ages 18 to 22 (and up). Look around your college classroom and you'll probably spy at least one A&F item—a cap, a shirt, a pair of jeans. Abercrombie & Fitch, a line of "casual luxury" apparel and other products, is actually one of five brands owned by Ohio-based A&F Corporation. The company's other brands include abercrombie ("classic cool" for preteens), Hollister ("SoCal" for teenagers), RUEHL 925 (a higher-priced brand for post-collegiates that recently closed), and Gilly Hicks (Australian-themed lounge and underwear for women).

Obviously, A&F's businesses are related, and its overall corporate strategy is best characterized as one of *related diversification*. Based on this strategy, one would assume that A&F's organizational design reflects a *divisional* structure, a form favored by companies that operate multiple related businesses. It is interesting, however, that A&F relies instead on a *functional* design based on functional departments (groups responsible for specific company functions).

In general, some form of divisional structure is preferred by most firms that pursue strategies of related diversification. Limited Brands, for example, a close competitor (and one-time parent) of A&F, uses a divisional structure to coordinate

Nano Calvo/Alamy

Abercrombie & Fitch has been a fashion mainstay for younger consumers for years. Although the firm has grown to be a huge retailer, it still uses a form of organization design more commonly found in much smaller businesses.

brands such as Victoria's Secret, Bath & Body Works, Pink, and the White Barn Candle Company. Each unit is empowered to make autonomous decisions but can also access companywide staff support in areas such as logistics, information technology, real estate, and store design. At A&F, on the other hand, every employee is assigned to one of eight basic business functions, such as planning, purchasing, distribution, or stores, each of which is headed by a president. Why this design? Basically, A&F wants every employee to develop highly specialized skills within a functional area. This design is also more effective in coordinating activities within a function.

The company's history also accounts in part for its choice of a functional structure. From its founding in 1892 until a bankruptcy in 1977, Abercrombie & Fitch was a high-end sporting-goods retailer. In 1978, Oshman's, a Houston-based sporting-goods chain, purchased the company brand and trademark and, for 11 years, operated a combination retail chain and catalog company, selling an eclectic line of products ranging from tweed jackets to exercise machines. Limited Brands purchased the brand in 1988, putting it on preppy, upscale clothing for young adults. Nine years later, Limited sold 16 percent of the company through a public stock sale, and when the remaining shares were sold to the public in 1998, A&F became an independent company. In its current incarnation, then, A&F started out as a division of a larger firm, so it makes sense that its structure would be much like that of one division in a multidivisional corporation.

It's also interesting to note that, even before the spinoff from Limited, A&F had begun to establish its own culture and its own pattern of growth. Michael Jeffries, a retail-industry veteran, became president in 1992 and undertook to transform the company into the retailer of choice for younger consumers. Jeffries quickly managed to attach the brand to an idealized lifestyle, emphasizing apparel that complemented youth, good looks, and good times. The transformation turned out to be highly profitable, with sales increasing from $85 million in 1992 to $165 million in just two years. During the same period, the number of stores in the chain grew from 36 to 67, and in 1999, with 212 stores nationwide, A&F topped $1 billion in sales. In the same year, A&F started its abercrombie division for children and preteens, and a year later, it launched Hollister, the first of its "lifestyle" chains. By the end of 2002, the multidivision company was running 485 A&F stores, 144 abercrombie shops, and 32 Hollister outlets. Sales for the year were just under $1.4 billion. RUEHL opened in 2004 and Gilly Hicks in 2008. Today, A&F Corporation operates around 1,100 stores.

And yet A&F is still organized as if it were one big company with one big brand and a single division. The main advantage of this choice can be explained as a desire to exercise top-down control over each brand by separating and controlling all the functions on which every brand—that is, every store type—depends. Regardless of how A&F is organized and otherwise managed, one thing is clear: It's the way it is because that's the way CEO Jeffries wants it. Jeffries took over a firm that was losing $25 million a year, declared that survival depended on becoming a "young, hip, spirited company," and engineered a reversal of fortunes by turning it into something completely new, a retailer that celebrates what one observer calls "the vain, highly constructed male." (A&F has had much less influence on women's fashion.)

Like many other retailers, A&F struggled during 2009 and 2010. The firm had always refused to discount, so some customers began to look elsewhere. To help combat the downturn, A&F closed RUEHL and started offering some limited discounting. These measures, along with the rebounding economy, helped A&F start to turn things around recently. In 2013, the firm reported sales of $3.5 billion and a modest profit. Jeffries is under contract through 2014 but will likely retire when the contract expires.[1]

All managers need the assistance of others to succeed and so must trust the members of their team to do their jobs and carry out their responsibilities. And the team members themselves need the support of their boss and a clear understanding of their role in the organization. Indeed, the working relationship between managers and their subordinates is one of the most critical elements comprising an organization. As you will see in this chapter, managing the basic frameworks that organizations use to get their work done—structure and design—is a fundamental part of the management process.

This chapter, the first of three devoted to organizing, discusses many of the critical elements of organization structure and design that managers can control. We first identify and describe the various elements of organizing. Next, we explore how those elements can be combined to create an overall design for the organization. Next, we introduce situational factors and how they impact organization design. We conclude by presenting emerging issues in organization design.

THE BASIC ELEMENTS OF ORGANIZING

The term *organization structure and design* refers to the overall set of elements that can be used to configure an organization. This section introduces and describes these elements: job specialization, departmentalization, reporting relationships, distribution of authority, and coordination.

Job Specialization

job specialization
The degree to which the overall task of the organization is broken down and divided into smaller component parts

The first building block of organization structure is job specialization. **Job specialization** is the degree to which the overall task of the organization is broken down and divided into smaller component parts. For example, when Walt Disney started his company, he did everything himself—wrote cartoons, drew them, added character voices, and then marketed them to theaters. As the business grew, though, he eventually hired others to perform many of these same functions. As growth continued, so, too, did specialization. For example, as animation artists work on Disney movies today, they may specialize in generating computer images of a single character or doing only background scenery. Others provide voices, and marketing specialists develop promotional campaigns. Today, the Walt Disney Company has literally thousands of different specialized jobs. Clearly, no one person could perform them all.

Benefits and Limitations of Specialization
Job specialization provides four benefits to organizations.[2] First, workers performing small, simple tasks will become very proficient at each task. Second, transfer time between tasks decreases. If employees perform several different tasks, some time is lost as they stop doing the first task and start doing the next. Third, the more narrowly defined a job is, the easier it is to develop specialized equipment to assist with that job. Fourth, when an employee who performs a highly specialized job is absent or resigns, the manager is able to train someone new at relatively low cost. Although specialization is generally thought of in terms of operating jobs, many organizations have extended the basic elements of specialization to managerial and professional levels.[3]

On the other hand, job specialization can have negative consequences. The foremost criticism is that workers who perform highly specialized jobs may become bored and dissatisfied. The job may be so specialized that it offers no challenge or stimulation. Boredom and monotony set in, absenteeism rises, and the quality of the work may suffer. Furthermore, the anticipated benefits of specialization do not always occur. For example, a classic study conducted at Maytag found that the time spent moving work in process from one worker to another was greater than the time needed for the same individual to change from job to job.[4] Thus, although some degree of specialization is necessary, it should not be carried to extremes because of the possible negative consequences. Managers must be sensitive to situations in which extreme specialization should be avoided. And indeed, several alternative approaches to designing jobs have been developed in recent years.

job rotation
An alternative to job specialization that involves systematically moving employees from one job to another

Alternatives to Specialization
To counter the problems associated with specialization, managers have sought other approaches to job design that achieve a better balance between organizational demands for efficiency and productivity and individual needs for creativity and autonomy. Five alternative approaches are job rotation, job enlargement, job enrichment, job characteristics approach, and work teams.[5]

Job rotation involves systematically moving employees from one job to another. A worker in a warehouse might unload trucks on Monday, carry incoming inventory to storage on Tuesday, verify invoices on Wednesday, pull outgoing inventory from storage on Thursday, and load trucks on Friday. Thus, the jobs do not change, but instead workers move from job to job. Unfortunately, for this very reason, job rotation has not been very successful in enhancing employee motivation or satisfaction. Jobs that are amenable to rotation tend to be relatively standard and routine. Workers who are rotated to a "new" job may be more satisfied at first, but satisfaction soon wanes. Although many companies (among them Raytheon, Ford, and Prudential Insurance) have tried job rotation, it is most often used today as a training device to improve worker skills and flexibility. Similarly, the TSA rotates security screeners at airports several times a day to offset problems of boredom that might set in if the same task were being performed all the time. The Walt Disney World resort swimming pool lifeguards rotate stations every half hour to help them maintain focus on their task.

job enlargement
An alternative to job specialization that increases the total number of tasks that workers perform

Job enlargement was developed to increase the total number of tasks workers perform. As a result, all workers perform a wide variety of tasks, which presumably reduces the level of job dissatisfaction. Many organizations have used job enlargement, including IBM, Detroit Edison, AT&T, the U.S. Civil Service, and Maytag. At Maytag, for example, the assembly line for producing washing-machine water pumps was systematically changed so that work that had originally been performed by six workers, who passed the work sequentially from one person to another, was performed by four workers, each of whom assembled a complete pump.[6] Unfortunately, although job enlargement does have some positive consequences, those are often offset by some disadvantages: (1) training costs usually increase, (2) unions have argued that pay should increase because the worker is doing more tasks, and (3) in many cases the work remains boring and routine even after job enlargement.

Paulo Fridman/Corbis

Many products like Maytag washers and dryers are manufactured using job specialization and assembly line technology. While this approach promotes efficiency, it can also lead to monotony and worker boredom. To help counter these negative effects, Maytag has experimented with job enlargement and other alternatives to job specialization.

A more comprehensive approach, **job enrichment**, assumes that increasing the range and variety of tasks is not sufficient by itself to improve employee motivation.[7] Thus, job enrichment attempts to increase both the number of tasks a worker does and the control the worker has over the job. To implement job enrichment, managers remove some controls from the job, delegate more authority to employees, and structure the work in complete, natural units. These changes increase subordinates' sense of responsibility. Another part of job enrichment is to continually assign new and challenging tasks, thereby increasing employees' opportunity for growth and advancement. AT&T, Texas Instruments, IBM, and General Foods are among the firms that have used job enrichment. This approach, however, also has disadvantages. For example, work systems need to be analyzed before enrichment, but this seldom happens, and managers rarely ask for employee preferences when enriching jobs.

The **job characteristics approach** is an alternative to job specialization that does take into account the work system and employee preferences.[8] As illustrated in Figure 6.1, the job characteristics approach suggests that jobs should be diagnosed and improved along five core dimensions:

1. *Skill variety*, the number of things a person does in a job
2. *Task identity*, the extent to which the worker does a complete or identifiable portion of the total job
3. *Task significance*, the perceived importance of the task
4. *Autonomy*, the degree of control the worker has over how the work is performed
5. *Feedback*, the extent to which the worker knows how well the job is being performed

Increasing the presence of these dimensions in a job presumably leads to higher motivation, higher-quality performance, higher satisfaction, and lower absenteeism and turnover. A large number of studies have been conducted to test the usefulness of the job characteristics approach. The Southwestern Division of Prudential Insurance, for example, used this approach in its claims division. Results included moderate declines in turnover and a small but measurable improvement in work quality. Other research findings have not supported this approach as strongly. Thus, although the job characteristics approach is one of the most promising alternatives to job specialization, it is probably not the final answer.

Another alternative to job specialization is **work teams**. Under this arrangement, a group is given responsibility for designing the work system to be used in performing an interrelated set of tasks. In the typical assembly-line system, the work flows from one worker to the next, and each worker has a specified job to perform. In a work team, however, the group itself decides how jobs will be allocated. For example, the work team assigns specific tasks to members, monitors and controls its own performance, and has autonomy over work scheduling.[9]

Grouping Jobs: Departmentalization

The second element of organization structure is the grouping of jobs according to some logical arrangement. The process of grouping jobs is called **departmentalization**. When organizations are small, the owner-manager can personally oversee everyone who works there. As an organization grows, however, personally supervising all the employees becomes more and more difficult for the owner-manager. Consequently, new managerial positions are created to supervise the work of others. Employees are not assigned to particular managers randomly. Rather, jobs are grouped according to some plan. The logic embodied in such a plan is the basis for all departmentalization.[10]

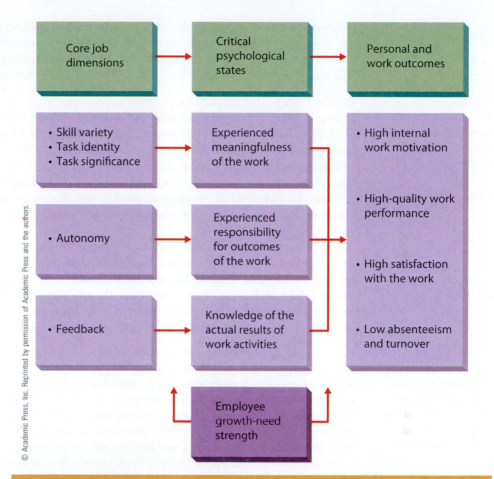

© Academic Press, Inc. Reprinted by permission of Academic Press and the authors.

FIGURE 6.1

The Job Characteristics Approach

The job characteristics approach to job design provides a viable alternative to job specialization. Five core job dimensions may lead to critical psychological states that, in turn, may enhance motivation, performance, and satisfaction while also reducing absenteeism and turnover.

Source: J. R. Hackman and G. R. Oldham, "Motivation through the Design of Work: Test of a Theory," *Organizational Behavior and Human Performance*, 1976, Vol. 16, pp. 250–279.

Functional Departmentalization   The most common base for departmentalization, especially among smaller organizations, is by function. **Functional departmentalization** groups together those jobs involving the same or similar activities. (The word *function* is used here to mean organizational functions such as finance and production, rather than the basic managerial functions, such as planning or controlling.) This approach, which is most common in smaller organizations, has three primary advantages. First, each department can be staffed by experts in that functional area. Marketing experts can be hired to run the marketing function, for example. Second, supervision is facilitated because an individual manager needs to be familiar with only a relatively narrow set of skills. And, third, coordinating activities inside each department is easier.

On the other hand, as an organization begins to grow in size, several disadvantages of this approach may emerge. For one, decision making tends to become slower and more

functional departmentalization
Grouping jobs involving the same or similar activities

bureaucratic. Employees may also begin to concentrate too narrowly on their own unit and lose sight of the total organizational system. Finally, accountability and performance become increasingly difficult to monitor. For example, determining whether a new product fails because of production deficiencies or a poor marketing campaign may not be possible.

product departmentalization
Grouping activities around products or product groups

Product Departmentalization   **Product departmentalization**, a second common approach, involves grouping and arranging activities around products or product groups. Most larger businesses adopt this form of departmentalization for grouping activities at the business or corporate level. Product departmentalization has three major advantages. First, all activities associated with one product or product group can be easily integrated and coordinated. Second, the speed and effectiveness of decision making are enhanced. Third, the performance of individual products or product groups can be assessed more easily and objectively, thereby improving the accountability of departments for the results of their activities.

Product departmentalization also has two major disadvantages. For one, managers in each department may focus on their own product or product group to the exclusion of the rest of the organization. For example, a marketing manager may see his or her primary duty as helping the group rather than helping the overall organization. For another, administrative costs rise because each department must have its own functional specialists for areas such as market research and financial analysis.

customer departmentalization
Grouping activities to respond to and interact with specific customers or customer groups

Customer Departmentalization   Under **customer departmentalization**, the organization structures its activities to respond to and interact with specific customers or customer groups. The lending activities in most banks, for example, are usually tailored to meet the needs of different kinds of customers (business, consumer, mortgage, and agricultural loans). The basic advantage of this approach is that the organization is able to use skilled specialists to deal with unique customers or customer groups. It takes one set of skills to evaluate a balance sheet and lend $5,000,000 for operating capital and a different set of skills to evaluate an individual's creditworthiness and lend $40,000 for a new car. However, a fairly large administrative staff is required to integrate the activities of the various departments. In banks, for example, coordination is necessary to make sure that the organization does not overcommit itself in any one area and to handle collections on delinquent accounts from a diverse set of customers.

location departmentalization
Grouping jobs on the basis of defined geographic sites or areas

Location Departmentalization   **Location departmentalization** groups jobs on the basis of defined geographic sites or areas. The defined sites or areas may range in size from a hemisphere to only a few blocks of a large city. Transportation companies, police departments (precincts represent geographic areas of a city), and the Federal Reserve Bank all use location departmentalization. The primary advantage of location departmentalization is that it enables the organization to respond easily to unique customer and environmental characteristics in the various regions. On the negative side, a larger administrative staff may be required if the organization must keep track of units in scattered locations.

Establishing Reporting Relationships

The third basic element of organizing is the establishment of reporting relationships among positions. The purpose of this activity is to clarify the chain of command and the span of management.

chain of command
A clear and distinct line of authority among the positions in an organization

Chain of Command   Chain of command is an old concept, first popularized in the early years of the twentieth century. For example, early writers about the **chain of command** argued that clear and distinct lines of authority need to be established among all positions in an organization. The chain of command actually has two components. The first, called *unity of command*, suggests that each person within an organization must have a clear reporting relationship to one and only one boss (as we see later, newer models of organization design routinely—and successfully—violate this premise). The second, called the *scalar principle*, suggests that there must be a clear and unbroken line of authority that extends from the lowest to the highest position in the organization. The popular saying "The buck stops here" is derived from this idea—someone in the organization must ultimately be responsible for every decision.

span of management

The number of people who report to a particular manager

Span of Management   Another part of establishing reporting relationships is determining how many people will report to each manager. This defines the **span of management** (sometimes called the *span of control*). For years, managers and researchers sought to determine the optimal span of management. Today, we recognize that the span of management is a crucial factor in structuring organizations but that there are no universal, cut-and-dried prescriptions for an ideal or optimal span.[11]

Tall Versus Flat Organizations   In recent years, managers have begun to focus attention on the optimal number of layers in their organizational hierarchy. Having more layers results in a taller organization, whereas having fewer layers results in a flatter organization. What difference does it make whether the organization is tall or flat? One early study at Sears found that a flat structure led to higher levels of employee morale and productivity.[12] Researchers have also argued that a tall structure is more expensive (because of the larger number of managers involved) and that it fosters more communication problems (because of the increased number of people through whom information must pass). On the other hand, a wide span of management in a flat organization may result in a manager having more administrative responsibility (because there are fewer managers) and more supervisory responsibility (because there are more subordinates reporting to each manager). If these additional responsibilities become excessive, the flat organization may suffer.[13]

Many experts agree that businesses can function effectively with fewer layers of organization than they currently have. The Franklin Mint, for example, reduced its number of management layers from 6 to 4. At the same time, the CEO increased his span of management from 6 to 12. The British firm Cadbury PLC, maker of Cadbury Dairy chocolates, Trident gum, and other confectionary products, recently eliminated a layer of management separating the CEO and the firm's operating units. The specific reasons for the change were to improve communication between the CEO and the operating unit heads and to speed up decision making.[14] The "Leading the Way" feature provides another recent example of a CEO leading a firm toward a flatter organization. One additional reason for this trend is that improved communication technologies such as e-mail and text messaging allow managers to stay in touch with a larger number of subordinates than was possible even just a few years ago.[15]

Distributing Authority

authority

Power that has been legitimized by the organization

Another important building block in structuring organizations is the determination of how authority is to be distributed among positions. **Authority** is power that has been legitimized by the organization.[16] Two specific issues that managers must address when distributing authority are delegation and decentralization.[17]

delegation

The process by which a manager assigns a portion of his or her total workload to others

The Delegation Process   Delegation is the establishment of a pattern of authority between a superior and one or more subordinates. Specifically, **delegation** is the process by which managers assign a portion of their total workload to others.[18] In theory, the delegation process involves three steps. First, the manager assigns responsibility or gives

LEADING THE WAY

Delayering as a Defense Mechanism

When Cynthia Carroll was appointed CEO of Anglo American PLC, the firm employed a rigid, bureaucratic structure. Ms. Carroll has been actively working to make Anglo American more responsive and flexible by eliminating layers of management.

AP Images/Dan Joling

Anglo American PLC, one of the world's largest diversified mining companies, recently announced that it was *delayering*—eliminating a layer of its organizational structure. Previously, the company had been organized into two global divisions—Coal and Ferrous Metals, each with its own CEO, both of whom reported directly to the CEO of Anglo American. Below the divisional level were Anglo's various global business operations, each dealing with a different commodity (e.g., coal, platinum, and iron ore) and each headed by its own CEO and functional support staff. The CEOs of these units reported directly to the CEO of his or her respective division.

As a result of "simplification and delayering," these businesses were reorganized into seven "commodity business units" (BUs), each of which is now "profit accountable"—that is, responsible for its own performance. The major criteria for this reorganization were geography and asset status. The platinum unit, for example, is headquartered in South Africa (which is also home to the parent company), the copper unit in Chile, and the metallurgical–coal unit in Australia.

Times have been hectic for Anglo. In February 2009, CEO Cynthia Carroll admitted that the organization, like many companies, was starting to feel the impact of the global recession. Her whirlwind campaign to cut costs by $450 million earned her the nickname "Cyclone Cynthia." Then the Swiss–British mining company Xstrata proposed a merger with Anglo. Carroll and the Anglo board quickly rejected Xstrata's offer as "totally unacceptable," and Carroll presented both Anglo's mid-year financial results and its argument for remaining independent. "Frankly," asserted Carroll,

> I know what it is that we need to do. … We have a strategy, we have clear goals, we have tremendous assets … in the most attractive commodities in the world. The opportunities are massive. … We're well aware of what Xstrata does, but I'm very confident of what we can do in the future.

Xstrata subsequently withdrew its offer in the face of resistance from the Anglo board. "Anglo," said a company spokesman, "can now move forward and run our business without further distraction." One analyst predicted that Anglo "will likely show a renewed sense of urgency … and pull out all the stops to win shareholders over," and exactly one week later, Carroll announced her "simplification and delayering" plan. In making the announcement, she asked shareholders for more time to develop the firm's assets and prove its value as an independent company. "The portfolio changes we have announced," she argued, "… will position Anglo American well for sustained, profitable growth in the commodities we have identified as being the most attractive."

References: Jeffrey Sparshott, "Miner Anglo to Sell Assets in Shake-Up," *Wall Street Journal*, October 22, 2009, http://www.dailytenders.co.za, accessed on November 13, 2013; Kate Holton et al., "Xstrata Seeks $68 Billion Merger with Anglo," *Reuters*, June 21, 2009, www.reuters.com, accessed on November 13, 2013; Julia Werdigier, "Xstrata Makes a New Move for Merger with Anglo," *New York Times*, June 25, 2009, www.nytimes.com, accessed on November 13, 2013; Martin Waller and David Robinson, "Business Big Shot: Cynthia Carroll of Anglo American," *The Times* (London) Online, August 1, 2009, www.thetimes.co.uk/tto/business, accessed on November 13, 2013; Andrew Cave, "Cynthia Carroll Digs Deep for Anglo," *Telegraph*, August 1, 2009, www.telegraph.co.uk, accessed on November 13, 2013; and Julia Werdigier, "Xstrata Ends Bid for Rival in London," *New York Times*, October 16, 2009, www.nytimes.com, accessed on November 13, 2013.

the subordinate a job to do. The assignment of responsibility might range from telling a subordinate to prepare a report to placing the person in charge of a task force. Along with the assignment, the individual is also given the authority to do the job. The manager may give the subordinate the power to requisition needed information from confidential files or to direct a group of other workers. Finally, the manager establishes the subordinate's accountability—that is, the subordinate accepts an obligation to carry out the task assigned by the manager. For instance, the CEO of AutoZone will sign off for the company on financial performance only when the individual manager responsible for each unit has certified his or her own results as being accurate. The firm believes that this high level of accountability will help it avoid the kind of accounting scandal that has hit many businesses in recent times.[19]

decentralization
The process of systematically delegating power and authority throughout the organization to middle- and lower-level managers

centralization
The process of systematically retaining power and authority in the hands of higher-level managers

Decentralization and Centralization

Just as authority can be delegated from one individual to another, organizations also develop patterns of authority across a wide variety of positions and departments. **Decentralization** is the process of systematically delegating power and authority throughout the organization to middle- and lower-level managers. It is important to remember that decentralization is actually one end of a continuum anchored at the other end by **centralization**, the process of systematically retaining power and authority in the hands of higher-level managers. Hence, a decentralized organization is one in which decision-making power and authority are delegated as far down the chain of command as possible. Conversely, in a centralized organization, decision-making power and authority are retained at higher levels in the organization.

What factors determine an organization's position on the decentralization–centralization continuum? One common determinant is the organization's external environment. Usually, the greater the complexity and uncertainty of the environment, the greater is the tendency to decentralize. Another crucial factor is the history of the organization. Firms have a tendency to do what they have done in the past, so there is likely to be some relationship between what an organization did in its early history and what it chooses to do today in terms of centralization or decentralization. The nature of the decisions being made is also considered. The costlier and riskier the decisions, the more pressure there is to centralize. In short, managers have no clear-cut guidelines for determining whether to centralize or decentralize. Many successful organizations, such as General Electric and Johnson & Johnson, are quite decentralized. Equally successful firms, such as McDonald's and Walmart, have remained centralized.

IBM has recently undergone a transformation from using a highly centralized approach to a much more decentralized approach to managing its operations. A great deal of decision-making authority was passed from the hands of a select group of top executives down to six product and marketing groups. The reason for the move was to speed up the company's ability to make decisions, introduce new products, and respond to customers. Similarly, Toyota recently announced its intent to provide more autonomy to country managers, especially those in the United States. This move came in part because of poor and slow decision making during a recent quality crisis involving Toyota products.[20]

In contrast, Royal Dutch Shell, long operated in a highly decentralized manner, has recently gone through several major changes all intended to make the firm more centralized. New CEO Peter Voser went so far as to note that "fewer people will make strategic decisions."[21] Yahoo! Inc. has also initiated a change to become more centralized.[22] The "At Your Service" feature provides an interesting example of how Best Buy created authority for its chief ethics officer.

AT YOUR SERVICE

A Panel of Your Peers

Kathleen Edmond is chief ethics officer at Best Buy, the world's largest consumer-electronics retailer. To help people better understand the role of ethics in a service business, Edmond posted the following exercise (which we've edited slightly) on her website at www.kathleenedmond.com:

A Best Buy Supervisor (a department manager responsible for seeing that merchandising and pricing standards are met) told a direct-report employee to put an "open item" tag on an unused, undamaged product. The tag would indicate that the product might later be priced at a markdown. The Supervisor explained that he was thinking about buying the product but wasn't sure and instructed the employee to put the "open item" price tag beneath a regular price tag until he'd made up his mind. The Supervisor did not buy this particular item but did buy other products at markdowns of 55–65 percent. As it happens, the employee who had been told to place the "open item" price tag on the new product rang up these purchases.

He reported that when another manager was called to the register to authorize the markdowns, he was assured by the Supervisor that the store's Product Process Manager (a higher-level manager responsible for merchandising, inventory, and loss prevention for the whole store) knew about the transaction. When questioned later about the purchases, the Supervisor confirmed that he'd spoken about them to the Product Process Manager. The Product Process Manager said that the Supervisor had indeed expressed an interest in buying some products but had provided no specifics about products or pricing.

At the end of this summary, Edmond addressed the following questions to Best Buy employees:

- What ethical missteps do you see in this story?
- Which of the Supervisor's actions were most alarming to you and why?

- Are there procedures in place that could prevent this from happening at your store?

Following established procedure, Edmond referred the dispute, at the Supervisor's request, to a Peer Review panel, which examined statements from all employees involved as well as the company's policy on Inappropriate Conduct. After a decision had been reached by the panel, Edmond posted its Decision Summary:

1. The discount applied was not consistent with other pricing of open-box items.
2. The pricing of the Supervisor's purchases seemed to be based on the fact that the Supervisor was purchasing them rather than on the condition of the products themselves.
3. Management was not involved in these pricing decisions.
4. The instructions to the subordinate to hide a price were considered.

So, what do you think? Given the factors considered by the Peer Review panel, what action should the company have taken?

References: Ethics and Compliance Officer Association, "Kathleen Edmond, Chief Ethics Officer, Best Buy," Board of Directors, 2011, www.theecoa.org, accessed on November 13, 2013; Best Buy Inc., "Code of Business Ethics," 2008, www.bestbuy.com, accessed on November 13, 2013; and Kathleen Edmond, "Supervisor Takes Massive Discounts," Kathleen Edmond, Best Buy's Chief Ethics Officer, January 13, 2009, www.kathleenedmond.com, accessed on November 13, 2013.

(*Note:* In the real situation, a decision to terminate the supervisor was originally made by his superiors, and his request for a hearing before the Peer Review panel was made as an appeal to this decision. The decision to terminate was upheld.)

Coordinating Activities

The fifth major element of organizing is coordination. As we discussed earlier, job specialization and departmentalization involve breaking down jobs into small units and then combining those jobs into departments. Once this has been accomplished, the activities of the departments must be linked—systems must be put into place to keep the activities of each department focused on the attainment of organizational goals. This is

coordination
The process of linking the activities of the various departments of the organization

accomplished by **coordination**—the process of linking the activities of the various departments of the organization.[23]

The Need for Coordination

The primary reason for coordination is that departments and work groups are interdependent—they depend on one another for information and resources to perform their respective activities. The greater the interdependence between departments, the more coordination the organization requires if departments are to be able to perform effectively. The three major forms of interdependence are pooled, sequential, and reciprocal.[24]

pooled interdependence
When units operate with little interaction; their output is pooled at the organizational level

Pooled interdependence represents the lowest level of interdependence. Units with pooled interdependence operate with little interaction—the output of the units is pooled at the organizational level. Old Navy clothing stores operate with pooled interdependence. Each store is considered a "department" by the parent corporation. Each has its own operating budget, staff, and so forth. The profits or losses from each store are "added together" at the organizational level. The stores are interdependent to the extent that the final success or failure of one store affects the others, but they do not generally interact on a day-to-day basis.

sequential interdependence
When the output of one unit becomes the input for another in a sequential fashion

In **sequential interdependence**, the output of one unit becomes the input for another in a sequential fashion. This creates a moderate level of interdependence. At Nissan, for example, one plant assembles engines and then ships them to a final assembly site at another plant, where the cars are completed. The plants are interdependent in that the final assembly plant must have the engines from engine assembly before it can perform its primary function of producing finished automobiles. But the level of interdependence is generally one way—the engine plant is not necessarily dependent on the final assembly plant.

reciprocal interdependence
When activities flow both ways between units

Reciprocal interdependence exists when activities flow both ways between units. This form is clearly the most complex. Within a Marriott hotel, for example, the reservations department, front-desk check-in, and housekeeping are all reciprocally interdependent. Reservations has to provide front-desk employees with information about how many guests to expect each day, and housekeeping needs to know which rooms require priority cleaning. If any of the three units does not do its job properly, all the others will be affected.

Structural Coordination Techniques

Because of the obvious coordination requirements that characterize most organizations, many techniques for achieving coordination have been developed. Some of the most useful devices for maintaining coordination among interdependent units are the managerial hierarchy, rules and procedures, liaison roles, task forces, and integrating departments.[25]

Organizations that use the hierarchy to achieve coordination place one manager in charge of interdependent departments or units. In Walmart distribution centers, major activities include receiving and unloading bulk shipments from railroad cars and loading other shipments onto trucks for distribution to retail outlets. The two groups (receiving and shipping) are interdependent in that they share the loading docks and some equipment. To ensure coordination and minimize conflict, one manager is in charge of the whole operation.

Routine coordination activities can be handled through rules and standard procedures. In the Walmart distribution center, an outgoing truck shipment has priority over an incoming rail shipment. Thus, when trucks are to be loaded, the shipping unit is given access to all of the center's auxiliary forklifts. This priority is specifically stated in a rule. But, as useful as rules and procedures often are in routine situations, they are not particularly effective when coordination problems are complex or unusual.

As a device for coordination, a manager in a liaison role coordinates interdependent units by acting as a common point of contact. This individual may not have any formal authority over the groups but instead simply facilitates the flow of information between units. Two engineering groups working on component systems for a large project might interact through a liaison. The liaison maintains familiarity with each group as well as with the overall project. She can answer questions and otherwise serve to integrate the activities of all the groups.

A task force may be created when the need for coordination is acute. When interdependence is complex and several units are involved, a single liaison person may not be sufficient. Instead, a task force might be assembled by drawing one representative from each group. The coordination function is thus spread across several individuals, each of whom has special information about one of the groups involved. When the project is completed, task force members return to their original positions. For example, a college overhauling its degree requirements might establish a task force made up of representatives from each department affected by the change. Each person not only retains his or her regular departmental affiliation and duties but also serves on the special task force. After the new requirements are agreed on, the task force is dissolved.

Integrating departments are occasionally used for coordination. These are somewhat similar to task forces but are more permanent. An integrating department generally has some permanent members as well as members who are assigned temporarily from units that are particularly in need of coordination. One study found that successful firms in the plastics industry, which is characterized by complex and dynamic environments, used integrating departments to maintain internal integration and coordination.[26] An integrating department usually has more authority than a task force and may even be given some budgetary control by the organization.

Electronic Coordination   Advances in information technology are also providing useful mechanisms for coordination. E-mail, for example, makes it easier for people to communicate with one another. This communication, in turn, enhances coordination. Similarly, many people in organizations today use electronic scheduling, at least some of which is accessible to others. Hence, if someone needs to set up a meeting with two colleagues, he or she can often check their electronic schedules to determine their availability, making it easier to coordinate their activities.

Local networks, increasingly managed by handheld electronic devices, are also making it easier to coordinate activities. Bechtel, for example, now requires its contractors, subcontractors, and suppliers to use a common web-based communication system to improve coordination among their myriad activities. The firm estimates that this improved coordination technology routinely saves it thousands of dollars on every big construction project it undertakes.

THE BUREAUCRATIC MODEL OF ORGANIZATION DESIGN

bureaucracy
A model of organization design based on a legitimate and formal system of authority

Max Weber, an influential German sociologist, was a pioneer of classical organization theory. At the core of Weber's writings was the bureaucratic model of organizations.[27] The Weberian perspective suggests that a **bureaucracy** is a model of organization design based on a legitimate and formal system of authority. Many people associate bureaucracy with "red tape," rigidity, and passing the buck. For example, how many times have you heard people refer disparagingly to "the federal bureaucracy"? Many U.S. managers believe that bureaucracy in the Chinese government is a major impediment to U.S. firms' ability to do business there.

Weber viewed the bureaucratic form of organization as logical, rational, and efficient. He offered the model as a framework to which all organizations should aspire—the "one best way" of doing things. According to Weber, the ideal bureaucracy exhibits five basic characteristics:

1. The organization should adopt a distinct division of labor, and each position should be filled by an expert.
2. The organization should develop a consistent set of rules to ensure that task performance is uniform.
3. The organization should establish a hierarchy of positions or offices that creates a chain of command from the top of the organization to the bottom.
4. Managers should conduct business in an impersonal way and maintain an appropriate social distance between themselves and their subordinates.
5. Employment and advancement in the organization should be based on technical expertise, and employees should be protected from arbitrary dismissal.

Perhaps the best examples of bureaucracies today are government agencies and universities. Consider, for example, the steps you must go through and the forms you must fill out to apply for admission to college, request housing, register each semester, change majors, submit a degree plan, substitute a course, and file for graduation. Even when paper is replaced with electronic media, the steps are often the same. The reason these procedures are necessary is that universities deal with large numbers of people who must be treated equally and fairly. Hence, rules, regulations, and standard operating procedures are needed. Large labor unions are also usually organized as bureaucracies.[28]

Some bureaucracies, such as the U.S. Postal Service, have been trying to portray themselves as less mechanistic and impersonal. The strategy of the Postal Service is to become more service oriented as a way to fight back against competitors such as FedEx and UPS.

A primary strength of the bureaucratic model is that several of its elements (such as reliance on rules and employment based on expertise) do, in fact, often improve efficiency. Bureaucracies also help prevent favoritism (because everyone must follow the rules) and make procedures and practices very clear to everyone. Unfortunately, however, this approach also has several disadvantages. One major disadvantage is that the bureaucratic model results in inflexibility and rigidity. Once rules are created and put in place, making exceptions or changing them is often difficult. In addition, the bureaucracy often results in the neglect of human and social processes within the organization.

situational view of organization design
Based on the assumption that the optimal design for any given organization depends on a set of relevant situational factors

SITUATIONAL INFLUENCES ON ORGANIZATION DESIGN

The **situational view of organization design** is based on the assumption that the optimal design for any given organization depends on a set of relevant situational factors. In other words, situational factors play a role in determining the best organization design for any particular circumstance.[29] Four basic situational factors—technology, environment, size, and organizational life cycle—are discussed here.

Fidelity Investments uses technology to transform investment dollars into growth and income for investors. This technology, in turn, plays a significant role in the kind of organization design that best serves Fidelity. Other firms that use different technologies, meanwhile, will likely use different forms of organization design.

NetPhotos/Alamy

Core Technology

technology
Conversion process used to transform inputs into outputs

Technology consists of the conversion processes used to transform inputs (such as materials or information) into outputs (such as products or services). Most organizations use multiple technologies, but an organization's most important one is called its core *technology*. Although most people visualize assembly lines and machinery when they think of technology, the term can also be applied to service organizations. For example, an investment firm like Fidelity uses technology to transform investment dollars into income in much the same way that Union Carbide uses natural resources to manufacture chemical products.

The link between technology and organization design was first recognized by Joan Woodward.[30] Woodward studied 100 manufacturing firms in southern England. She collected information about aspects such as the history of each organization, its manufacturing processes, its forms and procedures, and its financial performance. Woodward expected to find a relationship between the size of an organization and its design, but no such relationship emerged. As a result, she began to seek other explanations for differences. Close scrutiny of the firms in her sample led her to recognize a potential relationship between technology and organization design. This follow-up analysis led Woodward to first classify the organizations according to their technology. Three basic forms of technology were identified by Woodward:

1. *Unit or small-batch technology.* The product is custom-made to customer specifications or produced in small quantities. Organizations using this form of technology include a tailor shop specializing in custom suits, a printing shop that produces business cards and company stationery, and a photography studio.

2. *Large-batch or mass-production technology.* The product is manufactured in assembly-line fashion by combining component parts into another part or finished product. Examples include automobile manufacturers like Subaru, appliance makers like Whirlpool Corporation, and electronics firms like Philips.
3. *Continuous-process technology.* Raw materials are transformed to a finished product by a series of machine or process transformations. The composition of the materials themselves is changed. Examples include petroleum refineries like ExxonMobil and Shell, and chemical refineries like Dow Chemical and Hoechst AG.

These forms of technology are listed in order of their assumed levels of complexity. In other words, unit or small-batch technology is presumed to be the least complex and continuous-process technology the most complex. Woodward found that different configurations of organization design were associated with each technology.

Specifically, Woodward found that the two extremes (unit or small-batch and continuous-process) tended to have very little bureaucracy, whereas the middle-range organizations (large-batch or mass-production) were much more bureaucratic. The large-batch and mass-production organizations also had a higher level of specialization.[31] Finally, she found that organizational success was related to the extent to which organizations followed the typical pattern. For example, successful continuous-process organizations tended to have less bureaucracy, whereas less successful firms with the same technology tended to be more bureaucratic.

Environment

Environmental elements and organization design are specifically linked in a number of ways.[32] The first widely recognized analysis of environment–organization design linkages was provided by Tom Burns and G. M. Stalker.[33] Like Woodward, Burns and Stalker worked in England. Their first step was identifying two extreme forms of organizational environment: stable (one that remains relatively constant over time) and unstable (subject to uncertainty and rapid change). Next, they studied the designs of organizations in each type of environment. It was no surprise that they found that organizations in stable environments tended to have a different kind of design than organizations in unstable environments. The two kinds of design that emerged were called mechanistic and organic organization.

mechanistic organization
Similar to the bureaucratic model, most frequently found in stable environments

A **mechanistic organization**, quite similar to the bureaucratic model, was most frequently found in stable environments. Free from uncertainty, organizations structured their activities in rather predictable ways by means of rules, specialized jobs, and centralized authority. Mechanistic organizations are also quite similar to bureaucracies. Although no environment is completely stable, Abercrombie & Fitch and Wendy's use mechanistic designs. Each A&F store, for example, has prescribed methods for store design and merchandise-ordering processes. Little or no deviation is allowed from these methods. An **organic organization**, on the other hand, was most often found in unstable and unpredictable environments, in which constant change and uncertainty usually dictate a much higher level of fluidity and flexibility. Motorola (facing rapid technological change) and Apple (facing both technological change and constant change in consumer tastes) both use organic designs. A manager at Motorola, for example, has considerable discretion over how work is performed and how problems can be solved.

organic organization
Very flexible and informal model of organization design, most often found in unstable and unpredictable environments

These ideas were extended in the United States by Paul R. Lawrence and Jay W. Lorsch.[34] They agreed that environmental factors influence organization design but believed that this influence varies between different units of the same organization. In fact, they predicted that each organizational unit has a unique environment and responds by developing unique attributes. Lawrence and Lorsch suggested that organizations could be characterized along two primary dimensions.

differentiation
Extent to which the organization is broken down into subunits

One of these dimensions, **differentiation**, is the extent to which the organization is broken down into subunits. A firm with many subunits is highly differentiated; one with few subunits has a low level of differentiation. The second dimension, **integration**, is the degree to which the various subunits must work together in a coordinated fashion. For example, if each unit competes in a different market and has its own production facilities, they may need little integration. Lawrence and Lorsch reasoned that the degree of differentiation and integration needed by an organization depends on the stability of the environments that its subunits face.

integration
Degree to which the various subunits must work together in a coordinated fashion

Organizational Size and Life Cycle

organizational size
Total number of full-time or full-time–equivalent employees

The size and life cycle of an organization may also affect its design.[35] Although several definitions of size exist, we define **organizational size** as the total number of full-time or full-time–equivalent employees. A team of researchers at the University of Aston in Birmingham, England, believed that Woodward had failed to find a size–structure relationship (which was her original expectation) because almost all the organizations she studied were relatively small (three-fourths had fewer than 500 employees).[36] Thus, they decided to undertake a study of a wider array of organizations to determine how size and technology both individually and jointly affect an organization's design.

Their primary finding was that technology did in fact influence structural variables in small firms, probably because all their activities tend to be centered on their core technologies. In large firms, however, the strong technology–design link broke down, most likely because technology is not as central to ongoing activities in large organizations. The Aston studies yielded a number of basic generalizations: When compared to small organizations, large organizations tend to be characterized by higher levels of job specialization, more standard operating procedures, more rules, more regulations, and a greater degree of decentralization. Walmart is a good case in point. The firm expects to continue its dramatic growth for the foreseeable future, adding several thousand new jobs in the next few years. But, as it grows, the firm acknowledges that it will have to become more decentralized for its first-line managers to stay in tune with their customers.[37] Of course, size is not constant. As we noted in Chapter 5, for example, some small businesses are formed but soon disappear. Others remain as small, independently operated enterprises as long as their owner-manager lives. A few, such as Dell Computer, JetBlue, and Starbucks, skyrocket to become organizational giants. And occasionally, large organizations reduce their size through layoffs or divestitures. Marathon Oil, for instance, recently announced that it would be spinning off its downstream business, creating two independent businesses and significantly reducing the size of its business.[38] Consequently, Marathon is becoming a much smaller organization.

organizational life cycle
Progression through which organizations evolve as they grow and mature

Although no clear pattern explains changes in size, many organizations progress through a four-stage **organizational life cycle**.[39] The first stage is the birth of the organization. The second stage, youth, is characterized by growth and the expansion of organizational resources. Midlife is a period of gradual growth evolving eventually into stability. Finally, maturity is a period of stability, perhaps eventually evolving into decline. Firms like Netflix and Starbucks, for instance, are still in their youth stage; Halliburton and Chevron are in midlife; and Ford and Boeing are in maturity. (A key challenge for managers, of course, is to avoid allowing a mature organization to begin to decline. Hence, they must be alert for opportunities to reenergize the organization with new products and new markets.)

Managers must confront a number of organization design issues as the organization progresses through these stages. In general, as an organization passes from one stage to the next, it becomes bigger, more mechanistic, and more decentralized. It also becomes more specialized, devotes more attention to planning, and takes on an increasingly large staff component. Finally, coordination demands increase, formalization increases, organizational units become geographically more dispersed, and control systems become more extensive. Thus, an organization's size and design are clearly linked, and this link is dynamic because of the organizational life cycle.[40]

BASIC FORMS OF ORGANIZATION DESIGN

Because technology, environment, size, and life cycle can all influence organization design, it should come as no surprise that organizations adopt many different kinds of designs. Most designs, however, fall into one of four basic categories. Others are hybrids based on two or more of the basic forms.

Functional (U-Form) Design

functional design
Based on the functional approach to departmentalization

The **functional design** is an arrangement based on the functional approach to departmentalization. This design has been termed the *U-form* (for unitary) approach.[41] Under the U-form arrangement, the members and units in the organization are grouped into functional departments such as marketing and production.

For the organization to operate efficiently in this design, there must be considerable coordination across departments. This integration and coordination are most commonly the responsibility of the CEO and members of senior management. Figure 6.2 shows the U-form design applied to the corporate level of a small manufacturing company. In a U-form organization, none of the functional areas can survive without the others. Marketing, for example, needs products from operations to sell and funds from finance

© Cengage Learning

FIGURE 6.2

Functional (U-Form) Design for a Small Manufacturing Company

The U-form design is based on functional departmentalization. This small manufacturing firm uses managers at the vice presidential level to coordinate activities within each functional area of the organization. Note that each functional area is dependent on the others.

to pay for advertising. The WD-40 Company, which makes a popular lubricating oil, and the McIlhenny Company, which makes tabasco sauce, are both examples of firms that use the U-form design.

In general, this approach shares the basic advantages and disadvantages of functional departmentalization. Thus, it allows the organization to staff all important positions with functional experts, and it facilitates coordination and integration. On the other hand, it also promotes a functional, rather than an organizational, focus and tends to promote centralization. Functionally based designs are most commonly used in small organizations because an individual CEO can easily oversee and coordinate the entire organization. As an organization grows, the CEO finds staying on top of all functional areas increasingly difficult.

Conglomerate (H-Form) Design

conglomerate design

Used by an organization made up of a set of unrelated businesses

Another common form of organization design is the conglomerate, or *H-form* (for holding, as in holding company), approach.[42] The **conglomerate design** is used by an organization made up of a set of unrelated businesses. Thus, the H-form design is essentially a holding company that results from unrelated diversification.

This approach is based loosely on the product form of departmentalization. Each business or set of businesses is operated by a general manager who is responsible for its profits or losses, and each general manager functions independently of the others. Samsung Electronics Company, a South Korean firm, uses the H-form design. As illustrated in Figure 6.3, Samsung consists of four basic business groups. Other firms that use the H-form design include General Electric (aircraft engines, appliances, medical equipment, financial services, lighting products, plastics, and other unrelated businesses) and Tenneco (pipelines, auto parts, financial services, and other unrelated businesses). Honeywell has also recently adopted the H-form design.[43]

In an H-form organization, a corporate staff usually evaluates the performance of each business, allocates corporate resources across companies, and shapes decisions about buying and selling businesses. The basic shortcoming of the H-form design is the complexity associated with holding diverse and unrelated businesses. Managers usually find it difficult to compare and integrate activities across a large number of diverse operations. Research suggests that many organizations following this approach achieve only average-to-weak financial performance.[44] Thus, although some U.S. firms are still using the H-form design, many have abandoned it for other approaches.

© Cengage Learning

FIGURE 6.3

Conglomerate (H-Form) Design at Samsung

Samsung Electronics Company, a South Korean firm, uses the conglomerate form of organization design. This design, which results from a strategy of unrelated diversification, is a complex one to manage. Managers find that comparing and integrating activities among the dissimilar operations are difficult. Companies may abandon this design for another approach, such as the M-form design.

© Cengage Learning

FIGURE 6.4

Multidivisional (M-Form) Design at Hilton Hotels

Hilton Hotels uses the multidivisional approach to organization design. Although each unit operates with relative autonomy, all units function in the same general market. This design resulted from a strategy of related diversification. Other firms that use M-form designs include PepsiCo and the Walt Disney Company.

Divisional (M-Form) Design

divisional design
Based on multiple businesses in related areas operating within a larger organizational framework

In the **divisional design**, which is becoming increasingly popular, a product form of organization is also used; in contrast to the H-form approach, however, the divisions are related. Thus the divisional design, or *M-form* (for multidivisional) approach, is based on multiple businesses in related areas operating within a larger organizational framework. This design results from a strategy of related diversification.

Some activities are extremely decentralized down to the divisional level; others are centralized at the corporate level.[45] For example, as shown in Figure 6.4, Hilton Hotels uses this approach. Each of its divisions is headed by a president or executive vice president and operates with reasonable autonomy, but the divisions also coordinate their activities as is appropriate. Other firms that use this approach are the Walt Disney Company (theme parks, movies, and merchandising units, all interrelated) and Hewlett-Packard (computers, printers, scanners, electronic medical equipment, and other electronic instrumentation).

The opportunities for coordination and shared resources represent one of the biggest advantages of the M-form design. Hilton's market research and purchasing departments are centralized. Thus, a site selector can visit a city and look for possible locations for different Hilton brands, and a buyer can purchase bed linens for multiple Hilton brands from the same supplier. The M-form design's basic objective is to optimize internal competition and cooperation. Healthy competition for resources among divisions can enhance effectiveness, but cooperation should also be promoted. Research suggests that the M-form organization that can achieve and maintain this balance will outperform large U-form and all H-form organizations.[46]

Matrix Design

matrix design
Based on two overlapping bases of departmentalization

The **matrix design**, another common approach to organization design, is based on two overlapping bases of departmentalization.[47] The foundation of a matrix is a set of functional departments. A set of product groups, or temporary departments, is then superimposed across the functional departments. Employees in a matrix are simultaneously members of a functional department (such as engineering) and of a project team.

Figure 6.5 shows a basic matrix design. At the top of the organization are functional units headed by vice presidents of engineering, production, finance, and marketing. Each of these managers has several subordinates. Along the side of the organization are a number of positions called *project manager*. Each project manager heads a project

© Cengage Learning

FIGURE 6.5

A Matrix Organization

A matrix organization design is created by superimposing a product form of departmentalization on an existing functional organization. Project managers coordinate teams of employees drawn from different functional departments. Thus, a matrix relies on a multiple-command structure.

group composed of representatives or workers from the functional departments. Note from the figure that a matrix reflects a *multiple-command structure*—any given individual reports to both a functional superior and one or more project managers.

The project groups, or teams, are assigned to designated projects or programs. For example, the company might be developing a new product. Representatives are chosen from each functional area to work as a team on the new product. They also retain membership in the original functional group. At any given time, a person may be a member of several teams as well as a member of a functional group. Ford used this approach in creating its popular Focus automobile. It formed a group called *Team Focus* made up of designers, engineers, production specialists, marketing specialists, and other experts from different areas of the company. This group facilitated getting a very successful product to the market at least a year earlier than would have been possible using Ford's previous approaches.

Martha Stewart also uses a matrix organization for her lifestyle business. The company was first organized broadly into media and merchandising groups, each of which has specific products and product groups. Layered on top of this structure are teams of lifestyle experts organized into groups such as cooking, crafts, and weddings. Each of these groups is targeted toward specific customer needs, but they work as necessary across all of the product groups. For example, a wedding expert might contribute to an article on wedding planning for a *Martha Stewart Living* magazine, contribute a story idea for a cable TV program, and supply content for a Martha Stewart website. This same individual might also help select fabrics suitable for wedding gowns for retailing.[48]

The matrix form of organization design is most often used in one of three situations.[49] First, a matrix may work when there is strong pressure from the environment. For example, intense external competition may dictate the sort of strong marketing thrust that is best spearheaded by a functional department, but the diversity of a company's products may argue for product departments. Second, a matrix may be appropriate when large amounts of information need to be processed. For example, creating lateral relationships by means of a matrix is one effective way to increase the organization's capacity for processing information. Third, the matrix design may work when there is pressure for shared resources. For example, a company with ten product departments may have resources for only three marketing specialists. A matrix design would allow all the departments to share the company's scarce marketing resources.

Both advantages and disadvantages are associated with the matrix design. Researchers have observed six primary advantages of matrix designs. First, they enhance flexibility because teams can be created, redefined, and dissolved as needed. Second, because they assume a major role in decision making, team members are likely to be highly motivated and committed to the organization. Third, employees in a matrix organization have considerable opportunity to learn new skills. Fourth, the matrix design provides an efficient way for the organization to take full advantage of its human resources. Fifth, team members retain membership in their functional unit so that they can serve as a bridge between the functional unit and the team, enhancing cooperation. Sixth, the matrix design gives top management a useful vehicle for decentralization. Once the day-to-day operations have been delegated, top management can devote more attention to areas such as long-range planning.

On the other hand, the matrix design also has some major disadvantages. Employees may be uncertain about reporting relationships, especially if they are simultaneously assigned to a functional manager and to several project managers. To complicate matters, some managers see the matrix as a form of anarchy in which they have unlimited freedom. Another set of problems is associated with the dynamics of group behavior. Groups take longer than individuals to make decisions, may be dominated by one individual, and may compromise too much. They may also get bogged down in discussion and not focus on their primary objectives. Finally, in a matrix, more time may also be required for coordinating task-related activities.[50]

Hybrid Designs

Some organizations use a design that represents a hybrid of two or more of the common forms of organization design.[51] For example, an organization may have five related divisions and one unrelated division, making its design a cross between an M form and an H form. Indeed, few companies use a design in its pure form; most firms have one basic organization design as a foundation for managing the business but maintain sufficient flexibility so that temporary or permanent modifications can be made for strategic purposes. Ford, for example, used the matrix approach to design the Focus and the newest Mustang, but the company is basically a U-form organization showing signs of moving to an M-form design. As we noted earlier, any combination of factors may dictate the appropriate form of design for any particular company.

EMERGING ISSUES IN ORGANIZATION DESIGN

In today's complex and ever-changing environment, it should come as no surprise that managers continue to explore and experiment with new forms of organization design. Many organizations are creating designs for themselves that maximize their ability to adapt to changing circumstances and to a changing environment. They try to accomplish this by not becoming too compartmentalized or too rigid. As we noted earlier, bureaucratic organizations are hard to change, slow, and inflexible. To avoid these problems, then, organizations can try to be as different from bureaucracies as possible—relatively few rules, general job descriptions, and so forth. This final section highlights some of the most important emerging issues.[52]

The Team Organization

team organization
An approach to organization design that relies almost exclusively on project-type teams, with little or no underlying hierarchy

Some organizations today are using the **team organization**, an approach to organization design that relies almost exclusively on project-type teams, with little or no underlying functional hierarchy. Within such an organization, people float from project to project as necessitated by their skills and the demands of those projects. At Cypress Semiconductor, T. J. Rodgers refuses to allow the organization to grow so large that it cannot function this way. Whenever a unit or group starts getting too large, he simply splits it into smaller units. Consequently, all units within the organization are small. This allows them to change direction, explore new ideas, and try new methods without dealing with a rigid bureaucratic organizational context. Although few organizations have actually reached this level of adaptability, Apple Computer and Xerox are among those moving toward it.[53]

The Virtual Organization

virtual organization
One that has little or no formal structure

Closely related to the team organization is the **virtual organization** that has little or no formal structure. Such an organization typically has only a handful of permanent employees and a very small staff and administrative headquarters facility. As the needs of the organization change, its managers bring in temporary workers, lease facilities, and outsource basic support services to meet the demands of each unique situation. As the situation changes, the temporary workforce changes in parallel, with some people leaving the organization and others entering. Facilities and the services subcontracted to others change as well. Thus, the organization exists only in response to its needs. And, increasingly, virtual organizations are conducting most—if not all—of their businesses online.[54]

For example, TLG Research Inc. was founded as a virtual organization focused on marketing research for automotive, aviation, marine, and industrial markets for original equipment and replacement parts. Currently, the company consists of an in-house project management staff of ten people and a virtual network of industry professionals. It also has a global business and research sources in Europe, Latin America, and Asia–Pacific to which it refers for consulting and research services as needed.

The Learning Organization

learning organization
One that works to facilitate the lifelong learning and personal development of all its employees while continually transforming itself to respond to changing demands and needs

Another recent approach to organization design is the so-called learning organization. Organizations that adopt this approach work to integrate continuous improvement with continuous employee learning and development. Specifically, a **learning organization** is one that works to facilitate the lifelong learning and personal development of all its employees while continually transforming itself to respond to changing demands and needs.[55]

Although managers might approach the concept of a learning organization from a variety of perspectives, improved quality, continuous improvement, and performance measurement are frequent goals. The idea is that the most consistent and logical strategy for achieving continuous improvement is by constantly upgrading employee talent, skill, and knowledge. For example, if each employee in an organization learns one new thing each day and can translate that knowledge into work-related practice, continuous improvement will logically follow. Indeed, organizations that wholeheartedly embrace this approach believe that only through constant learning by employees can continuous improvement really occur.[56]

In recent years, many different organizations have implemented this approach. For example, Shell Oil purchased an executive conference center north of its headquarters in Houston. The center boasts state-of-the-art classrooms and instructional technology, lodging facilities, a restaurant, and recreational amenities such as a golf course, a swimming pool, and tennis courts. Line managers at the firm rotate through the Shell Learning Center, as the facility has been renamed, and serve as teaching faculty. Such teaching assignments last anywhere from a few days to several months. At the same time, all Shell employees routinely attend training programs, seminars, and related activities, all the while learning the latest information they need to contribute more effectively to the firm. Recent seminar topics have ranged from time management, to the implications of the Americans with Disabilities Act, to balancing work and family demands, to international trade theory. The idea is that by continuously immersing people in shared learning experiences, the firm will promote an organic design populated by people with common knowledge, goals, and expectations.

SUMMARY OF LEARNING OUTCOMES AND KEY POINTS

1. Identify the basic elements of organizations.

   - Organizations are made up of a series of elements:

     - designing jobs
     - grouping jobs
     - establishing reporting relationships
     - distributing authority
     - coordinating activities
     - differentiating between positions

2. Describe the bureaucratic perspective on organization design.

   - The bureaucratic model attempted to prescribe how all organizations should be designed.
   - It is based on the presumed need for legitimate, logical, and formal rules, regulations, and procedures.

3. Identify and explain key situational influences on organization design.

   - The situational view of organization design is based on the assumption that the optimal organization design is a function of situational factors.
   - Four important situational factors are the following:

     - technology
     - environment
     - size
     - organizational life cycle

4. Describe the basic forms of organization design that characterize many organizations.

   - Many organizations today adopt one of four basic organization designs:

     - functional (U form)
     - conglomerate (H form)
     - divisional (M form)
     - matrix

   - Other organizations use a hybrid design derived from two or more of these basic designs.

5. Identify and describe emerging issues in organization design.

   - Three emerging issues in organization design are the following:

     - team organization
     - virtual organization
     - learning organization

DISCUSSION QUESTIONS

Questions for Review

1. What is job specialization? What are its advantages and disadvantages?
2. What is departmentalization? What are its most common forms?
3. Distinguish between centralization and decentralization, and comment on their relative advantages and disadvantages.
4. Describe the basic forms of organization design. What are the advantages and disadvantages of each?
5. Compare and contrast the matrix organization and the team organization, citing their similarities and differences.

Questions for Analysis

1. How is specialization applied in settings such as a hospital, restaurant, and church?
2. Learn how your school or business is organized. Analyze the advantages and disadvantages of this form of departmentalization, and then comment on how well or how poorly other forms of organization might work.
3. Identify five ways in which electronic coordination affects your daily life.
4. Each of the organization designs is appropriate for some firms but not for others. Describe the characteristics that a firm using the U form should have. Then do the same for the H form, the M form, and the matrix design. For each item, explain the relationship between that set of characteristics and the choice of organization design.
5. What are the benefits of using the learning organization approach to design? Now consider that, to learn, organizations must be willing to tolerate many mistakes because it is only through the effort of understanding mistakes that learning can occur. With this statement in mind, what are some of the potential problems with the use of the learning organization approach?

BUILDING EFFECTIVE CONCEPTUAL SKILLS

Exercise Overview

Conceptual skills require you to think in the abstract. In this exercise, you'll use your conceptual skills in analyzing organizational structure.

Exercise Background

Looking at its organization chart allows you to understand a company's structure, including its distribution of authority, its divisional breakdown, its levels of hierarchy, and its reporting relationships. The reverse is also true: When you understand the elements of a company's structure, you can draw up an organization chart to reflect it. In this exercise, that's just what you'll do: You'll use the Internet to research a firm's structure and then draw an appropriate organization chart.

Exercise Task

1. Alone or with a partner, go online to research a publicly traded U.S. firm in which you're interested.

Focus on information that will help you understand the company's structure. If you research Ford Motor Company, for example, you should look for information about different types of vehicles, different regions in which Ford products are sold, and different functions that the company performs. (*Hint*: The firm's annual report is usually available online and typically contains a great deal of helpful information. In particular, take a look at the section containing an editorial message from the chairman or CEO and the section summarizing financial information. In many cases, "segment" data reveal a lot about divisional structure.)

2. Draw an organization chart based on your research.

3. Share your results with another group or with the class as a whole. Be prepared to explain and justify the decisions that you made in determining the firm's structure.

BUILDING EFFECTIVE DIAGNOSTIC SKILLS

Exercise Overview

Diagnostic skills enable a manager to visualize the most appropriate response to a situation. In this exercise, you're asked to apply your diagnostic skills to the question of centralization versus decentralization in an organization.

Exercise Background

Managers often find it necessary to change an organization's degree of centralization or decentralization. Begin this exercise by reflecting on two very different scenarios in which this issue has arisen:

Scenario A. You're the top manager in a large organization with a long and successful history of centralized operations. For valid reasons beyond the scope of this exercise, however, you've decided to make the firm much more decentralized.

Scenario B. Assume the exact opposite of the situation in Scenario A: You still occupy the top spot in your firm, but this time you're going to centralize operations in an organization that's always been decentralized.

Exercise Task

Now do the following:

1. For Scenario A, list the major barriers to decentralization that you foresee.
2. For Scenario B, list the major barriers to centralization that you foresee.
3. In your opinion, which scenario would be easier to implement in reality? In other words, is it probably easier to move from centralization to decentralization or vice versa? Whatever your opinion in the matter, be ready to explain it.
4. Given a choice of starting your career in a firm that's either highly centralized or highly decentralized, which would you prefer? Why?

SKILLS SELF-ASSESSMENT INSTRUMENT

Delegation Aptitude Survey

Purpose: Help students gain insight into the process of and the attitudes important to delegation.

Introduction: Delegation has a number of advantages for managers, workers, and organizations, but it also presents challenges. Managers who understand the benefits of delegation, who trust their subordinates, and who have the emotional maturity to allow others to succeed are more likely to be effective delegators.

Instructions:

1. Complete the following Delegation Aptitude Survey. You should think of work-related or group situations in which you have had the opportunity to delegate responsibility to others. If you have not had such experiences, try to imagine how you would respond in such a situation. Circle the response that best typifies your attitude or behavior.
2. Score the survey according to the directions that follow. Calculate your overall score.
3. Working with a small group, compare individual scores and prepare group responses to the discussion questions.
4. Calculate a class-average score. Have one member of the group present the group's responses to the discussion questions.

Delegation Aptitude Survey

Statement	Strongly Agree	Slightly Agree	Not Sure	Slightly Disagree	Strongly Disagree
1. I don't think others can do the work as well as I can.	1	2	3	4	5
2. I often take work home with me.	1	2	3	4	5
3. Employees who can make their own decisions tend to be more efficient.	5	4	3	2	1
4. I often have to rush to meet deadlines.	1	2	3	4	5

(continued)

Statement	Strongly Agree	Slightly Agree	Not Sure	Slightly Disagree	Strongly Disagree
5. Employees with more responsibility tend to have more commitment to group goals.	5	4	3	2	1
6. When I delegate, I always explain precisely how the task is to be done.	1	2	3	4	5
7. I always seem to have too much to do and too little time to do it in.	1	2	3	4	5
8. When employees have the responsibility to do a job, they usually do it well.	5	4	3	2	1
9. When I delegate, I make clear the end results I expect.	5	4	3	2	1
10. I usually only delegate simple, routine tasks.	1	2	3	4	5
11. When I delegate, I always make sure everyone concerned is so informed.	5	4	3	2	1
12. If I delegate, I usually wind up doing the job over again to get it right.	1	2	3	4	5
13. I become irritated watching others doing a job I can do better.	1	2	3	4	5
14. When I delegate, I feel I am losing the control I need.	1	2	3	4	5
15. When I delegate, I always set specific dates for progress reports.	5	4	3	2	1
16. When I do a job, I do it to perfection.	1	2	3	4	5
17. I honestly feel that I can do most jobs better than my subordinates can.	1	2	3	4	5
18. When employees make their own decisions, it tends to cause confusion.	1	2	3	4	5
19. It's difficult for subordinates to make decisions because they don't know the organization's goals.	1	2	3	4	5
20. When employees are given responsibility, they usually do what is asked of them.	5	4	3	2	1

Discussion Questions

1. In what respects do the survey responses agree or disagree?
2. What might account for some of the differences in individual scores?
3. How can you make constructive use of the survey results?

Source: From GRIFFIN, *Exercises for Griffin's Management*, 8E. © 2005 Cengage Learning.

EXPERIENTIAL EXERCISE

Purpose: *Organization design* refers to the overall set of elements used to configure an organization. The purpose of this exercise is to give you insights into how managers must make decisions within the context of creating an organization design.

Introduction: Whenever a new enterprise is started, the owner must make decisions about how to structure the organization. For example, he or she must decide what functions are required, how those functions will be broken down into individual jobs, how those jobs will be grouped back together into logical departments, and how authority and responsibility will be allocated across positions.

Instructions: Assume that you have decided to open a handmade chocolate business in your local community. Your products will be traditional bars and novelty-shaped chocolates, truffles, other chocolate products such as ice cream, and gift baskets and boxes featuring chocolates. You have hired a talented chef and believe that her expertise, coupled with your unique designs and high-quality ingredients, will make your products very popular. You have also inherited enough money to get your business up and running and to cover about one year of living expenses (in other words, you do not need to pay yourself a salary).

You intend to buy food items, including chocolate, cocoa, white chocolate, nuts, and fruit, from suppliers who deliver to your area. Your chef will then turn those ingredients into luscious products that will then be attractively packaged. Local grocery store owners and restaurant chefs have seen samples of your products and indicated a keen interest in selling them. You know, however, that you will still need to service accounts and keep your customers happy. At the present time, you are trying to determine how many people you need to get your business going and how to group them most effectively into an organization. You realize that you can start out quite small and then expand as sales warrant. However, you also worry that if you are continually adding people and rearranging your organization, confusion and inefficiency may result.

Under each of the following scenarios, decide how best to design your organization. Sketch a basic organization chart to show your thoughts.

- *Scenario 1.* You will design and sell the products yourself, as well as oversee production. You will start with a workforce of five people.
- *Scenario 2.* You intend to devote all of your time to sales to increase revenues, leaving all other functions to others. You will start with a workforce of nine people.
- *Scenario 3.* You do not intend to handle any one function yourself but will instead oversee the entire operation and will start with a workforce of 15 people.

1. After you have created your organization chart, form small groups of four to five people each. Compare your various organization charts, focusing on similarities and differences.
2. Working in the same group, assume that five years have passed and that your business has been a big success. You have a large factory for making your chocolates and are shipping them to 15 states. You employ almost 500 people. Create an organization design that you think fits this organization best.

Discussion Questions

1. How clear (or how ambiguous) were the decisions about organization design?
2. What are your thoughts about starting out too large to maintain stability, as opposed to starting small and then growing?
3. What basic factors did you consider in choosing a design?

MANAGEMENT AT WORK
The Alliance Maze

Let's say you're a businessperson in New York who needs to fly to Hong Kong. Logging on to Orbitz, you find that American Airlines (AMR) offers a nonstop round-trip flight for $2,692. Because Orbitz recommends that you "Act Fast! Only 1 ticket left at this price!" you buy your ticket online. On your departure date, you arrive at the American Airlines ticket desk, only to be referred to the Cathay Pacific Airways counter. Your flight, the ticket agent informs you, is actually operated by Cathay, and she points to the four-digit "codeshare number" on your ticket.

Bewildered but hoping that you're still booked on a flight to Hong Kong, you hustle to the Cathay counter, where your ticket is in fact processed. Settled into your seat a few hours later, you decide to get on your laptop to see if you can figure out why you are and aren't on the flight that you booked. Going back to Orbitz, you find that, like American, Cathay does indeed offer a nonstop round-trip flight to and from its home city of Hong Kong—for $1,738. It dawns on you that if you'd bought your ticket directly from Cathay, you'd be sitting in the same seat on the same airplane for almost $1,000 less.

If this scenario sounds confusing, that's because it is, even to veteran flyers. What's confusing about it is the practice of *code sharing*, which works like this: You buy a ticket from Airline A for a flight operated by Airline B on a route that Airline A doesn't otherwise serve. This practice is possible if both airlines, like AMR and Cathay, belong to the same *airline alliance* (in this case, Oneworld).

On the surface, the advantages to the airlines may seem mostly a matter of perception: An airline *seems* to be serving certain markets that it doesn't actually serve and flying certain routes more frequently than it actually does. The networks formed by codesharing agreements, however, are real, and the breadth of an airline's network is a real factor in attracting high-margin corporate travelers. In fact, the spread of codesharing has led directly to the formation of much larger "alliances" of carriers who cooperate on a substantial level, including codesharing and shared frequent-flyer programs. The three largest airline alliances are the Star Alliance, which includes United Airlines, Lufthansa, Air Canada, Air China, and Scandinavian Airlines; SkyTeam, which includes Delta, Air France, Alitalia, and Dutch-based KLM; and Oneworld, which includes AMR, Cathay, Qantas, British Airways, and Japan's JAL.

An airline alliance is one form of a *virtual organization*—in this case, a temporary alliance formed by two or more organizations to pursue a specific venture or to exploit a specific opportunity. Although each member remains an independently owned and managed organization, alliance members can save money by sharing sales, maintenance, and operational facilities and staff (such as check-in, boarding, and other on-the-ground personnel), and they can also cut costs on purchases and investments by negotiating volume discounts. The chief advantages, however, are breadth of service and geographical reach—in short, size (both perceived and real). Star Alliance, for example, operates over 21,000 daily flights to 1,200 airports in 181 countries. According to the most recent data, its members carried 665.4 million passengers for a total of nearly 1 trillion *revenue passenger kilometers* (1 *rpk* means that 1 paying passenger was flown 1 kilometer). Based on *rpk* (which is really a measure of sales volume), Star commands 29.8 percent of global market share in the airline industry—greater than the combined market share of all airlines that don't belong to any of the three major alliances.

Note that our definition of a *virtual organization* indicates a "*temporary* alliance," and shifts by members of airline alliances are not unheard of. In January 2009,

for example, a few months after merger talks had broken down with United Airlines, Continental Airlines, a member of SkyTeam since 2004, announced that it was joining United in the Star Alliance. According to one analyst, the move, which took effect in October 2009, "was obviously a precursor to a full-blown merger," and, sure enough, Continental and United merged in May 2010 under a parent company called United Continental Holdings. The new airline, retaining the United Airlines name, remains a member of the Star Alliance.

The Continental–United merger was particularly bad news for both AMR, a member of Oneworld and the country's largest stand-alone airline, and US Airways Group, a member of the Star Alliance and the fifth-largest U.S. carrier. With the merger of Continental and United, says Vaughn Cordle, chief analyst at Airline Forecasts, a specialist in industry investment research, "the odds of … bankruptcy for US Airways and American increase because it will be too difficult, if not impossible, for them to remain viable as stand-alone businesses … . [W]ithout a new strategic direction and significant changes in the industry's structure," Cordle predicts, AMR and US Airways "will continue on the slow … path to failure."

And as predicted, American soon declared bankruptcy. Several months later, US Airways proposed a merger. And after a protracted legal battle, the U.S. Department of Justice approved the merger plans in late 2013. The new airline will retain the American Airlines name but be run by top executives formerly at US Airways. When the merger is finalized, the new airline will be the largest in the world.

Case Questions

1. Take a *situational view of organization design*: What roles have *technology* and *environment* played in the development of alliances and virtual organizations in the airline industry? In what ways does the *corporate-level strategy* of joining an alliance affect an airline's *organizational functions*?

2. In what ways might the *divisional (M-form) designs* of most airlines lend themselves to the requirements of alliance membership? In what ways might they be compatible with the organizational needs of the alliances themselves?

3. According to one industry analyst, "in a scale business … size does matter." What does he mean by "a scale business"? Why is the airline industry "a scale business"? Once you've thought about these

two questions, how would you describe the "specific opportunity" which, as *virtual organizations*, airline alliances are designed to exploit?

4. Have you ever been on a flight that involved a *codesharing* arrangement? Did you notice then—or do you realize now—that there were advantages to the practice of codesharing? Based on what you know about airline travel, list a few of the possible advantages of codesharing for passengers.

Case References

"Orbitz: Flightstit," Orbitz.com, May 3, 2010, www.orbitz.com, accessed on November 13, 2013; David Grossman, "The Anomalies of Code Share," *USA Today*, June 23, 2006, www.usatoday.com, accessed on November 13, 2013; Star Alliance, "Star Alliance Statistics," July 2013, www.staralliance.com, accessed on November 13, 2013; Andrew Clark, "United and Continental Merge to Create World's Biggest Airline," *The Guardian*, September 17, 2010, www.guardian.co.uk, accessed on November 13, 2013; Susanna Ray, "AMR May Seek Alliances as Mergers Erase Lead in Size," *Bloomberg Businessweek*, May 3, 2010, www.businessweek.com, accessed on November 13, 2013; and "The Winners and Losers of the US Airways, American Merger," forbes.com, accessed on November 13, 2013.

Authority & Function at A&F

1. If you were hired to advise Michael Jeffries on A&F's current organizational design, what weaknesses and potential threats would you identify? What strengths and opportunities?

2. What kind of organizational design do you think would be best suited to Jeffries's managerial style?

3. What differences might you expect to see between the organizational designs of such traditional retailers as A&F and American Eagle and those at online retailers such as Amazon.com and eBay?

4. Assuming that you wanted a career in retailing, would you want to work for A&F? Why or why not?

ENDNOTES

1 Robert Berner, "Flip-Flops, Torn Jeans—And Control," *BusinessWeek*, May 30, 2005, www.businessweek.com, accessed on November 13, 2013; Jess Cartner-Morley, "History of Abercrombie & Fitch: Tracing a Line from JFK's Blazer," *The Guardian*, June 24, 2009, https://www.guardian.com, accessed on November 13, 2013; Benoit Denizet-Lewis, "The Man Behind Abercrombie & Fitch," *Salon.com*, January 24, 2006, www.salon.com, accessed on November 13, 2013; Andria Cheng, "Abercrombe & Fitch Clothed in Green," *MarketWatch*, February 13, 2009, www.marketwatch.com, accessed on November 13, 2013.

2 Ricky W. Griffin, *Task Design* (Glenview, Ill.: Scott, Foresman, 1982).

3 Anne S. Miner, "Idiosyncratic Jobs in Formal Organizations," *Administrative Science Quarterly*, September 1987, pp. 327–351.

4 Maurice D. Kilbridge, "Reduced Costs through Job Enlargement: A Case," *Journal of Business*, 1960, Vol. 33, No. 4, pp. 357–362.

5 Ricky W. Griffin and Gary C. McMahan, "Motivation through Job Enrichment," in Jerald Greenberg (ed.), *Organizational Behavior: State of the Science* (New York: Lawrence Erlbaum and Associates, 1994), pp. 23–44.

6 Maurice D. Kilbridge, "Reduced Costs through Job Enlargement: A Case," *Journal of Business*, 1960, Vol. 33, No. 4, pp. 357–362.

7 Frederick Herzberg, *Work and the Nature of Man* (Cleveland, Ohio: World Press, 1966).

8 J. Richard Hackman and Greg R. Oldham, *Work Redesign* (Reading, Mass.: Addison-Wesley, 1980).

9 Jerry Useem, "What's That Spell? Teamwork!" *Fortune*, June 12, 2006, pp. 64–66.

10 Richard L. Daft, *Organization Theory and Design*, 11th ed. (Cincinnati, Ohio: South-Western, 2013).

11 David D. Van Fleet and Arthur G. Bedeian, "A History of the Span of Management," *Academy of Management Review*, 1977, pp. 356–372.

12 James C. Worthy, "Factors Influencing Employee Morale," *Harvard Business Review*, January 1950, pp. 61–73.

13 Dan R. Dalton, William D. Todor, Michael J. Spendolini, Gordon J. Fielding, and Lyman W. Porter, "Organization Structure and Performance: A Critical Review," *Academy of Management Review*, January 1980, pp. 49–64.

14 "Cadbury Gives Its CEO More Control," *Wall Street Journal*, October 15, 2008, p. B2.

15 See Jerry Useem, "Welcome to the New Company Town," *Fortune*, January 10, 2000, pp. 62–70, for a related discussion. See also "Wherever You Go, You're on the Job," *Business Week*, June 20, 2005, pp. 87–90.

16 See Daft, *Organization Theory and Design*.

17 William Kahn and Kathy Kram, "Authority at Work: Internal Models and Their Organizational Consequences," *Academy of Management Review*, 1994, Vol. 19, No. 1, pp. 17–50.

18 Carrie R. Leana, "Predictors and Consequences of Delegation," *Academy of Management Journal*, December 1986, pp. 754–774.

[19] Jerry Useem, "In Corporate America It's Cleanup Time," *Fortune*, September 16, 2002, pp. 62–70.

[20] "Toyota Overhauls Management, Gives More Autonomy to North America," *LA Times*, March 7, 2013, p. 3B; "Toyota Shake-Up to Speed Decisions," *USA Today*, March 7, 2013, p. 1B.

[21] "New Shell CEO Begins Shake-Up," *Wall Street Journal*, May 28, 2009, p. B4.

[22] "Yahoo CEO to Install Top-Down Management," *Wall Street Journal*, February 23, 2009, p. B1.

[23] Kevin Crowston, "A Coordination Theory Approach to Organizational Process Design," *Organization Science*, March–April 1997, pp. 157–166.

[24] James Thompson, *Organizations in Action* (New York: McGraw-Hill, 1967). For a recent discussion, see Bart Victor and Richard S. Blackburn, "Interdependence: An Alternative Conceptualization," *Academy of Management Review*, July 1987, pp. 486–498.

[25] Jay R. Galbraith, *Designing Complex Organizations* (Reading, Mass.: Addison-Wesley, 1973) and *Organizational Design* (Reading, Mass.: Addison-Wesley, 1977).

[26] Paul R. Lawrence and Jay W. Lorsch, "Differentiation and Integration in Complex Organizations," *Administrative Science Quarterly*, March 1967, pp. 1–47.

[27] Max Weber, *Theory of Social and Economic Organizations*, trans. T. Parsons (New York: Free Press, 1947).

[28] Paul Jarley, Jack Fiorito, and John Thomas Delany, "A Structural Contingency Approach to Bureaucracy and Democracy in U.S. National Unions," *Academy of Management Journal*, 1997, Vol. 40, No. 4, pp. 831–861.

[29] See N. Anand and Richard L. Daft, "What Is the Right Organization Design?" *Organizational Dynamics*, 2007, Vol. 36, No 4, pp. 329–344, for a recent review.

[30] Joan Woodward, *Industrial Organization: Theory and Practice* (London: Oxford University Press, 1965).

[31] Joan Woodward, *Management and Technology, Problems of Progress Industry*, Series no. 3 (London: Her Majesty's Stationery Office, 1958).

[32] For example, see Michael Russo and Niran Harrison, "Organizational Design and Environmental Performance: Clues from the Electronics Industry," *Academy of Management Journal*, 2005, Vol. 48, No. 4, pp. 582–593. See also Sebastian Raisch and Julian Birkinshaw, "Organizational Ambidexterity: Antecedents, Outcomes, and Moderators," *Journal of Management*, 2008, Vol. 34, No.3, pp. 375–409.

[33] Tom Burns and G. M. Stalker, *The Management of Innovation* (London: Tavistock, 1961).

[34] Paul R. Lawrence and Jay W. Lorsch, *Organization and Environment* (Homewood, Ill.: Irwin, 1967).

[35] Edward E. Lawler III, "Rethinking Organization Size," *Organizational Dynamics*, Autumn 1997, pp. 24–33. See also Henrich R. Greve, "A Behavioral Theory of Firm Growth: Sequential Attention to Size and Performance Goals," *Academy of Management Journal*, 2008, Vol. 51, No. 3, pp. 476–494.

[36] Derek S. Pugh and David J. Hickson, *Organization Structure in Its Context: The Aston Program I* (Lexington, Mass.: D. C. Heath, 1976).

[37] Can Wal-Mart Get Any Bigger?" *Time*, January 13, 2003, pp. 38–43.

[38] "Marathon Oil to Split in Two," *New York Times*, January 13, 2011.

[39] Robert H. Miles and Associates, *The Organizational Life Cycle* (San Francisco: Jossey-Bass, 1980). See also "Is Your Company Too Big?" *BusinessWeek*, March 27, 1989, pp. 84–94.

[40] Douglas Baker and John Cullen, "Administrative Reorganization and Configurational Context: The Contingent Effects of Age, Size, and Change in Size," *Academy of Management Journal*, 1993, Vol. 36, No. 6, pp. 1251–1277. See also Kevin Crowston, "A Coordination Theory Approach to Organizational Process Design," *Organization Science*, March–April 1997, pp. 157–168.

[41] Oliver E. Williamson, *Markets and Hierarchies* (New York: Free Press, 1975).

[42] Williamson, Markets and Hierarchies.

[43] "The Real Winner of GE's CEO Bake-Off," *Bloomberg Businessweek*, May 6–May 12, 2013, pp. 19–20.

[44] Michael E. Porter, "From Competitive Advantage to Corporate Strategy," *Harvard Business Review*, May–June 1987, pp. 43–59.

[45] Williamson, *Markets and Hierarchies.*

[46] Jay B. Barney and William G. Ouchi (eds.), *Organizational Economics* (San Francisco: Jossey-Bass, 1986); and Robert E. Hoskisson, "Multidivisional Structure and Performance: The Contingency of Diversification Strategy," *Academy of Management Journal*, December 1987, pp. 625–644. See also Bruce Lamont, Robert Williams, and James Hoffman, "Performance during 'M-Form' Reorganization and Recovery Time: The Effects of Prior Strategy and Implementation Speed," *Academy of Management Journal*, 1994, Vol. 37, No. 1, pp. 153–166.

[47] Stanley M. Davis and Paul R. Lawrence, *Matrix* (Reading, Mass.: Addison-Wesley, 1977).

[48] "Martha, Inc.," *BusinessWeek*, January 17, 2000, pp. 63–72.

[49] Davis and Lawrence, *Matrix.*

[50] See Lawton Burns and Douglas Wholey, "Adoption and Abandonment of Matrix Management Programs: Effects of Organizational Characteristics and Interorganizational Networks," *Academy of Management Journal*, 1993, Vol. 36, No. 1, pp. 106–138.

[51] See Michael Hammer and Steven Stanton, "How Process Enterprises Really Work," *Harvard Business Review*, November–December 1999, pp. 108–118.

[52] Raymond E. Miles, Charles C. Snow, John A. Mathews, Grant Miles, and Henry J. Coleman, Jr., "Organizing in the Knowledge Age: Anticipating the Cellular Form," *Academy of Management Executive*, November 1997, pp. 7–24.

[53] John Mathieu, Travis M. Maynard, Tammy Rapp, and Lucy Gibson, "Team Effectiveness 1997–2007: A Review of Recent Advancements and a Glimpse into the Future," *Journal of Management*, 2008, Vol. 34, No. 3, p. 410–476.

[54] "Management by Web," *BusinessWeek*, August 28, 2000, pp. 84–96.

[55] Peter Senge, *The Fifth Discipline* (New York: Free Press, 1993). See also David Lei, John W. Slocum, and Robert A. Pitts, "Designing Organizations for Competitive Advantage: The Power of Unlearning and Learning," *Organizational Dynamics*, Winter 1999, pp. 24–35.

[56] Amy C. Edmondson, "The Competitive Imperative of Learning," *Harvard Business Review*, July–August 2008, pp. 60–70.

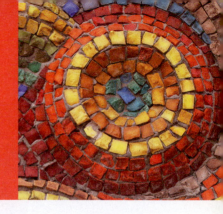

CHAPTER 7

Organization Change and Innovation

Learning Outcomes

After studying this chapter, you should be able to:

1 Describe the nature of organization change, including forces for change and planned versus reactive change.

2 Discuss the steps in organization change and how to manage resistance to change.

3 Identify and describe major areas of organization change and discuss the assumptions, techniques, and effectiveness of organization development (OD).

4 Describe the innovation process, forms of innovation, the failure to innovate, and how organizations can promote innovation.

Management in Action

Cultivating Innovation at IKEA

"Designing beautiful-but-expensive products is easy. Designing beautiful products that are inexpensive and functional is a huge challenge."

—IKEA Executive

According to *Businessweek* magazine, IKEA "is the quintessential cult brand," and its customers belong to "a like-minded cost/design/environmentally sensitive global tribe." The founder of this global "cult" is a Swedish entrepreneur named Ingvar Kamprad. Kamprad has always referred to his targeted customers as "the many," and his plan has been to bring affordable, well-designed furniture to this target market. "The many," then, is hardly a "mass" market: In reality, it's a profitable niche consisting primarily of consumers who want stylish furniture at a low cost. Its goal, says the company, is to offer "affordable solutions for better living," with "better living" referring to a range of well-designed furniture and furnishings and "affordable" referring to the price range of consumers who are starting up their own homes and/or expanding their families.

IKEA's marketing strategy depends on constant innovation, and the company's ability to innovate successfully depends in part on an organizational structure that encourages creativity and communication. In order to understand how it's all designed to work, however, we first need to break down the elements of "the IKEA way"—the factors which, *taken in combination*, have made the IKEA approach so successful. The *target market* that we've just described is the first of

IKEA is known for its innovative approach to retailing and its ability to implement change efficiently and effectively.

these factors, and we can identify four others in terms that any marketer would recognize:

- *Product*. With over 12,000 items, the IKEA product line is quite large, and because smaller products complement larger products, customers can experiment with ensembles that satisfy their own needs and tastes while calculating total costs as they proceed through the store or catalog. The company didn't pay much attention to product design at first, but today, admits one expert, "you will always find some pieces which are good designs and very reasonable in pricing." IKEA also wants consumers—especially Americans—to stop thinking of furniture as durable goods. Older Americans, says one company marketing manager, "keep a sofa longer than a car" because they believe that it's going to be the long-term "icon of the living room." IKEA wants to appeal to the willingness of younger consumers to experiment with changes, and its price structure makes it possible for them to do it.
- *Price*. "Designing beautiful-but-expensive products is easy," says one IKEA executive. "Designing beautiful products that are inexpensive and functional is a huge challenge." Nevertheless, IKEA prices are typically from 20 percent to 50 percent below those of stores selling fully assembled furniture. "When we decide about a product, we always start with the price," reports one product developer, and after starting with an original competitive price, IKEA then proceeds to drive it even lower. The company maintains price leadership not only by purchasing in large quantities but also by constantly looking for cheaper suppliers; nearly 50 percent of IKEA's outsourcing partners are located in developing economies.
- *Distribution*. In addition to a global network of thousands of manufacturers and nearly 1,400 suppliers in 54 countries, IKEA maintains a system of 27 distribution centers (which ship products to stores) and 11 customer-distribution centers

(which ship goods to consumers) in 16 countries. Its stores, too, are an important facet of IKEA's distribution strategy. A key innovation is the way they're laid out. Unlike the traditional furniture outlet, which directs customers to separate sections to view multiple versions of one product (e.g., beds) or one room (e.g., bedrooms), IKEA stores are laid out around a wide one-way path—the "natural path," according to the company—that carries customers directly from one section to the next. The "natural path" not only exposes them to the whole range of IKEA offerings but also encourages them to extend their in-store visits.

- *Promotion.* Promotion at IKEA revolves around the near-legendary annual catalog, a 300-page compendium of color photos and blurbs for about 12,000 products. Boasting a circulation of 175 million copies worldwide, the catalog covers the whole range of the company's new products, focuses on ideas for innovations in the customer's home, and relies on word-of-mouth publicity among the faithful. It is no surprise that IKEA stores are arranged to accomplish essentially the same goals. Like the IKEA catalog, for example, they're designed to encourage repeat visits by showcasing the company's regular turnover in new products (about one-third per year).

The IKEA store is also the company's most obvious and most important process innovation. Averaging around 300,000 square feet, most box-like blue-and-yellow stores feature both the series of showrooms arranged along the "natural path" and an in-store self-serve warehouse. After choosing items from the Showroom, customers collect trolleys for transporting their purchases and pass into the Market Hall, where they can pick up smaller items, such as linen, lighting, glassware, and rugs. Next along the path is the Self-Serve Warehouse, where they collect their furniture purchases in flat-pack form and then proceed to the rows of cashier's stations to pay for everything. Once they've paid for their purchases, customers can arrange for delivery or roll them to the loading dock, pack them in or on their vehicles, and take them home.

As important as process innovation has been to the company's success, the IKEA engine is powered by the introduction of new products and a constant stream of product innovations. Finding new products from outside sources, however, isn't the same thing as innovating within the company. At IKEA, innovation from within signals the company's commitment not only to respond to changes in the needs of customers all around the world but also to maintain a global brand identity and convey an ongoing sense of excitement among the brand-loyal faithful.

About 50 designers at the company's Swedish workshop are always busy creating new products, but designers aren't the only people in the organization who are responsible for innovative ideas. "[E]veryone contributes," says Bill Agee, head of marketing at IKEA United States. "Whoever you are within the IKEA organization, you're expected to contribute your ideas—your new ideas, your old ideas, or whatever it may be—and every idea is welcome." The concept works, explains Agee, because "we're a very process-oriented company.... [W]e have three basic processes: creating, communicating, and selling the home-furnishings offer. Each of these processes," he adds, "has a matrix structure": Working as members of what amounts to a companywide team, designers design products, marketers like Agee communicate the product message, and "coworkers" in the company's warehouses and stores deliver the product to the customer. "Our independence," Agee thinks, "has a lot to do with our innovation because we don't know any better.... We feel that we are, to a certain extent, operating outside of standard operating procedures."[1]

Managers at IKEA are fueling growth and profitability through the astute management of innovation. In particular, the company relies on the development and marketing of innovative products to grow and prosper. At a broader level, IKEA also relies heavily on change. As we will see, understanding when and how to implement change is a vital part of management. This chapter describes how organizations manage change. We first examine the nature of organization change and identify the basic issues of managing change. We then identify and describe major areas of change, including business process change, a major type of change undertaken by many firms recently. We then examine organization development and conclude by discussing organizational innovation as a vital form of change.

THE NATURE OF ORGANIZATION CHANGE

organization change

Any substantive modification to some part of the organization

Organization change is any substantive modification to some part of the organization.[2] Thus, change can involve virtually any aspect of an organization: work schedules, bases for departmentalization, span of management, machinery, organization design, people themselves, and so on. It is important to keep in mind that any change in an organization may have effects extending beyond the actual area where the change is implemented. For example, when General Motors recently installed a new automated production system at one of its plants, employees were trained to operate new equipment, the compensation system was adjusted to reflect new skill levels, the span of management for supervisors was altered, and several related jobs were redesigned. Selection criteria for new employees were also changed, and a new quality control system was installed. In addition, it is quite common for multiple organization change activities to be going on simultaneously.

Forces for Change

Why do organizations find change necessary? The basic reason is that something relevant to the organization either has changed or is likely to change in the foreseeable future. The organization therefore may have little choice but to change as well. Indeed, a primary reason for the problems that organizations often face is failure to anticipate or respond properly to changing circumstances. The forces that compel change may be external or internal to the organization.[3]

External Forces   External forces for change come from the organization's general and task environments. For example, two energy crises, an aggressive Japanese automobile industry, floating currency exchange rates, and floating international interest rates—all manifestations of the international dimension of the general environment—profoundly influenced U.S. automobile companies. New rules of production and competition forced them to dramatically alter the way they do business. In the political area, new laws, court decisions, and regulations affect organizations. The technological dimension may yield new production techniques that the organization needs to explore. The economic dimension is affected by inflation, the cost of living, and money supplies. The sociocultural dimension, reflecting societal values, determines what kinds of products or services will be accepted in the market.

Because of its proximity to the organization, the task environment is an even more powerful force for change. Competitors influence an organization through their price structures and product lines. When Dell lowers the prices it charges for computers, Hewlett-Packard may have little choice but to follow suit. Because customers determine what products can be sold at what prices, organizations must be concerned with consumer tastes and preferences. Suppliers affect organizations by raising or lowering prices or changing product lines. Regulators can have dramatic effects on an organization. For example, if OSHA rules that a particular production process is dangerous to workers, it can force a firm to close a plant until it meets higher safety standards. Unions can force change when they have the clout to negotiate for higher wages or if they go on strike.

Internal Forces   A variety of forces inside the organization may cause change. If top management revises the organization's strategy, organization change is likely to result. A decision by an electronics company to enter the home computer market or a decision to increase a ten-year product sales goal by 3 percent would occasion many organization changes. Other internal forces for change may be reflections of external forces. As sociocultural values shift, for example, workers' attitudes toward their job may also shift—and workers may demand a change in working hours or working conditions. In such a case, even though the force is rooted in the external environment, the organization must respond directly to the internal pressure it generates.[4]

Planned Versus Reactive Change

Some change is planned well in advance; other change comes about as a reaction to unexpected events. **Planned change** is designed and implemented in an orderly and timely fashion in anticipation of future events. **Reactive change** is a piecemeal response to circumstances as they develop. Because reactive change may be hurried, the potential for poorly conceived and executed change is increased. Planned change is almost always preferable to reactive change.[5]

Georgia-Pacific, a large forest products business, is an excellent example of a firm that went through a planned and well-managed change process. When A. D. Correll became CEO, he quickly became alarmed at the firm's high accident rate—9 serious injuries per 100 employees each year, and 26 deaths during the most recent 5-year period. Although the forest products business is inherently dangerous, Correll believed that the accident rate was far too high and set out on a major change effort to improve things. He and other top managers developed a multistage change program intended to educate workers about safety, improve safety equipment in the plant, and eliminate a long-standing part of the firm's culture that made injuries almost a badge of courage. As a result, Georgia-Pacific achieved the best safety record in the industry, with relatively few injuries.

On the other hand, Caterpillar was caught flat-footed by a worldwide recession in the construction industry, suffered enormous losses, and took several years to recover. Had managers at Caterpillar anticipated the need for change earlier, they might have been able to respond more quickly. The importance of approaching change from a planned perspective is reinforced by the frequency of organization change. Most companies or divisions of large companies implement some form of moderate change at least every year and one or more major changes every four to five years. Managers who sit back and respond only when they have to are likely to spend a lot of time hastily changing and rechanging things. A more effective approach is to anticipate forces urging change and plan ahead to deal with them.[6]

MANAGING CHANGE IN ORGANIZATIONS

Organization change is a complex phenomenon. A manager cannot simply wave a wand and implement a planned change like magic. Instead, any change must be systematic and logical to have a realistic opportunity to succeed.[7] To carry this off, the manager needs to understand the steps of effective change and how to counter employee resistance to change.[8]

---

planned change
Change that is designed and implemented in an orderly and timely fashion in anticipation of future events

reactive change
A piecemeal response to circumstances as they develop

Steps in the Change Process

Researchers have over the years developed a number of models or frameworks outlining steps for change. The Lewin model was one of the first, although a more comprehensive approach is usually more useful in today's complex business environment.

The Lewin Model   Kurt Lewin, a noted organizational theorist, suggested that every change requires three steps.[9] The first step is unfreezing—individuals who will be affected by the impending change must be led to recognize why the change is necessary. The second step is the *implementation* of the change itself. The third step is refreezing, which involves reinforcing and supporting the change so that it becomes a part of the system.[10] For example, one of the changes that Caterpillar faced in response to the recession noted earlier involved a massive workforce reduction. The first step (unfreezing) was convincing the United Auto Workers (UAW) to support the reduction because of its importance to long-term effectiveness. After this unfreezing was accomplished, 30,000 jobs were eliminated (implementation). Then it worked to improve its damaged relationship with its workers (refreezing) by guaranteeing future pay hikes and promising no more cutbacks. As interesting as the Lewin model is, it unfortunately lacks operational specificity. Thus, a more comprehensive perspective is often needed.

A Comprehensive Approach to Change   The comprehensive approach to change takes a systems view and delineates a series of specific steps that often leads to successful change. This expanded model is illustrated in Figure 7.1. The first step is recognizing the need for change. Reactive change might be triggered by employee complaints, declines in productivity or turnover, court injunctions, sales slumps, or labor strikes. Recognition may simply be managers' awareness that change in a certain area is inevitable. For example, managers may be aware of the general frequency of organizational change undertaken by most organizations and recognize that their organization should probably follow the same pattern. The immediate stimulus might be the result of a forecast indicating new market potential, the accumulation of a cash surplus for possible investment, or an opportunity to achieve and capitalize on a major technological breakthrough. Managers might also initiate change today because indicators suggest that it will be necessary in the near future.[11]

Second, managers must set goals for the change: to increase market share, to enter new markets, to restore employee morale, to settle a strike, and to identify investment opportunities—all might be goals for change. Third, managers must diagnose what brought on the need for change. Turnover, for example, might be caused by low pay, poor working conditions, poor supervisors, or employee dissatisfaction. Thus, although turnover may be the immediate stimulus for change, managers must understand its causes to make the right changes.

The next step is to select a change technique that will accomplish the intended goals. If turnover is caused by low pay, a new reward system may be needed. If the cause is poor supervision, interpersonal skills training may be called for. (Various change techniques are summarized later in this chapter.) After the appropriate technique has been chosen, its implementation must be planned. Issues to consider include the costs of the change, its effects on other areas of the organization, and the degree of employee participation appropriate for the situation. If the change is implemented as planned, the results should then be evaluated. If the change was intended to reduce turnover, managers must check turnover after the change has been in effect for a while. If turnover is still too high, other changes may be necessary.[12]

© Cengage Learning

Steps in the Change Process

Managers must understand how and why to implement change. A manager who, when implementing change, follows a logical and orderly sequence like the one shown here is more likely to succeed than a manager whose change process is haphazard and poorly conceived.

Understanding Resistance to Change

Another element in the effective management of change is understanding the resistance that often accompanies change.[13] Managers need to know why people resist change and what can be done about their resistance. When Schlumberger first provided all its managers with smartphones, most people responded favorably. One manager, however, resisted the change to the point where he maintained two telephone numbers, one on his new smartphone (which he left with his assistant) and his old standard cell phone that he continued to use. Such resistance is common for a variety of reasons.[14] The "Leading the Way" feature illustrates resistance to change.

Uncertainty   Perhaps the biggest cause of employee resistance to change is uncertainty. In the face of impending change, employees may become anxious and nervous. They may worry about their ability to meet new job demands, they may think that their job security is threatened, or they may simply dislike ambiguity. Nabisco was once the target of an extended and confusing takeover battle, and during the entire time, employees were nervous about the impending change. The *Wall Street Journal* described them this way: "Many are angry at their leaders and fearful for their jobs. They are swapping rumors and spinning scenarios for the ultimate outcome of the battle for the tobacco and food giant. Headquarters staffers in Atlanta know so little about what's happening in New York that some call their office 'the mushroom complex,' where they are kept in the dark."[15] More recently, 13,500 British Airways cabin crew members voted to participate in a strike over a heavily traveled holiday season. The action against the airlines was spurred by high levels of uncertainty as British Airways planned to merge with another airline and proposed cutting 1,700 jobs and freezing employee wages in the process.[16]

Threatened Self-Interests   Many impending changes threaten the self-interests of some managers within the organization. A change might diminish their power or influence within the company, so they fight it. Managers at Sears once developed a plan calling for a new type of store. The new stores would be somewhat smaller than a typical Sears store and would not be located in large shopping malls. Instead, they would be located in smaller strip centers. They would carry clothes and other "soft goods," but not hardware, appliances, furniture, or automotive products. When executives in charge of the excluded product lines heard about the plan, they raised such strong objections that the plan was cancelled.

Different Perceptions   A third reason that people resist change is due to different perceptions. A manager may make a decision and recommend a plan for change on the basis of her own assessment of a situation. Others in the organization may resist the change because they do not agree with the manager's assessment or perceive the situation differently.[17] Executives at 7-Eleven battled this problem as they attempted to enact a major organizational change. The corporation wanted to take its convenience stores a bit "upscale" and begin selling fancy fresh foods to go, the newest hardcover novels, some gourmet products, and higher-quality coffee. But many franchisees balked because they saw this move as taking the firm away from its core blue-collar customers.

Feelings of Loss   Many changes involve altering work arrangements in ways that disrupt existing social networks. Because social relationships are important, most people resist any change that might adversely affect those relationships. Other intangibles threatened by change include power, status, security, familiarity with existing procedures, and self-confidence.

Overcoming Resistance to Change

Of course, a manager should not give up in the face of resistance to change. Although there are no surefire cures, there are several techniques that at least have the potential to overcome resistance.[18]

Participation   Participation is often the most effective technique for overcoming resistance to change. Employees who participate in planning and implementing a change are better able to understand the reasons for the change. Uncertainty is reduced, and self-interests and social relationships are less threatened. Having had an opportunity to express their ideas and assume the perspectives of others, employees are more likely to accept the change gracefully. A classic study of participation monitored the introduction of a change in production methods among four groups in a Virginia pajama factory.[19] The two groups that were allowed to fully participate in planning and implementing the change improved significantly in their productivity and satisfaction, relative to the two groups that did not participate. 3M Company recently attributed several million dollars in cost savings to employee participation in several organization change activities.

LEADING THE WAY

Charting a "New" Old Course

Lenovo was started in Beijing by Liu Chuanzhi in 1984. Initially, Lenovo made computers for other companies. In 1990, the firm launched its own brand of PC and by 1997 Lenovo was the top-selling PC in its home country. Unfortunately, however, the company was not successful in gaining market share outside China. One reason for this was the lack of brand recognition. Another was that Lenovo simply did not have many top managers with global experience. But that changed in 2005. When IBM decided to sell its PC operation that year, Lenovo was quick to jump on the opportunity and bought IBM's entire PC business for $1.75 billion. Lenovo was allowed to continue using the IBM name through 2007 but then started to brand all of its PCs with the Lenovo name. Along with the PC business itself, Lenovo also got a team of skilled top managers well-versed in global PC markets.

Senior IBM executives were quickly integrated throughout the top management structure, and one of them, Stephen Ward, was appointed chief executive officer (CEO) of Lenovo. Liu Chuanzhi, meanwhile, moved into the background but remained a director—he felt that Lenovo's best opportunity for the firm to gain international market share would be under the leadership of a seasoned global manager like Ward.

But almost from the start, problems began to surface. Ward was extremely autocratic and believed that Lenovo should function in a highly centralized, command-and-control fashion. This alienated his new Chinese colleagues who assumed that their roles were being diminished because they spent less time with the CEO. Chuanzhi, for instance, had relied on a senior leadership team that worked together to make decisions, whereas Ward made

Doug Kanter/Bloomberg/Getty Images

Lenovo is a leading Chinese technology products company best known for the line of ThinkPad personal computers it purchased from IBM. For years, the company has struggled with balancing traditional Chinese approaches to management with contemporary management practices more widely practiced in global businesses. Lenovo's founder, Liu Chuanzhi, recently took back control of the firm in an effort to improve its competitiveness.

(continued)

LEADING THE WAY (Continued)

most of the major decisions by himself. And at a more general level, the U.S. managers tried to impose a rigid, centralized, and bureaucratic structure throughout the new Lenovo. The Chinese, meanwhile, were highly resistant to these efforts, strongly preferring the more consensus-style structure that they had used previously.

Within a matter of months, things came to a head. Among other changes, Ward was pushed out and replaced with William Amelio, a senior executive recruited from Dell Computer's Asia/Pacific operations. Amelio immediately indicated his intent to try to move Lenovo back toward the traditional Chinese structure. He also thought that the firm could benefit from an infusion of additional perspectives, so he began to aggressively recruit new executives from other high-tech firms such as Dell, Motorola, Samsung, and Toshiba. He also softened the rigid functional structure and tried building more coordination across areas by creating cross-functional teams. Unfortunately, though, Amelio never carried through on his plan to change how decisions were made, retaining much of the decision-making authority himself and continuing the command-and-control approach that had been Ward's downfall. Lenovo also began to lose market share and profits began to drop.

Finally, Chuanzhi decided that he had to take action. He pushed Amelio to resign and took control of the firm himself. He then quickly restructured the upper ranks of Lenovo to fall more in line with the traditional Chinese approach. Chuanzhi formed the eight top managers at Lenovo into a close-knit team and then brought them together regularly to make decisions and formulate plans. After decisions and plans were made by consensus, the team continued to work together to ensure that they were implemented effectively and with buy-in from others throughout the organization. Today Lenovo is headquartered in Hong Kong but has major operations in Beijing, Singapore, and Morrisville, North Carolina. The firm's products include PCs, workstations, servers, storage devices, and information technology (IT) services. Lenovo has also entered the mobile phone business, citing increased convergence between the PC and handheld wireless technologies. In 2012, Lenovo generated profits of $273 million on revenues of $21.6 billion and employed more than 27,000 workers. Right now, it's still too soon to know if the changes at Lenovo will improve its fortunes or not. But Chuanzhi believes that his new approach, which he calls a "blend of old Chinese thinking and modern global thinking," will soon carry the day.

References: "Lenovo's Legend Returns," *Time*, May 10, 2010, pp. 65–68; "Lenovo: A Company Without a Country," *Businessweek*, January 23, 2010, pp. 49–50; "Lenovo's Turnaround Man," *Forbes*, May 4, 2010, p. 88; *Hoover's Handbook of World Business 2013*, Austin: Hoover's Business Press, 2013, pp. 236–237; "IBM Shows Secret to Corporate Longevity," *USA Today*, June 16, 2011, pp. 1B, 3B; Miguel Helft, "Can Lenovo Do It?" *Fortune*, June 10, 2013, pp. 100–111.

Education and Communication   Educating employees about the need for and the expected results of an impending change should reduce their resistance. If open communication is established and maintained during the change process, uncertainty can be minimized. Caterpillar used these methods during many of its cutbacks to reduce resistance. First, it educated UAW representatives about the need for and potential value of the planned changes. Then management told all employees what was happening, when it would happen, and how it would affect them individually.

Facilitation   Several facilitation procedures are also advisable. For instance, making only necessary changes, announcing those changes well in advance, and allowing time for people to adjust to new ways of doing things can help reduce resistance to change.[20] One manager at a Prudential regional office spent several months systematically planning a change in work procedures and job design. He then became too impatient, coming in over the weekend with a work crew and rearranging the office layout. When employees walked in on Monday morning and saw what he had done, they were hostile, anxious,

Reasons for Closing	Plant closing	Reasons Against Closing
Need to cut costs		Resistance from unions
Excess capacity		Concern about worker welfare
Outmoded production facilities		Possible future needs

© Cengage Learning

FIGURE 7.2

Force-Field Analysis for Plant Closing at General Motors

A force-field analysis can help a manager facilitate change. A manager who is able to identify forces acting both for and against a change can see where to focus efforts to remove barriers to change (such as offering training and relocation to displaced workers). Removing the forces against the change can at least partially overcome resistance.

and resentful. What was a promising change became a disaster, and the manager had to scrap the entire plan.

Force-Field Analysis   Although force-field analysis may sound like something out of a *Star Trek* movie, it can help overcome resistance to change. In almost any change situation, forces are acting for and against the change. To facilitate the change, managers start by listing each set of forces and then trying to tip the balance so that the forces facilitating the change outweigh those hindering the change. It is especially important to try to remove or at least minimize some of the forces acting against the change. Suppose, for example, that General Motors (GM) is considering a plant closing as part of a change. As shown in Figure 7.2, three factors are reinforcing the change: GM needs to cut costs, it has excess capacity, and the plant has outmoded production facilities. At the same time, there is resistance from the UAW, concern for workers being put out of their jobs, and a feeling that the plant might be needed again in the future. GM might start by convincing the UAW that the closing is necessary by presenting profit-and-loss figures. It could then offer relocation and retraining to displaced workers. And it might shut down the plant and put it in "mothballs" so that it can be renovated later. The three major factors hindering the change are thus eliminated or reduced in importance.[21]

AREAS OF ORGANIZATION CHANGE

We noted earlier that change can involve virtually any part of an organization. In general, however, most change interventions involve organization structure and design, technology and operations, or people. The most common areas of change within each of these broad categories are listed in Table 7.1. In addition, many organizations have gone through massive and comprehensive business process change programs.

Changing Organization Structure and Design

Organization change might be focused on any of the basic components of organization structure or on the organization's overall design. Thus, the organization might change the way it designs its jobs or its bases of departmentalization. Likewise, it might change reporting relationships or the distribution of authority. For example, we noted in

Organization change can affect any part, area, or component of an organization. Most change, however, fits into one of three general areas: organization structure and design, technology and operations, and people.

Table 7.1	Areas of Organization Change	
Organization Structure and Design	**Technology and Operations**	**People**
Job design	Information technology	Abilities and skills
Departmentalization	Equipment	Performance
Reporting relationships	Work processes	Perceptions
Authority distribution	Work sequences	Expectations
Coordination mechanisms	Control systems	Attitudes
Line-staff structure	Enterprise resource planning	Values
Overall design		
Culture		
Human resource management		

© Cengage Learning

Chapter 6 the trend toward flatter organizations. Coordination mechanisms and line-and-staff configurations are also subject to change. On a larger scale, the organization might change its overall design. For example, a growing business could decide to drop its functional design and adopt a divisional design. Or it might transform itself into a matrix. Changes in culture usually involve the structure and design of the organization as well (recall that we discussed changing culture back in Chapter 2). Finally, the organization might change any part of its human resource management system, such as its selection criteria, its performance appraisal methods, or its compensation package.[22]

Changing Technology and Operations

Technology is the conversion process used by an organization to transform inputs into outputs. Because of the rapid rate of all technological innovation, technological changes are becoming increasingly important to many organizations. Table 7.1 lists several areas where technological change is likely to be experienced. One important area of change today revolves around information technology. The adoption and institutionalization of information technology innovations are almost constant in most firms. Sun Microsystems, for example, adopted a very short-range planning cycle to be best prepared for environmental changes. Another important form of technological change involves equipment. To keep pace with competitors, firms periodically find that replacing existing machinery and equipment with newer models is necessary.

A change in work processes or work activities may be necessary if new equipment is introduced or new products are manufactured. In manufacturing industries, the major reason for changing a work process is to accommodate a change in the materials used to produce a finished product. Consider a firm that manufactures battery-operated flashlights. For many years, flashlights were made of metal, but now most are made of plastic. A firm might decide to move from metal to plastic flashlights because of consumer preferences, raw materials' costs, or other reasons. Whatever the reason, the technology necessary to make flashlights from plastic differs importantly from that used to make flashlights from metal. Work process changes may occur in service organizations as well as in manufacturing firms. As traditional barbershops and beauty parlors are replaced by hair salons catering to both sexes, for example, the hybrid organizations have to develop new methods for handling appointments and setting prices.

A change in work sequence may or may not accompany a change in equipment or a change in work processes. Making a change in work sequence means altering the order or sequence of the workstations involved in a particular manufacturing process. For example, a manufacturer might have two parallel assembly lines producing two similar sets of machine parts. The lines might converge at one central quality-control unit, where inspectors verify tolerances. The manager, however, might decide to change to periodic rather than final inspection. Under this arrangement, one or more inspections are established farther up the line.

Work sequence changes can also be made in service organizations. The processing of insurance claims, for example, could be changed. The sequence of logging and verifying claims, requesting checks, getting countersignatures, and mailing checks could be altered in several ways, such as combining the first two steps or routing the claims through one person while another handles checks. Organizational control systems may also be targets of change. For example, a firm attempting to improve the quality of its products might develop and implement a set of more rigorous and comprehensive quality-control procedures.

Finally, many businesses have been working to implement technological and operations change by installing and using complex and integrated software systems. Such systems—called *enterprise resource planning* (ERP)—link virtually all facets of the business, making it easier for managers to keep abreast of related developments. **ERP** is a large-scale information system for integrating and synchronizing the many activities in the extended enterprise. In most cases, these systems are purchased from external vendors who then tailor their products to the client's unique needs and requirements. Companywide processes—such as materials management, production planning, order management, and financial reporting—can all be managed through ERP. In effect, these are the processes that cut across product lines, departments, and geographic locations.

Developing the ERP system starts by identifying the key processes that need critical attention, such as supplier relationships, material flows, or customer order fulfillment. The system could result, for instance, in sales processes being integrated with production planning and then integrating both of these into the firm's financial accounting system. For example, a customer in Rome can place an order that is to be produced in Ireland, schedule it to be shipped through air cargo to Rome, and then have it picked up by a truck at the airport and delivered to the customer's warehouse by a specified date. All of these activities are synchronized by activities linkages in one massive database.

The ERP integrates all activities and information flows that relate to the firm's critical processes. It also keeps updated real-time information on their current status, reports recent past transactions and upcoming planned transactions, and provides electronic notices that action is required on some items if planned schedules are to be met. It coordinates internal operations with activities by outside suppliers and notifies business partners and customers of current status and upcoming deliveries and billings. It can integrate financial flows among the firm, its suppliers, its customers, and commercial bank deposits for up-to-the-minute status reports that can be used to create real-time financial reports at a moment's notice, rather than in the traditional one-month (or longer) time span for producing a financial statement. ERP's multilanguage capabilities also allow real-time correspondence in various languages to facilitate international transactions.

Changing People, Attitudes, and Behaviors

A third area of organization change has to do with human resources. For example, an organization might decide to change the skill level of its workforce. This change might

ERP
A large-scale information system for integrating and synchronizing the many activities in the extended enterprise

be prompted by changes in technology or by a general desire to upgrade the quality of the workforce. Thus, training programs and new selection criteria might be needed. The organization might also decide to improve its workers' performance level. In this instance, a new incentive system or performance-based training might be in order. *Reader's Digest* recently eliminated 17 percent of its employees, reduced retirement benefits, and took away many of the "perks" (perquisites, or job benefits) that employees once enjoyed. Part of the reason for the changes was to instill in the remaining employees a sense of urgency and the need to adopt a new perspective on how they do their jobs. Similarly, Saks Fifth Avenue changed its entire top management team as a way to breathe new life into the luxury retailer.

Perceptions and expectations are also a common focus of organization change. Workers in an organization might believe that their wages and benefits are not as high as they should be. Management, however, might have evidence that shows the firm is paying a competitive wage and providing a superior benefit package. The change, then, would be centered on informing and educating the workforce about the comparative value of its compensation package. A common way to do this is to publish a statement that places an actual dollar value on each benefit provided and compares that amount to what other local organizations are providing their workers.

Change might also be directed at employee attitudes and values. In many organizations today, managers are trying to eliminate adversarial relationships with workers and to adopt a more collaborative relationship. In many ways, changing attitudes and values is perhaps the hardest thing to do.[23]

Changing Business Processes

Many organizations today have also gone through massive and comprehensive change programs involving all aspects of organization design, technology, and people. Although various descriptions are used, the terms currently in vogue for these changes are **business process change**, or **reengineering**, which is the radical redesign of all aspects of a business to achieve major gains in cost, service, or time.[24] ERP, as described earlier, is a common platform for changing business processes. However, business process change is a more comprehensive set of changes that goes beyond software and information systems.

Corning, for example, has undergone major reengineering. Whereas the 150-year-old business once manufactured cookware and other durable consumer goods, it has transformed itself into a high-tech powerhouse making products such as the ultra-thin screens used in products such as smartphones and laptops. Similarly, the dramatic overhauls of Yellow into a sophisticated freight delivery firm and of UPS into a major international delivery giant all required business process changes throughout these organizations.

The Need for Business Process Change   Why are so many organizations finding it necessary to undergo business process change? We noted in Chapter 1 that all systems, including organizations, are subject to entropy—a normal process leading to system decline. An organization is behaving most typically when it maintains the status quo, does not change in synch with its environment, and starts consuming its own resources to survive. In a sense, that is what happened to Kmart. In the early and mid-1970s, Kmart was in such a high-flying growth mode that it passed first J. C. Penney and then Sears to become the world's largest retailer. But then the firm's managers grew complacent and assumed that the discount retailer's prosperity would continue and that they

business process change (reengineering)
The radical redesign of all aspects of a business to achieve major gains in cost, service, or time

TOUGH TIMES, TOUGH CHOICES

To Offshore or Not to Offshore

From computer programmers in the Philippines and molecular biologists in Russia to customer-service agents in India, the practice of *offshoring* is bringing workers from around the world into the workforces of U.S. corporations in a broad range of industries. When U.S. firms "offshore," they're hiring foreign firms and foreign personnel to perform their business functions. In so doing, they're not only increasing the diversity of their workforces but also altering the processes by which they conduct organizational business. At Penske Truck Leasing, for instance, drivers submit their paper logs for data entry to a facility in Mexico, which forwards them to Hyderabad, India, where they're analyzed, and the results are reported to Penske management back in the United States. How does a company function with far-flung operations? As in most other decisions, companies choose operational partners according to the value-creation capabilities that they bring to the overall process.

Ideally, of course, offshoring should benefit the contractor as well as the contracting firm. Take, for example, the case of Wisconsin-based PCMC, which

designs and makes paper packaging. PCMC had a problem with its engineering function: Although it had a large base of potential customers, it often lost them because its engineering group was too small to create new designs fast enough to keep pace with customer needs. Nor could the company afford to expand its engineering department. To solve the problem, PCMC entered into an offshoring contract with an Indian company that agreed to provide a 160-member staff to support PCMC's engineering function. The result? Not only 160 new jobs in India but more orders and more jobs in Wisconsin as well.

Obviously, offshoring arrangements don't always work out as well as the one established by PCMC and its Indian partner. For one thing, language and culture differences can make communication difficult, especially when it's conducted by e-mail or phone. When 1-800-FLOWERS tried to expand its customer-service operation by outsourcing customer calls to India, the results were disastrous. Why? When customers call, florists have to do more than merely process orders: They're often called upon to

ZUMA Press/Alamy

Many businesses today have offshored various operations to foreign countries. These offshoring initiatives often involve call centers, and many businesses have found this approach to be very effective. But others, like 1-800-FLOWERS, have experienced problems with offshoring and some have even moved operations back to their home country.

(*continued*)

TOUGH TIMES, TOUGH CHOICES (Continued)

offer interior-design tips and relationship counseling and even to console the grieving. Indian workers could neither fully understand the psychology of U.S. flower buyers nor communicate the nuances necessary to serve their needs. After a few weeks, 1-800-FLOWERS terminated the experiment. "The folks were difficult to understand," admitted one company executive. "We were afraid that we would lose sales, and we couldn't risk that."

The decision made sense: Typically, it costs six times as much to replace a customer as to keep one. Fortunately, the company had a plan B—*homeshoring*, or hiring in-country contract workers. Homeshoring

employees are more expensive than overseas contractors, but they're less expensive than full-time on-site employees. They connect with American customers, and they also alleviate the concerns that some U.S. consumers have about their private data being shipped overseas.

References: Michelle Conlin, "Call Centers in the Rec Room," *Businessweek*, www.businessweek.com, accessed on November 15, 2013; Pete Engardio, "The Future of Outsourcing," *Businessweek*, www.businessweek.com, accessed on November 15, 2013; and Manjeet Kripalani with Brian Grow, "Offshoring: Spreading the Gospel," *Businessweek*, www.businessweek.com, accessed on November 15, 2013.

need not worry about environmental shifts, the growth of Walmart, and so forth—and entropy set in. The key is to recognize the beginning of the decline and immediately move toward changing relevant business processes. Major problems occur when managers either do not recognize the onset of entropy until it is well advanced or are complacent in taking steps to correct it.

Approaches to Business Process Change   Figure 7.3 shows general steps in reengineering. The first step is setting goals and developing a strategy for the changes. The organization must know in advance what new business processes are supposed to accomplish and how those accomplishments will be achieved. Next, top managers must begin and direct the reengineering effort. If a CEO simply announces that business process change is to occur but does nothing else, the program is unlikely to be successful. But, if the CEO is constantly involved in the process, underscoring its importance and taking the lead, business process change stands a much better chance of success.

Most experts also agree that successful business process change is usually accompanied by a sense of urgency. People in the organization must see the clear and present need for the changes being implemented and appreciate their importance. In addition, most successful reengineering efforts start with a new, clean slate. In other words, rather than assuming that the existing organization is a starting point and then trying to modify it, business process change usually starts by asking questions such as how customers are best served and competitors best neutralized. New approaches and systems are then created and imposed in place of existing ones.

Finally, business process change requires a careful blend of top-down and bottom-up involvement. On the one hand, strong leadership is necessary, but too much involvement by top management can make the changes seem autocratic. On the other hand, employee participation is also important, but too little involvement by leaders can undermine the program's importance and create a sense that top managers do not care. Thus, care must be taken to carefully balance these two countervailing forces. Our next section explores more fully one related but distinct approach called organization development (OD).

© Cengage Learning

FIGURE 7.3

The Reengineering Process

Reengineering is a major redesign of all areas of an organization. To be successful, reengineering requires a systematic and comprehensive assessment of the entire organization. Goals, top management support, and a sense of urgency help the organization re-create itself and blend both top-down and bottom-up perspectives.

Organization Development

We noted in several places the importance of people and change. Beyond those change interests discussed earlier, a special area of interest that focuses almost exclusively on people is OD.

OD Assumptions   OD is concerned with changing attitudes, perceptions, behaviors, and expectations. More precisely, **organization development** is a planned effort that is organization-wide, managed from the top, and intended to increase organizational effectiveness and health through planned interventions in the organization's process, using behavioral science knowledge.[25] The theory and practice of OD are based on several very important assumptions. The first is that employees have a desire to grow and develop. Another is that employees have a strong need to be accepted by others within the organization. Still another critical assumption of OD is that the total organization and the way it is designed will influence the way individuals and groups within the organization behave. Thus, some form of collaboration between managers and their employees is necessary to (1) take advantage of the skills and abilities of the employees and (2) eliminate aspects of the organization that retard employee growth, development, and group acceptance. Because of the intense personal nature of many OD activities, many large organizations rely on one or more OD consultants (either full-time employees assigned to this function or outside experts hired specifically for OD purposes) to implement and manage their OD program.[26]

OD Techniques   Several kinds of interventions or activities are generally considered part of OD. Some OD programs may use only one or a few of these; other programs use several of them at once.

organization development

A planned effort that is organization-wide, managed from the top, and intended to increase organizational effectiveness and health through planned interventions in the organization's process, using behavioral science knowledge

- *Diagnostic activities.* Just as a physician examines patients to diagnose their current condition, an OD diagnosis analyzes the current condition of an organization. To carry out this diagnosis, managers use questionnaires, opinion or attitude surveys, interviews, archival data, and meetings to assess various characteristics of the organization. The results of this diagnosis may generate profiles of the organization's activities, which can then be used to identify problem areas in need of correction.

- *Team building.* Team-building activities are intended to enhance the effectiveness and satisfaction of individuals who work in groups or teams and to promote overall group effectiveness. Given the widespread use of teams today, these activities have taken on increased importance. An OD consultant might interview team members to determine how they feel about the group; then an off-site meeting could be held to discuss the issues that surfaced and iron out any problem areas or member concerns. Caterpillar used team building as one method for changing the working relationships between workers and supervisors from confrontational to cooperative. One interesting new approach to team building involves having executive teams participate in group cooking classes to teach them the importance of interdependence and coordination.

- *Survey feedback.* In survey feedback, each employee responds to a questionnaire intended to measure perceptions and attitudes (for example, satisfaction and supervisory style). Everyone involved, including the supervisor, receives the results of the survey. The aim of this approach is usually to change the behavior of supervisors by showing them how their subordinates view them. After the feedback has been provided, workshops may be conducted to evaluate results and suggest constructive changes.

- *Third-party peacemaking.* Another approach to OD is through third-party peacemaking, which is most often used when substantial conflict exists within the organization. Third-party peacemaking can be appropriate on the individual, group, or organizational level. The third party, usually an OD consultant, uses a variety of mediation or negotiation techniques to resolve any problems or conflicts among individuals or groups.

- *Process consultation.* In process consultation, an OD consultant observes groups in the organization to develop an understanding of their communication patterns, decision-making and leadership processes, and methods of cooperation and conflict resolution. The consultant then provides feedback to the involved parties about the processes he or she has observed. The goal of this form of intervention is to improve the observed processes. A leader who is presented with feedback outlining deficiencies in his or her leadership style, for example, might be expected to change to overcome them.

- *Life and career planning.* Life and career planning helps employees formulate their personal goals and evaluate strategies for integrating their goals with the goals of the organization. Such activities might include specification of training needs and plotting a career map. General Electric has a reputation for doing an outstanding job in this area.

- *Coaching and counseling.* Coaching and counseling provide nonevaluative feedback to individuals. The purpose is to help people develop a better sense of how others see them and learn behaviors that will assist others in achieving their work-related goals. The focus is not on how the individual is performing today; instead, it is on how the person can perform better in the future.

The Effectiveness of OD   Given the diversity of activities encompassed by OD, it is not surprising that managers have reported mixed results from various OD interventions. Organizations that actively practice some form of OD include American Airlines,

Texas Instruments, Procter & Gamble, and BF Goodrich. Goodrich, for example, has trained 60 persons in OD processes and techniques. These trained experts have subsequently become internal OD consultants to assist other managers in applying the techniques. Many other managers, in contrast, report that they have tried OD but discarded it.

OD will probably remain an important part of management theory and practice. Of course, there are no sure things when dealing with social systems such as organizations, and the effectiveness of many OD techniques is difficult to evaluate. Because all organizations are open systems interacting with their environments, an improvement in an organization after an OD intervention may be attributable to the intervention, but it may also be attributable to changes in economic conditions, luck, or other factors.

ORGANIZATIONAL INNOVATION

innovation
The managed effort of an organization to develop new products or services or new uses for existing products or services

A final element of organization change that we address is **innovation**, which is the managed effort of an organization to develop new products or services or new uses for existing products or services. Innovation is clearly important because, without new products or services, any organization will fall behind its competition.

The Innovation Process

The organizational innovation process consists of developing, applying, launching, growing, and managing the maturity and decline of creative ideas.[27] This process is depicted in Figure 7.4.

Innovation Development   Innovation development involves the evaluation, modification, and improvement of creative ideas. It can transform a product or service with only modest potential into a product or service with significant potential. Parker Brothers, for example, decided during innovation development not to market an indoor volleyball game but instead to sell separately the appealing little foam ball designed for the game. The firm will never know how well the volleyball game would have sold, but the Nerf ball and numerous related products generated millions of dollars in revenues.

Development
Organization evaluates, modifies, and improves on a creative idea.

Application
Organization uses developed idea in design, manufacturing, or delivery of new products, services, or processes.

Launch
Organization introduces new products or services to the marketplace.

Decline
Demand for an innovation decreases, and substitute innovations are developed and applied.

Maturity
Most competing organizations have access to the idea.

Growth
Demand for new products or services grows.

© Cengage Learning

FIGURE 7.4

The Innovation Process

Organizations actively seek to manage the innovation process. These steps illustrate the general life cycle that characterizes most innovations. Of course, as with creativity, the innovation process will suffer if it is approached too mechanically and rigidly.

Innovation Application Innovation application is the stage in which an organization takes a developed idea and uses it in the design, manufacturing, or delivery of new products, services, or processes. At this point, the innovation emerges from the laboratory and is transformed into tangible goods or services. Business incubators and similar concepts are often used to facilitate innovation application.

Application Launch Application launch is the stage at which an organization introduces new products or services to the marketplace. The important question is not "Does the innovation work?" but "Will customers want to purchase the innovative product and service?" History is full of creative ideas that did not generate enough interest among customers to be successful. Some notable innovation failures include a portable seat warmer from Sony, "New" Coke, the revival of the Ford Thunderbird, and the Flip video recorder. Thus, despite development and application, new products and services can still fail at the launch phase.

Application Growth Once an innovation has been successfully launched, it then enters the stage of application growth. This is a period of high economic performance for an organization because demand for the product or service is often greater than supply. Organizations that fail to anticipate this stage may unintentionally limit their growth, as Apple did by not anticipating demand for the first iPhones. At the same time, overestimating demand for a new product can be just as detrimental to performance. Unsold products can sit in warehouses for years.

Innovation Maturity After a period of growing demand, an innovative product or service often enters a period of maturity. Innovation maturity is the stage at which most organizations in an industry have access to an innovation and are applying it in approximately the same way. The technological application of an innovation during this stage of the innovation process can be very sophisticated. Because most firms have access to the innovation, however, as a result of either developing the innovation on their own or copying the innovation from others, it does not provide competitive advantage to any one of them. The time that elapses between innovation development and innovation maturity varies notably depending on the particular product or service. Whenever an innovation involves the use of complex skills (such as a complicated manufacturing process or highly sophisticated teamwork), moving from the growth phase to the maturity phase will take longer. In addition, if the skills needed to implement these innovations are rare and difficult to imitate, then strategic imitation may be delayed, and the organization may enjoy a period of sustained competitive advantage.

Innovation Decline Every successful innovation bears its own seeds of decline. Because an organization does not gain a competitive advantage from an innovation at maturity, it must encourage its creative scientists, engineers, and managers to begin looking for additional innovations. This continued search for competitive advantage usually leads new products and services to move from the creative process through innovation maturity, and finally to innovation decline. Innovation decline is the stage during which demand for an innovation decreases and substitute innovations are developed and applied.

Forms of Innovation

Each creative idea that an organization develops poses a different challenge for the innovation process. Innovations can be radical or incremental, technical or managerial, and product or process innovations.

© iStockphoto.com/Saturated

The original iPhones and iPads were in many ways radical innovations in that they redefined product categories. Each subsequent generation of these products, however, such as the iPad Air shown here, are incremental innovations that take previous versions and introduce relatively minor improvements and/or new design features.

Radical Versus Incremental Innovations

Radical innovations are new products, services, or technologies developed by an organization that completely replace the existing products, services, or technologies in an industry.[28] **Incremental innovations** are new products, services, or processes that modify existing ones. Firms that implement radical innovations fundamentally shift the nature of competition and the interaction of firms within their environments. Firms that implement incremental innovations alter, but do not fundamentally change, competitive interaction in an industry.

Over the last several years, organizations have introduced many radical innovations. For example, compact disc (CD) technology replaced long-playing vinyl records in the recording industry and now digital downloading is replacing CDs, DVDs have replaced videocassettes but are now being supplanted by Blu-ray DVDs and online downloading, and high-definition television is replacing regular television technology. Whereas radical innovations like these tend to be very visible and public, incremental innovations actually are more numerous. For instance, each new generation of the iPhone and the iPad represents relatively minor changes over previous versions.

radical innovations
A new product, service, or technology that completely replaces an existing one

incremental innovations
A new product, service, or technology that modifies an existing one

Technical Versus Managerial Innovations

Technical innovations are changes in the physical appearance or performance of a product or service or of the physical processes through which a product or service is manufactured. Many of the most important innovations over the last 50 years have been technical. For example, the serial replacement of the vacuum tube with the transistor, the transistor with the integrated circuit, and the integrated circuit with the microchip have greatly enhanced the power, ease of use, and speed of operation of a wide variety of electronic products. Not all innovations developed by organizations are technical, however. **Managerial innovations** are changes in the management process by which products and services are conceived, built, and delivered to customers.[29] They do not necessarily affect the physical appearance or performance of products or services directly. In effect, reengineering, as we discussed earlier, represents a managerial innovation.

Product Versus Process Innovations

Perhaps the two most important types of technical innovations are **product innovations** and process innovations. Product innovations are changes in the physical characteristics or performance of existing products or services or the creation of brand-new products or services. **Process innovations** are changes in the way products or services are manufactured, created, or distributed. Whereas managerial innovations generally affect the broader context of development, process innovations directly affect manufacturing.

technical innovations

A change in the appearance or performance of a product or service or of the physical processes through which a product or service is manufactured

managerial innovations

A change in the management process in an organization

product innovations

A change in the physical characteristics or performance of an existing product or service or the creation of a new one

process innovations

A change in the way a product or service is manufactured, created, or distributed

The implementation of robotics is a process innovation. The effect of product and process innovations on economic return depends on the stage of the innovation process that a new product or service occupies. At first, during development, application, and launch, the physical attributes and capabilities of an innovation mostly affect organizational performance. Thus, product innovations are particularly important during these beginning phases. Later, as an innovation enters the phases of growth, maturity, and decline, an organization's ability to develop process innovations, such as fine-tuning manufacturing, increasing product quality, and improving product distribution, becomes important to maintaining economic return.

Japanese organizations have often excelled at process innovation. The market for SLR cameras was dominated by German and other European manufacturers when, in the early 1960s, Japanese organizations such as Canon and Nikon began making cameras. Some of these early Japanese products were not very successful, but these companies continued to invest in their process technology and eventually were able to increase quality and decrease manufacturing costs. The Japanese organizations came to dominate the worldwide market for SLR cameras, and the German companies, because they were not able to maintain the same pace of process innovation, struggled to maintain market share and profitability. And as film technology gave way to digital photography, the same Japanese firms effectively transitioned to leadership in this market as well.

The Failure to Innovate

To remain competitive in today's economy, organizations must be innovative. And yet many organizations that should be innovative are not successful at bringing out new products or services, or they do so only after innovations created by others are very mature. Organizations may fail to innovate for at least three reasons.

Lack of Resources   Innovation is expensive in terms of money, time, and energy. If a firm does not have sufficient money to fund a program of innovation or does not currently employ the kinds of employees it needs to be innovative, it may lag behind in innovation. Even highly innovative organizations cannot become involved in every new product or service its employees think up. For example, numerous other commitments in the electronic instruments and computer industry forestalled Hewlett-Packard (HP) from investing in Steve Jobs and Steve Wozniak's original idea for a personal computer. With infinite resources of money, time, and technical and managerial expertise, HP might have entered this market early. Because the firm did not have this flexibility, however, it had to make some difficult choices regarding in which innovations to invest.[30]

Failure to Recognize Opportunities   Because firms cannot pursue all innovations, they need to develop the capability to carefully evaluate innovations and to select the ones that hold the greatest potential. To obtain a competitive advantage, an organization must usually make investment decisions before the innovation process reaches the mature stage. The earlier the investment, however, the greater the risk. If organizations are not skilled at recognizing and evaluating opportunities, they may be overly cautious and fail to invest in innovations that later turn out to be successful for other firms.

Resistance to Change   As we discussed earlier, many organizations tend to resist change. Innovation means giving up old products and old ways of doing things in favor of new products and new ways of doing things. These kinds of changes can be personally difficult for managers and other members of an organization. Thus, resistance to change can slow the innovation process.

Promoting Innovation in Organizations   A wide variety of ideas for promoting innovation in organizations has been developed over the years. Three specific ways for promoting innovation are through the reward system, through the organizational culture, and through a process called *intrapreneurship.*[31]

The Reward System   A firm's reward system is the means by which it encourages and discourages certain behaviors by employees. Major components of the reward system include salaries, bonuses, and perquisites. Using the reward system to promote innovation is a fairly mechanical but nevertheless effective management technique. The idea is to provide financial and nonfinancial rewards to people and groups who develop innovative ideas. Once the members of an organization understand that they will be rewarded for such activities, they are more likely to work creatively. With this end in mind, Monsanto gives a $50,000 award each year to the scientist or group of scientists who develop the biggest commercial breakthrough.

It is important for organizations to reward creative behavior, but it is vital to avoid punishing creativity when it does not result in highly successful innovations. It is the nature of the creative and innovative processes that many new-product ideas will simply not work out in the marketplace. Each process is fraught with too many uncertainties to generate positive results every time. An individual may have prepared herself to be creative, but an insight may not be forthcoming. Or managers may attempt to apply a developed innovation, only to recognize that it does not work. Indeed, some organizations operate according to the assumption that, if all their innovative efforts succeed, then they are probably not taking enough risks in research and development. At 3M, nearly 60 percent of the creative ideas suggested each year do not succeed in the marketplace.

Managers need to be very careful in responding to innovative failure. If innovative failure is due to incompetence, systematic errors, or managerial sloppiness, then a firm should respond appropriately, for example, by withholding raises or reducing promotion opportunities. People who act in good faith to develop an innovation that simply does not work out, however, should not be punished for failure. If they are, they probably will not be creative in the future. A punitive reward system will discourage people from taking risks and therefore reduce the organization's ability to obtain competitive advantages.

Organization Culture   As we discussed in Chapter 2, an organization's culture is the set of values, beliefs, and symbols that help guide behavior. A strong, appropriately focused organizational culture can be used to support innovative activity. A well-managed culture can communicate a sense that innovation is valued and will be rewarded and that occasional failure in the pursuit of new ideas is not only acceptable but even expected. In addition to reward systems and intrapreneurial activities, firms such as Apple, Google, LG Electronics, Tata, Amazon, and HP are all known to have strong, innovation-oriented cultures that value individual creativity, risk taking, and inventiveness.[32]

intrapreneurs
Similar to entrepreneurs except that they develop new businesses in the context of a large organization

Intrapreneurship in Larger Organizations   In recent years, many large businesses have realized that the entrepreneurial spirit that propelled their growth becomes stagnant after they transform themselves from a small but growing concern into a larger one.[33] To help revitalize this spirit, some firms today encourage intrapreneurship. **Intrapreneurs** are similar to entrepreneurs except that they develop a new business in the context of a

Bernhard Classen/Alamy

Amazon.com is known for its innovative business practices. The firm's culture helps promote individual creativity, risk taking, and inventiveness. This Amazon.com distribution center, for example, was developed using new methods devised by Amazon employees.

large organization. There are three intrapreneurial roles in large organizations.[34] To successfully use intrapreneurship to encourage creativity and innovation, the organization must find one or more individuals to perform these roles.

The *inventor* is the person who actually conceives of and develops the new idea, product, or service by means of the creative process. Because the inventor may lack the expertise or motivation to oversee the transformation of the product or service from an idea into a marketable entity, however, a second role comes into play. A *product champion* is usually a middle manager who learns about the project and becomes committed to it. He helps overcome organizational resistance and convinces others to take the innovation seriously. The product champion may have only limited understanding of the technological aspects of the innovation. Nevertheless, product champions are skilled at knowing how the organization works, whose support is needed to push the project forward, and where to go to secure the resources necessary for successful development. A *sponsor* is a top-level manager who approves of and supports a project. This person may fight for the budget needed to develop an idea, overcome arguments against a project, and use organizational politics to ensure the project's survival. With a sponsor in place, the inventor's idea has a much better chance of being successfully developed.

Several firms have embraced intrapreneurship as a way to encourage creativity and innovation. Colgate-Palmolive has created a separate unit, Colgate Venture Company, staffed with intrapreneurs who develop new products. General Foods developed Culinova as a unit to which employees can take their ideas for possible development. S.C. Johnson & Son established a $250,000 fund to support new-product ideas, and Texas Instruments refuses to approve an innovative project unless it has an acknowledged inventor, champion, and sponsor.

SUMMARY OF LEARNING OUTCOMES AND KEY POINTS

1. Describe the nature of organization change, including forces for change and planned versus reactive change.

   - Organization change is any substantive modification to some part of the organization.
   - Change may be prompted by forces internal or external to the organization.
   - In general, planned change is preferable to reactive change.

2. Discuss the steps in organization change and how to manage resistance to change.

   - The Lewin model provides a general perspective on the steps involved in change.
   - A comprehensive model is usually more effective.
   - People tend to resist change because of uncertainty, threatened self-interests, different perceptions, and feelings of loss.
   - Participation, education and communication, facilitation, and force-field analysis are methods for overcoming this resistance.

3. Identify and describe major areas of organization change and discuss the assumptions, techniques, and effectiveness of OD.

   - The most common areas of change involve changing organizational structure and design, technology, and people.

   - Business process change is a more massive and comprehensive change.
   - OD is concerned with changing attitudes, perceptions, behaviors, and expectations. Its effective use relies on an important set of assumptions.
   - There are conflicting opinions about the effectiveness of several OD techniques.

4. Describe the innovation process, forms of innovation, the failure to innovate, and how organizations can promote innovation.

   - The innovation process has six steps: development, application, launch, growth, maturity, and decline.
   - Basic categories of innovation include radical, incremental, technical, managerial, product, and process innovations.
   - Despite the importance of innovation, many organizations fail to innovate because they lack the required creative individuals or are committed to too many other creative activities, fail to recognize opportunities, or resist the change that innovation requires.
   - Organizations can use a variety of tools to overcome these problems, including the reward system, organizational culture, and intrapreneurship.

DISCUSSION QUESTIONS

Questions for Review

1. What forces or kinds of events lead to organization change? Identify each force or event as the primary determinant of a planned or a reactive change.
2. Compare planned and reactive change. What are the advantages of planned change, as compared to reactive change?
3. Identify the primary reasons people resist change, and then summarize the primary methods managers can use to overcome this resistance.
4. In a brief sentence or just a phrase, describe each of the OD techniques.
5. Consider the following list of products. Categorize each along all three dimensions of innovation, if possible (radical versus incremental, technical versus managerial, and product versus process). Explain your answers.

   - Teaching college courses by digitally recording the instructor and then making the digital file available online
   - The rise in popularity of virtual organizations (discussed in Chapter 6)
   - Checking the security of packages on airlines with the type of magnetic resonance imaging (MRI) scanning devices that are common in health care
   - Smartphone devices such as the iPhone
   - Robotic arms that can perform surgery that is too precise for a human surgeon's hands
   - Hybrid automobiles, which run on both batteries and gasoline
   - Using video games to teach soldiers how to plan and execute battles

Questions for Analysis

1. What symptoms should a manager look for in determining whether an organization needs to change? What symptoms indicate that an organization has been through too much change?

2. Assume that you are the manager of an organization that has a routine way of performing a task and now faces a major change in how it performs that task. Using the Lewin model, tell what steps you would take to implement the change. Using the comprehensive approach, tell what steps you would take. For each step, give specific examples of actions you would take at that step.

3. Think back to a time when a professor announced a change that you, the student, did not want to adopt. What were the reasons for your resistance to change? Was the professor able to overcome your resistance? If so, tell what he or she did. If not, tell what he or she could have done that might have been successful.

4. Some people resist change, whereas others welcome it enthusiastically. To deal with the first group, one needs to overcome resistance to change; to deal with the second, one needs to overcome resistance to stability. What advice can you give a manager facing the latter situation?

5. Can a change made in one area of an organization—in technology, for instance—not lead to change in other areas? If you think that change in one area must lead to change in other areas, describe an example of an organization change to illustrate your point. If you think that change can occur in just one area without causing change in other areas, describe an example of an organization change that illustrates your point.

BUILDING EFFECTIVE DECISION-MAKING SKILLS

Exercise Overview

Decision-making skills refer to the ability to recognize and define problems and opportunities correctly and then to select an appropriate course of action for solving problems or capitalizing on opportunities. This exercise gives you some practice in making decisions about organizational innovation.

Exercise Background

You're a manager at a venture capital firm that seeks out companies with promising new ideas for technological improvements and then provides financing, advice, and expertise in exchange for part ownership. Your firm makes money when an idea is successfully brought to market, and the value of your ownership shares increases. Your personal compensation—not to mention your continued employment—are therefore based on your ability to choose the right ideas and to provide entrepreneurs with the right support.

Exercise Task

1. Use the Internet to locate information about at least five promising new technologies. (*Hint*: The websites of publications that report technology news, such as *TechWeb*, are good sources, as are the corporate websites of innovative companies like 3M. Or search the term *technology venture capital* to locate firms that invest in new technologies, and then find out what you can about their clients.) Then choose the new technology that interests you the most.

2. Next, describe the current status of your chosen technology in the innovation process. Explain how you arrived at your decision about where to place the technology in the process.

3. Finally, discuss the kinds of advice and expertise that this idea and its company need to grow into a successful start-up.

BUILDING EFFECTIVE DIAGNOSTIC SKILLS

Exercise Overview

Diagnostic skills, which enable a manager to visualize the most appropriate response to a situation, are especially important during periods of organizational change.

Exercise Background

You're the general manager of a hotel situated along a beautiful stretch of beach on a tropical island. One of the oldest of six large resorts in the immediate area, your hotel is owned by a group of foreign investors.

For several years, it's been operated as a franchise unit of a large international hotel chain, as have all the other hotels on the island.

For the past few years, the hotel's franchisee-owners have been taking most of the profits for themselves and putting relatively little back into the hotel. They've also let you know that their business is not in good financial health and that the revenue from the hotel is being used to offset losses incurred elsewhere. In contrast, most of the other hotels on the island have recently been refurbished, and plans for two brand-new hotels have been announced for the near future.

A team of executives from franchise headquarters has just visited your hotel. They're quite disappointed in the property, particularly because it's failed to keep pace with other resorts on the island. They've informed you that if the property isn't brought up to standards, the franchise agreement, which is up for review in a year, will be revoked. You realize that this move would be a potential disaster because you can ill afford to lose the franchisor's brand name, access to its reservation system, or any other benefits of the franchise arrangement.

Sitting alone in your office, you've identified several seemingly viable courses of action:

1. Convince the franchisee-owners to remodel the hotel. You estimate that it will take $10 million to meet the franchisor's minimum standards and another $15 million to bring the hotel up to the standards of the island's top resort.
2. Convince the franchisor to give you more time and more options for upgrading the facility.
3. Allow the franchise agreement to terminate and try to succeed as an independent hotel.
4. Assume that the hotel will fail and start looking for another job. You have a pretty good reputation, but you're not terribly happy about the possibility of having to accept a lower-level position (say, as an assistant manager) with another firm.

Exercise Task

Having mulled over your options, do the following:

1. Rank-order your four alternatives in terms of probable success. Make any necessary assumptions.
2. Identify alternatives other than the four that you first identified.
3. Can more than one alternative be pursued simultaneously? Which ones?
4. Develop an overall strategy for trying to save the hotel while protecting your own interests.

SKILLS SELF-ASSESSMENT INSTRUMENT

Innovation and Learning Styles

Introduction: David Kolb, a professor at Case Western University, has described a learning model that tells about different learning styles. While individuals move through all four activities, most express a preference for either hands-on learning or learning by indirect observation, and most express a preference for either learning about abstract concepts or learning about concrete experience. When these two dimensions are combined, the following learning styles are created.

Instructions: Fill out the following tables.

	Active Experimentation	Reflective Observation
Concrete Experience	Accommodator	Diverger
Abstract Conceptualization	Converger	Assimilator

Individuals with any of these styles can be creative and your learning innovative, although the way they will approach creativity and the contribution they can make to the innovation process differ. If you understand style, you'll be better equipped to participate in innovation.

Rank from 1 to 4
(1 = least like you,
4 = most like you)

1. a. I want to try something out first.
   b. I need to feel personally involved with things.
   c. I focus on useful practical applications.
   d. I look for differences and distinctions.

(continued)

	Active Experimentation	Reflective Observation
		Rank from 1 to 4 (1 = least like you, 4 = most like you)

2. a. I work mainly by intuition.
   b. I tend to ask myself questions.
   c. I always try to think logically.
   d. I am very result oriented.

		Rank from 1 to 4 (1 = least like you, 4 = most like you)

3. a. I let everything filter through my head and think about it.
   b. I am interested in the here and now.
   c. I mainly have a practical nature.
   d. I am mostly interested in the future.

		Rank from 1 to 4 (1 = least like you, 4 = most like you)

4. a. I consider the facts, and then I act.
   b. I act.
   c. I ponder until I have evaluated every option, and then I act.
   d. I would rather dream or imagine than think about the facts.

Interpretation: Add scores for 1a, 2d, 3b, and 4b. This is your Accommodator score.

Add scores for 1b, 2a, 3d, and 4d. This is your Diverger score.

Add scores for 1c, 2c, 3c, and 4a. This is your Converger score.

Add scores for 1d, 2b, 3a, and 4c. This is your Assimilator score.

While everyone uses each of the four styles at times, whichever score is higher is your preferred mode.

EXPERIENTIAL EXERCISE

Team Innovation

Purpose: To give you practice related to innovation as a team activity.

Introduction: Assume that your group is a team of professionals who are in charge of new-product design at your company.

Instructions: *Step 1*: Using *only* the materials your professor will give to you, design and construct a new product. This product can be something wholly new or an improvement on an existing product.

Step 2: Present your product to the class. Explain its use, features, and appeal to consumers.

Follow-Up Questions

How much influence did the selection of materials have on your design?

1. What, if anything, does this suggest to you about organization resources and their effect on innovation?

2. Explain the process your group used to come up with the design. Describe the number of people who participated, how they participated, how any disagreements were resolved, and so on. What, if anything, does this suggest to you about some of the potential advantages as well as the challenges of team-based innovation in organizations?

3. Describe the various roles played by members of your group. For example, did anyone function primarily as a "voice of caution"? Did anyone serve as a devil's advocate? Did anyone work as a facilitator, smoothing over feelings and resolving conflicts? Were some members better at design or at implementation? What, if anything, does this tell you regarding the various roles that individuals take in the innovation process in organizations?

MANAGEMENT AT WORK
The Science of the Deal

Over a decade ago, OSI Pharmaceuticals, a small bio-technology company based on Long Island, New York, was looking for a partner to share in the development of a newly invented drug for the treatment of lung and pancreatic cancer. The drug was extremely promising, and with 42 companies bidding on a piece of the action, the OSI deal was the year's most competitive in the pharmaceuticals industry. The winner was San Francisco–based Genentech, a highly successful pioneer in the biotech field. In order to lock up the deal, both Genentech and its largest shareholder (and eventual parent), the Swiss pharmaceuticals company Roche Group, purchased $35 million in OSI stock and offered up-front fees totaling another $117 million.

It was certainly an attractive offer, but it wasn't actually the highest bid. OSI went with Genentech because it had more than money to offer. Joe McCracken, who negotiated the deal for Genentech, argues that OSI accepted his bid because his company paid attention to what OSI wanted (in addition to a healthy infusion of capital): "They wanted to build a company," he recalls, "and you were not going to help them build a company by giving them a whole bunch of cash. … What we proposed … was a partner-ship where we would really work together and share the science and be partners in development." The agreement called for Genentech and OSI to share development costs and profits from U.S. sales and Roche to pay royalties on sales in all other markets.

According to McCracken (who was vice president of business development at the time), deals like the one with OSI are mostly about the science and the organizational processes that transform scientific resources into profitable products: At Genentech, he says, "we emphasize scientific rationale and probability of approval much more than we emphasize market size. A strong underlying scientific rationale or a probability of approval will trump market size any time."

For example, McCracken negotiated a deal with a biotech firm called Seattle Genetics Inc. to partner in the commercialization of a cancer drug known as SGN-40. Under the terms of the arrangement, Genentech made an up-front payment of $60 million and agreed to pay for future research, development, and manufacturing through "milestone" payments of more than $800 million based on Seattle Genetics' clinical and regulatory progress in developing the drug. It was

an expensive deal, but McCracken had good reason to make it: "[F]or us to do these larger deals," he explains, "… we have to believe we have synergies we can exploit in maximizing the development of [the products]. In this case, we really believe we have some good insights and expertise in basic research and in development and manufacturing that we can leverage. … This product," he adds, "has the opportunity to address an important disease that we don't have anything else in our pipeline to address. We put a big premium on that." As of 2012, SGN-40 was performing well in clinical trials on patients with a form of blood cancer known as non-Hodgkin lymphoma.

In the pharmaceuticals industry, in addition to the usual run of joint ventures and mergers and acquisitions (M&As), deals come in a variety of forms. *In-licensing* ventures, for example, are partnerships between firms with shared goals, strategies, or fields of interest; like Genentech's deals with OSI and Seattle Genetics, they're often created to share the costs of developing products from which both partners can profit. *Out-licensing* refers to ventures in which a firm seeks a partner to continue the development of a product that's previously been developed internally. For instance, Genentech once took a drug called Raptiva through preclinical and midstage clinical trials but didn't have the financial wherewithal to take it any further. So it out-licensed the drug to a small biotech company called Xoma, which used its familiarity with similar antibodies to complete the development process ("better, faster, and cheaper," according to McCracken). Raptiva returned $500 million in revenue for Genentech during the first five years after its launch. (Unfortunately, Raptiva turned from an asset to a liability in 2009, when Genentech withdrew it from the market: Studies associated usage of the drug with the risk of a rare and usually fatal brain infection, and Genentech is now contending with a slew of lawsuits.)

"Never underestimate the value of a small company that has a singular focus," advises McCracken, who points out that while Genentech was strapped for both the necessary "human resources and management attention," Raptiva was Xoma's "most important project." In the long run, reasons McCracken, this approach to deal making means that "we have all these opportunities and [we] manage our internal growth. The way you maximize the value of the [biotech] business is by leveraging the resources of partners in manufacturing and development." It is interesting to note that McCracken's approach leaves little room for acquisition as a deal-making option; in fact, Genentech has only made one acquisition in its entire history. "We haven't had to do them to drive growth," he explains. "We've been able to sustain growth with our internal pipeline. We've been able to get access to the technologies and products that we needed through licensing activities."

As part of a major reorganization of Genentech's development, commercial, and manufacturing activities, McCracken was given additional responsibilities as head of a new unit called Strategic Pipeline Development. Among the goals of the reorganization was focusing the efforts of top managers on product innovation and the firm's *product pipeline*—the flow of new-product concepts through the process that transforms them into products available to end users. McCracken's new responsibilities included heading up a team to advise the president of the Product Development unit on the expansion of the company's product pipeline.

Following the reorganization, McCracken's team would negotiate anywhere from 40 to 50 deals annually, but hooking up with partners soon became a secondary aspect of his job. Following the reorganization, he spent most of his time with what he called "my customers"—the people *inside* Genentech who conduct the research necessary to develop products already in the pipeline. The shift in his job description, according to McCracken, was important "because business development [at Genentech] is so integrated with our internal customers in research [and] development." For the record, it wasn't long before McCracken was back at the job of making partnership deals, first as Roche's head of Pharma Partnering Asia and, currently, as its global head of business development.

Case Questions

1. You're an up-and-coming assistant to a manager at Roche Group. Your boss is being transferred to the company's recently acquired research facilities at the former Genentech headquarters in San Francisco. She's asked you to compile a brief report on Genentech's overall approach to product innovation. What will you say in your report? (*Hint*: Structure your report according to the three *forms of innovation* discussed in the text: *radical versus incremental*, *technical versus managerial*, and *product versus process*.)

2. Ex-Roche Chairman Franz Humer committed the parent company to sustaining Genentech's "innovative culture," and his successor, Severin Schwan, has stated that he intends to "keep the two respective research and early development organizations as independent units"; merging the two R&D units, he says, "would kill innovation" at Genentech. Schwan needs suggestions on how best to follow through on both Humer's commitment and his own. It is no surprise that your boss has asked you to furnish her with two or three ideas that she might pass on to the CEO. What will your suggestions be?

3. Despite the commitments made by its CEOs, Roche Group is an immense company: It employs more than 80,000 people in 150 countries and posted revenues of $48 billion in 2012. There will undoubtedly be changes at Genentech. Generally speaking, what sort of changes might you expect in the following areas—*organization structure and design, technology and operations*, and *people, attitudes, and behaviors*?

Case References

"Genentech's Joe McCracken Is on the Hunt," *The Burrill Report*, May 7, 2007, www.burrillreport.com, accessed on July 21, 2012; Querida Anderson, "OSI Pharma Needs to Expand Pipeline," *Genetic Engineering & Biotechnology News*, June 15, 2007, www.genengnews.com, accessed on July 21, 2012; "Seattle Genetics Reports Final SGN-40 Phase I Non-Hodgkin Lymphoma Data at International Conference on Malignant Lymphoma," *Drugs.com*, February 3, 2011, www.drugs.com, accessed on July 21, 2012; Genentech Inc., "Genentech Announces Voluntary Withdrawal of Raptiva from the U.S. Market," *Press Release*, April 8, 2009, www.gene.com, accessed on July 21, 2012; Maureen Martino, "CEO: Roche, Genentech R&D Won't Merge," *Fierce Biotech*, September 15, 2010, www.fiercebiotech.com, accessed on July 21, 2012; and "Business Development at Roche and Genentech: An Interview with Joe McCracken and Dan Zabrowski," *BioPharma Today*, July 28, 2009, www.biopharmatoday.com, accessed on July 21, 2012.

You Make the Call

Cultivating Innovation at IKEA

1. You're an IKEA store manager, and corporate headquarters has instructed you to change the layout of your store. The change must be "dramatic," but the details are up to you. What steps will you take to ensure that you'll be successful?

2. There's an IKEA TV ad that features a discarded lamp, forsaken on a rainy night in some American city. A man looks at the camera and says in a sympathetic Swedish accent, "Many of you feel bad for this lamp," and then, after a well-timed pause, "That's because you're crazy." What's the message of the commercial?

3. One IKEA executive says that the current global economic situation has "pushed innovation" at the company. In fact, he says, "This is a great time to be more innovative." Explain what he most likely means.

4. Would you want to manage an IKEA store? Why or why not?

ENDNOTES

1 Zachary Lewis, "IKEA Has Inspired a Cult of Devoted Fans," *NJ.com*, November 15, 2013; Kerry Capell, "Understanding IKEA: How the Swedish Company Turned into a Global Obsession," *Business Week*, November 8, 2005, www.msnbc.com, accessed on November 15, 2013; Colin White, "Strategic Management: The IKEA Way," *Business Innovation*, November 15, 2013; "Key of IKEA," *Hub*, January 1, 2009, www.hubmagazine.com, accessed on November 15, 2013; IKEA, "IKEA History: How It All Began," "The IKEA Concept," "Facts & Figures," 2012–2013, www.ikea.com, accessed on November 15, 2013; and "Bill Agee: IKEA, the Recession and Innovation," *Hub*, January 9, 2009, www.ikeafans.com, accessed on November 15, 2013.

2 For an excellent review of this area, see Achilles A. Armenakis and Arthur G. Bedeian, "Organizational Change: A Review of Theory and Research in the 1990s," *Journal of Management*, 1999, Vol. 25, No. 3, pp. 293–315. For a more recent review, see Luis L. Martins, "*Organizational Change and Development*," in Sheldon Zedeck (ed.), *Handbook of Industrial and Organizational Psychology*, Vol. 3: *Maintaining, Expanding, and Contracting the Organization* (Washington, DC: American Psychological Association, 2010), pp. 691–728.

3 Michael A. Hitt, "The New Frontier: Transformation of Management for the New Millennium," *Organizational Dynamics*, Winter 2000, pp. 7–15. See also Michael Beer and Nitin Nohria, "Cracking the Code of Change," *Harvard Business Review*, May–June 2000, pp. 133–144; and Clark Gilbert, "The Disruption Opportunity," *MIT Sloan Management Review*, Summer 2003, pp. 27–32.

4 Alan L. Frohman, "Igniting Organizational Change from Below: The Power of Personal Initiative," *Organizational Dynamics*, Winter 1997, pp. 39–53.

5 Nandini Rajagopalan and Gretchen M. Spreitzer, "Toward a Theory of Strategic Change: A Multi-Lens Perspective and Integrative Framework," *Academy of Management Review*, 1997, Vol. 22, No. 1, pp. 48–79.

6 Clayton M. Christensen and Michael Overdorf, "Meeting the Challenge of Disruptive Change," *Harvard Business Review*, March–April 2000, pp. 67–77.

7 "To Maintain Success, Managers Must Learn How to Direct Change," *Wall Street Journal*, August 13, 2002, p. B1. See also Andrew Van de Ven and Kangyong Sun, "Breakdowns in Implementing Models of Organization Change," *Academy of Management Perspectives*, August 2011, pp. 58–68.

8 See Eric Abrahamson, "Change without Pain," *Harvard Business Review*, July–August 2000, pp. 75–85. See also Gib Akin and Ian Palmer, "Putting Metaphors to Work for Change in Organizations," *Organizational Dynamics*, Winter 2000, pp. 67–76.

9 Kurt Lewin, "Frontiers in Group Dynamics: Concept, Method, and Reality in Social Science," *Human Relations*, June 1947, pp. 5–41.

10 Michael Roberto and Lynne Levesque, "The Art of Making Change Initiatives Stick," *MIT Sloan Management Review*, Summer 2005, pp. 53–62.

11 "Time for a Turnaround," *Fast Company*, January 2003, pp. 55–61.

12 See John P. Kotter and Leonard A. Schlesinger, "Choosing Strategies for Change," *Harvard Business Review*, July–August 2008, pp. 130–141.

13 See Mel Fugate, Angelo J. Kinicki, and Gregory E. Prussia, "Employee Coping with Organizational Change: An Examination of Alternative Theoretical Perspectives and Models," *Personnel Psychology*, 2008, Vol. 61, No. 1, pp. 1–36. See also Jeffrey D. Ford and Laurie W. Ford, "Decoding Resistance to Change," *Harvard Business Review*, April 2009, pp. 99–104.

14 See Clark Gilbert and Joseph Bower, "Disruptive Change," *Harvard Business Review*, May 2002, pp. 95–104.

15 "RJR Employees Fight Distraction Amid Buy-Out Talks," *Wall Street Journal*, November 1, 1988, p. A8.

16 "Flight Chaos Looms as BA Staff Vow to Strike," *Sydney Morning Herald*, December 16, 2010.

[17] Arnon E. Reichers, John P. Wanous, and James T. Austin, "Understanding and Managing Cynicism About Organizational Change," *Academy of Management Executive*, February 1997, pp. 48–59.

[18] For a classic discussion, see Paul R. Lawrence, "How to Deal with Resistance to Change," *Harvard Business Review*, January–February 1969, pp. 4–12, 166–176. For a more recent discussion, see Jeffrey D. Ford, Laurie W. Ford, and Angelo D'Amelio, "Resistance to Change: The Rest of the Story," *Academy of Management Review*, 2008, Vol. 33, No. 2, pp. 362–377.

[19] Lester Coch and John R. P. French, Jr., "Overcoming Resistance to Change," *Human Relations*, August 1948, pp. 512–532.

[20] Benjamin Schneider, Arthur P. Brief, and Richard A. Guzzo, "Creating a Climate and Culture for Sustainable Organizational Change," *Organizational Dynamics*, Spring 1996, pp. 7–19.

[21] "Troubled GM Plans Major Tuneup," *USA Today*, June 6, 2005, pp. 1B, 2B.

[22] Paul Bate, Raza Khan, and Annie Pye, "Towards a Culturally Sensitive Approach to Organization Structuring: Where Organization Design Meets Organization Development," *Organization Science*, March–April 2000, pp. 197–211.

[23] Gerard Bohner and Nina Dickel, "Attitudes and Attitude Change," in Susan T. Fiske, Daniel L. Schacter, and Shelley Taylor (eds.), *Annual Review of Psychology 2011* (Palo Alto, CA: Annual Reviews, 2011), pp. 391–418.

[24] Thomas A. Stewart, "Reengineering—the Hot New Managing Tool," *Fortune* August 23, 1993, pp. 41–48.

[25] Richard Beckhard, *Organization Development: Strategies and Models* (Reading, MA: Addison-Wesley, 1969), p. 9.

[26] W. Warner Burke, "The New Agenda for Organization Development," *Organizational Dynamics*, Summer 1997, pp. 7–20.

[27] L. B. Mohr, "Determinants of Innovation in Organizations," *American Political Science Review*, 1969, pp. 111–126; G. A. Steiner, *The Creative Organization* (Chicago: University of Chicago Press, 1965); R. Duncan and A. Weiss, "Organizational Learning: Implications for Organizational Design," in B. M. Staw (ed.), *Research in Organizational Behavior*, Vol. 1 (Greenwich, CT: JAI Press, 1979), pp. 75–123; and J. E. Ettlie, "Adequacy of Stage Models for Decisions on Adoption of Innovation," *Psychological Reports*, 1980, Vol. 46, pp. 991–995.

[28] See Willow A. Sheremata, "Centrifugal and Centripetal Forces in Radical New Product Development under Time Pressure," *Academy of Management Review*, 2000, Vol. 25, No. 2, pp. 389–408. See also Richard Leifer, Gina Colarelli O'Connor, and Mark Rice, "Implementing Radical Innovation in Mature Firms: The Role of Hobs," *Academy of Management Executive*, 2001, Vol. 15, No. 3, pp. 102–113.

[29] See Julian Birkinshaw, Gary Hamel, and Michael J. Mol, "Management Innovation," *Academy of Management Review*, 2008, Vol. 33, No. 4, pp. 825–845.

[30] See Clayton M. Christensen, Stephen P. Kaufman, and Willy C. Shih, "Innovation Killers," *Harvard Business Review*, January 2008, pp. 98–107.

[31] Dorothy Leonard and Jeffrey F. Rayport, "Spark Innovation Through Empathic Design," *Harvard Business Review*, November–December 1997, pp. 102–115.

[32] "The 50 Most Innovative Companies," *Businessweek*, April 25, 2010, pp. 34–42.

[33] Geoffrey Moore, "Innovating Within Established Enterprises," *Harvard Business Review*, July–August 2004, pp. 87–96. See also David A. Garvin and Lynne C. Levesque, "Meeting the Challenge of Corporate Entrepreneurship," *Harvard Business Review*, October 2006, pp. 102–113.

[34] See Gifford Pinchot III, *Intrapreneuring* (New York: Harper & Row, 1985).

CHAPTER 8

Managing Human Resources in Organizations

Sergii Tsololo/Photos.com

Learning Outcomes

After studying this chapter, you should be able to:

1 Describe the environmental context of human resource management, including its strategic importance and its relationship with legal and social factors.

2 Discuss how organizations attract human resources, including human resource planning, recruiting, and selecting.

3 Describe how organizations develop human resources, including training and development, performance appraisal, and performance feedback.

4 Discuss how organizations maintain human resources, including the determination of compensation and benefits and career planning.

5 Discuss the nature of diversity, including its meaning, associated trends, impact, and management.

6 Describe labor relations, including how employees form unions and the mechanics of collective bargaining.

7 Describe the issues associated with managing knowledge and contingent and temporary workers.

No Company for Old-Fashioned Management

"Anything that requires knowledge and service gives us a reason to be."

—Danny Wegman, CEO of Wegmans Food Markets

If you're looking for the best Parmesan cheese for your chicken parmigiana recipe, you might try Wegmans, especially if you happen to live in the vicinity of Pittsford, New York. Cheese department manager Carol Kent will be happy to recommend the best brand because her job calls for knowing cheese, as well as managing some 20 subordinates. Kent is a knowledgeable employee, and knowledgeable employees, says Wegmans CEO Danny Wegman, are "something our competitors don't have and our customers couldn't get anywhere else."

Wegmans Food Markets, a family-owned East Coast chain with nearly 80 outlets in six states, prides itself on its commitment to customers, and it shows: It ranks at the top of the latest *Consumer Reports* survey of the best national and regional grocery stores. But commitment to customers is only half of Wegmans's overall strategy, which calls for reaching its customers

The Washington Post/Getty Images

Wegmans has achieved success by building a long-term mutually beneficial relationship with its employees. This Wegmans fish department manager is explaining cooking options for wild-caught swordfish to a customer.

through its employees. "How do we differentiate ourselves?" asks Wegman, who then proceeds to answer his own question: "If we can sell products that require knowledge in terms of how you use them, that's our strategy. Anything that requires knowledge and service gives us a reason to be." That's the logic behind one of Carol Kent's recent assignments—one which she understandably regards as a perk: Wegmans sent her to Italy to conduct a personal study of Italian cheese. "We sat with the families" that make the cheeses, she recalls, and "broke bread with them. It helped me understand that we're not just selling a piece of cheese. We're selling a tradition, a quality."

Kent and the employees in her department also enjoy the best benefits package in the industry, including fully paid health insurance. And that includes part-timers, who make up about two-thirds of the company's workforce of more than 37,000. In part, the strategy of extending benefits to this large segment of the labor force is intended to make sure that stores have enough good workers for crucial peak periods, but there's no denying that the costs of employee-friendly policies can mount up. At 15 to 17 percent of sales, for example, Wegmans' labor costs are well above the 12 percent figure for most supermarkets. But according to one company HR executive, holding down labor costs isn't necessarily a strategic priority: "We would have stopped offering free health insurance [to part-timers] a long time ago," she admits, "if we tried to justify the costs."

Besides, employee turnover at Wegmans is about 6 percent—a mere fraction of an industry average that hovers around 19 percent (and can approach 100 percent for part-timers). And this is an industry in which total turnover costs have been known to outstrip total annual profits by 40 percent. Wegmans employees tend to be knowledgeable because about 20 percent of them have been with the company for at least ten years, and many have logged at least a quarter century. Says one 19-year-old college student who works at an upstate New York Wegmans while pursuing a career as a high school history teacher, "I love this place. If teaching doesn't work out, I would so totally work at Wegmans." Edward McLaughlin, who directs the Food Industry Management Program at Cornell University, understands this sort of attitude: "When you're a 16-year-old kid, the last thing you want to do is wear a geeky shirt and work for a supermarket," but at Wegmans, he explains, "it's a badge of honor. You're not a geeky cashier. You're part of the social fabric."

In 2012, Wegmans placed fifth in *Fortune* magazine's annual list of "100 Best Companies to Work For"—good for 14 consecutive years on the list and seven straight top-seven finishes. "It says that we're doing something right," says a company spokesperson, "and that there's no better way to take care of our customers than to be a great place for our employees to work." In addition to its health-care package, Wegmans has been cited for such perks as fitness center discounts, compressed workweeks, telecommuting, and domestic-partner benefits (which extend to same-sex partners).

Finally, under the company's Employee Scholarship Program, full-time workers can receive up to $2,200 a year for four years and part-timers up to $1,500. Since its inception in 1984, the program has handed out over $76 million in scholarships to more than 23,500 employees. Like most Wegman policies, this one combines employee outreach with long-term corporate strategy: "This program has made a real difference in the lives of many young people," says President Colleen Wegman, who adds that it's also "one of the reasons we've been able to attract the best and the brightest to work at Wegmans."

Granted, Wegmans, which has remained in family hands since its founding in 1915, has an advantage in being as generous with its resources as its family of top executives wants to be: It doesn't have to do everything with quarterly profits in mind, and the firm likes to point out that taking care of its employees is a long-standing priority. Profit sharing and fully funded medical coverage were introduced in 1950 by Robert Wegman, son and nephew of brothers Walter and John, who opened the firm's original flagship store in Rochester, New York, in 1930. Why did Robert Wegman make such generous gestures to his employees way back then? "Because," he says simply, "I was no different from them."[1]

This chapter is about how organizations manage the people that comprise them. That's why our opening story is about a company that's reaped big dividends from a strategy that integrates customer satisfaction with employee satisfaction. The set of processes by which Wegmans and other companies manage their people is called "*human resource management*," or HRM. We start by describing the environmental context of HRM. We then discuss how organizations attract human resources. Next, we describe how organizations seek to further develop the capacities of their human resources. We also examine how high-quality human resources are maintained by organizations. We conclude by discussing workforce diversity, labor relations, and new challenges in the changing workplace.

THE ENVIRONMENTAL CONTEXT OF HRM

human resource management (HRM)
The set of organizational activities directed at attracting, developing, and maintaining an effective workforce

Human Resource Management (HRM) is the set of organizational activities directed at attracting, developing, and maintaining an effective workforce.[2] HRM takes place within a complex and ever-changing environmental context. Three particularly vital components of this context are HRM's strategic importance and the legal and social environments of HRM.

The Strategic Importance of HRM

Human resources are critical for effective organizational functioning. HRM (or "*personnel*," as it is sometimes called) was once relegated to second-class status in many organizations, but its importance has grown dramatically in the last two decades. Its new importance stems from increased legal complexities, the recognition that human resources are a valuable means for improving productivity, and the awareness today of the costs associated with poor HRM.[3] For example, Microsoft recently announced that it was eliminating 5,000 jobs in business areas that are expected to shrink. At the same time, though, the firm began developing strategies for hiring high-talent people for jobs related to Internet search, an important growth area for the company.[4] This careful and systematic approach of reducing human resources in areas where they are no longer needed and adding new human resources to key growth areas reflects a strategic approach to HRM.

Indeed, managers now realize that the effectiveness of their HR function has a substantial impact on the bottom-line performance of the firm. Poor human resource planning can result in spurts of hiring followed by layoffs—costly in terms of unemployment compensation payments, training expenses, and morale. Haphazard compensation systems do not attract, keep, or motivate good employees, and outmoded recruitment practices can expose the firm to expensive and embarrassing discrimination lawsuits. Consequently, the chief human resource executive of most large businesses is a vice president directly accountable to the CEO, and many firms are developing strategic HR plans and integrating those plans with other strategic planning activities.[5]

Even organizations with as few as 200 employees usually have a human resource manager and a human resource department charged with overseeing these activities. Responsibility for HR activities, however, is shared between the HR department and line managers. The HR department may recruit and initially screen candidates, but the final selection is usually made by managers in the department where the new employee will work. Similarly, although the HR department may establish performance appraisal policies and procedures, the actual evaluation and coaching of employees are done by their immediate superiors.

human capital
Reflects the organization's investment in attracting, retaining, and motivating an effective workforce

The growing awareness of the strategic significance of HRM has even led to new terminology to reflect a firm's commitment to people. **Human capital** reflects the organization's investment in attracting, retaining, and motivating an effective workforce. Hence, just as the phrase *financial capital* is an indicator of a firm's financial resources and reserves, so, too, does human capital serve as a tangible indicator of the value of the people who comprise an organization.[6]

The Legal Environment of HRM

A number of laws regulate various aspects of employee–employer relations, especially in the areas of equal employment opportunity, compensation and benefits, labor relations, and occupational safety and health. Several major ones are summarized in Table 8.1.

As much as any area of management, HRM is subject to wide-ranging laws and court decisions. These laws and decisions affect the human resource function in many areas. For example, AT&T was once fined several million dollars for violating Title VII of the Civil Rights Act of 1964.

Table 8.1	The Legal Environment of Human Resource Management

Equal Employment Opportunity

Title VII of the Civil Rights Act of 1964 (as amended by the Equal Employment Opportunity Act of 1972): Forbids discrimination in all areas of the employment relationship

Age Discrimination in Employment Act: Outlaws discrimination against people older than 40 years.

Various executive orders, especially Executive Order 11246 in 1965: Requires employers with government contracts to engage in affirmative action

Pregnancy Discrimination Act: Specifically outlaws discrimination on the basis of pregnancy

Vietnam Era Veterans Readjustment Assistance Act: Extends affirmative action mandate to military veterans who served during the Vietnam War

Americans with Disabilities Act: Specifically outlaws discrimination against disabled persons

Civil Rights Act of 1991: Makes it easier for employees to sue an organization for discrimination but limits punitive damage awards if they win

Compensation and Benefits

Fair Labor Standards Act: Establishes minimum wage and mandated overtime pay for work in excess of 40 hours per week

Equal Pay Act of 1963: Requires that men and women be paid the same amount for doing the same job

Employee Retirement Income Security Act of 1974 (ERISA): Regulates how organizations manage their pension funds

Family and Medical Leave Act of 1993: Requires employers to provide up to 12 weeks of unpaid leave for family and medical emergencies

Labor Relations

National Labor Relations Act: Spells out procedures by which employees can establish labor unions and requires organizations to bargain collectively with legally formed unions; also known as the *Wagner Act*

Labor Management Relations Act: Limits union power and specifies management rights during union-organizing campaign; also known as the *Taft–Hartley Act*

Health and Safety

Occupational Safety and Health Act of 1970 (OSHA): Mandates the provision of safe working conditions

© Cengage Learning

Title VII of the Civil Rights Act of 1964
Forbids discrimination on the basis of sex, race, color, religion, or national origin in all areas of the employment relationship

adverse impact
When minority group members meet or pass a selection standard at a rate less than 80 percent of the pass rate of majority group members

Equal Employment Opportunity Commission
Charged with enforcing Title VII of the Civil Rights Act of 1964

Age Discrimination in Employment Act
Outlaws discrimination against people older than 40 years; passed in 1967, amended in 1978 and 1986

affirmative action
Intentionally seeking and hiring qualified or qualifiable employees from racial, sexual, and ethnic groups that are underrepresented in the organization

Americans with Disabilities Act
Forbids discrimination against people with disabilities

Equal Employment Opportunity Title VII of the Civil Rights Act of 1964   This law forbids discrimination in all areas of the employment relationship. The intent of **Title VII of the Civil Rights Act of 1964** is to ensure that employment decisions are made on the basis of an individual's qualifications rather than on the basis of personal biases. The law has reduced direct forms of discrimination (such as refusing to promote African Americans into management, failing to hire men as flight attendants, or refusing to hire women as construction workers) as well as indirect forms of discrimination (such as using employment tests that whites pass at a higher rate than African Americans).

Employment requirements such as test scores and other qualifications are legally defined as having an **adverse impact** on minorities and women when such individuals meet or pass the requirement at a rate less than 80 percent of the rate of majority group members. Criteria that have an adverse impact on protected groups can be used only when there is solid evidence that they effectively identify individuals who are better able than others to do the job. The **Equal Employment Opportunity Commission** is charged with enforcing Title VII as well as several other employment-related laws.

The **Age Discrimination in Employment Act**, passed in 1967, amended in 1978, and amended again in 1986, is an attempt to prevent organizations from discriminating against older workers. In its current form, it outlaws discrimination against people older than 40 years. Both the Age Discrimination in Employment Act and Title VII require passive nondiscrimination, or equal employment opportunity. Employers are not required to seek out and hire minorities, but they must treat all who apply fairly.

As much as any area of management, HRM is subject to wide-ranging laws and court decisions. These laws and decisions affect the human resource function in many areas. For example, AT&T was once fined several million dollars for violating Title VII of the Civil Rights Act of 1964.

Several executive orders, however, require that employers holding government contracts engage in **affirmative action**—intentionally seeking and hiring employees from groups that are underrepresented in the organization. These organizations must have a written affirmative action plan that spells out employment goals for underutilized groups and how those goals will be met. These employers are also required to act affirmatively in hiring Vietnam-era veterans (as a result of the Vietnam Era Veterans Readjustment Assistance Act) and qualified disabled individuals. Finally, the Pregnancy Discrimination Act forbids discrimination against women who are pregnant.

In 1990, Congress passed the **Americans with Disabilities Act**, which forbids discrimination on the basis of disabilities and requires employers to provide reasonable accommodations for disabled employees. More recently, the **Civil Rights Act of 1991** amended the original Civil Rights Act as well as other related laws by both making it easier to bring discrimination lawsuits (which partially explains the aforementioned backlog of cases) and limiting the amount of punitive damages that can be awarded in those lawsuits.

Compensation and Benefits   Certain laws also regulate compensation and benefits. The **Fair Labor Standards Act**, passed in 1938 and amended frequently since then, sets a minimum wage and requires the payment of overtime rates for work in excess of 40 hours per week. Salaried professional, executive, and administrative employees are exempt from the minimum hourly wage and overtime provisions. The **Equal Pay Act of 1963** requires that men and women be paid the same amount for doing the same job. Attempts to circumvent the law by having different job titles and pay rates for men and women who perform the same work are also illegal. Basing an employee's pay on seniority or performance is legal, however, even if it means that a man and woman are paid different amounts for doing the same job.

Civil Rights Act of 1991

Amends the original Civil Rights Act, making it easier to bring discrimination lawsuits while also limiting punitive damages

Fair Labor Standards Act

Sets a minimum wage and requires overtime pay for work in excess of 40 hours per week; passed in 1938 and amended frequently since then

Equal Pay Act of 1963

Requires that men and women be paid the same amount for doing the same job

Employee Retirement Income Security Act of 1974 (ERISA)

A law that sets standards for pension plan management and provides federal insurance if pension funds go bankrupt

Family and Medical Leave Act of 1993

Requires employers to provide up to 12 weeks of unpaid leave for family and medical emergencies

National Labor Relations Act

Passed in 1935 to set up procedures for employees to vote on whether to have a union; also known as the *Wagner Act*

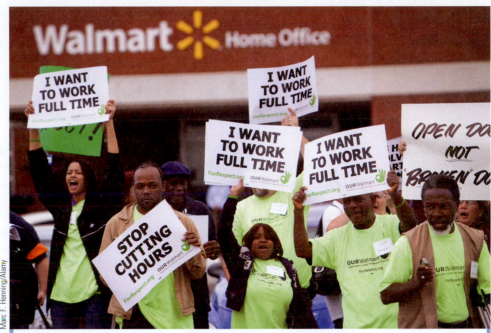

Marc F. Henning/Alamy

Walmart has been criticized in recent years for its low wages, weak health-care benefits, lack of full-time jobs, and other human resource practices. These Walmart employees are protesting some of these practices outside the retailer's home office in Bentonville, Arkansas.

The provision of benefits is also regulated in some ways by state and federal laws. Certain benefits are mandatory—for example, worker's compensation insurance for employees who are injured on the job. Employers who provide a pension plan for their employees are regulated by the **Employee Retirement Income Security Act of 1974 (ERISA)**. The purpose of this act is to help ensure the financial security of pension funds by regulating how they can be invested. The **Family and Medical Leave Act of 1993** requires employers to provide up to 12 weeks of unpaid leave for family and medical emergencies.

In the last few years, some large employers, most notably Walmart, have come under fire because they do not provide health care for all their employees. In response to this, the state of Maryland passed a law, informally called the Walmart Bill, that requires employers with more than 10,000 workers to spend at least 8 percent of their payrolls on health care or else pay a comparable amount into a general fund for uninsured workers. Walmart appealed this ruling and the case is still pending; meanwhile, several other states are considering the passage of similar laws.[7]

Labor Relations

Union activities and management's behavior toward unions constitute another heavily regulated area. The **National Labor Relations Act** (also known as the *Wagner Act*), passed in 1935, sets up a procedure for employees to vote on whether to have a union. If they vote for a union, management is required to bargain collectively with the union. The **National Labor Relations Board (NLRB)** was established by the Wagner Act to enforce its provisions. Following a series of severe strikes in 1946, the **Labor-Management Relations Act** (also known as the *Taft–Hartley Act*) was passed in 1947 to limit union power. The law increases management's rights during

National Labor Relations Board (NLRB)

Established by the Wagner Act to enforce its provisions

Labor-Management Relations Act

Passed in 1947 to limit union power; also known as the *Taft–Hartley Act*

Occupational Safety and Health Act of 1970 (OSHA)

Directly mandates the provision of safe working conditions

an organizing campaign. The Taft–Hartley Act also contains the National Emergency Strike provision, which allows the president of the United States to prevent or end a strike that endangers national security. Taken together, these laws balance union and management power. Employees can be represented by a legally created and managed union, but the business can make non-employee-related business decisions without interference.

Health and Safety   The **Occupational Safety and Health Act of 1970 (OSHA)** directly mandates the provision of safe working conditions. It requires that employers (1) provide a place of employment that is free from hazards that may cause death or serious physical harm, and (2) obey the safety and health standards established by the U.S. Department of Labor. Safety standards are intended to prevent accidents, whereas occupational health standards are concerned with preventing occupational disease. For example, standards limit the concentration of cotton dust in the air because this contaminant has been associated with lung disease in textile workers. The standards are enforced by OSHA inspections, which are conducted when an employee files a complaint of unsafe conditions or when a serious accident occurs. Spot inspections of plants in especially hazardous industries such as mining and chemicals are also made. Employers who fail to meet OSHA standards may be fined.

Investigators have been looking into claims that chemical agents in the butter flavoring used in microwave popcorn are harmful to workers where such products are made. At least 30 workers at one plant in Jasper, Missouri, contracted a rare lung disease, and some doctors believe that it resulted from conditions on their job site. Although federal health officials point out that there is no danger to those cooking or eating microwave popcorn, research is ongoing into potential hazards to those who work in the industry.[8]

Emerging Legal Issues   Several other areas of legal concern have emerged during the past few years. One is sexual harassment. Although sexual harassment is forbidden under Title VII, it has received additional attention in the courts recently, as more and more victims have decided to publicly confront the problem. Another emerging HRM issue is alcohol and drug abuse. Both alcoholism and drug dependence are major problems today. Recent court rulings have tended to define alcoholics and drug addicts as disabled, protecting them under the same laws that protect other disabled people. Finally, AIDS has emerged as an important legal issue as well. AIDS victims, too, are most often protected under various laws protecting the disabled.

ATTRACTING HUMAN RESOURCES

With an understanding of the environmental context of HRM as a foundation, we are now ready to address its first substantive concern—attracting qualified people who are interested in employment with the organization.

Human Resource Planning

The starting point in attracting qualified human resources is planning. HR planning, in turn, involves job analysis and forecasting the demand and supply of labor.

job analysis

A systematized procedure for collecting and recording information about jobs within an organization

Job Analysis   **Job analysis** is a systematic analysis of jobs within an organization. A job analysis is made up of two parts. The job description lists the duties of a job, the job's working conditions, and the tools, materials, and equipment used to perform it. The job specification lists the skills, abilities, and other credentials needed to do the job. Job analysis information is used in many human resource activities. For instance, knowing about job content and job requirements is necessary to develop appropriate selection methods and job-relevant performance appraisal systems and to set equitable compensation rates.

Forecasting Human Resource Demand and Supply After managers fully understand the jobs to be performed within the organization, they can start planning for the organization's future human resource needs. Figure 8.1 summarizes the steps most often followed. The manager starts by assessing trends in past human resource usage, future organizational plans, and general economic trends. A good sales forecast is often the foundation, especially for smaller organizations. Historical ratios can then be used to predict demand for employees such as operating employees and sales representatives. Of course, large organizations use much more complicated models to predict their future human resource needs. Several years ago, Walmart went through an exhaustive planning process that projected that the firm would need to hire 1 million people. Of this projected total, 800,000 were to be new positions created as the firm grows, and the other 200,000 were to replace current workers who were expected to leave for various reasons.[9] As time has passed, of course, Walmart adjusted these figures both up and down. But as things turned out, by the end of the forecast period, Walmart did indeed employ about 800,000 more people than when the plan was first completed.

© Cengage Learning

FIGURE 8.1

Human Resource Planning

Attracting human resources cannot be left to chance if an organization expects to function at peak efficiency. Human resource planning involves assessing trends, forecasting supply and demand of labor, and then developing appropriate strategies for addressing any differences.

Forecasting the supply of labor is really two tasks: forecasting the internal supply (the number and type of employees who will be in the firm at some future date) and forecasting the external supply (the number and type of people who will be available for hiring in the labor market at large).[10] The simplest approach merely adjusts present staffing levels for anticipated turnover and promotions. Again, though, large organizations use extremely sophisticated models to make these forecasts. At higher levels of the organization, managers plan for specific people and positions. The technique most commonly used is the **replacement chart**, which lists each important managerial position, who occupies it, how long he or she will probably stay in it before moving on, and who (by name) is now qualified or soon will be qualified to move into the position. This technique allows ample time to plan developmental experiences for persons identified as potential successors to critical managerial jobs.[11] In February 2012, Warren Buffett announced that he has a successor in mind to replace him as CEO of Berkshire Hathaway and stated the eventual transfer of power would be seamless.[12]

To facilitate both planning and identifying persons for current transfer or promotion, some organizations also have an **employee information system**, or **skills inventory**, which is usually computerized and contains information on each employee's education, skills, work experience, and career aspirations. Such a system can quickly locate all the employees in the organization who are qualified to fill a position requiring, for instance, a degree in chemical engineering, three years of experience in an oil refinery, and fluency in Spanish. Enterprise resource planning (ERP) systems, as described in Chapter 7, generally include capabilities for measuring and managing the internal supply of labor in ways that best fit the needs of the organization.

Forecasting the external supply of labor is a different problem altogether. How does a manager, for example, predict how many electrical engineers will be seeking work in Georgia three years from now? To get an idea of the future availability of labor, planners must rely on information from outside sources such as state employment commissions, government reports, and figures supplied by colleges on the number of students in major fields.

Matching Human Resource Supply and Demand   After comparing future demand and internal supply, managers can make plans to manage predicted shortfalls or overstaffing. If a shortfall is predicted, new employees can be hired, present employees can be retrained and transferred into the understaffed area, individuals approaching retirement can be convinced to stay on, or labor-saving or productivity-enhancing systems can be installed.

If the organization needs to hire, the external labor supply forecast helps managers plan how to recruit, based on whether the type of person needed is readily available or scarce in the labor market. As we noted earlier in this chapter, the trend in temporary workers also helps managers in staffing by affording them extra flexibility. If overstaffing is expected to be a problem, the main options are transferring the extra employees, not replacing individuals who quit, encouraging early retirement, and laying people off.

Recruiting Human Resources

Once an organization has an idea of its future human resource needs, the next phase is usually recruiting new employees.[13] **Recruiting** is the process of attracting qualified persons to apply for jobs that are open. Where do recruits come from? Some recruits are found internally; others come from outside the organization.

Internal recruiting means considering present employees as candidates for openings. Promotion from within can help build morale and keep high-quality employees from leaving the firm. In unionized firms, the procedures for notifying employees of internal

---

replacement chart
Lists each important managerial position, who occupies it, how long he or she will probably remain in the position, and who is or will be a qualified replacement

employee information system (skills inventory)
Contains information on each employee's education, skills, experience, and career aspirations; usually computerized

recruiting
The process of attracting individuals to apply for jobs that are open

internal recruiting
Considering current employees as applicants for higher-level jobs in the organization

job change opportunities are usually spelled out in the union contract. For higher-level positions, a skills inventory system may be used to identify internal candidates, or managers may be asked to recommend individuals who should be considered. Most businesses today routinely post job openings on their internal communication network, or intranet. One disadvantage of internal recruiting is its ripple effect. When an employee moves to a different job, someone else must be found to take his or her old job. In one organization, 454 job movements were necessary as a result of filling 195 initial openings.

External recruiting involves attracting persons outside the organization to apply for jobs. External recruiting methods include advertising, campus interviews, employment agencies or executive search firms, union hiring halls, referrals by present employees, and hiring "walk-ins" or "gate-hires" (people who show up without being solicited). Increasingly, firms are using the Internet to post job openings and to solicit applicants. Of course, a manager must select the most appropriate methods, using the state employment service to find maintenance workers but not a nuclear physicist, for example. Private employment agencies can be a good source of clerical and technical employees, and executive search firms specialize in locating top-management talent. In general, "help wanted" ads in newspapers and in online job posting sites are often used because they reach a wide audience and thus allow a large number of people to find out about and apply for job openings.

One generally successful method for facilitating a good person–job fit is the so-called **realistic job preview (RJP)**, which involves providing the applicant with a real picture of what it would be like to perform the job that the organization is trying to fill.[14] For example, it would not make sense for a firm to tell an applicant that the job is exciting and challenging when in fact it is routine and straightforward; yet some managers do this to hire the best people. The likely outcome will be a dissatisfied employee who will quickly be looking for a better job. If the company is more realistic about a job, though, the person hired will be more likely to remain in the job for a longer period of time.

external recruiting
Getting people from outside the organization to apply for jobs

realistic job preview (RJP)
Provides the applicant with a real picture of what it would be like to perform the job that the organization is trying to fill

validation
Determining the extent to which a selection device is really predictive of future job performance

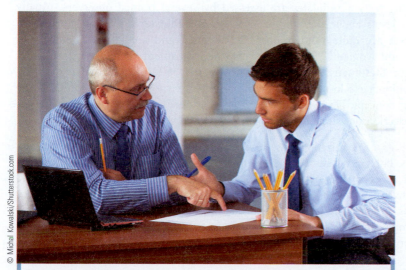

Realistic job previews play a big role in helping people better understand the nature of potential job opportunities. This senior manager, for example, is explaining the details of a potential new work assignment to one of his subordinates. By building familiarity and awareness in advance, businesses can reduce turnover and dissatisfaction later.

© Michal Kowalski/Shutterstock.com

Selecting Human Resources

Once the recruiting process has attracted a pool of applicants, the next step is to select whom to hire. The intent of the selection process is to gather from applicants information that will predict their job success and then to hire the candidates likely to be most successful.[15] Of course, the organization can gather information only about factors that are predictive of future performance. The process of determining the predictive value of information is called **validation**.

Application Blanks The first step in selection is usually asking the candidate to fill out an application blank. Application blanks are an efficient method of gathering information about the applicant's previous work history, educational background, and other job-related demographic data. They should not contain questions about areas not related to the job, such as gender, religion, or national origin. Application blank data are generally used informally to decide whether a candidate merits further evaluation, and interviewers use application blanks to familiarize themselves with candidates before interviewing them. Unfortunately, in recent years, there has been a trend toward job applicants' either falsifying or inflating their credentials to stand a better chance of getting a job. Indeed, one recent survey of 2.6 million job applications found that an astounding 44 percent of them contained some false information.[16]

Tests   Tests of ability, skill, aptitude, or knowledge that is relevant to the particular job are usually the best predictors of job success, although tests of general intelligence or personality are occasionally useful. In addition to being validated, tests should be administered and scored consistently. All candidates should be given the same directions, should be allowed the same amount of time, and should experience the same testing environment (temperature, lighting, and distractions).[17]

Interviews   Although a popular selection device, interviews are sometimes poor predictors of job success. For example, biases inherent in the way that people perceive and judge others at a first meeting affect subsequent evaluations by the interviewer. Interview validity can be improved by training interviewers to be aware of potential biases and by increasing the structure of the interview. In a structured interview, questions are written in advance, and all interviewers follow the same question list with each candidate they interview. This procedure introduces consistency into the interview procedure and allows the organization to validate the content of the questions to be asked.[18]

Assessment Centers   Assessment centers are a popular method used to select managers and are particularly good for selecting current employees for promotion. The assessment center is a content-valid simulation of major parts of the managerial job. A typical center lasts two to three days, with groups of 6 to 12 persons participating in a variety of managerial exercises. Centers may also include interviews, public speaking, and standardized ability tests. Candidates are assessed by several trained observers, usually managers several levels above the job for which the candidates are being considered. Assessment centers are quite valid if properly designed and are fair to members of minority groups and women.[19] For some firms, the assessment center is a permanent facility created for these activities. For other firms, the assessment activities are performed in a multipurpose location such as a conference room. AT&T pioneered the assessment center concept. For years, the firm has used assessment centers to make virtually all of its selection decisions for management positions.

Other Techniques   Organizations also use other selection techniques depending on the circumstances. Polygraph tests, once popular, are declining in popularity. On the other hand, more and more organizations are requiring that applicants in whom they are interested take physical exams. Organizations are also increasingly using drug tests, especially in situations in which drug-related performance problems could create serious safety hazards. For example, applicants for jobs in a nuclear power plant would likely be tested for drug use. Some organizations today even run credit checks on prospective employees.

DEVELOPING HUMAN RESOURCES

Regardless of how effective a selection system is, however, most employees need additional training if they are to grow and develop in their jobs. Evaluating their performance and providing feedback are also necessary.

Training and Development

training
Teaching operational or technical employees how to do the job for which they were hired

In HRM, **training** usually refers to teaching operational or technical employees how to do the job for which they were hired. **Development** refers to teaching managers and professionals the skills needed for both present and future jobs. Most organizations provide regular training and development programs for managers and employees. For example, IBM spends more than $700 million annually on programs and has a vice president in charge of employee education. U.S. businesses spend more than $125 billion annually on training and development programs away from the workplace. And this figure does not include wages and benefits paid to employees while they are participating in such programs.[20]

development
Teaching managers and professionals the skills needed for both present and future jobs

Assessing Training Needs The first step in developing a training plan is to determine what needs exist. For example, if employees do not know how to operate the machinery necessary to do their job, a training program on how to operate the machinery is clearly needed. On the other hand, when a group of office workers is performing poorly, training may not be the answer. The problem could be motivation, aging equipment, poor supervision, inefficient work design, or a deficiency of skills and knowledge. Only the last could be remedied by training. As training programs are being developed, the manager should set specific and measurable goals specifying what participants are to learn. The manager should also plan to evaluate the training program after employees complete it.

Common Training Methods Many different training and development methods are available. Selection of methods depends on many considerations, but perhaps the most important is training content. When the training content is factual material (such as company rules or explanations for how to fill out forms), assigned reading, programmed learning, and lecture methods work well. When the content is interpersonal relations or group decision making, however, firms must use a method that allows interpersonal contact, such as role-playing or case discussion groups. When employees must learn a physical skill, methods allowing practice and the actual use of tools and materials are needed, as in on-the-job training or vestibule training. (Vestibule training enables participants to focus on safety, learning, and feedback rather than on productivity.)

Web-based and other electronic-media–based training are becoming very popular. Such methods allow a mix of training content, are relatively easy to update and revise, let participants use a variable schedule, and lower travel costs.[21] On the other hand, they are limited in their capacity to simulate real activities and facilitate face-to-face interaction. Xerox, Massachusetts Mutual Life Insurance, and Ford have all reported tremendous success with these methods. In addition, most training programs actually rely on a mix of methods. Boeing, for example, sends managers to an intensive two-week training seminar involving tests, simulations, role-playing exercises, and DVD flight simulation exercises.[22]

Finally, some larger businesses have started creating their own self-contained training facility, often called a *corporate university*. McDonald's was among the first to start this practice with its so-called Hamburger University in Illinois. All management trainees of the firm attend training programs there to learn exactly how long to grill a burger, how to maintain good customer service, and so on. The cult hamburger chain In-N-Out Burger also has a similar training venue called In-N-Out University. Other firms using this approach include Shell Oil and General Electric.[23]

Evaluation of Training Training and development programs should always be evaluated. Typical evaluation approaches include measuring one or more relevant criteria (such as attitudes or performance) before and after the training, and determining whether the criteria changed. Evaluation measures collected at the end of training are easy to get, but actual performance measures collected when the trainee is on the job are more important. Trainees may say that they enjoyed the training and learned a lot, but the true test is whether their job performance improves after their training.

AT YOUR SERVICE

Darden Invests in Employee Development

ZUMA Press, Inc./Alamy

Darden Restaurants owns such popular brands as Olive Garden, LongHorn Steakhouse, and Capital Grill. Darden has a reputation for being one of the best places to work in America, in part because of its aggressive employee development and promote-from-within policies. Clarence Otis, the firm's CEO, believes that investing in Darden employees helps keep the business strong and profitable.

Some businesses see wages and salaries as an expense. But others see employees as vital resources that can give them a real competitive advantage. Darden Restaurants falls clearly in the second set. Darden operates such popular eateries

as Bahama Breeze, Olive Garden, LongHorn Steakhouse, and Capital Grill. All told, the firm has about 180,000 employees and 1,900 restaurants (all company owned, not franchised).

Darden was recently named the second-best company to work for in America (behind FedEx) by *Fortune* magazine, the only restaurant business that's ever made this list. The firm's annual employee turnover is about 20 percent lower than its industry average, and many Darden top managers started at the bottom and worked themselves up the corporate ladder. Indeed, that is one major reason that Darden's employees enjoy working there so much.

Take Mike Stroud, for example. Stroud started as a busboy at a Red Lobster (once a part of Darden) in Georgia in 1973. Today he is a senior vice president overseeing 215 locations. Likewise, Lisa Hoggs joined the company waiting tables at a LongHorn Steakhouse. Now she is a managing partner, running a $3 million location in Atlanta. About 42 percent of its employees are minorities, and 39 percent of its managers are women.

What's Darden's secret? For one thing it tries to impress upon its employees that working for Darden can be a career not just a job. The firm invests heavily in talent development and offers extensive career planning to all employees. The company also offers its employees an array of other meaningful benefits as well. For example, its supports a credit union that provides low-interest loans to employees, strong health-care packages, and substantial training and development opportunities.

Darden recently announced plans to open 500 new restaurants in the next five years and hire almost 50,000 new employees. Given its track record in hiring, nurturing, and promoting employees, there seems to be little question that it will succeed. And who knows—one day soon Bahama Breeze and Olive Garden may be as common as McDonalds and Starbucks.

References: "Serving Up the American Dream," *Fortune,* May 20, 2013, p. 34; *Hoover's Handbook of American Business 2013* (Austin: Mergent, Inc.), pp. 243–244; "Darden to Sell Red Lobster," *New York Times,* May 16, 2014, p. B1.

Performance Appraisal

performance appraisal
A formal assessment of how well an employee is doing his or her job

Once employees are trained and settled into their jobs, one of management's next concerns is performance appraisal. **Performance appraisal** is a formal assessment of how well employees are doing their jobs. Employees' performance should be evaluated regularly for many reasons. One reason is that performance appraisal may be necessary for validating selection devices or assessing the impact of training programs. A second reason is administrative—to aid in making decisions about pay raises, promotions, and training. Still another reason is to provide feedback to employees to help them improve their present performance and plan future careers.[24] Because performance evaluations often help determine wages and promotions, they must be fair and nondiscriminatory.

Common Appraisal Methods   Two basic categories of appraisal methods commonly used in organizations are objective methods and judgmental methods. Objective measures of performance include actual output (that is, number of units produced), scrap rate, dollar volume of sales, and number of claims processed. This may be contaminated by "opportunity bias" if some persons have a better chance to perform than others. For example, a sales representative selling snowblowers in Michigan has a greater opportunity than a colleague selling the same in Arkansas. Fortunately, adjusting raw performance figures for the effect of opportunity bias and thereby arriving at figures that accurately represent each individual's performance are often possible.

Another type of objective measure, the special performance test, is a method in which each employee is assessed under standardized conditions. This kind of appraisal also eliminates opportunity bias. For example, Verizon Southwest has a series of prerecorded calls that operators in a test booth answer. The operators are graded on speed, accuracy, and courtesy in handling the calls. Performance tests measure ability but do not measure the extent to which one is motivated to use that ability on a daily basis. (A high-ability person may be a lazy performer except when being tested.) Special performance tests must therefore be supplemented by other appraisal methods to provide a complete picture of performance.

Judgmental methods, including ranking and rating techniques, are the most common ways to measure performance. Ranking compares employees directly with one another and orders them from best to worst. Ranking has a number of drawbacks. Ranking is difficult for large groups because the persons in the middle of the distribution may be hard to distinguish from one another accurately. Comparisons of people in different work groups are also difficult. For example, an employee ranked third in a strong group may be more valuable than an employee ranked first in a weak group. Another criticism of ranking is that the manager must rank people on the basis of overall performance, although each person likely has both strengths and weaknesses. Furthermore, rankings do not provide useful information for feedback. To be told that one is ranked third is not nearly as helpful as to be told that the quality of one's work is outstanding, its quantity is satisfactory, one's punctuality could use improvement, or one's paperwork is seriously deficient.

Rating differs from ranking in that it compares each employee with a fixed standard rather than comparison with other employees. A rating scale provides the standard. Figure 8.2 gives examples of three graphic rating scales for a bank teller. Each consists of a performance dimension to be rated (punctuality, congeniality, and accuracy), followed by a scale on which to make the rating. In constructing graphic rating scales, performance dimensions that are relevant to job performance must be selected. In particular, they should focus on job behaviors and results rather than on personality traits or attitudes.

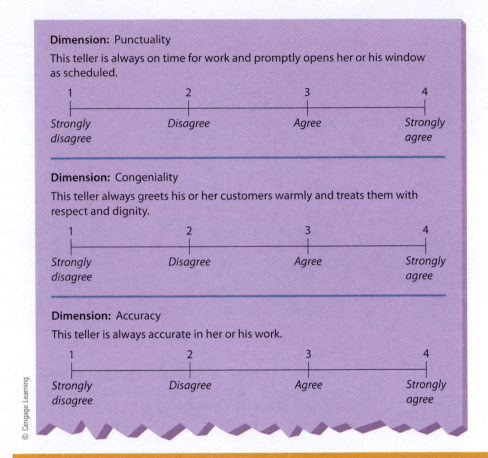

© Cengage Learning

Dimension: Punctuality

This teller is always on time for work and promptly opens her or his window as scheduled.

| 1 | 2 | 3 | 4 |

Strongly disagree   Disagree   Agree   Strongly agree

Dimension: Congeniality

This teller always greets his or her customers warmly and treats them with respect and dignity.

| 1 | 2 | 3 | 4 |

Strongly disagree   Disagree   Agree   Strongly agree

Dimension: Accuracy

This teller is always accurate in her or his work.

| 1 | 2 | 3 | 4 |

Strongly disagree   Disagree   Agree   Strongly agree

FIGURE 8.2

Graphic Rating Scales for a Bank Teller

Graphic rating scales are common methods for evaluating employee performance. The manager who is doing the rating circles the point on each scale that best reflects her or his assessment of the employee on that scale. Graphic rating scales are widely used for many different kinds of jobs.

Behaviorally Anchored Rating Scale (BARS)

A sophisticated rating method in which supervisors construct a rating scale associated with behavioral anchors

The **Behaviorally Anchored Rating Scale (BARS)** is a sophisticated and useful rating method. Supervisors construct rating scales associated with behavioral anchors. They first identify relevant performance dimensions and then generate anchors—specific, observable behaviors typical of each performance level. Figure 8.3 shows an example of a BARS for the dimension "Inventory control."

The other scales in this set, developed for the job of department manager in a chain of specialty stores, include "Handling customer complaints," "Planning special promotions," "Following company procedures," "Supervising sales personnel," and "Diagnosing and solving special problems." BARS can be effective because it requires that management takes proper care in constructing the scales and it provides useful anchors for supervisors to use in evaluating people. It is costly, however, because outside expertise is usually needed and because scales must be developed for each job within the organization.

Errors in Performance Appraisal   Errors or biases can occur in any kind of rating or ranking system.[25] One common problem is *recency error*—the tendency to base

Job: Specialty store manager
Dimension: Inventory control

7 Always orders in the right quantities and at the right time

6 Almost always orders at the right time but occasionally orders too much or too little of a particular item

5 Usually orders at the right time and almost always in the right quantities

4 Often orders in the right quantities and at the right time

3 Occasionally orders at the right time but usually not in the right quantities

2 Occasionally orders in the right quantities but usually not at the right time

1 Never orders in the right quantities or at the right time

© Cengage Learning

FIGURE 8.3

Behaviorally Anchored Rating Scale

Behaviorally anchored rating scales help overcome some of the limitations of standard rating scales. Each point on the scale is accompanied by a behavioral anchor—a summary of an employee behavior that fits that spot on the scale.

judgments on the subordinate's most recent performance because it is most easily recalled. Often a rating or ranking is intended to evaluate performance over an entire time period, such as six months or a year, so the recency error does introduce error into the judgment. Other errors include overuse of one part of the scale—being too lenient, being too severe, or giving everyone a rating of "average." *Halo error* is allowing the assessment of an employee on one dimension to "spread" to ratings of that employee on other dimensions. For instance, if an employee is outstanding on quality of output, a rater might tend to give him or her higher marks than deserved on other dimensions. Errors can also occur because of race, sex, or age discrimination, intentionally or unintentionally. The best way to offset these errors is to ensure that a valid rating system is developed at the outset and then to train managers in how to use it.

One interesting innovation in performance appraisal used in some organizations today is called **360-degree feedback**, in which managers are evaluated by everyone around them—their boss, their peers, and their subordinates. Such a complete and thorough approach provides people with a far richer array of information about their performance than does a conventional appraisal given just by the boss. Of course, such a system also takes considerable time and must be handled so as not to breed fear and mistrust in the workplace.[26]

Performance Feedback

The last step in most performance appraisal systems is giving feedback to subordinates about their performance. This is usually done in a private meeting between the person being evaluated and his or her boss. The discussion should generally be focused on the facts—the assessed level of performance, how and why that assessment was made, and how it can be improved in the future. Feedback interviews are not easy to conduct.

360-degree feedback

A performance appraisal system in which managers are evaluated by everyone around them—their boss, their peers, and their subordinates

Many managers are uncomfortable with the task, especially if feedback is negative and subordinates are disappointed by what they hear. Properly training managers, however, can help them conduct more effective feedback interviews.[27]

Some firms use a very aggressive approach to terminating people who do not meet expectations. General Electric has long used a system whereby each year the bottom 10 percent of its workforce is terminated and replaced with new employees. Company executives claim that this approach, although stressful for all employees, helps it to continuously upgrade its workforce. Other firms have started using this same approach. However, both Ford and Goodyear recently agreed to abandon similar approaches in response to age discrimination lawsuits.[28]

MAINTAINING HUMAN RESOURCES

After organizations have attracted and developed an effective workforce, they must also make every effort to maintain that workforce. To do so requires effective compensation and benefits as well as career planning. "Leading the Way" describes how one firm, Nucor Steel, uses compensation to maintain a strong workforce.

Determining Compensation

compensation

The financial remuneration given by the organization to its employees in exchange for their work

Compensation is the financial remuneration given by the organization to its employees in exchange for their work. There are three basic forms of compensation. *Wages* are the hourly compensation paid to operating employees. The minimum hourly wage paid in the United States today is $7.25 (some states have higher minimums). *Salary* refers to compensation paid for total contributions, as opposed to pay based on hours worked. For example, managers earn an annual salary, usually paid monthly. They receive the salary regardless of the number of hours they work. Some firms have started paying all their employees a salary instead of hourly wages. For example, all employees at Chaparral Steel earn a salary, starting at $30,000 a year for entry-level operating employees. Finally, *incentives* represent special compensation opportunities that are usually tied to performance. Sales commissions and bonuses are among the most common incentives.

Compensation is an important and complex part of the organization–employee relationship. Basic compensation is necessary to provide employees with the means to maintain a reasonable standard of living. Beyond this, however, compensation also provides a tangible measure of the value of the individual to the organization. If employees do not earn enough to meet their basic economic goals, they will seek employment elsewhere. Likewise, if they believe that their contributions are undervalued by the organization, they may leave or exhibit poor work habits, low morale, and little commitment to the organization. Thus, designing an effective compensation system is clearly in the organization's best interests.[29]

A good compensation system can help attract qualified applicants, retain present employees, and stimulate high performance at a cost reasonable for one's industry and geographic area. To set up a successful system, management must make decisions about wage levels, the wage structure, and the individual wage determination system. Some firms used the recent recession as an opportunity to refine their compensation systems. While many firms reduced their workforces through layoffs, others used targeted salary cuts to avoid layoffs. For instance, at Hewlett-Packard, the CEO first cut his own salary by 20 percent. The firm's very top performers kept their same pay levels. But others were given tiered salary cuts ranging from as little as 2.5 percent to as much as 20 percent. A few firms went even further. CareerBuilder.com, for instance, not only instituted pay cuts for all employees but also told everyone they only had to work half a day on Fridays.[30]

LEADING THE WAY

Holding True at Nucor Steel

Nucor Steel, the largest steelmaker in the United States, has achieved consistent profits and low employee turnover by using an innovative compensation model. Nucor Steel employees have a base guaranteed wage that is somewhat lower than the industry average but can earn considerably more than average wages by being productive. Compensation for every Nucor employee includes some form of incentive pay.

Nucor, the country's largest steelmaker, has never laid employees off or eliminated jobs. As a result of the recent recession, for example, the U.S. steel industry laid off some 10,000 workers in January 2009. But at its 11 U.S. facilities, Nucor employees were busy rewriting safety manuals, getting a head start on maintenance jobs, mowing the lawns, and cleaning the bathrooms—and still drawing paychecks. How has Nucor been able to pull this off? Experts point to two things: the firm's employees and culture. The firm's culture originated in the 1960s as the result of policies established by Ken Iverson, who brought a radical perspective on how to manage a company's human resources to the job of CEO. Iverson figured that workers would be much more productive if an employer went out of its way to share authority with them, respect what they accomplished, and compensate them as handsomely as possible. Today, the basics of the company's HR model are summed up in its "Employee Relations Principles":

- Management is obligated to manage Nucor in such a way that employees will have the opportunity to earn according to their productivity.
- Employees should feel confident that if they do their jobs properly, they will have a job tomorrow.
- Employees have the right to be treated fairly and must believe that they will be.
- Employees must have an avenue of appeal when they believe they are being treated unfairly.

The Iverson approach is based on a highly original pay system. Base pay is actually below the industry average, but the Nucor compensation plan is designed to pay more if employees perform better. For example, if a shift can turn out a defect-free batch of steel, every worker is entitled to a bonus that's paid weekly and that can potentially triple his or her take-home pay. In addition, there are one-time annual bonuses and profit-sharing payouts. In a good year, for example, the average steelworker can take home $79,000 in base pay and weekly bonuses, plus

(continued)

LEADING THE WAY (Continued)

a $2,000 year-end bonus and as much as $18,000 more in profit-sharing money. The system, however, cuts both ways. Take that defect-free batch of steel, for example. If there's a problem with a batch, workers on the shift obviously don't get any weekly bonus. And that's if they catch the problem before the batch leaves the plant. If it reaches the customer, they may *lose* up to three times what they would have received as a bonus.

Everybody in the company, from janitors to the CEO, is covered by some form of incentive plan tied to various goals and targets. Bonuses for department managers are based on a return-on-assets formula tied to divisional performance, as are bonuses under the Non-Production and Non-Department–Manager Plan, which covers everyone, except senior officers, not included in either of the first two plans; bonuses under both manager plans may increase base pay by 75 percent to 90 percent. Senior officers don't work under contracts or get

pension or retirement plans, and their base salaries are below industry average. In a world in which the typical CEO makes more than 400 times what a factory worker makes, Nucor's CEO makes considerably less. In 2012, for example, his combined salary and bonus (about $2.3 million) came to 23 times the total taken home by the average Nucor factory worker. His bonus and those of other top managers are based on a ratio of net income to stockholder's equity.

References: "Employee Relations Principles," NUCOR Corporation; "Pain, but No Layoffs at Nucor," *Business-Week*, www.businessweek.com, accessed on November 17, 2013; Byrnes with Michael Arndt, "The Art of Motivation," *BusinessWeek*, www.businessweek.com, accessed on November 17, 2013; "About Us," Nucor website, www.nucor.com, accessed on November 17, 2013; Kathy Mayer, "Nucor Steel: Pioneering Mill in Crawfordsville Celebrates 20 Years and 30 Million Tons," *AllBusiness*, www.allbusiness.com, accessed on November 17, 2013.

Wage-Level Decision The wage-level decision is a management policy decision about whether the firm wants to pay above, at, or below the going rate for labor in the industry or the geographic area. Most firms choose to pay near the average, although those that cannot afford more pay below average. Large, successful firms may like to cultivate the image of being "wage leaders" by intentionally paying more than average and thus attracting and keeping high-quality employees. IBM and Google, for example, pay top dollar to get the new employees they want. McDonald's and Walmart, on the other hand, often pay close to the minimum wage. The level of unemployment in the labor force also affects wage levels. Pay declines when labor is plentiful and increases when labor is scarce. Once managers make the wage-level decision, they need information to help set actual wage rates. Managers need to know what the maximum, minimum, and average wages are for particular jobs in the appropriate labor market. This information is collected by means of a wage survey. Area wage surveys can be conducted by individual firms or by local HR or business associations. Professional and industry associations often conduct surveys and make the results available to employers.

job evaluation
An attempt to assess the worth of each job relative to other jobs

Wage Structure Decision Wage structures are usually set up through a procedure called **job evaluation**—an attempt to assess the worth of each job relative to other jobs. At Ben & Jerry's Homemade, company policy once dictated that the highest-paid employee in the firm could not make more than seven times what the lowest-paid employee earned. But this policy had to be modified when the company found that it was simply unable to hire a new CEO without paying more than this amount. The simplest method for creating a wage structure is to rank jobs from those that should be paid the most (for example, the president) to those that should be paid the least (for example, a mail clerk or a janitor). In a smaller firm with few jobs (like Ben & Jerry's, for example), this method is quick and practical, but larger firms with many job titles require more sophisticated methods. The next step is setting actual wage rates based on a combination of survey data and the wage structure that results from job evaluation. Jobs of equal value are often grouped into wage grades for ease of administration.

Individual Wage Decisions   After wage-level and wage structure decisions are made, the individual wage decision must be addressed. This decision concerns how much to pay each employee in a particular job. Although the easiest decision is to pay a single rate for each job, more typically a range of pay rates is associated with each job. For example, the pay range for an individual job might be $10.00 to $14.40 per hour, with different employees earning different rates within the range.

A system is then needed for setting individual rates. This may be done on the basis of seniority (enter the job at $10.00, for example, and increase 50 cents per hour every six months on the job), initial qualifications (inexperienced people start at $10.00; more experienced people start at a higher rate), or merit (raises above the entering rate are given for good performance). Combinations of these bases may also be used.

The Internet is also playing a key role in compensation patterns today because both job seekers and current employees can more easily get a sense of their true market value. If they can document the claim that their value is higher than what their current employer now pays or is offering, they are in a position to demand a higher salary. Consider the case of one compensation executive who met recently with a subordinate to discuss her raise. He was surprised when she produced data from five different websites backing up her claim for a bigger raise than he had intended to offer.[31]

Determining Benefits

benefits
Things of value other than compensation that an organization provides to its workers

Benefits are things of value other than compensation that the organization provides to its workers. (Benefits are sometimes called *indirect compensation*.) The average company spends an amount equal to more than one-third of its cash payroll on employee benefits. Thus, an average employee who is paid, say, $30,000 per year averages a bit over $10,000 more per year in benefits. Benefits come in several forms. Pay for time not worked includes sick leave, vacation, holidays, and unemployment compensation. Insurance benefits often include life and health insurance for employees and their dependents. Workers' compensation is a legally required insurance benefit that provides medical care and disability income for employees injured on the job. Social Security is a government pension plan to which both employers and employees contribute. Many employers also provide a private pension plan to which they and their employees contribute. Employee service benefits include extras such as tuition reimbursement and recreational opportunities.

Some organizations have instituted *cafeteria benefit plans*, whereby basic coverage is provided for all employees but employees are then allowed to choose which additional benefits they want (up to a cost limit based on salary). An employee with five children might choose enhanced medical and dental coverage for dependents, a single employee might prefer more vacation time, and an older employee might elect increased pension benefits. Flexible systems are expected to encourage people to stay in the organization and even help the company attract new employees.[32]

In response to economic pressures, some firms have reduced employee benefits in the last few years. In 2002, for example, 17 percent of employees in the United States with employer health-care coverage saw their benefits cut; the 2008–2009 recession led to further reductions. Some employers have also reduced their contributions to employee retirement plans, cut the amount of annual leave they offer to employees, or both.[33] For instance, during the recession, 16 major companies announced that they would reduce or eliminate employer contributions to employee retirement plans. In recent years, several others followed suit. Among these were Wells Fargo, Anheuser-Busch,

Boise Cascade, Cooper Tire & Rubber, Kimberly-Clark, and Saks.[34] And in 2012, both Ford and General Motors offered lump-sum payoffs to retired workers currently drawing defined pensions. Meanwhile, although the Affordable Healthcare Act was supposed to provide more health-care coverage to more employees, major problems with its implementation raised new concerns.

MANAGING WORKFORCE DIVERSITY

Workforce diversity has become a very important issue in many organizations. The management of diversity is often seen as a key human resource function.

The Meaning of Diversity

diversity
A characteristic of a group or organization whose members differ from one another along one or more important dimensions, such as age, gender, or ethnicity

Diversity exists in a community of people when its members differ from one another along one or more important dimensions. In the business world, the term *diversity* is generally used to refer to demographic differences among people—differences in gender, age, ethnicity, and so forth. For instance, the average age of the U.S. workforce is gradually increasing, and so is the number of women in the labor force. Likewise, the labor force reflects growing numbers of African Americans, Latinos, and Asians, as well as more dual-career couples, same-gender couples, single parents, and physically challenged employees.

The Impact of Diversity

There is no question that organizations are becoming ever more diverse. But how does this affect organizations? Diversity provides both opportunities and challenges for organizations.

Diversity as a Competitive Advantage Many organizations are finding that diversity can be a source of competitive advantage in the marketplace (in addition to the fact that hiring and promoting in such a way as to enhance diversity are simply the right thing to do). For instance, organizations that manage diversity effectively often have higher levels of productivity and lower levels of turnover and absenteeism. Likewise, organizations that manage diversity effectively become known among women and minorities as good places to work. These organizations are thus better able to attract qualified employees from among these groups. Organizations with a diverse workforce are also better able to understand different market segments than are less diverse organizations. For example, a cosmetics firm such as Avon, which wants to sell its products to women and African Americans, can better understand how to create such products and effectively market them if women and African-American managers are available to provide and solicit inputs into product development, design, packaging, advertising, and so forth.[35] Finally, organizations with diverse workforces are generally more creative and innovative than other organizations.

Diversity as a Source of Conflict Unfortunately, diversity in an organization can also create conflict. This conflict can arise for a variety of reasons.[36] One potential source of conflict exists when an individual thinks that someone else has been hired, promoted, or fired because of his or her diversity status. Another source of conflict is when diversity is misunderstood or misinterpreted or as a result of inappropriate interactions among people of different groups.[37] Conflict may also arise if there is an environment of fear, distrust, or individual prejudice. Members of the dominant group in an organization may worry that newcomers from other groups pose a personal threat to their own position in the organization. For example, when U.S. firms have been taken over by Japanese firms, U.S. managers have sometimes been resentful about or hostile toward Japanese managers assigned to work with them. A final source of conflict exists when people are unwilling to accept people different from themselves. Personal bias and prejudices are still very real among some people today and can lead to potentially harmful conflict.

Managing Diversity in Organizations

Because of the tremendous potential that diversity holds for competitive advantage, as well as the importance of trying to avoid the negative consequences of associated conflict, much attention has been focused in recent years on how individuals and organizations can function more effectively in diverse contexts.

Individual Strategies   One important element of managing diversity and multiculturalism in an organization consists of things that individuals themselves can do. Understanding, of course, is the starting point. For instance, although people need to be treated fairly and equitably, managers must understand that differences among people do, in fact, exist. Thus, any effort to treat everyone the same, without regard for their fundamental human differences, will lead only to problems. People in an organization should also try to understand the perspectives of others. Further, even though people may learn to understand others, and even though they may try to empathize with others, the fact remains that they still may not accept or enjoy some aspect of their behavior. So, tolerance is also required. Finally, communication is also required. For example, suppose that a young employee has a habit of making jokes about the age of an older colleague. Perhaps the young colleague means no harm and is just engaging in what she sees as good-natured kidding. But the older employee may find the jokes offensive. If the two do not communicate, the jokes will continue, and the resentment will grow. Eventually, what started as a minor problem may erupt into a much bigger one.

Organizational Approaches   Whereas individuals are important in managing diversity and multiculturalism, the organization itself must play a fundamental role.[38] The starting point in managing diversity and multiculturalism is an organization's policies and how they directly or indirectly affect how people are treated. Another aspect of organizational policies that affects diversity and multiculturalism is how the organization addresses and responds to problems that arise from differences among people. For example, consider the example of a manager charged with sexual harassment. If the organization's policies put an excessive burden of proof on the individual being harassed and invoke only minor sanctions against the guilty party, it is sending a clear signal about the importance of such matters. But the organization that has a balanced set of policies for addressing concerns like sexual harassment sends its employees a message that diversity and individual rights and privileges are important.

Organizations can also help manage diversity and multiculturalism through a variety of ongoing practices and procedures. Avon's creation of networks for various groups represents one example of an organizational practice that fosters diversity. In general, the idea is that, because diversity and multiculturalism are characterized by differences among people, organizations can more effectively manage that diversity by following practices and procedures that are based on flexibility rather than on rigidity. Many organizations are finding that diversity and multicultural training is an effective means for managing diversity and minimizing its associated conflict. More specifically, **diversity and multicultural training** is designed to better enable members of an organization to

diversity and multicultural training

Training that is specifically designed to better enable members of an organization to function in a diverse and multicultural workforce function in a diverse and multicultural workplace.[39] Some organizations even go so far as to provide language training for their employees as a vehicle for managing diversity and multiculturalism. Motorola, for example, provides English-language training for its foreign employees on assignment in the United States. At Pace Foods in San Antonio, with a total payroll of over 450 employees, staff meetings and employee handbooks are translated into Spanish for the benefit of the company's 200 or so Latino employees.

MANAGING LABOR RELATIONS

labor relations
The process of dealing with employees who are represented by a union

Labor relations is the process of dealing with employees who are represented by a union.[40] At one time, almost one-third of the entire U.S. labor force belonged to a labor union. Unions enjoyed their largest membership between 1940 and 1955. Membership began to steadily decline in the mid-1950s, though, for several reasons: (1) increased standards of living made union membership seem less important, (2) traditionally unionized industries in the manufacturing sector began to decline, and (3) the globalization of business operations caused many unionized jobs to be lost to foreign workers. This downward trend continued until 2008, when union membership rose by the largest amount in over a quarter century, a gain of 428,000 members.[41] However, union membership again declined the following two years, dropping to 11.9 percent in 2010. Much of this fluctuation was attributable to fears of job insecurity due to the recession that hit in 2008; but as the economy bottomed out and started to rebound, membership again declined. Managing labor relations is an important part of HRM. However, most large firms have separate labor relations specialists to handle these activities apart from other human resource functions.

How Employees Form Unions

For employees to form a new local union, several things must occur. First, employees must become interested in having a union. Nonemployees who are professional organizers employed by a national union (such as the Teamsters or United Auto Workers [UAW]) may generate interest by making speeches and distributing literature outside the workplace. Inside, employees who want a union try to convince other workers of the benefits of a union.

The second step is to collect employees' signatures on authorization cards. These cards state that the signer wishes to vote to determine whether the union will represent him or her. To show the NLRB that interest is sufficient to justify holding an election, 30 percent of the employees in the potential

ON STRIKE

Int'l Association of
**MACHINISTS &
AEROSPACE WORKERS**
District 725
AFL-CIO Sanctioned

ROBYN BECK/AFP/Getty Images

A strike by a unionized workforce can be a debilitating event for any organization. Chris Langness is a machinist at the Boeing plant in Huntington Beach, California. He and 1,500 other members of the International Association of Machinists and Aerospace Workers (IAM) went on strike against Boeing when the two sides couldn't reach agreement over health insurance premiums and retirement benefits.

bargaining unit must sign these cards. Before an election can be held, however, the bargaining unit must be defined. The bargaining unit consists of all employees who will be eligible to vote in the election and to join and be represented by the union if one is formed.

The election is supervised by an NLRB representative (or, if both parties agree, the American Arbitration Association—a professional association of arbitrators) and is conducted by secret ballot. If a simple majority of those voting (not of all those eligible to vote) votes for the union, then the union becomes certified as the official representative of the bargaining unit.[42] The new union then organizes itself by officially signing up members and electing officers; it will soon be ready to negotiate the first contract. The union-organizing process is diagrammed in Figure 8.4. If workers become disgruntled with their union or if management presents strong evidence that the union is not representing workers appropriately, the NLRB can arrange a decertification election. The results of such an election determine whether the union remains certified.

© Cengage Learning

FIGURE 8.4

The Union-Organizing Process

If employees of an organization want to form a union, the law prescribes a specific set of procedures that both employees and the organization must follow. Assuming that these procedures are followed and the union is approved, the organization must engage in collective bargaining with the new union.

Organizations usually prefer that employees not be unionized because unions limit management's freedom in many areas. Management may thus wage its own campaign to convince employees to vote against the union. "Unfair labor practices" are often committed at this point. For instance, it is an unfair labor practice for management to promise to give employees a raise (or any other benefit) if the union is defeated. Experts agree that the best way to avoid unionization is to practice good employee relations all the time—not just when threatened by a union election. Providing absolutely fair treatment with clear standards in the areas of pay, promotion, layoffs, and discipline; having a complaint or appeal system for persons who feel unfairly treated; and avoiding any kind of favoritism will help make employees feel that a union is unnecessary. Walmart strives to avoid unionization through these practices.[43]

Collective Bargaining

collective bargaining

The process of agreeing on a satisfactory labor contract between management and a union

The intent of **collective bargaining** is to agree on a labor contract between management and the union that is satisfactory to both parties. The contract contains agreements about issues such as wages, work hours, job security, promotion, layoffs, discipline, benefits, methods of allocating overtime, vacations, rest periods, and the grievance procedure. The process of bargaining may go on for weeks, months, or longer, with representatives of management and the union meeting to make proposals and counterproposals. The resulting agreement must be ratified by the union membership. If it is not approved, the union may strike to put pressure on management, or it may choose not to strike and simply continue negotiating until a more acceptable agreement is reached. For example, Verizon workers went on strike in 2011 in order to protect their pensions and health-care benefits.[44]

Occasionally, circumstances cause management and labor to bargain over changes in existing contracts even before a new contract is needed. This is most likely to happen when unforeseen problems jeopardize the future of the business, and hence the jobs of union members. For example, when General Motors, Ford, and Chrysler were facing financial crisis in 2008–2009, the UAW agreed to contract concessions with the automakers to help give the firms the flexibility they claimed they needed to restructure their operations. Among others things, for instance, the UAW agreed to allow the companies to delay billions of dollars in payments for health-care costs for retirees and to eliminate a controversial job bank program that allowed workers to get most of their wages even when they had been laid off.[45]

grievance procedure

The means by which a labor contract is enforced

The **grievance procedure** is the means by which the contract is enforced. Most of what is in a contract concerns how management will treat employees. When employees feel that they have not been treated fairly under the contract, they file a grievance to correct the problem. The first step in a grievance procedure is for the aggrieved employee to discuss the alleged contract violation with her immediate superior. Often the grievance is resolved at this stage. If the employee still believes that she is being mistreated, however, the grievance can be appealed to the next level. A union official can help an aggrieved employee present her case. If the manager's decision is also unsatisfactory to the employee, additional appeals to successively higher levels are made until, finally, all in-company steps are exhausted. The final step is to submit the grievance to binding arbitration. An arbitrator is a labor law expert who is paid jointly by the union and management. The arbitrator studies the contract, hears both sides of the case, and renders a decision that both parties must obey. The grievance system for resolving disputes about contract enforcement prevents any need to strike during the term of the contract.

NEW CHALLENGES IN THE CHANGING WORKPLACE

As we have seen throughout this chapter, human resource managers face several ongoing challenges in their efforts to keep their organizations staffed with effective workforces. To complicate matters, new challenges arise as the economic and social environments of business change. We conclude this chapter with a look at two of the most important HRM issues facing business today.

Managing Knowledge Workers

Employees traditionally added value to organizations because of what they did or because of their experience. In the "information age," however, many employees add value because of what they know.[46]

knowledge workers
Workers whose contributions to an organization are based on what they know

The Nature of Knowledge Work   These employees are usually called **knowledge workers**, and the skill with which they are managed is a major factor in determining which firms will be successful in the future. Knowledge workers, including computer scientists, engineers, and physical scientists, provide special challenges for the HR manager. They tend to work in high-technology firms and are usually experts in some abstract knowledge base. They often like to work independently and tend to identify more strongly with their profession than with any organization—even to the extent of defining performance in terms recognized by other members of their profession.

As the importance of information-driven jobs grows, the need for knowledge workers continues to grow as well. But these employees require extensive and highly specialized training, and not every organization is willing to make the human capital investments necessary to take advantage of these jobs. In fact, even after knowledge workers are on the job, retraining and training updates are critical to prevent their skills from becoming obsolete. It has been suggested, for example, that the "half-life" of a technical education in engineering is about three years. The failure to update such skills will not only result in the loss of competitive advantage but also increase the likelihood that the knowledge worker will go to another firm that is more committed to updating them.

Knowledge Worker Management and Labor Markets   Even though overall demand for labor has slumped in recent years due to the economic downturn, the demand for knowledge workers remains strong. As a result, organizations that need these workers must introduce regular market adjustments (upward) to pay them enough to keep them. This is especially critical in areas in which demand is growing, as even entry-level salaries for these employees are high. Once an employee accepts a job with a firm, the employer faces yet another dilemma. Once hired, workers are more subject to the company's internal labor market, which is not likely to be growing as quickly as the external market for knowledge workers as a whole. Consequently, the longer an employee remains with a firm, the further behind the market his or her pay falls—unless, of course, it is regularly adjusted (upward).

It is no surprise that strong demand for these workers has inspired some fairly extreme measures for attracting them in the first place.[47] High starting salaries and sign-on bonuses are common. BP Exploration was recently paying starting petroleum engineers with undersea platform-drilling knowledge—not experience, just knowledge—salaries in the six figures, plus sign-on bonuses of over $50,000 and immediate profit sharing. Even with these incentives, HR managers complained that, in the Gulf Coast region, they cannot retain specialists because young engineers soon leave to accept sign-on bonuses with competitors.

Contingent and Temporary Workers

A final contemporary HR issue of note involves the use of contingent or temporary workers. Indeed, recent years have seen an explosion in the use of such workers by organizations. The FBI, for example, routinely employs a cadre of retired agents in various temporary jobs.[48]

Trends in Contingent and Temporary Employment In recent years, the number of contingent workers in the workforce has increased dramatically. A contingent worker is a person who works for an organization on something other than a permanent or full-time basis. Categories of contingent workers include independent contractors, on-call workers, temporary employees (usually hired through outside agencies), and contract and leased employees. Another category is part-time workers. The financial services giant Citigroup, for example, makes extensive use of part-time sales agents to pursue new clients. Roughly 1 in every 50 employed Americans held a temporary or contingent position in 2011.[49]

Managing Contingent and Temporary Workers Given the widespread use of contingent and temporary workers, HR managers must understand how to use such employees most effectively. In other words, they need to understand how to manage contingent and temporary workers. One key is careful planning. Even though one of the presumed benefits of using contingent workers is flexibility, it is still important to integrate such workers in a coordinated fashion. Rather than having to call in workers sporadically and with no prior notice, organizations try to bring in specified numbers of workers for well-defined periods of time. The ability to do so comes from careful planning.

A second key is understanding contingent workers and acknowledging both their advantages and their disadvantages. In other words, the organization must recognize what it can and cannot achieve from the use of contingent and temporary workers. Expecting too much from such workers, for example, is a mistake that managers should avoid. Third, managers must carefully assess the real cost of using contingent workers. We noted earlier, for example, that many firms adopt this course of action to save labor costs. The organization should be able to document precisely its labor-cost savings. How much would it be paying people in wages and benefits if they were on permanent staff? How does this cost compare with the amount spent on contingent workers? This difference, however, could be misleading. We also noted, for instance, that contingent workers might be less effective performers than permanent and full-time employees. Comparing employee for employee on a direct-cost basis, therefore, is not necessarily valid. Organizations must learn to adjust the direct differences in labor costs to account for differences in productivity and performance.

Finally, managers must fully understand their own strategies and decide in advance how they intend to manage temporary workers, specifically focusing on how to integrate them into the organization. On a very simplistic level, for example, an organization with a large contingent workforce must make some decisions about the treatment of contingent workers relative to the treatment of permanent, full-time workers. Should contingent workers be invited to the company holiday party? Should they have the same access to such employee benefits as counseling services and child care? There are no right or wrong answers to such questions. Managers must understand that they need to develop a strategy for integrating contingent workers according to some sound logic and then follow that strategy consistently over time.[50]

Indeed, this last point has become part of a legal battleground in recent years as some workers hired under the rubric of contingent workers have subsequently argued that this has been a title in name only, and that their employers use this title to discriminate against them in various ways. For instance, FedEx relies on over 13,000 "contract" drivers. These individuals wear FedEx uniforms, drive FedEx trucks, and must follow FedEx rules and procedures. However, because the firm has hired them under a different employment agreement than its "regular" employees, it does not provide them with benefits. Some of those individuals are currently suing FedEx on the grounds that, for all practical purposes, they are employees and should enjoy the same benefits as other drivers.[51]

SUMMARY OF LEARNING OUTCOMES AND KEY POINTS

1. Describe the environmental context of HRM, including its strategic importance and its relationship with legal and social factors.

   - HRM is concerned with attracting, developing, and maintaining the human resources that an organization needs.
   - Its environmental context consists of its strategic importance and the legal and social environments that affect HRM.

2. Discuss how organizations attract human resources, including human resource planning, recruiting, and selecting.

   - Attracting human resources is an important part of the HRM function.
   - Human resource planning starts with job analysis and then focuses on forecasting the organization's future need for employees, forecasting the availability of employees both within and outside the organization, and planning programs to ensure that the proper number and type of employees will be available when needed.
   - Recruitment and selection are the processes by which job applicants are attracted, assessed, and hired.
   - Methods for selecting applicants include application blanks, tests, interviews, and assessment centers.
   - Any method used for selection should be properly validated.

3. Describe how organizations develop human resources, including training and development, performance appraisal, and performance feedback.

   - Organizations must also work to develop their human resources.

   - Training and development enable employees to perform their present job effectively and to prepare for future jobs.
   - Performance appraisals are important for validating selection devices, assessing the impact of training programs, deciding pay raises and promotions, and determining training needs.
   - Both objective and judgmental methods of appraisal can be applied, and a good system usually includes several methods.
   - The validity of appraisal information is always a concern because it is difficult to accurately evaluate the many aspects of a person's job performance.

4. Discuss how organizations maintain human resources, including the determination of compensation and benefits and career planning.

   - Maintaining human resources is also important.
   - Compensation rates must be fair compared with rates for other jobs within the organization and with rates for the same or similar jobs in other organizations in the labor market.
   - Properly designed incentive or merit pay systems can encourage high performance, and a good benefits program can help attract and retain employees.
   - Career planning is also a major aspect of HRM.

5. Discuss the nature of diversity, including its meaning, associated trends, impact, and management.

   - Diversity exists in an organization when its members differ from one another along one or more important dimensions, including gender, age, and ethnicity.

- Individual strategies for managing diversity include being understanding, tolerant, and communicative with those who are different.
- Organizational strategies include having fair policies, practices, and procedures; providing diversity training; and maintaining a tolerant culture.

6. Discuss labor relations, including how employees form unions and the mechanics of collective bargaining.

- If a majority of a company's nonmanagement employees so desire, they have the right to be represented by a union.

- Management must engage in collective bargaining with the union in an effort to agree on a contract.
- While a union contract is in effect, the grievance system is used to settle disputes with management.

7. Describe the issues associated with managing knowledge, contingent, and temporary workers.

- Two important new challenges in the workplace include the following:
- Management of knowledge workers
- Issues associated with the use of contingent and temporary workers

DISCUSSION QUESTIONS

Questions for Review

1. Describe the steps in the process of human resource planning. Explain the relationships between the steps.
2. Describe the common selection methods. Which method or methods are the best predictors of future job performance? Which are the worst? Why?
3. Compare training and development, noting any similarities and differences. What are some commonly used training methods?
4. Define wages and benefits. List different benefits that organizations can offer. What three decisions must managers make to determine compensation and benefits? Explain each decision.
5. What are the potential benefits of diversity? How can individuals and organizations more effectively manage diversity?

Questions for Analysis

1. The Family and Medical Leave Act of 1993 is seen as providing much-needed flexibility and security for families and workers. Others think that it places an unnecessary burden on business. Yet another opinion is that the act hurts women,

who are more likely to ask for leave, and shuffles them off to a low-paid "mommy track" career path. In your opinion, what are the likely consequences of the act? You can adopt one of the viewpoints just expressed or develop another. Explain your answer.

2. How do you know a selection device is valid? What are the possible consequences of using invalid selection methods? How can an organization ensure that its selection methods are valid?
3. Consider a job that you have held or with which you are familiar. Describe how you think an organization could best provide an RJP for that position. What types of information and experiences should be conveyed to applicants? What techniques should be used to convey the information and experiences?
4. How would managing nonunionized workers differ from managing workers who elected to be in a union? Which would be easier? Why?
5. In what ways would managing temporary workers be easier than managing traditional permanent employees? In what ways would it be more difficult? What differences would likely exist in your own behavior if you were in a contingent or temporary job versus a traditional permanent job?

BUILDING EFFECTIVE DECISION-MAKING SKILLS

Exercise Overview

Decision-making skills refer to the ability to recognize and define problems and opportunities correctly and then to select an appropriate course

of action for solving problems or capitalizing on opportunities. For obvious reasons, these skills should be important to you in making career choices.

Exercise Background

If you're in the process of making a career choice, you need to have a firm grip on your own abilities, preferences, and limitations. This is particularly true for recent college graduates, who are often preparing to enter career fields that are largely unknown to them. Fortunately, many sources of helpful information are available. The BLS, for example, maintains data about occupations, employment prospects, compensation, working conditions, and many other issues of interest to job seekers. Information is available by industry, occupation, employer type, and region.

Exercise Task

1. Access a summary of the Department of Labor's National Compensation Survey at http://stats.bls .gov/ncs/ocs/sp/ncbl0449.pdf. (If the page has moved, search by the survey title.) Find detailed data related to the occupation that you regard as your most likely career choice when you graduate. Then locate detailed data about two other occupa-

tions that you might consider—one with a salary that's higher than that of your number-one career choice and one with a salary that's lower.

2. Record the hourly salary data for each of your three choices, and then use the hourly salary to project an expected annual income. (*Hint:* Full-time jobs require about 2,000 hours annually.)
3. Based *purely on salary information*, which occupation would be "best" for you?
4. Now go to www.bls.gov/ooh and access job descriptions for various occupations. Review the description for each of the three career choices that you've already investigated.
5. Based *purely on job characteristics*, which occupation would be "best" for you?
6. Is there any conflict between your answers to questions 3 and 5? If so, how do you plan to resolve it?
7. Are there any job characteristics that you desire strongly enough to sacrifice compensation in order to get them? What are they? What are the limits, if any, on your willingness to sacrifice pay for these job characteristics?

BUILDING EFFECTIVE TECHNICAL SKILLS

Exercise Overview

Technical skills are necessary to understand or perform the specific kind of work that an organization does. In many organizations, this work includes hiring appropriate people to fill positions. This exercise will help you apply certain technical skills to the process of employee selection.

Exercise Background

You may choose either of the following exercise variations. We tend to favor Variation 1 because the exercise is usually more useful if you can relate to real job requirements on a personal level.

Variation 1. If you currently work or have worked in the past, select two jobs with which you have some familiarity. Try to select one job that entails relatively low levels of skill, responsibility, education, and pay and one job that entails relatively high levels in the same categories.

Variation 2. If you've never worked or you're not personally familiar with an array of jobs, assume that you're a manager of a small manufacturing

plant. You need to hire people to fill two jobs. One job is for a plant custodian to sweep floors, clean bathrooms, empty trash cans, and so forth. The other job is for an office manager who will supervise a staff of three clerks and secretaries, administer the plant payroll, and coordinate the administrative operations of the plant.

Exercise Task

Reviewing what you've done so far, now do the following:

1. Identify the most basic skills needed to perform each of the two jobs effectively.
2. Identify the general indicators or predictors of whether a given individual can perform each job.
3. Develop a brief set of interview questions that you might use to determine whether an applicant has the qualifications for each job.
4. How important is it for you, as a manager hiring an employee to perform a job, to possess the technical skills needed to perform the job that you're trying to fill?

SKILLS SELF-ASSESSMENT INSTRUMENT

What Do Students Want from Their Jobs?

Purpose: This exercise investigates the job values held by college students at your institution. Then it asks the students to speculate about employers' perceptions of college students' job values. This will help you understand how college students can be recruited effectively. It also gives you insight into the difficulties of managing and motivating individuals with different values and perceptions.

Introduction: Employees choose careers that match their job values. Employers try to understand employee values to better recruit, manage, and motivate them. Job values are important therefore, in every HR process, from job advertisements and interviews, to performance appraisals, to compensation planning.

Instructions:

1. Complete the following Job Values Survey. Consider what you want from your future career. Using Column 1, rank the 14 job values from 1 to 14, with 1 being the most important to you and 14 being the least important.
2. In your opinion, when potential employers try to attract students, how much importance do they think students give to each of the values? For Column 2, respond with a 1 (plus) if you think employers would rank it higher than students or with a 2 (minus) if you think employers would rate it lower. This is the employers' perception of students' values, not of their own values.
3. In small groups or a class, compute an average ranking for each value. Then discuss the results.

Discussion Questions

1. How much variation do you see in the job value rankings in Column 1—that is, are students' values quite different, moderately different, or very similar overall?
2. If there are significant differences between individuals, what impact might these differences have on the recruiting process? On the training process? On the performance evaluation and compensation process?
3. How much variation do you see in the responses for Column 2—that is, does your group or class agree on how employers perceive college students?
4. Is there a large difference between how you think employers perceive college students and your group's or class's reported job values? If the difference is large, what difficulties might this create for job seekers and potential employers? How might these difficulties be reduced or eliminated?

Job Values Survey

	Column 1 Your Ranking	Column 2 Employer Ranking
Working conditions		
Working with people		
Employee benefits		
Challenge		
Location of job		
Self-development		
Type of work		
Job title		
Training program		
Advancement		
Salary		
Company reputation		
Job security		
Autonomy on the job		

EXPERIENTIAL EXERCISE
Choosing a Compensation Strategy

Purpose: This exercise helps you better understand how internal and external market forces affect compensation strategies.

Introduction: Assume that you are the head of a large academic department in a major research university. Your salaries are a bit below external market averages. For example, your assistant professors make between $45,000 and $55,000 a year, your associate professors make between $57,000 and $65,000 a year, and your full professors make between $80,000 and $90,000 a year.

Faculty who have been in your department for a long time enjoy the work environment and appreciate the low cost of living in the area. They know that they are somewhat underpaid but have tended to regard the advantages of being in your department as offsetting this disadvantage. Recently, however, external market forces have caused salaries for people in your field to escalate rapidly. Unfortunately, although your university acknowledges this problem, you have been told that no additional funds will be provided to your department.

You currently have four vacant positions that need to be filled. One of these is at the rank of associate professor, and the other three are at the rank of assistant professor. You have surveyed other departments in similar universities, and you realize that to hire the best new assistant professors, you will need to offer at least $60,000 a year and that to get a qualified associate professor, you will need to pay at least $70,000. You have been given the budget to hire new employees at more competitive salaries but cannot do anything to raise the salaries of faculty currently in your department. You have identified the following options:

1. You can hire new faculty from lower-quality schools. They will likely accept salaries below market rate.
2. You can hire the best people available, pay market salaries, and deal with internal inequities later.
3. You can hire fewer new faculty, use the extra money to boost the salaries of your current faculty, and cut class offerings in the future.

Instructions:

Step 1: Working alone, decide how you will proceed.

Step 2: Form small groups with your classmates and compare solutions.

Step 3: Identify the strengths and weaknesses of each option.

Follow-Up Questions

1. Are there other options that might be pursued?
2. Assume that you chose Option 2. How would you go about dealing with the internal inequity problems?
3. Discuss with your instructor the extent to which this problem exists at your school.

MANAGEMENT AT WORK
The Temptations of Temping

Back in 2002, New Yorker Diana Bloom logged on to Craigslist, an online network that posts free classified ads, and offered her services as a tutor, editor, and translator. She's been making a living on the short-term jobs that come her way from the website ever since. A former English professor who couldn't find secure long-term employment, Bloom works out of her home in order to take care of a young son. Temp work is also appealing, she says, because "I'm not very outgoing, and getting my foot in the door to companies would have been hard."

Craigslist works in the other direction, too, with employers posting openings for jobs both permanent and temporary. Another New Yorker, Simone Sneed, scours the Craigslist "Gigs" section for jobs that last for perhaps a day, often for just a few hours. Whether as a backup singer or a grants writer, she's turned the strategy of patching together "gigs" into a convenient way to supplement the income from her full-time job. "I'll use the extra money to pay off my school loan," she says. "Every little bit helps."

In the current economic climate, unfortunately, overall job postings are down on Craigslist and everywhere else, except for short-term jobs—gigs that usually include no health benefits, sick days, or paid vacations. If you're employed short term or part-time for economic reasons (probably because you got laid off), the Bureau of Labor Statistics (BLS) classifies you as "underemployed."

Naturally, most people who are "underemployed" are, by definition, "overqualified." In fact, they often have years of professional experience but are willing to take jobs that don't call for their levels of training or experience. Take the case of Gloria Christ. As national project manager for an information technology company in the Chicago area, Christ used to coordinate the installation of Wi-Fi hot spots all over the country. She has nearly 20 years of managerial experience, but today she's willing to put it to use as a temporary office manager. Of course, she'd like something with a little more long-term promise: "At this point in time," she says, "I think even if there was something that was temporary it could become full-time later on…. Sometimes," she explains, "you can go in at a low level to interview just to get your foot in the door."

It may be small compensation (so to speak), but during the current recession, although many companies are reluctant to add costly permanent jobs, they are increasingly willing to open up temporary positions to tide them over. Often, of course, you'll have to take a job that isn't exactly what you've trained for or set your sights on, but as one employment-services manager observes, job seekers today "are more than willing to try new occupations—much more willing than they were even a year ago."

It is interesting that for a lot of people, the adjustment to current labor-market conditions isn't necessarily as traumatic as you might think. A recent survey conducted by the temporary-staffing agency Kelly Services found that as many as 26 percent of employed American adults regard themselves as "free agents" when it comes to the type of job that they're willing to take (up from 19 percent in 2006). Of all those polled, only 10 percent said that they're doing temporary work because they've been laid off from permanent jobs; 90 percent said that they're doing it because they like the variety and flexibility that temping affords them.

Kelly client Jaime Gacharna's first assignment was packaging products for a light-industrial wholesaler— "putting doorknobs into little bags," he recalls. Since then, he's worked for eight different employers, working at a job for a few days, a few weeks, or a few months. He doesn't mind the constant adjustments because the variety in his work life compensates for the drawbacks. "If I want to try something out, and I like it," says Gacharna, "I can stay with [the company].

If I don't, I can always just call up Kelly and say I want something different."

In fact, temping offers several advantages. It can, for example, provide income during career transitions, and it's a good way to exercise a little control over the balance between your work and the rest of your life. In 1995, for example, when she was seven months pregnant with her first child, veteran retail manager Stacey Schick accepted a two-week data-entry job with the Orange County (New York) Association of Realtors. "I didn't know how to turn on a computer," she remembers, but "they needed bodies." Now the mother of two, Schick is still with the Association as its education coordinator. "I would never have considered it," she says, if a job in her field had come up, but the job she landed in has turned out to be a much better fit with her lifestyle: "It's afforded me the opportunity to have a family and be able to have time with them."

The path taken by Schick is called *temp-to-perm*, and it offers employers several advantages as well. Companies that are hesitant to make commitments to untested employees can try before they buy—they get a chance to see employees in action before finalizing hiring decisions. Because there are no fees to pay when an employee goes from temp to perm, trying out temps is also cheaper than paying an agency outright to find a hire. The big savings, of course, come from benefits, which can amount to one-third of the total cost of compensating a permanent position.

And then there's the recession. While many employers are laying off full-time workers, many are also trying to compensate by turning over some of the work to temp staff. Ironically, of course, many of those who've been laid off are highly qualified, and as they hit the job market willing to accept lower-level positions, the ranks of job hunters are being joined by a substantial number of highly qualified (which is to say, overqualified) workers. "The quality of candidates," says Laura Long of Banner Personnel, a Chicago-area staffing agency, "is tremendous…. As an employer, you can get great employees for a great price."

As a matter of fact, if you're a U.S. employer, you've always been able to get temp workers at a relatively good price. As of December 2010, according to the BLS, the average cost of a full-time worker in private industry was $22.26 per hour in wages plus $9.75 in benefits, for a total of $32.01 in compensation. By contrast, the average wages for a temp were $12.14 and the average benefits were $3.42, for total compensation of $15.56. One of the results of this cost differential has been a long-term increase in the number of temp workers which, over the last 20 years, has far outstripped the increase in jobs occupied by full-time workers.

Case Questions

1. You're a senior manager at a growing business and you're ready to add employees. Your HR manager has recommended a temp-to-perm policy. You know the advantages of this approach, but what might be some of the disadvantages?
2. Assume that you're a prospective job seeker (which you may very well be). What do you personally see as the advantages and disadvantages of taking a temp-to-perm position? Under what circumstances are you most likely to take a temp-to-perm position?
3. What sort of challenges are likely to confront a manager who supervises a mix of temporary and permanent employees? In what ways might these challenges differ if the temporary workers have

been hired on a temp-to-perm basis rather than on a strictly temporary basis?

Case References

"For Some, a Patchwork of Jobs Pays the Bills," *Boston.com*, www.boston.com, accessed on November 17, 2013; Kristin Kridel, "Overqualified Applying for Temporary Work," *Spokesman.com*, www.spokesman.com, accessed on November 17, 2013; Anne Fisher, "Be a Manager and a Temp?" *CNN Money.com*, www.cmfassociates.com, accessed on November 17, 2013; Sital Patel, "Skill Level of Temp Workers Rises amid Recession," *Fox Business*, www.jobs-work-employment.com, accessed on November 17, 2013; U.S. Bureau of Labor Statistics (BLS), "Employer Costs for Employee Compensation," news release, December 2010, www.bls.gov/ooh, accessed on November 17, 2013; and BLS, "Table 12. Private Industry, by Industry Group and Full-Time and Part-Time Status," news release, www.bls.gov/ooh, accessed on November 17, 2013.

You Make the Call

No Company for Old-Fashioned Management

1. If you were an HR executive at Wegmans, would you focus more on *internal recruiting* or on *external recruiting*? Would your strategy for higher-level positions differ from your strategy for lower-level positions? How would current economic conditions influence your strategy?
2. As an HR executive at Wegmans, you need to hire a group of new employees as part of your management-trainee program—people who will

be put on a track leading, ultimately, to positions as store managers. Briefly outline your program for developing these employees.
3. If you were an employee at Wegmans, how would you expect your annual performance appraisal to be conducted? Given the company's customer-relations strategy, which appraisal methods do you think would be most appropriate?

ENDNOTES

1 Jon Springer, "Danny Wegman," *Supermarket News*, http://supermarketnews.com, accessed on November 17, 2013; Michael A. Prospero, "Employee Innovator: Wegmans," *Fast Company*, www.fastcompany.com, accessed on November 17, 2013; Dan Mitchell, "Wegmans Price War Against Itself," *The Big Money*, www.slate.com/articles/business.html, accessed on November 17, 2013; "100 Best Companies to Work For," http://money.cnn.com, accessed on November 17, 2013; Business Civic Leadership Center, "Wegmans," *2009 Corporate Citizenship Awards* (Washington, DC: U.S. Chamber of Commerce, 2009), www.bclc.uschamber.com, accessed on November 17, 2013; and "In 2010, Wegmans Announces Largest Group of Employee Scholar-

ship Recipients Yet," press release, www.wegmans.com, accessed on November 17, 2013.

2 For a complete review of HRM, see Angelo S. DeNisi and Ricky W. Griffin, *HRM*, 2nd ed. (Cincinnati, OH: Cengage, 2013).

3 Patrick Wright and Gary McMahan, "Strategic Human Resources Management: A Review of the Literature," *Journal of Management*, June 1992, pp. 280–319. See also Peter Cappelli, "Talent Management for the Twenty-First Century," *Harvard Business Review*, March 2008, pp. 74–84; and Edward E. Lawler III, "Make Human Capital a Source of Competitive Advantage," *Organizational Dynamics*, January–March 2009, Vol. 38, No. 1, pp. 1–7.

4 "From the Ashes, New Tech Start-Ups Can Bloom," *USA Today*, February 17, 2009, p. 1B.

5 Augustine Lado and Mary Wilson, "Human Resource Systems and Sustained Competitive Advantage: A Competency-Based Perspective," *Academy of Management Review*, 1994, Vol. 19, No. 4, pp. 699–727.

6 David Lepak and Scott Snell, "Examining the Human Resource Architecture: The Relationships among Human Capital, Employment, and Human Resource Configurations," *Journal of Management*, 2002, Vol. 28, No. 4, pp. 517–543. See also Wayne F. Cascio and Herman Aguinis, "Staffing Twenty-First Century Organizations," in James P. Walsh and Arthur P. Brief (eds.), *The Academy of Management Annals*, Vol. 2 (London: Routledge, 2008), pp. 133–166.

7 "Maryland First to OK 'Wal-Mart Bill,'" *USA Today*, January 13, 2006, p. 1B.

8 "Is Butter Flavoring Ruining Popcorn Workers' Lungs?" *USA Today*, June 20, 2002, pp. 1A, 8A.

9 "While Hiring at Most Firms Chills, WalMart's Heats Up," *USA Today*, August 26, 2002, p. 1B.

10 Peter Cappelli, "A Supply Chain Approach to Workforce Planning," *Organizational Dynamics*, January–March 2009, Vol. 38, No. 1, pp. 8–15.

11 John Beeson, "Succession Planning," *Across the Board*, February 2000, pp. 38–41.

12 "Buffett Says a Successor Is Lined Up to Replace Him," *BBC News*, www.bbc.co.uk/news/business, accessed on November 17, 2013

13 "Star Search," *BusinessWeek*, October 10, 2005, pp. 66–78. See also Claudio Fernandez-Araoz, Boris Groysberg, and Nitin Nohria, "The Definitive Guide to Recruiting in Good Times and Bad," *Harvard Business Review*, May 2009, pp. 74–85.

14 James A. Breaugh and Mary Starke, "Research on Employee Recruiting: So Many Studies, So Many Remaining Questions," *Journal of Management*, 2000, Vol. 26, No. 3, pp. 405–434.

15 See Paul R. Sackett and Filip Lievens, "Personnel Selection," in Susan T. Fiske, Daniel L. Schacter, and Robert Sternberg (eds.), *Annual Review of Psychology, 2008* (Palo Alto, CA: Annual Reviews, 2008), pp. 419–450.

16 "Pumping Up Your Past," *Time*, June 10, 2002, p. 96.

17 Frank L. Schmidt and John E. Hunter, "Employment Testing: Old Theories and New Research Findings," *American Psychologist*, October 1981, pp. 1128–1137.

18 Robert Liden, Christopher Martin, and Charles Parsons, "Interviewer and Applicant Behaviors in Employment Interviews," *Academy of Management Journal*, 1993, Vol. 36, No. 2, pp. 372–386.

19 Paul R. Sackett, "Assessment Centers and Content Validity: Some Neglected Issues," *Personnel Psychology*, 1987, Vol. 40, No. 1, pp. 13–25.

20 Stern, Gary M. "Company Training Programs: What Are They Really Worth?" *Fortune* 27, May 2012, pp. 58–64.

21 Renee DeRouin, Barbara Fritzsche, and Eduardo Salas, "E-Learning in Organizations," *Journal of Management*, 2005, Vol. 31, No. 6, pp. 920–940. See Fred Luthans, James B. Avey, and Jaime L. Patera, "Experimental Analysis of a Web-Based Training Intervention to Develop Positive Psychological Capital," *Academy of Management Learning & Education*, 2008, Vol. 7, No. 2, pp. 209–221, for a recent illustration.

22 "'Boeing U': Flying by the Book," *USA Today*, October 6, 1997, pp. 1B, 2B. See also "Is Your Airline Pilot Ready for Surprises?" *Time*, October 14, 2002, p. 72.

23 "The Secret Sauce at In-N-Out Burger," *BusinessWeek*, April 20, 2009, pp. 68–69; and "Despite Cutbacks, Firms Invest in Developing Leaders," *Wall Street Journal*, February 9, 2009, p. B4.

24 See Paul Levy and Jane Williams, "The Social Context of Performance Appraisal: A Review and Framework for the Future," *Journal of Management*, 2004, Vol. 30, No. 6, pp. 881–905.

25 See Michael Hammer, "The 7 Deadly Sins of Performance Measurement (and How to Avoid Them)," *MIT Sloan Management Review*, Spring 2007, pp. 19–30.

26 See Angelo S. De Nisi and Avraham N. Kluger, "Feedback Effectiveness: Can 360-Degree Appraisals Be Improved?" *Academy of Management Executive*, 2000, Vol. 14, No. 1, pp. 129–139.

27 Barry R. Nathan, Allan Mohrman, and John Milliman, "Interpersonal Relations as a Context for the Effects of Appraisal Interviews on Performance and Satisfaction: A Longitudinal Study," *Academy of Management Journal*, June 1991, Vol. 34, No. 2, pp. 352–369.

28 "Goodyear to Stop Labeling 10% of Its Workers as Worst," *USA Today*, September 12, 2002, p. 1B.

29 Jaclyn Fierman, "The Perilous New World of Fair Pay," *Fortune*, June 13, 1994, pp. 57–64. See also "The Best vs. the Rest," *Wall Street Journal*, January 30, 2006, pp. B1, B3.

30 "Pay Cuts Made Palatable," *BusinessWeek*, May 4, 2009, p. 67. See also "The Right Way to Pay," *Forbes*, May 11, 2009, pp. 78–80 and "Do Pay Cuts Pay Off?" *Time*, April 27, 2009, p. Global 6.

31 Stephanie Armour, "Show Me the Money, More Workers Say," *USA Today*, June 6, 2000, p. 1B.

32 "To Each According to His Needs: Flexible Benefits Plans Gain Favor," *Wall Street Journal*, September 16, 1986, p. 29.

33 See "Companies Chisel Away at Workers' Benefits," *USA Today*, November 18, 2002, pp. 1B, 2B. See also "The Benefits Trap," *BusinessWeek*, July 19, 2004, pp. 64–72.

34 "More Companies Freeze Pensions," *USA Today*, May 11, 2009, p. 1A.

35 For an example, see "A Female Executive Tells Furniture Maker What Women Want," *Wall Street Journal*, June 25, 1999, pp. A1, A11.

36 Patricia L. Nemetz and Sandra L. Christensen, "The Challenge of Cultural Diversity: Harnessing a Diversity of Views to Understand Multiculturalism," *Academy of Management Review*, 1996, Vol. 21, No. 2, pp. 434–462. See also "Generational Warfare," *Forbes*, March 22, 1999, pp. 62–66.

37 Christine M. Riordan and Lynn McFarlane Shores, "Demographic Diversity and Employee Attitudes: An Empirical Examination of Relational Demography within Work Units," *Journal of Applied Psychology*, 1997, Vol. 82, No. 3, pp. 342–358.

38 Sara Rynes and Benson Rosen, "What Makes Diversity Programs Work?" *HR Magazine*, October 1994, pp. 67–75.

39 Karen Hildebrand, "Use Leadership Training to Increase Diversity," *HR Magazine*, August 1996, pp. 53–59.

40 Barbara Presley Nobel, "Reinventing Labor," *Harvard Business Review*, July–August 1993, pp. 115–125.

41 "Big Gains for Unions," *New York Times*, January 29, 2009, p. C1.

42 John A. Fossum, "Labor Relations: Research and Practice in Transition," *Journal of Management*, Summer 1987, Vol. 13, No. 2, pp. 281–300.

43 "How Wal-Mart Keeps Unions at Bay," *BusinessWeek*, October 28, 2002, pp. 94–96.

44 "Verizon Strike 2011: A Sign of the Times as Americans Go Wireless," *ABC News*, August 9, 2011, abc.go.com, accessed on 28 April 2012.

45 "UAW Gives Concessions to Big Three," *Wall Street Journal*, December 4, 2008, pp. B1, B2.

46 Max Boisot, *Knowledge Assets* (Oxford, UK: Oxford University Press, 1998).

47 Thomas Stewart, "In Search of Elusive Tech Workers," *Fortune*, February 16, 1998, pp. 171–172.

48 "FBI Taps Retiree Experience for Temporary Jobs," *USA Today*, October 3, 2002, p. 1A.

49 "Larger Temporary Workforce Could Be New Normal," *US News and World Report*, November 17, 2011, pp. 35–38.

50 "When Is a Temp Not a Temp?" *BusinessWeek*, December 7, 1998, pp. 90–92.

51 "Drivers Deliver Trouble to FedEx by Seeking Employee Benefits," *Wall Street Journal*, January 7, 2005, pp. A1, A8.

CHAPTER 9

Basic Elements of Individual Behavior in Organizations

Sergii Tsololo/Photos.com

Learning Outcomes

After studying this chapter, you should be able to:

1 Explain the nature of the individual–organization relationship.

2 Define personality and describe personality attributes that affect behavior in organizations.

3 Discuss individual attitudes in organizations and how they affect behavior.

4 Describe basic perceptual processes and the role of attributions in organizations.

5 Discuss the causes and consequences of stress, and describe how it can be managed.

6 Describe creativity and its role in organizations.

7 Explain how workplace behaviors can directly or indirectly influence organizational effectiveness.

Management in Action

Putting In the Hours

"They told me I was a manager, but I spent a lot of time sweeping and emptying the trash."

—**Omar Belazi, former RadioShack Manager**

People who work for organizations all have certain understandings about what they are supposed to do for their employer and what they can expect in return. When these factors seem fair and reasonable, people tend to be happy and productive. But when the balance gets out of line, problems can start to set in. This is especially true when people think they are not getting fairly paid for their contributions.

For instance, Heather Jennings worked as a customer service representative for Verizon and was paid on an hourly basis. However, she was told that she needed to be at her workstation 10 to 15 minutes before her shift officially started in order to log into her computer, open databases, and get her equipment adjusted so she could start work precisely on time. All of the other employees in her department were given the same instructions.

Similarly, Jeffrey Allen was a sergeant in the Chicago police department. He left work each day at 5:00 p.m. but continued to receive dozens of text messages, e-mails, and calls on his department-issued Blackberry until 10:00 p.m. or so each day. Allen felt compelled to respond to each contact, sometimes taking a matter of a few minutes but other times needing an hour or more. No one at his precinct told him he had to do this, but he felt subtle pressure to do so.

RadioShack was recently sued by a large group of current and former store managers in California. The retailer was charged with requiring store managers to perform nonmanagerial work after regular hours for no additional pay.

For years, Omar Belazi, a former RadioShack store manager, logged 65-hour workweeks and stayed late to clean the store's restrooms and vacuum the floor. He also felt pressured to work all weekend each week just to help meet the store's sales goals. Regardless of the hours he worked, however, he received the same monthly salary. Belazi gradually tired of the long hours, extra work, and stress, and he left RadioShack.

Each of these cases has something in common: what an employer can expect of its employees in relation to what it pays them. They have also each been the subject of a lawsuit. At the heart of the argument is a decades-old law that mandates overtime payments for hourly operating workers who work more than 40 hours a week but allows firms to pay salaries to professionals regardless of how many hours they work. The Fair Labor Standards Act specifically exempts those in executive, administrative, or professional jobs from overtime payments.

But because so many jobs have shifted from the manufacturing setting to service settings, and because the nature of so many jobs has changed, the lines between different kinds of work have blurred. That is, when someone works on an assembly line, it's pretty simple to step up to the line and start work, and the tasks themselves are clearly defined. Service jobs, though, often have more subjective "boundaries" and may require more start-up time.

Heather Jennings acknowledges that she is an hourly worker, but lodged complaints in order to get paid for the extra 10 to 15 minutes she spends each day getting ready to work. Jeffrey Allen, meanwhile, has filed grievances and wants overtime for the extra hours he works each evening. RadioShack eventually settled a lawsuit filed by 1,300 current and former California store managers for $29.9 million. In similar fashion, Oracle recently paid $35 million to 1,666 workers who claimed they were misclassified. And Walmart was recently fined $4.8 million for denying overtime pay to employees working in store vision centers who were classified as managers but who were expected to work extra hours performing nonmanagerial jobs.[1]

The relationships between people and their employers are growing increasingly complex. Although most employees have relatively healthy and constructive relationships with their organization and other employees in that organization, some employees, however, reflect different profiles. Indeed, myriad different and unique characteristics reside in each and every employee (and employer). These affect how they feel about the organization, how they will alter their future attitudes about the firm, and how they perform their jobs. These characteristics reflect the basic elements of individual behavior in organizations.

This chapter describes several of these basic elements and is the first of several chapters designed to develop a more complete perspective on the leading function of management. In the next section, we investigate the psychological nature of individuals in organizations. The following section introduces the concept of personality and discusses several important personality attributes that can influence behavior in organizations. We then examine individual attitudes and their role in organizations. The role of stress in the workplace is then discussed, followed by a discussion of individual creativity. Finally, we describe a number of basic individual behaviors that are important to organizations.

UNDERSTANDING INDIVIDUALS IN ORGANIZATIONS

As a starting point in understanding human behavior in the workplace, we must consider the basic nature of the relationship between individuals and organizations. We must also gain an appreciation of the nature of individual differences.

The Psychological Contract

psychological contract
The overall set of expectations held by an individual with respect to what he or she will contribute to the organization and what the organization will provide in return

contributions
What the individual provides to the organization

inducements
What the organization provides to the individual

Most people have a basic understanding of a contract. Whenever we buy a house or sell a car, for example, both buyer and seller sign a contract that specifies the terms of the agreement. A psychological contract is similar in some ways to a standard legal contract but is less formal and well defined. In particular, a **psychological contract** is the overall set of expectations held by an individual with respect to what he or she will contribute to the organization and what the organization will provide in return.[2] Thus, a psychological contract is not written on paper, nor are all its terms explicitly negotiated.

The essential nature of a psychological contract is illustrated in Figure 9.1. The individual makes a variety of **contributions** to the organization—effort, skills, ability, time, loyalty, and so forth. These contributions presumably satisfy various needs and requirements of the organization. In other words, because the organization may have hired the person because of her skills, it is reasonable for the organization to expect that she will subsequently display those skills in the performance of her job.

In return for these contributions, the organization provides **inducements** to the individual. Some inducements, like pay and benefits, are tangible rewards. Others, like job security and recognition, are more intangible. Just as the contributions available from the individual must satisfy the needs of the organization, the inducements offered by the organization must serve the needs of the individual. Thus, if a person accepts employment with an organization because she thinks she will earn an attractive salary and have an opportunity to advance, she will subsequently expect that those rewards will actually be forthcoming.

FIGURE 9.1

The Psychological Contract

Psychological contracts are the basic assumptions that individuals have about their relationships with their organization. Such contracts are defined in terms of contributions by the individual relative to inducements from the organization.

If both the individual and the organization perceive that the psychological contract is fair and equitable, they will be satisfied with the relationship and will likely continue it. On the other hand, if either party sees an imbalance or inequity in the contract, it may initiate a change. For example, the individual may request a pay raise or promotion, decrease her contributed effort, or look for a better job elsewhere. The organization can also initiate change by requesting that the individual improve her skills through training, transfer the person to another job, or terminate the person's employment altogether.[3]

A basic challenge faced by the organization, then, is to manage psychological contracts. The organization must ensure that it is getting value from its employees. At the same time, it must be sure that it is providing employees with appropriate inducements. If the organization is underpaying its employees for their contributions, for example, they may perform poorly or leave for better jobs elsewhere. On the other hand, if they are being overpaid relative to their contributions, the organization is incurring unnecessary costs.[4]

The Person–Job Fit

person–job fit
The extent to which the contributions made by the individual match the inducements offered by the organization

One specific aspect of managing psychological contracts is managing the **person–job fit**—the extent to which the contributions made by the individual match the inducements offered by the organization. In theory, each employee has a specific set of needs that he wants to be fulfilled and a set of job-related behaviors and abilities to contribute. Thus, if the organization can take perfect advantage of those behaviors and abilities and exactly fulfill his needs, it will have achieved a perfect person–job fit.

Of course, such a precise level of person–job fit is seldom achieved. There are several reasons for this. For one thing, organizational selection procedures are imperfect. Organizations can make approximations of employee skill levels when making hiring decisions and can improve them through training. But even simple performance dimensions are often hard to measure in objective and valid ways.

Another reason for imprecise person–job fits is that both people and organizations change. An individual who finds a new job stimulating and exciting may find the same job boring and monotonous after a few years of performing it. And, when the organization adopts new technology, it has changed the skills it needs from its employees. Still another reason for imprecision in the person–job fit is that each individual is unique. Measuring skills and performance is difficult enough. Assessing needs, attitudes, and personality is far more complex. Each of these individual differences serves to make matching individuals with jobs a difficult and complex process.[5]

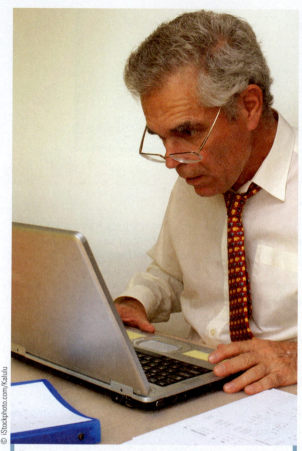

Person–job fit may change for a variety of reasons. For example, people change over time, as do jobs. New technology can also affect person–job fit. This manager, for example, is trying to master a new operating system his firm has adopted and is having trouble understanding it. While his confusion may be short-lived, more significant technological changes can lead to major problems with person–job fit.

The Nature of Individual Differences

Individual differences are personal attributes that vary from one person to another. Individual differences may be physical, psychological, or emotional. Taken together, all the individual differences that characterize any specific person serve to make that individual unique from everyone else. Much of the remainder of this chapter is devoted to individual differences. Before proceeding, however, we must also note the importance of the situation in assessing the behavior of individuals.

Are specific differences that characterize a given individual good or bad? Do they contribute to or detract from performance? The answer, of course, is that it depends on the circumstances. One person may be very dissatisfied, withdrawn, and negative in one job setting, but very satisfied, outgoing, and positive in another. Working conditions, coworkers, and leadership are all important ingredients.

Thus, whenever an organization attempts to assess or account for individual differences among its employees, it must also be sure to consider the situation in which behavior occurs. Individuals who are satisfied or productive workers in one context may prove to be dissatisfied or unproductive workers in another context. Attempting to consider both individual differences and contributions in relation to inducements and contexts, then, is a major challenge for organizations as they attempt to establish effective psychological contracts with their employees and achieve optimal fits between people and jobs.

individual differences
Personal attributes that vary from one person to another

personality
The relatively stable set of psychological and behavioral attributes that distinguish one person from another

PERSONALITY AND INDIVIDUAL BEHAVIOR

Personality traits represent some of the most fundamental sets of individual differences in organizations. **Personality** is the relatively stable set of psychological and behavioral attributes that distinguish one person from another.[6] Managers should strive to understand basic personality attributes and the ways they can affect people's behavior in organizational situations, not to mention their perceptions of and attitudes toward the organization.

The "Big Five" Personality Traits

Psychologists have identified literally thousands of personality traits and dimensions that differentiate one person from another. But, in recent years, researchers have identified five fundamental personality traits that are especially relevant to organizations. Because

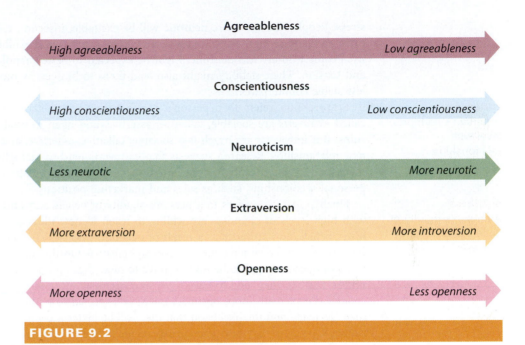

FIGURE 9.2

The "Big Five" Model of Personality

The Big Five personality model represents an increasingly accepted framework for understanding personality traits in organizational settings. In general, experts tend to agree that personality traits toward the left end of each dimension, as illustrated in this figure, are more positive in organizational settings, whereas traits closer to the right are less positive.

these five traits are so important and because they are currently the subject of so much attention, they are now commonly referred to as the **"Big Five" personality traits** and are illustrated in Figure 9.2.[7]

Agreeableness refers to a person's ability to get along with others. A high level of agreeableness in people causes them to be gentle, cooperative, forgiving, understanding, and good-natured in their dealings with others. Those with lower agreeableness can be irritable, short-tempered, uncooperative, and generally antagonistic toward other people.

Although research has not yet fully investigated the effects of agreeableness, it would seem likely that highly agreeable people will be better able to develop good working relationships with coworkers, subordinates, and higher-level managers than less agreeable people. This same pattern might also extend to relationships with customers, suppliers, and other key organizational constituents.

Conscientiousness refers to the person's ability to manage multiple tasks and to consistently meet deadlines. People who have high levels of conscientiousness are likely to be organized, systematic, careful, thorough, responsible, and self-disciplined as they work to accomplish tasks and meet goals. Others, however, tend to take on more tasks than they can manage and, as a result, are more disorganized, careless, and irresponsible, as well as less thorough and self-disciplined. Research has found that more conscientious people tend to be higher performers than less conscientious people across a variety of different jobs. This pattern seems logical, of course, because more conscientious people will take their jobs seriously and will approach the performance of their jobs in highly responsible fashions.

The third of the Big Five personality dimensions is **neuroticism**. People who are less neurotic will be relatively poised, calm, resilient, secure, and experience less anxiety and

"Big Five" personality traits
A popular personality framework based on five key traits

agreeableness
A person's ability to get along with others

conscientiousness
A person's ability to manage multiple tasks and consistently meet deadlines

Neuroticism
Extent to which a person experiences anxiety or is poised, calm, resilient, and secure

stress. People who are more neurotic will be excitable, insecure, reactive, and subject to extreme mood swings. They are also prone to be anxious and exhibit signs of vulnerability. People who are less neurotic might be expected to better handle job stress, pressure, and tension. Their stability might also lead them to be seen as more reliable than their less stable counterparts.

extraversion
A person's comfort level with relationships

Extraversion refers to a person's comfort level with relationships. People who are called *extraverts* are sociable, talkative, assertive, and open to establishing new relationships. But introverts are much less sociable, talkative, assertive, and open to establishing new relationships. Research suggests that extraverts tend to be higher overall job performers than introverts and that they are also more likely to be attracted to jobs based on personal relationships, such as sales and marketing positions.

openness
A person's rigidity of beliefs and range of interests

Finally, **openness** refers to a person's rigidity of beliefs and range of interests. People with high levels of openness are willing to listen to new ideas and to change their own ideas, beliefs, and attitudes as a result of new information. They also tend to have broad interests and to be curious, imaginative, and creative. On the other hand, people with low levels of openness tend to be less receptive to new ideas and be less willing to change their minds. Further, they tend to have fewer and narrower interests and to be less curious and creative. People with more openness might be expected to be better performers, owing to their flexibility and the likelihood that they will be better accepted by others in the organization. Openness may also encompass an individual's willingness to accept change. For example, people with high levels of openness may be more receptive to change, whereas people with low levels of openness may be more likely to resist change.

The Big Five framework continues to attract the attention of both researchers and managers. The potential value of this framework is that it encompasses an integrated set of traits that appear to be valid predictors of certain behaviors in certain situations. Thus, managers who can develop both an understanding of the framework and the ability to assess these traits in their employees will be in a good position to understand how and why employees behave as they do.[8] On the other hand, managers must also be careful not to overestimate their ability to assess the Big Five traits in others. Even assessment using the most rigorous and valid measures, for instance, is still likely to be somewhat imprecise. Another limitation of the Big Five framework is that it is based primarily on research conducted in the United States. Thus, there are unanswered questions as to how accurately it applies to workers in other cultures. And, even within the United States, a variety of other factors and traits are also likely to affect behavior in organizations.

The Myers–Briggs Framework

Another interesting approach to understanding personalities in organizations is the Myers–Briggs framework. This framework, based on the classic work of Carl Jung, differentiates people in terms of four general dimensions, defined as follows:

- *Extraversion (E) versus introversion (I).* Extraverts get their energy from being around other people, whereas introverts are worn out by others and need solitude to recharge their energy.
- *Sensing (S) versus intuition (N).* The sensing type prefers concrete things, whereas intuitives prefer abstract concepts.
- *Thinking (T) versus feeling (F).* Thinking individuals base their decisions more on logic and reason, whereas feeling individuals base their decisions more on feelings and emotions.
- *Judging (J) versus perceiving (P).* People who are the judging type enjoy completion or being finished, whereas perceiving types enjoy the process and open-ended situations.

To use this framework, people complete a questionnaire designed to measure their personality on each dimension. Higher or lower scores in each of the dimensions are used to classify people into one of sixteen different personality categories.

The Myers–Briggs Type Indicator (MBTI) is one popular questionnaire that some organizations use to assess personality types. Indeed, it is among the most popular selection instruments used today, with as many as 2 million people taking it each year. Research suggests that the MBTI is a useful method for determining communication styles and interaction preferences. In terms of personality attributes, however, questions exist about both the validity and the reliability of the MBTI.

Other Personality Traits at Work

Besides the Big Five and the Myers–Briggs framework, several other personality traits influence behavior in organizations. Among the most important are locus of control, self-efficacy, authoritarianism, Machiavellianism, self-esteem, and risk propensity.

Locus of control is the extent to which people believe that their behavior has a real effect on what happens to them.[9] Some people, for example, believe that, if they work hard, they will achieve their goals. They also may believe that people fail because they lack ability or motivation. People who believe that individuals are in control of their lives are said to have an *internal locus of control*. Other people think that fate, chance, luck, or other people's behavior determines what happens to them. For example, an employee who fails to get a pay raise may attribute that failure to a politically motivated boss or just bad luck, rather than to his or her own lack of skills or poor performance record. People who think that forces beyond their control dictate what happens to them are said to have an *external locus of control*.

Self-efficacy is a related but subtly different personality characteristic. It is a person's beliefs about his or her capabilities to perform a task.[10] People with high self-efficacy believe that they can perform well on a specific task, whereas people with low self-efficacy tend to doubt their ability to perform a specific task. Although self-assessments of ability contribute to self-efficacy, so, too, does the individual's personality. Some people simply have more self-confidence than do others. This belief in their ability to perform a task effectively results in their being more self-assured and more able to focus their attention on performance.

Another important personality characteristic is **authoritarianism**, the extent to which an individual believes that power and status differences are appropriate within hierarchical social systems like organizations.[11] For example, a person who is highly authoritarian may accept directives or orders from someone with more authority purely because the other person is "the boss." On the other hand, although a person who is not highly authoritarian may still carry out appropriate and reasonable directives from the boss, he or she is also more likely to question things, express disagreement with the boss, and even refuse to carry out orders if they are for some reason objectionable. A highly authoritarian manager may be autocratic and demanding, and highly authoritarian subordinates will be more likely to accept this behavior from their leader. On the other hand, a less authoritarian manager may allow subordinates a bigger role in making decisions, and less authoritarian subordinates will respond positively to this behavior.

Machiavellianism is another important personality trait. This concept is named after Niccolò Machiavelli, a sixteenth-century Italian political philosopher. In his book entitled *The Prince*, Machiavelli explained how the nobility could more easily gain and use power. *Machiavellianism* is now used to describe behavior directed at gaining power and controlling the behavior of others. Research suggests that Machiavellianism is a personality trait that varies from person to person. Individuals who are more

---

locus of control
The degree to which an individual believes that his or her behavior has a direct impact on the consequences of that behavior

self-efficacy
An individual's beliefs about his or her capabilities to perform a task

authoritarianism
The extent to which an individual believes that power and status differences are appropriate within hierarchical social systems like organizations

Machiavellianism
Behavior directed at gaining power and controlling the behavior of others

Machiavellian tend to be rational and nonemotional, may be willing to lie to attain their personal goals, may put little weight on loyalty and friendship, and may enjoy manipulating others' behavior. Individuals who are less Machiavellian are more emotional, are less willing to lie to succeed, value loyalty and friendship highly, and get little personal pleasure from manipulating others.

self-esteem
The extent to which a person believes that he or she is a worthwhile and deserving individual

Self-esteem is the extent to which a person believes that she is a worthwhile and deserving individual.[12] A person with high self-esteem is more likely to seek high-status jobs, be more confident in her ability to achieve higher levels of performance, and derive greater intrinsic satisfaction from her accomplishments. In contrast, a person with less self-esteem may be more content to remain in a lower-level job, be less confident of his ability, and focus more on extrinsic rewards. Among the major personality dimensions, self-esteem is the one that has been most widely studied in other countries. Although more research is clearly needed, the published evidence suggests that self-esteem as a personality trait does indeed exist in a variety of countries and that its role in organizations is reasonably important across different cultures.[13]

risk propensity
The degree to which an individual is willing to take chances and make risky decisions

Risk propensity is the degree to which an individual is willing to take chances and make risky decisions. A manager with a high risk propensity, for example, might be expected to experiment with new ideas and gamble on new products. She might also lead the organization in new and different directions. This manager might also be a catalyst for innovation. On the other hand, the same individual might also jeopardize the continued well-being of the organization if the risky decisions prove to be bad ones. A manager with low risk propensity might lead to a stagnant and overly conservative organization or help the organization successfully weather turbulent and unpredictable times by maintaining stability and calm. Thus, the potential consequences of risk propensity to an organization are heavily dependent on that organization's environment.

Emotional Intelligence

The concept of emotional intelligence (EQ) has been identified in recent years and provides some interesting insights into personality. **Emotional intelligence (EQ)** refers to the extent to which people are self-aware, manage their emotions, motivate themselves, express empathy for others, and possess social skills.[14] These various dimensions can be described as follows:

emotional intelligence (EQ)
The extent to which people are self-aware, manage their emotions, motivate themselves, express empathy for others, and possess social skills

- *Self-awareness.* This is the basis for the other components. It refers to a person's capacity for being aware of how they are feeling. In general, more self-awareness allows people to more effectively guide their own lives and behaviors.
- *Managing emotions.* This refers to a person's capacities to balance anxiety, fear, and anger so those emotions do not overly interfere with getting things accomplished.
- *Motivating oneself.* This refers to a person's ability to remain optimistic and to continue striving in the face of setbacks, barriers, and failure.
- *Empathy.* This refers to a person's ability to understand how others are feeling, even without being explicitly told.
- *Social skill.* This refers to a person's ability to get along with others and to establish positive relationships.

Preliminary research suggests that people with high EQs may perform better than others, especially in jobs that require a high degree of interpersonal interaction and that involve influencing or directing the work of others. Moreover, EQ appears to be something that is not biologically based but can be developed.[15]

ATTITUDES AND INDIVIDUAL BEHAVIOR

attitudes

Complexes of beliefs and feelings that people have about specific ideas, situations, or other people

Another important element of individual behavior in organizations is **attitudes**—complexes of beliefs and feelings that people have about specific ideas, situations, or other people. Attitudes are important because they are the mechanism through which most people express their feelings. An employee's statement that he feels underpaid by the organization reflects his feelings about his pay. Similarly, when a manager says that she likes the new advertising campaign, she is expressing her feelings about the organization's marketing efforts.

Attitudes have three components. The *affective component* of an attitude reflects feelings and emotions an individual has toward a situation. The *cognitive component* of an attitude is derived from knowledge an individual has about a situation. It is important to note that cognition is subject to individual perceptions (something we discuss more fully later). Thus, one person might "know" that a certain political candidate is better than another, whereas someone else might "know" just the opposite. Finally, the *intentional component* of an attitude reflects how an individual expects to behave toward or in the situation.

To illustrate these three components, consider the case of a manager who places an order for some supplies for his organization from a new office supply firm. Suppose many of the items he orders are out of stock, others are overpriced, and still others arrive damaged. When he calls someone at the supply firm for assistance, he is treated rudely and gets disconnected before his claim is resolved. When asked how he feels about the new office supply firm, he might respond, "I don't like that company [affective component]. They are the worst office supply firm I've ever dealt with [cognitive component]. I'll never do business with them again [intentional component]." The "Sustainability Matters" section explores the potential link between recycling behaviors and attitudes.

cognitive dissonance

Caused when an individual has conflicting attitudes

People try to maintain consistency among the three components of their attitudes as well as among all their attitudes. However, circumstances sometimes arise that lead to conflicts. The conflict individuals may experience among their own attitudes is called **cognitive dissonance.**[16] Say, for example, that an individual who has vowed never to work for a big, impersonal corporation intends instead to open her own business and be her own boss. Unfortunately, a series of financial setbacks leads her to have no choice but to take a job with a large company and work for someone else. Thus, cognitive dissonance occurs: The affective and cognitive components of the individual's attitude conflict with intended behavior. To reduce cognitive dissonance, which is usually an uncomfortable experience for most people, the individual might tell herself that the situation is only temporary and that she can go back out on her own in the near future. Or she might revise her cognitions and decide that working for a large company is more pleasant than she had expected.

Work-Related Attitudes

People in organizations form attitudes about many different things. For example, employees are likely to have attitudes about their salary, promotion possibilities, their boss, employee benefits, the food in the company cafeteria, and the color of the company softball team uniforms. Of course, some of these attitudes are more important than others. Especially important attitudes are job satisfaction or dissatisfaction and organizational commitment.[17]

job satisfaction or dissatisfaction

An attitude that reflects the extent to which an individual is gratified by or fulfilled in his or her work

Job Satisfaction or Dissatisfaction   **Job satisfaction or dissatisfaction** is an attitude that reflects the extent to which an individual is gratified by or fulfilled in his or her work. Extensive research conducted on job satisfaction has indicated that personal factors, such

SUSTAINABILITY MATTERS

Toss It, or Recycle It?

© Yobidaba/Shutterstock.com

Recycling has become increasingly common because people now have heightened understanding of the importance of sustainability. But while some people are conscientious and consistent recyclers, others have much less regard for recycling and make little or no effort to do so.

In most large public venues today—shopping malls, parks, athletic stadiums, theme parks—an abundance of trash receptacles and recycling bins are available. If you stand for a little while and watch, you'll also likely notice an array of behaviors exhibited by people. Some will conscientiously deposit various recyclable materials in the proper containers, and others will indiscriminately just toss everything into the trash cans. And when people see others discarding things inappropriately, some will encourage them to recycle and others may just look the other way.

What accounts for these differences? In part it may be personality. For instance, a highly conscientious person may be more capable of adding recycling to his or her daily routine than a less conscientious person, and a person with high levels of openness may be more prone to learn more about the benefits of recycling. Also, it seems likely that an individual with an internal locus of control may be more apt to recycle than will be a person with an external locus of control. People who are more authoritarian also may be prone to recycling because authority figures tell us that we should do so.

Attitudes may also play a big role. For instance, if a person knows the importance of recycling (cognition), believes that protecting the environment is important (affect), and therefore intends to recycle (behavioral intention), she or he is obviously more likely to recycle. On the other hand, some people believe that the costs of recycling outweigh the benefits. Others think that much of what is recycled still ends up in landfills. These people may be less likely to recycle because their cognitions are different.

as an individual's needs and aspirations, determine this attitude, along with group and organizational factors, such as relationships with coworkers and supervisors, working conditions, work policies, and compensation.[18]

A satisfied employee also tends to be absent less often, to make positive contributions, and to stay with the organization.[19] In contrast, a dissatisfied employee may be absent more often, may experience stress that disrupts coworkers, and may be continually looking for another job. Contrary to what many managers believe, however, high levels of job satisfaction do not necessarily lead to higher levels of performance. One survey has also indicated that, contrary to popular opinion, Japanese workers are less satisfied with their jobs than their counterparts in the United States.[20]

organizational commitment
An attitude that reflects an individual's identification with and attachment to the organization itself

Organizational Commitment **Organizational commitment** is an attitude that reflects an individual's identification with and attachment to the organization itself. A person with a high level of commitment is likely to see herself as a true member of the organization (for example, referring to the organization in personal terms like "We make high-quality products"), to overlook minor sources of dissatisfaction with the organization, and to see herself remaining a member of the organization. In contrast, a person with less organizational commitment is more likely to see himself as an outsider (for example, referring to the organization in less personal terms like "They don't pay their employees very well"), to express more dissatisfaction about things, and to not see himself as a long-term member of the organization. Some research has suggested that Japanese workers may be more committed to their organizations than American workers.[21] As the results from Japan suggest, although job satisfaction and organizational commitment would seem to be related (and are, in most instances), there are times when a person may be very satisfied with his job but less committed to his employer. For instance, All-Star baseball player Robinson Cano was satisfied playing second base for the New York Yankees but still chose to leave his employer to join the Seattle Mariners. Likewise, there may be times when a person may be less satisfied with her job but remain highly committed to the organization itself.

Research also suggests that commitment strengthens with an individual's age, years with the organization, sense of job security, and participation in decision making.[22] Employees who feel committed to an organization have highly reliable habits, plan a long tenure with the organization, and muster more effort in performance. Although there are few definitive things that organizations can do to create or promote commitment, a few specific guidelines are available.[23] For one thing, if the organization treats its employees fairly and provides reasonable rewards and job security, those employees will more likely be satisfied and committed. Allowing employees to have a say in how things are done can also promote all three attitudes.[24]

Affect and Mood in Organizations

Researchers have recently started to focus renewed interest on the affective component of attitudes. Recall from our earlier discussion that the affective component of an attitude reflects our feelings and emotions. Although managers once believed that emotion and feelings varied among people from day to day, research now suggests that, although some short-term fluctuation does indeed occur, there are also underlying stable predispositions toward fairly constant and predictable moods and emotional states.[25]

positive affectivity
A tendency to be relatively upbeat and optimistic, have an overall sense of well-being, see things in a positive light, and seem to be in a good mood

Some people, for example, tend to have a higher degree of **positive affectivity**, which means that they are relatively upbeat and optimistic, have an overall sense of well-being, and usually see things in a positive light. Thus, they always seem to be in a good mood. It's recently been proposed that positive affectivity may also play a role in entrepreneurial success.[26] Other people, those with more **negative affectivity**, are just the opposite. They are generally downbeat and pessimistic, and they usually see things in a negative way. Thus, they seem to be in a bad mood most of the time.

negative affectivity
A tendency to be generally downbeat and pessimistic, see things in a negative way, and seem to be in a bad mood

Of course, as noted earlier, short-term variations can occur among even the most extreme types. People with a lot of positive affectivity, for example, may still be in a bad mood if they have just received some bad news—such as being passed over for a promotion, getting extremely negative performance feedback, or being laid off or fired. Similarly, those with negative affectivity may still be in a good mood—at least for a short time—if they have just been promoted, have received very positive performance feedback, or had other good things befall them. After the initial impact of these events wears off, however, those with positive affectivity will generally return to their normal positive mood, whereas those with negative affectivity will gravitate back to their normal bad mood.

PERCEPTION AND INDIVIDUAL BEHAVIOR

As noted earlier, an important element of an attitude is the individual's perception of the object about which the attitude is formed. Because perception plays a role in a variety of other workplace behaviors, managers need to have a general understanding of basic perceptual processes.[27] The role of attributions is also important.

Basic Perceptual Processes

Perception is the set of processes by which an individual becomes aware of and inter-prets information about the environment. As shown in Figure 9.3, basic perceptual pro-cesses that are particularly relevant to organizations are selective perception and stereotyping.

Selective Perception   **Selective perception** is the process of screening out information that we are uncomfortable with or that contradicts our beliefs. For example, suppose a manager is exceptionally fond of a particular worker. The manager has a very positive atti-tude about the worker and thinks he is a top performer. One day the manager notices that the worker seems to be goofing off. Selective perception may cause the manager to quickly forget what he observed. Similarly, suppose a manager has formed a very negative image of a particular worker. She thinks this worker is a poor performer and never does a good job. When she happens to observe an example of high performance from the worker, she may not remember it for very long. In one sense, selective perception is beneficial because it allows us to disregard minor bits of information. Of course, this holds true only if our basic perception is accurate. If selective perception causes us to ignore important information, however, it can become quite detrimental.

Stereotyping   **Stereotyping** is the process of categorizing or labeling people on the basis of a single attribute. Common attributes from which people often stereotype are race, gender, and age.[28] Of course, stereotypes along these lines are inaccurate and can

perception
The set of processes by which an individual becomes aware of and interprets information about the environment

selective perception
The process of screening out information that we are uncomfortable with or that contradicts our beliefs

stereotyping
The process of categorizing or labeling people on the basis of a single attribute

© Cengage Learning

FIGURE 9.3

Perceptual Processes

Two of the most basic perceptual processes are selective perception and stereotyping. As shown here, selective perception occurs when we screen out information (represented by the – symbols) that causes us discomfort or that contradicts our beliefs. Stereotyping occurs when we categorize or label people on the basis of a single attribute, illustrated here by color.

be harmful. For example, suppose a manager forms the stereotype that women can perform only certain tasks and that men are best suited for other tasks. To the extent that this affects the manager's hiring practices, the manager is (1) costing the organization valuable talent for both sets of jobs, (2) violating federal law, and (3) behaving unethically. On the other hand, certain forms of stereotyping can be useful and efficient. Suppose, for example, that a manager believes that communication skills are important for a particular job and that speech communication majors tend to have exceptionally good communication skills. As a result, whenever he interviews candidates for jobs, he pays especially close attention to speech communication majors. To the extent that communication skills truly predict job performance and that majoring in speech communication does indeed provide those skills, this form of stereotyping can be efficient.

Perception and Attribution

attribution

The process of observing behavior and attributing causes to it

Perception is also closely linked with another process called **attribution**, which is a mechanism through which we observe behavior and then attribute causes to it.[29] The behavior that is observed may be our own or that of others. For example, suppose someone realizes one day that she is working fewer hours than before, that she talks less about her work, and that she calls in sick more frequently. She might conclude from this that she must have become disenchanted with her job and subsequently decide to quit. Thus, she observed her own behavior, attributed a cause to it, and developed what she thought was a consistent response.

More common is attributing cause to the behavior of others. For example, if the manager of the individual just described has observed the same behavior, he might form exactly the same attribution. On the other hand, he might instead decide that she has a serious illness, that he is driving her too hard, that she is experiencing too much stress, that she has a drug problem, or that she is having family problems.

The basic framework around which we form attributions is *consensus* (the extent to which other people in the same situation behave the same way), *consistency* (the extent to which the same person behaves in the same way at different times), and *distinctiveness* (the extent to which the same person behaves in the same way in other situations). For example, suppose a manager observes that an employee is late for a meeting. The manager might further realize that he is the only one who is late (low consensus), recall that he is often late for other meetings (high consistency), and subsequently realize that he is sometimes late for work and returning from lunch (low distinctiveness). This pattern of attributions might cause the manager to decide that the individual's behavior is something that should be changed. As a result, the manager might meet with the subordinate and establish some punitive consequences for future tardiness.

STRESS AND INDIVIDUAL BEHAVIOR

stress

An individual's response to a strong stimulus, which is called a *stressor*

General Adaptation Syndrome (GAS)

General cycle of the stress process

Another important element of behavior in organizations is **stress**—an individual's response to a strong stimulus called a *stressor*.[30] Stress generally follows a cycle referred to as the **General Adaptation Syndrome (GAS)**,[31] shown in Figure 9.4. According to this view, when an individual first encounters a stressor, the GAS is initiated, and stage 1, alarm, is activated. He may feel panic, wonder how to cope, and feel helpless. For example, suppose a manager is told to prepare a detailed evaluation of a plan by his firm to buy one of its competitors. His first reaction may be, "How will I ever get this done by tomorrow?"

FIGURE 9.4

The General Adaptation Syndrome

The GAS represents the normal process by which we react to stressful events. At stage 1—alarm—we feel panic and alarm, and our level of resistance to stress drops. Stage 2—resistance—represents our efforts to confront and control the stressful circumstance. If we fail, we may eventually reach stage 3—exhaustion—and just give up or quit.

If the stressor is too intense, the individual may feel unable to cope and never really try to respond to its demands. In most cases, however, after a short period of alarm, the individual gathers some strength and starts to resist the negative effects of the stressor. For example, the manager with the evaluation to write may calm down, call home to say he is working late, roll up his sleeves, order out for coffee, and get to work. Thus, at stage 2 of the GAS, the person is resisting the effects of the stressor.

In many cases, the resistance phase may end the GAS. If the manager is able to complete the evaluation earlier than expected, he may drop it in his briefcase, smile to himself, and head home tired but satisfied. On the other hand, prolonged exposure to a stressor without resolution may bring on stage 3 of the GAS—exhaustion. At this stage, the individual literally gives up and can no longer resist the stressor. The manager, for example, might fall asleep at his desk at 3:00 a.m. and never finish the evaluation.

We should note that stress is not all bad. In the absence of stress, we may experience lethargy and stagnation. An optimal level of stress, on the other hand, can result in motivation and excitement. Too much stress, however, can have negative consequences. It is also important to understand that stress can be caused by "good" as well as "bad" things. Excessive pressure, unreasonable demands on our time, and bad news can all cause stress. But even receiving a bonus and then having to decide what to do with the money can be stressful. So, too, can receiving a promotion, gaining recognition, and similar good things.

One important line of thinking about stress focuses on **Type A** and **Type B** personalities.[32] Type A individuals are extremely competitive, are very devoted to work, and have a strong sense of time urgency. They are likely to be aggressive, impatient, and very work oriented. They have a lot of drive and want to accomplish as much as possible as quickly as possible. Type B individuals are less competitive, are less devoted to work, and have a weaker sense of time urgency. Such individuals are less likely to experience conflict with other people and more likely to have a balanced, relaxed approach to life. They are able to work at a constant pace without time urgency. Type B people are not necessarily more or less successful than Type A people, but they are less likely to experience stress.

Type A
Individuals who are extremely competitive, are very devoted to work, and have a strong sense of time urgency

Type B
Individuals who are less competitive, are less devoted to work, and have a weaker sense of time urgency

© Cengage Learning

FIGURE 9.5

Causes of Work Stress

There are several causes of work stress in organizations. Four general sets of organizational stressors are task demands, physical demands, role demands, and interpersonal demands.

Causes and Consequences of Stress

Stress is obviously not a simple phenomenon. As listed in Figure 9.5, several different things can cause stress. Note that this list includes only work-related conditions. We should keep in mind that stress can also be the result of personal circumstances.[33]

Causes of Stress   Work-related stressors fall into one of four categories—task, physical, role, and interpersonal demands. *Task demands* are associated with the task itself. Some occupations are inherently more stressful than others. Having to make fast decisions, decisions with less than complete information, or decisions that have relatively serious consequences are some of the things that can make some jobs stressful. The jobs of surgeon, airline pilot, and stockbroker are relatively more stressful than the jobs of general practitioner, baggage handler, and office receptionist. Although a general practitioner makes important decisions, he is also likely to have time to make a considered diagnosis and fully explore a number of different treatments. But, during surgery, the surgeon must make decisions quickly while realizing that the wrong one may endanger her patient's life.

Physical demands are stressors associated with the job setting. Working outdoors in extremely hot or cold temperatures, or even in an improperly heated or cooled office, can lead to stress. Likewise, jobs that have rotating work shifts make it difficult for people to have stable sleep patterns. A poorly designed office, which makes it difficult for people to have privacy or promotes too little social interaction, can result in stress, as can poor lighting and inadequate work surfaces. Even more severe are actual threats to health. Examples include jobs such as coal mining, poultry processing, and toxic waste handling. Similarly, some jobs carry risks associated with higher incident rates of violence, for example, law enforcement officers, or those at risk of armed robberies, such as taxi drivers, and convenience store clerks.

Role demands can also cause stress. (Roles are discussed more fully in Chapter 13.) A role is a set of expected behaviors associated with a position in a group or organization. Stress can result from either role conflict or role ambiguity that people can experience in groups. For example, an employee who is feeling pressure from her boss to work longer hours or to travel more, while also being asked by her family for more time at home, will almost certainly experience stress as a result of role conflict.[34] Similarly, a new employee experiencing role ambiguity because of poor orientation and training practices by the organization will also suffer from stress. Excessive meetings and mobile communication devices that keep people connected to their jobs are also potential sources of stress.[35] Although job cuts and layoffs during the 2008–2009 recession focused on the stress experienced by those losing their jobs (and appropriately so), it's also the case that many of the managers imposing the layoffs experienced stress.[36]

Interpersonal demands are stressors associated with relationships that confront people in organizations. For example, group pressures regarding restriction of output and norm conformity can lead to stress. Leadership styles may also cause stress. An employee who feels a strong need to participate in decision making may feel stress if his boss refuses to allow participation. And individuals with conflicting personalities may experience stress if required to work too closely together. For example, a person with an internal locus of control might be frustrated when working with someone who prefers to wait and just let things happen.

Consequences of Stress   As noted earlier, the results of stress may be positive or negative. The negative consequences may be behavioral, psychological, or medical. Behaviorally, for example, stress may lead to detrimental or harmful actions, such as smoking, alcohol or drug abuse, and overeating. Other stress-induced behaviors are accident proneness, violence toward self or others, and appetite disorders. Substance abuse is also a potential consequence.[37]

The psychological consequences of stress can interfere with an individual's mental health and well-being. Problems include sleep disturbances, depression, family problems, and sexual dysfunction. Managers are especially prone to sleep disturbances when they experience stress at work.[38] Medical consequences of stress affect an individual's physiological well-being. Heart disease and stroke have been linked to stress, as have headaches, backaches, and skin conditions such as acne and hives.[39]

Individual stress also has direct consequences for businesses. For an operating employee, stress may translate into poor-quality work and lower productivity. For a manager, it may mean faulty decision making and disruptions in working relationships.[40] Withdrawal behaviors can also result from stress. People who are having difficulties with stress in their jobs are more likely to call in sick or to leave their positions. More subtle forms of withdrawal may also occur. A manager may start missing deadlines, for example, or taking longer lunch breaks. Employees may also withdraw by developing feelings of indifference. The irritation displayed by people under great stress can make them difficult to get along with. Job satisfaction, morale, and commitment can all suffer as a result of excessive levels of stress. So, too, can motivation to perform.

Another consequence of stress is **burnout**—a feeling of exhaustion that may develop when someone experiences too much stress for an extended period of time. Burnout results in constant fatigue, frustration, and helplessness. Increased rigidity follows, as do a loss of self-confidence and psychological withdrawal. The individual dreads going to work, often puts in longer hours but gets less accomplished than before, and exhibits mental and physical exhaustion. Because of the damaging effects of burnout, some firms are taking steps to help avoid it. For example, British Airways provides all of its employees with training designed to help them recognize the symptoms of burnout and develop strategies for avoiding it. The "Tough Times, Tough Choices" feature discusses other damaging consequences of stress.

Managing Stress

Given the potential consequences of stress, it follows that both people and organizations should be concerned about how to limit its more damaging effects. Numerous ideas and approaches have been developed to help manage stress. Some are strategies for individuals; others are strategies for organizations.[41]

burnout
A feeling of exhaustion that may develop when someone experiences too much stress for an extended period of time

TOUGH TIMES, TOUGH CHOICES

When Stress Becomes Too Tough to Handle

© micro10x/Shutterstock.com

Excessive stress can become very debilitating. This executive, for example, is clearly experiencing anxiety and frustration due to the pressures of her job—deadlines, tight budgets, problems with subordinates, and increased business competition. Occasionally, stress becomes so great that some people react with aggression and violence.

In November 2009, Jason Rodriguez, a former employee of an engineering firm in Orlando, Florida, entered the company's offices and opened fire with a handgun, killing one person and wounding five others. Rodriguez had been fired from Reynolds, Smith & Hills less than two years earlier and told police that he thought the firm was hindering his efforts to collect unemployment benefits. "They left me to rot," he told a reporter who asked him about his motive.

According to the U.S. Department of Labor, the incidence of workplace violence has actually been trending down over the past few years, in part because employers have paid more attention to the problem and taken successful preventive measures. More and more companies, for example, have set up *employee assistance programs* (*EAPs*) to help workers deal with various sources of stress, but EAP providers report that, in the current climate of economic uncertainty, they're being asked to deal with a different set of problems than the ones they've typically handled in the past.

In particular, financial problems have replaced emotional problems as employees' primary area of concern, and with unemployment totals approaching 27-year highs, American workers appear to be more worried about the future than about such conventional stressors as pressing deadlines and demanding bosses. Today, says Sandra Naiman, a Denver-based career coach, "off- and on-the-job stresses feed into one another" to elevate stress levels all around, and workplace stress during the current recession may reflect this unfamiliar convergence of stressors.

As yet, no hard data exist to connect workplace violence with economic downturns, but many professionals and other experts in the field are convinced that the connection is real. ComPsych Corp.,

(continued)

an EAP provider in Chicago, reports that calls are running 30 percent above normal, and according to Rick Kronberg of Perspectives Ltd., another Chicago-based EAP provider, "with the layoffs and the general financial picture, we're getting a lot of reaction…[from] people with a high degree of stress." Adds Tim Horner, a managing director at Kroll, Inc., a security consulting firm: "There are signs out there that something's going on. It's not unusual that somebody snaps." Kenneth Springer, another security specialist whose job now includes keeping an eye on potentially dangerous ex-employees for their former employers, agrees: "Tough times," he says, "will cause people to do crazy things."

By the same token, says Laurence Miller, a forensic psychologist and author of *From Difficult to Disturbed: Understanding and Managing Dysfunctional Employees*, economic stress alone won't turn someone into a killer, nor is the average coworker likely to turn violent without warning. "People shouldn't be sitting around wondering if someone they've been

working with for years who's been a regular guy [with] no real problems is going to suddenly snap and go ballistic on them," says Miller. "It's usually somebody," he warns, "that's had a long streak of problems." Unfortunately, that profile fits Jason Rodriguez, who'd been struggling for years with marital and mental-health problems, unemployment, debt, and smoldering anger. "He was a very, very angry man," reports his former mother-in-law.

References: Mark Trumbull, "Orlando Shooting Comes as Trend in Workplace Violence Drops," *Christian Science Monitor*, November 7, 2009, www.csmonitor.com, accessed on December 6, 2013; Ellen Wulhorst, "Recession Fuels Worries of Workplace Violence," *Reuters*, www.reuters.com, accessed on December 6, 2013; Scott Powers and Fernando Quintero, "Jason Rodriguez Profile: 'He Was a Very, Very Angry Man,'" *OrlandoSentinel.com*, November 6, 2009, www.orlandosentinel.com, accessed on December 6, 2013; Laurence Miller, *From Difficult to Disturbed: Understanding and Managing Dysfunctional Employees* (New York: AMACOM, 20138), http://books.google.com, accessed on December 6, 2013.

One way people manage stress is through exercise. People who exercise regularly feel less tension and stress, are more self-confident, and feel more optimistic. Their better physical condition also makes them less susceptible to many common illnesses. People who do not exercise regularly, on the other hand, tend to feel more stress and are more likely to be depressed. They are also more likely to have heart attacks. And, because of their physical condition, they are more likely to contract illnesses.

Another method people use to manage stress is relaxation. Relaxation allows individuals to adapt to, and therefore better deal with, their stress. Relaxation comes in many forms, such as taking regular vacations. A recent study found that people's attitudes toward a variety of workplace characteristics improved significantly following a vacation. People can also learn to relax while on the job. For example, some experts recommend that people take regular rest breaks during their normal workday.

People can also use time management to control stress. The idea behind time management is that many daily pressures can be reduced or eliminated if individuals do a better job of managing time. One approach to time management is to make a list every morning of the things to be done that day. The items on the list are then grouped into three categories: critical activities that must be performed, important activities that should be performed, and optional or trivial things that can be delegated or postponed. The individual performs the items on the list in their order of importance.

Finally, people can manage stress through support groups. A support group can be as simple as a group of family members or friends with whom to enjoy leisure time. Going out after work with a couple of coworkers to a basketball game or a movie, for example, can help relieve stress built up during the day. Family and friends can help people cope with stress on an ongoing basis and during times of crisis. For example, an employee who has just learned that she did not get the promotion she has been working toward for months may find it helpful to have a good friend to lean on, talk to, or yell at. People may also make use of more elaborate and formal support groups. Community centers or churches, for example, may sponsor support groups for people who have recently gone through a divorce, the death of a loved one, or some other tragedy.

Organizations are also beginning to realize that they should be involved in helping employees cope with stress. One argument for this is that because the business is at least partially responsible for stress, it should also help relieve it. Another is that stress-related insurance claims by employees can cost the organization considerable sums of money. Still another is that workers experiencing lower levels of detrimental stress will be able to function more effectively. AT&T has initiated a series of seminars and work-shops to help its employees cope with the stress they face in their jobs. The firm was prompted to develop these seminars for all three of the reasons noted earlier.

A wellness stress program is a special part of an organization specifically created to help deal with stress. Organizations have adopted stress management programs, health promotion programs, and other kinds of programs for this purpose. The AT&T seminar program noted earlier is similar to this idea, but true wellness programs are ongoing activities that have a number of different components. They commonly include exercise-related activities as well as classroom instruction programs dealing with smoking cessation, weight reduction, and general stress management.

Some companies are developing their own programs or using existing programs of this type. Johns Manville, for example, has a gym at its corporate headquarters. Other firms negotiate discounted health club membership rates with local establishments. For the instructional part of the program, the organization can again either sponsor its own training or perhaps jointly sponsor seminars with a local YMCA, civic organization, or church. Organization-based fitness programs facilitate employee exercise, a very positive consideration, but such programs are also quite costly. Still, more and more companies are developing fitness programs for employees. Similarly, some companies are offering their employees periodic sabbaticals—extended breaks from work that presumably allow people to get revitalized and reenergized. Intel and McDonald's are among the firms offering the benefit.[42]

CREATIVITY IN ORGANIZATIONS

creativity
The ability of an individual to generate new ideas or to conceive of new perspectives on existing ideas

Creativity is yet another important component of individual behavior in organizations. **Creativity** is the ability of an individual to generate new ideas or to conceive of new perspectives on existing ideas. What makes a person creative? How do people become creative? How does the creative process work? Although psychologists have not yet discovered complete answers to these questions, examining a few general patterns can help us understand the sources of individual creativity within organizations.[43]

The Creative Individual

Numerous researchers have focused their efforts on attempting to describe the common attributes of creative individuals. These attributes generally fall into three categories: background experiences, personal traits, and cognitive abilities.

Background Experiences and Creativity   Researchers have observed that many creative individuals were raised in environments in which creativity was nurtured. Mozart was raised in a family of musicians and began composing and performing music at age six. Pierre and Marie Curie, great scientists in their own right, also raised a daughter, Irene, who won the Nobel Prize in chemistry. Thomas Edison's creativity was nurtured by his mother. However, people with background experiences very different from theirs have also been creative. Frederick Douglass was born into slavery in Tuckahoe, Maryland, and had very limited opportunities for education. Nonetheless, his powerful oratory and creative thinking helped lead to the Thirteenth Amendment to the U.S. Constitution, which outlawed slavery in the United States.

Personal Traits and Creativity   Certain personal traits have also been linked to creativity in individuals. The traits shared by most creative people are openness, an attraction to complexity, high levels of energy, independence and autonomy, strong self-confidence, and a strong belief that one is, in fact, creative. Individuals who possess these traits are more likely to be creative than those who do not have them.

Cognitive Abilities and Creativity   Cognitive abilities are an individual's power to think intelligently and to analyze situations and data effectively. Intelligence may be a precondition for individual creativity—although most creative people are highly intelligent, not all intelligent people are necessarily creative. Creativity is also linked with the ability to think divergently and convergently. *Divergent thinking* is a skill that allows people to see differences among situations, phenomena, or events. *Convergent thinking* is a skill that allows people to see similarities among situations, phenomena, or events. Creative people are generally very skilled at both divergent and convergent thinking.

It is interesting to note that Japanese managers have come to question their own creative abilities. The concern is that their emphasis on group harmony may have stifled individual initiative and hampered the development of individual creativity. As a result, many Japanese firms, including Omron Corporation, Fuji Photo, and Shimizu Corporation, have launched employee training programs intended to boost the creativity of their employees.[44]

The Creative Process

Although creative people often report that ideas seem to come to them "in a flash," individual creative activity actually tends to progress through a series of stages. Not all creative activity has to follow these four stages, but much of it does.

Preparation   The creative process normally begins with a period of preparation. To make a creative contribution to business management or business services, individuals must usually receive formal training and education in business. Formal education and training are usually the most efficient ways of becoming familiar with this vast amount of research and knowledge. This is one reason for the strong demand for undergraduate- and master's-level business education.

Formal business education can be an effective way for an individual to get "up to speed" and begin making creative contributions quickly. Experiences that managers have on the job after their formal training has finished can also contribute to the creative process. In an important sense, the education and training of creative people never really end. They continue as long as people remain interested in the world and curious about the way things work. Bruce Roth earned a PhD in chemistry and then spent years working in the pharmaceutical industry learning more and more about chemical compounds and how they work in human beings.

Incubation   The second phase of the creative process is *incubation*—a period of less intense conscious concentration during which the knowledge and ideas acquired during preparation mature and develop. A curious aspect of incubation is that it is often helped along by pauses in concentrated rational thought. Some creative people rely on physical activity such as jogging or swimming to provide a break from thinking. Others may read or listen to music. Sometimes sleep may even supply the needed pause. Bruce Roth eventually joined Warner-Lambert, an up-and-coming drug company, to help develop a new medication to lower cholesterol. In his spare time, Roth read mystery novels and hiked in the mountains. He later acknowledged that this was when he did his best thinking. Similarly, Jeff Bezos, founder and CEO of Amazon.com, sets aside at least one day a week with no scheduled appointments or meetings and uses this time to allow ideas to incubate.

Insight   Usually occurring after preparation and incubation, insight is a spontaneous breakthrough in which the creative person achieves a new understanding of some problem or situation. Insight represents a coming together of all the scattered thoughts and ideas that were maturing during incubation. It may occur suddenly or develop slowly over time. Insight can be triggered by some external event, such as a new experience or an encounter with new data, which forces the individual to think about old issues and problems in new ways, or it can be a completely internal event in which patterns of thought finally coalesce in ways that generate new understanding. One day, Bruce Roth was reviewing results from statistical analyses from some earlier studies that had found the new medication under development to be no more effective than other drugs already available. But Roth recognized that there were better ways to analyze the data using different statistical methods. When he reanalyzed the data using the more appropriate methods, he found some significant statistical relationships that had not been identified previously. He knew then that he had a major breakthrough on his hands.

Verification   Once an insight has occurred, verification determines the validity or truthfulness of the insight. For many creative ideas, verification includes scientific experiments to determine whether the insight actually leads to the results expected. Verification may also include the development of a product or service prototype. A prototype is one product or a very small number of products built just to see if the ideas behind this new product actually work. Product prototypes are rarely sold to the public but are very valuable in verifying the insights developed in the creative process. Once the new product or service is developed, verification in the marketplace is the ultimate test of the creative idea behind it. Bruce Roth and his colleagues set to work testing the new drug compound and eventually won FDA approval. The drug, named Lipitor, is already the largest-selling pharmaceutical in history. And Pfizer, the firm that bought Warner-Lambert in a hostile takeover, is expected to earn more than $10 billion a year on the drug.[45]

PAUL J. RICHARDS/AFP/Getty Images/Newscom

Lipitor, a cholesterol-fighting drug, is one of the most successful pharmaceutical innovations in history. The scientist who first demonstrated the potential effectiveness of Lipitor was fully engaged in the creative process during the development and testing of the drug.

Enhancing Creativity in Organizations

Managers who wish to enhance and promote creativity in their organizations can do so in a variety of ways.[46] One important method for enhancing creativity is to make it a part of the organization's culture, often through explicit goals. Firms that truly want to stress creativity, like 3M and Rubbermaid, for example, state goals that some percentage of future revenues are to be gained from new products. This clearly communicates that creativity and innovation are valued. Best Buy recently picked four groups of salespeople in their twenties and early thirties and asked them to spend ten weeks living together in a Los Angeles apartment complex (with expenses paid by the company and still earning their normal pay). Their job was to sit around and brainstorm new business ideas that could be rolled out quickly and cheaply.[47]

Another important part of enhancing creativity is to reward creative successes, while being careful not to punish creative failures. Many ideas that seem worthwhile on paper fail to pan out in reality. If the first person to come up with an idea that fails is fired or otherwise punished, others in the organization will become more cautious in their own work. And, as a result, fewer creative ideas will emerge.

TYPES OF WORKPLACE BEHAVIOR

workplace behavior
A pattern of action by the members of an organization that directly or indirectly influences organizational effectiveness

Now that we have looked closely at how individual differences can influence behavior in organizations, let's turn our attention to what we mean by workplace behavior. **Workplace behavior** is a pattern of action by the members of an organization that directly or indirectly influences organizational effectiveness. Important workplace behaviors include performance and productivity, absenteeism and turnover, and organizational citizenship. Unfortunately, a variety of dysfunctional behaviors can also occur in organizational settings.

Performance Behaviors

performance behaviors
The total set of work-related behaviors that the organization expects the individual to display

Performance behaviors are the total set of work-related behaviors that the organization expects the individual to display. Thus, they derive from the psychological contract. For some jobs, performance behaviors can be narrowly defined and easily measured. For example, an assembly-line worker who sits by a moving conveyor and attaches parts to a product as it passes by has relatively few performance behaviors. He or she is expected to remain at the workstation and correctly attach the parts. Performance can often be assessed quantitatively by counting the percentage of parts correctly attached.

For many other jobs, however, performance behaviors are more diverse and much more difficult to assess. For example, consider the case of a research and development scientist at Merck. The scientist works in a lab trying to find new scientific breakthroughs that have commercial potential. The scientist must apply knowledge learned in graduate school with experience gained from previous research. Intuition and creativity are also important elements. And the desired breakthrough may take months or even years to accomplish. As we discussed in Chapter 8, organizations rely on a number of different methods for evaluating performance. The key, of course, is to match the evaluation mechanism with the job being performed.

Withdrawal Behaviors

absenteeism
When an individual does not show up for work

Another important type of work-related behavior is that which results in withdrawal—absenteeism and turnover. **Absenteeism** occurs when an individual does not show up for work. The cause may be legitimate (illness, jury duty, death in the family, and so forth) or feigned (reported as legitimate but actually just an excuse to stay home). When an employee is absent, his or her work does not get done at all, or a substitute must be hired to do it. In either case, the quantity or quality of actual output is likely to suffer. Obviously, some absenteeism is expected. The key concern of organizations is to minimize feigned absenteeism and to reduce legitimate absences as much as possible. High absenteeism may be a symptom of other problems as well, such as job dissatisfaction and low morale.

turnover
When people quit their jobs

Turnover occurs when people quit their jobs. An organization usually incurs costs in replacing individuals who have quit, but if turnover involves especially productive people, it is even more costly. Turnover seems to result from a number of factors, including aspects of the job, the organization, the individual, the labor market, and family influences. In general, a poor person–job fit is also a likely cause of turnover.[48] The current high levels of unemployment reduce employee-driven turnover, given that fewer jobs are available. But when unemployment is low (and there are many open jobs), turnover may naturally increase as people seek better opportunities, higher pay, and so forth.

Efforts to directly manage turnover are frequently fraught with difficulty, even in organizations that concentrate on rewarding good performers. Of course, some turnover is inevitable, and in some cases it may even be desirable. For example, if the organization is trying to cut costs by reducing its staff, having people voluntarily choose to leave is preferable to having to terminate their jobs. And, if the people who choose to leave are low performers or express high levels of job dissatisfaction, the organization may also benefit from turnover.

Organizational Citizenship

organizational citizenship
The behavior of individuals that makes a positive overall contribution to the organization

Organizational citizenship is the behavior of individuals that makes a positive overall contribution to the organization.[49] Consider, for example, an employee who does work that is acceptable in terms of both quantity and quality. However, she refuses to work overtime, will not help newcomers learn the ropes, and is generally unwilling to make any contribution to the organization beyond the strict performance of her job. Although this person may be seen as a good performer, she is not likely to be seen as a good organizational citizen.

Another employee may exhibit a comparable level of performance. In addition, however, he will always work late when the boss asks him to, takes time to help newcomers learn their way around, and is perceived as being helpful and committed to the organization's success. Although his level of performance may be seen as equal to that of the first worker, he is also likely to be seen as a better organizational citizen.

The determinant of organizational citizenship behaviors is likely to be a complex mosaic of individual, social, and organizational variables. For example, the personality, attitudes, and needs of the individual will have to be consistent with citizenship behaviors. Similarly, the social context in which the individual works, or the work group, will need to facilitate and promote such behaviors (we discuss group dynamics in Chapter 13). And the organization itself, especially its culture, must be capable of promoting, recognizing, and rewarding these types of behaviors if they are to be maintained. Although the study of organizational citizenship is still in its infancy, preliminary research suggests that it may play a powerful role in organizational effectiveness.[50]

Dysfunctional Behaviors

dysfunctional behaviors
Those that detract from, rather than contribute to, organizational performance

Some work-related behaviors are dysfunctional in nature. **Dysfunctional behaviors** are those that detract from, rather than contribute to, organizational performance.[51] Two of the more common ones, absenteeism and turnover, were discussed earlier. But other forms of dysfunctional behavior may be even more costly for an organization. Theft and sabotage, for example, result in direct financial costs for an organization. Sexual and racial harassment also cost an organization, both indirectly (by lowering morale, producing fear, and driving off valuable employees) and directly (through financial liability if the organization responds inappropriately). So, too, can costs result from politicized behavior, intentionally misleading others in the organization, spreading malicious rumors, and similar activities. Incivility and rudeness can result in conflict and damage to morale and the organization's culture.[52] Workplace violence is also a growing concern in many organizations. Violence by disgruntled workers or former workers results in dozens of deaths and injuries each year.[53]

SUMMARY OF LEARNING OUTCOMES AND KEY POINTS

1. Explain the nature of the individual–organization relationship.

   - A basic framework that can be used to facilitate this understanding is the psychological contract—the set of expectations held by people with respect to what they will contribute to the organization and what they expect to get in return.
   - Organizations strive to achieve an optimal person–job fit, but this process is complicated by the existence of individual differences.

2. Define personality and describe personality attributes that affect behavior in organizations.

   - Personality is the relatively stable set of psychological and behavioral attributes that distinguish one person from another.
   - The "Big Five" personality traits follow:

   - Agreeableness
   - Conscientiousness
   - Neuroticism
   - Extraversion
   - Openness

   - The Myers–Briggs framework can also be a useful mechanism for understanding personality.
   - Other important traits are the following:

   - Locus of control
   - Self-efficacy
   - Authoritarianism
   - Machiavellianism
   - Self-esteem
   - Risk propensity

   - EQ, a fairly new concept, may provide additional insights into personality.

3. Discuss individual attitudes in organizations and how they affect behavior.

   - Attitudes are based on emotion, knowledge, and intended behavior.
   - Whereas personality is relatively stable, some attitudes can be formed and changed easily. Others are more constant.
   - Job satisfaction or dissatisfaction and organizational commitment are important work-related attitudes.

4. Describe basic perceptual processes and the role of attributions in organizations.

   - Perception is the set of processes by which an individual becomes aware of and interprets information about the environment.
   - Basic perceptual processes include selective perception and stereotyping.
   - Perception and attribution are also closely related.

5. Discuss the causes and consequences of stress and describe how it can be managed.

   - Stress is an individual's response to a strong stimulus.
   - The GAS outlines the basic stress process.
   - Stress can be caused by task, physical, role, and interpersonal demands.
   - Consequences of stress include organizational and individual outcomes, as well as burnout.
   - Several things can be done to manage stress.

6. Describe creativity and its role in organizations.

   - Creativity is the capacity to generate new ideas.
   - Creative people tend to have certain profiles of background experiences, personal traits, and cognitive abilities.
   - The creative process itself includes preparation, incubation, insight, and verification.

7. Explain how workplace behaviors can directly or indirectly influence organizational effectiveness.

- Workplace behavior is a pattern of action by the members of an organization that directly or indirectly influences organizational effectiveness.
- Performance behaviors are the set of work-related behaviors that the organization expects the individual to display to fulfill the psychological contract.

- Basic withdrawal behaviors are absenteeism and turnover.
- Organizational citizenship refers to behavior that makes a positive overall contribution to the organization.
- Dysfunctional behaviors can be very harmful to an organization.

DISCUSSION QUESTIONS

Questions for Review

1. What is a psychological contract? List the things that might be included in individual contributions. List the things that might be included in organizational inducements.
2. Describe the three components of attitudes and tell how the components are related. What is cognitive dissonance? How do individuals resolve cognitive dissonance?
3. Identify and discuss the steps in the creative process. What can an organization do to increase employees' creativity?
4. Identify and describe several important workplace behaviors.

Questions for Analysis

1. Organizations are increasing their use of personality tests to screen job applicants. What are the advantages and disadvantages of this approach? What can managers do to avoid some of the potential pitfalls?
2. As a manager, how can you tell that an employee is experiencing job satisfaction? How can you tell that employees are highly committed to the organization? If a worker is not satisfied, what can a manager do to improve satisfaction? What can a manager do to improve organizational commitment?
3. Managers cannot pay equal attention to every piece of information, so selective perception is a fact of life. How does selective perception help managers? How does it create difficulties for them? How can managers increase their "good" selective perception and decrease the "bad"?
4. Write the psychological contract you have in this class. In other words, what do you contribute, and what inducements are available? Ask your professor to tell the class about the psychological contract that he or she intended to establish with the students in your class. How does the professor's intended contract compare with the one you wrote? If there are differences, why do you think the differences exist? Share your ideas with the class.
5. Assume that you are going to hire three new employees for the department store you manage. One will sell shoes, one will manage the toy department, and one will work in the stockroom. Identify the basic characteristics you want in each of the people, to achieve a good person–job fit.

BUILDING EFFECTIVE INTERPERSONAL SKILLS

Exercise Overview

Interpersonal skills refer to the ability to communicate with, understand, and motivate individuals and groups. This exercise introduces you to a widely used tool for personality assessment and shows how an understanding of personality can be of use in developing effective interpersonal relationships within organizations.

Exercise Background

Of the many different ways of interpreting personality, the widely used MBTI categorizes individual personality types along four dimensions, which were discussed earlier.

Using the MBTI, researchers use survey answers to classify individuals into 16 personality types—all the possible combinations of the four Myers–Briggs dimensions. The resulting personality type is then expressed as a four-character code, such as *ESTP* for *extravert, sensing, thinking,* and *perceiving*. These four-character codes are then used to describe an individual's preferred way of interacting with others.

Exercise Task

1. Use a Myers–Briggs assessment form to determine your own personality type. You can find a form at www.keirsey.com/sorter/register.aspx, a website that also contains additional information about personality type. (*Note*: There are no fees for taking the Temperament Sorter, nor must you agree to receive e-mail.)

2. When you've determined the four-letter code for your personality type, you can get a handout from your instructor that will explain how your personality type affects not only your preferred style of working but your leadership style as well.

3. Conclude by responding to the following questions:

    - How easy is it to measure personality?
    - Do you feel that the online test accurately assessed your personality?
    - Why or why not? Share your assessment results and your responses with the class.

BUILDING EFFECTIVE TIME MANAGEMENT SKILLS

Exercise Overview

Time management skills refer to the ability to prioritize tasks, to work efficiently, and to delegate appropriately. Among other reasons, they're important because poor time management skills may result in stress. This exercise shows you how effective time management skills can help reduce stress.

Exercise Background

List several of the major events or expectations that tend to be stressful for you. Common stressors include school (classes and exams), work (finances and schedules), and personal circumstances (friends, romance, and family). Try to be as specific as possible, and try to identify at least ten different stressors.

Exercise Task

Using your list, do each of the following:

1. Evaluate the extent to which poor time management skills on your part play a role in the way each stressor affects you. Do exams cause stress, for example, because you tend to put off studying?

2. For each stressor that's affected by your time management habits, develop a strategy for using your time more efficiently.

3. Note the interrelationships among different kinds of stressors to see if they revolve around time-related problems. For example, financial pressures may cause you to work, and work may interfere with school. Can you manage any of these interrelationships more effectively by managing your time more effectively?

4. How do you typically manage the stress in your life? Can you manage stress in a more time-effective manner?

SKILLS SELF-ASSESSMENT INSTRUMENT

Personality Types at Work

Interpersonal skills reflect the ability to communicate with, understand, and motivate individuals and groups. This exercise focuses on personality traits and how they relate to interpersonal processes in organizations. It shows how an understanding of personality can aid in developing effective interpersonal relationships within organizations.

Introduction: There are many different ways of viewing personality. One common framework is based on the Big Five model discussed early in this chapter. According to the Big Five model, our personalities can be assessed along five different dimensions. Our position on each dimension may help determine the kinds of jobs that we are best suited to perform and our effectiveness in performing those jobs.

Instructions

_____ 1. Search for an online assessment form to measure your personality on each of the Big Five dimensions. An abundance of such measures are available free of charge. Select any one of these, complete the assessment, and score your results.

_____ 2. Interpret your results as they compare to recent job experiences, your choice of major, and your long-term career goals. Critique the value of the Big Five model as it relates to your own personal job-related choices and experiences.

_____ 3. Form a small group with three to four of your classmates and share your individual critiques from Step 2. Does this additional information change your assessment of the Big Five model in either a more positive or more negative direction?

EXPERIENTIAL EXERCISE

Stress Test

Job-related stress is very common in organizations—almost everyone experiences stress some of the time. Stress can also occur in nonwork settings, such as school or family life. While a moderate level of stress can have positive effects, too much stress can lead to physical and mental health problems, absenteeism and turnover, low productivity and morale, and eventually burnout.

Investigate the demands of your Management class to assess the extent of factors that increase stress, writing down your answers individually. Discuss your perceptions with a small group of classmates. Then, as a group, suggest changes that would make your class less stressful.

Step 1: Working alone, assess the task demands associated with your Management class. In this category, include items such as the extent to which you are fully informed and can therefore make informed decisions. Also consider the time pressure and the possible consequences of your actions.

Assess the physical demands associated with your Management class. In this category, include items such as the location and facilities available in the classroom. Also include lighting, heating, ventilation, seating, amount of space, flexibility of the space, and so on. Assess the role demands associated with your Management class. In this category, consider the role you play as a student. Do you understand what is expected of you in this role? Are you comfortable in this role? Does your role as a student conflict with any of the other important roles that you play?

Assess the interpersonal demands associated with your Management class. In this category, consider your relationships with the instructor and your fellow students. Any personality conflicts or pressure to conform to group norms would tend to increase stress.

Step 2: In a small group, discuss your answers. Try to recognize patterns of similarities and differences. Then discuss changes that could be made that would reduce stress. Be sure to consider changes that could be made by your institution or department, by your instructor, and by the students.

Step 3: Discuss your conclusions with the class and your instructor.

MANAGEMENT AT WORK

Is Anybody in Control Here?

The media called it the "Miracle on the Hudson." On the wintry afternoon of January 15, 2009, just minutes after takeoff from New York's LaGuardia Airport, US Airways Flight 1549 struck a flock of birds. Both engines were knocked out, and pilot Chesley "Sully" Sullenberger had no choice but to land his 81-ton Airbus A320 in the frigid Hudson River on the west side of Manhattan. It was the first crash-landing of a major aircraft in the water in some 50 years, but all of the 155 people on board survived. "It was intense," said one passenger. "You've got to give it to the pilot."

Fortunately, Sullenberger had 40 years of flying experience, and at least one other US Airways pilot wasn't all that surprised at his extraordinary feat. "He held his cool," said Rick Kurner, who'd flown with Sullenberger for more than 20 years.

As for Sullenberger, he remembered "the worst sickening, pit-of-your stomach, falling-through-the-floor feeling" that he'd ever experienced. For weeks after the crash, he suffered symptoms of post-traumatic stress, including sleeplessness and flashbacks, but acknowledged that his condition had improved after a month or two. No wonder Sullenberger experienced some repercussion from the stress, says Patrick Harten, the LaGuardia air traffic controller who was on the other end of the line when Sullenberger radioed his intention to put down in the river. "I thought it was his own death sentence," recalled Harten. "I believed at that moment I was going to be the last person to talk to anyone on that plane alive…. I felt like I'd been hit by a bus." For his own part, says Harten, "the trauma of working an airplane that crash-landed" didn't begin to subside until about a year later.

It is interesting to note that if Sullenberger, who was 57 at the time of the crash, had been an air traffic controller instead of a pilot, he would probably have been required to retire a year before Flight 1549 took off. Both jobs, of course, are extremely stressful, and the Federal Aviation Administration (FAA) mandates retirement ages for both. Pilots, however, can stay on the job until they're 65, while controllers must in most cases call it quits at age 56. Why? Because being an air traffic controller, it seems, is *more* stressful than being a pilot.

At any given moment, about 5,000 airplanes are in the skies over the United States. The National Air Traffic Controllers Association (NATCA) reports that, on an average day, controllers handle 87,000 flights. In a year, they manage 64 million takeoffs and landings. And that's just sheer volume of traffic. Needless to say, all that traffic is also very complex. "Air traffic control is like playing chess at high speed," says Pete Rogers, who helps manage 52,000 flights a year to and from (and over) Martha's Vineyard, Massachusetts. Melvin Davis, who's been directing air traffic in Southern California for more than 20 years, agrees: "My daily routine," he reports, "is dealing with aircraft that have anywhere between two and four hundred people on board and are traveling at about 600 miles an hour."

In addition, not all aircraft are traveling at the same speed or at the same altitude, and very few of them are traveling at a steady perpendicular to the ground. Once they learn to "see traffic," according to New York controller Christopher Tucker, controllers "have to learn how to solve the conflicts, preferably in the simplest … manner. It can be as simple as stopping someone's climb or descent to pass below or above converging traffic or issuing speed assignments to ensure constant spacing." Often, of course, it's not that simple. For example, explains Tucker, "newer aircraft with highly efficient wings cannot descend quickly while going slow, so that has to be taken into account when setting up an intrail operation where arrivals must be descended as well as slowed down."

And then there's the weather. Controllers record weather data every hour and have to be constantly aware of changing conditions. "We have to make sure we don't launch somebody into a thunderstorm," says Rogers. Moreover, because storm systems often appear on radar with little or no notice, controllers must also be able to make quick decisions. According to Tucker, "The ability to run through possible solutions and quickly choose the best one" is a necessary skill for any controller, and so is "being able to make a bad situation work after having made a poor decision."

At present, there are about 11,000 fully trained air traffic controllers in the United States—the lowest number in 17 years. The total number of positions is slated to increase by 13 percent between now and 2018, but that rate won't keep pace with the projected increase in the number of aircraft that will be in the skies—not to mention vying for air and runway space at the nation's airports. At lower-traffic airports, cost considerations already require controllers to work eight-hour shifts by themselves, performing the jobs of all tower positions, communicating with aircraft in the sky and on the ground, and coordinating the activities of perhaps three separate facilities.

"And so we have a rise in operational errors," both at regional and national airports, admits Melvin Davis. In 2007, for instance, there were 370 *runway incursions* at U.S. airports—incidents in which planes invaded one another's ground space—and according to the FAA's risk–severity matrix, the potential for catastrophic accident at that rate was "unacceptable." The next year, however, there were 951 such incidents, and the total rose to 1,009 in 2009. This alarming increase, charges Davis, can be traced to the kind of working conditions that have made air traffic control more stressful than ever, especially the policy of assigning controllers to long shifts during which many of them work alone. "It's a business decision," he says, arguing that the current situation at the nation's airports is

> *clearly the result of a reduction in staffing, a decline in experience, and an increase in the use of employee overtime, which leads to increased fatigue. The result is a 300 percent to 400 percent increase in operational errors … which results in two bullet trains coming together at 600 miles an hour.*

Case Questions

1. What about you? Do you think that you could handle the kind of stress that air traffic controllers face on the job? Why or why not?

2. In your opinion, which causes of work stress, or *organizational stressors*, are likely to be among the most common experienced by air traffic controllers? Explain your reasoning.

3. Controller Pete Rogers says that any gathering of air traffic controllers is "almost like a mini-convention of Type A personalities." Does this assessment surprise you or make sense to you? In what ways is it perhaps a good thing? A not-so-good thing?

4. "This business of people saying they 'thrive on stress'? It's nuts," says one eminent psychiatrist who goes so far as to say that such people are in danger of slipping into a pathological state. Nevertheless, some people say that they like getting into chaotic situations and putting them back in order. What about you? Are there times when you seem to be motivated and satisfied by circumstances that most people would call stressful? If your answer is yes, what kinds of circumstances are they, and why do you think you react the way you do? If your answer is no, what do you normally do when faced with such circumstances?

Case References

"'Miracle on the Hudson': All Safe in Jet Crash," *MSNBC.com*, January 15, 2009, www.msnbc.com, accessed on December 6, 2013; Phil Derner, Jr., "One Year after the 'Miracle on the Hudson,' an Exclusive Interview with Air Traffic Controller Patrick Harten," *NYCAviation.com*, January 18, 2010, http://nycaviation.com, accessed on December 6, 2013; Steve Myrick, "Air Traffic Control—'Chess at High Speed,'" *Martha's Vineyard Times*, December 24, 2009, www.mvtimes.com, accessed on December 6, 2013; Alex Altman and Tiffany Sharples, "Air Traffic Controller Sounds Alarm," *Time*, time.com, accessed on December 6, 2013; Christopher Tucker, "I Am an Air Traffic Controller," *Daily Speculations*, www.dailyspeculations.com, accessed on December 6, 2013; and Mary Carmichael, "Who Says Stress Is Bad for You?" *Newsweek*, www.newsweek.com, accessed on December 6, 2013.

You Make the Call

Putting In the Hours

1. From a management perspective, what are the key issues in this chapter's opening case?

2. How would you respond if one of your employees wanted to come in early and get set up for their job but said they did not want to get paid for this extra time?

3. How might you respond if your employer (current or future) directly or indirectly requires you to work extra hours with no additional compensation?

4. What might you as a manager do to ensure your employees never feel compelled to work "off the clock?"

ENDNOTES

[1] *Hoover's Handbook of American Business 2013* (Austin; Mergent, 2013), pp. 642–642 "Overworked and Underpaid?" *USA Today*, April 16, 2012, pp. 1A, 2A, www.usatoday.com, accessed on December 6, 2013; "10 Tricks Employers Use to Cheat Workers Out of Overtime," www.jobs.com, accessed on December 6, 2013; "Walmart Fined by Labor Department for Denying Workers Overtime," *Huffington Post*, March 2, 2012, www.huffingtonpost.com, accessed on December 6, 2013; "Overworked and Underpaid?" *USA Today*, April 16, 2013, pp. 1A, 2A.

[2] Lynn McGarlane Shore and Lois Tetrick, "The Psychological Contract as an Explanatory Framework in the Employment Relationship," in C. L. Cooper and D. M. Rousseau (eds.), *Trends in Organizational Behavior* (London: Wiley, 1994). See also Jacqueline Coyle-Shapiro and Neil Conway, "Exchange Relationships: Examining Psychological Contracts and Perceived Organizational Support," *Journal of Applied Psychology*, 2005, Vol. 90, No.4, pp. 774–781; and Denise M. Rousseau, "The Individual–Organization Relationship: The Psychological Contract," in Sheldon Zedeck (ed.), *Handbook of Industrial and Organizational Psychology*, Vol. 3: *Maintaining, Expanding, and Contracting the Organization* (Washington, DC: American Psychological Association, 2010), pp. 191–220.

[3] See Reid Hoffman, Ben Casnocha, and Chris Yeh, "The new Employer-Employee Compact," *Harvard Business Review*, June 2013, pp. 49–58.

[4] Elizabeth Wolfe Morrison and Sandra L. Robinson, "When Employees Feel Betrayed: A Model of How Psychological Contract Violation Develops," *Academy of Management Review*, January 1997, Vol. 22, No. 1, pp. 226–256.

5 See Arne Kalleberg, "The Mismatched Worker: When People Don't Fit Their Jobs," *Academy of Management Perspectives*, 2008, Vol. 22, No. 1, pp. 24–40.

6 See Dan McAdams and Bradley Olson, "Personality Development: Continuity and Change over the Life Course," in Susan Fiske, Daniel Schacter, and Robert Sternberg (eds.), *Annual Review of Psychology*, Vol. 61 (Palo Alto, Calif.: Annual Reviews, 2010), pp. 517–542.

7 L. R. Goldberg, "An Alternative 'Description of Personality': The Big Five Factor Structure," *Journal of Personality and Social Psychology*, 1990, Vol. 59, pp.1216–1229.

8 Michael K. Mount, Murray R. Barrick, and J. Perkins Strauss, "Validity of Observer Ratings of the Big Five Personality Factors," *Journal of Applied Psychology*, 1994, Vol. 79, No. 2, pp. 272–280; and Timothy A. Judge, Joseph J. Martocchio, and Carl J. Thoreson, "Five-Factor Model of Personality and Employee Absence," *Journal of Applied Psychology*, 1997, Vol. 82, No. 5, pp. 745–755.

9 J. B. Rotter, *"Generalized Expectancies for Internal vs. External Control of Reinforcement," Psychological Monographs*, 1966, Vol. 80, pp. 1–28. See also Simon S. K. Lam and John Schaubroeck, "The Role of Locus of Control in Reactions to Being Promoted and to Being Passed Over: A Quasi Experiment," *Academy of Management Journal*, 2000, Vol. 43, No. 1, pp. 66–78.

10 Marilyn E. Gist and Terence R. Mitchell, "Self-Efficacy: A Theoretical Analysis of Its Determinants and Malleability," *Academy of Management Review*, April 1992, pp. 183–211.

11 T. W. Adorno, E. Frenkel-Brunswick, D. J. Levinson, and R. N. Sanford, *The Authoritarian Personality* (New York: Harper & Row, 1950).

12 Jon L. Pierce, Donald G. Gardner, and Larry L. Cummings, "Organization-Based Self-Esteem: Construct Definition, Measurement, and Validation," *Academy of Management Journal*, 1989, Vol. 32, No. 3, pp. 622–648.

13 Michael Harris Bond and Peter B. Smith, "Cross-Cultural Social and Organizational Psychology," in Janet Spence (ed.), *Annual Review of Psychology*, Vol. 47 (Palo Alto, Calif.: Annual Reviews, 1996), pp. 205–235.

14 See Daniel Goleman, *Emotional Intelligence: Why It Can Matter More Than IQ* (New York: Bantam, 1995).

15 Daniel Goleman, "Leadership That Gets Results," *Harvard Business Review*, March–April 2000, pp. 78–90. See also Kenneth Law, Chi-Sum Wong, and Lynda Song, "The Construct and Criterion Validity of Emotional Intelligence and Its Potential Utility for Management Studies," *Journal of Applied Psychology*, 2004, Vol. 87, No. 3, pp. 483–496; Joseph C. Rode, Christine H. Mooney, Marne L. Arthaud-Day, Janet P. Near, Timothy T. Baldwin, Robert S. Rubin, and William H. Bommer, "Emotional Intelligence and Individual Performance: Evidence of Direct and Indirect Effects," *Journal of Organizational Behavior*, 2007, Vol. 28, No. 4, pp. 399–421; and John D. Mayer, Richard D. Roberts, and Sigal G. Barsade, "Human Abilities: Emotional Intelligence," in Susan T. Fiske, Daniel L. Schacter, and Robert Sternberg (eds.), *Annual Review of Psychology 2008* (Palo Alto, CA: Annual Reviews, 2008), pp. 507–536.

16 Leon Festinger, *A Theory of Cognitive Dissonance* (Palo Alto, Calif.: Stanford University Press, 1957).

17 See John J. Clancy, "Is Loyalty Really Dead?" *Across the Board*, June 1999, pp. 15–19.

18 Patricia C. Smith, L. M. Kendall, and Charles Hulin, *The Measurement of Satisfaction in Work and Behavior* (Chicago: Rand-McNally, 1969). See also Steven Currall, Annette Towler, Tomothy Judge, and Laura Kohn, "Pay Satisfaction and Organizational Outcomes," *Personnel Psychology*, 2005, Vol. 58, pp.613–640.

19 "Companies Are Finding Real Payoffs in Aiding Employee Satisfaction," *Wall Street Journal*, October 11, 2000, p. B1.

20 James R. Lincoln, "Employee Work Attitudes and Management Practice in the U.S. and Japan: Evidence from a Large Comparative Study," *California Management Review*, Fall 1989, pp. 89–106.

21 Lincoln, "Employee Work Attitudes and Management Practice in the U.S. and Japan."

22 Richard M. Steers, "Antecedents and Outcomes of Organizational Commitment," *Administrative Science Quarterly*, 1977, Vol. 22, pp.46–56.

23 See Timothy R. Clark, "Engaging the Disengaged," *HR Magazine*, April 2008, pp. 109–115.

24 Omar N. Solinger, Woody van Olffen, and Robert A. Roe, "Beyond the Three-Component Model of Organizational Commitment," *Journal of Applied Psychology*, 2008, Vol. 93, No. 1, pp. 70–83. See also Steven M. Elias, "Employee Commitment in Times of Change: Assessing the Importance of Attitudes toward Organizational Change," *Journal of Management*, 2009, Vol. 35, No. 1, pp. 37–55.

25 For research work in this area, see Jennifer M. George and Gareth R. Jones, "The Experience of Mood and Turnover Intentions: Interactive Effects of Value Attainment, Job Satisfaction, and Positive Mood," *Journal of Applied Psychology*, 1996, Vol. 81, No. 3, pp. 318–325; and Larry J. Williams, Mark B. Gavin, and Margaret Williams, "Measurement and Nonmeasurement Processes with Negative Affectivity and Employee Attitudes," *Journal of Applied Psychology*, 1996, Vol. 81, No. 1, pp. 88–101.

26 See Robert A. Baron, "The Role of Affect in the Entrepreneurial Process," *Academy of Management Review*, 2008, Vol. 33, No. 2, pp. 328–340.

27 Kathleen Sutcliffe, "What Executives Notice: Accurate Perceptions in Top Management Teams," *Academy of Management Journal*, 1994, Vol. 37, No. 5, pp. 1360–1378.

28 Richard A. Posthuma and Michael A. Campion, "Age Stereotypes in the Workplace: Common Stereotypes, Moderators, and Future Research Directions," *Journal of Management*, 2009, Vol. 35, No. 1, pp. 158–188.

29 For a classic treatment of attribution, see H. H. Kelley, *Attribution in Social Interaction* (Morristown, NJ: General Learning Press, 1971). For a recent application, see Edward C. Tomlinson and Roger C. Mayer, "The Role of Causal Attribution Dimensions in Trust Repair," *Academy of Management Review*, January 2009, Vol. 34, No. 1, pp. 85–104.

30 For a recent overview of the stress literature, see Frank Landy, James Campbell Quick, and Stanislav Kasl, "Work, Stress, and Well-Being," *International Journal of Stress Management*, 1994, Vol. 1, No. 1, pp. 33–73. See also Mark A. Griffin and Sharon Clarke, "Stress and Well-Being at Work," in Sheldon Zedeck (ed.), *Handbook of Industrial and Organizational Psychology*, Vol. 3: *Maintaining, Expanding, and Contracting the Organization* (Washington, DC: American Psychological Association, 2010), pp. 359–397.

31 Hans Selye, *The Stress of Life* (New York: McGraw-Hill, 1976).

[32] M. Friedman and R. H. Rosenman, *Type A Behavior and Your Heart* (New York: Knopf, 1974).

[33] "Work & Family," *BusinessWeek*, June 28, 1993, pp. 80–88.

[34] Richard S. DeFrank, Robert Konopaske, and John M. Ivancevich, "Executive Travel Stress: Perils of the Road Warrior," *Academy of Management Executive*, 2000, Vol. 14, No. 2, pp. 58–67.

[35] Steven Rogelberg, Desmond Leach, Peter Warr, and Jennifer Burnfield, "'Not Another Meeting!' Are Meeting Time Demands Related to Employee Well-Being?" *Journal of Applied Psychology*, 2006, Vol. 91, No. 1, pp. 86–96. See also "Always Working," *USA Today*, March 7, 2013, pp. 1A, 2A.

[36] "Those Doing Layoffs Can Feel the Pain," *USA Today*, April 23, 2009, p. 5D.

[37] Michael R. Frone, "Are Work Stressors Related to Employee Substance Abuse? The Importance of Temporal Context in Assessments of Alcohol and Illicit Drug Use," *Journal of Applied Psychology*, 2008, Vol. 93, No. 1, pp. 199–296.

[38] "Breaking Point," *Newsweek*, March 6, 1995, pp. 56–62. See also "Rising Job Stress Could Affect Bottom Line," *USA Today*, July 28, 2003, p. 18.

[39] Thomas Wright, "Much More Than Meets the Eye: The Role of Psychological Well-Being in Job Performance, Employee Retention, and Cardiovascular Health," *Organizational Dynamics*, January–March 2010, Vol. 39, No. 1, pp. 13–23.

[40] See Christopher M. Barnes and John R. Hollenbeck, "Sleep Deprivation and Decision-Making Teams: Burning the Midnight Oil or Playing with Fire?" *Academy of Management Review*, January 2009, Vol. 34, No. 1, pp. 56–66.

[41] John M. Kelly, "Get a Grip on Stress," *HR Magazine*, February 1997, pp. 51–58. See also Marilyn Macik-Frey, James Campbell Quick, and Debra Nelson, "Advances in Occupational Health: From a Stressful Beginning to a Positive Future," *Journal of Management*, 2007, Vol. 33, No. 6, pp. 809–840.

[42] "Nice Work If You Can Get It," *BusinessWeek*, January 9, 2006, pp. 56–57. See also "Wellness," *Time*, February 23, 2009, pp. 78–79.

[43] See Richard W. Woodman, John E. Sawyer, and Ricky W. Griffin, "Toward a Theory of Organizational Creativity," *Academy of Management Review*, April 1993, pp. 293–321. See also Beth Henessey and Teresa Amabile, "Creativity," in Susan Fiske, Daniel Schacter, and Robert Sternberg (eds.), *Annual Review of Psychology*, Vol. 61 (Palo Alto, CA: Annual Reviews, 2010), pp. 569–598; and Jing Zhou and Christina E. Shalley, "Deepening Our Understanding of Creativity in the Workplace: A Review of Different Approaches to Creativity Research," in Sheldon Zedeck (ed.), *Handbook of Industrial and Organizational Psychology*, Vol. 1: *Building and Developing the Organization* (Washington, DC: American Psychological Association, 2010), pp. 275–302.

[44] Emily Thornton, "Japan's Struggle to Be Creative," *Fortune*, April 19, 1993, pp. 129–134.

[45] John Simons, "The $10 Billion Pill," *Fortune*, January 20, 2003, pp. 58–68.

[46] Christina E. Shalley, Lucy L. Gilson, and Terry C. Blum, "Matching Creativity Requirements and the Work Environment: Effects on Satisfaction and Intentions to Leave," *Academy of Management Journal*, 2000, Vol. 43, No. 2, pp. 215–223. See also Filiz Tabak, "Employee Creative Performance: What Makes It Happen?" *Academy of Management Executive*, 1997, Vol. 11, No. 1, pp. 119–122; and Giles Hirst, Daan van Knippenberg, and Jing Zhou, "A Cross-Level Perspective on Employee Creativity: Goal Orientation, Team Learning Behavior, and Individual Creativity," *Academy of Management Journal*, 2009, Vol. 52, No. 2, pp. 280–293.

[47] "Real Life Imitates *Real World*," *BusinessWeek*, March 23/30, 2009, p. 42.

[48] See Ryan D. Zimmerman, "Understanding the Impact of Personality Traits on Individuals' Turnover Decisions: A Meta-Analytic Path Model," *Personnel Psychology*, 2008, Vol. 61, 309–348. See also Jean Martin and Conrad Schmidt, "How to Keep Your Top Talent," *Harvard Business Review*, May 2010, pp. 54–61.

[49] For recent findings regarding this behavior, see Philip M. Podsakoff, Scott B. MacKenzie, Julie Beth Paine, and Daniel G. G. Bacharah, "Organizational Citizenship Behaviors: A Critical Review of the Theoretical and Empirical Literature and Suggestions for Future Research," *Journal of Management*, 2000, Vol. 26, No. 3, pp. 513–563; and Dennis W. Organ, Philip M. Podsakoff, and Nathan P. Podsakoff, *"Expanding the Criterion Domain to Include Organizational Citizenship Behavior: Implications for Employee Selection,"* in Sheldon Zedeck (ed.), *Handbook of Industrial and Organizational Psychology*, Vol. 2: *Selecting and Developing Members for the Organization* (Washington, DC: American Psychological Association, 2010), pp. 281–323.

[50] Dennis W. Organ "Personality and Organizational Citizenship Behavior," *Journal of Management*, 1994, Vol. 20, No. 2, pp. 465–478; Mary Konovsky and S. Douglas Pugh, "Citizenship Behavior and Social Exchange," *Academy of Management Journal*, 1994, Vol. 37, No. 3, pp. 656–669; and Jacqueline A.-M. Coyle-Shapiro, "A Psychological Contract Perspective on Organizational Citizenship," *Journal of Organizational Behavior*, 2002, Vol. 23, pp. 927–946.

[51] Ricky Griffin and Yvette Lopez, "'Bad Behavior' in Organization: A Review and Typology for Future Research," *Journal of Management*, 2005, Vol. 31, No. 6, pp. 988–1005.

[52] For an illustration, see Sandy Lim, Lilia M. Cortina, and Vicki J. Magley, "Personal and Workgroup Incivility: Impact on Work and Health Outcomes," *Journal of Applied Psychology*, 2008, Vol. 93, No. 1, pp. 95–107. See also Christine Porath and Christine Pearson, "The Cost of Bad Behavior," *Organizational Dynamics*, January–March 2010, Vol. 39, No. 1, pp. 64–71.

[53] See Anne O'Leary-Kelly, Ricky W. Griffin, and David J. Glew, "Organization-Motivated Aggression: A Research Framework," *Academy of Management Review*, January 1996, Vol. 21, No. 1, pp. 225–253. See also Ricky W. Griffin and Anne M. O'Leary Kelly, *The Dark Side of Organizational Behavior* (San Francisco: Jossey-Bass, 2004); and Scott C. Douglas, Christian Kiewitz, Mark J. Martinko, Paul Harvey, Younhee Kim, and Jae Uk Chun, "Cognitions, Emotions, and Evaluations: An Elaboration Likelihood Model for Workplace Aggression," *Academy of Management Review*, 2008, Vol. 33, No. 2, pp. 425–451. See also Laurie J. Barclay and Karl Aquino, "Workplace Aggression and Violence," in Sheldon Zedeck (ed.), *Handbook of Industrial and Organizational Psychology*, Vol. 3: *Maintaining, Expanding, and Contracting the Organization* (Washington, DC: American Psychological Association, 2010), pp. 615–640.

CHAPTER 10

Managing Employee Motivation and Performance

Sergii Tsololo/Photos.com

Learning Outcomes

After studying this chapter, you should be able to:

1 Characterize the nature of motivation, including its importance and basic historical perspectives.

2 Identify and describe the major content perspectives on motivation.

3 Identify and describe the major process perspectives on motivation.

4 Describe reinforcement perspectives on motivation.

5 Identify and describe popular motivational strategies.

6 Describe the role of organizational reward systems in motivation.

Motivating the Whole Person

"If I put our mission in simple terms, it would be, No. 1, to change the way the world eats and, No. 2, to create a workplace based on love and respect."

—**Whole Foods co-CEO Walter Robb**

Whole Foods is often recognized as a great place to work. Employees such as this one are motivated by Whole Foods' competitive pay and benefits, although some criticism has been directed at the firm's health-care plan.

Jim West/Alamy

Whole Foods Market (WFM) started out in 1980 as 1 store with 19 employees in Austin, Texas. Today, with 350 stores and 54,000 employees in North America and Great Britain, it's the leading natural and organic foods supermarket (and ninth-largest food and drug chain in the United States). Along the way, it's also gained a considerable reputation as a socially responsible company and a good place to work. WFM's motto is "Whole Foods, Whole People, Whole Planet," and its guiding "core value," according to co-CEO Walter Robb, is "customers first, then team members, balanced with what's good for other stakeholders.... If I put our mission in simple terms," Robb continues, "it would be, No. 1, to change the way the world eats and, No. 2, to create a workplace based on love and respect."

WFM made *Fortune* magazine's very first list of the "100 Best Companies to Work For" in 1998 and is one of 13 organizations to have made it every year since. Citations have acknowledged the company's growth (which means more jobs), salary-cap limits (the top earner gets no more than 19 times the average full-time salary), and generous health plan. The structure of the company's current health-care program, which revolves around high deductibles and so-called *health savings accounts (HSAs)*, was first proposed in 2003. Under such a plan, an employee (a "team member," in WFM parlance) pays a deductible before his or her expenses are covered. Meanwhile, the employer funds a special account (an HSA) for each employee, who can spend the money to cover health-related expenditures. The previous WFM plan had covered 100 percent of all expenses, and when some employees complained about the proposed change, the company decided to put it to a vote. Nearly 90 percent of the workforce went to the polls, with 77 percent voting for the new plan. In 2006, employees voted to retain the plan, which now carries a deductible of around $1,300; HSAs may go as high as $1,800 (and accrue for future use). The company pays 100 percent of the premiums for eligible employees (about 89 percent of the workforce).

High-deductible plans save money for the employer (the higher the deductible, the lower the premium), and more important—at least according to founder and co-CEO John Mackey—they also make employees more responsible consumers. When the first $1,300 of their medical expenses comes out of their own pockets (or their own HSAs), he argues, people "start asking how much things cost. Or they get a bill and say, 'Wow, that's expensive.' They begin to ask questions. They may not want to go to the emergency room if they wake up with a hangnail in the middle of the night. They may schedule an appointment now."

Mackey believes that "the individual is the best judge of what's right for the individual," and he's so convinced of the value of plans like the one offered by his company that in August 2009 he wrote an op-ed in the *Wall Street Journal* in which he recommended "The Whole Foods Alternative to ObamaCare." Health care, he wrote, "is a service that we all need, but just like food and shelter, it is best provided through voluntary and mutually beneficial market exchanges." Going a step further, Mackey argued against an "intrinsic right to health care," and on this point he stirred up a reaction among his customers that ran the gamut from surprise to boycotting. "I'm boycotting [Whole Foods]," said one customer who'd been shopping WFM several times a week, "because all Americans need health care. While Mackey is worried about health-care and stimulus spending, he doesn't seem too worried about expensive wars and tax breaks for the wealthy and big businesses such as his own that contribute to the [national] deficit."

Consumer advocates and HR specialists also attacked Mackey's proposals and policies. "High-deductible plans for low-wage workers," says Judy Dugan, research director of Consumer Watchdog, "are the next best thing to being uninsured: The up-front costs are so high that workers have to weigh getting health care against paying the rent (to the detriment of their health)." A former WFM executive points out, for example, that the firm's plan entails "astronomical deductibles and co-pays." As for the HSA, it has to cover all co-pays and all expenses not covered by the plan (such as mental health care). "There's way more going on here than 'health insurance,'" concludes the anonymous former exec. "... [The] system has massive hidden charges that routinely threaten and undermine the financial stability and, ultimately, [the] well-being of the employees."

Responding to the backlash against Mackey's *WSJ* piece, the WFM Customer Communications Team hastened to point out that "our team members vote on our plan ... to make sure they continue to have a voice in our benefits." Mackey's intent, said the press release, "was to express his personal opinions—not those of Whole Foods Market team members or our company as a whole." The release also offered an apology for having "offended some of our customers," but for many onetime WFM loyalists, the apology was too little too late. "I will no longer be shopping at Whole Foods," announced one New Jersey shopper, explaining that "a CEO should take care that if he speaks about politics, his beliefs reflect at least the majority of his clients." In fact, WFM had become, in the words of one reporter, "the granola set's chain of choice," and much of its customer base consists of people whose opinions on such issues as health-care reform are quite different from Mackey's. His *WSJ* article, declared a contributor to the company's online forum, was "an absolute slap in the face to the millions of progressive-minded consumers that have made [Whole Foods] what it is today."

The potential repercussions weren't lost on the WFM board. In late August, following the appearance of the *WSJ* op-ed piece, shareholder activists called for Mackey's removal. The CEO, they charged, had "attempted to capitalize on the brand reputation of Whole Foods to champion his personal political views but has instead deeply offended a key segment of Whole Foods consumer base." The company's stock had also slipped 30 percent over the previous five-year period. The board eventually compromised by convincing Mackey to step down as chairman of the board.[1]

Obviously, managers can't always motivate people to perform in ways that are in the best interests of the organization. But managers are responsible for encouraging high performance from their employees, so it's always worthwhile trying to figure out what makes employees more (or less) productive. Whether it's pay, benefits, or job security, the issue almost invariably comes down to motivation, which is the subject of this chapter. We first examine the nature of employee motivation and then explore the major perspectives on motivation. Newly emerging approaches are then discussed. We conclude with a description of rewards and their role in motivation.

THE NATURE OF MOTIVATION

motivation
The set of forces that cause people to behave in certain ways

Motivation is the set of forces that cause people to behave in certain ways.[2] On any given day, an employee may choose to work as hard as possible at a job, work just hard enough to avoid a reprimand, or do as little as possible. The goal for the manager is to maximize the likelihood of the first behavior and minimize the likelihood of the last. This goal becomes all the more important when we understand how important motivation is in the workplace.

Individual performance is generally determined by three things: motivation (the desire to do the job), ability (the capability to do the job), and the work environment (the resources needed to do the job). If an employee lacks ability, the manager can provide

FIGURE 10.1

The Motivation Framework

The motivation process progresses through a series of discrete steps. Content, process, and reinforcement perspectives on motivation address different parts of this process.

training or replace the worker. If there is a resource problem, the manager can correct it. But, if motivation is the problem, the task for the manager is more challenging.[3] Individual behavior is a complex phenomenon, and the manager may be hard pressed to figure out the precise nature of the problem and how to solve it. Thus, motivation is important because of its significance as a determinant of performance and because of its intangible character.[4]

The motivation framework in Figure 10.1 is a good starting point for understanding how motivated behavior occurs. The motivation process begins with a need deficiency.

For example, when a worker feels that she is underpaid, she experiences a need for more income. In response, the worker searches for ways to satisfy the need, such as working harder to try to earn a raise or seeking a new job. Next, she chooses an option to pursue. After carrying out the chosen option—working harder and putting in more hours for a reasonable period of time, for example—she then evaluates her success. If her hard work resulted in a pay raise, she probably feels good about things and will continue to work hard. But, if no raise has been provided, she is likely to try another option.

CONTENT PERSPECTIVES ON MOTIVATION

content perspectives
Approach to motivation that tries to answer the question "What factors motivate people?"

Content perspectives on motivation deal with the first part of the motivation process—needs and need deficiencies. More specifically, **content perspectives** address the question "What factors in the workplace motivate people?" Labor leaders often argue that workers can be motivated by more pay, shorter working hours, and improved working conditions. Meanwhile, some experts suggest that motivation can be more effectively enhanced by providing employees with more autonomy and greater responsibility.[5] Both of these views represent content views of motivation. The former asserts that motivation is a function of pay, working hours, and working conditions; the latter suggests that autonomy and responsibility are the causes of motivation. Two widely known content perspectives on motivation are the needs hierarchy and the two-factor theory.

The Needs Hierarchy Approach

The needs hierarchy approach has been advanced by many theorists. Needs hierarchies assume that people have different needs that can be arranged in a hierarchy of importance. The best known is Maslow's hierarchy of needs.

Abraham Maslow, a human relationist, argued that people are motivated to satisfy five need levels.[6] **Maslow's hierarchy of needs** is shown in Figure 10.2. At the bottom of the hierarchy are the *physiological needs*—things such as food, sex, and air, which represent basic issues of survival and biological function. In organizations, survival needs are generally satisfied by adequate wages and the work environment itself, which provides restrooms, adequate lighting, comfortable temperatures, and ventilation.

Next are the *security needs* for a secure physical and emotional environment. Examples include the desire for housing and clothing and the need to be free from worry about money and job security. These needs can be satisfied in the workplace by assured job continuity (no layoffs), an effective grievance system (to protect against arbitrary supervisory actions), and an adequate insurance and retirement benefit package (for security against illness and provision of income in later life). Even today, however, depressed industries and economic decline can put people out of work and restore the primacy of security needs.

Belongingness needs relate to social processes. They include the need for love and companionship and the need to be accepted by one's peers. These needs are satisfied for most people by family and community relationships outside work and by friendships on the job. A manager can help satisfy these needs by allowing social interaction and by making employees feel like part of a team or work group.

Maslow's hierarchy of needs

Suggests that people must satisfy five groups of needs in order—physiological, security, belongingness, esteem, and self-actualization

FIGURE 10.2

Maslow's Hierarchy of Needs

Maslow's hierarchy suggests that human needs can be classified into five categories and that these categories can be arranged in a hierarchy of importance. A manager should understand that an employee may not be satisfied with only a salary and benefits; he or she may also need challenging job opportunities to experience self-growth and satisfaction.

Source: Adapted from Abraham H. Maslow, "A Theory of Human Motivation," *Psychology Review*, 1943, Vol. 50, pp. 370–396.

Esteem needs actually comprise two different sets of needs: the need for a positive self-image and self-respect and the need for recognition and respect from others. A manager can help address these needs by providing a variety of extrinsic symbols of accomplishment, such as job titles, nice offices, and similar rewards as appropriate. At a more intrinsic level, the manager can provide challenging job assignments and opportunities for the employee to feel a sense of accomplishment.

At the top of the hierarchy are the *self-actualization needs*. These involve realizing one's potential for continued growth and individual development. The self-actualization needs are perhaps the most difficult for a manager to address. In fact, it can be argued that these needs must be met entirely from within the individual. But a manager can help by promoting a culture wherein self-actualization is possible. For instance, a manager could give employees a chance to participate in making decisions about their work and the opportunity to learn new things.

Maslow suggests that the five need categories constitute a hierarchy. An individual is motivated first and foremost to satisfy physiological needs. As long as they remain unsatisfied, the individual is motivated to fulfill only them. When satisfaction of physiological needs is achieved, they cease to act as primary motivational factors, and the individual moves "up" the hierarchy and becomes concerned with security needs. This process continues until the individual reaches the self-actualization level. Maslow's concept of the needs hierarchy has a certain intuitive logic and has been accepted by many managers. But research has revealed certain shortcomings and defects in the theory. Some research has found that five levels of need are not always present and that the order of the levels is not always the same, as postulated by Maslow.[7] In addition, people from different cultures are likely to have different need categories and hierarchies.

The Two-Factor Theory

two-factor theory of motivation

Suggests that people's satisfaction and dissatisfaction are influenced by two independent sets of factors—motivation factors and hygiene factors

Another popular content perspective is the **two-factor theory of motivation**.[8] Frederick Herzberg developed his theory by interviewing a group of accountants and engineers. He asked them to recall occasions when they had been satisfied and motivated and occasions when they had been dissatisfied and unmotivated. Surprisingly, he found that different sets of factors were associated with satisfaction and with dissatisfaction—that is, a person might identify "low pay" as causing dissatisfaction but would not necessarily mention "high pay" as a cause of satisfaction. Instead, different factors—such as recognition or accomplishment—were cited as causing satisfaction and motivation.

This finding led Herzberg to conclude that the traditional view of job satisfaction was incomplete. That view assumed that satisfaction and dissatisfaction are at opposite ends of a single continuum. People might be satisfied, dissatisfied, or somewhere in between. But Herzberg's interviews had identified two different dimensions altogether: one ranging from satisfaction to no satisfaction and the other ranging from dissatisfaction to no dissatisfaction. This perspective, along with several examples of factors that affect each continuum, is shown in Figure 10.3. Note that the factors influencing the satisfaction continuum—called *motivation factors*—are related specifically to the work content. The factors presumed to cause dissatisfaction—called *hygiene factors*—are related to the work environment.

Based on these findings, Herzberg argued that there are two stages in the process of motivating employees. First, managers must ensure that the hygiene factors are not deficient. Pay and security must be appropriate, working conditions must be safe, technical supervision must be acceptable, and so on. By providing hygiene factors at an appropriate level, managers do not stimulate motivation but merely ensure that employees are "not dissatisfied." Employees whom managers attempt to "satisfy" through hygiene

FIGURE 10.3

The Two-Factor Theory of Motivation

The two-factor theory suggests that job satisfaction has two dimensions. A manager who tries to motivate an employee using only hygiene factors, such as pay and good working conditions, will likely not succeed. To motivate employees and produce a high level of satisfaction, managers must also offer factors such as responsibility and the opportunity for advancement (motivation factors).

factors alone will usually do just enough to get by. Thus, managers should proceed to stage 2—giving employees the opportunity to experience motivation factors such as achievement and recognition. The result is predicted to be a high level of satisfaction and motivation. Herzberg also went a step further than most other theorists and described exactly how to use the two-factor theory in the workplace. Specifically, he recommended job enrichment, as discussed in Chapter 6. He argued that jobs should be redesigned to provide higher levels of the motivation factors.

Although widely accepted by many managers, Herzberg's two-factor theory is not without its critics. One criticism is that the findings in Herzberg's initial interviews are subject to different explanations. Another charge is that his sample was not representative of the general population and that subsequent research often failed to uphold the theory[9]. At the present time, Herzberg's theory is not held in high esteem by researchers in the field. The theory has had a major impact on managers, however, and has played a key role in increasing their awareness of motivation and its importance in the workplace.

Individual Human Needs

In addition to these theories, research has focused on specific individual human needs that are important in organizations. The three most important individual needs, sometimes referred to as *manifest needs*, are achievement, affiliation, and power.[10]

need for achievement

The desire to accomplish a goal or task more effectively than in the past

The **need for achievement**, the best known of the three, is the desire to accomplish a goal or task more effectively than in the past. People with a high need for achievement have a desire to assume personal responsibility, a tendency to set moderately difficult goals, a desire for specific and immediate feedback, and a preoccupation with their task. David C. McClelland, the psychologist who first identified this need, argues that only about 10 percent of the U.S. population has a high need for achievement. In contrast, almost 25 percent of the workers in Japan have a high need for achievement.

need for affiliation

The desire for human companionship and acceptance

The **need for affiliation** is less well understood. Like Maslow's belongingness need, the need for affiliation is a desire for human companionship and acceptance. People with a strong need for affiliation are likely to prefer (and perform better in) a job that entails a lot of social interaction and offers opportunities to make friends. One recent survey found that workers with one or more good friends at work are much more likely to be committed to their work. American Airlines, for instance, allows flight attendants to form their own teams; those who participate tend to form teams with their friends.[11]

need for power
The desire to be influential in a group and to control one's environment

The **need for power** is the desire to be influential in a group and to control one's environment. Research has shown that people with a strong need for power are likely to be superior performers, have good attendance records, and occupy supervisory positions. The need for power has also received considerable attention as an important ingredient in managerial success. One study found that managers as a group tend to have a stronger power motive than the general population and that successful managers tend to have stronger power motives than less successful managers.[12] The need for power might explain why Mark Hurd, the former CEO of Hewlett-Packard, recently took advantage of his power and role as head of the company. Hurd was forced to resign after a sexual harassment claim by a female contractor alleging that Hurd had used corporate funds for personal gains in attempts to woo her. The former CEO had submitted personal receipts ranging from $1,000 to $20,000 over a two-year period.[13]

PROCESS PERSPECTIVES ON MOTIVATION

process perspectives
Approaches to motivation that focus on why people choose certain behavioral options to satisfy their needs and how they evaluate their satisfaction after they have attained those goals

Process perspectives are concerned with how motivation occurs. Rather than attempting to identify motivational stimuli, **process perspectives** focus on why people choose certain behavioral options to satisfy their needs and how they evaluate their satisfaction after they have attained those goals. Three useful process perspectives on motivation are the expectancy, equity, and goal-setting theories.

Expectancy Theory

expectancy theory
Suggests that motivation depends on two things—how much we want something and how likely we think we are to get it

Expectancy theory suggests that motivation depends on two things—how much we want something and how likely we think we are to get it.[14] Assume that you are approaching graduation and looking for a job. You see online that Ford Motor Company is seeking a new vice president with a starting salary of $900,000 per year. Even though you might want the job, you will not apply because you realize that you have little chance of getting it. You also find a job posting for someone to scrape bubble gum from underneath theater seats for a starting wage of $8 an hour. Even though you could probably get this job, you do not apply because you do not want it. Then you see a posting for a management trainee at a big company, with a starting salary of $60,000. You will probably apply for this job because you want it and because you think you have a reasonable chance of getting it.

Expectancy theory rests on four basic assumptions. First, it assumes that behavior is determined by a combination of forces in the individual and in the environment. Second, it assumes that people make decisions about their own behavior in organizations. Third, it assumes that different people have different types of needs, desires, and goals. Fourth, it assumes that people make choices from among alternative plans of behavior, based on their perceptions of the extent to which a given behavior will lead to desired outcomes.

Figure 10.4 summarizes the basic expectancy model. The model suggests that motivation leads to effort and that effort, combined with employee ability and environmental factors, results in performance. Performance, in turn, leads to various outcomes, each of which has an associated value, called its *valence*. The most important parts of the expectancy model cannot be shown in the figure, however. These are the individual's expectation that effort will lead to high performance, that performance will lead to outcomes, and that each outcome will have some kind of value.

© Cengage Learning

FIGURE 10.4

The Expectancy Model of Motivation

The expectancy model of motivation is a complex but relatively accurate portrayal of how motivation occurs. According to this model, a manager must understand what employees want (such as pay, promotions, or status) to begin to motivate them.

---

effort-to-performance expectancy
The individual's perception of the probability that effort will lead to high performance

performance-to-outcome expectancy
The individual's perception that performance will lead to a specific outcome

outcomes
Consequences of behaviors in an organizational setting, usually rewards

valence
An index of how much an individual values a particular outcome; the attractiveness of the outcome to the individual

---

Effort-to-Performance Expectancy   The **effort-to-performance expectancy** is the individual's perception of the probability that effort will lead to high performance. When the individual believes that effort will lead directly to high performance, expectancy will be quite strong (close to 1.00). When the individual believes that effort and performance are unrelated, expectancy is very weak (close to 0). The belief that effort is somewhat but not strongly related to performance carries with it a moderate expectancy (somewhere between 0 and 1.00).

Performance-to-Outcome Expectancy   The **performance-to-outcome expectancy** is the individual's perception that performance will lead to a specific outcome. For example, the individual who believes that high performance will result in a pay raise has a high expectancy (approaching 1.00). The individual who believes that high performance may lead to a pay raise has a moderate expectancy (between 1.00 and 0). The individual who believes that performance has no relationship to rewards has a low expectancy (close to 0).

Outcomes and Valences   Expectancy theory recognizes that an individual's behavior results in a variety of **outcomes**, or consequences, in an organizational setting. A high performer, for example, may get bigger pay raises, faster promotions, and more praise from the boss. On the other hand, she may also be subject to more stress and incur resentment from coworkers. Each of these outcomes also has an associated value, or **valence**—an index of how much an individual values a particular outcome. If the individual wants the outcome, its valence is positive; if the individual does not want the outcome, its valence is negative; and if the individual is indifferent to the outcome, its valence is zero.

It is this part of expectancy theory that goes beyond the content perspectives on motivation. Different people have different needs, and they will try to satisfy these needs in different ways. For an employee who has a high need for achievement and a low need for affiliation, the pay raise and promotions cited earlier as outcomes of high performance might have positive valences, the praise and resentment zero valences, and the stress a negative valence. For a different employee, one with a low need for achievement and a high need for affiliation, the pay raise, promotions, and praise might all have positive valences, whereas both resentment and stress could have negative valences.

For motivated behavior to occur, three conditions must be met. First, the effort-to-performance must be greater than 0 (the individual must believe that if effort is expended, high performance will result). The performance-to-outcome expectancy must also be greater than 0 (the individual must believe that if high performance is achieved, certain outcomes will follow). And the sum of the valences for the outcomes must be greater than 0. (One or more outcomes may have negative valences if they are more than offset by the positive valences of other outcomes. For example, the attractiveness of a pay raise, a promotion, and praise from the boss may outweigh the unattractiveness of more stress and resentment from coworkers.) Expectancy theory suggests that when these conditions are met, the individual is motivated to expend effort.

Starbucks credits its unique stock ownership program with maintaining a dedicated and motivated workforce. Based on the fundamental concepts of expectancy theory, Starbucks employees earn stock as a function of their seniority and performance. Thus, their hard work helps them earn shares of ownership in the company.[15]

The Porter–Lawler Extension   An interesting extension of expectancy theory has been proposed by Porter and Lawler.[16] Recall from Chapter 1 that the human relationists assumed that employee satisfaction causes good performance. We also noted that research has not supported such a relationship. Porter and Lawler suggested that there may indeed be a relationship between satisfaction and performance but that it goes in the opposite direction—that is, high performance may lead to high satisfaction. Figure 10.5 summarizes Porter and Lawler's logic. Performance results in rewards for an individual. Some of these are extrinsic (such as pay and promotions); others are intrinsic (such as self-esteem and accomplishment). The individual evaluates the equity, or fairness, of the rewards relative to the effort expended and the level of performance attained. If the rewards are perceived to be equitable, the individual is satisfied.

FIGURE 10.5

The Porter–Lawler Extension of Expectancy Theory

The Porter–Lawler extension of expectancy theory suggests that if performance results in equitable rewards, people will be more satisfied. Thus, performance can lead to satisfaction. Managers must therefore be sure that any system of motivation includes rewards that are fair, or equitable, for all.

Source: "The Effect of Performance on Job Satisfaction," *Industrial Relations*, p. 23, Edward E. Lawler III and Lyman W. Porter. © 1967. Reproduced with permission of John Wiley & Sons Ltd.

Equity Theory

After needs have stimulated the motivation process and the individual has chosen an action that is expected to satisfy those needs, the individual assesses the fairness, or equity, of the resultant outcome. **Equity theory** contends that people are motivated to seek social equity in the rewards they receive for performance.[17] Equity is an individual's belief that the treatment he or she is receiving is fair relative to the treatment received by others. According to equity theory, outcomes from a job include pay, recognition, promotions, social relationships, and intrinsic rewards. To get these rewards, the individual makes inputs to the job, such as time, experience, effort, education, and loyalty. The theory suggests that people view their outcomes and inputs as a ratio and then compare it to someone else's ratio. This other "person" may be someone in the work group or some sort of group average or composite. The process of comparison looks like this:

$$\frac{\text{Outcomes (self)} = \text{Outcomes (other)}}{\text{Inputs (self)} = \text{Inputs (other)}}$$

Both the formulation of the ratios and comparisons between them are very subjective and based on individual perceptions. As a result of comparisons, three conditions may result: The individual may feel equitably rewarded, underrewarded, or overrewarded. A feeling of equity will result when the two ratios are equal. This may occur even though the other person's outcomes are greater than the individual's own outcomes—provided that the other's inputs are also proportionately greater. Suppose that Mark has a high school education and earns $35,000. He may still feel equitably treated relative to Susan, who earns $50,000, because she has a college degree.

People who feel underrewarded try to reduce the inequity. Such an individual might decrease her inputs by exerting less effort, increase her outcomes by asking for a raise, distort the original ratios by rationalizing, try to get the other person to change her or his outcomes or inputs, leave the situation, or change the object of comparison. An individual may also feel overrewarded relative to another person. This is not likely to be terribly disturbing to most people, but research suggests that some people who experience inequity under these conditions are somewhat motivated to reduce it. Under such a circumstance, the person might increase his inputs by exerting more effort, reduce his outcomes by producing fewer units (if paid on a per-unit basis), distort the original ratios by rationalizing, or try to reduce the inputs or increase the outcomes of the other person.

Managers today may need to pay even greater attention to equity theory and its implications. Many firms, for example, are moving toward performance-based reward systems (discussed later in this chapter) as opposed to standard or across-the-board salary increases. Hence, they must ensure that the bases for rewarding some people more than others are clear and objective. Beyond legal issues such as discrimination, managers need to be sure that they are providing fair rewards and incentives to those who do the best work.[18] Moreover, they must be sensitive to cultural differences that affect how people may perceive and react to equity and inequity.[19]

Goal-Setting Theory

The goal-setting theory of motivation assumes that behavior is a result of conscious goals and intentions.[20] Therefore, by setting goals for people in the organization, a manager should be able to influence their behavior. Given this premise, the challenge is to develop a thorough understanding of the processes by which people set goals and then work to reach them. In the original version of goal-setting theory, two specific goal characteristics—goal difficulty and goal specificity—were expected to shape performance.

Goal Difficulty   *Goal difficulty* is the extent to which a goal is challenging and requires effort. If people work to achieve goals, it is reasonable to assume that they will work harder to achieve more difficult goals. But a goal must not be so difficult that it is unattainable. If a new manager asks her sales force to increase sales by 300 percent, the group may become disillusioned. A more realistic but still difficult goal—perhaps a 30 percent increase—would be a better incentive. A substantial body of research supports the importance of goal difficulty. In one study, for example, managers at Weyerhauser set difficult goals for truck drivers hauling loads of timber from cutting sites to wood yards. Over a nine-month period, the drivers increased the quantity of wood they delivered by an amount that would have required $250,000 worth of new trucks at the previous per-truck average load.[21]

Goal Specificity   *Goal specificity is* the clarity and precision of the goal. A goal of "increasing productivity" is not very specific; a goal of "increasing productivity by 3 percent in the next six months" is quite specific. Some goals, such as those involving costs, output, profitability, and growth, are readily amenable to specificity. Other goals, however, such as improving employee job satisfaction, morale, company image and reputation, ethics, and socially responsible behavior, may be much harder to state in specific terms. Like difficulty, specificity has been shown to be consistently related to performance. The study of timber truck drivers just mentioned, for example, also examined goal specificity. The initial loads the truck drivers carried were found to be 60 percent of the maximum weight each truck could haul. The managers set a new goal for drivers of 94 percent, which the drivers were soon able to reach. Thus, the goal was both specific and difficult.

Because the theory attracted so much widespread interest and research support from researchers and managers alike, an expanded model of the goal-setting process was eventually proposed. The expanded model, shown in Figure 10.6, attempts to capture more fully the complexities of goal setting in organizations.

FIGURE 10.6

The Expanded Goal-Setting Theory of Motivation

One of the most important emerging theories of motivation is goal-setting theory. This theory suggests that goal difficulty, specificity, acceptance, and commitment combine to determine an individual's goal-directed effort. This effort, when complemented by appropriate organizational support and individual abilities and traits, results in performance. Finally, performance is seen as leading to intrinsic and extrinsic rewards that, in turn, result in employee satisfaction.

Source: Reprinted from *Organizational Dynamics*, Autumn 1979, Gary P. Latham and Edwin A. Locke, A Motivational Technique That Works, p. 79, © 1979, with permission from Elsevier.

The expanded theory argues that goal-directed effort is a function of four goal attributes: difficulty and specificity, as already discussed, and acceptance and commitment. *Goal acceptance* is the extent to which a person accepts a goal as his or her own. *Goal commitment* is the extent to which he or she is personally interested in reaching the goal. The manager who vows to take whatever steps are necessary to cut costs by 10 percent has made a commitment to achieve the goal. Factors that can foster goal acceptance and commitment include participating in the goal-setting process, making goals challenging but realistic, and believing that goal achievement will lead to valued rewards.

The interaction of goal-directed effort, organizational support, and individual abilities and traits determines actual performance. Organizational support is whatever the organization does to help or hinder performance. Positive support might mean making available adequate personnel and a sufficient supply of raw materials; negative support might mean failing to fix damaged equipment. Individual abilities and traits are the skills and other personal characteristics necessary for doing a job. As a result of performance, a person receives various intrinsic and extrinsic rewards, which in turn influence satisfaction. Note that the latter stages of this model are quite similar to the Porter–Lawler expectancy model discussed earlier.[22]

reinforcement theory
Approach to motivation that argues that behavior that results in rewarding consequences is likely to be repeated, whereas behavior that results in punishing consequences is less likely to be repeated

positive reinforcement
A method of strengthening behavior with rewards or positive outcomes after a desired behavior is performed

avoidance
Used to strengthen behavior by avoiding unpleasant consequences that would result if the behavior were not performed

punishment
Used to weaken undesired behaviors by using negative outcomes or unpleasant consequences when the behavior is performed

REINFORCEMENT PERSPECTIVES ON MOTIVATION

A third element of the motivational process addresses why some behaviors are maintained over time and why other behaviors change. As we have seen, content perspectives deal with needs, whereas process perspectives explain why people choose various behaviors to satisfy needs and how they evaluate the equity of the rewards they get for those behaviors. Reinforcement perspectives explain the role of those rewards as they cause behavior to change or remain the same over time. Specifically, **reinforcement theory** argues that behavior that results in rewarding consequences is likely to be repeated, whereas behavior that results in punishing consequences is less likely to be repeated.[23] The "Leading the Way" feature highlights an interesting perspective on reinforcement.

Kinds of Reinforcement in Organizations

Four basic kinds of reinforcement can result from behavior—positive reinforcement, avoidance, punishment, and extinction.[24] Two kinds of reinforcement strengthen or maintain behavior, whereas the other two weaken or decrease behavior.

Positive reinforcement, one method of strengthening behavior, is a reward or a positive outcome after a desired behavior is performed. When a manager observes an employee doing an especially good job and offers praise, the praise serves to positively reinforce the behavior of good work. Other positive reinforcers in organizations include pay raises, promotions, and awards. Employees who work at General Electric's customer service center receive clothing, sporting goods, and even all-expenses-paid vacations as rewards for outstanding performance.

The other method of strengthening desired behavior is through **avoidance**. An employee may come to work on time to avoid a reprimand. In this instance, the employee is motivated to perform the behavior of punctuality to avoid an unpleasant consequence that is likely to follow tardiness.

Punishment is used by some managers to weaken undesired behaviors. When an employee is loafing, coming to work late, doing poor work, or interfering with the work of others, the manager might resort to reprimands, discipline, or fines. The logic is that the unpleasant consequence will reduce the likelihood that the employee will choose that

LEADING THE WAY

To Reward or To Punish? ... That Is the Question

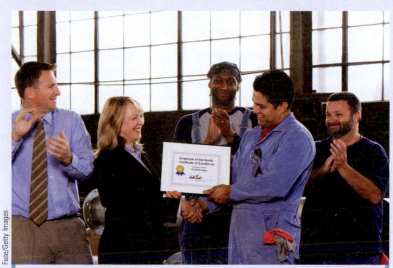

Organizations use a variety of rewards to motivate their employees. This employee, for example, is receiving an award recognizing his high performance. His facial expression clearly communicates his sense of accomplishment and happiness at being recognized for his contributions.

Suppose you are the general manager of a supermarket and you've just finished a department-by-department year-end review of your managers' performance. Every department—meats, dairy, seafood, deli, bakery, and so forth—has performed up to or beyond expectations. All except one: Produce fell 12 percent short of your forecast. You decide to reward all your managers with healthy bonuses except for your produce manager. In other words, you plan to use *punishment* to motivate your produce manager and *positive reinforcement* to motivate all of your other managers. You congratulate yourself for having reached a fair and logical decision.

According to Daniel Kahneman, a psychologist who won the Nobel Prize in economics for his work on behavioral and decision-making models, your decision is probably not fair (at least not altogether), and it's certainly not logical—at least not when the reality of the situation is taken into consideration. Here's how Kahneman sees your two-pronged decision-making model:

- *Manager's department performs well → You reward manager → Department continues to perform well*

- *Manager's department performs poorly → You punish manager → Department performs better*

The key to Kahneman's perspective is called *regression to the mean*—the principle that, from one performance measurement to the next, the change in performance will be toward the overall average level of performance. Say, for example, that you're a par golfer and that par for your course is 72. If you shoot 68 in one round, your next round will probably be *in the direction* of 72—not necessarily 72 exactly, which is your average, or 76, which would bring you exactly back to a two-round average of 72. Technically, regression to the mean is a *law*, and not a *rule*: You could shoot a second round of 70 or even 67, but *most of the time*, your second-round score won't be as good as your first-round score.

Why does regression to the mean occur? Because a complex combination of factors usually determines any outcome. And because this combination is complex, it's not likely that the same combination will repeat itself the next time you measure the outcome. Which brings us back to your produce manager: *It's not likely that his managerial performance was the sole (or even necessarily the primary) factor in his department's poor performance.* Other factors might include variations in competition, economic and market conditions, and decisions made by managers above him—all of which are largely random and which will undoubtedly be different from one performance measurement to the next.

Now that you understand a little about the reality of regression to the mean, compare your decision-making model to a model that reflects reality:

- *Manager's department performs well → Department probably does not perform as well*
- *Manager's department performs poorly → Department probably performs better*

(continued)

LEADING THE WAY (Continued)

Your reinforcement decision will *probably* have little or nothing to do with next year's outcome in any of your store's departments. And you've *probably* been unfair to your produce manager. Kahneman isn't inclined to be overly critical of your mistaken belief that you've made a logical, fair, and effective decision: "It's very difficult for people to detect their own errors," he admits. "You're too busy making a mistake to detect it at the same time." He does, however, reserve the right to be pessimistic: "The failure to recognize the import of regression," he warns,

can have pernicious consequences.... We normally reinforce others when their behavior is good and punish them when their behavior is bad. By regression alone [however], they are most likely to improve after being punished and most likely to deteriorate after being rewarded. Consequently, we are exposed to a lifetime schedule in which we are most often rewarded for punishing others and punished for rewarding [them].

References: Bryan Burke, "Fighter Pilots and Firing Coaches," *Advanced NFL Stats*, www.advancedfootball analytics.com, accessed on December 7, 2013; David Hall, "Daniel Kahneman Interview," *New Zealand Listener*, www.listener.co.nz, accessed on December 7, 2013; Steve Miller, "We're Not Very Good Statisticians," *Information Management*, www.information-management.com, accessed on December 7, 2013; Galen Strawson, "*Thinking, Fast and Slow* by Daniel Kahneman—Review," *The Guardian*, www.guardian.co.uk, accessed on December 7, 2013; and *Judgment under Uncertainty: Heuristics and Biases*, ed. Daniel Kahneman, Paul Slovic, and Amos Tversky (Cambridge, UK: Cambridge University Press, 1982), http://books.google.com, accessed on December 7, 2013.

extinction
Used to weaken undesired behaviors by simply ignoring or not reinforcing them

fixed-interval schedule
Provides reinforcement at fixed intervals of time, such as regular weekly paychecks

variable-interval schedule
Provides reinforcement at varying intervals of time, such as occasional visits by the supervisor

fixed-ratio schedule
Provides reinforcement after a fixed number of behaviors regardless of the time interval involved, such as a bonus for every fifth sale

particular behavior again. Given the counterproductive side effects of punishment (such as resentment and hostility), it is often advisable to use the other kinds of reinforcement if at all possible. **Extinction** can also be used to weaken behavior, especially behavior that has previously been rewarded. When an employee tells an offensive joke and the boss laughs, the laughter reinforces the behavior and the employee may continue to tell offensive jokes. By simply ignoring this behavior and not reinforcing it, the boss can cause the behavior to subside and eventually become "extinct."

Providing Reinforcement in Organizations

The kind of reinforcement is important, but when or how often it occurs also is important. Various strategies are possible for providing reinforcement. The **fixed-interval schedule** provides reinforcement at fixed intervals of time, regardless of behavior. A good example of this schedule is the weekly or monthly paycheck. This method provides the least incentive for good work because employees know they will be paid regularly regardless of their efforts. A **variable-interval schedule** also uses time as the basis for reinforcement, but the time interval varies from one reinforcement to the next. This schedule is appropriate for praise or other rewards based on visits or inspections. When employees do not know when the boss is going to drop by, they tend to maintain a reasonably high level of effort all the time.

A **fixed-ratio schedule** gives reinforcement after a fixed number of behaviors, regardless of the time that elapses between behaviors. This results in an even higher level of effort. For example, when Sears is recruiting new credit-card customers, salespersons get a small bonus for every fifth application returned from their department. Under this arrangement, motivation will be high because each application gets the person closer to the next bonus. The **variable-ratio schedule**, the most powerful schedule in terms of maintaining desired behaviors, varies the number of behaviors needed for each reinforcement. A supervisor who praises an employee for her second order, the seventh order after that, the ninth after that, then the fifth, and then the third is using a variable-ratio

variable-ratio schedule
Provides reinforcement after varying numbers of behaviors are performed, such as the use of compliments by a supervisor on an irregular basis

organizational behavior modification (OB Mod)
Method for applying the basic elements of reinforcement theory in an organizational setting

schedule. The employee is motivated to increase the frequency of the desired behavior because each performance increases the probability of receiving a reward. Of course, a variable-ratio schedule is difficult (if not impossible) to use for formal rewards such as pay because it would be too complicated to keep track of who was rewarded when.

Managers wanting to explicitly use reinforcement theory to motivate their employees generally do so with a technique called **organizational behavior modification (OB Mod)**.[25] An OB Mod program starts by specifying behaviors that are to be increased (such as producing more units) or decreased (such as coming to work late). These target behaviors are then tied to specific forms or kinds of reinforcement. Although many organizations (such as Procter & Gamble and Ford) have used OB Mod, the best-known application was at Emery Air Freight (now a part of UPS). Management felt that the containers used to consolidate small shipments into fewer, larger shipments were not being packed efficiently. Through a system of self-monitored feedback and rewards, Emery increased container usage from 45 percent to 95 percent and saved over $3 million during the first three years of the program.[26]

POPULAR MOTIVATIONAL STRATEGIES

Although the various theories discussed thus far provide a solid explanation for motivation, managers must use various techniques and strategies to actually apply them. Among the most popular motivational strategies today are empowerment and participation and alternative forms of work arrangements. Various forms of performance-based reward systems, discussed in the next section, also reflect efforts to boost motivation and performance.

Empowerment and Participation

empowerment
The process of enabling workers to set their own work goals, make decisions, and solve problems within their sphere of responsibility and authority

participation
The process of giving employees a voice in making decisions about their own work

Empowerment and participation represent important methods that managers can use to enhance employee motivation. **Empowerment** is the process of enabling workers to set their own work goals, make decisions, and solve problems within their sphere of responsibility and authority. **Participation** is the process of giving employees a voice in making decisions about their own work. Thus, empowerment is a somewhat broader concept that promotes participation in a wide variety of areas, including but not limited to work itself, work context, and work environment.[27]

The role of participation and empowerment in motivation can be expressed in terms of both content perspectives and expectancy theory. Employees who participate in decision making may be more committed to executing decisions properly. Furthermore, the successful process of making a decision, executing it, and then seeing the positive consequences can help satisfy one's need for achievement, provide recognition and responsibility, and enhance self-esteem. Simply being asked to participate in organizational decision making may also enhance an employee's self-esteem. In addition, participation should help clarify expectancies; that is, by participating in decision making, employees may better understand the linkage between their performance and the rewards they want most. The "At Your Service" feature highlights the importance of empowerment in service organizations.

Alternative Forms of Work Arrangements

Many organizations today are also experimenting with a variety of alternative work arrangements. These alternative arrangements are generally intended to enhance employee motivation and performance by providing employees with greater

AT YOUR SERVICE

Service with a Smile

© Norman Pogson/Shutterstock.com

More and more people are working in service jobs. Service employees are often a critical point of contact with customers so it is important that they feel good about their jobs and convey a sense of trust. Empowering service employees to make decisions and solve problems can go a long way toward building excellent customer relationships.

Service organizations generally rely on their employees' ability to figure out what the customer wants, needs, and expects and then provide it during that experience. This means that empowerment is a necessity in services because there is no way to fully prepare, train, or teach an employee how to perform the tasks required in the way that each customer expects. So, most service organizations use empowerment extensively. Empowerment works because supervisors can't be everywhere all the time to answer questions, coach correct employee behavior, or prepare their employees for every possible variation that customers will bring to the service encounter.

An even more critical reason that empowerment is necessary is that service failures are inevitable. Thus, employees have to be ready, willing, and able to correct those situations in which the service hasn't gone the way the customer expected and something must be done to fix the service failure. The research on service failures tells us that the faster a service failure is resolved, the better the outcome for company and customer. The customer is

happier when the problem is resolved quickly—and sometimes is even happier than if there had been no problem in the first place. The company is also happier because happy customers are more likely to return as repeat customers. Best of all, the server is happier because most customer encounters with failures are not pleasant, and having the ability to resolve a failure in a positive, quick way leads to a more positive experience for the employee as well as the customer. As one final benefit, most people feel that when they are hired they are supposed to do the jobs for which they were employed and greatly appreciate the opportunity to do them well. When empowered to add value to the customer's experience by personalizing the transaction, service employees feel they have more control over how to perform their jobs, more awareness of the business and their contribution to its success, and more accountability for their own performance.

Successful empowerment requires satisfying five assumptions. First, the employee must have the training, capability, and motivation to do what is needed in the service experience. Second, the outcome must be measureable in some way. Third, the employee must be committed to the organization's mission to provide excellent service and care about sustaining his or her role in the organization's success. Fourth, the manager must be comfortable with allowing the employee to use discretion in performing the job. Finally, the organization needs a strong culture that can guide the employee on doing the right thing when the right thing is an on-the-spot decision the employee must make as to what should be done to respond to a customer. Thus, both company and employee have to be ready, willing, and able to do what the customer wants when the customer wants it.

flexibility in how and when they work. Among the more popular alternative work arrangements are variable work schedules, flexible work schedules, job sharing, and telecommuting.[28]

Variable Work Schedules Although there are many exceptions, of course, the traditional work schedule starts at 8:00 or 9:00 in the morning and ends at 5:00 in the evening, five days a week (of course, many managers work additional hours outside these times). Unfortunately, this schedule makes it difficult to attend to routine personal business—going to the bank, seeing a doctor or dentist for a routine checkup, having a parent–teacher conference, getting an automobile serviced, and so forth. At a surface level, then, employees locked into this sort of arrangement may find it necessary to take a sick day or a vacation day to handle these activities. At a more unconscious level, some people may also feel powerless and constrained by their job schedule and develop resentment and frustration.

compressed work schedule

Working a full forty-hour week in fewer than the traditional five days

To help counter these problems, some businesses have adopted a **compressed work schedule**, working a full forty-hour week in fewer than the traditional five days.[29] One approach involves working ten hours a day for four days, leaving an extra day off. Another alternative is for employees to work slightly fewer than ten hours a day, but to complete the forty hours by lunchtime on Friday. A few firms have tried having employees work twelve hours a day for three days, followed by four days off. Organizations that have used these forms of compressed workweeks include Chevron, BP Amoco, Kraft Foods, and Philip Morris. One problem with this schedule is that when employees put in too much time in a single day, they tend to get tired and perform at a lower level later in the day.

A schedule that some organizations today are beginning to use is what they call a "nine-eighty" schedule. Under this arrangement, an employee works a traditional schedule one week and a compressed schedule the next, getting every other Friday off. In other words, they work eighty hours (the equivalent of two weeks of full-time work) in nine days. By alternating the regular and compressed schedules across half of its workforce, the organization can be fully staffed at all times, while still giving employees two extra full days off each month. Shell Oil and BP Amoco Chemicals are two of the firms that currently use this schedule.

flexible-work schedules

Work schedules that allow employees to select, within broad parameters, the hours they work

Flexible Work Schedules Another promising alternative work arrangement is **flexible work schedules**, sometimes called *flextime*. Flextime gives employees more personal control over the times they work. The workday is broken down into two categories: flexible time and core time. All employees must be at their workstation during core time, but they can choose their own schedules during flexible time. Thus, one employee may choose to start work early in the morning and leave in mid-afternoon, another to start in the late morning and work until late afternoon, and still another to start early in the morning, take a long lunch break, and work until late afternoon. Organizations that have used the flexible-work schedule method for arranging work include Hewlett-Packard, Microsoft, and Texas Instruments.

job sharing

When two part-time employees share one full-time job

Job Sharing Yet another potentially useful alternative work arrangement is job sharing. In **job sharing**, two part-time employees share one full-time job. One person may perform the job from 8:00 a.m. to noon, and the other from 1:00 p.m. to 5:00 p.m. Job sharing may be desirable for people who want to work only part-time or when job markets are tight. For its part, the organization can accommodate the preferences of a broader range of employees and may benefit from the talents of more people.

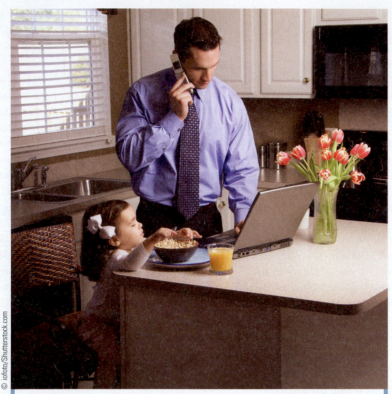

Telecommuting is becoming more and more common and can often help enhance employee commitment and motivation. This man is spending his morning working from home. He has served breakfast to his daughter and is now discussing a work issue with a colleague. The flexibility afforded to him by his employer helps him function more effectively as both a parent and an employee.

Telecommuting An increasingly popular approach to alternative work arrangements is **telecommuting**—allowing employees to spend part of their time working offsite, usually at home. By using various forms of digital communication, many employees can maintain close contact with their organization and still get just as much—or even more—work done at home as if they were in their office.

The increased power and sophistication of modern communication technology are making telecommuting easier and easier. One recent study found that nearly 40 percent of the U.S. workforce (33 million workers) are in jobs that allow for partial or complete telecommuting. Nearly half of AT&T's employees have received mobile and remote access technologies that provide them with the flexibility to work from various locations. And 40 percent of IBM's employees currently telecommute. (In the case of IBM, not only are employees more satisfied with the arrangement but the firm also has saved close to $2.9 billion in office space needs.[30])

telecommuting
Allowing employees to spend part of their time working offsite, usually at home

reward system
The formal and informal mechanisms by which employee performance is defined, evaluated, and rewarded

USING REWARD SYSTEMS TO MOTIVATE PERFORMANCE

Aside from these types of motivational strategies, an organization's reward system is its most basic tool for managing employee motivation. An organizational **reward system** is the formal and informal mechanisms by which employee performance is defined, evaluated, and rewarded. Rewards that are tied specifically to performance, of course, have the greatest impact on enhancing both motivation and actual performance. But managing rewards and motivation is not always as easy as it might first seem.

Performance-based rewards play a number of roles and address a variety of purposes in organizations. The major purposes involve the relationship of rewards to motivation and to performance. Specifically, organizations want employees to perform at relatively high levels and need to make it worth their effort to do so. When rewards are associated with higher levels of performance, employees will presumably be motivated to work harder to achieve those awards. At that point, their own self-interests coincide with the organization's interests. Performance-based rewards are also relevant regarding other employee behaviors, such as retention and citizenship.

Merit Reward Systems

merit pay
Pay awarded to employees on the basis of the relative value of their contributions to the organization

Merit reward systems are one of the most fundamental forms of performance-based rewards. **Merit pay** generally refers to pay awarded to employees on the basis of the relative value of their contributions to the organization. Employees who make greater contributions are given higher pay than those who make lesser contributions. **Merit pay plans**, then, are compensation plans that formally base at least some meaningful portion of compensation on merit. The most general form of merit pay plan is to provide annual salary increases to individuals in the organization based on their relative merit. Merit, in turn, is usually determined or defined based on the individual's performance and overall contributions to the organization. For example, an organization using such a traditional merit pay plan might instruct its supervisors to give all their employees an average pay raise of, say, 4 percent. But the individual supervisor is further instructed to differentiate among high, average, and low performers. Under a simple system, for example, a manager might give the top 20 percent of her employees a 7 percent pay raise, the middle 60 percent a 5 percent or average pay raise, and the bottom 20 percent a 3 percent pay raise.

merit pay plan
Compensation plan that formally bases at least some meaningful portion of compensation on merit

Incentive Reward Systems

piece-rate incentive plan
Reward system wherein the organization pays an employee a certain amount of money for every unit he or she produces

Incentive reward systems are among the oldest forms of performance-based rewards. For example, some companies were using individual piece-rate incentive plans over 100 years ago.[31] Under a **piece-rate incentive plan**, the organization pays an employee a certain amount of money for every unit he or she produces. For example, an employee might be paid $5 for every dozen units of products that are successfully completed. But such simplistic systems fail to account for facts such as minimum wage levels and rely very heavily on the assumptions that performance is totally under an individual's control and that the individual employee does a single task continuously throughout his or her work time. Thus, most organizations today that try to use incentive compensation systems use more sophisticated methodologies.

Incentive Pay Plans   Generally speaking, *individual incentive plans* reward individual performance on a real-time basis. In other words, rather than increasing a person's base salary at the end of the year, an individual instead receives some level of salary increase or financial reward in conjunction with demonstrated outstanding performance in close proximity to when that performance occurred. Individual incentive systems are most likely to be used in cases in which performance can be objectively assessed in terms of number of units of output or similar measures, rather than on a subjective assessment of performance by a superior.

Some variations on a piece-rate system are still fairly popular. Although many of these still resemble the early plans in most ways, a well-known piece-rate system at Lincoln Electric illustrates how an organization can adapt the traditional model to achieve better results. For years, Lincoln's employees were paid individual incentive payments based on their performance. However, the amount of money shared (or the incentive pool) was based on the company's profitability. There was also a well-organized system whereby employees could make suggestions for increasing productivity. There was motivation to do this because the employees received one-third of the profits (another third went to the stockholders, and the last share was retained for improvements and seed money). Thus, the pool for incentive payments was determined by profitability, and an employee's share of this pool was a function of his or her base pay and rated performance based on the piece-rate system. Lincoln Electric was most famous, however, because of the stories (which were apparently typical) of production workers receiving a year-end bonus payment that equaled their yearly base pay.[32]

In recent years, Lincoln has partially abandoned its famous system for business reasons, but it still serves as a benchmark for other companies seeking innovative piece-rate pay systems.

Perhaps the most common form of individual incentive is *sales commissions* that are paid to people engaged in sales work. For example, sales representatives for consumer products firms and retail sales agents may be compensated under this type of commission system. In general, the person might receive a percentage of the total volume of attained sales as his or her commission for a period of time. Some sales jobs are based entirely on commission, whereas others use a combination of base minimum salary with additional commission as an incentive. Notice that these plans put a considerable amount of the salespersons' earnings "at risk." In other words, although organizations often have drawing accounts to allow the salesperson to live during lean periods (the person then "owes" this money back to the organization), if he or she does not perform well, he or she will not be paid much. The portion of salary based on commission is simply not guaranteed and is paid only if sales reach some target level.

Other Forms of Incentive   Occasionally, organizations may also use other forms of incentives to motivate people. For example, a nonmonetary incentive, such as additional time off or a special perk, might be a useful incentive. For example, a company might establish a sales contest in which the sales group that attains the highest level of sales increase over a specified period of time will receive an extra week of paid vacation, perhaps even at an arranged place, such as a tropical resort or a ski lodge.[33]

A major advantage of incentives relative to merit systems is that incentives are typically a one-shot reward and do not accumulate by becoming part of the individual's base salary. Stated differently, an individual whose outstanding performance entitles him or her to a financial incentive gets the incentive only one time, based on that level of performance. If the individual's performance begins to erode in the future, then the individual may receive a lesser incentive or perhaps no incentive in the future. As a consequence, his or her base salary remains the same or is perhaps increased at a relatively moderate pace; he or she receives one-time incentive rewards as recognition for exemplary performance. Furthermore, because these plans, by their very nature, focus on one-time events, it is much easier for the organization to change the focus of the incentive plan. At a simple level, for example, an organization can set up an incentive plan for selling one product during one quarter, but then shift the incentive to a different product the next quarter, as the situation requires.

Daniel Acker/Bloomberg/Getty Images

Automobile makers like Ford routinely offer sales incentives on vehicles that are selling at a slower rate than projected. Common consumer incentives include price cuts, rebates, and low interest rate financing. Incentives are also offered to dealerships and individual sales people who "push" these vehicles. Extra commissions and bonuses, for example, are often used in addition to consumer incentives.

Team and Group Incentive Reward Systems

The merit compensation and incentive compensation systems described in the preceding sections deal primarily with performance-based reward arrangements for individuals. There also exists a different set of performance-based reward programs that are targeted for teams and groups. These programs are particularly important for managers to understand today, given the widespread trends toward team- and group-based methods of work and organizations.[34]

Common Team and Group Reward Systems

There are two commonly used types of team and group reward systems. One type used in many organizations is an approach called *gainsharing*. **Gainsharing programs** are designed to share the cost savings from productivity improvements with employees. The underlying assumption of gainsharing is that employees and the employer have the same goals and thus should appropriately share in incremental economic gains.[35]

gainsharing programs
Designed to share the cost savings from productivity improvements with employees

In general, organizations that use gainsharing start by measuring team- or group-level productivity. It is important that this measure be valid and reliable and that it truly reflects current levels of performance by the team or group. The team or work group itself is then given the charge of attempting to lower costs or otherwise improve productivity through any measures that its members develop and its manager approves. Resulting cost savings or productivity gains that the team or group is able to achieve are then quantified and translated into dollar values. A predetermined formula is then used to allocate these dollar savings between the employer and the employees themselves. A typical formula for distributing gainsharing savings is to provide 25 percent to the employees and 75 percent to the company.

One specific type of gainsharing plan is an approach called the Scanlon plan. This approach was developed by Joseph Scanlon in 1927. The **Scanlon plan** has the same basic strategy as gainsharing plans, in that teams or groups of employees are encouraged to suggest strategies for reducing costs. However, the distribution of these gains is usually tilted much more heavily toward employees, with employees usually receiving between two-thirds and three-fourths of the total cost savings that the plan achieves. Furthermore, the distribution of cost savings resulting from the plan is given not just to the team or group that suggested and developed the ideas, but across the entire organization.

Scanlon plan
Similar to gainsharing, but the distribution of gains is tilted much more heavily toward employees

Other Types of Team and Group Rewards   Although gainsharing and Scanlon-type plans are among the most popular group incentive reward systems, there are other systems that are used by some organizations. Some companies, for example, have begun to use true incentives at the team or group level. Just as with individual incentives, team or group incentives tie rewards directly to performance increases. And, like individual incentives, team or group incentives are paid as they are earned rather than being added to employees' base salary. The incentives are distributed at the team or group level, however, rather than at the individual level. In some cases, the distribution may be based on the existing salary of each employee, with incentive bonuses being given on a proportionate basis. In other settings, each member of the team or group receives the same incentive pay.

Some companies also use nonmonetary rewards at the team or group level—most commonly in the form of prizes and awards. For example, a company might designate the particular team in a plant or subunit of the company that achieves the highest level of productivity increase, the highest level of reported customer satisfaction, or a similar index of performance. The reward itself might take the form of additional time off, as described earlier in this chapter, or a tangible award, such as a trophy or plaque. In any event, the idea is that the reward is at the team level and serves as recognition of exemplary performance by the entire team.

There are also other kinds of team or group level incentives that go beyond the contributions of a specific work group. These are generally organization-wide kinds of incentives. One long-standing method for this approach is *profit sharing*. In a profit-sharing approach, at the end of the year, some portion of the company's profits is paid into a profit-sharing pool that is then distributed to all employees. If the amount is not distributed at that time, it is put into an escrow account and payment is deferred until the employee retires.

Employee stock ownership plans (ESOPs) also represent a group-level reward system that some companies use. Under the ESOP, employees are gradually given a major stake in ownership of a corporation. The typical form of this plan involves the company's taking out a loan, which is then used to buy a portion of its own stock in the open market. Over time, company profits are then used to pay off this loan. Employees, in turn, receive a claim on ownership of some portion of the stock held by the company, based on their seniority and perhaps on their performance. Eventually, each individual becomes an owner of the company.

Executive Compensation

The top-level executives of most companies have separate compensation programs and plans. These are intended to reward these executives for their performance and for the performance of the organization.

Standard Forms of Executive Compensation   Most senior executives receive their compensation in two forms. One form is a *base salary*. As with the base salary of any staff member or professional member of an organization, the base salary of an executive is a guaranteed amount of money that the individual will be paid. For example, in 2013 Kraft Foods paid its CEO, Irene Rosenfeld, $3,600,000 million in base salary.[36]

Above and beyond this base salary, however, most executives also receive one or more forms of incentive pay. The traditional method of incentive pay for executives is in the form of bonuses. Bonuses, in turn, are usually determined by the performance of the organization. Thus, at the end of the year, some portion of a corporation's profits may be diverted into a bonus pool. Senior executives then receive a bonus expressed as a percentage of this bonus pool. The CEO and president are obviously likely to get a larger percentage bonus than a vice president. The exact distribution of the bonus pool is usually specified ahead of time in the individual's employment contract. Some organizations intentionally leave the distribution unspecified, so that the board of directors has the flexibility to give larger rewards to those individuals deemed to be most deserving. Kraft Foods' Irene Rosenfeld received a cash bonus of about $6.5 million in 2013.[37]

Special Forms of Executive Compensation   Beyond base salary and bonuses, many executives receive other kinds of compensation as well. A form of executive compensation that has received a lot of attention in recent years has been various kinds of stock options. A **stock option plan** is established to give senior managers the option to buy company stock in the future at a predetermined fixed price. The basic idea underlying stock option plans is that if the executives contribute to higher levels of organizational performance, then the company stock should increase in value. Then the executive will be able to purchase the stock at the predetermined price, which theoretically should be lower than its future market price. The difference then becomes profit for the individual. Kraft Foods awarded Irene Rosenfeld stock options with a potential value of $14.4 million.[38]

stock option plan
Established to give senior managers the option to buy company stock in the future at a predetermined fixed price

Stock options continue to grow in popularity as a means of compensating top managers. Options are seen as a means of aligning the interests of the manager with those of the stockholders, and given that they do not cost the organization much (other than some possible dilution of stock values), they will probably be even more popular in the future. In fact, a recent study by KPMG Peat Marwick indicates that for senior management whose salary exceeds $250,000, stock options represent the largest share of the salary mix (relative to salary and other incentives). Furthermore, when we consider all of top management (annual salary over $750,000), stock options comprise a full 60 percent of their total compensation. And the Peat Marwick report indicates that even among exempt employees at the $35,000-a-year level, stock options represent 13 percent of total compensation.

But events in recent years have raised serious questions about the use of stock options as incentives for executives. For example, several executives at Enron allegedly withheld critical financial information from the markets, cashed in their stock options (while Enron stock was trading at $80 a share), and then watched as the financial information was made public and the stock fell to less than $1 a share. Of course, such actions (if proven) are illegal, but they raise questions in the public's mind about the role of stock options and about the way organizations treat stock options from an accounting perspective. Most organizations have *not* treated stock options as liabilities, even though, when exercised, they are exactly that. There is concern that by not carrying stock options as liabilities, the managers are overstating the value of the company, which, of course, can help raise the stock price. Finally, when stock markets generally fell during the middle of 2002, many executives found that their options were worthless because the price of the stock fell below the option price. When stock options go "underwater" in this way, they have no value to anyone.

Aside from stock option plans, other kinds of executive compensation are also used by some companies. Among the more popular are perquisites such as memberships in private clubs, access to company recreational facilities, and similar considerations. Some organizations also make available to senior executives low- or no-interest loans. These are often given to new executives whom the company is hiring from other companies and serve as an incentive for the individual to leave his or her current job to join a new organization. Kraft Food's Irene Rosenfeld received slightly more than $400,000 in other compensation during 2013 for things such as perks and payment of life insurance.[39]

Criticisms of Executive Compensation   In recent years, executive compensation has come under fire for a variety of reasons. One major reason is that the levels of executive compensation attained by some managers seem simply too large for the average shareholder to understand. It is not uncommon, for instance, for a senior executive of a major corporation to earn total income from his or her job in a given year of well in excess of $1 million. Sometimes the income of CEOs can be substantially more than this. Thus, just as the typical person has difficulty comprehending the astronomical salaries paid to some movie stars and sports stars, so, too, would the average person be aghast at the astronomical salaries paid to some senior executives.

Compounding the problem created by perceptions of executive compensation is the fact that there often seems to be little or no relationship between the performance of the organization and the compensation paid to its senior executives.[40] Certainly, if an organization is performing at an especially high level and its stock price is increasing consistently, then most observers would agree that the senior executives responsible for this growth should be entitled to attractive rewards.[41] However, it is more difficult to understand a case in which executives are paid huge salaries and other forms of rewards when their company is performing at only a marginal level, yet this is fairly common today.

Finally, we should note that the gap between the earnings of the CEO and the earnings of a typical employee is enormous. First of all, the size of the gap has been increasing in the United States. In 1980, the typical CEO earned 42 times the earnings of an ordinary worker; by 1990, this ratio had increased to 85 times the earnings of an ordinary worker; in 2009, the ratio was 263 times the earnings of a typical worker. In Japan, on the other hand, the CEO-to-worker pay ratio is 16 times; in Germany, the ratio is 13 times.[42]

New Approaches to Performance-Based Rewards

Some organizations have started to recognize that they can leverage the value of the incentives that they offer to their employees and to groups in their organization by allowing those individuals and groups to have a say in how rewards are distributed. For example, at the extreme, a company could go so far as to grant salary increase budgets to work groups and then allow the members of those groups themselves to determine how the rewards are going to be allocated among the various members of the group. This strategy would appear to hold considerable promise if everyone understands the performance arrangements that exist in the work group and if everyone is committed to being fair and equitable. Unfortunately, it can also create problems if people in a group feel that rewards are not being distributed fairly.[43]

Organizations are also getting increasingly innovative in their incentive programs. For example, some now offer stock options to all their employees, rather than just top executives. In addition, some firms are looking into ways to purely individualize reward systems. For instance, a firm might offer one employee a paid three-month sabbatical every two years in exchange for a 20 percent reduction in salary. Another employee in the same firm might be offered a 10 percent salary increase in exchange for a 5 percent reduction in company contributions to the person's retirement account. Corning, General Electric, and Microsoft are among the firms closely studying this option.[44]

Regardless of the method used, however, it is also important that managers in an organization effectively communicate what rewards are being distributed and the basis for that distribution. In other words, if incentives are being distributed on the basis of perceived individual contributions to the organization, then members of the organization should be informed of that fact. This will presumably better enable them to understand the basis on which pay increases and other incentives and performance-based rewards have been distributed.

SUMMARY OF LEARNING OUTCOMES AND KEY POINTS

1. Characterize the nature of motivation, including its importance and basic historical perspectives.

   - Motivation is the set of forces that causes people to behave in certain ways.
   - Motivation is an important consideration for managers because it, along with ability and environmental factors, determines individual performance.

2. Identify and describe the major content perspectives on motivation.

   - Content perspectives on motivation are concerned with what factors cause motivation.
   - Popular content theories include Maslow's hierarchy of needs, the ERG theory, and Herzberg's two-factor theory.
   - Other important needs are the needs for achievement, affiliation, and power.

3. Identify and describe the major process perspectives on motivation.

   - Process perspectives on motivation deal with how motivation occurs.

- Expectancy theory suggests that people are motivated to perform if they believe that their effort will result in high performance, that this performance will lead to rewards, and that the positive aspects of the outcomes outweigh the negative aspects.
- Equity theory is based on the premise that people are motivated to achieve and maintain social equity.
- Goal-setting theory assumes people are motivated by goals that are challenging and specific.

4. Describe reinforcement perspectives on motivation.

- The reinforcement perspective focuses on how motivation is maintained.
- Its basic assumption is that behavior that results in rewarding consequences is likely to be repeated, whereas behavior resulting in negative consequences is less likely to be repeated.
- Reinforcement contingencies can be arranged in the form of positive reinforcement, avoidance, punishment, and extinction, and they can be provided on fixed-interval, variable-interval, fixed-ratio, or variable-ratio schedules.

5. Identify and describe popular motivational strategies.

- Managers use a variety of motivational strategies derived from the various theories of motivation.
- Common strategies include empowerment and participation and alternative forms of work arrangements, such as variable work schedules, flexible work schedules, and telecommuting.

6. Describe the role of organizational reward systems in motivation.

- Reward systems also play a key role in motivating employee performance.
- Popular methods include merit reward systems, incentive reward systems, and team and group incentive reward systems.
- Executive compensation is also intended to serve as motivation for senior managers but has currently come under close scrutiny and criticism.

DISCUSSION QUESTIONS

Questions for Review

1. Summarize Maslow's hierarchy of needs and the two-factor theory. In what ways are they similar and in what ways are they different?
2. Compare and contrast content, process, and reinforcement perspectives on motivation.
3. Using equity theory as a framework, explain how a person can experience inequity because he or she is paid too much. What are the potential outcomes of this situation?
4. Explain how goal-setting theory works. How is goal setting different from merely asking a worker to "do your best"?
5. Describe some new forms of working arrangements. How do these alternative arrangements increase motivation?

Questions for Analysis

1. Choose one theory from the content perspectives and one from the process perspectives. Describe actions that a manager might take to increase worker motivation under each of the theories. What differences do you see between the theories in terms of their implications for managers?
2. Can factors from both the content and the process perspectives be acting on a worker at the same time? Explain why or why not. Whether you answered yes or no to the previous question, explain the implications for managers.
3. How do rewards increase motivation? What would happen if an organization gave too few rewards? What would happen if it gave too many?
4. Think about the worst job you have held. What approach to motivation was used in that organization? Now think about the best job you have held. What approach to motivation was used there? Can you base any conclusions on this limited information? If so, what are they?
5. Consider a class you have taken. Using just that one class, offer examples of times when the professor used positive reinforcement, avoidance, punishment, and extinction to manage students' behavior.

BUILDING EFFECTIVE INTERPERSONAL AND COMMUNICATION SKILLS

Exercise Overview

Interpersonal skills refer to the ability to communicate with, understand, and motivate individuals and groups, and *communication skills* refer to the ability to send and receive information effectively. This exercise is designed to demonstrate the essential roles played in employee motivation by an understanding of what motivates people and an ability to communicate that understanding.

Exercise Background

One implication of reinforcement theory is that both positive reinforcement (reward) and punishment can be effective in altering employee behavior. The use of punishment, however, may result in resentment on the employee's part, and over the long term, that resentment can diminish the effectiveness of punishment. By and large, positive reinforcement is more effective over time.

Exercise Task

Your instructor will ask for volunteers to perform a demonstration in front of the class. Consider volunteering, but if you don't want to participate, observe the behavior of the volunteers closely. When the demonstration is over, respond to the following questions:

1. Based on what you saw, which is more effective—positive reinforcement or punishment?
2. How did positive reinforcement and punishment affect the "employee" in the demonstration? How did it affect the "boss"?
3. What, in your opinion, are the likely long-term consequences of positive reinforcement and punishment?

BUILDING EFFECTIVE DECISION-MAKING SKILLS

Exercise Overview

Decision-making skills refer to the ability to recognize and define problems and opportunities correctly and then to select an appropriate course of action for solving problems or capitalizing on opportunities. This exercise allows you to build your decision-making skills while applying goal-setting theory to the task of planning your career.

Exercise Background

Lee Iacocca started his career at Ford in 1946 in an entry-level engineering job. By 1960, he was a vice president and in charge of the group that designed the Mustang, and ten years later, he was a president of the firm. After being fired from Ford in 1978, he then became a president at Chrysler and eventually rose to the CEO spot, a job he held until he retired in 1992. What's really remarkable about Iacocca's career arc—at least the upward trajectory—is the fact that he apparently had it all planned out, even before he finished college.

The story goes that, while he was still an undergraduate, Iacocca wrote out a list of all the positions that he'd like to hold during his career. Number one was "engineer at an automaker," followed by all the career steps that he planned to take until he was a CEO. He also included a timetable for his climb up the corporate ladder. Then he put his list on a three-by-five-inch card that he folded and stowed in his wallet, and we're told that every time he took out that card and looked at it, he gained fresh confidence and drive. He apparently reached the top several years ahead of schedule, but otherwise he followed his career path and timetable faithfully.

As you can see, Iacocca used goal-setting theory to motivate himself, and there's no reason you can't do the same.

Exercise Task

1. Consider the position that you'd like to hold at the peak of your career. It may be CEO, owner of a chain of clothing stores, partner in a law or accounting firm, or president of a university. Then again, it may be something less lofty. Whatever it is, write it down.
2. Now describe a career path that will lead you toward that goal. It may help to work "backward"—that is, start with your final position and work backward in time to some entry-level job. If you aren't sure about the career path that will lead to your ultimate goal, do some research. Talk to

someone in your selected career field, ask an instructor who teaches in it, or go online. The website of the American Institute of Certified Public Accountants, for example, has a section on Career Resources, which includes information about career paths and position descriptions for accounting.

3. Write down each step in your path on a card or a sheet of paper.
4. If, like Lee Iacocca, you were to carry this piece of paper with you and refer to it often as you pursued your career goals, do you think it would help you achieve them? Why or why not?

SKILLS SELF-ASSESSMENT INSTRUMENT

Assessing Your Needs

Introduction: Needs are one factor that influences motivation. The following assessment surveys your judgments about some of your personal needs that might be partially shaping your motivation.

Instructions: Judge how descriptively accurate each of the following statements is about you. You may find making a decision difficult in some cases, but you should force yourself to make a choice. Record your answers next to each statement according to the following scale:

Rating Scale

5 Very descriptive of me
4 Fairly descriptive of me
3 Somewhat descriptive of me
2 Not very descriptive of me
1 Not descriptive of me at all

_____ 1. I aspire to accomplish difficult tasks and maintain high standards and am willing to work toward distant goals.

_____ 2. I enjoy being with friends and people in general and accept people readily.

_____ 3. I am easily annoyed and am sometimes willing to hurt people to get my way.

_____ 4. I try to break away from restraints or restrictions of any kind.

_____ 5. I want to be the center of attention and enjoy having an audience.

_____ 6. I speak freely and tend to act on the spur of the moment.

_____ 7. I assist others whenever possible, giving sympathy and comfort to those in need.

_____ 8. I believe in the saying that "there is a place for everything and everything should be in its place." I dislike clutter.

_____ 9. I express my opinions forcefully, enjoy the role of leader, and try to control my environment as much as I can.

_____ 10. I want to understand many areas of knowledge and value synthesizing ideas and generalization.

EXPERIENTIAL EXERCISE

Motivation at Bluefield

Bob works for a fast-growing manufacturer of cosmetics at their oldest plant in Bluefield, West Virginia. Bob has an MBA from State University and began his career at Bluefield in the Human Resource Department. He got his first big chance when the company, facing increased problems with the local minority community, put Bob in charge of a new affirmative action program. Bob is proud of his success in that position. His supervisors were also impressed and promoted him to the position of Manager of Machine Operations. He managed a workforce of 74 employees through seven supervisors. He's held this job for only one year.

There is a new program to revitalize operations at Bluefield. Bob, because of his earlier success, has been assigned the task of developing a motivation plan for his seven subordinate supervisors. Bob needs to review the personnel files and try to identify the needs or motivators for each supervisor. To provide a working framework for the study, Bob decides to use both Maslow's hierarchy of needs and Herzberg's two-factor theory, as shown on the Need/Motivation Worksheet.

Bob divides the worksheet into three sections: (1) Maslow's Needs, (2) Motivation Factors, and (3) Hygiene Factors. In each category, he plans to rank the appropriate items for each supervisor, using a 1 for the top ranking, a 2 for the second ranking, and so on.

Instructions:

1. Read the following personnel files. In addition to other data, each profile contains a supervisor's Performance Measure (PM). This is a score assigned by a computer-based productivity program developed by Industrial Engineering. The program uses a variety of cost and output figures to calculate a PM for each supervisor on a scale ranging from 0 (representing very poor performance) to 100 (nearly perfect performance).

2. Then, as a small group, use the following Need/Motivation Worksheet to rank the relative importance of each of the motivators for each supervisor. Rank within groups—1 to 5 for Maslow's Needs, then 1 to 5 for Motivation Factors, and then 1 to 6 for Hygiene Factors.

3. Present your group findings to the class and discuss.

Bluefield Plant Supervisor Profiles

JOHN MILLER is the senior supervisor with 21 years of seniority. He is 60 years old and has only a sixth-grade education. His most recent PM score is 50, which is lower than it used to be. John's past appraisals suggest that he has done an average job in the past, and Bob thinks his performance is still average and is sorry to see John's performance declining. His peers are convinced that John is too old to cut the mustard. Bob thinks that John has the easiest job in the group. John is a widower who spends a lot of time at his cabin by the lake. His current salary is $45,000.

MOHAMMAD NAJEED is 52 with 16 years with the firm. His PM is 70 and his salary is $38,000. Mohammad is a high-school graduate, and his wife is quite wealthy. Bob believes that Mohammad has the best overall experience in the group and is a very capable supervisor, although his peers rank him average, the same as his past evaluations. Mohammad supervises a group that has about average responsibilities.

TANIKA FORESTER is 36 with 10 years of seniority. She has a BS in Management, a PM of 80, and a salary of $31,000. Bob feels she has one of the easier jobs and is doing only a so-so job. He is surprised to find that her earlier appraisals have been very good, an evaluation shared by her peers. Tanika's husband was killed in a car accident, and she has three dependent children.

TOM WILSON is 44 with 1 year with the company. Tom has a high-school diploma, a PM of 50, and a salary of $28,000. Tom has the hardest group to supervise, but his earlier appraisals have only been average, an opinion shared by Tom's peers. Bob agrees that Tom's performance is average and is concerned that it might get worse as Tom seems to be having too many personal problems lately.

SIDNEY BENTON is 35 and has 8 years of seniority, a PM of 80, and a salary of $26,000. Sidney has a BS in Industrial Technology and is enrolled in State's night MBA program. Sidney has a difficult job, requiring specialized skills, and he would be very hard to replace. Bob believes Sidney to be a top supervisor, an opinion shared by his peers. But Bob is troubled by past appraisals that vary from outstanding to poor.

LI TRAN is 32 with 5 years at the plant, a PM of only 30, and a salary of $22,000. She is a high-school dropout who quit school to have her first child. She is a single parent with four children and works very hard to support them. Li represents one of the affirmative action promotions that Bob arranged when he was the Affirmative Action Officer, and he is disappointed to find that her past and present appraisals are quite poor. Although her present job is perceived to require average skill, her peers consider her to be an incompetent troublemaker who constantly complains about the need for more affirmative action efforts at the plant.

LUIS FUENTES is 26, has only 2 years with the company, a PM of only 20, and a salary of $19,000. He dropped out of school to take care of his sick mother and two younger sisters. Bob hired Luis as part of the Affirmative Action Program. Luis's first appraisal was low, but Bob believes that was because he was in a job requiring too much experience. So Bob moved him to a job with more average demands. Bob thinks that Luis is doing a bit better in the new job and, in time, will be a good supervisor. Peer evaluations are somewhat mixed but above average.

Need/Motivation Worksheet

(In each category, rank the appropriate items for each supervisor. Top rank = 1, second rank = 2, and so forth.)

Need/Factor	John Miller	Mohammed Najeed	Tanika Forester	Tom Wilson	Sidney Benton	Li Tran	Luis Fuentes
Maslow's Needs							
Physiological							
Security							
Belongingness							
Esteem							
Self-Actualization							
Motivation Factors							
Achievement							
Recognition							
Work Itself							
Responsibility							
Advancement/ Growth							
Hygiene Factors							
Supervision							
Working conditions							
Interpersonal							
Pay							
Security							
Policy and Administration							

Adapted from Morable, *Exercises in Management*, to accompany Griffin, *Management*, 8th edition.

MANAGEMENT AT WORK

The Law of Diminishing Motivation

The enrollment of women in U.S. law schools took off after 1970, and women have been graduating at the same rate as men for more than 25 years. Today, however, the census of American law firms still counts relatively few women *partners*—typically, the veteran lawyers who are joint owners and directors. Currently, for example, 32.4 percent of all lawyers are women, yet only 19.2 percent of law firm partners are women. Most female lawyers are *associates*—paid employees with the prospect of becoming partners. Moreover, the further up the law-firm ladder you look, the greater the disparity. According to the National Association of Women Lawyers, 92 percent of all managing partners (partners who run the business end of a firm) are men; men occupy 85 percent of the seats on the governing committees that control a firm's policies, and they hold 84 percent of all equity partnerships (which come with ownership and profit sharing). At this rate, women will achieve parity with their male colleagues in approximately 2088.

So what happens between the time women get job offers and the time firms hand out partnerships and promotions? Bettina B. Plevan, an employment law specialist and partner in the Manhattan firm of Proskauer Rose, believes that, somewhere along the way, female lawyers lose the kind of motivation necessary to get ahead in a law office. "You have a given population of people," she observes, "who were significantly motivated to go through law school with a certain career goal in mind. What de-motivates them," she asks, "to want to continue working in the law?"

The problem, says Karen M. Lockwood, a partner in the Washington, DC, firm Howrey, is neither discrimination nor lack of opportunity. "Law firms," she says, "are way beyond discrimination. Problems with advancement and retention are grounded in biases, not discrimination." In part, these biases issue from institutional inertia. Lauren Stiller Rikleen, a partner in the Worcester, Massachusetts, firm of Bowditch & Dewey, points out that most law firms are "running on an institutional model that's about 200 years old." Most of them, she adds, "do a horrible job of managing their personnel, in terms of training them and communicating with them." Such problems, of course, affect men as well as women, but because of lingering preconceptions about women's attitudes, values, and goals, women bear the brunt of the workplace burden. In practical terms, they face less adequate mentoring, poorer networking opportunities, lower-grade case assignments, and unequal access to positions of committee control.

To all of these barriers to success, Lockwood adds the effect of what she calls the "maternal wall": Male partners, she says, assume that women who return to the firm after having children will be less willing to work hard and less capable of dedicating themselves to their jobs. As a result, men get the choice assignments and senior positions. Jane DiRenzo Pigott, a onetime law-firm partner who now owns a consultancy firm, agrees but thinks the issues run deeper than maternity leave. "People explain it simply as the fact that women have children," she explains,

but so many other factors play into it. Women self-promote in a different way than men, and because women don't get their success acknowledged in the same way as men who more aggressively self-promote, it creates a high level of professional dissatisfaction for women. Saying these two words "I want" is not something women are used to doing. They're not saying, "I want the top bonus" or "I want that position." … [W]omen need to learn how to be comfortable saying "I want" and how to say it effectively.

The fact remains that, according to a study of "Women in Law" conducted by Catalyst, a New York research firm, one in eight female lawyers work only part-time, compared to just one in fifty males. Why? According to Plevan, most female attorneys would prefer to work and raise children at the same time but find that they can't do both effectively. "I organized my personal life so I was able to move toward my goals," she says, but admits that it helped to have a gainfully employed spouse (also a lawyer), dual incomes sufficient to hire household help, and nearby relatives to pick up the slack in home–life responsibilities. In most cases, of course, although dual incomes are an advantage to a household, it's difficult for either spouse to devote time to child rearing when they're both working. The Catalyst study shows that 44 percent of male lawyers have spouses who are employed full-time—and are thus unavailable for such household duties as attending to children. Among women, nearly twice as many—84 percent—have spouses with full-time jobs.

Like firms in many other industries, law firms have experimented with such options as flexible scheduling and parental leave. More and more, however, they report that such measures have not been as effective as they'd hoped. Says Edith R. Matthai, founder with her husband of the Los Angeles firm Robie & Matthai, "We're very accommodating with leaves and flexible schedules, and even with that we still lose women…. [The] pressures on women from spouses, family, peers, schools, and others is huge," she adds. The situation has improved over the last 30 years, but "we have a long way to go…. I think the real solution is a reassessment of the role that women play in the family. One thing we need is a sense of shared responsibilities for the household and, most importantly, shared responsibilities for taking care of the kids."

Case Questions

1. Among the various approaches to enhancing workplace satisfaction and productivity discussed in the chapter, which ones might you take under the circumstances described in the case? Why are

some of the other approaches less likely to be effective (or even relevant)?

2. You're the managing partner in a law firm with 55 male associates and 45 female associates, and you agree with the argument that women lawyers need to "self-promote" more effectively. Which approach to motivation would you apply in order to encourage female associates in your firm to "self-promote" more actively? Explain your choice of approach.

3. What about your own values when it comes to balancing your home and work life? Assume that you're about to graduate from law school and about to marry someone who's also about to graduate from law school. When you sit down with your future husband/wife to discuss your plans for married life ever after, what do you want to do about raising a family? What kind of adjustments will you propose if it turns out that your intended's ideas on the matter are more or less the opposite of your own? Be sure

to consider such factors as the debt you've racked up while in law school and the standard of living that you'd like to achieve.

Case References

Patricia Gillette, "Lack of Self-Promotion Hurts Women in Large Firms," *Law.com*, http://amlaw daily.typepad.com, accessed on December 7, 2013; Lizz O'Donnell, "Women in Law Firms: Stuck in the Middle," *The Glass Hammer*, www.theglas shammer.com, accessed on December 7, 2013; Timothy L. O'Brien, "Why Do So Few Women Reach the Top of Big Law Firms?" *New York Times*, www.nytimes.com, accessed on December 7, 2013; Catalyst, "Women in Law," www.catalyst.org, accessed on December 7, 2013; and Lynne Marek, "Women Lawyers Find Their Own Paths as Law Firms Struggle to Keep Them," *Law.com*, www.law .com, accessed on December 7, 2013.

You Make the Call

Motivating the Whole Person

1. If you worked at WFM, how would you vote when the company's current health-care plan came up for an employee vote? Explain your reasoning.

2. To underscore WFM's relatively high prices, some sceptics point out that, despite discounts of 15 percent or more, many of the firm's employees can't afford to shop where they work. If you were a team member at WFM, how would this fact affect your motivation?

3. John Mackey now takes $1 a year in pay. In the last year in which he received a regular paycheck as CEO,

his pay package totalled $436,000—about 14 times the average WFM worker's salary of $32,000 and relatively low for the industry. In the same year, however, he exercised nearly $2 million in stock options, bringing his total earnings to about $2.5 million. The company acknowledges that Mackey also holds more money invested stock options but prefers to publicize its worker-friendly pay cap. If you were a team member at WFM, would this fact affect your motivation? How about your attitude toward your job?

ENDNOTES

[1] John Stossel et al., "Health Savings Accounts: Putting Patients in Control," *ABC News*, http://abcnews.go.com, accessed on December 7, 2013; John Mackey, "The Whole Foods Alternative to ObamaCare," *Wall Street Journal,* August 11, 2009, http:// online.wsj.com, accessed on December 7, 2013; Judy Dugan, "Whole Foods' Crummy Insurance: What John Mackey Means by 'Choice,'" *Consumer Watchdog*, www.consumerwatchdog.org, accessed on December 7, 2013; Emily Friedman, "Health Care Stirs Up Whole Foods CEO John Mackey, Customers Boycott Organic Grocery Store," *ABC News*, http://abcnews.go.com, accessed on December 7, 2013; Nick Paumgarten, "Food

Fighter," *The New Yorker*, www.newyorker.com, accessed on December 7, 2013; and "Whole Foods CEO John Mackey Stepping Down as Chairman," *Huffington Post*, www.huffington post.com, accessed on December 7, 2013.

[2] Richard M. Steers, Gregory A. Bigley, and Lyman W. Porter, *Motivation and Leadership at Work*, 7th ed. (New York: McGraw-Hill, 2002). See also Edwin Locke and Gary Lartham, "What Should We Do About Motivation Theory? Six Recommendations for the Twenty-First Century," *Academy of Management Review*, 2004, Vol. 29, No. 3, pp. 388–403; and Robert Lord,

James Diefendorff, Aaron Schmidt, and Rosalie Hall, "Self-Regulation at Work," in Susan Fiske, Daniel Schacter, and Robert Sternberg (eds.), *Annual Review of Psychology*, Vol. 61 (Palo Alto, CA: Annual Reviews, 2010), pp. 543–568.

3   See Nigel Nicholson, "How to Motivate Your Problem People," *Harvard Business Review*, January 2003, pp. 57–67. See also James M. Diefendorff and Megan M. Chandler, "Motivating Employees," in Sheldon Zedeck (ed.), *Handbook of Industrial and Organizational Psychology*, Vol. 3: *Maintaining, Expanding, and Contracting the Organization* (Washington, DC: American Psychological Association, 2010), pp. 635–655.

4   See Jeffrey Pfeffer, *The Human Equation* (Cambridge, MA: Harvard Business School Press, 1998). See also Nitin Nohria, Boris Groysberg, and Linda-Eling Lee, "Employee Motivation—a Powerful New Model," *Harvard Business Review*, July–August 2008, pp. 78–89; and Adrienne Fox, "Raising Engagement," *HR Magazine*, May 2010, pp. 35–40.

5   For a recent discussion of these questions, see Teresa Amabile and Steven Kramer, "What Really Motivates Workers," *Harvard Business Review*, January–February 2010, pp. 44–45.

6   Abraham H. Maslow, "A Theory of Human Motivation," *Psychological Review*, 1943, Vol. 50, pp. 370–396; and Abraham H. Maslow, *Motivation and Personality* (New York: Harper & Row, 1954). Maslow's most recent work is Abraham H. Maslow and Richard Lowry, *Toward a Psychology of Being* (New York: Wiley, 1999).

7   For a review, see Craig Pinder, *Work Motivation in Organizational Behavior*, 2nd ed. (Upper Saddle River, NJ: Prentice Hall, 2008).

8   Frederick Herzberg, Bernard Mausner, and Barbara Snyderman, *The Motivation to Work* (New York: Wiley, 1959); and Frederick Herzberg, "One More Time: How Do You Motivate Employees?" *Harvard Business Review*, January–February 1987, pp. 109–120 (reprinted in *Harvard Business Review*, January 2003, pp. 87–98).

9   Robert J. House and Lawrence A. Wigdor, "Herzberg's Dual-Factor Theory of Job Satisfaction and Motivation: A Review of the Evidenceanda Criticism," *Personnel Psychology*, Winter 1967, Vol. 20, No. 4, pp. 369–389; and Victor H. Vroom, *Work and Motivation* (New York: Wiley, 1964). See also Pinder, *Work Motivation in Organizational Behavior*.

10   David C. McClelland, *The Achieving Society* (Princeton, NJ: Van Nostrand, 1961); and David C. McClelland, *Power: The Inner Experience* (New York: Irvington, 1975).

11   "Best Friends Good for Business," *USA Today*, December 1, 2004, pp. 1B, 2B.

12   David McClelland and David H. Burnham, "Power Is the Great Motivator," *Harvard Business Review*, March–April 1976, pp. 100–110 (reprinted in *Harvard Business Review*, January 2003, pp. 117–127).

13   "HP Chief Executive Hurd Resigns after Sexual Harrassment Probe," *Bloomberg Businessweek*, August 7, 2010.

14   Victor H. Vroom, *Work and Motivation* (New York: Wiley, 1964).

15   "Starbucks' Secret Weapon," *Fortune*, September 29, 1997, p. 268.

16   Lyman W. Porter and Edward E. Lawler III, *Managerial Attitudes and Performance* (Homewood, IL: Dorsey, 1968).

17   J. Stacy Adams, "Towards an Understanding of Inequity," *Journal of Abnormal and Social Psychology*, November 1963, Vol. 67, No. 5, pp. 422–436.

18   "The Best vs. the Rest," *Wall Street Journal*, January 30, 2006, pp. B1, B3.

19   Mark C. Bolino and William H. Turnley, "Old Faces, New Places: Equity Theory in Cross-Cultural Contexts," *Journal of Organizational Behavior*, 2008, Vol. 29, pp. 29–50.

20   See Edwin A. Locke, "Toward a Theory of Task Performance and Incentives," *Organizational Behavior and Human Performance*, 1968, Vol. 3, pp. 157–189.

21   Gary P. Latham and J. J. Baldes, "The Practical Significance of Locke's Theory of Goal Setting," *Journal of Applied Psychology*, 1975, Vol. 60, pp. 187–191.

22   For a recent extension of goal-setting theory, see Yitzhak Fried and Linda Haynes Slowik, "Enriching Goal-Setting Theory with Time: An Integrated Approach," *Academy of Management Review*, 2004, Vol. 29, No. 3, pp. 404–422.

23   B. F. Skinner, *Beyond Freedom and Dignity* (New York: Knopf, 1971). See also Raymond A. Noe, Michael J. Tews, and Alison McConnell Dachner, "Learner Engagement: A New Perspective for Enhancing Our Understanding of Learner Motivation and Workplace Learning," in James P. Walsh and Arthur P. Brief (eds.), *The Academy of Management Annals 2010* (Philadelphia: Taylor and Francis, 2010), pp. 279–316.

24   Fred Luthans and Robert Kreitner, *Organizational Behavior Modification and Beyond: An Operant and Social Learning Approach* (Glenview, IL: Scott, Foresman, 1985).

25   Luthans and Kreitner, *Organizational Behavior Modification and Beyond*; and W. Clay Hamner and Ellen P. Hamner, "Behavior Modification on the Bottom Line," *Organizational Dynamics*, Spring 1976, pp. 2–21.

26   "At Emery Air Freight: Positive Reinforcement Boosts Performance," *Organizational Dynamics*, Winter 1973, pp. 41–50; and, for a recent update, see Alexander D. Stajkovic and Fred Luthans, "A Meta-Analysis of the Effects of Organizational Behavior Modification on Task Performance, 1975–95," *Academy of Management Journal*, 1997, Vol. 40, No. 5, pp. 1122–1149.

27   David J. Glew, Anne M. O'Leary-Kelly, Ricky W. Griffin, and David D. Van Fleet, "Participation in Organizations: A Preview of the Issues and Proposed Framework for Future Analysis," *Journal of Management*, 1995, Vol. 21, No. 3, pp. 395–421.

28   Baxter W. Graham, "The Business Argument for Flexibility," *HR Magazine*, May 1996, pp. 104–110.

29   A. R. Cohen and H. Gadon, *Alternative Work Schedules: Integrating Individual and Organizational Needs* (Reading, MA: Addison Wesley, 1978). See also Ellen Ernst Kossek and Jesse S. Michel, "Flexible Work Schedules," in Sheldon Zedeck (ed.), *Handbook of Industrial and Organizational Psychology*, Vol. 1: *Building and Developing the Organization* (Washington, DC: American Psychological Association, 2010), pp. 535–572.

30   "How Telecommuting Lets Workers Mobilize for Sustainability," *GreenBiz.com*, February 17, 2011; and "Study: Telecommuting Can Save American Households $1.7 Billion per Year," *SmartPlanet.com*, March 16, 2011.

31   Daniel Wren, *The Evolution of Management Theory*, 4th ed. (New York: Wiley, 1994).

32 C. Wiley, "Incentive Plan Pushes Production," *Personnel Journal*, August 1993, p. 91.

33 "When Money Isn't Enough," *Forbes*, November 18, 1996, pp. 164–169.

34 Jacquelyn DeMatteo, Lillian Eby, and Eric Sundstrom, "Team-Based Rewards: Current Empirical Evidence and Directions for Future Research," in L. L. Cummings and Barry Staw (eds.), *Research in Organizational Behavior*, Vol. 20 (Greenwich, CT: JAI, 1998), pp. 141–183. See also Barry Gerhart, Sara L. Rynes, and Ingrid Smithey Fulmer, "Pay and Performance: Individuals, Groups, and Executives," in James P. Walsh and Arthur P. Brief (eds.), *The Academy of Management Annals 2009* (Philadelphia: Taylor and Francis, 2009), pp. 251–316; and Joseph J. Martocchio, "Strategic Reward and Compensation Plans," in Sheldon Zedeck (ed.), *Handbook of Industrial and Organizational Psychology*, Vol. 1: *Building and Developing the Organization* (Washington, DC: American Psychological Association, 2010), pp. 343–372.

35 Theresa M. Welbourne and Luis R. Gomez-Mejia, "Gainsharing: A Critical Review and a Future Research Agenda," *Journal of Management*, 1995, Vol. 21, No. 3, pp. 559–609.

36 Associated Press, "Kraft Gave CEO Raise in 2013," www.cnn.com, accessed on March 30, 2014.

37 Associated Press, "Kraft Gave CEO Raise in 2013."

38 Associated Press, "Kraft Gave CEO Raise in 2013."

39 Associated Press, "Kraft Gave CEO Raise in 2013."

40 Harry Barkema and Luis Gomez-Mejia, "Managerial Compensation and Firm Performance: A General Research Framework," *Academy of Management Journal*, 1998, Vol. 41, No. 2, pp. 135–145.

41 Rajiv D. Banker, Seok-Young Lee, Gordon Potter, and Dhinu Srinivasan, "Contextual Analysis of Performance Impacts of Outcome-Based Incentive Compensation," *Academy of Management Journal*, 1996, Vol. 39, No. 4, pp. 920–948.

42 "Average Japanese CEO Earns One-Sixth as Much as American CEOs," thinkprogress.org, July 8, 2010.

43 Steve Kerr, "The Best-Laid Incentive Plans," *Harvard Business Review*, January 2003, pp. 27–40.

44 "Now It's Getting Personal," *Businessweek*, December 16, 2002, pp. 90–92.

CHAPTER 11

Leadership and Influence Processes

Sergii Tsololo/Photos.com

Learning Outcomes

After studying this chapter, you should be able to:

1 Describe the nature of leadership and relate leadership to management.

2 Discuss and evaluate the two generic approaches to leadership.

3 Identify and describe the major situational approaches to leadership.

4 Identify and describe three related approaches to leadership.

5 Describe three emerging approaches to leadership.

6 Discuss political behavior in organizations and how it can be managed.

Management in Action

When to Stand on Your Head and Other Tips from the Top

"[Leadership is] a game of pinball, and you're the ball."

—U.S. Senator John McCain

It isn't easy leading a U.S. business these days. Leaving aside the global recession, the passion for "lean-and-mean" operations means that there are fewer workers to do more work. Globalization means keeping abreast of cross-cultural differences. Knowledge industries present unique leadership challenges requiring better communication skills and greater flexibility. Advances in technology have opened unprecedented channels of communication. Now, more than ever, leaders must be able to do just about everything and more of it. As U.S. Senator and former presidential candidate John McCain puts it, "[Leadership is] a game of pinball, and you're the ball." Fortunately, a few of corporate America's veteran leaders have some tips for those who still want to follow their increasingly treacherous path.

First of all, if you think you're being overworked—if your hours are too long and your schedule is too demanding—odds are, you're right: Most people—including executives—*are* overworked. And in some industries, they're *particularly* overworked. Airlines in the United States, for example, now service 100 million more passengers annually than they did just five years ago—with 70,000 fewer workers. "I used to manage my time," quips one airline executive. "Now I manage my energy." In fact, many high-ranking managers have realized

Carlos Ghosn is CEO of Nissan/Renault. He uses a variety of strategies to keep his life in balance while leading a major international automobile company.

ZUMA Press, Inc./Alamy

that energy is a key factor in their ability to complete tasks on tough schedules. Most top corporate leaders work 80 to 100 hours a week, and a lot of them have found that regimens that allow them to refuel and refresh make it possible for them to keep up the pace.

Carlos Ghosn, who's currently president of Renault *and* CEO of Nissan, believes in regular respites from his work-week routine. "I don't bring my work home. I play with my four children and spend time with my family on weekends," says Ghosn. "I come up with good ideas as a result of becoming stronger after being recharged." Yahoo! CEO Marissa Mayer admits that "I can get by on four to six hours of sleep," but she also takes a weeklong vacation three times a year. Global HR consultant Robert Freedman devotes two minutes every morning to doodling on napkins. Not only does it give him a chance to meditate, but he's also thinking about publishing both his doodles and his meditations in a coffee-table book.

Many leaders report that playing racquetball, running marathons, practicing yoga, or just getting regular exercise helps them to recover from overwork. Hank Greenberg, who's currently CEO of the financial-services firm C. V. Starr & Co., plays tennis for most of the year and skis in the winter months. "I'm addicted to exercise," he says, because it "unwinds me." Max Levchin, founder of Slide, which makes widgets for social-networking sites, prefers "80 or 90 hard miles on a road bike … starting early on Saturday mornings." Eighty-eight-year-old Viacom CEO Sumner Redstone rises at 5 a.m. and hits both the exercise bike and treadmill before the markets open. (Redstone also recommends "lots of fish and plenty of antioxidants.") Finally, Strauss Zelnick, CEO and chairman of Take-Two Interactive Software, is *really* serious about exercise: he takes a weekly exercise class at a gym, works with a personal trainer once or twice a week, cycles with friends for an hour three times a week, and lifts weights two or three times a week.

Effective leaders also take control of information flow—which means managing it, not reducing the flow until it's as close to a trickle as they can get it. Like most executives, for example, Mayer can't get by without multiple sources of information: "I always have my laptop with me," she reports, and "I adore my cell phone." Starbucks CEO Howard Schultz receives a morning voicemail summarizing the previous day's sales results and reads three newspapers a day. Mayer watches the news all day, and Bill Gross, a securities portfolio manager, keeps on eye on six monitors displaying real-time investment data.

On the other hand, Gross stands on his head to force himself to take a break from communicating. When he's upright again, he tries to find time to concentrate. "Eliminating the noise," he says, "is critical.... I only pick up the phone three or four times a day.... I don't want to be connected—I want to be disconnected." Ghosn, whose schedule requires weekly intercontinental travel, uses bilingual assistants to screen and translate information—one assistant for information from Europe (Renault's location), one for information from Japan (Nissan's location), and one for information from the United States (where Ghosn often must be when he doesn't have to be in Europe or Japan). Clothing designer Vera Wang also uses an assistant to filter information. "The barrage of calls is so enormous," she says, "that if I just answered calls I'd do nothing else.... If I were to go near e-mail, there'd be even more obligations, and I'd be in [a mental hospital] with a white jacket on."

It is no surprise that Microsoft founder Bill Gates integrates the role of his assistant into a high-tech information-organizing system. He uses three screens synchronized to form a single desktop. His e-mails are displayed on one, his browser is open in another, and whatever he is working on is on the third. As he notes, "This setup gives me the ability to glance and see what new has come in while I'm working on something and to bring up a link that's related to an e-mail and look at it while the e-mail is still in front of me." Like most managers, Gates says that his biggest challenges relate to managing the flow of information that directly affects him.[1]

This chapter examines people like Bill Gates, Carlos Ghosn, and Strauss Zelnick to find out not only how they manage their physical and mental health but also how they focus on the tasks of leadership and how they see its role in management. We characterize the nature of leadership and trace through the three major approaches to studying leadership—traits, behaviors, and situations. After examining other perspectives on leadership, we conclude by describing another approach to influencing others—political behavior in organizations.

THE NATURE OF LEADERSHIP

In Chapter 10, we described various models and perspectives on employee motivation. From the manager's standpoint, trying to motivate people is an attempt to influence their behavior. In many ways, leadership, too, is an attempt to influence the behavior of others. In this section, we first define leadership, then differentiate it from management, and conclude by relating it to power.

The Meaning of Leadership

leadership
As a process, the use of noncoercive influence to shape the group's or organization's goals, motivate behavior toward the achievement of those goals, and help define group or organizational culture; as a property, the set of characteristics attributed to individuals who are perceived to be leaders

Leadership is both a process and a property.[2] As a process—focusing on what leaders actually do—leadership is the use of noncoercive influence to shape the group's or organization's goals, motivate behavior toward the achievement of those goals, and help define group or organizational culture.[3] As a property, leadership is the set of characteristics attributed to individuals who are perceived to be leaders. Thus, **leaders** are (1) people who can influence the behaviors of others without having to rely on force, or (2) people whom others accept as leaders.

Leadership and Management

leaders
People who can influence the behaviors of others without having to rely on force; those accepted by others as leaders

From these definitions, it should be clear that leadership and management are related, but they are not the same. A person can be a manager, a leader, both, or neither.[4] Some of the basic distinctions between the two are summarized by John Kotter in Table 11.1. In the first column of the table are four elements that differentiate leadership from management. The other two columns show how each element differs when considered from a management and from a leadership point of view. For example, when executing plans, managers focus on monitoring results, comparing them with goals, and correcting deviations. In contrast, the leader focuses on energizing people to overcome bureaucratic hurdles to reach goals.

Organizations need both management and leadership if they are to be effective. Leadership is necessary to create change, and management is necessary to achieve orderly results. Management in conjunction with leadership can produce orderly change, and leadership in conjunction with management can keep the organization properly aligned with its environment. Indeed, perhaps part of the reason executive compensation has soared in recent years is the belief that management and leadership skills reflect a critical but rare combination that can lead to organizational success.

Leadership and Power

power
The ability to affect the behavior of others

To fully understand leadership, it is necessary to understand **power**—the ability to affect the behavior of others. One can have power without actually using it. For example, a football coach has the power to bench a player who is not performing up to par. The coach seldom has to use this power because players recognize that the power exists and work hard to keep their starting positions. Managers and leaders often have to actually use power but should do so only in ways that are ethical and appropriate. In organizational settings, there are usually five kinds of power: legitimate, reward, coercive, referent, and expert power.[5]

Management and leadership are related, but distinct, constructs. Managers and leaders differ in how they create an agenda, develop a rationale for achieving the agenda, and execute plans, and in the types of outcomes they achieve.

legitimate power
Power granted through the organizational hierarchy; the power defined by the organization to be accorded to people occupying a particular position

Legitimate Power   **Legitimate power** is power granted through the organizational hierarchy; it is the power defined by the organization to be accorded to people occupying a particular position. A manager can assign tasks to a subordinate, and a subordinate who refuses to do them can be reprimanded or even fired. Such outcomes stem from the manager's legitimate power as defined and vested in him or her by the organization. Legitimate power, then, is authority. All managers have legitimate power over their subordinates. The mere possession of legitimate power, however, does not by itself make someone a leader. Some subordinates follow only orders that are strictly within the letter of organizational rules and policies. If asked to do something not in their job descriptions, they refuse or do a poor job. The manager of such employees is exercising authority but not leadership.

Table 11.1	Distinctions Between Management and Leadership	
Activity	**Management**	**Leadership**
Creating an agenda	*Planning and budgeting*: Establishing detailed steps and timetables for achieving needed results and allocating the resources necessary to make those needed results happen	*Establishing direction*: Developing a vision of the future, often the distant future, and strategies for producing the changes needed to achieve that vision
Developing a human network for achieving the agenda	*Organizing and staffing*: Establishing some structure for accomplishing plan requirements, staffing that structure with individuals, delegating responsibility and authority for carrying out the plan, providing policies and procedures to help guide people, and creating methods or systems to monitor implementation	*Aligning people*: Communicating the direction by words and deeds to everyone whose cooperation may be needed to influence the creation of teams and coalitions that understand the visions and strategies and accept their validity
Executing plans	*Controlling and problem solving*: Monitoring results versus planning in some detail, identifying deviations, and then planning and organizing to solve these problems	*Motivating and inspiring*: Energizing people to overcome major political, bureaucratic, and resource barriers by satisfying very basic, but often unfulfilled, human needs
Outcomes	Produces a degree of predictability and order and has the potential to produce consistently major results expected by various stakeholders (for example, for customers, always being on time; or, for stockholders, being on budget)	Produces change, often to a dramatic degree, and has the potential to produce extremely useful change (for example, new products that customers want, or new approaches to labor relations that help make a firm more competitive)

Source: Reprinted with the permission of Free Press, a Division of Simon & Schuster, Inc., from *A Force for Change: How Leadership Differs from Management*, by John P. Kotter. Copyright © 1990 by John P. Kotter, Inc. All rights reserved.

reward power
The power to give or withhold rewards, such as salary increases, bonuses, promotions, praise, recognition, and interesting job assignments

Reward Power   **Reward power** is the power to give or withhold rewards. Rewards that a manager may control include salary increases, bonuses, promotion recommendations, praise, recognition, and interesting job assignments. In general, the greater the number of rewards a manager controls and the more important the rewards are to subordinates, the greater is the manager's reward power. If the subordinate sees as valuable only the formal organizational rewards provided by the manager, then the manager is not a leader. If the subordinate also wants and appreciates the manager's informal rewards, such as praise, gratitude, and recognition, then the manager is also exercising leadership.

coercive power
The power to force compliance by means of psychological, emotional, or physical threat

Coercive Power   **Coercive power** is the power to force compliance by means of psychological, emotional, or physical threat. In the past, physical coercion in organizations was relatively common. In most organizations today, however, coercion is limited to verbal reprimands, written reprimands, disciplinary layoffs, fines, demotion, and termination. Some managers occasionally go so far as to use verbal abuse, humiliation, and psychological coercion in an attempt to manipulate subordinates. (Of course, most people would agree that these are not appropriate managerial behaviors.) The more punitive the elements under a manager's control and the more important they are to subordinates, the more coercive power the manager possesses. On the other hand, the more a manager uses coercive power, the more likely he is to provoke resentment and hostility and the less likely he is to be seen as a leader.[6] Charlie Ergen, founder and CEO of Dish Network, often uses coercive power. One former Dish executive says that Ergen gets his way by "Pounding people into submission." For instance, he requires long hours, provides few paid holidays, routinely yells at employees, and commonly berates people in meetings who disagree with him.[7]

referent power
The personal power that accrues to someone based on identification, imitation, loyalty, or charisma

Referent Power   Compared with legitimate, reward, and coercive power, which are relatively concrete and grounded in objective facets of organizational life, **referent power** is abstract. It is based on identification, imitation, loyalty, or charisma. Followers may react favorably because they identify in some way with a leader, who may be like them in personality, background, or attitudes. In other situations, followers might choose to imitate a leader with referent power by wearing the same kind of clothes, working the same hours, or espousing the same management philosophy. Referent power may also take the form of charisma, an intangible attribute of the leader that inspires loyalty and enthusiasm. Thus, a manager might have referent power, but it is more likely to be associated with leadership.

expert power
The personal power that accrues to someone based on the information or expertise that they possess

Expert Power   **Expert power** is derived from information or expertise. A manager who knows how to interact with an eccentric but important customer, a scientist who is capable of achieving an important technical breakthrough that no other company has dreamed of, and a secretary who knows how to unravel bureaucratic red tape all have expert power over anyone who needs that information. The more important the information and the fewer the people who have access to it, the greater is the degree of expert power possessed by any one individual. In general, people who are both leaders and managers tend to have a lot of expert power.

GENERIC APPROACHES TO LEADERSHIP

Early approaches to the study of leadership adopted what might be called a *universal* or *generic* perspective. Specifically, they assumed that there was one set of answers to the leadership puzzle. One generic approach focused on leadership traits, and the other looked at leadership behavior.

Leadership Traits

The first organized approach to studying leadership analyzed the personal, psychological, and physical traits of strong leaders. The trait approach assumed that some basic trait or set of traits existed that differentiated leaders from nonleaders. If those traits could be defined, potential leaders could be identified. Researchers thought that leadership traits might include intelligence, assertiveness, above-average height, good vocabulary, attractiveness, self-confidence, and similar attributes.[8]

During the first half of the twentieth century, hundreds of studies were conducted in an attempt to identify important leadership traits. For the most part, the results of the studies were disappointing. For every set of leaders who possessed a common trait, a long list of exceptions was also found, and the list of suggested traits soon grew so long that it had little practical value. Alternative explanations usually existed even for relationships between traits and leadership that initially appeared valid. For example, it was observed that many leaders have good communication skills and are assertive. Rather than those traits being the cause of leadership, however, successful leaders may begin to display those traits after they have achieved a leadership position.

Although most researchers gave up trying to identify traits as predictors of leadership ability, many people still explicitly or implicitly adopt a trait orientation.[9] For example, politicians are all too often elected on the basis of personal appearance, speaking ability, or an aura of self-confidence. In addition, honesty and integrity may very well be fundamental leadership traits that do serve an important purpose. Intelligence also seems to play a meaningful role in leadership.[10]

Leadership Behaviors

Spurred on by their lack of success in identifying useful leadership traits, researchers soon began to investigate other variables, especially the behaviors or actions of leaders. The new hypothesis was that effective leaders somehow behaved differently from less effective leaders. Thus, the goal was to develop a fuller understanding of leadership behaviors.

Michigan Studies   Researchers at the University of Michigan, led by Rensis Likert, began studying leadership in the late 1940s.[11] Based on extensive interviews with both leaders (managers) and followers (subordinates), this research identified two basic forms of leader behavior: job centered and employee centered. Managers using **job-centered leader behavior** pay close attention to subordinates' work, explain work procedures, and are keenly interested in performance. Managers using **employee-centered leader behavior** are interested in developing a cohesive work group and ensuring that employees are satisfied with their jobs. Their primary concern is the welfare of subordinates.

The two styles of leader behavior were presumed to be at the ends of a single continuum. Although this suggests that leaders may be extremely job centered, extremely employee centered, or somewhere in between, Likert studied only the two end styles for contrast. He argued that employee-centered leader behavior generally tends to be more effective. We should also note the similarities between Likert's leadership research and his Systems 1 through 4 organization designs (discussed in Chapter 12). Job-centered leader behavior is consistent with the System 1 design (rigid and bureaucratic), whereas employee-centered leader behavior is consistent with the System 4 design (organic and flexible). When Likert advocates moving organizations from System 1 to System 4, he is also advocating a transition from job- to employee-centered leader behavior.

Ohio State Studies   At about the same time that Likert was beginning his leadership studies at the University of Michigan, a group of researchers at Ohio State University began studying leadership.[12] The extensive questionnaire surveys conducted during the Ohio State studies also suggested that there are two basic leader behaviors or styles: initiating-structure behavior and consideration behavior. When using **initiating-structure behavior**, the leader clearly defines the leader–subordinate role so that everyone knows what is expected, establishes formal lines of communication, and determines how tasks will be performed. Leaders using **consideration behavior** show concern for

initiating-structure behavior
The behavior of leaders who define the leader–subordinate role so that everyone knows what is expected, establish formal lines of communication, and determine how tasks will be performed

consideration behavior
The behavior of leaders who show concern for subordinates and attempt to establish a warm, friendly, and supportive climate

subordinates and attempt to establish a warm, friendly, and supportive climate. The behaviors identified at Ohio State are similar to those described at Michigan, but there are important differences. One major difference is that the Ohio State researchers did not interpret leader behavior as being one-dimensional; each behavior was assumed to be independent of the other. Presumably, then, a leader could exhibit varying levels of initiating structure and at the same time varying levels of consideration.

At first, the Ohio State researchers thought that leaders who exhibit high levels of both behaviors would tend to be more effective than other leaders. A study at International Harvester (now Navistar International), however, suggested a more complicated pattern.[13] The researchers found that employees of supervisors who ranked high on initiating structure were high performers but expressed low levels of satisfaction and had a higher absence rate. Conversely, employees of supervisors who ranked high on consideration had low performance ratings but high levels of satisfaction and few absences from work. Later research isolated other variables that make consistent prediction difficult and determined that situational influences also occurred. (This body of research is discussed in "Situational Approaches to Leadership."[14])

Managerial Grid   Another behavioral approach to leadership is the Managerial Grid.[15] The Managerial Grid provides a means for evaluating leadership styles and then training managers to move toward an ideal style of behavior. The Managerial Grid is shown in Figure 11.1. The horizontal axis represents **concern for production** (similar to job-centered and initiating-structure behaviors), and the vertical axis represents **concern for people** (similar to employee-centered and consideration behaviors). Note the five extremes of managerial behavior: the 1,1 manager (impoverished management), who exhibits minimal concern for both production and people; the 9,1 manager (authority-compliance), who is highly concerned about production but exhibits little concern for people; the 1,9 manager (country club management), who has exactly opposite concerns from the 9,1 manager; the 5,5 manager (middle-of-the-road management), who maintains adequate concern for both people and production; and the 9,9 manager (team management), who exhibits maximum concern for both people and production.

According to this approach, the ideal style of managerial behavior is 9,9. There is a six-phase program to assist managers in achieving this style of behavior. A. G. Edwards, Westinghouse, the FAA, Equicor, and other companies have used the Managerial Grid with reasonable success. However, there is little published scientific evidence regarding its true effectiveness.

The leader-behavior theories have played an important role in the development of contemporary thinking about leadership. In particular, they urge us not to be preoccupied with who leaders are (the trait approach) but to concentrate on what leaders do (their behaviors). Unfortunately, these theories also make universal generic prescriptions about what constitutes effective leadership. However, when we are dealing with complex social systems composed of complex individuals, few, if any, relationships are consistently predictable, and certainly no formulas for success are infallible. Yet, the behavior theorists tried to identify consistent relationships between leader behaviors and employee responses in the hope of finding a dependable prescription for effective leadership. As we might expect, they often failed. Other approaches to understanding leadership were therefore needed. The catalyst for these new approaches was the realization that although interpersonal and task-oriented dimensions might be useful for describing the behavior of leaders, they were not useful for predicting or prescribing it. The next step in the evolution of leadership theory was the creation of situational models.

concern for production
The part of the Managerial Grid that deals with the job and task aspects of leader behavior

concern for people
The part of the Managerial Grid that deals with the human aspects of leader behavior

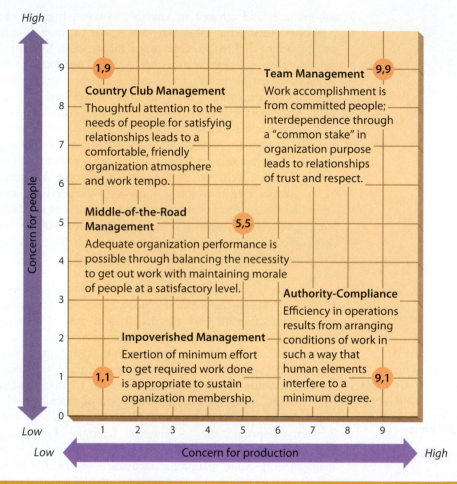

High

Concern for people

9 **1,9**

Country Club Management

Thoughtful attention to the needs of people for satisfying relationships leads to a comfortable, friendly organization atmosphere and work tempo.

Team Management   **9,9**

Work accomplishment is from committed people; interdependence through a "common stake" in organization purpose leads to relationships of trust and respect.

Middle-of-the-Road Management   **5,5**

Adequate organization performance is possible through balancing the necessity to get out work with maintaining morale of people at a satisfactory level.

Authority-Compliance

Efficiency in operations results from arranging conditions of work in such a way that human elements interfere to a minimum degree.

Impoverished Management

Exertion of minimum effort to get required work done is appropriate to sustain organization membership.

1,1   **9,1**

Low

Low   Concern for production   High

FIGURE 11.1

The Managerial Grid

The Managerial Grid® is a method of evaluating leadership styles. The overall objective of an organization using the Grid® is to train its managers using organization development techniques so that they are simultaneously more concerned for both people and production (the 9,9 style on the Grid®).

Source: Robert R. Blake and Anne Adams McCanse, Leadership Dilemmas—Grid Solutions (Houston, TX: Gulf Publishing Company, 1997), p. 29. (Formerly Robert R. Blake and Jane S. Mouton, The Managerial Grid.) © 1997 by Grid International, Inc. Reproduced by permission of the owners.

SITUATIONAL APPROACHES TO LEADERSHIP

Situational models assume that appropriate leader behavior varies from one situation to another. For instance, the "Tough Times, Tough Choices" feature illustrates how economic factors might influence leader behavior. The goal of a situational theory, then, is to identify key situational factors and to specify how they interact to determine appropriate leader behavior. In the following sections, we describe four of the most important and widely accepted situational theories of leadership: the least-preferred coworker (LPC) theory, the path-goal theory, Vroom's decision tree approach, and the leader–member exchange (LMX) approach.

TOUGH TIMES, TOUGH CHOICES

Leadership Tips for Tough Times

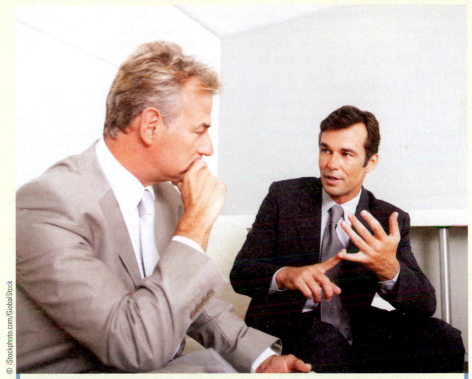

A key part of effective leadership is communication. This is especially true when an organization is going through tough times. By sharing information as openly and candidly as possible, leaders can help maintain the trust of their employees and keep morale from eroding.

How does one go about leading in a stagnant economy with a continued threat of recession? What adjustments do you have to make when money is scarce, markets are volatile, and morale needs boosting? Dennis Carey, vice chairman of Korn Ferry International, an executive-search firm, suggests that top managers start by acknowledging that leading in extreme circumstances means calling into question everything they do under normal circumstances. "You can't rely on a peacetime general to fight a war," he reminds fellow executives. "The wartime CEO prepares for the worst so that his or her company can take market share away from players who haven't." Hire away your competitors' best people, advises Carey, and keep them from grabbing yours. Or buy up their assets while they can be had at bargain prices.

Jack Hayhow, consultant and founder of Opus Training and ReallyEasyHR, adds that leaders need to make sure their employees know why they're making changes. Specifically, Hayhow argues that managers need to explain why reductions are necessary, that old business models no longer work, and that everyone must adapt to the changing business world. He also suggests that managers tell their employees that if they truly want job security they should concentrate on finding so many ways to contribute that the business cannot afford to let them go.

Hayhow also stresses the importance of creating an environment in which people motivate themselves. How do you create such an environment? "Start by matching talent with the task," he says. "Play to your employees' strengths. Figure out who

(Continued)

TOUGH TIMES, TOUGH CHOICES (Continued)

does what and make sure they're spending their time where they can best utilize their talents." Finally, Hayhow also recommends giving people some control over their jobs—that is, by letting people decide how best to perform their jobs, they will likely feel more commitment to their work and perform at a higher level.

Ex-Starbucks CEO Jim Donald makes a fairly simple recommendation: "Communicate, communicate, communicate. Especially at a time of crisis," he advises, "make sure your message reaches all levels, from the very lowest to the uppermost." Kip Tindell, who's been CEO of the Container Store since its founding in 1978, agrees. That's why his managers "run around like chickens relentlessly trying to communicate everything to every single employee at all times." He admits that it's an impossible task, but he's also convinced that the effort is more important than ever in times of crisis. He also contends that his company is in a better position to ride out

the economic storm "because we're so dedicated to the notion that communication and leadership are the same thing." At the very least, he says, "we're fortunate to be minus the paranoia that goes with employees who feel they don't know what's going on."

References: Emily Thornton, "Managing Through a Crisis: The New Rules," *BusinessWeek*, www.businessweek .com, accessed on January 1, 2014; Anthony Portuesi, "Leading in a Recession: An Interview with Jack Hayhow," *Driven Leaders*, February 24, 2009, http://drivenleaders.com, accessed on January 1, 2014; Jim Donald, "Guest Post: Former Starbucks CEO's Tips for Tough Times," *Fortune*, http://postcards.blogs.fortune.cnn.com, accessed on January 1, 2014; Ellen Davis, "Retail Execs Offer Insights on Leadership in Tough Economic Times," *NRF Annual 2009 Convention Blog*, January 15, 2009, http://blog.nrf.com, accessed on January 1, 2014; and "In Tough Times, Bosses Need to Get Out and Talk to Employees," *USA Today*, August 4, 2012, p. B1.

LPC Theory

LPC theory
A theory of leadership that suggests that the appropriate style of leadership varies with situational favorableness

LPC measure
The measuring scale that asks leaders to describe the person with whom he or she is able to work least well (the *least-preferred coworker,* or LPC)

The **LPC theory**, developed by Fred Fiedler, was the first truly situational theory of leadership.[16] Beginning with a combined trait and behavioral approach, Fiedler identified two styles of leadership: task oriented (analogous to job-centered and initiating-structure behaviors) and relationship oriented (similar to employee-centered and consideration behaviors). He went beyond the earlier behavioral approaches by arguing that the style of behavior is a reflection of the leader's personality and that most personalities fall into one of his two categories—task oriented or relationship oriented by nature. Fiedler measures leadership style by means of a controversial questionnaire called the **LPC measure**. To use the measure, a manager or leader is asked to describe the specific person with whom he or she is able to work least well—the LPC—by filling in a set of 16 scales anchored at each end by a positive or negative adjective. For example, 3 of the 16 scales are as follows:

Helpful __ __ __ __ __ __ __ __ Frustrating

8 7 6 5 4 3 2 1

Tense __ __ __ __ __ __ __ __ Relaxed

1 2 3 4 5 6 7 8

Boring __ __ __ __ __ __ __ __ Interesting

1 2 3 4 5 6 7 8

The leader's LPC score is then calculated by adding up the numbers below the line checked on each scale. Note in these three examples that the higher numbers are associated with positive qualities (helpful, relaxed, and interesting), whereas the negative qualities (frustrating, tense, and boring) have low point values. A high total score is assumed to reflect a relationship orientation on the part of the leader, and a low score a task orientation on his or her part. The LPC measure is controversial because researchers disagree about its validity. Some question exactly what an LPC measure reflects and whether the score is an index of behavior, personality, or some other factor.[17]

Favorableness of the Situation　　The underlying assumption of situational models of leadership is that appropriate leader behavior varies from one situation to another. According to Fiedler, the key situational factor is the favorableness of the situation from the leader's point of view. This factor is determined by leader–member relations, task structure, and position power. *Leader–member relations* refer to the nature of the relationship between the leader and the work group. If the leader and the group have a high degree of mutual trust, respect, and confidence, and if they like one another, relations are assumed to be good. If there is little trust, respect, or confidence, and if they do not like one another, relations are poor. Naturally, good relations are more favorable.

Task structure is the degree to which the group's task is well defined. The task is structured when it is routine, easily understood, and unambiguous and when the group has standard procedures and precedents to rely on. An unstructured task is nonroutine, ambiguous, and complex, with no standard procedures or precedents. You can see that high structure is more favorable for the leader, whereas low structure is less favorable. For example, if the task is unstructured, the group will not know what to do, and the leader will have to play a major role in guiding and directing its activities. If the task is structured, the leader will not have to get so involved and can devote time to nonsupervisory activities.

Position power is the power vested in the leader's position. If the leader has the power to assign work and to reward and punish employees, position power is assumed to be strong. But, if the leader must get job assignments approved by someone else and does not administer rewards and punishment, position power is weak, and it is more difficult to accomplish goals. From the leader's point of view, strong position power is clearly preferable to weak position power. However, position power is not as important as task structure and leader–member relations.

Favorableness and Leader Style　　Fiedler and his associates conducted numerous studies linking the favorableness of various situations to leader style and the effectiveness of the group.[18] The results of these studies—and the overall framework of the theory—are shown in Figure 11.2. To interpret the model, look first at the situational factors at the top of the figure. Good or bad leader–member relations, high or low task structure, and strong or weak leader position power can be combined to yield six unique situations. For example, good leader–member relations, high task structure, and strong leader position power (at the far left) are presumed to define the most favorable situation; bad leader–member relations, low task structure, and weak leader power (at the far right) are the least favorable situation. The other combinations reflect intermediate levels of favorableness.

Below each set of situations are shown the degree of favorableness and the form of leader behavior found to be most strongly associated with effective group performance for those situations. When the situation is most and least favorable, Fiedler found that a task-oriented leader is most effective. When the situation is only moderately favorable, a relationship-oriented leader is predicted to be most effective.

Contingency Factors	Situations							
Leader–member relations	Good				Bad			
Task structure	High		Low		High		Low	
Position power	Strong	Weak	Strong	Weak	Strong	Weak	Strong	Weak

Favorableness of Situation: Most favorable　Moderately favorable　Most unfavorable

Appropriate Leader Behavior: Task-oriented　Relationship-oriented　Task-oriented

© Cengage Learning

FIGURE 11.2

The Least-Preferred Coworker Theory of Leadership

Fiedler's LPC theory of leadership suggests that appropriate leader behavior varies as a function of the favorableness of the situation. Favorableness, in turn, is defined by task structure, leader–member relations, and the leader's position power. According to the LPC theory, the most and least favorable situations call for task-oriented leadership, whereas moderately favorable situations suggest the need for relationship-oriented leadership.

Flexibility of Leader Style　Fiedler argued that, for any given individual, leader style is essentially fixed and cannot be changed; leaders cannot change their behavior to fit a particular situation because it is linked to their particular personality traits. Thus, when a leader's style and the situation do not match, Fiedler argued that the situation should be changed to fit the leader's style. When leader–member relations are good, task structure low, and position power weak, the leader style that is most likely to be effective is relationship oriented. If the leader is task oriented, a mismatch exists. According to Fiedler, the leader can make the elements of the situation more congruent by structuring the task (by developing guidelines and procedures, for instance) and increasing power (by requesting additional authority or by other means).

Fiedler's LPC theory has been attacked on the grounds that it is not always supported by research, that his findings are subject to other interpretations, that the LPC measure lacks validity, and that his assumptions about the inflexibility of leader behavior are unrealistic.[19] However, Fiedler's theory was one of the first to adopt a situational perspective on leadership. It has helped many managers recognize the important situational factors they must contend with, and it has fostered additional thinking about the situational nature of leadership. Moreover, in recent years, Fiedler has attempted to address some of the concerns about his theory by revising it and adding additional elements such as cognitive resources.

Path-Goal Theory

The **path-goal theory** of leadership—associated most closely with Martin Evans and Robert House—is a direct extension of the expectancy theory of motivation discussed in Chapter 10.[20] Recall that the primary components of expectancy theory included the likelihood of attaining various outcomes and the value associated with those outcomes. The path-goal theory of leadership suggests that the primary functions of a leader are to make valued or desired rewards available in the workplace and to clarify for the

path-goal theory A theory of leadership suggesting that the primary functions of a leader are to make valued or desired rewards available in the workplace and to clarify for the subordinate the kinds of behavior that will lead to those rewards subordinate the kinds of behavior that will lead to goal accomplishment and valued rewards—that is, the leader should clarify the paths to goal attainment.

Leader Behavior   The most fully developed version of path-goal theory identifies four kinds of leader behavior. *Directive leader behavior* lets subordinates know what is expected of them, gives guidance and direction, and schedules work. *Supportive leader behavior* is being friendly and approachable, showing concern for subordinate welfare, and treating members as equals. *Participative leader behavior* includes consulting with subordinates, soliciting suggestions, and allowing participation in decision making. *Achievement-oriented leader* behavior means setting challenging goals, expecting subordinates to perform at high levels, encouraging subordinates, and showing confidence in subordinates' abilities.

In contrast to Fiedler's theory, path-goal theory assumes that leaders can change their style or behavior to meet the demands of a particular situation. For example, when encountering a new group of subordinates and a new project, the leader may be directive in establishing work procedures and in outlining what needs to be done. Next, the leader may adopt supportive behavior to foster group cohesiveness and a positive climate. As the group becomes familiar with the task and as new problems are encountered, the leader may exhibit participative behavior to enhance group members' motivation. Finally, achievement-oriented behavior may be used to encourage continued high performance.

Situational Factors   Like other situational theories of leadership, path-goal theory suggests that the appropriate leader style depends on situational factors. Path-goal theory focuses on the situational factors of the personal characteristics of subordinates and environmental characteristics of the workplace.

Important personal characteristics include the subordinates' perception of their own abilities and their locus of control. If people perceive that they are lacking in abilities, they may prefer directive leadership to help them understand path-goal relationships better. If they perceive themselves to have a lot of abilities, employees may resent directive leadership. Locus of control is a personality trait. People who have an internal locus of control believe that what happens to them is a function of their own efforts and behavior. Those who have an external locus of control assume that fate, luck, or "the system" determines what happens to them. A person with an internal locus of control may prefer participative leadership, whereas a person with an external locus of control may prefer directive leadership. Managers can do little or nothing to influence the personal characteristics of subordinates, but they can shape the environment to take advantage of these personal characteristics by, for example, providing rewards and structuring tasks.

Environmental characteristics include factors outside the subordinates' control. Task structure is one such factor. When structure is high, directive leadership is less effective than when structure is low. Subordinates do not usually need their boss to continually tell them how to do an extremely routine job. The formal authority system is another important environmental characteristic. Again, the higher the degree of formality, the less directive is the leader behavior that will be accepted by subordinates. The nature of the work group also affects appropriate leader behavior. When the work group provides the employee with social support and satisfaction, supportive leader behavior is less critical. When social support and satisfaction cannot be derived from the group, the worker may look to the leader for this support.

The basic path-goal framework as illustrated in Figure 11.3 shows that different leader behaviors affect subordinates' motivation to perform. Personal and environmental characteristics are seen as defining which behaviors lead to which outcomes. The path-goal theory of leadership is a dynamic and incomplete model. The original intent was to

© Cengage Learning

© Cengage Learning

FIGURE 11.3

The Path-Goal Framework

The path-goal theory of leadership suggests that managers can use four types of leader behavior to clarify subordinates' paths to goal attainment. Both personal characteristics of the subordinate and environmental characteristics within the organization must be taken into account when determining which style of leadership will work best for a particular situation.

state the theory in general terms so that future research could explore a variety of interrelationships and modify the theory. Research that has been done suggests that the path-goal theory is a reasonably good description of the leadership process and that future investigations along these lines should enable us to discover more about the link between leadership and motivation.[21]

Vroom's Decision Tree Approach

Vroom's decision tree approach

Predicts what kinds of situations call for different degrees of group participation

The third major contemporary approach to leadership is **Vroom's decision tree approach**. The earliest version of this model was proposed by Victor Vroom and Philip Yetton and later revised and expanded by Vroom and Arthur Jago.[22] Most recently, Vroom has developed yet another refinement of the original model.[23] Like the path-goal theory, this approach attempts to prescribe a leadership style appropriate to a given situation. It also assumes that the same leader may display different leadership styles. But Vroom's approach concerns itself with only a single aspect of leader behavior: subordinate participation in decision making.

Basic Premises   Vroom's decision tree approach assumes that the degree to which subordinates should be encouraged to participate in decision making depends on the characteristics of the situation. In other words, no one decision-making process is best for all situations. After evaluating a variety of problem attributes (characteristics of the problem or decision), the leader determines an appropriate decision style that specifies the amount of subordinate participation.

Vroom's current formulation suggests that managers use one of two different decision trees.[24] To do so, the manager first assesses the situation in terms of several factors. This assessment involves determining whether the given factor is high or low for the decision that is to be made. For instance, the first factor is decision significance. If the decision is extremely important and may have a major impact on the organization (such as choosing a location for a new plant), its significance is high. But, if the decision is routine and its consequences are not terribly important (selecting a color for the firm's softball team uniforms), its significance is low.

This assessment guides the manager through the paths of the decision tree to a recommended course of action. One decision tree is to be used when the manager is interested primarily in making the decision as quickly as possible; the other is to be used when time is less critical and the manager is interested in helping subordinates to improve and develop their own decision-making skills.

The two decision trees are shown in Figures 11.4 and 11.5. The problem attributes (situational factors) are arranged along the top of the decision tree. To use the model,

Decision Significance	Importance of Commitment	Leader Expertise	Likelihood of Commitment	Group Support	Group Expertise	Team Competence	
P R O B L E M S T A T E M E N T H	H	H	H	—	—	—	**Decide**
			L	H	H	H	**Delegate**
						L	**Consult (group)**
					L	—	
				L	—	—	
		L	H	H	H	H	**Facilitate**
						L	**Consult (individually)**
					L	—	
				L	—	—	
			L	H	H	H	**Facilitate**
						L	**Consult (group)**
					L	—	
				L	—	—	
	L	H	—	—	—	—	**Decide**
		L	—	H	H	H	**Facilitate**
						L	**Consult (individually)**
					L	—	
				L	—	—	
L	H	—	H	—	—	—	**Decide**
			L	—	—	H	**Delegate**
						L	**Facilitate**
	L	—	—	—	—	—	**Decide**

FIGURE 11.4

Vroom's Time-Driven Decision Tree

This matrix is recommended for situations where time is of the highest importance in making a decision. The matrix operates like a funnel. You start at the left with a specific decision problem in mind. The column headings denote situational factors that may or may not be present in that problem. You progress by selecting high or low (H or L) for each relevant situational factor. Proceed down the funnel, judging only those situational factors for which a judgment is called, until you reach the recommended process.

Source: Reprinted from *Organizational Dynamics*, Vol. 28, No. 4, Victor H. Vroom, "Leadership and the Decision-Making Process," pp. 82–94. Copyright 2000, with permission from Elsevier.

Decision Significance	Importance of Commitment	Leader Expertise	Likelihood of Commitment	Group Support	Group Expertise	Team Competence	
H	H	—	H	H	H	H	Decide
						L	Facilitate
					L	—	Consult (group)
				L	—	—	Consult (group)
			L	H	H	H	Delegate
						L	Facilitate
					L	—	Facilitate
				L	—	—	Consult (group)
H	L	—	—	H	H	H	Delegate
						L	Facilitate
					L	—	Consult (group)
				L	—	—	Consult (group)
L	H	—	H	—	—	—	Decide
			L	—	—	—	Delegate
	L	—	—	—	—	—	Decide

(Row label at left: P R O B L E M   S T A T E M E N T)

FIGURE 11.5

Vroom's Development-Driven Decision Tree

This matrix is to be used when the leader is more interested in developing employees than in making the decision as quickly as possible. Just as with the time-driven tree shown in Figure 11.4, the leader assesses up to seven situational factors. These factors, in turn, funnel the leader to a recommended process for making the decision.

Source: Reprinted from *Organizational Dynamics*, Vol. 28, No. 4, Victor H. Vroom, "Leadership and the Decision-Making Process," pp. 82–94. Copyright 2000, with permission from Elsevier.

the decision maker starts at the left side of the diagram and assesses the first problem attribute (decision significance). The answer determines the path to the second node on the decision tree, where the next attribute (importance of commitment) is assessed. This process continues until a terminal node is reached. In this way, the manager identifies an effective decision-making style for the situation.

Decision-Making Styles   The various decision-making styles reflected at the ends of the tree branches represent different levels of subordinate participation that the manager should attempt to adopt in a given situation. The five styles are defined as follows:

- *Decide*. The manager makes the decision alone and then announces or "sells" it to the group.
- *Consult (individually)*. The manager presents the program to group members individually, obtains their suggestions, and then makes the decision.
- *Consult (group)*. The manager presents the problem to group members at a meeting, gets their suggestions, and then makes the decision.

- *Facilitate.* The manager presents the problem to the group at a meeting, defines the problem and its boundaries, and then facilitates group member discussion as they make the decision.
- *Delegate.* The manager allows the group to define for itself the exact nature and parameters of the problem and then to develop a solution.

Vroom's decision tree approach represents a very focused but quite complex perspective on leadership. To compensate for this difficulty, Vroom has developed elaborate expert system software to help managers assess a situation accurately and quickly and then to make an appropriate decision regarding employee participation.[25] Many firms, including Halliburton Company, Litton Industries, and Borland International, have provided their managers with training in how to use the various versions of this model.

Evaluation and Implications   Because Vroom's current approach is relatively new, it has not been fully scientifically tested. The original model and its subsequent refinement, however, attracted a great deal of attention and were generally supported by research.[26] For example, there is some support for the idea that individuals who make decisions consistent with the predictions of the model are more effective than those who make decisions inconsistent with it. The model, therefore, appears to be a tool that managers can apply with some confidence in deciding how much subordinates should participate in the decision-making process.

The LMX Approach

LMX model
Stresses that leaders have different kinds of relationships with different subordinates

Because leadership is such an important area, managers and researchers continue to study it. As a result, new ideas, theories, and perspectives are continuously being developed. The **LMX model** of leadership, conceived by George Graen and Fred Dansereau, stresses the importance of variable relationships between supervisors and each of their subordinates.[27] Each superior–subordinate pair is referred to as a *vertical dyad*. The model differs from earlier approaches in that it focuses on the differential relationship that leaders often establish with different subordinates. Figure 11.6 shows the basic concepts of the LMX theory.

© Cengage Learning

FIGURE 11.6

The Leader–Member Exchange Model

The LMX model suggests that leaders form unique independent relationships with each of their subordinates. As illustrated here, a key factor in the nature of this relationship is whether the individual subordinate is in the leader's out-group or in-group.

The model suggests that supervisors establish a special relationship with a small number of trusted subordinates, referred to as the *in-group*. The in-group usually receives special duties requiring responsibility and autonomy; they may also receive special privileges. Subordinates who are not a part of this group are called the *out-group*, and they receive less of the supervisor's time and attention. Note in Figure 11.6 that the leader has a dyadic, or one-to-one, relationship with each of the five subordinates.

Early in his or her interaction with a given subordinate, the supervisor initiates either an in-group or an out-group relationship. It is not clear how a leader selects members of the in-group, but the decision may be based on personal compatibility and subordinates' competence. Research has confirmed the existence of in-groups and out-groups. In addition, studies generally have found that in-group members have a higher level of performance and satisfaction than do out-group members.[28]

RELATED APPROACHES TO LEADERSHIP

Because of its importance to organizational effectiveness, leadership continues to be the focus of a great deal of research and theory building. New approaches that have attracted much attention are the concepts of substitutes for leadership and transformational leadership.[29]

Substitutes for Leadership

substitutes for leadership
A concept that identifies situations in which leader behaviors are neutralized or replaced by characteristics of the subordinate, the task, and the organization

The concept of **substitutes for leadership** was developed because existing leadership models and theories do not account for situations in which leadership is not needed.[30] They simply try to specify what kind of leader behavior is appropriate. The substitutes concept, however, identifies situations in which leader behaviors are neutralized or replaced by characteristics of the subordinate, the task, and the organization. For example, when a patient is delivered to a hospital emergency room, the professionals on duty do not wait to be told what to do by a leader. Nurses, doctors, and attendants all go into action without waiting for directive or supportive leader behavior from the emergency room supervisor.

Characteristics of the subordinate that may serve to neutralize leader behavior include ability, experience, need for independence, professional orientation, and indifference toward organizational rewards. For example, employees with a high level of ability and experience may not need to be told what to do. Similarly, a subordinate's strong need for independence may render leader behavior ineffective. Task characteristics that may substitute for leadership include routineness, the availability of feedback, and intrinsic satisfaction. When the job is routine and simple, the subordinate may not need direction. When the task is challenging and intrinsically satisfying, the subordinate may not need or want social support from a leader.

Organizational characteristics that may substitute for leadership include formalization, group cohesion, inflexibility, and a rigid reward structure. Leadership may not be necessary when policies and practices are formal and inflexible, for example. Similarly, a rigid reward system may rob the leader of reward power and thereby decrease the importance of the role. Preliminary research has provided support for the concept of substitutes for leadership.[31]

Charismatic Leadership

charismatic leadership
Assumes that charisma is an individual characteristic of the leader

charisma
A form of interpersonal attraction that inspires support and acceptance

The concept of **charismatic leadership**, like trait theories, assumes that charisma is an individual characteristic of the leader. **Charisma** is a form of interpersonal attraction that inspires support and acceptance. All else being equal, then, someone with charisma is more likely to be able to influence others than someone without charisma. For example, a highly charismatic supervisor will be more successful in influencing subordinate behavior than a supervisor who lacks charisma. Thus, influence is again a fundamental element of this perspective.

Robert House first proposed a theory of charismatic leadership, based on research findings from a variety of social science disciplines.[32] His theory suggests that charismatic leaders are likely to have a lot of self-confidence, a firm conviction in their beliefs and ideals, and a strong need to influence people. They also tend to communicate high expectations about follower performance and express confidence in followers. Donald Trump is an excellent example of a charismatic leader. Even though he has made his share of mistakes and generally is perceived as only an "average" manager, many people view him as larger than life.[33]

Most experts acknowledge three elements of charismatic leadership in organizations today.[34] First, the leader needs to be able to envision the future, set high expectations, and model behaviors consistent with meeting those expectations. Next, the charismatic leader must be able to energize others through a demonstration of personal excitement, personal confidence, and patterns of success. Finally, the charismatic leader enables others by supporting them, empathizing with them, and expressing confidence in them.[35]

Charismatic leadership ideas are quite popular among managers today and are the subject of numerous books and articles. Unfortunately, few studies have attempted to specifically test the meaning and impact of charismatic leadership. There are also lingering ethical issues about charismatic leadership that trouble some people. For instance, President Bill Clinton was a charismatic leader. But some of his critics argued that this very charisma caused his supporters to overlook his flaws and to minimize some of his indiscretions. In contrast, President George W. Bush did not possess a high level of charisma, and this may have enabled some critics to magnify his shortcomings.

Transformational Leadership

Another new perspective on leadership has been called by a number of labels: charismatic leadership, inspirational leadership, symbolic leadership, and transformational leadership. We use the term **transformational leadership** and define it as leadership that goes beyond ordinary expectations by transmitting a sense of mission, stimulating learning experiences, and inspiring new ways of thinking.[36] Because of rapid change and turbulent environments, transformational leaders are increasingly being seen as vital to the success of business.[37]

A recent article in the popular press identified seven keys to successful leadership: trusting one's subordinates, developing a vision, keeping cool, encouraging risk, being an expert, inviting dissent, and simplifying things.[38] Although this list was the result of a simplistic survey of the leadership literature, it is nevertheless consistent with the premises underlying transformational leadership. So, too, are recent examples cited as effective leadership. Take the case of 3M: CEO George Buckley is working to make the firm more efficient and profitable while simultaneously keeping its leadership role in new-product innovation. He has also changed the reward system, overhauled procedures, and restructured the entire firm. And so far, at least, analysts have applauded these changes.[39]

transformational leadership

Leadership that goes beyond ordinary expectations by transmitting a sense of mission, stimulating learning experiences, and inspiring new ways of thinking

C. LEBEDINSKY/Challenges-REA/Redux

During his tenure as CEO of 3M, George Buckley has worked to make the firm more efficient and profitable while maintaining its leadership role in new-product innovation. Buckley has relied on transformational leadership to help move 3M toward these goals.

EMERGING APPROACHES TO LEADERSHIP

Recently, three potentially very important new approaches to leadership have emerged. One is called *strategic leadership*; the others deal with *cross-cultural leadership* and *ethical leadership*.

Strategic Leadership

strategic leadership
The capability to understand the complexities of both the organization and its environment and to lead change in the organization to achieve and maintain a superior alignment between the organization and its environment

Strategic leadership is a new concept that explicitly relates leadership to the role of top management. We define **strategic leadership** as the capability to understand the complexities of both the organization and its environment and to lead change in the organization to achieve and maintain a superior alignment between the organization and its environment. This definition reflects an integration of the leadership concepts covered in this chapter with our discussion of strategic management in Chapter 3. Its board of directors, of course, is a key element in any firm's strategic leadership.

To be effective in this role, a manager needs to have a thorough and complete understanding of the organization—its history, its culture, its strengths, and its weaknesses. In addition, the leader needs a firm grasp of the organization's environment. This understanding must encompass current conditions and circumstances as well as significant trends and issues on the horizon. The strategic leader also needs to recognize how the firm is currently aligned with its environment—where it relates effectively and where it relates less effectively with that environment. Finally, looking at environmental trends and issues, the strategic leader works to improve both the current alignment and the future alignment.[40]

Since taking the reins at Apple following the death of Steve Jobs, Tim Cook has been systematically changing the firm's organization design by rearranging functions and reassigning top managers.[41] Jeffrey Immelt (CEO of General Electric), Hector Ruiz (CEO of Advanced Micro Devices), John Chambers (CEO of Cisco), Michael Dell (founder and CEO of Dell Computer), and Irene Rosenfeld (CEO of Kraft Foods) are generally seen as strong strategic leaders.[42] On the other hand, Ken Lewis (former CEO of Bank of America) and Mike Jeffries (CEO of Abercrombie & Fitch) have recently been cited as less effective strategic leaders.[43]

Cross-Cultural Leadership

Another new approach to leadership is based on cross-cultural issues. In this context, *culture* is used as a broad concept to encompass both international differences and diversity-based differences within one culture. For instance, when a Japanese firm sends an executive to head the firm's operations in the United States, that person will need to become acclimated to the cultural differences that exist between the two countries and to change his or her leadership style accordingly. Japan is generally characterized by collectivism (the view that the group is more important than any individual within the group), whereas the United States is based more on individualism (the belief that individuals are more important than the group). The Japanese executive, then, will find it necessary to recognize the importance of individual contributions and rewards, as well as the differences in individual and group roles, that exist in Japanese and U.S. businesses.

Similarly, cross-cultural factors play a growing role in organizations as their workforces become more and more diverse. Most leadership research, for instance, has been conducted on samples or case studies involving white male leaders (until several years ago, most business leaders were white males). But, as more females, African Americans, and Latinos achieve leadership positions, it may be necessary to reassess how applicable current theories and models of leadership are when applied to an increasingly diverse pool of leaders.[44] At the same time, though, as discussed more fully in the "Leading the Way" feature, diversity continues to lag in some settings.

LEADING THE WAY

Diversity Still Lagging in the Boardroom

Most experts agree that diversity among group members can contribute to better decisions and solutions. But while many organizations strive to promote diversity within teams and work groups such as this one, most boards of directors of large businesses still have relatively little diversity.

"It's been proven again and again," says Carl Brooks, CEO of the Executive Leadership Council, a network of senior African American executives, "that companies with board members who reflect gender and ethnic diversity also tend to have better returns on equity and sales." According to Marc H. Morial, CEO of the National Urban League, which promotes economic empowerment for African Americans, a minority presence on corporate boards is also necessary to protect the interests of minority consumers and other stakeholders: "African American voices and perspectives," he argues, "are needed on corporate boards to ensure that business decisions affecting Black America are both responsible and sensitive to the needs of our communities."

Unfortunately, says Morial, "African Americans still represent a miniscule fraction of board-level corporate leadership in America." Citing a recent study by the Executive Leadership Council, Morial points out that the number of blacks on Fortune 500 boards has actually *declined* in recent years: Even though blacks comprise 13 percent of the U.S. population,

representation on corporate boards stands at "a meager 7 percent."

The same trend was confirmed with the release of the U.S. Senate Democratic Hispanic Task Force report on minority and women representation on *Fortune 500* boards and executive teams (CEOs plus their direct reports). Here are some of the survey's findings:

- Women comprise 18 percent of all board members and just under 20 percent of executive team members (roughly one in five). Those figures, of course, are far below the 50-percent proportion of women in the population.

- Minorities comprise 14.5 percent of all directors—about one out of every seven—and an even smaller percentage of executive-team members. That's less than half of their 35-percent proportion of the population.

- Although African Americans boast the highest minority representation on boards—8.8 percent—that's equivalent to only 69 percent of their total

(Continued)

© Andrey_Popov/Shutterstock.com

LEADING THE WAY (Continued)

proportion of the population. Representation on executive teams is only 4.2 percent.

- Hispanics fared worse than any other minority. Although they represent 15 percent of the U.S. population, they comprise only 3.3 percent of board members and 3 percent of executive-team members.

The report, says task force chair Robert Menendez (one of a small number of Hispanic members of the U.S. Senate),

clearly confirms what we had suspected all along—that American corporations need to do better when it comes to having the boardrooms on Wall Street reflect the reality on Main Street. We need to change the dynamic and make it commonplace for minorities to be part of the American corporate structure. It is not just about doing what's right, but it's a good business decision that will benefit both corporations and the communities they're tapping into and making investments in.

References: "African Americans Lose Ground on Fortune 500 Boards," *Savoy*, January 1, 2014; Marc H. Morial, "National Urban League Trains African Americans for Corporate Boards," *Philadelphia Tribune*, January 1, 2014; "Results of Menendez's Major *Fortune 500* Diversity Survey: Representation of Women and Minorities on Corporate Boards Still Lags Far Behind National Population," August 4, 2010, Senator Robert Menendez's website (press release), www.menendez.senate.gov, accessed on January 1, 2014.

Ethical Leadership

Most people have long assumed that top managers are ethical people. But in the wake of recent corporate scandals, faith in top managers has been shaken. Perhaps now more than ever, high standards of ethical conduct are being held up as a prerequisite for effective leadership. More specifically, top managers are being called on to maintain high ethical standards for their own conduct, to exhibit ethical behavior unfailingly, and to hold others in their organization to the same standards.

The behaviors of top leaders are being scrutinized more than ever, and those responsible for hiring new leaders for a business are looking more and more closely at the background of those being considered. And the emerging pressures for stronger corporate governance models are likely to further increase commitment to selecting only those individuals with high ethical standards and to holding them more accountable than in the past for both their actions and the consequences of those actions.[45]

POLITICAL BEHAVIOR IN ORGANIZATIONS

political behavior
The activities carried out for the specific purpose of acquiring, developing, and using power and other resources to obtain one's preferred outcomes

Another common influence on behavior is politics and political behavior. **Political behavior** describes activities carried out for the specific purpose of acquiring, developing, and using power and other resources to obtain one's preferred outcomes.[46] Political behavior may be undertaken by managers dealing with their subordinates, subordinates dealing with their managers, and managers and subordinates dealing with others at the same level. In other words, it may be directed upward, downward, or laterally. Decisions ranging from where to locate a manufacturing plant to where to put the company coffeemaker are subject to political action. In any situation, individuals may engage in political behavior to further their own ends, to protect themselves from others, to further goals they sincerely believe to be in the organization's best interests, or simply to acquire and exercise power. And power may be sought by individuals, by groups of individuals, or by groups of groups.[47]

Although political behavior is difficult to study because of its sensitive nature, one early survey found that many managers believed that politics influenced salary and hiring decisions in their firm. Many also believed that the incidence of political behavior was greater at the upper levels of their organization and lesser at the lower levels. More than half of the respondents felt that organizational politics were bad, unfair, unhealthy, and irrational, but most suggested that successful executives have to be good politicians and be political to get ahead.[48]

Common Political Behaviors

Research has identified four basic forms of political behavior widely practiced in organizations.[49] One form is *inducement*, which occurs when a manager offers to give something to someone else in return for that individual's support. For example, a product manager might suggest to another product manager that she will put in a good word with his boss if he supports a new marketing plan that she has developed. By most accounts, former WorldCom CEO Bernard Ebbers made frequent use of this tactic to retain his leadership position in the company. For example, he allowed board members to use the corporate jet whenever they wanted and invested heavily in their pet projects.

A second tactic is *persuasion*, which relies on both emotion and logic. An operations manager wanting to construct a new plant on a certain site might persuade others to support his goal on grounds that are objective and logical (for example, it is less expensive and taxes are lower) as well as subjective and personal. Ebbers also used this approach. For instance, when one board member attempted to remove him from his position, he worked behind the scenes to persuade the majority of board members to allow him to stay on.

A third political behavior involves the *creation of an obligation*. For example, one manager might support a recommendation made by another manager for a new advertising campaign. Although he might really have no opinion on the new campaign, he might think that by going along, he is incurring a debt from the other manager and will be able to "call in" that debt when he wants to get something done and needs additional support. Ebbers loaned WorldCom board members money, for example, but then forgave the loans in exchange for their continued support.

Coercion, a fourth political behavior, is the use of force to get one's way. For example, a manager may threaten to withhold support, rewards, or other resources as a way to influence someone else. This, too, was a common tactic used by Ebbers. He reportedly belittled any board member who dared question him, for example. In the words of one former director, "Ebbers treated you like a prince—as long as you never forgot who was king."[50]

Impression Management

impression management
A direct and intentional effort by someone to enhance his or her image in the eyes of others

Impression management is a subtle form of political behavior that deserves special mention. **Impression management** is a direct and intentional effort by someone to enhance his or her image in the eyes of others. People engage in impression management for a variety of reasons. For one thing, they may do so to further their own careers. By making themselves look good, they think they are more likely to receive rewards, to be given attractive job assignments, and to receive promotions. They may also engage in impression management to boost their self-esteem. When people have a solid image in an organization, others make them aware of it through compliments, respect, and so forth. Still another reason people use impression management is in an effort to acquire more power and hence more control.

People attempt to manage how others perceive them through a variety of mechanisms. Appearance is one of the first things that people think of. Hence, a person motivated by

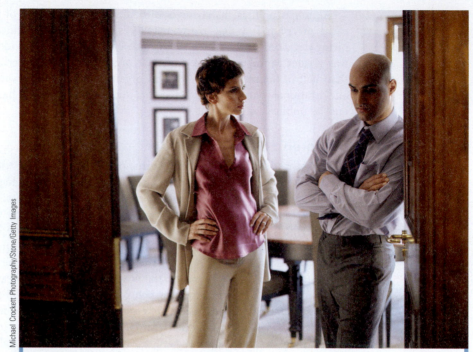

Michael Crockett Photography/Stone/Getty Images

Coercion is sometimes used in organizations to pressure people to do something they might not want to do. This manager, for example, is pressuring one of her colleagues to support a recommendation she is making to their boss. He is clearly reluctant to comply, but she is pushing aggressively to get her way.

impression management will pay close attention to choice of attire, selection of language, and use of manners and body posture. People interested in impression management are also likely to jockey for association only with successful projects. By being assigned to high-profile projects led by highly successful managers, a person can begin to link his or her own name with such projects in the minds of others.

Sometimes people too strongly motivated by impression management become obsessed with it and may resort to dishonest or unethical means. For example, some people have been known to take credit for others' work in an effort to make themselves look better. People have also been known to exaggerate or even falsify their personal accomplishments in an effort to build an enhanced image.[51] For instance, one Silicon Valley entrepreneur recently noted, "Every time I turn around, there is someone sticking their head in my office reminding me what they are doing for me."[52]

Managing Political Behavior

By its very nature, political behavior is tricky to approach in a rational and systematic way. But managers can handle political behavior so that it does not do excessive damage.[53] First, managers should be aware that, even if their actions are not politically motivated, others may assume that they are. Second, by providing subordinates with autonomy, responsibility, challenge, and feedback, managers reduce the likelihood of political behavior by subordinates. Third, managers should avoid using power if they want to avoid charges of political motivation. Fourth, managers should get disagreements out in the open so that subordinates will have less opportunity for political behavior through using conflict for their own purposes. Finally, managers should avoid covert activities. Behind-the-scenes activities give the impression of political intent, even if none really exists.[54] Other guidelines include clearly communicating the bases and processes for performance evaluation, tying rewards directly to performance, and minimizing competition among managers for resources.[55]

Of course, these guidelines are much easier to list than they are to implement. The well-informed manager should not assume that political behavior does not exist or, worse yet, attempt to eliminate it by issuing orders or commands. Instead, the manager must recognize that political behavior exists in virtually all organizations and that it cannot be ignored or stamped out. It can, however, be managed in such a way that it will seldom inflict serious damage on the organization. It may even play a useful role in some situations.[56] For example, a manager may be able to use his or her political influence to stimulate a greater sense of social responsibility or to heighten awareness of the ethical implications of a decision.

SUMMARY OF LEARNING OUTCOMES AND KEY POINTS

1. Describe the nature of leadership and relate leadership to management.

   - As a process, leadership is the use of noncoercive influence to shape the group's or organization's goals, motivate behavior toward the achievement of those goals, and help define group or organization culture.
   - As a property, leadership is the set of characteristics attributed to those who are perceived to be leaders.
   - Leadership and management are often related but are also different.
   - Managers and leaders use legitimate, reward, coercive, referent, and expert power.

2. Discuss and evaluate the two generic approaches to leadership.

   - The trait approach to leadership assumed that some basic trait or set of traits differentiated leaders from nonleaders.
   - The leadership behavior approach to leadership assumed that the behavior of effective leaders was somehow different from the behavior of nonleaders.
   - Research at the University of Michigan and Ohio State University identified two basic forms of leadership behavior—one concentrating on work and performance, and the other concentrating on employee welfare and support.
   - The Managerial Grid attempts to train managers to exhibit high levels of both forms of behavior.

3. Identify and describe the major situational approaches to leadership.

   - Situational approaches to leadership recognize that appropriate forms of leadership behavior are not universally applicable and attempt to specify situations in which various behaviors are appropriate.
   - The LPC theory suggests that a leader's behaviors should be either task oriented or relationship oriented, depending on the favorableness of the situation.
   - The path-goal theory suggests that directive, supportive, participative, or achievement-oriented leader behaviors may be appropriate, depending on the personal characteristics of subordinates and the environment.
   - Vroom's decision tree approach maintains that leaders should vary the extent to which they allow subordinates to participate in making decisions as a function of problem attributes.
   - The LMX model focuses on individual relationships between leaders and followers and on in-group versus out-group considerations.

4. Identify and describe three related approaches to leadership.

   - Related leadership perspectives are as follows:
     - The concept of substitutes for leadership
     - Charismatic leadership
     - The role of transformational leadership in organizations

5. Describe three emerging approaches to leadership.

   - Emerging approaches include the following:
     - Strategic leadership

- Cross-cultural leadership
- Ethical leadership

6. Discuss political behavior in organizations and how it can be managed.

  - Political behavior is another influence process frequently used in organizations.

- Impression management, one especially important form of political behavior, is a direct and intentional effort by someone to enhance his or her image in the eyes of others.
- Managers can take steps to limit the effects of political behavior.

DISCUSSION QUESTIONS

Questions for Review

1. What activities do managers perform? What activities do leaders perform? Do organizations need both managers and leaders? Why or why not?
2. What are the two generic approaches to leadership? What can managers today learn from these approaches?
3. What are the situational approaches to leadership? Briefly describe each and compare and contrast their findings.
4. Describe the subordinate's characteristics, leader behaviors, and environmental characteristics used in path-goal theory. How do these factors combine to influence motivation?
5. In your own words, define political behavior. Describe four political tactics and give an example of each.

Questions for Analysis

1. Even though the trait approach to leadership has no empirical support, it is still widely used. In your opinion, why is this so? In what ways is the use of the trait approach helpful to those who use it? In what ways is it harmful to those who use it?
2. The behavioral theories of leadership claim that an individual's leadership style is fixed. Do you agree or disagree? Give examples to support your position. The behavioral theories also claim that the ideal style is the same in every situation. Do you agree or disagree? Again, give examples.

3. Consider the following list of leadership situations. For each situation, describe in detail the kinds of power the leader has. If the leader were the same but the situation changed—for example, if you thought of the president as the head of his family rather than of the military—would your answers change? Why?
   - The president of the United States is commander in chief of the U.S. military.
   - An airline pilot is in charge of a particular flight.
   - Fans look up to a movie star.
   - Your teacher is the head of your class.

4. Think about a decision that would affect you as a student. Use Vroom's decision tree approach to decide whether the administrator making that decision should involve students in the decision. Which parts of the model seem most important in making that decision? Why?

5. Describe a time when you or someone you know was part of an in-group or an out-group. What was the relationship between each of the groups and the leader? What was the relationship between the members of the two different groups? What was the outcome of the situation for the leader? For the members of the two groups? For the organization?

BUILDING EFFECTIVE DIAGNOSTIC SKILLS

Exercise Overview

Diagnostic skills enable a manager to visualize the most appropriate response to a situation. This exercise shows how they can be useful when a manager must decide which type of power is most appropriate in different situations.

Exercise Background

William Shakespeare's play *Henry V*, which was performed for the first time in 1599, explores the themes of war, leadership, brotherhood, and treachery in a way that remains relevant today. The play contains the famous "St. Crispin's Day" speech that, despite its brevity, many people, Shakespearean scholars and non-experts alike, regard as one of the most inspiring speeches ever written.

First, we need to set the scene: In 1415, England, under the leadership of King Henry IV, has invaded France to regain control of some disputed lands. Bear in mind that, to Shakespeare's audience, the legitimacy of Henry's claim makes both his cause and his war "just." Having won several hard-fought battles, the English army of 6,000 has marched from the coast into the interior of France and is encamped outside the French town of Agincourt. At this point in the campaign, they are sick, cold, hungry, and dispirited, and to make matters worse, they face an army of 25,000 well-rested, well-equipped soldiers and armored knights on horseback. Through a combination of courage, strategy, and plain luck, they win one of history's most renowned battles, losing only 200 men while inflicting more than 5,000 casualties on the enemy.

The short scene in which Henry delivers his St. Crispin's Day speech occurs just before the Battle of Agincourt. Henry's officers are understandably disheartened and fearful of the coming battle, and Henry

must motivate them. That's the purpose of his St. Crispin's Day speech.

Exercise Task

Read the transcript of the speech that your professor will provide you. Then answer the following questions:

1. What types of power does Henry exert in this speech? Give specific examples of each type.
2. It is interesting that Henry had been a notoriously wayward youth before turning his life around and living up to his royal responsibilities. In what ways might knowledge of his past tend to increase or decrease his referent power?
3. In Shakespeare's play, of course, Henry's speech inspires his soldiers to almost impossible victory. You may or may not find it inspiring, but you should be able to see why audiences have long praised it as sufficiently stirring to account for such an improbable achievement. What elements of the speech do the most to make it inspirational? If you find the speech inspiring, explain why. If you don't, explain why not.

BUILDING EFFECTIVE INTERPERSONAL SKILLS

Exercise Overview

Interpersonal skills refer to your ability to communicate with, understand, and motivate both individuals and groups. This exercise asks you to examine in what ways your attitudes toward work relationships reflect your political behavior in the workplace.

Exercise Task

A series of 20 statements follows. To what extent does each statement describe your use—actual or planned—of the described behavior when you're on the job? To address this question, rate your response to each statement according to the following scale:

1	2	3	4	5
Rarely		Occasionally	Usually	

_____ 1. I use personal contacts to get jobs and promotions.

_____ 2. I try to find out what's going on in every organizational department.

_____ 3. I dress the same way as the people in power and develop the same interests (e.g., watch or play sports, or join the same clubs).

_____ 4. I purposely seek contacts and network with higher-level managers.

_____ 5. If upper management offered me a raise and promotion requiring me to move to a new location, I'd say yes even if I didn't want to move.

_____ 6. I get along with everyone, even people regarded as difficult to get along with.

_____ 7. I try to make people feel important by complimenting them.

_____ 8. I do favors for other people and ask for favors in return; and I thank people, often sending thank-you notes.

_____ 9. I work at developing a good working relationship with my supervisor.

_____ 10. I ask my supervisor and other people for advice.

_____ 11. When someone opposes me, I still work to maintain a positive working relationship with that person.

_____ 12. I'm courteous, positive, and pleasant in my relationships with other people.

_____ 13. When my supervisor makes a mistake, I never point it out publicly.

_____ 14. I'm more cooperative (I compromise) than competitive (I try to get my own way).

_____ 15. I tell the truth.

_____ 16. I avoid saying negative things about my supervisor or other people behind their backs.

_____ 17. I work at getting people to know me by name and face by continually introducing myself.

_____ 18. I ask satisfied customers and other people familiar with my work to let my supervisor know how good a job I'm doing.

_____ 19. I try to win contests and get prizes, pins, and other awards.

_____ 20. I send notices of my accomplishments to higher-level managers and such outlets as company newsletters.

Scoring

1. Add up the 20 numbers in the blanks before all the questions. Your total will range between 20 and 100. This number reflects your overall political behavior: _The higher your score, the greater your political behavior._

2. Record your score here and on the following scale:

20—30—40—50—60—70—80—90—100

Nonpolitical   _Political_

3. Now you want to determine your use of political power in _four different areas_ (e.g., learning organizational culture or being a team player). To do this, add up your numbers for each of the following _sets of questions_, and then divide by 5. You will then have your average score for each area:

   A. _Learning the organizational culture and getting to know the power players:_
      Questions 1–5 total divided by 5 = _____

   B. _Developing good working relationships, especially with your boss:_
      Questions 6–12 total divided by 5 = _____

   C. _Being a loyal, honest team player:_
      Questions 13–16 total divided by 5 = _____

   D. _Gaining recognition:_
      Questions 17–20 total divided by 5 = _____

4. _The higher your average score for each set of questions, the greater your use of political power in that area._ Do you rate about the same in each area, or do you rate more highly in some areas more than others? Discuss your findings with some of your classmates and develop an interpretation of the pattern of results you and they have identified for yourselves.

Source: From Lussier/Achua, _Leadership_, 4E. © 2010 Cengage Learning.

SKILLS SELF-ASSESSMENT INSTRUMENT

Managerial Leader Behavior Questionnaire

Introduction: Leadership is now recognized as consisting of a set of characteristics that is important for everyone in an organization to develop. The following assessment surveys the practices or beliefs that you would apply in a management role—that is, your managerial leadership.

Instructions: The following statements refer to different ways you might behave in a managerial leadership role. For each statement, indicate how you do behave or how you think you would behave. Describing yourself may be difficult in some cases, but you should force yourself to make a selection. Record your answers next to each statement according to the following scale:

Rating Scale

5 Very descriptive of me
4 Fairly descriptive of me
3 Somewhat descriptive of me
2 Not very descriptive of me
1 Not descriptive of me at all

_____ 1. I emphasize the importance of performance and encourage everyone to make a maximum effort.

_____ 2. I am friendly, supportive, and considerate toward others.

_____ 3. I offer helpful advice to others on how to advance their careers and encourage them to develop their skills.

_____ 4. I stimulate enthusiasm for the work of the group and say things to build the group's confidence.

_____ 5. I provide appropriate praise and recognition for effective performance and show appreciation for special efforts and contributions.

_____ 6. I reward effective performance with tangible benefits.

_____ 7. I inform people about their duties and responsibilities, clarify rules and policies, and let people know what is expected of them.

_____ 8. Either alone or jointly with others, I set specific and challenging but realistic performance goals.

_____ 9. I provide any necessary training and coaching, or arrange for others to do it.

_____ 10. I keep everyone informed about decisions, events, and developments that affect their work.

_____ 11. I consult with others before making work-related decisions.

_____ 12. I delegate responsibility and authority to others and allow them discretion in determining how to do their work.

_____ 13. I plan in advance how to efficiently organize and schedule the work.

_____ 14. I look for new opportunities for the group to exploit, propose new undertakings, and offer innovative ideas.

_____ 15. I take prompt and decisive action to deal with serious work-related problems and disturbances.

_____ 16. I provide subordinates with the supplies, equipment, support services, and other resources necessary to work effectively.

_____ 17. I keep informed about the activities of the group and check on its performance.

_____ 18. I keep informed about outside events that have important implications for the group.

_____ 19. I promote and defend the interests of the group and take appropriate action to obtain necessary resources for the group.

_____ 20. I emphasize teamwork and try to promote cooperation, cohesiveness, and identification with the group.

_____ 21. I discourage unnecessary fighting and bickering within the group and help settle conflicts and disagreements in a constructive manner.

_____ 22. I criticize specific acts that are unacceptable, find positive things to say, and provide an opportunity for people to offer explanations.

_____ 23. I take appropriate disciplinary action to deal with anyone who violates a rule, disobeys an order, or has consistently poor performance.

Source: Reprinted with permission from David D. Van Fleet and Gary A. Yukl, *Military Leadership: An Organizational Behavior Perspective*, pp. 38–39. © Emerald Group Publishing.

EXPERIENTIAL EXERCISE

The Leadership/Management Interview Experiment

Purpose: Leadership and management are in some ways the same, but more often they are different. This exercise offers you an opportunity to develop a conceptual framework for leadership and management.

Introduction: Most management behaviors and leadership behaviors are a product of individual work experience, so each leader/manager tends to have a unique leadership/management style. Analyzing leadership/management styles, comparing such styles, and relating them to different organizational contexts are often rewarding experiences in learning.

Instructions: *Fact Finding and Execution of the Experiment*

1. Develop a list of questions related to issues you have studied in this chapter that you want to ask a practicing manager and leader during a face-to-face interview. Prior to the actual interview, submit your list of questions to your instructor for approval.

2. Arrange to interview a practicing manager and a practicing leader. For purposes of this assignment, a manager or leader is a person whose job priority involves supervising the work of other people. The

leader/manager may work in a business or in a public or private agency.

3. Interview at least one manager and at least one leader, using the questions you developed. Take good notes on their comments and on your own observations. Do not take more than one hour of each leader or manager's time.

Oral Report

Prepare an oral report using the questions here and your interview information. Complete the following report after the interview. (Attach a copy of your interview questions.)

The Leadership/Management Interview Experiment Report

1. How did you locate the leader(s) and manager(s) you interviewed? Describe your initial contacts.

2. Describe the level and responsibilities of your leader(s) and manager(s). Do not supply names—their responses should be anonymous.

3. Describe the interview settings. How long did the interview last?

4. In what ways were the leaders/managers similar or in agreement about issues?

5. What were some of the major differences between the leaders/managers and between the ways in which they approached their jobs?

6. In what ways would the managers agree or disagree with ideas presented in this course?

7. Describe and evaluate your own interviewing style and skills.

8. How did your managers feel about having been interviewed? How do you know that?

MANAGEMENT AT WORK

Abuse of Power

At first glance, it doesn't seem too hard to figure out what sort of behavior constitutes *sexual harassment* in the workplace. The U.S. Equal Employment Opportunity Commission (EEOC), the federal agency that investigates complaints of workplace discrimination, offers the following explanation:

> Unwelcome sexual advances, requests for sexual favors, and other verbal or physical conduct of a sexual nature constitutes sexual harassment when submission to or rejection of this conduct explicitly or implicitly affects an individual's employment, unreasonably interferes with an individual's work performance, or creates an intimidating, hostile, or offensive work environment.

If you still have questions, the EEOC is happy to clarify a few of the legal fine points. Sexual harassment, for example, can occur in a variety of circumstances, including but not limited to the following:

- The victim as well as the harasser may be a woman or a man. The victim does not have to be of the opposite sex.
- The harasser can be the victim's supervisor, an agent of the employer, a supervisor in another area, a coworker, or a nonemployee.
- The victim does not have to be the person harassed but could be anyone affected by the offensive conduct.
- Unlawful sexual harassment may occur without economic injury to or discharge of the victim.

What does all of this mean in a practical sense—if, let's say, you're a woman who must go to court to assert your rights against workplace discrimination, as defined by Title VII of the Civil Rights Act of 1964 (and subsequent court decisions)? According to employee-rights attorney Ellen Simon, you'll have to establish four facts:

1. That you're a member of a protected class (female)
2. That you were subjected to harassment through either words or actions, based on gender
3. That the harassment had the effect of unreasonably interfering with your work performance and creating an objectively intimidating, hostile, or offensive work environment
4. That there exists some basis for liability on the part of your employer

Consider the case of Julie Gallagher, who held a sales position in the Cleveland office of C. H. Robinson Worldwide, Inc., which provides freight transportation and other supply chain–management services. According to Gallagher, a typical workday in the Robinson office included the widespread use of foul language and what one employee-rights lawyer familiar with the case calls "male arrested-development behavior." Women were regularly called "sluts," "bitches," and other epithets that most people would find unacceptable in the workplace and coworkers displayed nude photos of girlfriends, traded dirty jokes, and engaged in graphic discussions of sexual fantasies and preferences. Gallagher herself was often referred to as a "bitch" and once as a "heifer with milking udders." The work space consisted of cubicles separated by short dividers and grouped in pods on an open floor plan, making it impossible for her to avoid exposure to such behavior. When she complained to the branch manager —who not only had witnessed some of this behavior but had actually participated in it—things only got worse.

"I have been hearing these stories—and they haven't seemed to change that much—for the past 30 years," says Simon. "This stuff happens all the time." Like about 12,000 other female workers that year, Gallager sought a legal resolution to her story and filed charges of sexual harassment against C. H. Robinson. Judge Dan A. Polster of the U.S. District Court for the Northern District of Ohio threw her case out of court. Why? "For reasons that I am at a complete loss to genuinely understand," says Simon, who nevertheless boils down the judge's reasoning to three key points:

1. The conduct in the Robinson office was not "based on sex." Both men and women were regularly present, and because the behavior in question was "indiscriminate," Gallagher could not argue that it discriminated against her.
2. The behavior in the office was not severe enough to satisfy the legal requirements of sexual harassment: Most of it wasn't directed at Gallagher, her work performance didn't suffer, and it wasn't "objectively" hostile. In other words, Gallagher was being "unreasonable" or "hypersensitive" in perceiving the level of hostility.
3. The actions that took place in its office did not make the employer, C. H. Robinson, liable for sexual harassment. Gallagher had not followed the firm's established harassment policies; the company itself received no notice of her complaints, and she was being unreasonable in expecting things to change after complaining only to the branch manager.

Gallagher appealed the district court's ruling. The appeals court sided with her, and sent the case back to district court for further consideration. As of our publication date, the case was still pending.

Case Questions

1. What is the role of power in sexual harassment?
2. What should leaders do when sexual harassment is alleged?
3. What is your opinion of the situation cited in this case?
4. Do some online research and see if the case has been resolved.

Case References

U.S. Equal Employment Opportunity Commission, "Sexual Harassment," "Facts about Sexual Harassment" (Washington, DC, 2012), www.eeoc.gov, accessed on January 1, 2014; EEOC, "Sexual Harassment Charges EEOC & FEPAs Combined: FY 1997–FY 2009" (Washington, DC, 2010), www1.eeoc.gov, accessed on January 1, 2014; Ellen Simon, "Harassed Female Wins 'Locker Room' Hostile Environment Case," *Employee Rights Post*, www.employeerightspost.com, accessed on January 1, 2014; Paul Mollica, "*Gallagher v. C. H. Robinson Worldwide, Inc.*, No. 08-3337 (6th Cir., May 22, 2009)," *Daily Developments in EEO Law*, May 21, 2009, www.employmentlawblog.info, accessed on January 1, 2014; and Simon, "Gender-Based Profanity Constitutes Sexual Harassment," *Employee Rights Post*, www.employeerightspost.com, accessed on January 1, 2014.

When to Stand on Your Head and Other Tips from the Top

1. Studies indicate that good leaders are typically positive and enthusiastic. In what ways do the tips cited in the vignette suggest the possession of these qualities by the various leaders who offer them? Based on their suggestions for managing stress and information flow, what other qualities might you assign, in general, to the leaders cited in the vignette?
2. Recall our discussion, in Chapter 9, of *locus of control*, which we defined as the degree to which an

individual believes that his or her behavior has a direct impact on the consequences of that behavior. In what ways do the attitudes expressed or implied in the vignette suggest the degree of locus control possessed by the leaders who are cited?

3. We discussed *delegation*—the process by which managers assign work to subordinates—in Chapter 6. It is no surprise that effective delegation eases the stress on managers. Judging from their advice on managing information flow, what sort of tasks do you think these managers delegate to others? What sort of tasks do they *not* delegate? As a result of your efforts to address these questions, can you think of a good rule of thumb for what a successful leader should and should not delegate?

ENDNOTES

1 Geoffrey Colvin, "Catch a Rising Star," *Fortune*, http://money. cnn.com, on January 1, 2014; Klaus Kneale, "Stress Management for the CEO," *Forbes.com*, www.forbes.com, accessed on January 1, 2014; Susan Berfield, "The Real Effects of Workplace Anxiety," *BusinessWeek*, www.businessweek.com, accessed on January 1, 2014; Susan Berfield, "How Executives Manage Stress," *BusinessWeek*, http://images.businessweek.com, accessed on January 1, 2014; Jerry Useem, "Making Your Work Work for You," *Fortune*, http://money.cnn.com, accessed on April 23, 2011; and Bill Gates, "How I Work," *Fortune*, http://money.cnn.com, accessed on January 1, 2014.

2 See Ronald A. Heifetz and Donald L. Laurie, "The Work of Leadership," *Harvard Business Review*, January–February 1997, pp. 124–134. See also Arthur G. Jago, "Leadership: Perspectives in Theory and Research," *Management Science*, March 1982, pp. 315–336; and "The New Leadership," *BusinessWeek*, August 28, 2000, pp. 100–187.

3 Gary A. Yukl, *Leadership in Organizations*, 7th ed. (Englewood Cliffs, NJ: Prentice Hall, 2010), p. 5. See also Gregory G. Dess and Joseph C. Pickens, "Changing Roles: Leadership in the 21st Century," *Organizational Dynamics*, Winter 2000, pp. 18–28; and Julian Barling, Amy Christie, and Colette Hoption, "Leadership," in Sheldon Zedeck (ed.), *Handbook of Industrial and Organizational Psychology*, Vol. 1: *Building and Developing the Organization* (Washington, DC: American Psychological Association, 2010), pp. 183–240.

4 John P. Kotter, "What Leaders Really Do," *Harvard Business Review*, May–June 1990, pp. 103–111 (reprinted in *Harvard Business Review*, December 2001, pp. 85–93). See also Daniel Goleman, "Leadership That Gets Results," *Harvard Business Review*, March–April 2000, pp. 78–88; and Keith Grints, *The Arts of Leadership* (Oxford: Oxford University Press, 2000).

5 John R. P. French and Bertram Raven, "The Bases of Social Power," in Dorwin Cartwright (ed.), *Studies in Social Power* (Ann Arbor: University of Michigan Press, 1959), pp. 150–167.

6 Bennett J. Tepper, "Consequences of Abusive Supervision," *Academy of Management Journal*, 2000, Vol. 43, No. 2, pp. 178–190. See also Bennett J. Tepper, "Abusive Supervision in Work Organizations: Review, Synthesis, and Research Agenda," *Journal of Management*, 2007, Vol. 33, No. 3, pp. 261–289.

7 "Management Secrets from the Meanest Company in America," *Bloomberg Businessweek*, January 2, 2013, pp. 46–51.

8 Bernard M. Bass, *Bass & Stogdill's Handbook of Leadership*, 3rd ed. (Riverside, NJ: Free Press, 1990).

9 Shelley A. Kirkpatrick and Edwin A. Locke, "Leadership: Do Traits Matter?" *Academy of Management Executive*, May 1991, Vol. 5, No. 2, pp. 48–60. See also Robert J. Sternberg, "Managerial Intelligence: Why IQ Isn't Enough," *Journal of Management*, 1997, Vol. 23, No. 3, pp. 475–493.

10 Timothy Judge, Amy Colbert, and Remus Ilies, "Intelligence and Leadership: A Quantitative Review and Test of Theoretical Propositions," *Journal of Applied Psychology*, 2004, Vol. 89, No. 3, pp. 542–552.

11 Rensis Likert, *New Patterns of Management* (New York: McGraw-Hill, 1961); and Rensis Likert, *The Human Organization* (New York: McGraw-Hill, 1967).

12 The Ohio State studies stimulated many articles, monographs, and books. A good overall reference is Ralph M. Stogdill and A. E. Coons (eds.), *Leader Behavior: Its Description and Measurement* (Columbus: Bureau of Business Research, Ohio State University, 1957).

13 Edwin A. Fleishman, E. F. Harris, and H. E. Burt, *Leadership and Supervision in Industry* (Columbus: Bureau of Business Research, Ohio State University, 1955).

14 See Timothy Judge, Ronald Piccolo, and Remus Ilies, "The Forgotten One? The Validity of Consideration and Initiating Structure in Leadership Research," *Journal of Applied Psychology*, 2004, Vol. 89, No. 1, pp. 36–51.

15 Robert R. Blake and Jane S. Mouton, *The Managerial Grid* (Houston, TX: Gulf Publishing, 1964); and Robert R. Blake and Jane S. Mouton, *The Versatile Manager: A Grid Profile* (Homewood, IL: Dow Jones-Irwin, 1981).

16 Fred E. Fiedler, *A Theory of Leadership Effectiveness* (New York: McGraw-Hill, 1967).

17 Chester A. Schriesheim, Bennett J. Tepper, and Linda A. Tetrault, "Least Preferred Co-Worker Score, Situational Control, and Leadership Effectiveness: A Meta-Analysis of Contingency Model Performance Predictions," *Journal of Applied Psychology*, 1994, Vol. 79, No. 4, pp. 561–573.

18 Fiedler, *A Theory of Leadership Effectiveness*; and Fred E. Fiedler and M. M. Chemers, *Leadership and Effective Management* (Glenview, IL: Scott, Foresman, 1974).

19 For recent reviews and updates, see Lawrence H. Peters, Darrell D. Hartke, and John T. Pohlmann, "Fiedler's Contingency Theory of Leadership: An Application of the Meta-Analysis Procedures of Schmidt and Hunter," *Psychological Bulletin*, Vol. 97, 2002, pp. 274–285; and Fred E. Fiedler, "When to Lead, When to Stand Back," *Psychology Today*, September 1987, pp. 26–27.

20 Martin G. Evans, "The Effects of Supervisory Behavior on the Path-Goal Relationship," *Organizational Behavior and Human Performance*, May 1970, pp. 277–298; and Robert J. House and Terence R. Mitchell, "Path-Goal Theory of Leadership," *Journal of Contemporary Business*, Autumn 1974, pp. 81–98. See also Yukl, *Leadership in Organizations*, p. 5.

21 For a recent review, see J. C. Wofford and Laurie Z. Liska, "Path-Goal Theories of Leadership: A Meta-Analysis," *Journal of Management*, 1993, Vol. 19, No. 4, pp. 857–876.

22 See Victor H. Vroom and Philip H. Yetton, *Leadership and Decision Making* (Pittsburgh, PA: University of Pittsburgh Press, 1973); and Victor H. Vroom and Arthur G. Jago, *The New Leadership* (Englewood Cliffs, NJ: Prentice Hall, 1988).

23 Victor Vroom, "Leadership and the Decision-Making Process," *Organizational Dynamics*, 2000, Vol. 28, No. 4, pp. 82–94.

24 Vroom and Jago, *The New Leadership*.

25 Vroom and Jago, *The New Leadership*.

26 See Madeline E. Heilman, Harvey A. Hornstein, Jack H. Cage, and Judith K. Herschlag, "Reaction to Prescribed Leader Behavior as a Function of Role Perspective: The Case of the Vroom-Yetton Model," *Journal of Applied Psychology*, February 1984, Vol. 69, No. 1, pp. 50–60; and R. H. George Field, "A Test of the Vroom-Yetton Normative Model of Leadership," *Journal of Applied Psychology*, February 1982, Vol. 67, No. 5, pp. 523–532.

27 George Graen and J. F. Cashman, "A Role-Making Model of Leadership in Formal Organizations: A Developmental Approach," in J. G. Hunt and L. L. Larson (eds.), *Leadership Frontiers* (Kent, OH: Kent State University Press, 1975), pp. 143–165; and Fred Dansereau, George Graen, and W. J. Haga, "A Vertical Dyad Linkage Approach to Leadership within Formal Organizations: A Longitudinal Investigation of the Role-Making Process," *Organizational Behavior and Human Performance*, 1975, Vol. 15, pp. 46–78.

28 See Kathryn Sherony and Stephen Green, "Coworker Exchange: Relationships between Coworkers, Leader-Member Exchange, and Work Attitudes," *Journal of Applied Psychology*, 2002, Vol. 87, No. 3, pp. 542–548.

29 See Bruce J. Avolio, Fred O. Walumbwa, and Todd J. Weber, "Leadership: Current Theories, Research, and Future Directions," in Susan T. Fiske, Daniel L. Schacter, and Robert Sternberg (eds.), *Annual Review of Psychology 2009* (Palo Alto, CA: Annual Reviews, 2009), pp. 421–450.

30 Steven Kerr and John M. Jermier, "Substitutes for Leadership: Their Meaning and Measurement," *Organizational Behavior and Human Performance*, December 1978, Vol. 22, No. 3, pp. 375–403.

31 See Charles C. Manz and Henry P. Sims, Jr., "Leading Workers to Lead Themselves: The External Leadership of Self-Managing Work Teams," *Administrative Science Quarterly*, March 1987, Vol. 32, No. 1, pp. 106–129. See also "Living without a Leader," *Fortune*, March 20, 2000, pp. 218–219.

32 See Robert J. House, "A 1976 Theory of Charismatic Leadership," in J. G. Hunt and L. L. Larson (eds.), *Leadership: The Cutting Edge* (Carbondale: Southern Illinois University Press, 1977), pp. 189–207. See also Jay A. Conger and Rabindra N. Kanungo,

"Toward a Behavioral Theory of Charismatic Leadership in Organizational Settings," *Academy of Management Review*, October 1987, Vol. 12, No. 4, pp. 637–647.

33 Stratford P. Sherman, "Donald Trump Just Won't Die," *Fortune*, August 13, 1990, pp. 75–79.

34 David A. Nadler and Michael L. Tushman, "Beyond the Charismatic Leader: Leadership and Organizational Change," *California Management Review*, Winter 1990, Vol. 32, No. 2, pp. 77–97.

35 Jane Howell and Boas Shamir, "The Role of Followers in the Charismatic Leadership Process: Relationships and Their Consequences," *Academy of Management Review*, 2005, Vol. 30, No. 1, pp. 96–112.

36 James MacGregor Burns, *Leadership* (New York: Harper & Row, 1978). See also A. N. Pieterse, D. van Knippenberg, M. Schippers, and D. Stam, "Transformational and Transactional Leadership and Innovative Behavior: The Role of Psychological Empowerment," *Journal of Organizational Behavior*, May 2010, Vol. 32, No. 4, pp. 609–623.

37 Robert Rubin, David Munz, and William Bommer, "Leading from Within: The Effects of Emotion Recognition and Personality on Transformational Leadership Behaviors," *Academy of Management Journal*, 2005, Vol. 48, No. 5, pp. 845–858.

38 Kenneth Labich, "The Seven Keys to Business Leadership" *Fortune*, October 1988, pp. 97–104.

39 Jerry Useem, "Tape+Light Bulbs=?" *Fortune*, August 12, 2002, pp. 127–132.

40 Dusya Vera and Mary Crossan, "Strategic Leadership and Organizational Learning," *Academy of Management Review*, 2004, Vol. 29, No. 2, pp. 222–240. See also Cynthia A. Montgomery, "Putting Leadership Back into Strategy," *Harvard Business Review*, January 2008, pp. 54–63.

41 "CEO Cook Continues Redesign of Executive Ranks at Apple," *USA Today*, November 12, 2013, p. 3B.

42 "The Best Performing CEOs in the World," *Harvard Business Review*, January–February 2013.

43 "Which of These 9 Grossly Overpaid CEOs Are Worth It?" *seekingalpha.com*, April 20, 2011; and "CEO Mike Jeffries Overvalues His Own Brand and Loses His Cool," *About.com*, September 7, 2012.

44 Tamara Erickson, "The Leaders We Need Now," *Harvard Business Review*, May 2010, pp. 62–67.

45 See Kurt Dirks and Donald Ferrin, "Trust in Leadership," *Journal of Applied Psychology*, 2002, Vol. 87, No. 4, pp. 611–628. See also Russell A. Eisenstat, Michael Beer, Nathanial Foote, Tobias Fredberg, and Flemming Norrgren, "The Uncompromising Leader," *Harvard Business Review*, July–August 2008, pp. 51–59; and Christopher Meyer and Julia Kirby, "Leadership in the Age of Transparency," *Harvard Business Review*, April 2010, pp. 38–46.

46 Jeffrey Pfeffer, *Power in Organizations* (Marshfield, MA: Pitman, 1981), p. 7. See also Gerald R. Ferris and Wayne A. Hochwarter, "Organizational Politics," in Sheldon Zedeck (ed.), *Handbook of Industrial and Organizational Psychology*, Vol. 3: *Maintaining, Expanding, and Contracting the Organization* (Washington, DC: American Psychological Association, 2010), pp. 435–459.

47 Timothy Judge and Robert Bretz, "Political Influence Behavior and Career Success," *Journal of Management*, 1994, Vol. 20, No. 1, pp. 43–65.

48 Victor Murray and Jeffrey Gandz, "Games Executives Play: Politics at Work," *Business Horizons*, December 1980, pp. 11–23; and Jeffrey Gandz and Victor Murray, "The Experience of Workplace Politics," *Academy of Management Journal*, June 1980, Vol. 23, No. 2, pp. 237–251.

49 Don R. Beeman and Thomas W. Sharkey, "The Use and Abuse of Corporate Power," *Business Horizons*, March–April 1987, pp. 26–30.

50 "How Ebbers Kept the Board in His Pocket," *BusinessWeek*, October 14, 2002, pp. 138–139.

51 See William L. Gardner, "Lessons in Organizational Dramaturgy: The Art of Impression Management," *Organizational Dynamics*, Summer 1992, Vol. 21, No. 1, pp. 51–63; Elizabeth Wolf Morrison and Robert J. Bies, "Impression Management in the Feedback-Seeking Process: A Literature Review and Research Agenda," *Academy of Management Review*, July 1991, pp. 522–541; and Mark C. Bolino, K. Michele Kacmar, William H. Turnley, and J. Bruce Gilstrap, "A Multi-Level Review of Impression Management Motives and Behaviors," *Journal of Management*, 2008, Vol. 34, No. 6, pp. 1080–1109.

52 *BusinessWeek*, April 13, 2009, p. 54.

53 See Chad Higgins, Timothy Judge, and Gerald Ferris, "Influence Tactics and Work Outcomes: A Meta-Analysis," *Journal of Organizational Behavior*, 2003, Vol. 24, pp. 89–106; and Gerald R. Ferris, Darren C. Treadway, Pamela L. Perrewe, Robyn L. Brour, Ceasar Douglas, and Sean Lux, "Political Skill in Organizations," *Journal of Management*, 2007, Vol. 33, No. 3, pp. 290–320.

54 Murray and Gandz, "Games Executives Play."

55 Beeman and Sharkey, "The Use and Abuse of Corporate Power."

56 Stefanie Ann Lenway and Kathleen Rehbein, "Leaders, Followers, and Free Riders: An Empirical Test of Variation in Corporate Political Involvement," *Academy of Management Journal*, December 1991, Vol. 34, No. 4, pp. 893–905.

CHAPTER 12

Communication in Organizations

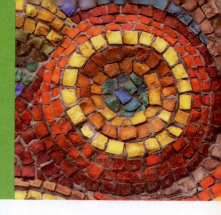

Sergii Tsololo/Photos.com

Learning Outcomes

After studying this chapter, you should be able to:

1 Describe the role and importance of communication in the manager's job.

2 Identify the basic forms of communication in organizations.

3 Describe the role of digital communication in organizations.

4 Discuss informal communication, including its various forms and types.

5 Describe how the communication process can be managed to recognize and overcome barriers.

Management in Action

¿*Qué Pasa* in the Ad Agency?

"… it's the current best-in-class companies that are spending more in the Hispanic market in an effort to turn around those businesses."

—AHAA chair Gisela Girard

A recent Toyota television ad: A father is explaining Toyota's hybrid engine to his son. "[The car] runs on gas and electricity," he says. "Mira. Mira aquí. [Look. Look here.] It uses both." The son replies, "Like you, with English and Spanish." "Sí," replies the father.

As the makeup of U.S. society changes, organizations have realized that they need to change the ways in which they communicate with diverse customer bases. It might come as something of a surprise, but this Toyota TV spot reflects a virtually revolutionary change in the way American companies address potential buyers from different cultures. Once, for example, they assumed that Hispanics living in the United States were immigrants, spoke no English, and clung to old-world values. Today, however, they're well aware of the fact that over half of the country's 50 million Hispanics were born in this country. Like the father and son in Toyota's depiction of Hispanic life, most Spanish speakers know English and mix elements not only of both languages but also of both U.S. and Latino culture. "This group is not about nostalgia for the home country," says Jaime Fortuño, managing partner of Azafrán, a New York–based ad agency.

There was also a time when advertisers relied on mainstream ads—ads aimed at the center of the market where they expected to find the "typical" consumer.

Don Mason/Blend Images/Getty Images

Most businesses today recognize that they must have the capability to communicate with customers, employees, and other stakeholders in multiple languages. This automobile dealer is conversing with a customer in Spanish.

But as the purchasing power of minorities has increased, companies have put more energy into developing targeted ads—ads aimed at specific groups of consumers and often delivered through language-targeted media. Today, for example, a corporation thinks nothing of budgeting $100 million a year for Hispanic-themed ads. Since 2004, about one-third of ads targeted to Hispanics have been presented in Spanish, and that proportion is growing—for good reason. The buying power of Hispanics grew from $490 billion in 2000 to $1 trillion in 2010—a rate of 108 percent over the decade (compared to a 49 percent rate for the majority market). By 2015, Hispanic buying power will hit $1.5 trillion and will account for 11 percent of the national total.

Although advertising slumped across the board in 2008 and 2009, the decline in Spanish-language media was more moderate than in the industry as a whole. And although Spanish-language advertising in 2009 was down from 2008, the Association of Hispanic Advertising Agencies (AHAA) reports a rebound in 2010, especially among its "best-in-class" Spanish-language advertisers—those that allocate more than 11.8 percent of their ad budgets to Hispanic audiences. "Our 2009 report," says AHAA chair Gisela Girard, "revealed that many corporations 'don't get it,' [but] our 2010 … findings indicate that it's the current best-in-class companies that are spending more in the Hispanic market in an effort to turn around those businesses."

An ad for Southwest Airlines: A virile young Hispanic rollerblades up to a parked car to admire his image in the tinted window. The window unexpectedly rolls down to reveal two men inside the car who are also admiring him. "Want to get away?" reads the punchline, which is followed by a low airfare price.

"In advertising," observes Juan Pablo Oubiña, art director at Grupo Gallegos, an LA-area agency, "it's not easy to be different. It takes ten times as much work." And getting the language right isn't really the hardest part of making Spanish-language ads. Like the Southwest ad from the Hispanic-owned agency Dieste Harmel & Partners, many of the latest-vintage Spanish-language ads have succeeded in appealing to Hispanic audiences by playing with and against stereotypes, but as one Hispanic marketing consultant observes, it's a tricky balancing act. "Not only are Americans comfortable with positive stereotypes as a means to be politically correct," says Jennifer Woodard, "but so are many Hispanics." The problem of stereotyping, she reminds us, is usually twofold: Advertisers tend to rely on stereotypes because they assume that they're somehow reflective of the mainstream, and the consumers being stereotyped tend to settle for stereotypes because they dominate the images of themselves that are available to them in the media.

An ad for Fox Sports Net: Returning home from a shopping trip, a Hispanic woman detects an unpleasant odor in the house. The camera pursues her as she follows her nose from room to room until she reaches the living room, where she realizes that her husband is so thoroughly immersed in a televised soccer game that he's been watching through the open door of a nearby toilet.

This ad—a Grupo Gallegos creation—does a good job of playing *with and against* stereotypes because it bounces off the stereotype of the soccer-obsessed Latino in what Woodard describes as "a great example of taking a slice of life from a husband and wife, no matter the culture, and pushing the ad into entertainment." Contrast this ad, however, with the far more common appropriation of the same stereotype in TV advertising aimed at Hispanics. Advertising agency executive Tommy Thompson thinks that far too many ads targeted at Hispanic viewers use soccer as a connecting point. "What does soccer have to do with life insurance?" he argues. "Are there really no other insights as relates to Hispanics' need for life insurance that can be communicated without soccer?" Thompson, founder and president of Dallas-based iNSPIRE!, argues that advertisers should focus less on playing to stereotypes and more on understanding the cultures being targeted.

It's advice that Gallegos put to good use in an ad for Energizer batteries. Gallegos was originally given the task of making the brand "iconic" for Hispanic consumers—giving it immediately familiar symbolic value so that Spanish speakers would think of perpetual motion and say "*como el conejito Energizer*" the same way that English speakers think of perpetual motion and say "like the Energizer bunny." At Grupo Gallegos, however, brainstorming on a new account always starts with "Okay, *aquí está el problema que tenemos* when we really start looking at the brand," and the Gallegos team realized early on that most Hispanics don't associate batteries with perpetual motion (or anything else): For them, a battery is a battery. So Gallegos came up with an ad in which a Mexican man walks down the street and shares his realization that he's immortal—whereupon a two-story commercial sign falls on his head. Among other things, he observes, being immortal means that you need a very long-lasting battery for your camera.[1]

Businesses continue to look for effective ways to communicate with their customers, employees, job seekers, customers, and investors. Adopting multiple languages is one increasingly common method for getting messages to different stakeholders. Communication has always been a vital part of managerial work. Indeed, managers around the world agree that communication is one of their most important tasks. It is important for them to communicate with others to convey their vision and goals of the organization. And it is important for others to communicate with them so that they will better understand what is going on in their environment and how they and their organization can become more effective.

This chapter discusses communication, one of the most basic forms of interaction among people. We begin by examining communication in the context of the manager's job. We then identify and discuss forms of interpersonal, group, and organizational communication. After discussing informal means of communication, we describe how organizational communication can be effectively managed.

COMMUNICATION AND THE MANAGER'S JOB

A typical day for a manager includes doing desk work, attending scheduled meetings, placing and receiving phone calls, reading and answering correspondence (both print and electronic), attending unscheduled meetings, and making tours.[2] Most of these activities involve communication. In fact, managers usually spend over half their time on some form of communication. Communication always involves two or more people, so other behavioral processes, such as motivation, leadership, and group and team interactions, all come into play. Top executives must handle communication effectively if they are to be true leaders.

A Definition of Communication

communication
The process of transmitting information from one person to another

Imagine three managers working in an office building. The first is all alone but is nevertheless yelling for a subordinate to come help. No one appears, but he continues to yell. The second is talking on the phone to a subordinate, but a poor network connection causes the subordinate to misunderstand some important numbers being provided by the manager. As a result, the subordinate sends 1,500 crates of eggs to 150 Fifth Street, when he should have sent 150 crates of eggs to 1500 Fifteenth Street. The third manager is talking in her office with a subordinate who clearly hears and understands what is being said. Each of these managers is attempting to communicate, but with different results.

effective communication
The process of sending a message in such a way that the message received is as close in meaning as possible to the message intended

Communication is the process of transmitting information from one person to another.[3] Did any of our three managers communicate? The last did, and the first did not. How about the second? In fact, she did communicate. She transmitted information, and information was received. The problem was that the message transmitted and the message received were not the same. The words spoken by the manager were distorted by static and noise. **Effective communication**, then, is the process of sending a message in such a way that the message received is as close in meaning as possible to the message intended. Although the second manager engaged in communication, it was not effective.

data
Raw figures and facts reflecting a single aspect of reality

A key element in effective communication is differentiating between data and information. **Data** are raw figures and facts reflecting a single aspect of reality. The facts that a plant has 35 machines, that each machine is capable of producing 1,000 units of output per day, that current and projected future demand for the units is 30,000 per day, and that workers sufficiently skilled to run the machines make $20 an hour are data. **Information**,

information
Data presented in a way or form that has meaning

meanwhile, is data presented in a way or form that has meaning.[4] Thus, combining and summarizing the four pieces of data just given provides information: The plant has excess capacity and is therefore incurring unnecessary costs. Information has meaning to a manager and provides a basis for action. The plant manager might use the information and decide to sell four machines (perhaps keeping one as a backup) and transfer five operators to other jobs.

Characteristics of Useful Information

What characteristics make the difference between information that is useful and information that is not useful? In general, information is useful if it is accurate, timely, complete, and relevant.

accurate information
Provides a valid and reliable reflection of reality

Accurate   For information to be of real value to a manager, it must be **accurate information**. Accuracy means that the information must provide a valid and reliable reflection of reality. One of the first major mergers between a traditional bricks-and-mortar business and a dot-com business took place when Time Warner, an old-line media conglomerate, merged with AOL, one of the biggest dot-com businesses at the time. Unfortunately, it soon became clear that the value of AOL had been inflated by improper accounting practices and revenue overstatements. It was no surprise, then, that the new firm struggled to develop a unified strategy and culture while enduring multiple government investigations and write-downs of corporate assets. Finally, Time Warner sold its AOL division in 2009.[5]

timely information
Available in time for appropriate managerial action

Timely   Information also needs to be **timely**. Timeliness does not necessarily mean speediness; it means only that information needs to be available in time for appropriate managerial action. What constitutes timeliness is a function of the situation facing the manager. When Marriott was gathering information for a new hotel project, managers allowed themselves a six-month period for data collection. They felt this would give them an opportunity to do a good job of getting the information they needed while not delaying things too much. In contrast, Marriott's reservation and accounting systems can provide a manager today with last night's occupancy level at any Marriott facility. United Airlines once filed for bankruptcy protection while it restructured its finances. Several years later, an error led a South Florida newspaper to post an old story about the earlier filing on its website in a way that made it appear as a current event. The resulting panic among investors caused United Airlines shares to drop from $12.50 a share to less than $3 a share before the error was caught and corrected.[6]

complete information
Provides the manager with all the information that he or she needs

Complete   Information must tell a complete story for it to be useful to a manager. If it is less than **complete information**, the manager is likely to get an inaccurate or distorted picture of reality. For example, managers at Kroger used to think that house-brand products were more profitable than national brands because they yielded higher unit profits. On the basis of this information, they gave house brands a great deal of shelf space and centered promotional activities around them. As Kroger's managers became more sophisticated in understanding their information, however, they realized that national brands were actually more profitable over time because they sold many more units than house brands during any given period of time. Hence, although a store might sell 10 cans of Kroger coffee in a day, with a profit of 50 cents per can (total profit of $5), it would sell 15 cans of Maxwell House with a profit of 40 cents per can (total profit of $6) and 10 vacuum bags of Starbucks coffee with a profit of $1 per bag (total profit of $10). With this more complete picture, managers could do a better job of selecting the right mix of Kroger, Maxwell House, and Starbucks coffee to display and promote.

Relevant   Finally, information must be relevant if it is to be useful to managers. **Relevant information**, like timely information, is defined according to the needs and circumstances of a particular manager. Operations managers need information on costs and productivity, human resource managers need information on hiring needs and turnover rates, and marketing managers need information on sales projections and advertising rates. As Walmart contemplates countries as possible expansion opportunities, it gathers information about local regulations, customs, and so forth. But the information about any given country is not as relevant before a decision is made to enter that market than it is after the firm has made a decision to enter the market.

The Communication Process

Figure 12.1 illustrates how communication generally takes place between people. The process of communication begins when one person (the sender) wants to transmit a fact, idea, opinion, or other information to someone else (the receiver). This fact, idea, or opinion has meaning to the sender, whether it is simple and concrete or complex and abstract.

The next step is to encode the meaning into a form appropriate to the situation. The encoding might take the form of words, facial expressions, gestures, or even artistic expressions and physical actions. After the message has been encoded, it is transmitted through the appropriate channel or medium. The channel by which this encoded

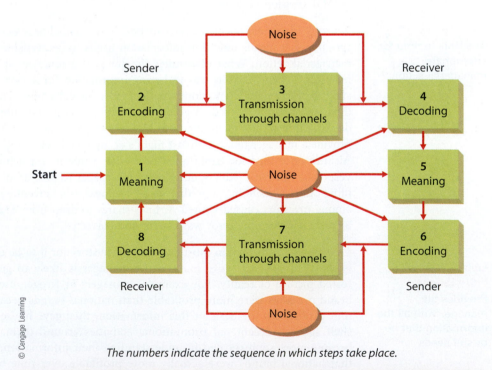

© Cengage Learning

The numbers indicate the sequence in which steps take place.

FIGURE 12.1

The Communication Process

As the figure shows, noise can disrupt the communication process at any step. Managers must therefore understand that a conversation in the next office, a fax machine out of paper, and the receiver's smartphone being out of service may all thwart the manager's best attempts to communicate.

message is being transmitted to you is the printed page. Common channels in organizations include meetings, e-mails, memos, letters, reports, and phone calls. After the message is received, it is decoded back into a form that has meaning for the receiver. As noted earlier, the consistency of this meaning can vary dramatically. In many cases, the meaning prompts a response, and the cycle is continued when the same steps are used to send a new message back to the original sender.

"Noise" may disrupt communication anywhere along the way. Noise can be the sound of someone coughing, a loud truck driving by, or two people talking close at hand. It can also include disruptions such as a letter lost in the mail, a dropped cell phone call, an e-mail misrouted or infected with a virus, or one of the participants in a conversation being called away before the communication process is completed.

FORMS OF COMMUNICATION IN ORGANIZATIONS

Managers need to understand several kinds of communication that are common in organizations today.[7] These include interpersonal communication, communication in networks and work teams, organizational communication, and electronic communication.

Interpersonal Communication

Interpersonal communication generally takes one of two forms: oral and written. As we will see, each has clear strengths and weaknesses.

oral communication
Face-to-face conversation, group discussions, telephone calls, and other circumstances in which the spoken word is used to transmit meaning

Oral Communication   **Oral communication** takes place in conversations, group discussions, phone calls, and other situations in which the spoken word is used to express meaning. One study (conducted before the advent of e-mail) demonstrated the importance of oral communication by finding that most managers spent between 50 and 90 percent of their time talking to people.[8] Oral communication is so prevalent for several reasons. The primary advantage of oral communication is that it promotes prompt feedback and interchange in the form of verbal questions or agreement, facial expressions, and gestures. Oral communication is also easy (all the sender needs to do is talk), and it can be done with little preparation (though careful preparation is advisable in certain situations). The sender does not need pencil and paper, a computer, or other equipment. In another survey, 55 percent of the executives sampled felt that their own written communication skills were fair or poor, so they chose oral communication to avoid embarrassment![9]

However, oral communication also has drawbacks. It may suffer from problems of inaccuracy if the speaker chooses the wrong words to convey meaning or leaves out pertinent details, if noise disrupts the process, or if the receiver forgets part of the message.[10] In a two-way discussion, there is seldom time for a thoughtful, considered response or for introducing many new facts, and there is no permanent record of what has been said. In addition, although most managers are comfortable talking to people individually or in small groups, fewer enjoy speaking to larger audiences.[11]

written communication
Memos, letters, reports, notes, and other circumstances in which the written word is used to transmit meaning

Written Communication   "Putting it in writing" in a letter, report, memorandum, handwritten note, or e-mail can solve many of the problems inherent in oral communication. Nevertheless, and perhaps surprisingly, **written communication** is not as common as one might imagine, nor is it a mode of communication much respected by managers. One sample of managers indicated that only 13 percent of the printed mail they received was of immediate use to them.[12] Over 80 percent of the managers who responded to another survey indicated that the written communication they received was of fair or poor quality.[13]

The biggest single drawback of traditional forms of written communication is that they inhibit feedback and interchange. When one manager sends another manager a letter, it must be written or dictated, typed, mailed, received, routed, opened, and read. If there is a misunderstanding, it may take several days for it to be recognized, let alone rectified. Although the use of e-mail, texts, or instant messaging is, of course, much faster, both sender and receiver must still have access to a computer or smartphone, and the receiver must open and read the message for it to actually be received. A phone call could settle the whole matter in just a few minutes. Thus, written communication often inhibits feedback and interchange and is usually more difficult and time consuming than oral communication.

Of course, written communication offers some advantages. It is often quite accurate and provides a permanent record of the exchange. The sender can take the time to collect and assimilate the information and can draft and revise it before it is transmitted. The receiver can take the time to read it carefully and can refer to it repeatedly, as needed. For these reasons, written communication is generally preferable when important details are involved. At times, it is important to one or both parties to have a written record available as evidence of exactly what took place. Julie Regan, founder of Toucan-Do, an importing company based in Honolulu, relies heavily on formal business letters in establishing contacts and buying merchandise from vendors in Southeast Asia. She believes that such letters give her an opportunity to carefully think through what she wants to say, tailor her message to each individual, and avoid later misunderstandings.

Choosing the Right Form   Which form of interpersonal communication should the manager use? The best medium is determined by the situation. Oral communication or e-mail or text may be preferred when the message is personal, nonroutine, and brief. More formal written communication is usually best when the message is more impersonal, routine, and longer. And, given the prominent role that e-mails have played in several recent court cases, managers should always use discretion when sending messages electronically.[14] For example, private e-mails made public during legal proceedings have played major roles in litigation involving Enron, Tyco, WorldCom, and Morgan Stanley.[15]

The manager can also combine media to capitalize on the advantages of each. For example, a quick phone call to set up a meeting is easy and gets an immediate response. Following up the call with a reminder e-mail or handwritten note helps ensure that the recipient will remember the meeting, and it provides a record of the meeting having been called. Digital communication, discussed more fully later in this chapter, blurs the differences between oral and written communication and can help each be more effective.

Communication in Networks and Work Teams

Although communication among team members in an organization is clearly interpersonal in nature, substantial research also focuses specifically on how people in networks and work teams communicate with one another. A **communication network** is the pattern through which the members of a group or team communicate. Researchers studying group dynamics have discovered several typical networks in groups and teams consisting of three, four, and five members. Representative networks among members of five-member teams are shown in Figure 12.2.[16]

In the wheel pattern, all communication flows through one central person, who is probably the group's leader. In a sense, the wheel is the most centralized network because one person receives and disseminates all information. The Y pattern is slightly less centralized—two people are close to the center. The chain offers a more even flow of information among members, although two people (the ones at each end) interact

communication network

The pattern through which the members of a group communicate

Wheel	Y	Chain	Circle	All channel

FIGURE 12.2

Types of Communication Networks

Research on communication networks has identified five basic networks for five-person groups. These networks vary in terms of information flow, position of the leader, and effectiveness for different types of tasks. Managers might strive to create centralized networks when group tasks are simple and routine. Alternatively, managers can foster decentralized groups when group tasks are complex and nonroutine.

with only one other person. This path is closed in the circle pattern. Finally, the all-channel network, the most decentralized, allows a free flow of information among all group members. Everyone participates equally, and the group's leader, if there is one, is not likely to have excessive power.

Research conducted on networks suggests some interesting connections between the type of network and group performance. For example, when the group's task is relatively simple and routine, centralized networks tend to perform with greatest efficiency and accuracy. The dominant leader facilitates performance by coordinating the flow of information. When a group of accounting clerks is logging incoming invoices and distributing them for payment, for example, one centralized leader can coordinate things efficiently. When the task is complex and nonroutine, such as making a major decision about organizational strategy, decentralized networks tend to be most effective because open channels of communication permit more interaction and a more efficient sharing of relevant information. Managers should recognize the effects of communication networks on group and organizational performance and should try to structure networks appropriately.

Organizational Communication

Still other forms of communication in organizations are those that flow among and between organizational units or groups. Each of these involves oral or written communication, but each also extends to broad patterns of communication across the organization.[17] As shown in Figure 12.3, two of these forms of communication follow vertical and horizontal linkages in the organization.

vertical communication
Communication that flows up and down the organization, usually along formal reporting lines; takes place between managers and their superiors and subordinates and may involve several different levels of the organization

Vertical Communication   **Vertical communication** is communication that flows up and down the organization, usually along formal reporting lines—that is, it is the communication that takes place between managers and their superiors and subordinates. Vertical communication may involve only two people, or it may flow through several different organizational levels.

Upward communication consists of messages from subordinates to superiors. This flow is usually from subordinates to their direct superior, then to that person's direct superior, and so on up the hierarchy. Occasionally, a message might bypass a particular superior. The typical content of upward communication is requests, information that the lower-level manager thinks is of importance to the higher-level manager, responses to requests from the higher-level manager, suggestions, complaints, and financial information. Research has shown that upward communication is more subject to distortion than

© Cengage Learning

← Vertical communication

←----- Horizontal communication

© Cengage Learning

FIGURE 12.3

Formal Communication in Organizations

Formal communication in organizations follows official reporting relationships or prescribed channels. For example, vertical communication, shown here with solid lines, flows between levels in the organization and involves subordinates and their managers. Horizontal communication, shown with dashed lines, flows between people at the same level and is usually used to facilitate coordination.

downward communication. Subordinates are likely to withhold or distort information that makes them look bad. The greater the degree of difference in status between superior and subordinate and the greater the degree of distrust, the more likely the subordinate is to suppress or distort information.[18] For example, subordinates might choose to withhold information about problems from their boss if they think the news will make him angry and if they think they can solve the problem themselves without his knowledge.

Downward communication occurs when information flows down the hierarchy from superiors to subordinates. The typical content of these messages is directives on how something is to be done, the assignment of new responsibilities, performance feedback, and general information that the higher-level manager thinks will be of value to the lower-level manager. Vertical communication can and usually should be two-way in nature. In other words, give-and-take communication with active feedback is generally likely to be more effective than one-way communication.[19]

Horizontal Communication   Whereas vertical communication involves a superior and a subordinate, **horizontal communication** involves colleagues and peers at the same level of the organization. For example, an operations manager might communicate to a marketing manager that inventory levels are running low and that projected delivery dates should be extended by two weeks. Horizontal communication probably occurs more among managers than among nonmanagers.

This type of communication serves a number of purposes.[20] It facilitates coordination among interdependent units. For example, a manager at Motorola was once researching the strategies of Japanese semiconductor firms in Europe. He found a great deal of information that was relevant to his assignment. He also uncovered some additional information that was potentially important to another department, so he passed it along to a colleague in that department, who used it to improve his own operations. Horizontal communication can also be used for joint problem solving, as when two plant managers at Northrop Grumman got together to work out a new method to improve productivity. Finally, horizontal communication plays a major role in work teams with members drawn from several departments.

horizontal communication

Communication that flows laterally within the organization; involves colleagues and peers at the same level of the organization and may involve individuals from several different organizational units

Digital Communication

An increasingly important form of organizational communication relies on digital communication technology. **Information technology (IT)** consists of the resources used by an organization to manage information that it needs to carry out its mission. IT may consist of computers, computer networks, telephones, fax machines, smartphones, and other pieces of hardware. In addition, IT involves software that facilitates the system's ability to manage information in a way that is useful for managers. Both formal information systems and personal information technology have reshaped how managers communicate with one another. The Tough Times, Tough Choices feature, The Brutally-Honest-Opinion Business, shows how some corporations are making use of blogs, one form of digital electronic communication.

Information Systems   Advances in IT have made it increasingly easy for managers to use many different kinds of information systems. In this section, we discuss the most common kinds of information systems used by businesses today.

Transaction-processing systems (TPSs) are applications of information processing for basic day-to-day business transactions. Customer order taking by online retailers, approval of claims at insurance companies, receipt and confirmation of reservations by airlines, payroll processing and bill payment at almost every company—all are routine business processes. Typically, the TPS for first-level (operational) activities is well defined, with predetermined data requirements, and follows the same steps to complete all transactions in the system.

Systems for knowledge workers and office applications support the activities of both knowledge workers and employees in clerical positions. They provide assistance for data processing and other office activities, including the creation of communications documents. Like other departments, the information systems (IS) department includes both knowledge workers and data workers. *Systems for operations and data workers* make sure that the right programs are run in the correct sequence, and they monitor equipment to ensure that it is operating properly. Many organizations also have employees who enter data into the system for processing. *Knowledge-level and office systems* are also increasingly widespread. The widespread availability of text processing, document imaging, desktop publishing, computer-aided design, simulation modeling, and similar tools has increased the productivity of both knowledge and office workers. Desktop publishing combines graphics and word-processing text to publish professional-quality print and web documents. Document-imaging systems can scan paper documents and images, convert them into digital form, store them, retrieve them, manipulate them, and/or transmit them to workstations throughout the network, all without generating any additional paper.

Management information systems (MISs) support an organization's managers by providing daily reports, schedules, plans, and budgets. Each manager's information activities vary according to his or her functional area (say, accounting or marketing) and management level. Whereas midlevel managers focus mostly on internal activities and information, higher-level managers are also engaged in external activities. Middle managers, the largest MIS user group, need networked information to plan upcoming activities such as personnel training, materials movements, and cash flows. They also need to know the current status of the jobs and projects being carried out in their department: What stage is it at now? When will it be finished? Is there an opening so we can start the next job? Many of a firm's MISs—cash flow, sales, production scheduling, and shipping—are indispensable in helping managers find answers to such questions.

Decision support systems (DSSs) are interactive systems that locate and present information needed to support the decision-making process. Whereas some DSSs are devoted to specific problems, others serve more general purposes, allowing managers to

---

information technology (IT)

The resources used by an organization to manage information that it needs to carry out its mission

transaction-processing systems (TPSs)

An application of information processing for basic day-to-day business transactions

management information systems (MISs)

An information system that supports an organization's managers by providing daily reports, schedules, plans, and budgets

decision support systems (DSSs)

An interactive system that locates and presents information needed to support the decision-making process

TOUGH TIMES, TOUGH CHOICES

The Brutally-Honest-Opinion Business

Cell phones and fax machines? Your grandfather's technology. Video conferencing? Been there, done that. The Internet? Old news. E-mail? Business as usual. PDA? Smartphone? Standard issue for today's manager.

Obviously, the explosion in digital-communication technology over the last 25 years has created many new media. Corporations now rely extensively on these new technologies, and they've changed the way we work. Virtual teams, global workforces, outsourcing, just-in-time inventory—these are just a few of the widely accepted business tools and methods that could never have existed without new developments in communication technology. Today, yet another new technology is at the cutting edge of business-communication strategies: *web logs*, or so-called blogs.

A *blog* is any web-based publication consisting mainly of periodically posted articles, usually in reverse chronological order. They're similar to journals in that bloggers express thoughts or opinions over a period of time, but most blogs allow readers to add their own comments in response to original posts. Blogs allow groups of people, whether or not

they're otherwise connected, to share thoughts, and for some readers, professionally (or semiprofessionally) posted blogs actually supplement or replace traditional news media. Blogs can also function much like face-to-face grapevines to communicate information that's suppressed elsewhere.

Nowadays, organizations as disparate as General Motors, the Dallas Cowboys, and Stonyfield Farm (an organic dairy) maintain popular corporate blogs; Microsoft supports 237 blogs (at last count). What do corporations do with blogs? Naturally, they use them to communicate with customers and employees, but they've found a variety of other uses for them, too. A consumer-research firm called Umbria, for example, charges companies such as Electronic Arts, SAP, and Sprint $60,000 a year to conduct routine scans of 20 million blogs. The data is valuable to corporate marketers, in particular because bloggers are often early product adopters, and blog opinions show up quickly. Marketers, however, should be prepared for the kind of input they're going to get for their money: "The blogosphere," warns Umbria CEO Howard Kaushansky, "is overflowing with brutally honest opinion."

© Alexey Boldin/Shutterstock.com

Communication technology continues to change at a very rapid clip. While smartphones and tablets are slowing making laptop computers seem old-fashioned, so-called "wearable" technology like this smartwatch may soon become the standard.

(continued)

TOUGH TIMES, TOUGH CHOICES (Continued)

With a survey list of nearly 20 million blogs and a 10 percent share, Umbria is actually a fairly small player in the blog-research market. Larger competitors in the $20 million market include Intelliseek, with about a third of the market, and Buzz Metrics, which doesn't reveal how much business it does. There appears to be room for more competitors, however. According to the search engine Technorati, there are at least 112.8 million blogs out there (not counting another 72.8 million in China), with about 175,000 new blogs popping up every day. Bloggers put up more than 1.6 million posts per day, or more than 18 updates a second.

References: Matthew Boyle, "Do's and Don'ts of Corporate Blogging," *Fortune*, http://money.cnn.com, accessed on January 1, 2014; Justin Martin, "What Bloggers Think of Your Business," *Fortune*, http://money.cnn.com, accessed on January 1, 2014; Anne Helmond, "How Many Blogs Are There? Is Someone Still Counting?" *The Blog Herald*, www.blogherald.com, accessed on January 1, 2014; and Adam Thierer, "Need Help ... How Many Blogs Are There Out There?" *The Technology Liberation Front*, http://tech liberation.com, accessed on January 1, 2014.

analyze different types of problems. Thus, a firm that often faces decisions on plant capacity, for example, may have a capacity DSS: The manager inputs data on anticipated levels of sales, working capital, and customer delivery requirements. Then the DSS's built-in transaction processors manipulate the data and make recommendations on the best levels of plant capacity for each future time period. In contrast, a general-purpose system, such as a marketing DSS, might respond to a variety of marketing-related problems. It may be programmed to handle "What if ... ?" questions, such as "When is the best time to introduce a new product if my main competitor introduces one in 3 months, our new product has an 18-month expected life, demand is seasonal with a peak in autumn, and my goal is to gain the largest possible market share?" The DSS can help managers make decisions for which predetermined solutions are unknown by using sophisticated modeling tools and data analysis.

executive support system (ESS)
A quick-reference, easy-access application of information systems specially designed for instant access by upper-level managers

An **executive support system (ESS)** is a quick-reference, easy-access application of information systems specially designed for instant access by upper-level managers. ESSs are designed to assist with executive-level decisions and problems, ranging from "What lines of business should we be in five years from now?" to "Based on forecasted developments in digital technologies, to what extent should our firm be globalized in five years? In ten years?" The ESS also uses a wide range of both internal information and external sources, such as industry reports, global economic forecasts, and reports on competitors' capabilities. Because senior-level managers do not usually possess advanced computer skills, they prefer systems that are easily accessible and adaptable. Accordingly, ESSs are not designed to address only specific, predetermined problems. Instead, they allow the user some flexibility in attacking a variety of problem situations. They are easily accessible by means of simple keyboard strokes or even voice commands.

artificial intelligence (AI)
The construction of computer systems, both hardware and software, to imitate human behavior— that is, to perform physical tasks, use thought processes, and learn

Artificial intelligence (AI) can be defined as the construction of computer systems, both hardware and software, to imitate human behavior—in other words, systems that perform physical tasks, use thought processes, and learn. In developing AI systems, knowledge workers (business specialists, modelers, and IT experts) try to design computer-based systems capable of reasoning, so that computers, instead of people, can perform certain business activities. One simple example is a credit evaluation system that decides which loan applicants are creditworthy and which ones are risky and then composes acceptance and rejection letters accordingly. One special form of AI, the *expert system*, is designed to imitate the thought processes of human experts in a particular field. Expert systems incorporate the rules that an expert applies to specific types of problems, such as the judgments a physician makes in diagnosing illnesses. In effect, expert systems supply everyday users with "instant expertise." A system called *maintenance operations center advisor* (MOCA), by imitating the thought processes of a maintenance manager, schedules routine maintenance for American Airlines's entire fleet.

intranets
A communication network similar to the Internet but operating within the boundaries of a single organization

Intranets, or private Internet networks, are accessible only to employees via entry through electronic firewalls. Firewalls are used to limit access to an intranet. Ford's intranet connects over 100,000 workstations in Asia, Europe, and the United States to thousands of Ford websites containing private information on Ford activities in production, engineering, distribution, and marketing. Sharing such information has helped reduce the lead time for getting models into production from 36 to 24 months. Ford's latest project in improving customer service through internal information sharing is called *manufacturing on demand*. Now, for example, the Mustang that required 50 days' delivery time in 1996 is available in fewer than 2 weeks. The savings to Ford, of course, will be billions of dollars in inventory and fixed costs.

extranets
A communication network that allows selected outsiders limited access to an organization's internal information system, or intranet

Extranets allow outsiders limited access to a firm's intranet. The most common application allows buyers to enter the seller's system to see which products are available for sale and delivery, thus providing product availability information quickly to outside buyers. Industrial suppliers, too, are often linked into their customers' intranets so that they can see planned production schedules and make supplies ready as needed for customers' upcoming operations.

Personal Digital Technology   In recent years, the nature of organizational communication has changed dramatically, mainly because of breakthroughs in personal electronic communication technology, and the future promises even more change. It has become common, for instance, to have teleconferences in which managers stay at their own location (such as offices in different cities) but are seen on monitors as they "meet." A manager in New York can keyboard a letter or memorandum at her personal computer, point and click with a mouse, and have it delivered to hundreds or even thousands of colleagues around the world in a matter of seconds. Highly detailed information can be retrieved with ease from large electronic databanks. This has given rise to a new version of an old work arrangement—the cottage industry. In a cottage industry, people work at home (in their "cottage") and periodically bring the products of their labors in to the company. *Telecommuting* is the label given to a new digital cottage industry. In telecommuting, people work at home on their computers and communicate with colleagues and coworkers using electronic media.

Smartphones have made it even easier for managers to communicate with one another. Many now use such phones to make calls while commuting to and from work and carry them in their briefcases so that they can receive calls while at lunch. In addition, of course, they can also send and receive documents and other information. And related personal computing devices such as the iPad are revolutionizing how people communicate with one another. Wi-Fi technology is further extending the impact of these devices.

AP Images/Ariel Schalit

Personal digital technology continues to change the way people communicate. Take this unusual image, for example. Tourists in northern Israel can ride Wi-Fi–outfitted donkeys and use iPads or similar devices to see biblical reenactments as they ride through Old Testament landscapes. Visitors can then like, share, or snap their experiences instantly to their friends around the world.

Psychologists, however, are beginning to associate some problems with these communication advances. For one thing, managers who are seldom in their "real" office are likely to fall behind in their field and to be victimized by organizational politics because they are not present to keep in touch with what is going on and to protect themselves. They drop out of the organizational grapevine and miss out on much of the informal communication that takes place. Moreover, the use of digital communication at the expense of face-to-face meetings and conversations makes it hard to build a strong culture, develop solid working relationships, and create a mutually supportive atmosphere of trust and cooperativeness. Finally, electronic communication is opening up new avenues for dysfunctional employee behavior, such as the passing of lewd or offensive materials to others. For example, a few years ago, the *New York Times* fired almost 10 percent of its workers at one of its branch offices for sending inappropriate e-mails at work.

INFORMAL COMMUNICATION IN ORGANIZATIONS

The forms of organizational communication discussed in the previous section all represent planned and relatively formal communication mechanisms. However, in many cases, some of the communication that takes place in an organization transcends these formal channels and instead follows any of several informal methods. Figure 12.4 illustrates numerous examples of informal communication. Common forms of informal communication in organizations include the grapevine, management by wandering around, and nonverbal communication.

The Grapevine

grapevine
An informal communication network among people in an organization

The **grapevine** is an informal communication network that can permeate an entire organization. Grapevines are found in all organizations except the very smallest, but they do not always follow the same patterns as, nor do they necessarily coincide with, formal channels of authority and communication. Research has identified several kinds of

© Cengage Learning

FIGURE 12.4

Informal Communication in Organizations

Informal communication in organizations may or may not follow official reporting relationships or prescribed channels. It may cross different levels and different departments or work units, and it may or may not have anything to do with official organizational business.

Gossip Chain
(One person tells many)

Cluster Chain
(Many people tell a few)

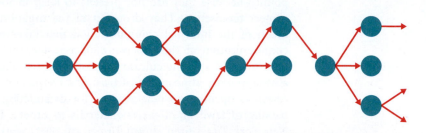

FIGURE 12.5

Common Grapevine Chains Found in Organizations

The two most common grapevine chains in organizations are the gossip chain (in which one person communicates messages to many others) and the cluster chain (in which many people pass messages to a few others).

Source: Based on Keith Davis and John W. Newstrom, *Human Behavior at Work: Organizational Behavior,* 8th ed., 1989. The McGraw-Hill Companies, Inc.

grapevines.[21] The two most common are illustrated in Figure 12.5. The gossip chain occurs when one person spreads the message to many other people. Each one, in turn, may either keep the information confidential or pass it on to others. The gossip chain is likely to carry personal information. The other common grapevine is the cluster chain, in which one person passes the information to a selected few individuals. Some of the receivers pass the information to a few other individuals; the rest keep it to themselves.

There is some disagreement about whether the information carried by the grapevine is accurate, but research is increasingly finding it to be fairly accurate, especially when the information is based on fact rather than speculation. One study found that the grapevine may be between 75 and 95 percent accurate.[22] That same study also found that informal communication is increasing in many organizations for two basic reasons. One contributing factor is the recent increase in merger, acquisition, and takeover activity. Because such activity can greatly affect the people within an organization, it follows that they may spend more time talking about it.[23] The second contributing factor is that as more and more corporations move facilities from inner cities to suburbs, employees tend to talk less and less to others outside the organization and more and more to one another.

Attempts to eliminate the grapevine are fruitless, but fortunately the manager does have some control over it. By maintaining open channels of communication and responding vigorously to inaccurate information, the manager can minimize the damage the grapevine can do. The grapevine can actually be an asset. By learning who the key people in the grapevine are, for example, the manager can partially control the information they receive and use the grapevine to sound out employee reactions to new ideas, such as a change in human resource policies or benefit packages. The manager can also get valuable information from the grapevine and use it to improve decision making.[24]

Forms of social media such as Twitter and Facebook often mimic the traditional grapevine. Messages can be formatted quickly and transmitted rapidly to thousands of other people. Of course, there may also be accuracy issues if the original messages are ill-informed or contain incorrect information. Most experts today suggest that firms develop a social media strategy, although many businesses have not yet done this.

Management by Wandering Around

management by wandering around

An approach to communication that involves the manager literally wandering around and having spontaneous conversations with others

Another increasingly popular form of informal communication is called, interestingly enough, **management by wandering around**.[25] The basic idea is that some managers keep in touch with what is going on by wandering around and talking with people—immediate subordinates, subordinates far down the organizational hierarchy, delivery people, customers, or anyone else who is involved with the company in some way. Bill Marriott, for example, frequently visits the kitchens, loading docks, and custodial work areas whenever he tours a Marriott hotel. He claims that, by talking with employees throughout the hotel, he gets new ideas and has a better feel for the entire company. And, when United Airlines CEO Jeff Smisek travels, he makes a point of talking to flight attendants and other passengers to gain continuous insights into how the business can be run more effectively.

A related form of organizational communication that really has no specific term is the informal interchange that takes place outside the normal work setting. Employees attending the company picnic, playing on the company softball team, or taking fishing trips together will almost always spend part of their time talking about work. For example, Texas Instruments (TI) engineers at TI's Lewisville, Texas, facility often frequent a local bar in town after work. On any given evening, they talk about the Dallas Cowboys, the newest government contract received by the company, the weather, their boss, the company's stock price, local politics, and problems at work. There is no set agenda, and the key topics of discussion vary from group to group and from day to day. Still, the social gatherings serve an important role. They promote a strong culture and enhance understanding of how the organization works.

Nonverbal Communication

nonverbal communication

Any communication exchange that does not use words or uses words to carry more meaning than the strict definition of the words themselves

Nonverbal communication is a communication exchange that does not use words or uses words to carry more meaning than the strict definition of the words themselves. Nonverbal communication is a powerful but little-understood form of communication in organizations. It often relies on facial expressions, body movements, physical contact, and gestures. One study found that as much as 55 percent of the content of a message is transmitted by facial expressions and body posture and that another 38 percent derives from inflection and tone. Words themselves account for only 7 percent of the content of the message.[26] The At Your Service feature highlights the role of nonverbal communication in service settings.

Research has identified three kinds of nonverbal communication practiced by managers—images, settings, and body language.[27] In this context, images are the kinds of words people elect to use. "Damn the torpedoes, full speed ahead" and "Even though there are some potential hazards, we should proceed with this course of action" may convey the same meaning. Yet, the person who uses the first expression may be perceived as a maverick, a courageous hero, an individualist, or a reckless and foolhardy adventurer. The person who uses the second might be described as aggressive, forceful, diligent, or narrow minded and resistant to change. In short, our choice of words conveys much more than just the strict meaning of the words themselves.

The setting for communication also plays a major role in nonverbal communication. Boundaries, familiarity, the home turf, and other elements of the setting are all important. Much has been written about the symbols of power in organizations. The size and location of an office, the kinds of furniture in the office, and the accessibility of the person in the office all communicate useful information. For example, when H. Ross Perot ran Electronic Data Systems (EDS), he positioned his desk so that it is always between

AT YOUR SERVICE

Say It with a Smile

Isn't it great when someone smiles at you? That simple facial expression communicates a number of important things to the person receiving the smile. It says, "Welcome," "I'm glad you're here," and "I am anxious to listen and help if I can." Service organizations spend considerable time and effort encouraging their employees to smile at their customers. This simple act can be an important part of the success of almost any service experience. The question arises, though: Why is this so important? The answer can be attributed to several human characteristics. The most discussed answer is based on our tendency to like those who like us.

Thus, a person who smiles at us is sending a nonverbal signal that the person finds us to be like him or her and is a friend, not a foe. If a service employee smiles at us, we tend to smile back. In other words, we use mimicry to enhance the quality and value of the service experience. There is some interesting research that gives us some insight into the value of mimicry. People being mimicked will like those who mimic them. Moreover, they respond more generously toward people who mimic them. This has been termed the "chameleon effect." Service employees such as restaurant servers can increase the amount of their tips by mimicking the behaviors of their customers in rate of speech, accents, word choice, and syntax. Even mimicking behaviors such as rubbing their face, laughing, and other behaviors when mimicked influence our liking of others.

The second aspect of service with a smile is based on its impact on our emotions. If we see the smile as authentic, it has more impact on us than if it is seen as somehow fake. A "fake" smile will affect our feelings about the person smiling at us. In other words, we have both a mimicking reaction to someone smiling at us because we automatically and subconsciously respond to behaviors of those with whom we want to interact, and we will make judgments as to the authenticity of those behaviors. Thus, service managers seek to find ways to encourage their employees to smile in ways that feel authentic to their customers. These strategies can be simple as posting small mirrors on checkout cash registers so that employees can self-monitor their behaviors and be happily smiling when customers enter their work space. Another strategy puts considerable emphasis on creating fun work environments so that employees have fun that leads them to be genuinely smiling when customers appear.

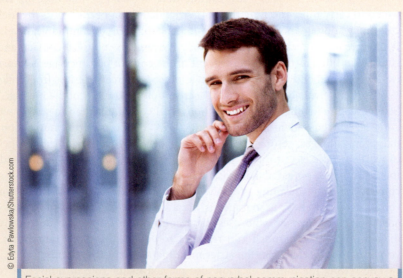

© Edyta Pawlowska/Shutterstock.com

Facial expressions and other forms of nonverbal communication can convey a lot of information. In service settings, it is especially important that employees use appropriate nonverbal communication. This man's smile, for example, seems to be genuine and sincere. This will make a customer feel much better than if he were scowling or unauthentic.

In addition to smiling, eye contact is another important form of nonverbal communication. An unwillingness to maintain eye contact, for instance, may signal that an individual is hiding information or is being untruthful. Prolonged eye contact, meanwhile, can have several different meanings. These two executives are locked in a tough negotiation and may be using eye contact to establish that each feels strongly about their position and may not be open to compromise.

him and a visitor. This signaled that he was in charge. When he wanted a less formal dialogue, he moved around to the front of the desk and sat beside his visitor. Michael Dell of Dell Computer, in contrast, has his desk facing a side window so that, when he turns around to greet a visitor, there is never anything between them.

A third form of nonverbal communication is body language.[28] The distance we stand from someone as we speak has meaning. In the United States, standing very close to someone you are talking to generally signals either familiarity or aggression. The English and Germans stand farther apart than Americans when talking, whereas the Arabs, Japanese, and Mexicans stand closer together.[29] Eye contact is another effective means of nonverbal communication. For example, prolonged eye contact might suggest either hostility or romantic interest. Other kinds of body language include body and hand movement, pauses in speech, and mode of dress.

The manager should be aware of the importance of nonverbal communication and recognize its potential impact. Giving an employee good news about a reward with the wrong nonverbal cues can destroy the reinforcement value of the reward. Likewise, reprimanding an employee but providing inconsistent nonverbal cues can limit the effectiveness of the sanctions. The tone of the message, where and how the message is delivered, facial expressions, and gestures can all amplify or weaken the message or change the message altogether. E-mails and other digital communication may be misinterpreted based on actual content, so some people use "emoticons" to reinforce the notion that the message is "happy" or "sad."

MANAGING ORGANIZATIONAL COMMUNICATION

In view of the importance and pervasiveness of communication in organizations, it is vital for managers to understand how to manage the communication process.[30] Managers should understand how to maximize the potential benefits of communication and minimize the potential problems. We begin our discussion of communication management by considering the factors that might disrupt effective communication and how to deal with them.

Barriers to Communication

Several factors may disrupt the communication process or serve as barriers to effective communication.[31] As shown in Table 12.1, these may be divided into two classes: individual barriers and organizational barriers.

Individual Barriers   Several individual barriers may disrupt effective communication. One common problem is conflicting or inconsistent signals. A manager is sending

Numerous barriers can disrupt effective communication. Some of these barriers involve individual characteristics and processes. Others are functions of the organizational context in which communication is taking place.

Table 12.1	Barriers to Effective Communication
Individual Barriers	**Organizational Barriers**
Conflicting or inconsistent signals	Semantics
Credibility about the subject	Status or power differences
Reluctance to communicate	Different perceptions
Poor listening skills	Noise
Predispositions about the subject	Overload
	Language differences

© Cengage Learning

conflicting signals when she says on Monday that things should be done one way, but then prescribes an entirely different procedure on Wednesday. Inconsistent signals are being sent by a manager who says that he has an "open-door" policy and wants his subordinates to drop by, but keeps his door closed and becomes irritated whenever someone stops in.

Numerous barriers can disrupt effective communication. Some of these barriers involve individual characteristics and processes. Others are functions of the organizational context in which communication is taking place.

Another barrier is lack of credibility. Credibility problems arise when the sender is not considered a reliable source of information. He may not be trusted or may not be perceived as knowledgeable about the subject at hand. When a politician is caught withholding information or when a manager makes a series of bad decisions, the extent to which he or she will be listened to and believed thereafter diminishes. In extreme cases, people may talk about something they obviously know little or nothing about.

Some people are simply reluctant to initiate a communication exchange. This reluctance may occur for a variety of reasons. A manager may be reluctant to tell subordinates about an impending budget cut because he knows they will be unhappy about it. Likewise, a subordinate may be reluctant to transmit information upward for fear of reprisal or because it is felt that such an effort would be futile.

Poor listening habits can be a major barrier to effective communication. Some people are simply poor listeners. When someone is talking to them, they may be daydreaming, looking around, reading, texting, or listening to another conversation. Because they are not concentrating on what is being said, they may not comprehend part or all of the message. They may even think that they really are paying attention, only to realize later that they cannot remember parts of the conversation.

Receivers may also bring certain predispositions to the communication process. They may already have their minds made up, firmly set in a certain way. For example, a manager may have heard that his new boss is unpleasant and hard to work with. When she calls him in for an introductory meeting, he may go into that meeting predisposed to dislike her and discount what she has to say.

Organizational Barriers   Other barriers to effective communication involve the organizational context in which the communication occurs. Semantics problems arise when words have different meanings for different people. Words and phrases such as *profit, increased output*, and *return on investment* may have positive meanings for managers but less positive meanings for labor.

Communication problems may also arise when people of different power or status try to communicate with each other. The company president may discount a suggestion from an operating employee, thinking, "How can someone at that level help me run my business?" Or, when the president goes out to inspect a new plant, workers may be reluctant to offer suggestions because of their lower status. The marketing vice president may have more power than the human resource vice president and consequently may not pay much attention to a staffing report submitted by the human resource department.

If people perceive a situation differently, they may have difficulty communicating with one another. When two managers observe that a third manager has not spent much time in her office lately, one may believe that she has been to several important meetings, and the other may think she is "hiding out." If they need to talk about her in some official capacity, problems may arise because one has a positive impression and the other a negative impression.

Environmental factors may also disrupt effective communication. As mentioned earlier in this chapter, noise may affect communication in many ways. Similarly, overload may be a problem when the receiver is being sent more information than he or she can effectively handle. For more than a decade, many managers have reported getting so many messages each day as to sometimes feel overwhelmed.[32] As a result, many senior executives have two e-mail accounts: one is their "public" account that is actually monitored by a subordinate who only passes along truly important messages, and the other is a "private" account available only to a few critical contacts. And, when the manager gives a subordinate many jobs on which to work and at the same time the subordinate is being told by family and friends to do other things, overload may result and communication effectiveness diminishes. An HR executive at Aviva Investors recently intended to send an e-mail to a single individual informing him that he was fired, but the e-mail ended up going to all 1,300 of the firm's employees![33]

Finally, as businesses become more and more global, different languages can create problems. To counter this problem, some firms are adopting an "official language." For example, when the German chemical firm Hoechst merged with the French firm Rhone-Poulenc, the new company adopted English as its official language. Indeed, English is generally considered to be the standard business language around the world.[34]

Improving Communication Effectiveness

Considering how many factors can disrupt communication, it is fortunate that managers can resort to several techniques for improving communication effectiveness.[35] As shown in Table 12.2, these techniques include both individual and organizational skills.

Because communication is so important, managers have developed several methods of overcoming barriers to effective communication. Some of these methods involve individual skills, whereas others are based on organizational skills.

Table 12.2	Overcoming Barriers to Communication
Individual Skills	**Organizational Skills**
Develop good listening skills	Follow up
Encourage two-way communication	Regulate information flows
Be aware of language and meaning	Understand the richness of media
Maintain credibility	
Be sensitive to the receiver's perspective	
Be sensitive to the sender's perspective	

More Effective Listening		Less Effective Listening
Stays active, focused		Is passive, laid back
Pays attention		Is easily distracted
Asks questions		Asks no questions
Keeps an open mind		Has preconceptions
Assimilates information		Disregards information

© Cengage Learning

FIGURE 12.6

More and Less Effective Listening Skills

Effective listening skills are a vital part of communication in organizations. There are several barriers that can contribute to poor listening skills by individuals in organizations. Fortunately, there are also several practices for improving listening skills.

Individual Skills   The single most important individual skill for improving communication effectiveness is being a good listener.[36] Being a good listener requires that the individual be prepared to listen, not interrupt the speaker, concentrate on both the words and the meaning being conveyed, be patient, and ask questions as appropriate.[37] Avoiding checking e-mail or texts when someone is talking is also a wise idea. So important are good listening skills that companies such as Delta, IBM, and Boeing conduct programs to train their managers to be better listeners. Figure 12.6 illustrates the characteristics of poor listeners versus good listeners.

Because communication is so important, managers have developed several methods of overcoming barriers to effective communication. Some of these methods involve individual skills, whereas others are based on organizational skills.

In addition to being a good listener, several other individual skills can promote effective communication. Feedback, one of the most important, is facilitated by two-way communication. Two-way communication allows the receiver to ask questions, request clarification, and express opinions that let the sender know whether he or she has been understood. In general, the more complicated the message, the more useful is two-way communication. In addition, the sender should be aware of the meanings that different receivers might attach to various words. For example, when addressing stockholders, a manager might use the word *profits* often (because most stockholders, of course, see profits in a positive light). When addressing labor leaders, however, she may choose to use *profits* less often (because those individuals might see excessive profit as coming at the expense of employee welfare).

Furthermore, the sender should try to maintain credibility. This can be accomplished by not pretending to be an expert when one is not, by "doing one's homework" and checking facts, and by otherwise being as accurate and honest as possible. The sender should also try to be sensitive to the receiver's perspective. A manager who must tell a subordinate that she has not been recommended for a promotion should recognize that the subordinate will be frustrated and unhappy. Therefore, the content of the message and its method of delivery should be chosen accordingly. The manager should be primed to accept a reasonable degree of hostility and bitterness without getting angry in return.[38]

Finally, the receiver should also try to be sensitive to the sender's point of view. Suppose that a manager has just received some bad news—for example, that his position is being eliminated next year. Others should understand that he may be disappointed, angry, or even depressed for a while. Thus, they might make a special effort not to take too much offense if he snaps at them, and they might look for signals that he needs someone to talk to.[39]

Organizational Skills   Three useful organizational skills can also enhance communication effectiveness for both the sender and the receiver—following up, regulating information flow, and understanding the richness of different media. Following up simply involves checking at a later time to be sure that a message has been received and understood. After a manager e-mails a report to a colleague, she might call a few days later to ask whether the colleague has had an opportunity to review it or has any questions about it.

Regulating information flow means that the sender or receiver takes steps to ensure that overload does not occur. For the sender, this could mean not passing too much information through the system at one time. For the receiver, it might mean calling attention to the fact that he is being asked to do too many things at once. Many managers limit the influx of information by periodically weeding out the list of journals and routine reports they receive, or they train their assistant to screen phone calls and visitors. Indeed, some executives now get so much e-mail that they have it routed to an assistant. That person reviews the e-mails, discards those that are not useful (such as spam), responds to those that are routine, and passes on to the executive only those that require his or her personal attention.

Both parties should also understand the richness associated with different media. When a manager is going to lay off a subordinate temporarily, the message should be delivered in person. A face-to-face channel of communication gives the manager an opportunity to explain the situation and answer questions. When the purpose of the message is to grant a pay increase, written communication may be appropriate because it can be more objective and precise. The manager could then follow up the written notice with personal congratulations.

SUMMARY OF LEARNING OUTCOMES AND KEY POINTS

1. Describe the role and importance of communication in the manager's job.

   - Communication is the process of transmitting information from one person to another.
   - Effective communication is the process of sending a message in such a way that the message received is as close in meaning as possible to the message intended.
   - For information to be useful, it must be accurate, timely, complete, and relevant.

   - The communication process consists of a sender encoding meaning and transmitting it to one or more receivers, who receive the message and decode it into meaning.
   - In two-way communication, the process continues with the roles reversed.
   - Noise can disrupt any part of the overall process.

2. Identify the basic forms of communication in organizations.

   - Interpersonal communication focuses on communication among a small number of people.

     - Two important forms of interpersonal communication, oral and written, offer both unique advantages and disadvantages.
     - The manager should weigh the pros and cons of each when choosing a medium for communication.

   - Communication networks are recurring patterns of communication among members of a group or work team.
   - Vertical communication between superiors and subordinates may flow upward or downward.
   - Horizontal communication involves peers and colleagues at the same level in the organization.

3. Describe the role of digital communication in organizations.

   - There are several basic levels of information systems:

     - Transaction-processing systems
     - Systems for various types of workers
     - Basic management information systems
     - Decision support systems and executive support systems
     - Artificial intelligence, including expert systems

   - Intranets and extranets are also growing in popularity.
   - Electronic communication is having a profound effect on managerial and organizational communication.

4. Discuss informal communication, including its various forms and types.

   - The grapevine is the informal communication network among people in an organization.
   - Management by wandering around is also a popular informal method of communication.
   - Nonverbal communication is expressed through images, settings, and body language.

5. Describe how the communication process can be managed to recognize and overcome barriers.

   - Managing the communication process entails recognizing the barriers to effective communication and understanding how to overcome them.
   - Barriers can be identified at both the individual and organizational levels.
   - Likewise, both individual and organizational skills can be used to overcome these barriers.

DISCUSSION QUESTIONS

Questions for Review

1. Describe the difference between communication and effective communication. How can a sender verify that a communication was effective? How can a receiver verify that a communication was effective?
2. Which form of interpersonal communication is best for long-term retention? Why? Which form is best for getting across subtle nuances of meaning? Why?
3. What are the similarities and differences of oral and written communication? What kinds of situations call for the use of oral methods? What situations call for written communication?
4. What forms of digital communication do you use regularly?
5. Describe the individual and organizational barriers to effective communication. For each barrier, describe one action that a manager could take to reduce the problems caused by that barrier.

Questions for Analysis

1. At what points in the communication process can problems occur? Give examples of how noise can interfere with the communication process. What can managers do to reduce problems and noise?
2. How are digital communication devices (cell phones, e-mail, and websites) affecting the communication process? Describe both the advantages and the disadvantages of these three devices over traditional communication methods, such as face-to-face conversations, written notes, and phone calls.
3. What forms of communication have you experienced today? What form of communication is involved in a face-to-face conversation with a friend? A phone call from a customer? A traffic light or crossing signal? A picture of a cigarette in a circle with a slash across it? An area around machinery defined by a yellow line painted on the floor?

4. Keep track of your own activities over the course of a few hours of leisure time to determine what forms of communication you encounter. Which forms were most common? If you had been tracking your communications while at work, how would the list be different? Explain why the differences occur.

5. For each of the following situations, tell which form of communication you would use. Then ask the same question to someone who has been in the workforce for at least ten years. For any differences that occur, ask the worker to explain why his or her choice is better than yours. Do you agree with his or her assessment? Why or why not?

   - Describing complex changes in how health-care benefits are calculated and administered to every employee of a large firm
   - Asking your boss a quick question about how she wants something done
   - Telling customers that a new two-for-one promotion is available at your store
   - Reprimanding an employee for excessive absences on the job
   - Reminding workers that no smoking is allowed in your facility

BUILDING EFFECTIVE TECHNICAL SKILLS

Exercise Overview

Technical skills are the skills necessary to perform the work of the organization. This exercise will help you develop and apply technical skills involving the Internet and its potential for gathering information relevant to making important decisions.

Exercise Background

Assume that you are a manager for a large national retailer. You have been assigned the responsibility for identifying potential locations for the construction of a warehouse and distribution center. The idea behind such a center is that the firm can use its enormous purchasing power to buy many products in bulk quantities at relatively low prices. Individual stores can then order the specific quantities they need from the warehouse.

The location will need an abundance of land. The warehouse itself, for example, will occupy more than four square acres of land. In addition, it must be close to railroads and major highways because shipments will be arriving by both rail and truck, although outbound shipments will be exclusively by truck. Other important variables are that land prices and the cost of living should be relatively low and weather conditions should be mild (to minimize disruptions to shipments).

The firm's general experience is that small to mid-sized communities work best. Moreover, warehouses are already in place in the western and eastern parts of the United States, so this new one will most likely be in the central or south-central area. Your boss has asked you to identify three or four possible sites.

Exercise Task

With the aforementioned information as a framework, do the following:

1. Use the Internet to identify as many as ten possible locations.
2. Using additional information from the Internet, narrow the set of possible locations to three or four.
3. Again using the Internet, find out as much as possible about the potential locations.

BUILDING EFFECTIVE INTERPERSONAL SKILLS

Exercise Overview

A manager's interpersonal skills include his or her abilities to understand and to motivate individuals and groups. This in-class demonstration gives you practice in understanding the nonverbal and verbal behavior of a pair of individuals.

Exercise Background

Nonverbal communication conveys more than half of the information in any face-to-face exchange, and body language is a significant part of our nonverbal behavior. Consider, for example, the impact of a yawn or a frown or a shaking fist. At the same time, however, nonverbal communication is often neglected by managers. The result can be confusing and misleading signals.

In this exercise, you will examine interactions between two people without sound, with only visual clues to meaning. Then you will examine those same interactions with both visual and verbal clues.

Exercise Task

1. Observe the silent video segments that your professor shows to the class. For each segment, describe the nature of the relationship and interaction between the two individuals. What nonverbal clues did you use in reaching your conclusions?

2. Next, observe the same video segments, but this time with audio included. Describe the interaction again, along with any verbal clues you used.

3. How accurate were your assessments when you had only visual information? Explain why you were or were not accurate.

4. What does this exercise show you about the nature of nonverbal communication? What advice would you now give managers about their nonverbal communication?

SKILLS SELF-ASSESSMENT INSTRUMENT

Gender Communications Quiz

Introduction: Research shows that men and women sometimes have trouble communicating effectively with one another at work because they have contrasting values and beliefs about differences between the sexes. The following assessment surveys your beliefs and values about each sex.

Instructions: How much do you know about how men and women communicate? If you think a statement is an accurate description of communication patterns, mark it true. If you think it isn't, mark it false.

True/False

_____ 1. Men talk more than women.

_____ 2. Men are more likely to interrupt women than to interrupt other men.

_____ 3. During conversations, women spend more time looking at their partner than men do.

_____ 4. Nonverbal messages carry more weight than verbal messages.

_____ 5. Female managers communicate with more emotional openness and drama than male managers.

_____ 6. Men not only control the content of conversations, they also work harder in keeping conversations going.

_____ 7. When people hear generic words, such as "mankind" and "he," they respond inclusively, indicating that the terms apply to both sexes.

_____ 8. In classroom communications, male students receive more reprimands and criticism.

_____ 9. Women are more likely than men to disclose information about intimate personal concerns.

_____ 10. Female speakers are more animated in their style than are males.

_____ 11. Women use less personal space than men.

_____ 12. When a male speaks, he is listened to more carefully than a female speaker, even when she makes the identical presentation.

_____ 13. In general, women speak in a more tentative style than do men.

_____ 14. Women are more likely to answer questions that are not addressed to them.

_____ 15. There is widespread gender segregation in schools, and it hinders effective classroom communication.

_____ 16. Female managers are seen by both male and female subordinates as better communicators than male managers.

_____ 17. In classroom communications, teachers are more likely to give verbal praise to female than to male students.

_____ 18. In general, men smile more often than women.

Source: From Myra Sadker and Joyce Kaser, The Communications Gender Gap, Mid-Atlantic Center for Sex Equity, 5010 Wisconsin Avenue, N.W., Suite 308, Washington, D.C. 20016, 1984.

EXPERIENTIAL EXERCISE
Nonverbal Communication in Groups

Purpose: The role of nonverbal communication in organizations can be just as important as oral or written communication, but is often overlooked. This activity will make you more aware of the power of nonverbal communication and give you some practice in using it.

Instructions:

Step 1: Your instructor will break your class into groups of about 20. Change your seat as needed until the group members are sitting fairly close and facing each other. Count the exact number of members and agree upon the count as a group.

Step 2: Count out loud, one at a time, from 1 up to the total number of group members. The group must do this without discussion or planning about who will say each number. Members may not use any verbal or physical signals, for example no pointing, nodding, or touching. Each member must say exactly one number, and no number may be repeated. No two people may speak simultaneously.

Step 3: If any of the rules are violated, begin the task again from the number 1. Continue until the group successfully completes the task. Then answer the follow-up questions.

Follow-Up Questions:

1. What methods of communication did you use to determine who would say each number? How effective was this method?
2. How did the group arrive at this method? For example, did the group try several methods before settling on one?
3. What does this exercise demonstrate to you about the power of nonverbal communication?
4. Can you think of examples of situations that you have experienced in which nonverbal communication played an important role?
5. Can you think of examples of situations that could occur in business organizations in which nonverbal communication might play an important role?

MANAGEMENT AT WORK
The Converse of In-Person Communication

News flash: *Interviews are stressful.* The uncomfortable dress clothes, the need to make an instant good impression, the unexpected questions. Surely phone interviews are easier, right? Wrong. A job interview is a job interview, and interviews conducted on the phone pose all the challenges of a face-to-face interview—and then some. You need to take phone interviewing seriously because nowadays many corporations use them to pre-screen applicants and, more important, because many HR departments rely on phone interviews exclusively.

Remember first of all that talking on the phone is a certain type of communication and that, as such, it poses certain communication challenges and requires certain communication skills. It also requires a little common sense, so here are a few tips on how to solve some of the common problems that tend to accompany phone interviews.

Problem 1: Scheduling. Interviewers usually call at mutually agreed-upon times. Sometimes, however, they want to assess a candidate's ability to think on his or her feet and are looking for unscripted responses. In that case, the call may come at an unscheduled or even inconvenient time—say, when the kids are screaming for dinner or your roommate's throwing a party.

Solution: If the interviewer calls at a time when conversation is truly out of the question, you'll have to call back. Bear in mind, however, that some interviewers are put off by the request, so if the call is merely difficult but not impossible, you're better off following through with the interview.

Problem 2: Preparation. Phone interviews require the same preparation as in-person interviews, but they do have a potential benefit: "You cannot be seen," points out an advisor at CollegeGrad.com, a leading website for entry-level job seekers. "Use this [fact] to your advantage." Even while you're on the phone, for example, do what you can to relax.

Solution: Prepare notes (yes, it's OK to use notes) on the points that you want to cover, and be sure to arrange them near the phone so that you can actually make use of them. It's also OK to say, "Could I have just a moment to look at my notes?" Referring to your notes reminds the interviewer that you're prepared. You should also have paper and pen handy so that you can *take* notes.

Problem 3: Noise. When it comes to the process of communicating, "noise" means any sort of distraction—like trying to talk while multitasking at your computer as well as having to put up with the sounds of a nearby television. Phone conversations are especially subject to all sorts of noise, including a poor connection or the sudden demise of a cell phone battery as well as plain environmental noise.

Solution: Shut the door and try to make as little unnecessary noise of your own as possible. If you have a poor connection, ask the interviewer to speak up. If your cell phone battery isn't charged, you aren't prepared for any kind of phone communication, much less an interview for the job you want or need. (In other words, keep your phone charged.) Focus on the activity at hand and pay attention to the conversation.

Problem 4: Lack of context cues. For good or ill, an in-person conversation is affected by all sorts of nonverbal "context cues"—gesture, body language, facial expression, dress, and so forth. In fact, only a small portion of conversational meaning is determined solely by words. A phone interview, on the other hand, allows for just one nonverbal element—tone of voice.

Solution: Even though the interviewer can't see you, smile: The information that you're conveying will come across as personal and intended for the person on the other end of the line. Many experts also recommend that you feel free to use gestures, expressions, and body language, just as if you were in a face-to-face interview. Take a tip from phone-sales professionals, who often stand or walk around the room in order to sound more comfortable and more energetic.

Now that you're properly equipped to solve the most common problems that come up in phone interviews, let's run over a few do's and don'ts. First, some tips on what you should do from Job Application and Interview Advice, a website written by management and HR professionals:

- *Be positive.* Talk about the positive aspects of your present job and what you're looking forward to in a new one.
- *Know what you're talking about and be specific.* In other words, hold the interviewer's interest by taking charge of context cues. "Because [interviewers] don't have an image of your face to set you apart from others," says one job counselor, "you need to draw pictures with your words." Back up general

statements with good examples; people prefer good (economical) stories to dissertations, and they get a better impression of what you've done in your work life.

- *Refer to your notes.* Don't be embarrassed about asking to look at your notes. It shows confidence and preparation to ask to refer to notes.
- *Take the initiative.* If there's something that you feel it's important to talk about but that doesn't come up, bring it up. Don't waste any opportunity to sell yourself.
- *Know when a topic's been covered (and when the conversation's over).* Don't be tempted to fill in silences by simply continuing to talk.

Finally, let's review a few things to avoid. Matt Aberham, who interviews would-be program managers and engineers for Microsoft's Online Services Business, offers the following list of five good ways to avoid failing a telephone interview (at least one that he's in charge of):

- *Keep track of the time.* Because most interviews are slated for 30–45 minutes, there's time to cover several topics thoroughly and a couple in fairly deep detail. But no matter what you're talking about, be conscious of how long you've been talking about it. Err on the side of conciseness—if the interviewer wants to know more, he or she will be sure to let you know.
- *Answer the question instead of trying to sell yourself.* Don't be afraid to discuss areas where you need (and want) further development. "I'm not looking to be sold," says Aberham. "[I want] to get an accurate view of your experience."
- *Talk about "me," not "we."* Don't get into the habit of saying "we" instead of "I" throughout the interview unless you're trying to show how you *led* a group in accomplishing its goals. Take "ownership" of what *you* did. "Showing ownership," explains Aberham, "helps me figure out if … your contributions are appropriate for the work we're thinking of having you do."
- *Be concrete instead of abstract.* Don't give a hypothetical answer to a specific question. "The quickest way to fail a 'Tell-me-about-a-time-when …' question," advises Aberham, "is to give me a 'Here's-what-I-would-do-in-that-situation …' answer … . If [I ask you] to describe a situation you've never handled, let me know and I'll pick a different question."
- *Don't ask, "How'd I do?"* Interviewers usually don't mind giving you some feedback about the match between your skills and experiences and the

employer's needs, but they're rarely ready at the end of a phone interview to tell you what they're going to do next about you. And Aberham particularly doesn't like it when something like "How'd I do?" is the only question you have for him.[40]

Businesses continue to look for effective ways to communicate with their employees, as well as job seekers, customers, and investors. The idea of phone interviews for job seekers may seem odd to some people, but many firms are finding this method of screening prospective employees to be both efficient and effective. Of course, as noted, there are both advantages and disadvantages to phone interviews.

Case Questions

1. Experts suggest that you dress professionally for a telephone interview even though the interviewer can't see you. Do you agree that this is important? Why or why not?

2. In getting ready for a telephone interview for a new job, what are the three or four things for which you most want to be prepared? If you were getting ready to interview someone else for a job, what are the three or four major things that you'd expect that person to be prepared for?

3. Matt Aberham warns against simply trying to "sell yourself" during a phone interview. You agree, but you also believe that selling yourself is one of the things that you have to do as a job seeker. What sort of strategies do you regard as legitimate and effective in trying to sell yourself to a phone interviewer (or an in-person interviewer, for that matter)?

4. Think of one or two experiences from your own life that you'd particularly like to come up in a job interview. What sort of questions might allow you to "take the initiative" in making sure that they didn't fall through the cracks? How much time do you think each incident would be worth in a 30–45-minute interview?

5. Using Skype and similar methods has become quite popular in setting up the complete online conversation. How would the use of this technology modify a telephone interviews? How about other forms of communication, such as text messaging?

"Que Pasa in the Ad Agency?"

1. You're assistant director of marketing for a maker of upscale furniture, and your company is preparing to enter new markets in California and the Southwest. Entering new markets, especially one of this size, is expensive, and your boss has decided to forgo Spanish-language advertising as part of the firm's market-entry strategy. You're inclined to disagree. What might you say to your boss to change her mind?

2. You're a top manager in a large factory whose workforce is approximately 40 percent Hispanic. Business is down because of the recession, and you've learned that there's a rumor about layoffs circulating in the grapevine. In particular, a lot of Hispanic-speaking employees seem to think that they'll be laid off first. How should you deal with the rumor?

3. Arnold Schwarzenegger, the Austrian-born ex-governor of California, which is home to 13.6 million Hispanics, advised Latino immigrants that if they wanted to learn English more quickly, "You've got to turn off Spanish[-language] television … . I know that when I came to this country, I very rarely spoke German to anyone." Do you agree with Schwarzenegger's advice to immigrants on learning English in the United States? Why or why not?

ENDNOTES

[1] Cynthia Gorney, "How Do You Say 'Got Milk' en Español?" *New York Times*, www.nytimes.com, accessed on January 1, 2014; Sam Fahmy, "Despite Recession, Hispanic and Asian Buying Power Expected to Surge in U.S., According to Annual UGA Selig Center Multicultural Economy Study," University of Georgia, Terry College of Business, November 4, 2010, www.terry.uga.edu, accessed on January 1, 2014; Aimee Valentine, "The State of

Spanish Language Media Industries: A Summary of Spanish Language Advertising 2010," *The State of Spanish Language Media: 2010 Annual Report* (Denton: Center for Spanish Language Media, University of North Texas), January 2011, www.spanishmedia.unt.edu, accessed on January 1, 2014; Mark Maier, "Breaking Down Hispanic Stereotypes," Luce Performance Group, January 11, 2009, www.luceperformance group.com, accessed on January 1, 2014; and Tommy Thompson, "The Problem with 'Hispanic Insights,'" *Advertising Age*, http://adage.com, accessed on January 1, 2014.

2 Henry Mintzberg, *The Nature of Managerial Work* (New York: Harper & Row, 1973).

3 Marshall Scott Poole, "Communication," in Sheldon Zedeck (ed.), *Handbook of Industrial and Organizational Psychology*, Vol. 3: *Maintaining, Expanding, and Contracting the Organization* (Washington, DC: American Psychological Association, 2010), pp. 249–270.

4 See Michael H. Zack, "Managing Codified Knowledge," *Sloan Management Review*, Summer 1999, Vol. 40, No. 4, pp. 45–58.

5 "It's Now Official: AOL, Time Warner to Split," *Wall Street Journal*, May 29, 2009, p. B1.

6 "UAL Shares Dive as Old News Surfaces on Net," *Wall Street Journal*, September 2008, pp. B1, B10.

7 Bruce Barry and Ingrid Fulmer, "The Medium and the Message: The Adaptive Use of Communication Media in Dyadic Influence," *Academy of Management Review*, 2004, Vol. 29, No. 2, pp. 272–292.

8 Mintzberg, *The Nature of Managerial Work*.

9 Reid Buckley, "When You Have to Put It to Them," *Across the Board*, October 1999, pp. 44–48.

10 "'Did I Just Say That?!' How to Recover from Foot-in-Mouth," *Wall Street Journal*, June 19, 2002, p. B1.

11 "Executives Who Dread Public Speaking Learn to Keep Their Cool in the Spotlight," *Wall Street Journal*, May 4, 1990, pp. B1, B6.

12 Henry Mintzberg, *The Nature of Managerial Work* (Englewood Cliffs, NJ: Prentice-Hall), 1973.

13 Reid Buckley, "When You Have to Put It to Them," *Across the Board*, October 1999, pp. 44–48.

14 See "Watch What You Put in That Office Email," *BusinessWeek*, September 30, 2002, pp. 114–115; see also Institute of Leadership and Management, "32% of People Making Inappropriate Use of Work Emails," April 20, 2011.

15 Nicholas Varchaver, "The Perils of E-mail," *Fortune*, February 17, 2003, pp. 96–102; "How a String of E-Mail Came to Haunt CSFB and Star Banker," *Wall Street Journal*, February 28, 2003, pp. A1, A6; and "How Morgan Stanley Botched a Big Case by Fumbling Emails," *Wall Street Journal*, May 16, 2005, pp. A1, A10.

16 A. Vavelas, "Communication Patterns in Task-Oriented Groups," *Journal of the Acoustical Society of America*, 1950, Vol. 22, pp. 725–730; and Jerry Wofford, Edwin Gerloff, and Robert Cummins, *Organizational Communication* (New York: McGraw-Hill, 1977).

17 Nelson Phillips and John Brown, "Analyzing Communications in and around Organizations: A Critical Hermeneutic Approach," *Academy of Management Journal*, 1993, Vol. 36, No. 6, pp. 1547–1576.

18 Walter Kiechel III, "Breaking Bad News to the Boss," *Fortune*, April 9, 1990, pp. 111–112.

19 Mary Young and James Post, "Managing to Communicate, Communicating to Manage: How Leading Companies Communicate with Employees," *Organizational Dynamics*, Summer 1993, pp. 31–43.

20 For one example, see Kimberly D. Elsbach and Greg Elofson, "How the Packaging of Decision Explanations Affects Perceptions of Trustworthiness," *Academy of Management Journal*, 2000, Vol. 43, No. 1, pp. 80–89.

21 Keith Davis, "Management Communication and the Grapevine," *Harvard Business Review*, September–October 1953, pp. 43–49.

22 Spread the Word: Gossip Is Good," *Wall Street Journal*, October 4, 1988, p. B1.

23 See David M. Schweiger and Angelo S. DeNisi, "Communication with Employees Following a Merger: A Longitudinal Field Experiment," *Academy of Management Journal*, March 1991, pp. 110–135.

24 Nancy B. Kurland and Lisa Hope Pelled, "Passing the Word: Toward a Model of Gossip and Power in the Workplace," *Academy of Management Review*, 2000, vol. 25, No. 2, pp. 428–438.

25 See Tom Peters and Nancy Austin, *A Passion for Excellence* (New York: Random House, 1985).

26 Albert Mehrabian, *Nonverbal Communication* (Chicago: Aldine, 1972).

27 Michael B. McCaskey, "The Hidden Messages Managers Send," *Harvard Business Review*, November–December 1979, pp. 135–148.

28 David Givens, "What Body Language Can Tell You That Words Cannot," *U.S. News & World Report*, November 19, 1984, p. 100.

29 Edward J. Hall, *The Hidden Dimension* (New York: Doubleday, 1966).

30 For a detailed discussion of improving communication effectiveness, see Courtland L. Bovee, John V. Thill, and Barbara E. Schatzman, *Business Communication Today*, 7th ed. (Upper Saddle River, NJ: Prentice Hall, 2003).

31 See Otis W. Baskin and Craig E. Aronoff, *Interpersonal Communication in Organizations* (Glenview, IL: Scott, Foresman, 1980).

32 See "You Have (Too Much) E-Mail," *USA Today*, March 12, 1999, p. 3B.

33 "Aviva Investors Accidentally Fires Entire Company Via Email," ibtimes.com, April 23, 2012.

34 Justin Fox, "The Triumph of English," *Fortune*, September 18, 2000, pp. 209–212.

35 Joseph Allen and Bennett P. Lientz, *Effective Business Communication* (Santa Monica, CA: Goodyear, 1979).

36 See "Making Silence Your Ally," *Across the Board*, October 1999, p. 11.

37 Boyd A. Vander Houwen, "Less Talking, More Listening," *HRMagazine*, April 1997, pp. 53–58.

38 For a discussion of these and related issues, see Eric M. Eisenberg and Marsha G. Witten, "Reconsidering Openness in Organizational Communication," *Academy of Management Review*, July 1987, pp. 418–426.

39 For a recent illustration, see Barbara Kellerman, "When Should a Leader Apologize—and When Not?" *Harvard Business Review*, April 2006, pp. 72–81.

40 Hugh Anderson, "Phone-Interview Tips for Savvy Candidates," *BNet*, 2010, http://www.techrepublic.com/, accessed on January 1, 2014; Anne Fisher, "Fear of Phoning," *Fortune*, http://money.cnn.com, accessed on January 1, 2014; Fisher, "How Can I Survive a Phone Interview?" *Fortune*, http://money.cnn.com, accessed on January 1, 2014; "Phone Interview Success," *CollegeGrad.com*, www.collegegrad.com, accessed on January 1, 2014; "Need Some Phone Interview Help? Score Big with Our 11 Top Tips," *BNet*, http://www.techrepublic.com/, accessed on January 1, 2014; and Matt Aberham, "JobsBlog Rewind: Five Ways to Fail My Phone Interview," *The JobsBlog*, http://microsoftjobsblog.com, accessed on January 1, 2014.

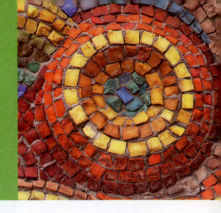

CHAPTER 13

Managing Work Groups and Teams

Learning Outcomes

After studying this chapter, you should be able to:

1 Define and identify types of groups and teams in organizations, discuss reasons people join groups and teams, and list the stages of group and team development.

2 Identify and discuss four essential characteristics of groups and teams.

3 Discuss interpersonal and intergroup conflict in organizations.

4 Describe how organizations manage conflict.

5 Describe the negotiation process.

Management in Action

Managing by Clowning Around

"It's difficult to be creative in isolation."

—Lyn Heward, former president of Cirque du Soleil's Creative Content Division

Fourteen-year-old Guy Laliberté dropped out of high school in Québec, Canada, because he wanted to see the world. "I decided to go into street performing because it was a traveling job," he recalls, and although his skills were limited to playing the accordion and telling stories, they were enough to get him to London by the time he was 18. From there, he not only extended his travels to Europe but also broadened his repertoire to include fire breathing, juggling, magic, and stilt walking. "It was just an adventure," he admits, "and I was planning to go back to school and have a regular life," but his nearly decade-long adventure had only deepened his passion for street performing. When he returned to Canada, he joined a stilt-walking troupe, and in 1984, when he was 23 years old, Laliberté partnered with another high school dropout to form their own street-performance company. Today, he still runs that company, and as 80 percent owner of Cirque du Soleil, he's one of the richest people in Canada.

Cirque du Soleil, which is French for *circus of the sun* ("The sun," explains Laliberté, "stands for energy and youth, which is what I thought the circus should be about"), has completely transformed the traditional three-ring spectacle with trapeze artists, clowns, and lion tamers. Laliberté calls Cirque a "transdiciplinary experience"—an amalgam of breathtaking stunt work, dazzling stagecraft, surreal costumes, and pulsing music. There are currently 20 different Cirque shows, each developed around a distinctive theme and story arc, such as

ITAR-TASS Photo Agency/Alamy

Cirque du Soleil makes extensive use of teams to plan, design, and execute its elaborate shows such as Varekai, shown here being performed in Moscow.

"the urban experience in all its myriad forms" (*Saltimbanco*) and "a tribute to the nomadic soul" (*Varekai*). Headquartered in Montreal, Canada, the company now employs 5,000 people, including more than 1,300 artists, and its shows have been seen by 100 million spectators. Profits for 2012 were $250 million on revenues of $1 billion.

The key to this success, according to Laliberté, is creativity: "I believe that the profits will come from the quality of your creative products," he says. "Since the beginning, I've always wanted to develop a self-feeding circle of creative productions: The positive financial returns from one show would be used to develop and create a new show, and so on." He's also convinced that his job is to provide a working environment that fosters collective creativity: "I believe in nurturing creativity and offering a haven for creators, enabling them to develop their ideas to the fullest. With more and more talented creators being drawn to Cirque in an environment that fulfills them, these [conditions] are ideal to continue developing great new shows."

Lyn Heward, former president of Cirque's Creative Content Division, calls the company's process of training and integrating talented people "creative transformation." "Everyone," she says, "when they come to Cirque as an employee, even an accountant, comes there because it's a creative and admired company, and they want to be able to contribute something creatively." From her experience at Cirque, Heward drew up a nine-point guide to "creative transformation," and at the heart of her list is a commitment to the value of teamwork. In fact, the fifth item on her list says, "Practice teamwork. True creativity requires stimulation and collaboration. It's difficult to be creative in isolation." Item 6 picks up the same theme: "Keep creativity fresh with hard-working bosses who constantly encourage and receive employees' ideas and feedback and accept that there are often different ways of getting the same end result."

"No matter what your product," Heward argues, "whether it's computers, cars, or anything else, your results [depend on] having a passionate strong team of people." In any workplace, she explains, "our most natural resource is the people we work with—the people we build our product with. Unless there's a strong commitment to teambuilding, passionate leadership, and creativity, even at Cirque it would not happen." Heward is willing to admit that "incredible freedom is a problem for most people because it requires us to think differently," but she's also confident that getting people committed to teamwork is the best way to get them to develop their creativity. Take Igor Jijikine, a Russian-born acrobat-actor who helped train performers for *Mystère*, Cirque's permanent show at Las Vegas's Treasure Island Hotel and Casino. "[T]he really challenging thing," he says,

> is to change the mentality of the performers I work with. Many of our performers are former competitive gymnasts. Gymnastics is essentially an individual sport. Gymnasts never have to think creatively or be a part of a true team. They got here by being strong individuals. So, right from the start, we really challenge ourselves to erase the lines between athletics and artistry, between individuals and the group. We need to transform an individual into a team player everyone else can count on, literally with their lives.

Finally, Heward acknowledges that you can't imbue employees with the Cirque du Soleil culture and "then tell them to go work in their cubicles." The space in which they work, she says, "has to reflect [Cirque's] values and vision." All Cirque du Soleil productions are created and developed by teams working at the Montreal facility, which the company calls "the Studio" and describes as "a full-fledged creation, innovation, and training laboratory." In addition to administrative space—"eight floors of uniquely designed office spaces and relaxation areas conducive to inspiration"—the complex boasts acrobatic, dance, and theatrical studios, and the effect of the whole, says Heward, is that of "a fantastical playground." Creativity, she explains,

> is fostered in work groups where people first get to know each other and then learn to trust one another. And in this playground, we recognize that a good idea can emerge from anywhere in the organization or from within a team. We make our shows from this collective creativity.

Cirque CEO Daniel Lamarre has a succinct way of explaining the company's success: "We let the creative people run it." As for Laliberté, he, too, is content to trust his creative people—an instinct, he says, that he learned in his days as a street performer: "In the street, you have to develop that instinct of trusting people and reading people because that instinct is your lifesaver." He lists himself as "Artistic Guide" in production notes and tries "not to be too involved in the beginning and during the process," the better to keep his perspective "fresh" and to "be able to give constructive recommendation on the final production." He also wants to do the same thing that he wanted to do when he was 14: "I still want to travel, I still want to entertain, and I most certainly still want to have fun."[1]

This chapter is about the processes that lead to and follow from successes like those enjoyed by Cirque de Soleil. More important, it's also about the processes leading to and following successful group and team dynamics. In Chapter 12, we established the interpersonal nature of organizations. We extend that discussion here by first introducing basic concepts of group and team dynamics. Subsequent sections explain the characteristics of groups and teams in organizations. We then describe interpersonal and intergroup conflict and discuss how conflict can be managed. We conclude with a brief discussion of negotiation.

GROUPS AND TEAMS IN ORGANIZATIONS

group
Consists of two or more people who interact regularly to accomplish a common purpose or goal

Groups are a ubiquitous part of organizational life. They are the basis for much of the work that gets done, and they evolve both inside and outside the normal structural boundaries of the organization. We define a **group** as two or more people who interact regularly to accomplish a common purpose or goal.[2] The purpose of a group or team may range from preparing a new advertising campaign, to informally sharing information, to making important decisions, to fulfilling social needs.

Types of Groups and Teams

In general, three basic kinds of groups are found in organizations—functional groups, informal or interest groups, and task groups and teams.[3] These are illustrated in Figure 13.1.

functional group
A permanent group created by the organization to accomplish a number of organizational purposes with an unspecified time horizon

Functional Groups   A **functional group** is a permanent group created by the organization to accomplish a number of organizational purposes with an unspecified time horizon. The advertising department at Starbucks, the management department at Iowa State University, and the nursing staff at the M.D. Anderson Cancer Center. The advertising department at Starbucks, for example, seeks to plan effective advertising campaigns, increase sales, run in-store promotions, and develop a unique identity for the company. It is assumed that the functional group will remain in existence after it attains its current objectives—those objectives will be replaced by new ones.

informal or interest group
Created by its members for purposes that may or may not be relevant to those of the organization

Informal or Interest Groups   An **informal or interest group** is created by its own members for purposes that may or may not be relevant to organizational goals. It also has an unspecified time horizon. A group of employees who lunch together every day may be discussing productivity, money embezzling, or local politics and sports. As long as the group members enjoy eating together, they will probably continue to do so. When lunches cease to be pleasant, they will seek other company or a different activity.

Informal groups can be a powerful force that managers cannot ignore.[4] One writer described how a group of employees at a furniture factory subverted their boss's efforts to increase production. They tacitly agreed to produce a reasonable amount of work but not to work too hard. One man kept a stockpile of completed work hidden as a backup in case he got too far behind. In another example, autoworkers described how they left out gaskets and seals and put soft-drink bottles inside doors.[5] Of course, informal groups can also be a positive force, such as when people work together to help out a colleague who has suffered a personal tragedy. For example, during and in the aftermath of Hurricane Sandy, the superstorm that devastated the northeast United States in 2012, literally dozens of incidents were reported portraying how informal groups emerged to help those in distress.

In recent years, the Internet has served as a platform for the emergence of more and different kinds of informal or interest groups. As one example, Google includes a wide array of interest groups that bring together people with common interests. And increasingly,

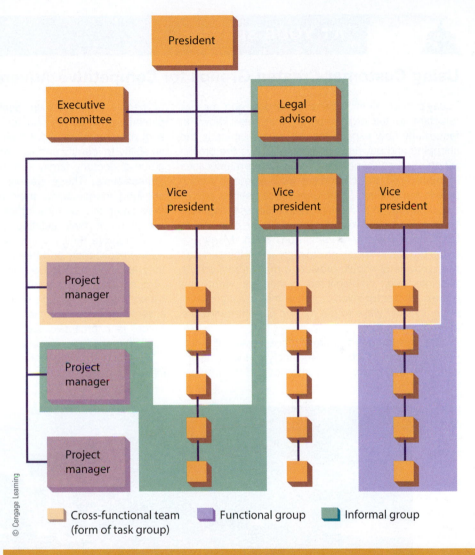

© Cengage Learning

Cross-functional team
(form of task group)   ■ Functional group   ■ Informal group

FIGURE 13.1

Types of Groups in Organizations

Every organization has many different types of groups. In this hypothetical organization, a functional group is shown within the purple area, a cross-functional team within the yellow area, and an informal group within the green area.

workers who lose their jobs as a result of layoffs are banding together electronically to offer moral support to one another and to facilitate networking as they all look for new jobs.[6] The "At Your Service" feature illustrates other new types of groups.

task group
A group created by the organization to accomplish a relatively narrow range of purposes within a stated or implied time horizon

Task Groups   A **task group** is a group created by the organization to accomplish a relatively narrow range of purposes within a stated or implied time horizon. Most committees and task forces are task groups. The organization specifies group membership and assigns a relatively narrow set of goals, such as developing a new product or evaluating a proposed grievance procedure. The time horizon for accomplishing these purposes is either specified (a committee may be asked to make a recommendation within 30 days) or implied (the project team will disband when the new product is developed).

AT YOUR SERVICE

Using Customer-Created Groups for Competitive Advantage

Today's customers know a great deal and are not reluctant to tell organizations what they know. In fact, many now expect not only to participate in the shopping and buying experience in ways the organization does not expect and for which in many cases is unprepared, but customers also expect to participate in the creation of the experience itself as part of the organization's creative team. Service organizations have long asked customers their opinions to learn what customers want from them. Many use focus groups to solicit information about the services they provide or should provide in the future. Today's well-informed, web-enabled customers want and expect far greater involvement in their buying experience and find ways to get it. Two current trends are examples of this.

The first trend is customer management of a networked team, which is increasingly found in health care. The availability of the Internet and the interest of people in their own health mean that many patients arrive at their doctor's office not only with a lot of information about their ailment but also with an ability to identify and assemble their own support group of doctors, family and friends, and health-care professionals. These people want to be actively engaged in managing their own health care and they enter the doctor's office expecting to involve members of their existing wellness group. They help integrate their primary care physician with any referred specialists and freely add in other specialists they learn about via chat rooms, public rankings of doctors, and disease-specific websites. While the historic model in health care had the family physician assembling a treatment and care team, the modern model is a proactive patient who assembles and actively manages a group of health-care providers.

The second example of customer groups collaborating with an organization can be seen in the phenomena

David Livingston/Getty Images

Some organizations creatively use customer-created groups to function more effectively. These people are gathered to watch a street performance in Los Angeles. Performers will gauge the audience response to their early performances and then tailor their later performances to best match what the audience wants.

(continued)

AT YOUR SERVICE (Continued)

of crowdsourcing. Although the practice of asking a crowd for help is as old as the wanted posters on post office walls, the web has expanded this concept greatly because it can connect people anywhere in the world who want to be involved. Many newer business models are built on their ability to provide platforms for participation. Many people use crowdsourced Wikipedia as their only encyclopedia and the customer recommendations provided by Amazon, TripAdvisor, OpenTable, and Yelp as their guide for what to read and where to go, eat, or shop.

In the simplest form of crowdsourcing, a group is assembled, usually online, to solve a problem or engineer a solution. One classic illustration is described by Tapscott and Williams in their book *Wikinomics*. They write of a struggling Canadian gold mining firm, Goldcorp, that decided to release all its proprietary geological data about its property to the public and offered a $575,000 prize for anyone who could develop a better way to locate gold on that property. The winning team from Australia gave them an answer that enabled them to increase their production of gold from just over 50,000 ounces annually at a cost of $360 an ounce to over a half million ounces annually at a cost of only $59 an ounce. Successful examples of crowdsourcing like this one have generated much interest among others seeking solutions to problems that traditional methods don't seem to solve well. By building a web platform and posing a problem in a way that will interest potential participants, a crowd can be attracted. For example, Threadless uses its website to engage anyone wishing

to participate in creating new shirt designs. The U.S. Department of Defense offers people an opportunity to help test its software, the Library of Congress asked Flickr users to help identify people in its photo collection, and Walmart asks customers to vote on which new products it should stock.

In all these cases, the organization is creating a nonemployee group that it must manage sometimes without even knowing who the members are. The company generally pays little or nothing for participation. The individuals participating often interact with each other to argue the merits of proposed solutions. IKEA manages a website where it not only solicits new ideas for its stores but also where customers can share solutions to each other's problems. Organizations using crowdsourcing must provide a problem in a manner that can be comprehended by potential participants, an interactive web platform that can be found by those knowledgeable and interested in the topic, and some process for identifying success and recognition of contribution when the problem is resolved. The point is that organizations increasingly must manage groups that they don't employ or groups of people who they don't even know. These groups are often customers involved in product innovation or their own health care but can also be computer gamers testing software or suggesting new code or anyone with an expertise and willingness to participate in the problem the organization wishes to solve. Crowd management will require learning new skills beyond those used for managing employees.

team
A group of workers that functions as a unit, often with little or no supervision, to carry out work-related tasks, functions, and activities

virtual teams
Teams composed of people from remote work sites who work together online

Teams are a special form of task group that have become increasingly popular.[7] In the sense used here, a **team** is a group of workers that functions as a unit, often with little or no supervision, to carry out work-related tasks, functions, and activities. Table 13.1 lists and defines some of the various types of teams that are being used today. Earlier forms of teams included autonomous work groups and quality circles. Today, teams are also sometimes called *self-managed teams*, *cross-functional teams*, or *high-performance teams*. Many firms today are routinely using teams to carry out most of their daily operations.[8] Further, **virtual teams**—teams composed of people from remote work sites who work together online—are also becoming more and more common.[9]

Organizations create teams for a variety of reasons. For one thing, they give more responsibility for task performance to the workers who are actually performing the tasks. They also empower workers by giving them greater authority and decision-making freedom. In addition, they allow the organization to capitalize on the knowledge and motivation of their workers. Finally, they enable the organization to shed its bureaucracy and promote flexibility and responsiveness. Ford used teams to design its newest

Table 13.1	Types of Teams
Problem-solving team	Most popular type of team; comprises knowledge workers who gather to solve a specific problem and then disband.
Management team	Consists mainly of managers from various functions like sales and production; coordinates work among other teams.
Work team	An increasingly popular type of team; work teams are responsible for the daily work of the organization; when empowered, they are self-managed teams.
Virtual team	A new type of work team that interacts digitally; members enter and leave the network as needed and may take turns serving as leader.
Quality circle	Declining in popularity; quality circles, comprising workers and supervisors who meet intermittently to discuss workplace problems.

Source: From *Fortune*, September 5, 1994. © 1994 Time Inc. All rights reserved.

Mustang and Focus models. Similarly, General Motors used a team to develop its newest model of the Chevrolet Corvette.

When an organization decides to use teams, it is essentially implementing a major form of organization change, as discussed in Chapter 7. Thus, it is important to follow a logical and systematic approach to planning and implementing teams in an existing organization design. It is also important to recognize that resistance may be encountered. This resistance is most likely from first-line managers, who will be giving up much of their authority to the team. Many organizations find that they must change the whole management philosophy of such managers to move away from being a supervisor and toward being a coach or facilitator.[10]

After teams are in place, managers should continue to monitor their contributions and how effectively they are functioning. In the best circumstances, teams will become very cohesive groups with high performance norms. To achieve this state, the manager can use any or all of the techniques described later in this chapter for enhancing cohesiveness. If implemented properly, and with the support of the workers themselves, performance norms will likely be relatively high. In other words, if the change is properly implemented, the team participants will understand the value and potential of teams and the rewards they may expect to get as a result of their contributions. On the other hand, poorly designed and implemented teams will do a less effective job and may detract from organizational effectiveness.[11]

Why People Join Groups and Teams

People join groups and teams for a variety of reasons. They join functional groups simply by virtue of joining organizations. People accept employment to earn money or practice their chosen professions. Once inside the organization, they are assigned to jobs and roles, and thus become members of functional groups. People in existing functional groups are told, are asked, or volunteer to serve on committees, task forces, and teams. People join informal or interest groups for a variety of reasons, most of which are quite complex.[12] Indeed, the need to be a team player has grown so strong today that many organizations will actively resist hiring someone who does not want to work with others.[13]

Interpersonal Attraction   One reason people choose to form informal or interest groups is that they are attracted to one another. Many different factors contribute to interpersonal attraction. When people see a lot of each other, pure proximity increases the likelihood that interpersonal attraction will develop. Attraction is increased when people have similar attitudes, personalities, or economic standings.

Group Activities   Individuals may also be motivated to join a group because the activities of the group appeal to them. Jogging, playing bridge or fantasy football, bowling, discussing poetry, playing war games, or flying model airplanes are all activities that some people enjoy. It is more enjoyable to participate in many of them as a member of a group, and most require more than one person. Many large firms such as Exxon Mobil and Apple have a football, softball, or bowling league. A person may join a bowling team, not because of any particular attraction to other group members, but simply because being a member of the group allows that person to participate in a pleasant activity. Of course, if the group's level of interpersonal attraction is very low, a person may choose to forgo the activity rather than join the team.

Group Goals   The goals of a group may also motivate people to join. The Sierra Club, which is dedicated to environmental conservation, is a good example of this kind of interest group. Various fund-raising groups are another illustration. Members may or may not be personally attracted to the other fund-raisers, and they probably do not enjoy the activity of knocking on doors asking for money, but they join the group because they subscribe to its goal. Workers join unions such as the United Auto Workers because they support their goals.

Need Satisfaction   Still another reason for joining a group is to satisfy the need for affiliation. New residents in a community may join the Newcomers Club partially as a

Jupiter images/Stone/Getty Images

People sometime join groups in order to engage in certain activities. These young men, for instance, are playing flag football in a city park. They may or may not have known each other before their game, and may or may not keep in contact with one another after the game. But for the moment, they are enjoying a group activity—a game that could not be played without others.

way to meet new people and partially just to be around other people. Likewise, newly divorced people often join support groups as a way to have companionship. This need also plays a role in why some people use Facebook and other social media venues.

Instrumental Benefits   A final reason people join groups is that membership is sometimes seen as instrumental in providing other benefits to the individual. For example, it is fairly common for college students entering their senior year to join several professional clubs or associations because listing such memberships on a résumé is thought to enhance the chances of getting a good job. Similarly, a manager might join a certain racquet club not because she is attracted to its members (although she might be) and not because of the opportunity to play tennis (although she may enjoy it). The club's goals are not relevant, and her affiliation needs may be satisfied in other ways. However, she may feel that being a member of this club will lead to important and useful business contacts. The racquet club membership is instrumental in establishing those contacts. Membership in civic groups such as the Junior League and Rotary may be solicited for similar reasons.

Stages of Group and Team Development

Imagine the differences between a collection of five people who have just been brought together to form a group or team and a group or team that has functioned like a well-oiled machine for years. Members of a new group or team are unfamiliar with how they will function together and are tentative in their interactions. In a group or team with considerable experience, members are familiar with one another's strengths and weaknesses and are more secure in their roles in the group. The former group or team is generally considered to be immature, whereas the latter is considered mature. To progress from the immature phase to the mature phase, a group or team must go through certain stages of development, as shown in Figure 13.2.[14]

The first stage of development is called *forming*. The members of the group or team get acquainted and begin to test which interpersonal behaviors are acceptable and which are unacceptable to the other members. The members are very dependent on others at this point to provide cues about what is acceptable. The basic ground rules for the group or team are established, and a tentative group structure may emerge.[15] At Reebok, for example, a merchandising team was created to handle its sportswear business. The team leader and his members were barely acquainted and had to spend a few weeks getting to know one another.

The second stage of development, often slow to emerge, is *storming*. During this stage, there may be a general lack of unity and uneven interaction patterns. At the same time, some members of the group or team may begin to exert themselves to become recognized as the group leader or at least to play a major role in shaping the group's agenda. In Reebok's team, some members advocated a rapid expansion into the marketplace; others argued for a slower entry. The first faction won, with disastrous results. Because of the rush, product quality was poor and deliveries were late. As a result, the team leader was fired and a new manager placed in charge.

The third stage of development, called *norming*, usually begins with a burst of activity. During this stage, each person begins to recognize and accept her or his role and to understand the roles of others. Members also begin to accept one another and to develop a sense of unity. There may also be temporary regressions to the previous stage. For example, the group or team might begin to accept one particular member as the leader. If this person later violates important norms or otherwise jeopardizes his or her claim to leadership, conflict might reemerge as the group rejects this leader and searches for another. Reebok's new leader transferred several people away from the team and set up

© Cengage Learning

FIGURE 13.2

Stages of Group Development

As groups mature, they tend to evolve through four distinct stages of development. Managers must understand that group members need time to become acquainted, accept one another, develop a group structure, and become comfortable with their roles in the group before they can begin to work directly to accomplish goals.

a new system and structure for managing things. The remaining employees accepted his new approach and settled into doing their jobs.

Performing, the final stage of group or team development, is also slow to develop. At this stage, the team really begins to focus on the problem at hand. The members enact the roles they have accepted, interaction occurs, and the efforts of the group are directed toward goal attainment. The basic structure of the group or team is no longer an issue but has become a mechanism for accomplishing the purpose of the group. Reebok's sportswear business is now growing consistently and has successfully avoided the problems that plagued it at first.

CHARACTERISTICS OF GROUPS AND TEAMS

As groups and teams mature and pass through the four basic stages of development, they begin to take on four important characteristics—a role structure, norms, cohesiveness, and informal leadership.[16]

Role Structures

role

The part an individual plays in a group that helps the group reach its goals

role structure

The set of defined roles and interrelationships among those roles that the group members define and accept

Each individual in a team has a part, or **role**, to play in helping the group reach its goals. Some people are leaders, some do the work, some interface with other teams, and so on. Indeed, a person may take on a *task specialist role* (concentrating on getting the group's task accomplished) or a *socioemotional role* (providing social and emotional support to others on the team). A few people, usually the leaders, perform both roles; a few others may do neither. The group's **role structure** is the set of defined roles and interrelationships among those roles that the group or team members define and accept. Each of us belongs to many groups and therefore plays multiple roles—in work groups, classes, families, and social organizations.[17]

Role structures emerge as a result of role episodes, as shown in Figure 13.3. The process begins with the expected role—what other members of the team expect the individual to do. The expected role gets translated into the sent role—the messages and cues that team members use to communicate the expected role to the individual. The perceived role is what the individual perceives the sent role to mean. Finally, the enacted role is what the individual actually does in the role. The enacted role, in turn, influences future expectations of the team. Of course, role episodes seldom unfold this easily. When major disruptions occur, individuals may experience role ambiguity, conflict, or overload.[18]

role ambiguity

Arises when the sent role is unclear and the individual does not know what is expected of him or her

Role Ambiguity **Role ambiguity** arises when the sent role is unclear. If your instructor tells you to write a term paper but refuses to provide more information, you will probably experience role ambiguity. You do not know what the topic is, how long the paper should be, what format to use, or when the paper is due. In work settings, role ambiguity can stem from poor job descriptions, vague instructions from a supervisor, or unclear cues from coworkers. The result is likely to be a subordinate

© Cengage Learning

Expected role → Sent role → Perceived role → Enacted role

FIGURE 13.3

The Development of a Role

Roles and role structures within a group generally evolve through a series of role episodes. The first two stages of role development are group processes, as the group members let individuals know what is expected of them. The other two parts are individual processes, as the new group members perceive and enact their roles.

who does not know what to do. Role ambiguity can be a significant problem for both the individual who must contend with it and the organization that expects the employee to perform.

role conflict
Occurs when the messages and cues composing the sent role are clear but contradictory or mutually exclusive

Role Conflict   **Role conflict** occurs when the messages and cues composing the sent role are clear but contradictory or mutually exclusive.[19] One common form is *interrole conflict*—conflict between roles. For example, if a person's boss says that one must work overtime and on weekends to get ahead, and the same person's coworkers say that you can succeed without working nights and weekends, conflict may result. In a matrix organization, interrole conflict often arises between the roles one plays in different teams as well as between team roles and one's permanent role in a functional group.

Intrarole conflict may occur when the person gets conflicting demands from different sources within the context of the same role. A manager's boss may tell the manager that she needs to put more pressure on subordinates to follow new work rules. At the same time, her subordinates may indicate that they expect her to get the rules changed. Thus, the cues are in conflict, and the manager may be unsure about which course to follow. *Intrasender conflict* occurs when a single source sends clear but contradictory messages. This might arise if the boss says one morning that there can be no more overtime for the next month but after lunch tells someone to work late that same evening. *Person–role conflict* results from a discrepancy between the role requirements and the individual's personal values, attitudes, and needs. If a person is told to do something unethical or illegal, or if the work is distasteful (for example, firing a close friend), person–role conflict is likely. Role conflict of all varieties is of particular concern to managers. Research has shown that conflict may occur in a variety of situations and lead to a variety of adverse consequences, including stress, poor performance, and rapid turnover.

role overload
Occurs when expectations for the role exceed the individual's capabilities to perform

Role Overload   A final consequence of a weak role structure is **role overload**, which occurs when expectations for the role exceed the individual's capabilities. When a manager gives an employee several major assignments at once, while increasing the person's regular workload, the employee will probably experience role overload. Role overload may also result when an individual takes on too many roles at one time. For example, a person trying to work extra hard at a job, run for election to the school board, serve on a committee in church, coach Little League baseball, maintain an active exercise program, and be a contributing member to her or his family will probably encounter role overload.

In a functional group or team, the manager can take steps to avoid role ambiguity, conflict, and overload. Having clear and reasonable expectations and sending clear and straightforward cues go a long way toward eliminating role ambiguity. Consistent expectations that take into account the employee's other roles and personal value system may minimize role conflict. Role overload can be avoided simply by recognizing the individual's capabilities and limits. In friendship and interest groups, role structures are likely to be less formal; hence, the possibility of role ambiguity, conflict, or overload may not be so great. However, if one or more of these problems does occur, they may be difficult to handle. Because roles in friendship and interest groups are less likely to be partially defined by a formal authority structure or written job descriptions, the individual cannot turn to those sources to clarify a role. The "Sustainability Matters" feature highlights how more and more research is being conducted by teams of researchers from different disciplines, each of whom adopts a specific role in the research project.

SUSTAINABILITY MATTERS

Measuring Carbon Footprints

If you're one of the world's 700 million richest people, you're probably a "high emitter" living a "carbon-intensive" lifestyle (at least statistically speaking). In plain English, because your lifestyle probably includes air travel, the use of a car, and a house to heat and cool, you're probably responsible for releasing more than your share of carbon dioxide (CO_2) into the Earth's atmosphere. "We estimate that … half the world's emissions come from just 700 million people," explains Shoibal Chakravarty, lead author of a recent study conducted by researchers at Princeton University. "It's mischievous," admits coauthor Robert Socolow, "but it's meant to be a logjam-breaking concept," and the proposals for cutting CO_2 emissions offered by the Princeton team have been widely praised for the fairness that they inject into a debate that's been stalemated for nearly 20 years.

The research team's report lists six coauthors. Shoibal Chakravarty, a physicist specializing in CO_2 emissions, is a research associate at the Princeton Environmental Institute (PEI), an interdisciplinary center for environmental research and education. Also associated with PEI is Massimo Tavoni, an economist who studies international policies on climate change. Stephen Pacala, who's the director of PEI, is a professor of ecology and evolutionary biology who focuses on the interactions of climate and the global biosphere. Robert Socolow, a professor of mechanical and aerospace engineering, studies global carbon management. Ananth Chikkatur, of Harvard's Belfer Center for Science and International Affairs, is a physicist who specializes in energy policy and technology innovation. Heleen de Coninck, a chemist, works on international climate policy and technology at the Energy Research Centre of the Netherlands.

Needless to say, the carbon footprint team was a diverse group in terms of academic discipline (not to mention nationality). Its innovative approach to the problem of CO_2 emissions—one which shows that it's possible to cut emissions and reduce poverty at the same time—resulted from an approach to high-level scientific problem solving that's typically called

Thomas Tolstrup/Iconica/Getty Images

The carbon footprint team is a diverse group of scientists working together to learn more about sustainability. More and more often, important scientific discoveries are being made by teams rather than by individuals working alone.

(continued)

SUSTAINABILITY MATTERS (Continued)

interdisciplinary or *multidisciplinary research*. The global footprint study, says Pacala, "represents a collaboration among young people from disparate disciplines—physics, economics, political science …. The team," he stresses, "worked together to formulate a novel approach to a long-standing and intractable problem," and its interdisciplinary approach to that problem reflects the prevailing model for the study of today's most complex and daunting issues, such as AIDS, terrorism, and global climate change.

To determine the extent to which team-based research has supplanted individual research among academics, a group at Northwestern University examined nearly 20 million papers published over a period of five decades. They found that

> teams increasingly dominate solo authors in the production of knowledge. Research is increasingly done in teams across virtually all fields. Teams typically produce more highly cited research than individuals do, and this advantage is increasing over time. Teams now also produce the exceptionally high-impact research …

The shift from the individual to the team-based model of research has been most significant in the sciences, where there's been, says the Northwestern study, "a substantial shift toward collective research." One reason for the shift, suggest the authors, may be "the increasing capital intensity of research" in laboratory sciences, where the growth of collaboration has been particularly striking. The increasing tendency toward specialization may be another reason. As knowledge grows in a discipline, scientists tend to devote themselves to specialty areas, the discipline itself becomes fragmented into "finer divisions of labor," and studies of larger issues in the discipline thus require greater collaboration.

What about collaboration that extends beyond the confines of academia? As it happens, Robert Socolow and Stephen Pacala, in addition to working on the carbon footprint team, are codirectors of the Carbon Mitigation Initiative (CMI), a partnership among Princeton, Ford, and BP, the world's third-largest oil company. BP picks up 75 percent of the tab for research that has as its goal, according to CMI's mission statement, "a compelling and sustainable solution of the carbon and climate change problem." CMI seeks "a novel synergy across fundamental science, technological development, and business principles that accelerates the pace of discovery," and collaboration is essential to its work because it crosses the borders between scientific, technological, and business interests. CMI is divided into research groups, including the Capture Group, which works on technologies for capturing emissions from fossil fuels, and the Storage Group, which investigates the potential risks of injecting CO_2 underground. Working through CMI, BP has been able to launch a CCS trial at a gas-development facility in Algeria.

References: Douglas Fischer, "Solving the Climate Dilemma One Billion Emitters at a Time," *Daily Climate*, http://www.goodhousekeeping.com/home/green-living/the-daily-green, accessed on January 1, 2014; Kitta McPherson, "New Princeton Method May Help Allocate Carbon Emissions Responsibility among Nations," *News at Princeton*, July 6, 2009, www.princeton.edu, accessed on January 1, 2014; Shoibal Chakravarty et al., "Sharing Global CO_2 Emission Reductions among One Billion High Emitters," *Proceedings of the National Academy of Sciences*, Vol. 106 (July 2009), www.pnas.org, accessed on January 1, 2014; Stefan Wuchty et al., "The Increasing Dominance of Teams in Production of Knowledge," *Sciencexpress*, www.kellogg.northwestern.edu, accessed on January 1, 2014; and Carbon Mitigation Initiative, "About the Carbon Mitigation Initiative," Princeton University, February 24, 2011, http://cmi.princeton.edu, accessed on January 1, 2014.

Behavioral Norms

norms
Standards of behavior that the group accepts for and expects of its members

Norms are standards of behavior that the group or team accepts and expects of its members. Most committees, for example, develop norms governing their discussions. A person who talks too much is perceived as doing so to make a good impression or to get his or her own way. Other members may not talk much to this person, may not sit nearby, may glare at the person, and may otherwise "punish" the individual for violating the norm. Norms, then, define the boundaries between acceptable and unacceptable behavior.[20] Some groups develop norms that limit the upper bounds of behavior to "make life easier" for the group—for example, do not make more than two comments in a committee discussion or do not produce any more than you have to. In general, these norms are counterproductive. Other groups may develop norms that limit the lower bounds of behavior—for example, do not come to meetings unless you have read the reports to be discussed or have produced as much as you can. These norms tend to reflect motivation, commitment, and high performance. Managers can sometimes use norms for the betterment of the organization. For example, Kodak successfully used group norms to reduce injuries in some of its plants.[21]

Norm Generalization   The norms of one group cannot always be generalized to another group. Some academic departments, for example, have a norm that suggests that faculty members dress up on teaching days. People who fail to observe this norm are "punished" by sarcastic remarks or even formal reprimands. In other departments, the norm may be casual clothes, and the person unfortunate enough to wear dress clothes may be punished just as vehemently. Even within the same work area, similar groups or teams can develop different norms. One team may strive always to produce above its assigned quota; another may maintain productivity just below its quota. The norm of one team may be to be friendly and cordial to its supervisor; that of another team may be to remain aloof and distant. Some differences are due primarily to the composition of the teams.

Norm Variation   In some cases, norm variation also can occur within a group or team. A common norm is that the least senior member of a group is expected to perform unpleasant or trivial tasks for the rest of the group. These tasks might be to wait on customers who are known to be small tippers (in a restaurant), to deal with complaining customers (in a department store), or to handle the low-commission line of merchandise (in a sales department). Another example is when certain individuals, especially informal leaders, may violate some norms. If the team is going to meet at 8 a.m., anyone arriving late will be chastised for holding things up. Occasionally, however, the informal leader may arrive a few minutes late. As long as this does not happen too often, the group probably will not do anything about it.

Norm Conformity   Four sets of factors contribute to norm conformity. First, factors associated with the group are important. For example, some groups or teams may exert more pressure for conformity than others. Second, the initial stimulus that prompts behavior can affect conformity. The more ambiguous the stimulus (for example, news that the team is going to be transferred to a new unit), the more pressure there is to conform. Third, individual traits determine the individual's propensity to conform (for example, more intelligent people are often less susceptible to pressure to conform). Finally, situational factors, such as team size and unanimity, influence conformity. As an individual learns the group's norms, he can do several different things. The most obvious is to adopt the norms. For example, the new male professor who notices that all the other men in the department dress up to teach can also start wearing a suit. A variation is to try to obey the "spirit" of the norm while retaining individuality. The professor may recognize that the norm is actually to wear a tie; thus, he might succeed by wearing a tie with his sport shirt, jeans, and sneakers.

The individual may also ignore the norm. When a person does not conform, several things can happen. At first, the group may increase its communication with the deviant individual to try to bring her back in line. If this does not work, communication may decline. Over time, the group may begin to exclude the individual from its activities and, in effect, ostracize the person. Finally, we need to briefly consider another aspect of norm conformity—socialization. **Socialization** is generalized norm conformity that occurs as a person makes the transition from being an outsider to being an insider.

socialization
Generalized norm conformity that occurs as a person makes the transition from being an outsider to being an insider in the organization

A newcomer to an organization, for example, gradually begins to learn about such norms as dress, working hours, and interpersonal relations. As the newcomer adopts these norms, she is being socialized into the organizational culture. Some organizations, such as Texas Instruments, work to actively manage the socialization process; others leave it to happenstance.

Cohesiveness

cohesiveness

The extent to which members are loyal and committed to the group; the degree of mutual attractiveness within the group

A third important team characteristic is cohesiveness. **Cohesiveness** is the extent to which members are loyal and committed to the group. In a highly cohesive team, the members work well together, support and trust one another, and are generally effective at achieving their chosen goals.[22] In contrast, a team that lacks cohesiveness is not very coordinated, its members do not necessarily support one another fully, and it may have a difficult time reaching goals. Of particular interest are the factors that increase and reduce cohesiveness and the consequences of team cohesiveness. These are listed in Table 13.2.

Several different factors can influence the cohesiveness of a group. For example, a manager can establish intergroup competition, assign compatible members to the group, create opportunities for success, establish acceptable goals, and foster interaction to increase cohesiveness. Other factors can be used to decrease cohesiveness.

Factors That Increase Cohesiveness   Five factors can increase the level of cohesiveness in a group or team. One of the strongest is intergroup competition. When two or more groups are in direct competition (for example, three sales groups competing for top sales honors or two football teams competing for a conference championship), each group is likely to become more cohesive. Second, just as personal attraction plays a role in causing a group to form, so, too, does attraction seem to enhance cohesiveness. Third, favorable evaluation of the entire group by outsiders can increase cohesiveness. Thus, a group's winning a sales contest or a conference title or receiving recognition and praise from a superior tends to increase cohesiveness.

Similarly, if all the members of the group or team agree on their goals, cohesiveness is likely to increase.[23] And the more frequently members of the group interact with one another, the more likely the group is to become cohesive. A manager who wants to foster a high level of cohesiveness in a team might do well to establish some form of intergroup competition, assign members to the group who are likely to be attracted to one another, provide opportunities for success, establish goals that all members are likely to accept, and allow ample opportunities for interaction.[24]

Table 13.2	Factors That Influence Group Cohesiveness	
Factors That Increase Cohesiveness	**Factors That Reduce Cohesiveness**	
Intergroup competition	Group size	
Personal attraction	Disagreement on goals	
Favorable evaluation	Intragroup competition	
Agreement on goals	Domination	
Interaction	Unpleasant experiences	

Factors That Reduce Cohesiveness   There are also five factors that are known to reduce team cohesiveness. First of all, cohesiveness tends to decline as a group increases in size. Second, when members of a team disagree on what the goals of the group should be, cohesiveness may decrease. For example, when some members believe the group should maximize output and others think output should be restricted, cohesiveness declines. Third, intragroup competition reduces cohesiveness. When members are competing among themselves, they focus more on their own actions and behaviors than on those of the group.

Fourth, domination by one or more persons in the group or team may cause overall cohesiveness to decline. Other members may feel that they are not being given an opportunity to interact and contribute, and they may become less attracted to the group as a consequence. Finally, unpleasant experiences that result from group membership may reduce cohesiveness. A sales group that comes in last in a sales contest, an athletic team that sustains a long losing streak, and a work group reprimanded for poor-quality work may all become less cohesive as a result of their unpleasant experiences.

Consequences of Cohesiveness   In general, as teams become more cohesive, their members tend to interact more frequently, conform more to norms, and become more satisfied with the team. Cohesiveness may also influence team performance. However, performance is also influenced by the team's performance norms. Figure 13.4 shows how cohesiveness and performance norms interact to help shape team performance.

When both cohesiveness and performance norms are high, high performance should result because the team wants to perform at a high level (norms) and its members are working together toward that end (cohesiveness). When norms are high and cohesiveness is low, performance will be moderate. Although the team wants to perform at a high level, its members are not necessarily working well together. When norms are low, performance will be low, regardless of whether group cohesiveness is high or low. The least desirable situation occurs when low performance norms are combined with high cohesiveness. In this case, all team members embrace the standard of restricting performance (owing to the low performance norm), and the group is united in its efforts to maintain that standard (owing to the high cohesiveness). If cohesiveness were low, the manager might be able to raise performance norms by establishing high goals and rewarding goal attainment or by bringing in new group members who are high performers. But a highly cohesive group is likely to resist these interventions.[25]

FIGURE 13.4

The Interaction Between Cohesiveness and Performance Norms

Group cohesiveness and performance norms interact to determine group performance. From the manager's perspective, high cohesiveness combined with high performance norms comprise the best situation, and high cohesiveness combined with low performance norms create the worst situation. Managers who can influence the level of cohesiveness and performance norms can greatly improve the effectiveness of a work group.

© Cengage Learning

Formal and Informal Leadership

Most functional groups and teams have a formal leader—that is, one appointed by the organization or chosen or elected by the members of the group. Because friendship and interest groups are formed by the members themselves, however, any formal leader must be elected or designated by the members. Although some groups do designate such a leader (a softball team may elect a captain, for example), many do not. Moreover, even when a formal leader is designated, the group or team may also look to others for leadership. An **informal leader** is a person who engages in leadership activities but whose right to do so has not been formally recognized. The formal and the informal leader in any group or team may be the same person, or they may be different people. We noted earlier the distinction between the task specialist and socioemotional roles within groups. An informal leader is likely to be a person capable of carrying out both roles effectively. If the formal leader can fulfill one role but not the other, an informal leader often emerges to supplement the formal leader's functions. If the formal leader can fill neither role, one or more informal leaders may emerge to carry out both sets of functions.

Is informal leadership desirable? In many cases, informal leaders are quite powerful because they draw from referent or expert power. When they are working in the best interests of the organization, they can be a tremendous asset. Notable athletes like Peyton Manning and Abby Wambach are examples of informal leaders. However, when informal leaders work counter to the goals of the organization, they can cause significant difficulties. Such leaders may lower performance norms, instigate walkouts or wildcat strikes, or otherwise disrupt the organization.

informal leader
A person who engages in leadership activities but whose right to do so has not been formally recognized by the organization or group

INTERPERSONAL AND INTERGROUP CONFLICT

Of course, when people work together in an organization, things do not always go smoothly. Indeed, conflict is an inevitable element of interpersonal relationships in organizations. In this section, we look at how conflict affects overall performance. We also explore the causes of conflict between individuals, between groups, and between an organization and its environment.

The Nature of Conflict

Conflict is a disagreement among two or more individuals, groups, or organizations. This disagreement may be relatively superficial or very strong. It may be short-lived or exist for months or even years, and it may be work related or personal. Conflict may manifest itself in a variety of ways. People may compete with one another, glare at one another, shout, or withdraw. Groups may band together to protect popular members or oust unpopular members. Organizations may seek legal remedies.

Most people assume that conflict is something to be avoided because it connotes antagonism, hostility, unpleasantness, and dissension. Indeed, managers and management theorists have traditionally viewed conflict as a problem to be avoided.[26] In recent years, however, we have come to recognize that, although conflict can be a major problem, certain kinds of conflict may also be beneficial.[27] For example, when two members of a site selection committee disagree over the best location for a new plant, each may be forced to more thoroughly study and defend his or her preferred alternative. As a result of more systematic analysis and discussion, the committee may make a better decision and be better prepared to justify it to others than if everyone had agreed from the outset and accepted an alternative that was perhaps less well analyzed.

conflict
A disagreement among two or more individuals or groups

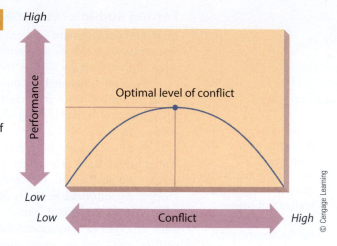

FIGURE 13.5

The Nature of Organizational Conflict

Either too much or too little conflict can be dysfunctional for an organization. In either case, performance may be low. However, an optimal level of conflict that sparks motivation, creativity, innovation, and initiative can result in higher levels of performance.

As long as conflict is handled in a cordial and constructive manner, it is probably serving a useful purpose in the organization. On the other hand, when working relationships are disrupted and the conflict has reached destructive levels, it has likely become dysfunctional and needs to be addressed.[28] We discuss ways of dealing with such conflict later in this chapter.

Figure 13.5 depicts the general relationship between conflict and performance for a group or an organization. If there is absolutely no conflict in the group or organization, its members may become complacent and apathetic. As a result, group or organizational performance and innovation may begin to suffer. A moderate level of conflict among group or organizational members, on the other hand, can spark motivation, creativity, innovation, and initiative and raise performance. Too much conflict, though, can produce such undesirable results as hostility and lack of cooperation, which lower performance. The key for managers is to find and maintain the optimal amount of conflict that fosters performance. Of course, what constitutes optimal conflict varies with both the situation and the people involved.[29]

Causes of Conflict

Conflict may arise in both interpersonal and intergroup relationships. Occasionally, conflict between individuals and groups may be caused by particular organizational strategies and practices. A third arena for conflict is between an organization and its environment.

Interpersonal Conflict   Conflict between two or more individuals is almost certain to occur in any organization, given the great variety in perceptions, goals, attitudes, and so forth among its members. Bill Gates, founder of Microsoft, and Kazuhiko Nishi, a former business associate from Japan, once ended a lucrative long-term business relationship because of interpersonal conflict. Nishi accused Gates of becoming too political, while Gates charged that Nishi became too unpredictable and erratic in his behavior.[30]

A frequent source of interpersonal conflict in organizations is what many people call a *personality clash*—when two people distrust each other's motives, dislike each other, or for some other reason simply cannot get along.[31] Conflict may also arise between people who have different beliefs or perceptions about some aspect of their work or their organization. For example, one manager might want the organization to require that all employees use Microsoft Office software, to promote standardization.

Another manager might believe that a variety of software packages should be allowed, in order to accommodate individuality. Similarly, a male manager may disagree with his female colleague over whether the organization is guilty of discriminating against women in promotion decisions. Conflict can also result from excess competitiveness among individuals. Two people vying for the same job, for example, may resort to political behavior in an effort to gain an advantage. If either competitor sees the other's behavior as inappropriate, accusations are likely to result. Even after the "winner" of the job is determined, such conflict may continue to undermine interpersonal relationships, especially if the reasons given in selecting one candidate are ambiguous or open to alternative explanations. Acer CEO and President Gianfranco Lanci resigned due to several months of unresolved conflict with the company's board of directors. Lanci and the board had differing views on organizational growth, customer value creation, brand position enhancement, and resource allocation. Lanci pushed strongly for a move into the mobile segment to compete with Apple's iPad, while the board wanted to maintain its core PC business.[32]

Intergroup Conflict   Conflict between two or more organizational groups is also quite common. For example, the members of a firm's marketing group may disagree with the production group over product quality and delivery schedules. Two sales groups may disagree over how to meet sales goals, and two groups of managers may have different ideas about how best to allocate organizational resources.

Many intergroup conflicts arise more from organizational causes than from interpersonal causes. In Chapter 6, we described three forms of group interdependence—pooled, sequential, and reciprocal. Just as increased interdependence makes coordination more difficult, it increases the potential for conflict. For example, recall that in sequential interdependence, work is passed from one unit to another. Intergroup conflict may arise if the first group turns out too much work (the second group will fall behind), too little work (the second group will not meet its own goals), or poor-quality work.

At one J. C. Penney department store, conflict arose between stockroom employees and sales associates. The sales associates claimed that the stockroom employees were slow in delivering merchandise to the sales floor where it could be priced and shelved. The stockroom employees, in turn, claimed that the sales associates were not giving them enough lead time to get the merchandise delivered and failed to understand that they had additional duties besides carrying merchandise to the sales floor.

Just like people, different departments often have different goals. Further, these goals may often be incompatible. A marketing goal of maximizing sales, achieved partially by offering many products in a wide variety of sizes, shapes, colors, and models, probably conflicts with a production goal of minimizing costs, achieved partially by long production runs of a few items. Reebok recently confronted this very situation. One group of managers wanted to introduce a new sportswear line as quickly as possible, but other managers wanted to expand more deliberately and cautiously. Because the two groups were not able to reconcile their differences effectively, conflict arose between the two factions, which led to quality problems and delivery delays that plagued the firm for months.

Competition for scarce resources can also lead to intergroup conflict. Most organizations—especially universities, hospitals, government agencies, and businesses in depressed industries—have limited resources. In one New England town, for example, the public works department and the library battled over funds from a federal construction grant. The Buick, Pontiac, GMC, and Chevrolet divisions of General Motors frequently fought over the right to manufacture various new products developed by the company. This infighting was identified as one of many factors that led to GM's recent problems. As part of the solution, the Pontiac brand was eventually discontinued.

Conflict Between Organization and Environment   Conflict that arises between one organization and another is called *interorganizational conflict*. A moderate amount of interorganizational conflict resulting from business competition is expected, of course, but sometimes conflict becomes more extreme. For example, the owners of Jordache Enterprises, Inc., and Guess?, Inc., battled in court for years over ownership of the Guess? label, allegations of design theft, and several other issues.[33] Similarly, General Motors and Volkswagen went to court to resolve a bitter conflict that spanned more than four years. It all started when a key GM executive, Jose Ignacio Lopez de Arriortua, left for a position at Volkswagen. GM claimed that he took with him key secrets that could benefit its German competitor. After the messy departure, dozens of charges and countercharges were made by the two firms, and only a court settlement was able to put the conflict to an end.[34]

Conflict can also arise between an organization and other elements of its environment. For example, an organization may conflict with a consumer group over claims it makes about its products. McDonald's faced this problem a few years ago when it published nutritional information about its products that omitted details about fat content. A manufacturer might conflict with a governmental agency such as the federal Occupational Safety and Health Administration (OSHA). For example, the firm's management may believe it is in compliance with OSHA regulations, whereas officials from the agency believe that the firm is not in compliance. Or a firm might conflict with a supplier over the quality of raw materials. The firm may think the supplier is providing inferior materials, while the supplier thinks the materials are adequate.

MANAGING CONFLICT IN ORGANIZATIONS

How do managers cope with all this potential conflict? Fortunately, as Table 13.3 shows, there are ways to stimulate conflict for constructive ends, to control conflict before it gets out of hand, and to resolve it if it does. We now look at ways of managing conflict.[35]

Conflict is a powerful force in organizations, and it has both negative and positive consequences. Thus managers can draw on several different techniques to stimulate, control, or resolve and eliminate conflict, depending on their unique circumstances.

Table 13.3	Methods for Managing Conflict
Stimulating Conflict	
Increase competition among individuals and teams.	
Hire outsiders to shake things up.	
Change established procedures.	
Controlling Conflict	
Expand resource base.	
Enhance coordination of interdependence.	
Set superordinate goals.	
Match personalities and work habits of employees.	
Resolving and Eliminating Conflict	
Avoid conflict.	
Convince conflicting parties to compromise.	
Bring conflicting parties together to confront and negotiate conflict.	

© Cengage Learning

Conflict is a powerful force in organizations, and it has both negative and positive consequences. Thus, managers can draw on several different techniques to stimulate, control, or resolve and eliminate conflict, depending on their unique circumstances.

Stimulating Conflict

In some situations, an organization may stimulate conflict by placing individual employees or groups in competitive situations. Managers can establish sales contests, incentive plans, bonuses, or other competitive stimuli to spark competition. As long as the ground rules are equitable and all participants perceive the contest as fair, the conflict created by the competition is likely to be constructive because each participant will work hard to win (thereby enhancing some aspect of organizational performance).

Another useful method for stimulating conflict is to bring in one or more outsiders who will shake things up and present a new perspective on organizational practices. Outsiders may be new employees, current employees assigned to an existing work group, or consultants or advisors hired on a temporary basis. Of course, this action can also provoke resentment from insiders who feel they were qualified for the position. The Beecham Group, a British company, once hired an executive from the United States for its CEO position, expressly to change how the company did business. His arrival brought with it new ways of doing things and a new enthusiasm for competitiveness. Unfortunately, some valued employees also chose to leave Beecham because they resented some of the changes that were made.

Changing established procedures, especially procedures that have outlived their usefulness, can also stimulate conflict. Such actions cause people to reassess how they perform their jobs and whether they perform them correctly. For example, one university president announced that all vacant staff positions could be filled only after written justification had received his approval. Conflict arose between the president and the department heads, who felt they were required to do more paperwork than was necessary. Most requests were approved, but because department heads now had to think through their staffing needs, a few unnecessary positions were appropriately eliminated.

Controlling Conflict

One method of controlling conflict is to expand the resource base. Suppose a top manager receives two budget requests for $300,000 each. If she has only $500,000 to distribute, the stage is set for conflict because each group will believe its proposal is worth funding and will be unhappy if it is not fully funded. If both proposals are indeed worthwhile, it may be possible for the manager to come up with the extra $100,000 from some other source and thereby avoid difficulty.

As noted earlier, pooled, sequential, and reciprocal interdependence can all result in conflict. If managers use an appropriate technique for enhancing coordination, they can reduce the probability that conflict will arise. Techniques for coordination (described in Chapter 6) include making use of the managerial hierarchy, relying on rules and procedures, enlisting liaison people, forming task forces, and integrating departments. At the J. C. Penney store mentioned earlier, the conflict was addressed by providing salespeople with clearer forms on which to specify the merchandise they needed and in what sequence. If one coordination technique does not have the desired effect, a manager might shift to another one.

Competing goals can also be a source of conflict among individuals and groups. Managers can sometimes focus employee attention on higher-level, or superordinate, goals as a way of eliminating lower-level conflict. When labor unions such as the United Auto Workers make wage concessions to ensure survival of the automobile industry, they are responding to a superordinate goal. Their immediate goal may be higher wages for members, but they realize that, without the automobile industry, their members would not even have jobs.

Finally, managers should try to match the personalities and work habits of employees so as to avoid conflict between individuals. For instance, two valuable subordinates, one a chain smoker and the other a vehement antismoker, probably should not be required to work together in an enclosed space. If conflict does arise between incompatible individuals, a manager might seek an equitable transfer for one or both of them to other units.

Resolving and Eliminating Conflict

Despite everyone's best intentions, conflict sometimes flares up. If it is disrupting the workplace, creating too much hostility and tension, or otherwise harming the organization, attempts must be made to resolve it.[36] Some managers who are uncomfortable dealing with conflict choose to avoid the conflict and hope it will go away. Avoidance may sometimes be effective in the short run for some kinds of interpersonal disagreements, but it does little to resolve long-run or chronic conflicts. Even more unadvisable, though, is "smoothing"—minimizing the conflict and telling everyone that things will "get better." Often, though, avoiding conflict may only make it worse as people continue to brood over it.

Compromise is striking a middle-range position between two extremes. This approach can work if it is used with care, but in most compromise situations, someone wins and someone loses. Budget problems are one of the few areas amenable to compromise because of their objective nature. Assume, for example, that additional resources are not available to the manager mentioned earlier. She has $500,000 to divide, and each of two groups claims to need $300,000. If the manager believes that both projects warrant funding, she can allocate $200,000 to each. The fact that the two groups have at least been treated equally may minimize the potential conflict.

The confrontational approach to conflict resolution—also called *interpersonal problem solving*—consists of bringing the parties together to confront the conflict. The parties discuss the nature of their conflict and attempt to reach an agreement or a solution. Confrontation requires a reasonable degree of maturity on the part of the participants, and the manager must structure the situation carefully. If handled well, this approach can be an effective means of resolving conflict. In recent years, many organizations have experimented with a technique called *alternative dispute resolution*, using a team of employees to arbitrate conflict in this way.[37] Negotiation, a closely related method, is discussed in our final section of this chapter.

Regardless of the approach, organizations and their managers should realize that conflict must be addressed if it is to serve constructive purposes and be prevented from bringing about destructive consequences. Conflict is inevitable in organizations, but its negative effects can be constrained with proper attention. For example, Union Carbide sent 200 of its managers to a three-day workshop on conflict management. The managers engaged in a variety of exercises and discussions to learn with whom they were most likely to come in conflict and how they should try to resolve it. As a result, managers at the firm later reported that hostility and resentment in the organization had been greatly diminished and that people in the firm reported more pleasant working relationships.[38]

negotiation
The process in which two or more parties (people or groups) reach agreement on an issue even though they have different preferences regarding that issue

NEGOTIATION

Negotiation is the process in which two or more parties (people or groups) reach agreement on an issue even though they have different preferences regarding that issue. In a sense, then, negotiation is also a form of conflict resolution. In its simplest form, the parties involved may be two individuals who are trying to decide who will pay for lunch. A little more complexity is involved when two people, such as an

Negotiations can take a variety of forms and deal with many different issues. For instance, people negotiate over salary, contract terms, job assignments, and a variety of other business activities. These representatives from different organizations have just reached an agreement to co-sponsor an advertising campaign and are "sealing the deal" with a symbolic handshake.

employee and a manager, sit down to decide on personal performance goals for the next year against which the employee's performance will be measured. Even more complex are the negotiations that take place between labor unions and the management of a company or between two companies as they negotiate the terms of a joint venture. The key issues in such negotiations are that at least two parties are involved, their preferences are different, and they need to reach agreement. Interest in negotiation has grown steadily in recent years. Four primary approaches to negotiation have dominated its study: individual differences, situational characteristics, game theory, and cognitive approaches.[39]

Early psychological approaches concentrated on the personality traits of the negotiators.[40] Traits investigated have included demographic characteristics and personality variables. Demographic characteristics have included age, gender, and race, among others. Personality variables have included risk taking, locus of control, tolerance for ambiguity, self-esteem, authoritarianism, and Machiavellianism. The assumption of this type of research was that the key to successful negotiation was selecting the right person to do the negotiating, one who had the appropriate demographic characteristics or personality. This assumption seemed to make sense because negotiation is such a personal and interactive process. However, the research rarely showed the positive results expected because situational variables negated the effects of the individual differences.[41]

Situational characteristics are the context within which negotiation takes place. They include such things as the types of communication between negotiators, the potential outcomes of the negotiation, the relative power of the parties (both positional and personal), the time frame available for negotiation, the number of people representing each side, and the presence of other parties. Some of this research has contributed to our understanding of the negotiation process. However, the shortcomings of the situational approach are similar to those of the individual characteristics approach. Many situational characteristics are external to the negotiators and beyond their control. Often the negotiators cannot change their relative power positions or the setting within which the negotiation occurs. So, although we have learned a lot from research on the situational issues, we still need to learn much more about the process.

Game theory was developed by economists using mathematical models to predict the outcome of negotiation situations (as illustrated in the Academy Award–winning movie *A Beautiful Mind*). It requires that every alternative and outcome be analyzed with probabilities and numerical outcomes reflecting the preferences of negotiating parties for each outcome. In addition, the order in which different parties can make choices and every possible move are predicted, along with associated preferences for outcomes. The outcomes of this approach are exactly what negotiators want: a predictive model of how negotiation should be conducted. One major drawback is that it requires the ability to describe all possible options and outcomes for every possible move in every situation before the negotiation starts. This is often very tedious, if possible at all. Another problem is that this theory assumes that negotiators are rational at all times. However, it is unlikely that negotiators will in fact always act rationally. Therefore, this approach, although elegant in its prescriptions, is usually unworkable in a real negotiation situation.

The fourth approach is the cognitive approach, which recognizes that negotiators often depart from perfect rationality during negotiation; it tries to predict how and when negotiators will make these departures. Howard Raiffa's decision analytic approach focuses on providing advice to negotiators actively involved in negotiation.[42] Bazerman and Neale have added to Raiffa's work by specifying eight ways in which negotiators systematically deviate from rationality.[43] The types of deviations they describe include escalating commitment to a previously selected course of action, overrelying on readily available information, assuming that the negotiations can produce fixed-sum outcomes, and anchoring negotiation in irrelevant information. These cognitive approaches have advanced the study of negotiation a long way beyond the early individual and situational approaches. Negotiators can use them to attempt to predict in advance how the negotiation might take place.

SUMMARY OF LEARNING OUTCOMES AND KEY POINTS

1. Define and identify types of groups and teams in organizations, discuss the reasons people join groups and teams, and list the stages of group and team development.

   - A group is two or more people who interact regularly to accomplish a common purpose or goal.
   - General kinds of groups in organizations are
     - functional groups.
     - task groups and teams.
     - informal or interest groups.
   - A team is a group of workers that functions as a unit, often with little or no supervision, to carry out organizational functions.

2. Identify and discuss four essential characteristics of groups and teams.

   - People join functional groups and teams to pursue a career.
   - Their reasons for joining informal or interest groups include interpersonal attraction, group activities, group goals, need satisfaction, and potential instrumental benefits.
   - The stages of team development include testing and dependence, intragroup conflict and hostility, development of group cohesion, and focusing on the problem at hand.
   - Four important characteristics of teams are role structures, behavioral norms, cohesiveness, and informal leadership.
     - Role structures define task and socioemotional specialists, and they may be disrupted by role ambiguity, role conflict, or role overload.

   - Norms are standards of behavior for group members.
   - Cohesiveness is the extent to which members are loyal and committed to the team and to one another.
   - Informal leaders are those leaders the group members themselves choose to follow.

3. Discuss interpersonal and intergroup conflict in organizations.

   - Conflict is a disagreement between two or more people, groups, or organizations.
   - Too little or too much conflict may hurt performance; an optimal level of conflict may improve performance.
   - Interpersonal and intergroup conflict in organizations may be caused by personality differences or by particular organizational strategies and practices.

4. Describe how organizations manage conflict.

   - Organizations may encounter conflict with one another and with various elements of the environment.
   - Three methods of managing conflict are
     - to stimulate it.
     - to control it.
     - to resolve and eliminate it.

5. Describe the negotiation process

   - Negotiation is the process in which two or more parties reach agreement on an issue, even though they have different preferences regarding that issue.

DISCUSSION QUESTIONS

Questions for Review

1. What is a group? Describe the several different types of groups and indicate the similarities and differences among them. What is the difference between a group and a team?
2. Identify the stages of group development. Do all teams develop through all the stages discussed in this chapter? Why or why not? How might the management of a mature team differ from the management of teams that are not yet mature?
3. Describe the development of a role within a group. Tell how each role leads to the next.
4. Identify two examples of informal leaders. Can a person be a formal and an informal leader at the same time?
5. Describe the causes of conflict in organizations. What can a manager do to control conflict? To resolve and eliminate conflict?

Questions for Analysis

1. Individuals join groups for a variety of reasons. Most groups contain members who joined for different reasons. What is likely to be the result when members join a group for different reasons? What can a group leader do to reduce the negative impact of a conflict in reasons for joining the group?
2. Consider the case of a developed group, where all members have been socialized. What are the benefits to the individuals of norm conformity? What are the benefits of not conforming to the group's norms? What are the benefits to an organization of conformity? What are the benefits to an organization of nonconformity?
3. Do you think teams are a valuable new management technique that will endure, or are they just a fad that will be replaced with something else in the near future?
4. Think of several groups of which you have been a member. Why did you join each? Did each group progress through the stages of development discussed in this chapter? If not, why do you think it did not?
5. Describe a case of interpersonal conflict that you have observed in an organization. Describe a case of intergroup conflict that you have observed. (If you have not observed any, interview a worker or manager to obtain examples.) In each case, was the conflict beneficial or harmful to the organization, and why?

BUILDING EFFECTIVE CONCEPTUAL SKILLS

Exercise Overview

Conceptual skills require you to think in the abstract. This exercise will allow you to practice your conceptual skills as they apply to the activities of work teams in organizations.

Exercise Background

Business organizations, of course, don't have a monopoly on effective groups. Basketball teams and military squadrons are teams, as is a government policy group such as the president's cabinet, the leadership of a church or civic organization, or even a student committee.

Exercise Task

1. Use the Internet to identify an example of a real-life team. Be sure to choose one that meets two criteria (1) It's not part of a for-profit business, and (2) you can argue that it's highly effective.
2. Determine the reasons for the team's effectiveness. (*Hint*: You might look for websites sponsored by the group itself, review online news sources for current articles about it, or enter the group name in a search engine.) Consider team characteristics and activities, such as role structures, norms, cohesiveness, and conflict management.
3. What can a manager learn from the characteristics and activities of this particular team? How might the factors that contribute to this team's success be adopted in a business setting?

BUILDING EFFECTIVE COMMUNICATION SKILLS

Exercise Overview

Communication skills refer to the ability to not only convey information and ideas to others but also to handle information and ideas received from them. They're essential to effective teamwork because teams depend on the ability of members to send and receive information that's accurate. This exercise invites you to play a game designed to demonstrate how good communication skills can lead to improved teamwork and team performance.

Exercise Background

You'll play this game in three separate rounds. In round 1, you're on your own. In round 2, you'll work in a small group and share information. You'll also work in a small group in round 3, but this time, you'll have the additional benefit of some suggestions for improving the group's performance. Typically, students find that performance improves over the course of the three rounds. In particular, they find that creativity is enhanced when information is shared.

Exercise Task

1. Play the Name Game that your professor will explain to you. In round 1, work out your answers individually and then report your individual score to the class.

2. For round 2, you'll join a group of three to five students. Work out your answers together and write your group answers on a single sheet of paper. Now, allow each group member to look at the answer sheet. If you can do so without being overheard by other groups, have each group member whisper the answers on the sheet to the group. Report your group score to the class.

3. Your professor will then ask the highest-performing individuals and groups to share their methods with the class. At this point, your professor will make some suggestions. Be sure to consider at least two strategies for improving your score.

4. Now play round 3, working together in the same small groups in which you participated in round 2. Report your group scores to the class.

5. Did average group scores improve upon average individual scores? Why or why not?

6. Did average group scores improve after methods for improvement were discussed at the end of round 2? Why or why not?

7. What has this game taught you about teamwork and effectiveness? Share your thoughts with the class.

SKILLS SELF-ASSESSMENT INSTRUMENT

Using Teams

Introduction: The use of groups and teams is becoming more common in organizations throughout the world. The following assessment surveys your beliefs about the effective use of teams in work organizations.

Instructions: You will agree with some of the statements and disagree with others. In some cases, you may find it difficult to make a decision, but you should force yourself to make a choice. Record your answers next to each statement according to the following scale:

Rating Scale

4 Strongly agree
3 Somewhat agree
2 Somewhat disagree
1 Strongly disagree

_____ 1. Each individual in a work team should have a clear assignment so that individual accountability can be maintained.

_____ 2. For a team to function effectively, the team must be given complete authority over all aspects of the task.

_____ 3. One way to get teams to work is simply to assemble a group of people, tell them in general what needs to be done, and let them work out the details.

_____ 4. Once a team gets going, management can turn its attention to other matters.

_____ 5. To ensure that a team develops into a cohesive working unit, managers should be especially careful not to intervene in any way during the initial start-up period.

_____ 6. Training is not critical to a team because the team will develop any needed skills on its own.

_____ 7. It's easy to provide teams with the support they need because they are basically self-motivating.

_____ 8. Teams need little or no structure to function effectively.

_____ 9. Teams should set their own direction, with managers determining the means to the selected end.

_____ 10. Teams can be used in any organization.

Source: Test adapted from J. Richard Hackman, ed., *Groups That Work (and Those That Don't)*, San Francisco: Jossey-Bass Publishers, 1990, pp. 493–504.

EXPERIENTIAL EXERCISE

Team Size and Performance

Purpose: Choosing the number of members in a team is an important decision that will affect team processes and outcomes. A team with too few members will have low performance because it is not receiving all the benefits of effective teamwork. A team that is too large won't be able to develop strong cohesion and, again, performance will suffer. The best team size in a particular situation depends on the members themselves, the tasks they will perform, and the nature of the interaction among them.

Instructions:

Step 1:   In a small class, the class will be divided into groups of four by the instructor. In a larger class, four students may be asked to volunteer to demonstrate in front of the whole group.

Step 2:   Each group will receive a regular deck of 52 playing cards from the instructor. One group member is chosen to be the "sorter." The cards should be shuffled thoroughly and placed in a stack on the desk in front of the sorter. Another group member is the timer.

Step 3:   At a signal from the instructor, the sorter or sorters pick up the cards. The timer notes the starting time. They must place the cards into four stacks by suit, arranging each stack from lowest to highest card. Aces are considered to be high. The task is done when the cards are in the four stacks. The timer records the elapsed time.

Step 4:   After thoroughly shuffling the cards, repeat Step 3. This time, however, the sorter will have a helper. The help may take any form—advice, encouragement, moving the cards, or anything else. After a brief discussion of the actions the helper will take to aid the sorter, begin timing and start the task. At the end, the timer notes the elapsed time.

Step 5:   After thoroughly shuffling the cards, repeat Step 3. This time, however, the sorter will have three helpers. The help may take any form—advice, encouragement, moving the cards, or anything else. After a brief discussion of the actions the helpers will take to aid the sorter, begin timing and start the task. At the end, the timer notes the elapsed time.

Follow-Up Questions:

1. Which of the three trials happened the most quickly? Which was the slowest? Which seemed to go the most smoothly for the sorter? Which seemed to be the most challenging for the sorter? Explain.
2. What was the impact of the help? Were three helpers better than one?
3. What types of help were effective, and what types were ineffective?
4. In what ways is this exercise similar to a situation in a business organization? In what ways is it dissimilar? What lessons might managers learn from this exercise?

MANAGEMENT AT WORK

On the One Hand (Or Maybe on the Other Hand)

Each of the following operating-room mishaps occurred in hospitals in the state of Rhode Island:

- A surgeon drilled into the wrong side of a patient's head in a procedure to drain blood.
- A surgeon operated on the wrong knee of a patient undergoing arthroscopic surgery.

- A surgeon operated on the wrong side of a child's mouth during surgery to correct a cleft palate.
- A surgeon anesthetized the wrong eye of a patient about to undergo eye surgery.
- A surgeon operated on the wrong finger of a patient during hand surgery.

One of the latest instances of so-called wrong-site surgery—an operation conducted on a body part other than the one intended by patient and surgeon—took place at Rhode Island Hospital, the state's largest and the main teaching hospital of prestigious Brown University. According to the chief quality officer of the hospital's parent company, Lifespan, the incident served to underscore how difficult it is to prevent such errors. The hospital, said Mary Reich Cooper, is committed to safety, and "every time one of these kinds of things happens, that commitment is just made stronger."

There's apparently some question, however, about how many times such errors have to happen before a hospital's commitment is strong enough. Only two years earlier, the state department of health had fined Rhode Island Hospital $50,000 for the occurrence of three wrong-site surgical errors in a one-year span—all of them involving procedures in which doctors drilled into the wrong side of a patient's head. "Frustrating—in capital letters—is probably the best way to describe the mood here," said department director David R. Gifford after the wrong-finger incident. Asked if there might be some fundamental flaw in the hospital's procedural system, Gifford replied, "I'm wondering that myself."

All the incidents of wrong-site surgery on our list occurred in one state during a period of just over two years, and the Joint Commission on Accreditation of Healthcare Organizations, which evaluates more than 15,000 health-care facilities and programs in the United States, estimates that wrong-site surgery occurs about 40 times a week around the country. A study in Pennsylvania conducted by the state's Patient Safety Authority added "near misses" into the mix and found that an "adverse event" (in other words, wrong-site surgery) or a "near miss" occurred every other day at Pennsylvania health-care facilities. "To be frank," says Dr. Stan Mullens, vice president of the Authority's board of directors, "wrong-site surgeries in Pennsylvania should never occur." But he hastens to add, "We're not alone. Wrong-site surgeries are no more common in Pennsylvania than they are in other states."

The Joint Commission has spent 15 years looking for ways to reduce the number of wrong-site surgical errors, but the results so far haven't been very promising; in fact, the rate of occurrence is the same as it was 15 years ago. So, what's the underlying problem? According to the Commission, it is communications breakdown, and some studies show that communications failure is a factor in two-thirds of all surgical mishaps resulting in serious patient harm or death. Surgery, of course, is performed by *teams*, and the typical surgical team has at least three core members: the surgeon, who performs the operation and leads the team; the anesthesiologist, whose responsibility is pain management and patient safety; and the operating nurse, who provides comprehensive care, assistance, and pain management at every stage of the operation. Perhaps the most logical question to start with, therefore, is: What are the barriers to communication among the core members of a surgical team?

According to some researchers, the most serious barrier results from team members' different perceptions about the nature and quality of the group's teamwork and communications. According to a study commissioned by the Department of Veterans Affairs, the "most common pattern" of differing perceptions reflects a disparity between the perceptions of nurses and anesthesiologists on the one hand and those of surgeons on the other. In particular, surgeons tend to believe that both teamwork and communications are more effective than nurses and anesthesiologists do. One item on the research questionnaire, for example, asked team members to respond to the statement "I am comfortable intervening in a procedure if I have concerns about what is occurring." While surgeons reported that the operating room (OR) environment did indeed support intervention, nurses and anesthesiologists generally did not. Surgeons were also more likely to report that "morale on our team is high." In assessing such results as these, the authors of the study wonder, "If surgical team members have disparate perceptions about how well they are communicating or collaborating with each other, how is it possible for them to be collaborating optimally with other members of the surgical team for the care of their patients?"

When the results of a study at Johns Hopkins revealed a similar breakdown in perceptions, the lead researcher, who is also a surgeon, admitted that "the study is somewhat humbling to me …. We need to balance out the captain-of-the-ship doctrine," suggested Dr. Martin A. Makary. Makary believes that a standardized OR briefing program is one way to improve surgical-team communication and has helped to make brief two-minute "team meetings" a regular step in surgical procedure at Johns Hopkins and other university hospitals. During the meeting, which is conducted just after anesthesia is administered, all members of the OR team state their names and roles and the surgeon verifies the critical aspects of the procedure, including the correct site.

Where the policy has been adopted, according to Makary, researchers have observed an increase in "the awareness of OR personnel with regard to the site and procedure and their perceptions of operating room safety." Without such a policy, Makary points out, many surgeons simply walk into the OR and start operating without even asking the names of the other medical personnel in the room. Such measures as team meetings hold some promise in the effort to reduce surgical error, as do checklists and time-outs, both of which require periodic confirmation of the critical components of a procedure. But "the unfortunate truth," cautions Dr. Mark R. Chassin, president of the Joint Commission, "is that no hospital today … can guarantee that [surgical errors] will never happen. We do not know how to perfect our processes…." In some hospitals, he admits, the Commission has even encountered "denial or serious avoidance of the potential for real problems," and he recommends that patients everywhere ask surgeons in advance what steps will be taken to prevent errors while they're in the OR.[44]

Case Question

1. Explain a surgical team as a kind of *functional group*. What features does it share with most functional groups? What features distinguish it from most functional groups?
2. Explain a surgical team in terms of its *role structures*. What factors might lead to *role ambiguity*? To *role conflict*? To *role overload*?
3. Explain a surgical team in terms of its *behavioral norms*. How might *norm variation* and *norm conformity* contribute to either effective or ineffective communications?
4. How do various strategies for improving surgical-team communications reflect a desire to achieve *cohesiveness*? Is increased cohesiveness always a desirable goal? Why or why not?

Case References

Felice J. Freyer, "Another Wrong-Site Surgery at R.I. Hospital," *Providence (RI) Journal*, October 28, 2009, www.providencejournal.com, accessed on January 1, 2014; " Wrong-Site Surgery Problems Common: Study," *Philadelphia Business Journal,* www.bizjournals.com, accessed on January 1, 2014; Steven Reinberg, "Errors in Surgical Procedure Persist," *HealthDay*, http://health.usnews.com, accessed on January 1, 2014; Peter Mills, Julia Neily, and Ed Dunn, "Teamwork and Communication in Surgical Teams: Implications for Patient Safety," *Journal of the American College of Surgeons*, Vol. 206 (January 2008), https://www.facs.org/education/nora-institute, accessed on January 1, 2014; and Johns Hopkins Medicine, "RX for Wrong-Site Surgery: Two Minutes of Conversation," press release, January 23, 2007, www.hopkinsmedicine.org, accessed on January 1, 2014.

Managing By Clowning Around

1. What role do groups play at Cirque du Soleil?
2. How easy or difficult would it be for a traditional organization to adopt the team-based methods used at Cirque Du Soleil?
3. If for some reason Cirque du Soleil decided to move away from team-based decision making, what difficulties might it encounter?
4. How do organizations like Cirque du Soleil most likely manage conflict?

ENDNOTES

[1] "Stick to Your Dream—Guy Laliberté," *Young Entrepreneur*, www.entrepreneur.com/topic/young-entrepreneurs, accessed on January 1, 2014; "Business Lessons from Poker—Guy Laliberté," *Young Entrepreneur*, www.entrepreneur.com/topic/young-entrepreneurs, accessed on January 1, 2014; Jason Zinoman, "Defiant Showman Demands His 'Wow,'" *New York Times*, June 3, 2011, www.nytimes.com, accessed on January 1, 2014; "Laliberté, Guy," *eNotes.com*, 2013, www.enotes.com, accessed on January 1, 2014; Cirque du Soleil,

"Cirque du Soleil at a Glance" (2012), http://www.cirquedusoleil.com/en/home/shows.aspx, accessed on January 1, 2014; Lyn Heward and John U. Bacon, *Spark: Igniting the Creative Fire That Lives within Us All* (Toronto: Doubleday Canada, 2006); Arupa Tesolin, "Igniting the Creative Spark at Cirque du Soleil," *SelfGrowth.com*, www.selfgrowth.com, accessed on January 1, 2014; Geoff Keighly, "The Phantasmagoria Factory," *CNNMoney.com*, http://money.cnn.com, accessed on January 1, 2014; Glenn Collins, "Run Away to the Circus? No Need. It's Staying Here," *New York Times*, April 29, 2009, www.nytimes.com, accessed on January 1, 2014.

2   For a review of definitions of groups, see Gregory Moorhead and Ricky W. Griffin, *Organizational Behavior*, 11th ed. (Boston: Houghton Mifflin, 2013).

3   Dorwin Cartwright and Alvin Zander, eds., *Group Dynamics: Research and Theory*, 3rd ed. (New York: Harper & Row, 1968).

4   Rob Cross, Nitin Nohria, and Andrew Parker, "Six Myths about Informal Networks—and How to Overcome Them," *Sloan Management Review*, Spring 2002, pp. 67–77. See also Richard McDermott and Douglas Archibald, "Harnessing Your Staff's Informal Networks," *Harvard Business Review*, March 2010, pp. 82–89.

5   Robert Schrank, *Ten Thousand Working Days* (Cambridge, Mass.: MIT Press, 1978); and Bill Watson, "Counter Planning on the Shop Floor," in Peter Frost, Vance Mitchell, and Walter Nord (eds.), *Organizational Reality*, 2nd ed. (Glenview, IL: Scott, Foresman, 1982), pp. 286–294.

6   "After Layoffs, More Workers Band Together," *Wall Street Journal*, February 26, 2002, p. B1.

7   Bradley L. Kirkman and Benson Rosen, "Powering Up Teams," *Organizational Dynamics*, Winter 2000, pp. 48–58.

8   John Mathieu, M. Travis Maynard, Tammy Rapp, and Lucy Gibson, "Team Effectiveness 1997–2007: A Review of Recent Advancements and a Glimpse into the Future," *Journal of Management*, 2008, Vol. 34, No. 3, pp. 410–476.

9   Arvind Malhotra, Ann Majchrzak, and Benson Rosen, "Leading Virtual Teams," *Academy of Management Perspectives*, 2007, Vol. 21, No. 1, pp. 60–70.

10   "Why Teams Fail," *USA Today*, February 25, 1997, pp. 1B, 2B.

11   Brian Dumaine, "The Trouble with Teams," *Fortune*, September 5, 1994, pp. 86–92. See also Susan G. Cohen and Diane E. Bailey, "What Makes Teams Work: Group Effectiveness Research from the Shop Floor to the Executive Suite," *Journal of Management*, 1997, Vol. 23, No. 3, pp. 239–290; and John Mathieu, Lucy Gilson, and Thomas Ruddy, "Empowerment and Team Effectiveness: An Empirical Test of an Integrated Model," *Journal of Applied Psychology*, 2006, Vol. 91, No. 1, pp. 97–108.

12   Marvin E. Shaw, *Group Dynamics: The Psychology of Small Group Behavior*, 4th ed. (New York: McGraw-Hill, 1985).

13   "How to Avoid Hiring the Prima Donnas Who Hate Teamwork," *Wall Street Journal*, February 15, 2000, p. B1.

14   See Connie Gersick, "Marking Time: Predictable Transitions in Task Groups," *Academy of Management Journal*, June 1989, Vol. 32, No. 2, pp. 274–309. See also Janis A. Cannon-Bowers and Clint Bowers, "Team Development and Functioning," in Sheldon Zedeck (ed.), *Handbook of Industrial and Organizational Psychology*, Vol. 1: *Building and Developing the Organization* (Washington, DC: American Psychological Association, 2010), pp. 597–650.

15   See Gilad Chen, "Newcomer Adaptation in Teams: Multilevel Antecedents and Outcomes," *Academy of Management Journal*, 2005, Vol. 48, No. 1, pp. 101–116.

16   For a review of other team characteristics, see Michael Campion, Gina Medsker, and A. Catherine Higgs, "Relations between Work Group Characteristics and Effectiveness: Implications for Designing Effective Work Groups," *Personnel Psychology*, Winter 1993, pp. 823–850.

17   David Katz and Robert L. Kahn, *The Social Psychology of Organizations*, 2nd ed. (New York: Wiley, 1978), pp. 187–221. See also Greg L. Stewart and Murray R. Barrick, "Team Structure and Performance: Assessing the Mediating Role of Intrateam Process and the Moderating Role of Task Type," *Academy of Management Journal*, 2000, Vol. 43, No. 2, pp. 135–148; and Michael G. Pratt and Peter O. Foreman, "Classifying Managerial Responses to Multiple Organizational Identities," *Academy of Management Review*, 2000, Vol. 25, No. 1, pp. 18–42.

18   See Travis C. Tubre and Judith M. Collins, "Jackson and Schuler (1985) Revisited: A Meta-Analysis of the Relationships between Role Ambiguity, Role Conflict, and Job Performance," *Journal of Management*, 2000, Vol. 26, No. 1, pp. 155–169. See also David M. Sluss, Rolf van Dick, and Bryant S. Thompson, "Role Theory in Organizations: A Relational Perspective," in Sheldon Zedeck (ed.), *Handbook of Industrial and Organizational Psychology*, Vol. 1: *Building and Developing the Organization* (Washington, DC: American Psychological Association, 2010), pp. 503–534.

19   Robert L. Kahn, D. M. Wolfe, R. P. Quinn, J. D. Snoek, and R. A. Rosenthal, *Organizational Stress: Studies in Role Conflict and Role Ambiguity* (New York: Wiley, 1964).

20   Daniel C. Feldman, "The Development and Enforcement of Group Norms," *Academy of Management Review*, January 1984, Vol. 9, No. 1, pp. 47–53.

21   "Companies Turn to Peer Pressure to Cut Injuries as Psychologists Join the Battle," *Wall Street Journal*, March 29, 1991, pp. B1, B3.

22   James Wallace Bishop and K. Dow Scott, "How Commitment Affects Team Performance," *HRMagazine*, February 1997, pp. 107–115.

23   Anne O'Leary-Kelly, Joseph Martocchio, and Dwight Frink, "A Review of the Influence of Group Goals on Group Performance," *Academy of Management Journal*, 1994, Vol. 37, No. 5, pp. 1285–1301.

24   For an interesting application of these ideas, see Anat Drach-Zahavy and Anat Freund, "Team Effectiveness under Stress: A Structural Contingency Approach," *Journal of Organizational Behavior*, 2007, Vol. 28, pp. 423–450.

25   Philip M. Podsakoff, Michael A. Hearne, and Scott B. MacKenzie, "Organizational Citizenship Behavior and the Quantity and Quality of Work Group Performance," *Journal of Applied Psychology*, 1997, Vol. 82, No. 2, pp. 262–270.

26   Suzy Wetlaufer, "Common Sense and Conflict," *Harvard Business Review*, January–February 2000, pp. 115–125.

27   Kathleen M. Eisenhardt, Jean L. Kahwajy, and L. J. Bourgeois III, "How Management Teams Can Have a Good Fight," *Harvard Business Review*, July–August 1997, pp. 77–89.

28   Thomas Bergmann and Roger Volkema, "Issues, Behavioral Responses and Consequences in Interpersonal Conflicts," *Journal of Organizational Behavior*, 1994, Vol. 15, pp. 467–471; see also Carsten K. W. De Dreu, "The Virtue and Vice of Workplace

Conflict: Food for (Pessimistic) Thought," *Journal of Organizational Behavior*, 2008, Vol. 29, pp. 5–18.

29 Robin Pinkley and Gregory Northcraft, "Conflict Frames of Reference: Implications for Dispute Processes and Outcomes," *Academy of Management Journal*, 1994, Vol. 37, No. 1, pp. 193–205.

30 "How 2 Computer Nuts Transformed Industry before Messy Breakup," *Wall Street Journal*, August 27, 1996, pp. A1, A10.

31 Bruce Barry and Greg L. Stewart, "Composition, Process, and Performance in Self-Managed Groups: The Role of Personality," *Journal of Applied Psychology*, 1997, Vol. 82, No. 1, pp. 62–78.

32 "Acer CEO Resigns Suddenly amid Conflict with Board," *Gadget News Today*, March 31, 2011.

33 "A 'Blood War' in the Jeans Trade," *BusinessWeek*, November 13, 1999, pp. 74–81.

34 Peter Elkind, "Blood Feud," *Fortune*, April 14, 1997, pp. 90–102.

35 See Patrick Nugent, "Managing Conflict: Third-Party Interventions for Managers," *Academy of Management Executive*, 2002, Vol. 16, No. 1, pp. 139–148.

36 See Kristin J. Behfar, Randall S. Peterson, Elizabeth A. Mannix, and William M. K. Trochim, "The Critical Role of Conflict Resolution in Teams: A Close Look at the Links between Conflict, Conflict Management Strategies, and Team Outcomes," *Journal of Applied Psychology*, 2008, Vol. 93, No. 1, pp. 170–188.

37 "Solving Conflicts in the Workplace without Making Losers," *Wall Street Journal*, May 27, 1997, p. B1.

38 "Teaching Business How to Cope with Workplace Conflicts," *BusinessWeek*, February 18, 1990, pp. 136, 139.

39 See Kimberly Wade-Benzoni, Andrew Hoffman, Leigh Thompson, Don Moore, James Gillespie, and Max Bazerman, "Barriers to Resolution in Ideologically Based Negotiations: The Role of Values and Institutions," *Academy of Management Review*, 2002, Vol. 27, No. 1, pp. 41–57.

40 J. Z. Rubin and B. R. Brown, *The Social Psychology of Bargaining and Negotiation* (New York: Academic Press, 1975).

41 R. J. Lewicki and J. A. Litterer, *Negotiation* (Homewood, IL: Irwin, 1985).

42 Howard Raiffa, *The Art and Science of Negotiation* (Cambridge, MA: Belknap, 1982).

43 K. H. Bazerman and M. A. Neale, *Negotiating Rationally* (New York: Free Press, 1992).

44 Felice J. Freyer, "Another Wrong-Site Surgery at R.I. Hospital," *Providence* (R.I.) *Journal*, October 28, 2009, www.providence journal.com, accessed on April 30, 2011; "Wrong-Site Surgery Problems Common: Study," *Philadelphia Business Journal*, June 26, 2007, www.bizjournals.com, accessed on August 15, 2012; Steven Reinberg, "Errors in Surgical Procedure Persist," *HealthDay*, November 19, 2009, http://health.usnews.com, accessed on August 15, 2012; Peter Mills, Julia Neily, and Ed Dunn, "Teamwork and Communication in Surgical Teams: Implications for Patient Safety," *Journal of the American College of Surgeons*, Vol. 206 (January 2008), https://www.facs.org/education/nora-institute, accessed on April 30, 2011; and Johns Hopkins Medicine, "RX for Wrong-Site Surgery: Two Minutes of Conversation," press release, January 23, 2007, www.hopkinsmedicine.org, accessed on August 15, 2012.

Sergii Tsololo/Photos.com

CHAPTER 14

Basic Elements of Control

Learning Outcomes

After studying this chapter, you should be able to:

1 Explain the purpose of control, identify different types of control, and describe the steps in the control process.

2 Identify and explain the three forms of operations control.

3 Describe budgets and other tools for financial control.

4 Identify and distinguish between two opposing forms of structural control.

5 Discuss the relationship between strategy and control.

6 Identify characteristics of effective control, why people resist control, and how managers can overcome this resistance.

Management in Action

Shifting Gears in the Auto Industry

"We've been sticking to our guns, and it's worked well so far."

—**Chrysler Group CEO Sergio Marchionne on his strategy for reviving Chrysler**

In November 2008, U.S. automaker Chrysler announced that it was cutting 25 percent of its workforce and acknowledged that domestic sales had dropped 35 percent in 12 months. Then-CEO Robert Nardelli also admitted that the company could survive only by means of an alliance with another automaker and an infusion of government cash. In December, Chrysler announced that it would shut down all production through January 2009, that it planned to file for bankruptcy, and that it ultimately expected to cease production permanently. Federal aid to both Chrysler and General Motors was authorized in the same month and had topped $17 billion by March 2009, when the Obama administration gave Chrysler 30 days to finalize a previously announced merger agreement with the Italian carmaker Fiat or face the loss of another $6 billion in government subsidies.

Fiat? Things, it seems, had changed since the days when, for many American car buyers, *Fiat* stood for "Fix It Again, Tony." As recently as 2005, GM had been only too happy to pay $2 billion to bail out of a joint venture with Fiat, which was wallowing in debt after accumulated losses of $14 billion. A year later, however, Fiat had actually shown a profit—its first since 2000—and its stock price had doubled. By 2009, it was on *Fortune* magazine's list of the "World's Most

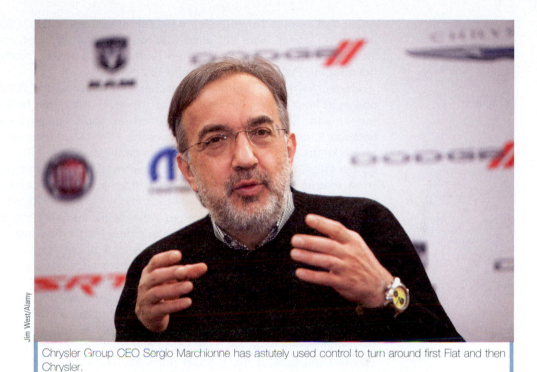

Chrysler Group CEO Sergio Marchionne has astutely used control to turn around first Fiat and then Chrysler.

Admired Companies." It's now Europe's third-largest car company, behind only Volkswagen and Peugeot Citroën and ahead of Renault, Daimler (Mercedes Benz), and BMW, and number nine in the world, producing more cars than Hyundai or Mitsubishi.

The credit for this remarkable turnaround goes to CEO Sergio Marchionne, an accountant and industry outsider who, in 2004, became Fiat's fifth CEO in two years. Billie Blair, a consultant specializing in corporate change management, reports that Marchionne brought an "unconventional approach" to the task of managing a car company in the twenty-first century. In the process, she says—citing Marchionne's own explanation of his success at Fiat—he "revolutionized the [Fiat] culture in a way that will keep the company competitive in the long term." Adds David Johnston, whose Atlanta-based marketing company has worked with Chrysler: Marchionne "has been able to garner respect for Fiat again after its down years and reestablish it as a business leader."

What was Marchionne's "unconventional approach"? It's the same approach that he's trying to bring to Chrysler. Taking over Fiat after nearly 15 years of continuously poor performance, Marchionne was forced to lay off employees, but he focused his job-cutting strategy on longer-term goals: He cut 10 percent of the company's white-collar workforce of about 20,000, stripping away layers of management and making room for a younger generation of managers with experience in brand marketing rather than engineering. Refocusing the company on market-driven imperatives, he cut the design-to-market process from 4 years to 18 months, and, even more important, he spurred the introduction of a slew of new products. The Grande Punto, which was launched in mid-2005, was the best-selling subcompact in Western Europe a year later and spearheaded the firm's resurgence. The Fiat Nuova 500, a subcompact with a distinctive retro look (think Volkswagen New Beetle), was first introduced in 2007. Both the car and its marketing launch were designed with heavy customer involvement, and the 500, like the Grande Punto, was an immediate success, with first-year sales outstripping Fiat's original target by 160 percent.

Under the merger agreement reached with Fiat in June 2009, the 500 became one of at least seven Fiat vehicles that Chrysler will begin building and selling in the United States by 2014. Produced in four versions—hatchback, sporty hatchback, convertible, and station wagon—the U.S. adaptation of the 500 went to market in 2011, and Marchionne was convinced that, with a full range of body styles, "the 500 … will be a smash if we do it right." Strategically, Marchionne knew that he had to reposition Chrysler from a maker of clunky gas-guzzlers to a marketer of stylish energy-efficient technology, and the 500, which one marketing association in Japan has declared "the sexiest car in the world," has been designated the flagship of Fiat Chrysler's new North American fleet.

Many analysts, however, remained skeptical about Marchionne's prospects for turning Chrysler around even if the 500 turned out to be "a smash." A big issue, they say, is time: Can "New Chrysler" (officially Chrysler Group LLC) hang on financially until projected new-product revenues start filling the company coffers? Completely new and improved Chryslers didn't hit showrooms until 2013, but the new management has managed to roll out some new products, including a revamped Jeep Compass and an all-new Chrysler 300 sedan. "We've attacked the bulk of the product portfolio," says Marchionne. "What we've got now is a commercially viable set of products in the marketplace." He also points out that Chrysler sales are ahead of internal targets and claims that he's more confident now about the prospects for a turnaround than he had been when the merger plans were being drawn up. "We've been sticking to our guns," he says, "and it's worked well so far."[1]

Sergio Marchionne has used control effectively first at Fiat and more recently at Chrysler. As we discussed in Chapter 1, control is one of the four basic managerial functions that provide the organizing framework for this book. This is the first of two chapters devoted to this important area. In the first section of this chapter, we explain the purpose of control. We then look at types of control and the steps in the control process. The rest of the chapter examines the four levels of control that most organizations must employ to remain effective: operations, financial, structural, and strategic control. We conclude by discussing the characteristics of effective control, noting why some people resist control and describing what organizations can do to overcome this resistance. The next chapter in this part focuses on managing operations, quality, and productivity.

THE NATURE OF CONTROL

control
The regulation of organizational activities in such a way as to facilitate goal attainment

Control is the regulation of organizational activities so that some targeted element of performance remains within acceptable limits. Without this regulation, organizations have no indication of how well they are performing in relation to their goals. Control, like a ship's rudder, keeps the organization moving in the proper direction. At any point in time, it compares where the organization is in terms of performance (financial, productive, or otherwise) to where it is supposed to be. Like a rudder, control provides an organization with a mechanism for adjusting its course if performance falls outside acceptable boundaries.

For example, FedEx has a performance goal of delivering 99.9 percent of its packages on time. If on-time deliveries fall to, say, 99.6 percent, control systems will signal the problem to managers so that they can make necessary adjustments in operations to regain the target level of performance. An organization without effective control procedures is not likely to reach its goals—or, if it does reach them, to know that it has!

The Purpose of Control

As Figure 14.1 illustrates, control provides an organization with ways to adapt to environmental change, to limit the accumulation of error, to cope with organizational complexity, and to minimize costs. These four functions of control are worth a closer look.

Adapting to Environmental Change   In today's complex and turbulent business environment, all organizations must contend with change.[2] If managers could establish goals and achieve them instantaneously, control would not be needed. But, between the time a goal is established and the time it is reached, many things can happen in the organization and its environment to disrupt movement toward the goal—or even to change the goal itself. A properly designed control system can help managers anticipate, monitor, and respond to changing circumstances.[3] In contrast, an improperly designed system can result in organizational performance that falls far below acceptable levels.

For example, Michigan-based Metalloy, a 60-year-old, family-run metal-casting company, signed a contract to make engine seal castings for NOK, a big Japanese auto parts maker. Metalloy was satisfied when its first 5,000-unit production run yielded 4,985 acceptable castings and only 15 defective ones. NOK, however, was quite unhappy with this performance and insisted that Metalloy raise its standards. In short, global quality standards in most industries are such that customers demand near perfection from their suppliers. A properly designed control system can help managers like those at Metalloy stay better attuned to rising standards.

Limiting the Accumulation of Error   Small mistakes and errors do not often seriously damage the financial health of an organization. Over time, however, small errors may accumulate and become very serious. For example, Whistler Corporation, a large

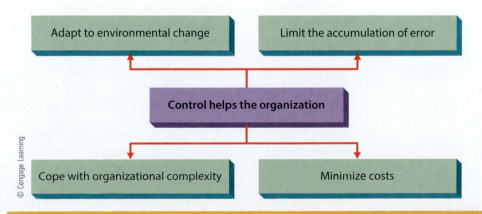

FIGURE 14.1

The Purpose of Control

Control is one of the four basic management functions in organizations. The control function, in turn, has four basic purposes. Properly designed control systems can fulfill each of these purposes.

radar detector manufacturer, was once faced with such rapidly escalating demand that quality essentially became irrelevant. The defect rate rose from 4 percent to 9 percent to 15 percent and eventually reached 25 percent. One day, a manager started paying more attention to this and realized that 100 of the plant's 250 employees were spending all their time fixing defective units and that $2 million worth of inventory was awaiting repair. Had the company adequately controlled quality as it responded to increased demand, the problem would never have reached such proportions. Similarly, a routine quality-control inspection of a prototype of Boeing's 787 Dreamliner revealed that a fastener had not been installed correctly. Closer scrutiny then revealed that literally thousands of fasteners had been installed incorrectly in each prototype under construction. As a result, the entire project was delayed several months. If the inspection process had been more rigorous, the error would likely have been found and corrected much earlier, rather than accumulating into a major problem for Boeing.[4]

Coping with Organizational Complexity   When a firm purchases only one raw material, produces one product, has a simple organization design, and enjoys constant demand for its product, its managers can maintain control with a very basic and simple system. But a business that produces many products from myriad raw materials and has a large market area, a complicated organization design, and many competitors needs a sophisticated system to maintain adequate control. When large firms merge, the short-term results are often disappointing. The typical reason for this is that the new enterprise is so large and complex that the existing control systems are simply inadequate. When United Airlines and Continental Airlines agreed to merge at the end of 2010, the two firms faced myriad challenges in how to merge two complex flight operations centers, their human resource practices, their frequent flyer programs, and so forth. As a result, it took over two years for the merger to be completed, in large part due to the complex nature of the two organizations and their industry. And when American Airlines agreed to merge with US Airways in 2013, experts predicted a similar time frame for completing the merger.

Minimizing Costs   When it is practiced effectively, control can also help reduce costs and boost output. For example, Georgia-Pacific Corporation, a large wood products company, learned of a new technology that could be used to make thinner blades for its saws. The firm's control system was used to calculate the amount of wood that could be saved from each cut made by the thinner blades relative to the costs used to replace the existing blades. The results have been impressive—the wood that is saved by the new blades each year fills 800 rail cars. As Georgia-Pacific discovered, effective control systems can eliminate waste, lower labor costs, and improve output per unit of input. Starbucks recently instructed its coffee shops to stop automatically brewing decaffeinated coffee after lunch. Sales of decaf plummet after lunch, and Starbucks realized that baristas were simply pouring most of it down the drain. Now, between noon and early evening, they brew decaf only by the cup and only when a customer orders it.[5] Similarly, many businesses are cutting back on everything from health insurance coverage to overnight shipping to business lunches for clients in their quest to lower costs.[6] The "Tough Times, Tough Choices" feature highlights how FedEx uses control as a central part of its business model.

Types of Control

The examples of control given thus far have illustrated the regulation of several organizational activities, from producing quality products to coordinating complex organizations. Organizations practice control in a number of different areas, and at different levels, and the responsibility for managing control is widespread.

TOUGH TIMES, TOUGH CHOICES

Engineering Time

Among the reasons for FedEx's long-term success are its commitments to customer service and prompt, accurate delivery. The company's information systems are critical to its ability to keep these commitments because they support the firm's complex operations (including over 90,000 vehicles, 677 airplanes, and 200,000 employees in 220 countries) and allow it to deliver 6 million packages daily.

"We engineer time," explains executive vice president and chief information officer Rob Carter. "We … allow you to engineer time to make things happen along time schedules that weren't possible [before]." Texas-based Motion Computing, for example, outsources assembly to a factory in China, and FedEx is able to transport a finished PC from the assembly plant directly to the consumer in about five days. Why is such speed so important to Motion? "We have no inventory tied up in the process anywhere," says CEO Scott Eckert. "Frankly, our business is enabled by FedEx."

FedEx founder and CEO Fred Smith once remarked that information about a package is as important as the package itself, and his company has for a long time been putting this insight into practice by means of an extensive online tracking system. Recently, the entire system has been reconfigured so that customers can stay ahead of deliveries rather than merely keeping up with them. "[We] took the whole tracking mechanism and turned it around," reports Carter, "so that as opposed to having to track a package, you say, 'I want to know what's coming to me today.' You can go out there now and see every inbound package, regardless of whether you knew someone was sending it."

It's important to FedEx that it was the first company in the package-delivery industry to recognize the strategic value of information systems. Rival UPS, asserts Carter, still lags behind even though "it's easier to copy than it is to innovate." While granting that UPS offers many of the same information services as FedEx, Carter hastens to underscore what

© iStockphoto.com/winhorse

FedEx is one of the world's most efficient businesses. A commitment to customer service and prompt, accurate deliveries, combined with continuous improvement in its operating systems has allowed FedEx to remain a leader in overnight delivery industry.

(continued)

he considers some significant differences between the two competitors. "We've been in a battle on customer-based technology," but FedEx, he explains, "tends to focus slightly less on operational technology. We focus a little more on revenue-generating, customer-satisfaction–generating, strategic-advantage technology.

"The key focus of my job," Carter adds, "is driving technology that increases the top line." As CIO, he puts the emphasis on effectiveness, quality, and satisfaction rather than on bottom-line efficiency and cost control. With a veteran team committed to innovation

and an annual budget of $1 billion, Carter expects FedEx's IT operations to be a source of both strategic control and advantage for some time to come.

References: Geoffrey Colvin, "The FedEx Edge," *Fortune*, http://money.cnn.com, accessed on January 1, 2014; Dean Foust, "FedEx: Taking Off Like 'A Rocket Ship,'" *BusinessWeek*, April 3, 2006, www.businessweek.com, accessed on January 1, 2014; "FedEx Recognized as One of *Fortune* Magazine's '100 Best Companies to Work For,'" Business Wire, www.businesswire.com, accessed on January 1, 2014; "100 Best Companies to Work For," *Fortune*, http://money.cnn.com, accessed on January 1, 2014.

Areas of Control   Control can focus on any area of an organization. Most organizations define areas of control in terms of the four basic types of resources they use: physical, human, information, and financial.[7] Control of physical resources includes inventory management (stocking neither too few nor too many units in inventory), quality control (maintaining appropriate levels of output quality), and equipment control (supplying the necessary facilities and machinery). Control of human resources includes selection and placement, training and development, performance appraisal, and compensation. Relatedly, organizations also attempt to control the behavior of their employees—directing them toward higher performance, for example, and away from unethical behaviors.[8] Control of information resources includes sales and marketing forecasting, environmental analysis, public relations, production scheduling, and economic forecasting.[9] Financial control involves managing the organization's financial obligations so that they do not become excessive, ensuring that the firm always has enough cash on hand to meet its obligations but does not have excess cash sitting idly in a checking account, and ensuring that receivables are collected and bills are paid on a timely basis.

In many ways, the control of financial resources is the most important area, because financial resources are related to the control of all the other resources in an organization. Too much inventory leads to storage costs; poor selection of personnel leads to termination and rehiring expenses; inaccurate sales forecasts lead to disruptions in cash flows and other financial effects. Financial issues tend to pervade most control-related activities.

The crisis in the U.S. airline industry precipitated by the terrorist attacks on September 11, 2001, the economic recession of 2009 that reduced business travel, and rising fuel costs can be fundamentally traced to financial issues. Essentially, airline revenues have dropped, while their costs have increased. Because of high labor costs and other expenses, the airlines faced major problems in making appropriate adjustments. Major long-haul U.S. airlines such as United spend nearly half of their revenues on labor; in contrast, JetBlue spends only about 25 percent of its revenues on labor.

Levels of Control   Just as control can be broken down by area, it can also be broken down by level within the organizational system, as shown in Figure 14.2. **Operations control** focuses on the processes the organization uses to transform resources into products or services.[10] Quality control is one type of operations control. **Financial control**

operations control
Focuses on the processes that the organization uses to transform resources into products or services

financial control
Concerned with the organization's financial resources

© Cengage Learning

FIGURE 14.2

Levels of Control

Managers use control at several different levels. The most basic levels of control in organizations are strategic, structural, operations, and financial. Each level must be managed properly if control is to be most effective.

structural control
Concerned with how the elements of the organization's structure are serving their intended purpose

strategic control
Focuses on how effectively the organization's strategies are succeeding in helping the organization meet its goals

controller
A position in organizations that helps line managers with their control activities

is concerned with the organization's financial resources. Monitoring receivables to make sure customers are paying their bills on time is an example of financial control. **Structural control** is concerned with how the elements of the organization's structure are serving their intended purpose. Monitoring the administrative ratio to make sure staff expenses do not become excessive is an example of structural control. Finally, **strategic control** focuses on how effectively the organization's corporate, business, and functional strategies are succeeding in helping the organization meet its goals. For example, if a corporation has been unsuccessful in implementing its strategy of related diversification, its managers need to identify the reasons for that lack of success and either change the strategy or renew their efforts to implement it. We discuss these four levels of control more fully later in this chapter.

Responsibilities for Control Traditionally, managers have been responsible for overseeing the wide array of control systems and concerns in organizations. They decide which types of control the organization will use, and they implement control systems and take actions based on the information provided by control systems. Thus, ultimate responsibility for control rests with all managers throughout an organization.

Most larger organizations also have one or more specialized managerial positions called *controller*. A **controller** is responsible for helping line managers with their control activities, for coordinating the organization's overall control system, and for gathering and assimilating relevant information. Many businesses that use an H-form or M-form organization design have several controllers: one for the corporation and one for each division. The job of controller is especially important in organizations where control systems are complex.[11]

In addition, many organizations are also beginning to use operating employees to help maintain effective control. Indeed, employee participation is often used as a vehicle for allowing operating employees an opportunity to help facilitate organizational effectiveness. For example, Whistler Corporation increased employee participation in an effort to turn its quality problems around. As a starting point, the quality control unit,

FIGURE 14.3

Steps in the Control Process

Having an effective control system can help ensure that an organization achieves its goals. Implementing a control system, however, is a systematic process that generally proceeds through four interrelated steps.

formerly responsible for checking product quality at the end of the assembly process, was eliminated. Next, all operating employees were encouraged to check their own work and told that they would be responsible for correcting their own errors. As a result, Whistler has eliminated its quality problems and is now highly profitable once again.

Steps in the Control Process

Regardless of the type or levels of control systems that an organization needs, each control process has four fundamental steps.[12] These are illustrated in Figure 14.3.

Establishing Standards   The first step in the control process is establishing standards. A **control standard** is a target against which subsequent performance will be compared.[13] Employees at a Taco Bell fast-food restaurant, for example, work toward the following service standards:

control standard
A target against which subsequent performance will be compared

1. A minimum of 95 percent of all customers will be greeted within 3 minutes of their arrival.
2. Preheated tortilla chips will not sit in the warmer more than 30 minutes before they are served to customers or discarded.
3. Empty tables will be cleaned within 5 minutes after being vacated.

Standards established for control purposes should be expressed in measurable terms. Note that standard 1 has a time limit of 3 minutes and an objective target of 95 percent of all customers. In standard 3, the objective target of "all" empty tables is implied.

Control standards should also be consistent with the organization's goals. Taco Bell has organizational goals involving customer service, food quality, and restaurant cleanliness. A control standard for a retailer like Best Buy should be consistent with its goal of increasing its annual sales volume by 25 percent within five years. A hospital trying to shorten the average hospital stay for a patient will have control standards that reflect current averages. A university reaffirming its commitment to academics might adopt a standard of graduating 80 percent of its student athletes within five years of their enrollment. Control standards can be as narrow or as broad as the level of activity to which they apply and must follow logically from organizational goals and objectives. When Airbus introduced the A380, the world's largest passenger airplane, managers indicated that the firm needed to ship 270 planes to break even, and set a goal of delivering 18 per year.

Managers also forecast that demand for very large aircraft like the A380 and Boeing's revamped 747 would exceed 1,200 planes during the next 20 years.[14]

A final aspect of establishing standards is to identify performance indicators. Performance indicators are measures of performance that provide information that is directly relevant to what is being controlled. For example, suppose an organization is following a tight schedule in building a new plant. Relevant performance indicators could be buying a site, selecting a building contractor, and ordering equipment. Monthly sales increases are not, however, directly relevant. On the other hand, if control is being focused on revenue, monthly sales increases are relevant, whereas buying land for a new plant is less relevant.

Measuring Performance   The second step in the control process is measuring performance. Performance measurement is a constant, ongoing activity for most organizations. For control to be effective, performance measures must be valid. Daily, weekly, and monthly sales figures measure sales performance, and production performance may be expressed in terms of unit cost, product quality, or volume produced. Employees' performance is often measured in terms of quality or quantity of output, but for many jobs, measuring performance is not so straightforward.

A research and development scientist at Texas Instruments, for example, may spend years working on a single project before achieving a breakthrough. A manager who takes over a business on the brink of failure may need months or even years to turn things around. Valid performance measurement, however difficult to obtain, is nevertheless vital in maintaining effective control, and performance indicators usually can be developed. The scientist's progress, for example, may be partially assessed by peer review, and the manager's success may be evaluated by her ability to convince creditors that she will eventually be able to restore profitability.

As Airbus completed the design and manufacture of its A380 jumbo jet, managers recognized that delays and cost overruns had changed its breakeven point. New calculations indicated that the company would need to sell 420 planes before it would become profitable. Its actual annual sales, of course, remained relatively easy to measure.

Designing and building new products requires managers to use a variety of control techniques. When the product is as complex as the Airbus 380, control becomes both more important and more complicated. Literally thousands of control-related activities were used throughout the stages of designing, engineering, manufacturing, testing, and selling the plane before the first commercial flight was ever made.

Comparing Performance Against Standards
The third step in the control process is comparing measured performance against established standards. Performance may be higher than, lower than, or identical to the standard. In some cases, comparison is easy. The goal of each product manager at General Electric is to make the product either number one or number two (on the basis of total sales) in its market. Because this standard is clear and total sales are easy to calculate, it is relatively simple to determine whether this standard has been met. Sometimes, however, comparisons are less clear-cut. If performance is lower than expected, the question is how much deviation from standards to allow before taking remedial action. For example, is increasing sales by 7.9 percent close enough when the standard was 8 percent?

The timetable for comparing performance to standards depends on a variety of factors, including the importance and complexity of what is being controlled. For longer-run and higher-level standards, annual comparisons may be appropriate. In other circumstances, more frequent comparisons are necessary. For example, a business with a severe cash shortage may need to monitor its on-hand cash reserves daily. In its first year of production, Airbus did indeed deliver 18 A380s, just as it had forecast.

Considering Corrective Action   The final step in the control process is determining the need for corrective action. Decisions regarding corrective action draw heavily on a manager's analytic and diagnostic skills. For example, as health-care costs have risen, many firms have sought ways to keep their own expenses in check. Some have reduced benefits; others have opted to pass on higher costs to their employees.[15]

After comparing performance against control standards, one of three actions is appropriate: Maintain the status quo (do nothing), correct the deviation, or change the standards. Maintaining the status quo is preferable when performance essentially matches the standards, but it is more likely that some action will be needed to correct a deviation from the standards.

Sometimes, performance that is higher than expected may also cause problems for organizations. For example, when highly anticipated new video games or game systems are first introduced, the demand may be so strong that customers are placed on waiting lists. And even some people who are among the first to purchase such products immediately turn around and list them for sale on eBay for an inflated price. The manufacturer may be unable to increase production in the short term, though, and also knows that demand will eventually drop. At the same time, however, the firm would not want to alienate potential customers. Consequently, it may decide to simply reduce its advertising. This may curtail demand a bit and limit customer frustration.

Changing an established standard usually is necessary if it was set too low or too high at the outset. This is apparent if large numbers of employees routinely beat the standard by a wide margin or if no employees ever meet the standard. Also, standards that seemed perfectly appropriate when they were established may need to be adjusted if circumstances have since changed.

As the 2008–2009 global recession began to take its toll, two major Airbus customers, Qantas and Emirates, indicated that they wanted to defer delivery of some previously ordered A380s. As a result, Airbus found it necessary to reduce its production in 2009 from 18 down to only 14. It also indicated that the plane's breakeven point had increased, but would not reveal the new target.

operations control
Focuses on the processes the organization use to transform resources into products or services

OPERATIONS CONTROL

One of the four levels of control practiced by most organizations, **operations control** is concerned with the processes that the organization uses to transform resources into products or services. As Figure 14.4 shows, the three forms of operations control—preliminary, screening, and postaction—occur at different points in relation to the transformation processes used by the organization.

Preliminary Control

preliminary control
Attempts to monitor the quality or quantity of financial, physical, human, and information resources before they actually become part of the system

Preliminary control concentrates on the resources—financial, material, human, and information—the organization brings in from the environment. Preliminary control attempts to monitor the quality or quantity of these resources before they enter the organization. Firms such as PepsiCo and General Mills hire only college graduates for their management training programs, and even then only after applicants satisfy several interviewers and selection criteria. In this way, they control the quality of the human resources entering the organization. When Sears orders merchandise to be manufactured under its own brand name, it specifies rigid standards of quality, thereby controlling physical inputs. Organizations also control financial and information resources. For example, closely held companies such as Toys "R" Us and Mars limit the extent to which outsiders can buy their stock, and television networks verify the accuracy of news stories before they are broadcast.

Screening Control

screening control
Relies heavily on feedback processes during the transformation process

Screening control focuses on meeting standards for product or service quality or quantity during the actual transformation process itself. Screening control relies heavily on feedback processes. For example, in a Dell assembly factory, computer system components are checked periodically as each unit is being assembled. This is done to ensure that all the components that have been assembled up to that point are working properly. The periodic quality checks provide feedback to workers so that they know what, if any, corrective actions to take. Because they are useful in identifying the cause of problems, screening controls tend to be used more often than other forms of control.

More and more companies are adopting screening controls because they are an effective way to promote employee participation and catch problems early in the overall transformation process. For example, Corning adopted screening controls for use in manufacturing television glass. In the past, finished television screens were inspected only after they were finished. Unfortunately, over 4 percent of them were later returned by customers because of defects. Now the glass screens are inspected at each step in the production process, rather than at the end, and the return rate from customers has dropped to .03 percent.

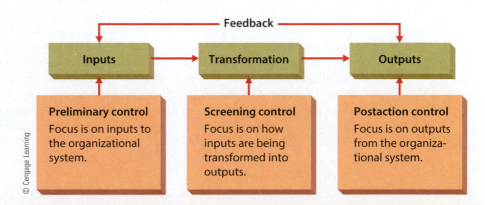

© Cengage Learning

FIGURE 14.4

Forms of Operations Control

Most organizations develop multiple control systems that incorporate all three basic forms of control. For example, the publishing company that produced this book screens inputs by hiring only qualified employees, typesetters, and printers (preliminary control). In addition, quality is checked during the transformation process, such as after the manuscript is typeset (screening control), and the outputs—printed and bound books—are checked before they are shipped from the bindery (postaction control).

Postaction Control

postaction control
Monitors the outputs or results of the organization after the transformation process is complete

Postaction control focuses on the outputs of the organization after the transformation process is complete. Corning's old system was postaction control—final inspection after the product was manufactured. Although Corning abandoned its postaction control system, it still may be an effective method of control, primarily if a product can be manufactured in only one or two steps or if the service is fairly simple and routine. Although postaction control alone may not be as effective as preliminary or screening control, it can provide management with information for future planning. For example, if a quality check of finished goods indicates an unacceptably high defect rate, the production manager knows that he or she must identify the causes and take steps to eliminate them. Postaction control also provides a basis for rewarding employees. Recognizing that an employee has exceeded personal sales goals by a wide margin, for example, may alert the manager that a bonus or promotion is in order.

Most organizations use more than one form of operations control. For example, Honda's preliminary control includes hiring only qualified employees and specifying strict quality standards when ordering parts from other manufacturers. Honda uses numerous screening controls in checking the quality of components during car assembly. A final inspection and test drive as each car rolls off the assembly line is part of the company's postaction control.[16] Indeed, most successful organizations employ a wide variety of techniques to facilitate operations control.

FINANCIAL CONTROL

financial control
Concerned with the organization's financial resources

Financial control is the control of financial resources as they flow into the organization (such as revenues and shareholder investments), are held by the organization (for example, working capital and retained earnings), and flow out of the organization (like pay and expenses). Businesses must manage their finances so that revenues are sufficient to cover costs and still return a profit to the firm's owners. Not-for-profit organizations such as universities have the same concerns: Their revenues (from tax dollars or tuition) must cover operating expenses and overhead. U.S. automakers Ford and General Motors have come to realize that they have to reduce the costs of paying employees they do not need but whom they are obligated to keep due to long-standing labor agreements. Ford has offered to cover the full costs of a college education for certain of its employees if they will resign; GM, for its part, has offered lump-sum payments of varying amounts to some of its workers in return for their resignations.[17] A complete discussion of financial management is beyond the scope of this book, but we will examine the control provided by budgets and other financial control tools.

Budgetary Control

budget
A plan expressed in numerical terms

A **budget** is a plan expressed in numerical terms. Organizations establish budgets for work groups, departments, divisions, and the whole organization. The usual time period for a budget is one year, although breakdowns of budgets by the quarter or month are also common. Budgets are generally expressed in financial terms, but they may occasionally be expressed in units of output, time, or other quantifiable factors. When Disney launches the production of a new animated cartoon feature, it creates a budget for how much the movie should cost. Several years ago, when movies such as *The Lion King* were raking in hundreds of millions of dollars, Disney executives were fairly flexible about budget overruns. But, on the heels of several

Weak financial control can be devastating to a business, especially when economic conditions change. General Motors, for example, did not have sufficient financial reserves to weather the 2008 economic recession and had to seek government assistance to remain afloat. The firm also had to lay off thousands of employees and close several plants. But just as the firm was regaining its financial health, allegations about ongoing product defects led to the largest recall in automobile history in 2014.

animated-movie flops, such as *Atlantis: The Lost Empire* and *Treasure Planet*, the company had to take a much harder line on budget overruns.[18] More recently, major losses on Disney live-action films like 2014's *The Lone Ranger* have prompted increased budget scrutiny on all future films.

Because of their quantitative nature, budgets provide yardsticks for measuring performance and facilitate comparisons across departments, between levels in the organization, and from one time period to another. Budgets serve four primary purposes. They help managers coordinate resources and projects (because they use a common denominator, usually dollars). They help define the established standards for control. They provide guidelines about the organization's resources and expectations. Finally, budgets enable the organization to evaluate the performance of managers and organizational units.

Types of Budgets Most organizations develop and make use of three kinds of budgets—financial, operating, and nonmonetary. Table 14.1 summarizes the characteristics of each of these.

A *financial budget* indicates where the organization expects to get its cash for the coming time period and how it plans to use it. Because financial resources are critically important, the organization needs to know where those resources will be coming from and how they are to be used. The financial budget provides answers to both these questions. Usual sources of cash include sales revenue, short- and long-term loans, the sale of assets, and the issuance of new stock.

For years, Exxon was very conservative in its capital budgeting. As a result, the firm amassed a huge financial reserve but was being overtaken in sales by Royal Dutch/Shell Group. But executives at Exxon were then able to use their reserves to help finance the firm's merger with Mobil, creating ExxonMobil, and to regain the number-one sales position. Since that time, the firm has become more aggressive in capital budgeting to stay ahead of its European rival.

An *operating budget* is concerned with planned operations within the organization. It outlines what quantities of products or services the organization intends to create and what resources will be used to create them. IBM creates an operating budget that specifies how many of each model of its personal computers will be produced each quarter.

A *nonmonetary budget* is simply a budget expressed in nonfinancial terms, such as units of output, hours of direct labor, machine hours, or square-foot allocations. Nonmonetary budgets are most commonly used by managers at the lower levels of an organization. For example, a plant manager can schedule work more effectively knowing that he or she has 9,000 labor hours to allocate in a week, rather than trying to determine how to best spend $96,485 in wages in a week.

Organizations use various types of budgets to help manage their control functions. The three major categories of budgets are financial, operating, and nonmonetary. There are several different types of budgets in each category. To be most effective, each budget must be carefully matched with the specific function being controlled.

Table 14.1	Developing Budgets in Organizations
Types of Budget	**What Budget Shows**
Financial Budget	*Sources and Uses of Cash*
Cash flow or cash budget	All sources of cash income and cash expenditures in monthly, weekly, or daily periods
Capital expenditures budget	Costs of major assets such as a new plant, machinery, or land
Balance sheet budget	Forecast of the organization's assets and liabilities in the event that all other budgets are met
Operating Budget	*Planned Operations in Financial Terms*
Sales or revenue budget	Income that the organization expects to receive from normal operations
Expense budget	Anticipated expenses for the organization during the coming time period
Profit budget	Anticipated differences between sales or revenues and expenses
Nonmonetary Budget	*Planned Operations in Nonfinancial Terms*
Labor budget	Hours of direct labor available for use
Space budget	Square feet or meters of space available for various functions

© Cengage Learning

Developing Budgets   Traditionally, budgets were developed by top management and the controller and then imposed on lower-level managers. Although some organizations still follow this pattern, many contemporary organizations now allow all managers to participate in the budget process. As a starting point, top management generally issues a call for budget requests, accompanied by an indication of overall patterns the budgets may take. For example, if sales are expected to drop in the next year, managers may be told up front to prepare for cuts in operating budgets.

As Figure 14.5 shows, the heads of each operating unit typically submit budget requests to the head of their division. An operating unit head might be a department manager in a manufacturing or wholesaling firm or a program director in a social service agency. The division heads might include plant managers, regional sales managers, or college deans. The division head integrates and consolidates the budget requests from operating unit heads into one overall division budget request. A great deal of interaction among managers usually takes place at this stage because the division head coordinates the budgetary needs of the various departments.

Division budget requests are then forwarded to a budget committee. The budget committee is usually composed of top managers. The committee reviews budget requests from several divisions, and once again, duplications and inconsistencies are corrected. Finally, the budget committee, the controller, and the CEO review and agree on the

Operating unit budget requests

Division budget requests

Organizational budget
• Prepared by budget committee
• Approved by budget committee, controller, and CEO

© Cengage Learning

FIGURE 14.5

Developing Budgets in Organizations

Most organizations use the same basic process to develop budgets. Operating units are requested to submit their budget requests to divisions. These divisions, in turn, compile unit budgets and submit their own budgets to the organization. An organizational budget is then compiled for approval by the budget committee, controller, and CEO.

overall budget for the organization, as well as specific budgets for each operating unit. These decisions are then communicated back to each manager.

Strengths and Weaknesses of Budgeting   Budgets offer a number of advantages, but they also have weaknesses. On the plus side, budgets facilitate effective control. Placing dollar values on operations enables managers to monitor operations better and pinpoint problem areas. Budgets also facilitate coordination and communication between departments because they express diverse activities in a common denominator (dollars). Budgets help maintain records of organizational performance and are a logical complement to planning. In other words, as managers develop plans, they should simultaneously consider control measures to accompany them. Organizations can use budgets to link plans and control by first developing budgets as part of the plan and then using those budgets as part of control.

On the other hand, some managers apply budgets too rigidly. Budgets are intended to serve as frameworks, but managers sometimes fail to recognize that changing circumstances may warrant budget adjustments. Also, the process of developing budgets can be very time consuming. Finally, budgets may limit innovation and change. When all available funds have been allocated to specific operating budgets, it may be impossible to procure additional funds to take advantage of an unexpected opportunity.

Indeed, for these very reasons, some organizations are working to scale back their budgeting systems. Although most organizations are likely to continue to use budgets, the goal is to make them less confining and rigid.

Other Tools for Financial Control

Although budgets are the most common means of financial control, other useful tools are financial statements, ratio analysis, and financial audits.

financial statement
A profile of some aspect of an organization's financial circumstances

Financial Statements A **financial statement** is a profile of some aspect of an organization's financial circumstances. Financial statements must be prepared and presented in commonly accepted and required ways. The two most basic financial statements prepared and used by virtually all organizations are a balance sheet and an income statement.

balance sheet
List of assets and liabilities of an organization at a specific point in time

The **balance sheet** lists the assets and liabilities of the organization at a specific point in time, usually the last day of an organization's fiscal year. For example, the balance sheet may summarize the financial condition of an organization on December 31, 2015. Most balance sheets are divided into current assets (assets that are relatively liquid or easily convertible into cash), fixed assets (assets that are longer term in nature and less liquid), current liabilities (debts and other obligations that must be paid in the near future), long-term liabilities (payable over an extended period of time), and stockholders' equity (the owners' claim against the assets).

income statement
A summary of financial performance over a period of time, usually one year

Whereas the balance sheet reflects a snapshot profile of an organization's financial position at a single point in time, the **income statement** summarizes financial performance over a period of time, usually one year. For example, the income statement might be for the period from January 1, 2015, through December 31, 2015. The income statement summarizes the firm's revenues less its expenses to report net income (profit or loss) for the period. Information from the balance sheet and income statement is used in computing important financial ratios.

ratio analysis
The calculation of one or more financial ratios to assess some aspect of the organization's financial health

Ratio Analysis Financial ratios compare different elements of a balance sheet or income statement to one another. **Ratio analysis** is the calculation of one or more financial ratios to assess some aspect of the financial health of an organization. Organizations use a variety of financial ratios as part of financial control. For example, *liquidity ratios* indicate how liquid (easily converted into cash) an organization's assets are. *Debt ratios* reflect ability to meet long-term financial obligations. *Return ratios* show managers and investors how much return the organization is generating relative to its assets. *Coverage ratios* help estimate the organization's ability to cover interest expenses on borrowed capital. *Operating ratios* indicate the effectiveness of specific functional areas rather than that of the total organization. Walt Disney is an example of a company that relies heavily on financial ratios to keep its financial operations on track.[19]

audits
An independent appraisal of an organization's accounting, financial, and operational systems

Financial Audits **Audits** are independent appraisals of an organization's accounting, financial, and operational systems. The two major types of financial audits are the external audit and the internal audit.

External audits are financial appraisals conducted by experts who are not employees of the organization. External audits are typically concerned with determining whether the organization's accounting procedures and financial statements are compiled in an objective and verifiable fashion. The organization contracts with a certified public accountant (CPA) for this service. The CPA's main objective is to verify for stockholders, the IRS, and other interested parties that the methods by which the organization's financial managers and accountants prepare documents and reports are legal and proper.

External audits are so important that publicly held corporations are required by law to have external audits regularly, as assurance to investors that the financial reports are reliable.

Unfortunately, flaws in the auditing process played a major role in the downfall of Enron and several other major firms. The problem can be traced back partially to the auditing groups' problems with conflicts of interest and eventual loss of objectivity. For instance, Enron was such an important client for its auditing firm, Arthur Andersen, that the auditors started letting the firm take liberties with its accounting systems for fear that if they were too strict, Enron might take its business to another auditing firm. In the aftermath of the resulting scandal, Arthur Andersen was forced to close its doors, Enron had to liquidate all of its assets, several top managers from both firms went to jail, and the entire accounting profession was forced to reexamine its basic businesses practices.[20]

Some organizations are also starting to employ external auditors to review other aspects of their financial operations. For example, some auditing firms now specialize in checking corporate legal bills. An auditor for the Fireman's Fund Insurance Company uncovered several thousands of dollars in legal-fee errors. Other auditors are beginning to specialize in real estate, employee benefits, and pension plan investments.

Whereas external audits are conducted by external accountants, an *internal audit* is handled by employees of the organization. Its objective is the same as that of an external audit—to verify the accuracy of financial and accounting procedures used by the organization. Internal audits also examine the efficiency and appropriateness of financial and accounting procedures. Because the staff members who conduct them are a permanent part of the organization, internal audits tend to be more expensive than external audits. But employees, who are more familiar with the organization's practices, may also point out significant aspects of the accounting system besides its technical correctness. Large organizations like Halliburton and Ford have an internal auditing staff that spends all its time conducting audits of different divisions and functional areas of the organization. Smaller organizations may assign accountants to an internal audit group on a temporary or rotating basis.

Satyam Computer Services in India falsely reported profits of over $1 billion when in reality it had only $66 million. The Indian affiliate of PricewaterhouseCoopers, PW India, was in charge of routinely auditing the firm, but failed to follow basic auditing procedures. Rather than confirming the supposed $1 billion cash balances with the banks, PW India relied solely on the information provided by the firm's management. In some cases, auditors failed to follow up on confirmations sent independently by the banks that showed significant differences from the balances reported by management. PW India was eventually fined $7.5 million—the largest penalty ever imposed by India on a foreign accounting firm.[21]

STRUCTURAL CONTROL

Organizations can create designs for themselves that result in very different approaches to control. Two major forms of structural control, bureaucratic control and decentralized control, represent opposite ends of a continuum, as shown in Figure 14.6.[22] The six dimensions shown in the figure represent perspectives adopted by the two extreme types of structural control. In other words, they have different goals, degrees of formality, performance expectations, organization designs, reward systems, and levels of participation. Although a few organizations fall precisely at one extreme or the other, most tend toward one end but may have specific characteristics of either.

Bureaucratic Control	Dimension	Decentralized Control
Employee compliance	Goal of control approach	Employee commitment
Strict rules, formal controls, rigid hierarchy	Degree of formality	Group norms, culture, self-control
Directed toward minimum levels of acceptable performance	Performance expectations	Directed toward enhanced performance above and beyond the minimum
Tall structure, top-down influence	Organization design	Flat structure, shared influence
Directed at individual performance	Reward system	Directed at group performance
Limited and formal	Participation	Extended and informal

© Cengage Learning

FIGURE 14.6

Organizational Control

Organizational control generally falls somewhere between the two extremes of bureaucratic and decentralized control. McDonald's uses bureaucratic control, whereas Starbucks uses decentralized control.

Bureaucratic Control

bureaucratic control
A form of organizational control characterized by formal and mechanistic structural arrangements

Bureaucratic control is an approach to organization design characterized by formal and mechanistic structural arrangements. As the term suggests, it follows the bureaucratic model. The goal of bureaucratic control is employee compliance. Organizations that use it rely on strict rules and a rigid hierarchy, insist that employees meet minimally acceptable levels of performance, and often have a tall structure. They focus their rewards on individual performance and allow only limited and formal employee participation.

McDonald's applies structural controls that reflect many elements of bureaucracy. The organization relies on numerous rules to regulate employee travel, expense accounts, and other expenses. A new performance appraisal system precisely specifies minimally acceptable levels of performance for everyone. The organization's structure is considerably taller than those of the other major networks, and rewards are based on individual contributions. In another example, a large oil company recently made the decision to allow employees to wear casual attire to work. But a committee then spent weeks developing a 20-page set of guidelines on what was and was not acceptable. For example, denim pants are not allowed. Similarly, athletic shoes may be worn as long as they are not white. And all shirts must have a collar. Nordstrom, the department store chain, is also moving toward bureaucratic control as it works to centralize all of its purchasing in an effort to lower costs. Similarly, Home Depot is moving more toward bureaucratic control to cut its costs and more effectively compete with its hard-charging rival, Lowe's.

Decentralized Control

decentralized control

An approach to organizational control based on informal and organic structural arrangements

Decentralized control, in contrast, is an approach to organizational control characterized by informal and organic structural arrangements. As Figure 14.6 shows, its goal is employee commitment to the organization. Accordingly, it relies heavily on group norms and a strong corporate culture, and gives employees the responsibility for controlling themselves. Employees are encouraged to perform beyond minimally acceptable levels. Organizations using this approach are usually relatively flat. They direct rewards at group performance and favor widespread employee participation.

Starbucks allows local managers considerable discretion in the décor of each coffee shop, as well as what merchandise is displayed. Another company that uses this approach is Southwest Airlines. When Southwest made the decision to "go casual," the firm resisted the temptation to develop dress guidelines. Instead, managers decided to allow employees to exercise discretion over their attire and to deal with clearly inappropriate situations on a case-by-case basis.

STRATEGIC CONTROL

Given the obvious importance of an organization's strategy, it is also important that the organization assess how effective that strategy is in helping the organization meet its goals.[23] To do this requires that the organization integrate its strategy and control systems. This is especially true for the global organization.

strategic control

Control aimed at ensuring that the organization is maintaining an effective alignment with its environment and moving toward achieving its strategic goals

Strategic control generally focuses on five aspects of organizations—structure, leadership, technology, human resources, and information and operational control systems. For example, an organization should periodically examine its structure to determine whether it is facilitating the attainment of the strategic goals being sought. Suppose a firm using a functional (*U-form*) design has an established goal of achieving a 20 percent sales growth rate per year. However, performance indicators show that it is currently growing at a rate of only 10 percent per year. Detailed analysis might reveal that the current structure is inhibiting growth in some way (for example, by slowing decision making and inhibiting innovation) and that a divisional (*M-form*) design is more likely to bring about the desired growth (by speeding decision making and promoting innovation).

In this way, strategic control focuses on the extent to which implemented strategy achieves the organization's strategic goals. If, as outlined earlier, one or more avenues of implementation are inhibiting the attainment of goals, that avenue should be changed. Consequently, the firm might find it necessary to alter its structure, replace key leaders, adopt new technology, modify its human resources, or change its information and operational control systems.

For several years, Pfizer, the world's largest pharmaceutical company, has invested billions of dollars in research and development. Recently, though, the firm acknowledged that it was not getting an adequate return on its investment and announced that it was laying off 800 senior researchers. The firm also signaled a strategic reorientation by suggesting it would look for other drug companies to buy in order to acquire new patents and drug formulas.[24] Kohl's department stores essentially redefined how to compete effectively in the midtier retailing market and was on trajectory to leave competitors such as Sears and Dillard's in its dust. But then the firm inexplicably stopped doing many of the very things that had led to its success—such as keeping abreast of current styles, maintaining low inventories, and keeping its stores neat and clean—and began to stumble. Now, managers are struggling to rejuvenate Kohl's strategic focus and get it back on track.[25]

Because of both their relatively large size and the increased complexity associated with international business, global organizations must take an especially pronounced strategic view of their control systems. One very basic question that has to be addressed is whether to manage control from a centralized or a decentralized perspective.[26] Under a centralized system, each organizational unit around the world is responsible for frequently reporting the results of its performance to headquarters. Managers from the home office often visit foreign branches to observe firsthand how the units are functioning.

BP, Unilever, Procter & Gamble, and Sony all use this approach. They believe centralized control is effective because it allows the home office to keep better informed of the performance of foreign units and to maintain more control over how decisions are made. For example, BP discovered that its Australian subsidiary was not billing its customers for charges as quickly as were its competitors. By shortening the billing cycle, BP now receives customer payments five days faster than before. Managers believe that they discovered this oversight only because of a centralized financial control system.

Organizations that use a decentralized control system require foreign branches to report less frequently and in less detail. For example, each unit may submit summary performance statements on a quarterly basis and provide full statements only once a year. Similarly, visits from the home office are less frequent and less concerned with monitoring and assessing performance. IBM, Ford, and Shell all use this approach. Because Ford practices decentralized control of its design function, European designers have developed several innovative automobile design features. Managers believe that if they had been more centralized, designers would not have had the freedom to develop their new ideas.

MANAGING CONTROL IN ORGANIZATIONS

Effective control, whether at the operations, financial, structural, or strategic level, successfully regulates and monitors organizational activities. To use the control process, managers must recognize the characteristics of effective control and understand how to identify and overcome occasional resistance to control.[27] The "Leading the Way" feature highlights one example of how to manage control.

Characteristics of Effective Control

Control systems tend to be most effective when they are integrated with planning and when they are flexible, accurate, timely, and objective.

Integration with Planning   Control should be linked with planning. The more explicit and precise this linkage, the more effective the control system is. The best way to integrate planning and control is to account for control as plans develop. In other words, as goals are set during the planning process, attention should be paid to developing standards that will reflect how well the plan is realized. Managers at Champion Spark Plug Company decided to broaden their product line to include a full range of automotive accessories—a total of 21 new products. As part of this plan, managers decided in advance what level of sales they wanted to realize from each product for each of the next five years. They established these sales goals as standards against which actual sales would be compared. Thus, by accounting for their control system as they developed their plan, managers at Champion did an excellent job of integrating planning and control.

Flexibility   The control system itself must be flexible enough to accommodate change. Consider, for example, an organization whose diverse product line requires 75 raw materials. The company's inventory control system must be able to manage and monitor current levels of inventory for all 75 materials. When a change in product line changes the number of raw materials needed, or when the required quantities of the existing materials change, the

LEADING THE WAY

Balancing Control with Fun

John Caparella was hired to be the opening manager of the 1,400-room Gaylord Palms resort in Orlando, Florida. He immediately decided to create a culture that would focus his employees on how to provide excellent customer service while also meeting organizational control standards. Caparella began by assembling a leadership team that shared his beliefs. When they started hiring new employees, they also looked for people who were interested in a fun work environment but who also understood the importance of performance and control standards. People who were selected were termed "10's" because they were the one out of ten candidates who were actually hired. To further build a language that would reinforce the cultural values, Caparella's team coined the acronym "STARS" as a word to ideal employees: Smiles, Teamwork, Attitude, Reliability, and Service with a passion. The idea was to use language to constantly remind employees about the cultural beliefs.

To teach employees the cultural values of what customers should expect at the Palms, Caparella used the power of telling stories. He wrote a letter that would represent what he hoped the hotel would get from guests once the hotel was opened. He knew the power of stories, legends, and heroes in teaching culture and wanted to provide a strong example of a service hero in the letter that would establish a benchmark of what excellent service looked like to a customer. Eventually, once the hotel had been open long enough to receive feedback from real guests, that benchmark would be adjusted based on their comments. He also knew the power of teaching culture through what was rewarded and what was punished. He provided bonuses to employees based on the percentage of positive comments from guests.

Perhaps one of the most unusual parts of balancing fun and control was the offer of an employment guarantee to every employee. Newly hired employees were told that if the job wasn't what was promised, they should call Caparella directly to tell him about it. Obviously, this promoted supervisory responsiveness to all employee concerns and consideration across the entire organization. The obvious question is whether all this culture building was worth it. It would seem so: The hotel was honored in multiple years as a best place to work, it was considered an outstanding place to hold meetings and events, and it made good profits. Building a service culture guided employees to fill in the gaps between what they could be trained to do and what needed to be done in successfully dealing with many different customers.

The Gaylord Palms resort in Orlando has a culture that emphasizes customer service. Top employees are called STARS, an acronym for Smiles, Teamwork, Attitude, Reliability, and Service.

© Yulia Glam/Shutterstock.com

control system should be flexible enough to handle the revised requirements. The expense associated with the alternative—designing and implementing a new control system—would then be avoided. Champion's control system, for example, included a mechanism that automatically shipped products to major customers to keep the inventories of those customers at predetermined levels. The firm had to adjust this system when one of its biggest customers decided not to stock the full line of Champion products. Because its control system was flexible, though, modifying it for the customer was relatively simple.

Accuracy   Managers make a surprisingly large number of decisions based on inaccurate information. Field representatives may hedge their sales estimates to make themselves look better. Production managers may hide costs to meet their targets. Human resource managers may overestimate their minority recruiting prospects to meet affirmative action goals. In each case, the information that other managers receive is inaccurate, and the results of inaccurate information may be quite dramatic. If sales projections are inflated, a manager might cut advertising (thinking it is no longer needed) or increase advertising (to further build momentum). Similarly, a production manager unaware of hidden costs may quote a sales price much lower than desirable. Or a human resources manager may speak out publicly on the effectiveness of the company's minority recruiting, only to find out later that these prospects have been overestimated. In each case, the result of inaccurate information is inappropriate managerial action.

Timeliness   Timeliness does not necessarily mean quickness. Rather, it describes a control system that provides information as often as is necessary. Because Champion has a wealth of historical data on its sparkplug sales, it does not need information on sparkplugs as frequently as it needs sales feedback for its newer products. Retail organizations usually need sales results daily so that they can manage cash flow and adjust advertising and promotion. In contrast, they may require information about physical inventory only quarterly or annually. In general, the more uncertain and unstable the circumstances, the more frequently measurement is needed.

Objectivity   The control system should provide information that is as objective as possible. To appreciate this, imagine the task of a manager responsible for control of his organization's human resources. He asks two plant managers to submit reports. One manager notes that morale at his plant is "OK," that grievances are "about where they should be," and that turnover is "under control." The other reports that absenteeism at her plant is running at 4 percent, that 16 grievances have been filed this year (compared with 24 last year), and that turnover is 12 percent. The second report will almost always be more useful than the first. Of course, managers also need to look beyond the numbers when assessing performance. For example, a plant manager may be boosting productivity and profit margins by putting too much pressure on workers and using poor-quality materials. As a result, impressive short-run gains may be overshadowed by longer-run increases in employee turnover and customer complaints.

Resistance to Control

Managers sometimes make the mistake of assuming that the value of an effective control system is self-evident to employees. This is not always so, however. Many employees resist control, especially if they feel overcontrolled, if they think control is inappropriately focused or rewards inefficiency, or if they are uncomfortable with accountability.

Overcontrol   Occasionally, organizations try to control too many things. This becomes especially problematic when the control directly affects employee behavior. An organization that instructs its employees when to come to work, where to park, when to have morning coffee, and when to leave for the day exerts considerable control over people's daily activities. Yet, many organizations attempt to control not only these but other aspects of work behavior as well. Of particular relevance in recent years are the efforts of some companies to control their employees' access to private e-mail and the Internet during work hours. Some companies have no policies governing these activities, some attempt to limit access, and some attempt to forbid it altogether.

Troubles arise when employees perceive these attempts to limit their behavior as being unreasonable. A company that tells its employees how to dress, how to arrange their desks, and how to wear their hair may meet with more resistance. Employees at Chrysler who drove non-Chrysler vehicles used to complain because they were forced to park in a distant parking lot. People felt that these efforts to control their personal behavior (what kind of car to drive) were excessive. Managers eventually removed these controls and now allow open parking. Some employees at Abercrombie & Fitch argue that the firm is guilty of overcontrol because of its strict dress and grooming requirements—for example, no necklaces or facial hair for men and only natural nail polish and earrings no larger than a dime for women. Likewise, Enterprise Rent-A-Car has a set of 30 dress-code rules for women and 26 rules for men. The firm was recently sued by one former employee who was fired because of the color of her hair.[28] UBS, the large Swiss bank, had (until recently) a 44-page dress code that prescribed, among other things, that employees should avoid eating garlic and onions (so as to not offend customers), keep their toenails trimmed (so as to not tear their stockings or socks), and wear only skin-colored underwear (so it could remain unseen). Men were instructed in how to knot a tie, and everyone was encouraged to keep their glasses clean. (When the dress code was made public in 2011, UBS indicated that it would be making some revisions![29])

Inappropriate Focus   A control system may be too narrow, or it may focus too much on quantifiable variables and leave no room for analysis or interpretation. A sales standard that encourages high-pressure tactics to maximize short-run sales may do so at the expense of goodwill from long-term customers. Such a standard is too narrow. A university reward system that encourages faculty members to publish large numbers of articles but fails to consider the quality of the work is also inappropriately focused. Employees resist the intent of the control system by focusing their efforts only on the performance indicators being used.

Rewards for Inefficiency   Imagine two operating departments that are approaching the end of their fiscal years. Department 1 expects to have $30,000 of its budget left over; department 2 is already $15,000 in the red. As a result, department 1 is likely to have its budget cut for the next year ("They had money left, so they obviously got too much to begin with"), and department 2 is likely to get a budget increase ("They obviously haven't been getting enough money"). Thus, department 1 is punished for being efficient, and department 2 is rewarded for being inefficient. (No wonder departments commonly hasten to deplete their budgets as the end of the year approaches!) As with inappropriate focus, people resist the intent of this control and behave in ways that run counter to the organization's intent.

Too Much Accountability   Effective controls allow managers to determine whether employees successfully discharge their responsibilities. If standards are properly set and performance accurately measured, managers know when problems arise and which departments and individuals are responsible. People who do not want to be answerable for their mistakes or who do not want to work as hard as their boss might, therefore, resist control. For example, American Express has a system that provides daily information on how many calls each of its customer service representatives handles. If one representative has typically worked at a slower pace and handled fewer calls than other representatives, that individual's deficient performance can now more easily be pinpointed.

Overcoming Resistance to Control

Perhaps the best way to overcome resistance to control is to create effective control to begin with. If control systems are properly integrated with organizational planning and if the controls are flexible, accurate, timely, and objective, the organization will be less likely to overcontrol, to focus on inappropriate standards, or to reward inefficiency. Two other ways to overcome resistance are encouraging employee participation and developing verification procedures.

Encourage Employee Participation   Chapter 13 noted that participation can help overcome resistance to change. By the same token, when employees are involved with planning and implementing the control system, they are less likely to resist it. For instance, employee participation in planning, decision making, and quality control at the Chevrolet Gear and Axle plant in Detroit resulted in increased employee concern for quality and a greater commitment to meeting standards.

Develop Verification Procedures   Multiple standards and information systems provide checks and balances in control and allow the organization to verify the accuracy of performance indicators. Suppose a production manager argues that she failed to meet a certain cost standard because of increased prices of raw materials. A properly designed inventory control system will either support or contradict her explanation. Suppose that an employee who was fired for excessive absences argues that he was not absent "for a long time." An effective human resource control system should have records that support the termination. Resistance to control declines because these verification procedures protect both employees and management. If the production manager's claim about the rising cost of raw materials is supported by the inventory control records, she will not be held solely accountable for failing to meet the cost standard, and some action probably will be taken to lower the cost of raw materials.

SUMMARY OF LEARNING OUTCOMES AND KEY POINTS

1. Explain the purpose of control, identify different types of control, and describe the steps in the control process.

   - Control is the regulation of organizational activities so that some targeted element of performance remains within acceptable limits.
   - Control provides ways to adapt to environmental change, to limit the accumulation of errors, to cope with organizational complexity, and to minimize costs.
   - Control can focus on financial, physical, information, and human resources and includes operations, financial, structural, and strategic levels.
   - Control is the function of managers, the controller, and, increasingly, operating employees.

     - Steps in the control process are
       - to establish standards of expected performance.
       - to measure actual performance.
       - to compare performance to the standards.
       - to evaluate the comparison and take appropriate action.

2. Identify and explain the three forms of operations control.

   - Operations control focuses on the processes the organization uses to transform resources into products or services.
   - Preliminary control is concerned with the resources that serve as inputs to the system.

   - Screening control is concerned with the transformation processes used by the organization.
   - Postaction control is concerned with the outputs of the organization.
   - Most organizations need multiple control systems because no one system can provide adequate control.

3. Describe budgets and other tools for financial control.

   - Financial control focuses on controlling the organization's financial resources.
   - The foundation of financial control is budgets, which are plans expressed in numerical terms.
   - Most organizations rely on financial, operating, and nonmonetary budgets.
   - Financial statements, various kinds of ratios, and external and internal audits are also important tools organizations use as part of financial control.

4. Identify and distinguish between two opposing forms of structural control.

   - Structural control addresses how well an organization's structural elements serve their intended purpose.
   - Two basic forms of structural control are bureaucratic and decentralized control.
   - Bureaucratic control is relatively formal and mechanistic.
   - Decentralized control is informal and organic.

- Most organizations use a form of organizational control somewhere between total bureaucratic and total decentralized control

5. Discuss the relationship between strategy and control.

   - Strategic control focuses on how effectively the organization's strategies are succeeding in helping the organization meet its goals.
   - The integration of strategy and control is generally achieved through organization structure, leadership, technology, human resources, and information and operational control systems.
   - International strategic control is generally a question of balance between centralization and decentralization.

6. Identify characteristics of effective control, why people resist control, and how managers can overcome this resistance.

   - One way to increase the effectiveness of control is to fully integrate planning and control.
   - The control system should also be as flexible, accurate, timely, and objective as possible.
   - Employees may resist organizational controls because of overcontrol, inappropriate focus, rewards for inefficiency, and a desire to avoid accountability.
   - Managers can overcome this resistance by improving the effectiveness of controls and by allowing employee participation and developing verification procedures.

DISCUSSION QUESTIONS

Questions for Review

1. What is the purpose of organizational control? Why is it important?
2. What are the different levels of control? What are the relationships between the different levels?
3. Describe how a budget is created in most organizations. How does a budget help a manager with financial control?
4. Describe the differences between bureaucratic and decentralized control. What are the advantages and disadvantages of each?
5. Why do some people resist control? How can managers help overcome this resistance?

Questions for Analysis

1. How can a manager determine whether his or her firm needs improvement in control? If improvement is needed, how can the manager tell what type of control needs improvement (operations, financial, structural, or strategic)? Describe some steps a manager can take to improve each of these types of control.

2. One company uses strict performance standards. Another has standards that are more flexible. What are the advantages and disadvantages of each system?

3. Are the differences in bureaucratic control and decentralized control related to differences in organization structure? If so, how? If not, why not? (The terms do sound similar to those used to discuss the organizing process.)

4. Many organizations today are involving lower-level employees in control. Give at least two examples of specific actions that a lower-level worker could do to help his or her organization better adapt to environmental change. Then do the same for limiting the accumulation of error, coping with organizational complexity, and minimizing costs.

5. Describe ways that the top management team, midlevel managers, and operating employees can participate in each step of the control process. Do all participate equally in each step, or are some steps better suited for personnel at one level? Explain your answer.

BUILDING EFFECTIVE TIME MANAGEMENT SKILLS

Exercise Overview

It is no surprise that *time management skills*—which are the ability to prioritize tasks, to work efficiently, and to delegate appropriately—play a major role in performing the control function: Managers can use time management skills to control their own work activities more effectively. The purpose of this exercise is to demonstrate the relationship between time management skills and the process of controlling workplace activities.

Exercise Background

You're a middle manager in a small manufacturing plant. Today is Monday, and you've just returned from a week's vacation. The first thing you discover is that your assistant won't be in today (his aunt died, and he's out of town at the funeral). He did, however, leave you the following note:

Dear Boss:

Sorry about not being here today. I will be back tomorrow. In the meantime, here are some things you need to know:

Ms. Hernandez [your boss] wants to see you today at 4:00.

The shop steward wants to see you as soon as possible about a labor problem.

Mr. Withers [one of your big customers] has a complaint about a recent shipment.

Ms. Howard [one of your major suppliers] wants to discuss a change in delivery schedules.

Mr. Zapata from the Chamber of Commerce wants you to attend a breakfast meeting on Wednesday to discuss our expansion plans.

The legal office wants to discuss our upcoming OSHA inspection.

Human resources wants to know when you can interview someone for the new supervisor's position.

Bill Woodman, the machinist you fired last month, has been hanging around the parking lot, and his presence is making some employees uncomfortable.

Exercise Task

Review the preceding information and then prioritize the work that needs to be done by sorting the information into three categories: *very timely, moderately timely,* and *less timely.* Then address the following questions:

1. Are *importance* and *timeliness* the same thing?
2. What additional information do you need before you can begin to prioritize all of these demands on your time?
3. How would your approach differ if your assistant were in the office?

BUILDING EFFECTIVE TECHNICAL SKILLS

Exercise Overview

Technical skills are necessary to understand or perform the specific kind of work that an organization does. This exercise allows you to develop the technical skills needed to construct and evaluate the effectiveness of a budget.

Exercise Background

Although corporate budgets are obviously much more complicated, the basic processes of creating a corporate budget on the one hand and a personal budget on the other share a few important features. Both, for instance, begin with estimations of inflow and outflow. In addition, both compare actual results with estimated results, and both culminate in plans for corrective action.

Exercise Task

1. Prepare lists of your *estimated* expenditures and income for one month. Remember: You're dealing with budgeted amounts, not the amounts that you actually spend and take in. You're also dealing with figures that represent a typical month or a reasonable

minimum. If, for example, you estimate that you spend $200 a month on groceries, you need to ask yourself whether that's a reasonable amount to spend on groceries for a month. If it's not, perhaps a more typical or reasonable figure is, say, $125. First, estimate your necessary monthly expenses for tuition, rent, car payments, childcare, food, utilities, and so on. Then estimate your income from all sources, such as wages, allowance, loans, and funds borrowed on credit cards. Calculate both totals.

2. Now write down all of your *actual* expenses and all your *actual* income over the last month. If you don't have exact figures, estimate as closely as you can. Calculate both totals.
3. Compare your *estimates* to your *actual* expenses and actual income. Are there any discrepancies? If so, what caused them?
4. Did you expect to have a surplus or a deficit for the month? Did you actually have a surplus or a deficit? What can you do to make up any deficit or manage any surplus?
5. Do you regularly use a personal budget? If yes, how is it helpful? If no, how might it be helpful?

SKILLS SELF-ASSESSMENT INSTRUMENT

Understanding Control

Introduction: Control systems must be carefully constructed for all organizations, regardless of their specific goals. The following assessment surveys your ideas about and approaches to control.

Instructions: You will agree with some of the statements and disagree with others. In some cases, making a decision may be difficult, but you should force yourself to make a choice. Record your answers next to each statement according to the following scale:

Rating Scale

4 Strongly agree
3 Somewhat agree
2 Somewhat disagree
1 Strongly disagree

_____ 1. Effective controls must be unbending if they are to be used consistently.

_____ 2. The most objective form of control is one that uses measures such as stock prices and rate of return on investment (ROI).

_____ 3. Control is restrictive and should be avoided if at all possible.

_____ 4. Controlling through rules, procedures, and budgets should not be used unless measurable standards are difficult or expensive to develop.

_____ 5. Overreliance on measurable control standards is seldom a problem for business organizations.

_____ 6. Organizations should encourage the development of individual self-control.

_____ 7. Organizations tend to try to establish behavioral controls as the first type of control to be used.

_____ 8. The easiest and least costly form of control is output or quantity control.

_____ 9. Short-run efficiency and long-run effectiveness result from the use of similar control standards.

_____ 10. Controlling by taking into account ROI and using stock prices in making control decisions are ways of ensuring that a business organization is responding to its external market.

_____ 11. Self-control should be relied on to replace other forms of control.

_____ 12. Controls such as ROI are more appropriate for corporations and business units than for small groups or individuals.

_____ 13. Control is unnecessary in a well-managed organization.

_____ 14. The use of output or quantity controls can lead to unintended or unfortunate consequences.

_____ 15. Standards of control do not depend on which constituency is being considered.

_____ 16. Controlling through the use of rules, procedures, and budgets can lead to rigidity and to a loss of creativity in an organization.

_____ 17. Different forms of control cannot be used at the same time. An organization must decide how it is going to control and stick to that method.

_____ 18. Setting across-the-board output or quantity targets for divisions within a company can lead to destructive results.

_____ 19. Control through rules, procedures, and budgets is generally not very costly.

_____ 20. Reliance on individual self-control can lead to problems with integration and communication.

Source: From Hill, *Strategic Management*, 4th Edition. © 1998 Cengage Learning.

EXPERIENTIAL EXERCISE

Control Systems at State University

Purpose: This exercise offers you an opportunity to practice analyzing an organization's need for controls. You also will describe likely challenges to implementation and list ways to overcome resistance to control.

Introduction: The following case represents an organization with seriously deficient control systems, which is rather unrealistic. However, most organizations do suffer from one or more control efforts that are lacking or ineffective. In addition, implementing controls is usually more difficult than simply diagnosing the need for controls, especially when organization members resist the control.

Instructions: *Step 1*: The instructor will divide the class into small groups. Read "The University Control Problem" short case, which follows.

The University Control Problem

You are on a committee appointed by the State University Student Council to help the new president deal with a number of problems that have plagued the campus for years. For example, the university regularly runs out of funds before the academic year ends, causing major disruptions of student services. In fact, some departments seem to have no knowledge of how much money they need or how much they have spent. Students are upset because tuition fees are constantly being changed in an effort to match the university's varying demands for money. Department chairs have no idea how many students are being admitted, so they never schedule the appropriate number of courses.

Some buildings are in bad physical shape. Classrooms are assigned to departments, and some classrooms seem to sit empty while others are overcrowded. There seems to be an oversupply of research equipment but a shortage of computer equipment for students. Some schools, such as the business school, don't have enough faculty to teach their classes, while some departments in liberal arts have surplus faculty with no students to teach.

Step 2: As a small group, reach consensus about how to complete the University Control Matrix, shown here. Identify the different controls that might be established for each of the four resources—physical, financial, human, and information—and remember to consider each type of control. Preliminary controls focus on inputs into the university. Screening controls act on the university's transformation processes. Postaction controls control the university's outputs.

Step 3: As a small group, develop responses to the following Discussion Questions. Discuss your responses with the class.

The University Control Matrix

System Stages	Physical Resources	Financial Resources	Human Resources	Information Resources
Preliminary Controls				
Screening Controls				
Postaction Controls				

Discussion Questions

1. Which of the recommended controls may be the hardest to implement? To manage?
2. Will the controls receive some form of resistance? If so, describe which organization members are likely to resist and the likely form of that resistance.

Source: Adapted from Morable, *Exercises in Management*, to accompany Griffin, *Management*, 8th Edition.

MANAGEMENT AT WORK

Using Control at J.P. Morgan

In October 2006, the head of the mortgage-servicing department, which collects payments on home loans, informed J.P. Morgan CEO Jamie Dimon that late payments were increasing at an alarming rate. When Dimon reviewed the report, he confirmed not only that late payments were a problem at Morgan but also that things were even worse for other lenders. "We concluded," recalls Dimon, "that underwriting standards were deteriorating across the industry." Shortly thereafter, Dimon was informed that the cost of insuring securities backed by subprime mortgages was going up, even though ratings agencies persisted in rating them AAA. At the time, creating securities backed by subprime mortgages was the hottest and most profitable business on Wall Street, but by the end of the year, Dimon had decided to get out of it. "We saw no profit, and lots of risk," reports Bill Winters, co-head of Morgan's investment arm. "It was Jamie," he adds, "who saw all the pieces."

Dimon's caution—and willingness to listen to what his risk-management people were telling him—paid off in a big way. Between July 2007 and July 2008, when the full force of the crisis hit the country's investment banks, Morgan recorded losses of $5 billion on mortgage-backed securities. That's a lot of money, but relatively little compared to the losses sustained by banks that didn't see the writing on the wall—$33 billion at Citibank, for example, and $26 billion at Merrill Lynch. Citi is still in business, thanks to $45 billion in cash infusions from the federal government, but Merrill Lynch isn't—it was forced to sell itself to Bank of America. Morgan, though hit hard, weathered the storm and is still standing on its own Wall Street foundations. "You know," said President-elect Barack Obama as he surveyed the damage sustained by the U.S. banking industry in 2008, "… there are a lot of banks that are actually pretty well managed, J.P. Morgan being a good example. Jamie Dimon … is doing a pretty good job managing an enormous portfolio."

Ironically, Dimon got his start in banking at Citibank, where he worked closely with legendary CEO Sandy Weill for 12 years, helping to transform what's now known as Citigroup into the largest financial institution in the United States. Dimon left Citi in 1998 and, two years later, became CEO of Bank One, then the country's fifth-largest bank. He sold a revitalized Bank One to J.P. Morgan Chase in 2004, and in 2006, he became CEO and chairman of J.P. Morgan Chase & Co., a financial-services institution, which includes J.P. Morgan Chase Bank, a commercial-retail bank, and J.P. Morgan Trust Company, an investment bank. With assets of $176.8 billion, J.P. Morgan Chase boasts the largest market-capitalization and deposit bases in the U.S. financial industry.

Dimon came to J.P. Morgan Chase with a few ideas about how to manage an enormous portfolio. Shortly after he took over, he increased oversight and control of Bank One's operations and expenses, using cost-saving measures to free up $3 billion annually by 2007. He then used the cash to finance the expansion of Morgan Chase operations, including the installation of more ATMs and the creation of new products. As improved fundamentals and expanded operations yielded greater revenues, the bank's stock price went up (at least until the subprime crisis hit), freeing up further funds for new growth. Once the basics are right, says Dimon, "you earn the right to do a deal," and he set about building a Citi-like financial empire, relying mostly on mergers to jump-start growth in underserved regional and international markets.

Experience had shown Dimon that a large organization "can get arrogant and … lose focus, like the Roman Empire." In 2006, for example, J.P. Morgan Chase was enjoying high sales but spending a lot more than Dimon was used to spending at Bank One. Moreover, Dimon had inherited a company that had engineered multiple mergers without making much effort to integrate operations. The twofold result was ho-hum profits and a loose collection of incompatible structures and systems. Financial results from different divisions, for instance, were simply being combined, and the upshot, according to CFO Michael Cavanagh, was that even though "strong businesses were subsidizing weak ones … the numbers didn't jump out at you. With the results mashed together, it was easy for managers to hide."

Dimon thus set out to exercise more effective operational oversight, and his control practices currently extend to virtually every aspect of J.P. Morgan Chase operations:

- Every month, managers must submit 50-page reports showing financial ratios and results, product sales, and even detailed expenses for every worker. Then Dimon and his top executives spend hours combing through the data, with the CEO asking tough questions and demanding frank answers.
- One of Dimon's top priorities is slashing bloated budgets. "Waste hurt[s] our customers," he reminds his management team. "Cars, phones, clubs, perks—what's that got to do with customers?" He's also eliminated such amenities as fresh flowers, lavish expense accounts, and oversized offices and closed the in-house gym. One time, he asked a line of limousine drivers outside company headquarters for the names

of the executives they were waiting for. Then he called up each one, asking, "Too good for the subway?" or "Why don't you try walking?" Dimon denies the story, but limo service at J.P. Morgan Chase is way down.

- Dimon also takes a close look at compensation. Regional bank managers at J.P. Morgan Chase once earned $2 million a year, compared with Bank One's modest salary of $400,000. "I'd tell people they were way overpaid," says Dimon, and, as he suspected, "they already knew it." He cut pay for most staff by 20 to 50 percent, but most people elected to stay with the company. Today, a strict pay-for-performance formula keeps compensation in line.

- "In a big company," Dimon advises, "it's easy for people to BS you. A lot of them have been practicing for decades." So he gathers outcome data from every manager, various forms of information from low-level staffers, and even candid performance critiques from suppliers. "If you just want to run your business on your own and report results," warns Steve Black, co-head of investment banking, "you won't like working for Jamie."

- Finally, Dimon is convinced that IT is critical to the bank's long-term strategy and once cancelled a long-running information-services contract with IBM. "When you're outsourcing," he explained, "… people don't care" about your performance. At J.P. Morgan Chase, "we want patriots, not mercenaries." Between 2007 and 2008, he invested $2 billion in technology developed in-house and considers it money well spent.

Dimon, however, doesn't like being thought of as a control freak. "It's offensive … to be called a cost cutter," he complains, and besides, his long-run goal isn't merely control—it's growth. "It's thousand-mile march," observes one J.P. Morgan analyst, "and not everyone will survive."

Case Questions

1. In what ways is Jamie Dimon's approach to management pretty much what you'd expect of a top-level manager in the financial industry? In what ways is it different from what you'd expect?

2. Under what circumstances might Dimon need to change his approach to organizational control?

3. Explain how Dimon has practiced each of the following *levels of control* at J.P. Morgan Chase: (a) *financial*, (b) *structural*, and (c) *strategic*. Then focus on *operations control*: What steps has Dimon taken to exercise each form of operations control—*preliminary, screening,* and *postaction*?

4. What aspects of Dimon's approach to control were important in steering J.P. Morgan Chase through the subprime crisis that crippled or toppled other financial institutions?

5. Under what circumstances might Dimon need to change his approach to organizational control?

Case References

Roger Lowenstein, "Jamie Dimon: America's Least-Hated Banker," *New York Times*, December 1, 2010, www.nytimes.com, accessed on January 1, 2014; Felix Salmon, "Dimon in the Rough: How J.P. Morgan's CEO Manages Risk," *Seeking Alpha*, September 3, 2008, http://seekingalpha.com/, accessed on January 1, 2014; Duff McDonald, "The Banker Who Saved Wall Street," *Newsweek*, September 11, 2009, www.newsweek.com, accessed on January 1, 2014; Shawn Tully, "How J. P. Morgan Steered Clear of the Credit Crunch," *CNNMoney.com*, http://money.cnn.com, accessed on January 1, 2014; Jamie Dimon, "No More 'Too Big to Fail,'" *Washington Post*, November 13, 2009, www.washingtonpost.com, accessed on January 1, 2014; and Mike Taylor, "Hardest-Hitting Jamie Dimon Profile Ever Still Concludes He's Pretty Great," *The New York Observer*, November 2, 2010, http://observer.com/, accessed on January 1, 2014.

You Make the Call

Shifting Gears in the Auto Industry

1. Identify as many examples and uses of control as you can that are especially relevant for an automobile manufacturer.

2. Sergio Marchionne's education and early training was in accounting. In what ways might this have helped him in turning around first Fiat and then Chrysler?

3. As planned, the Fiat 500 was launched in the U.S. market in 2014. Read recent reviews and sales data online and see if the car seems to be performing as well as projected. If not, what control actions might be necessary?

4. What automobile industry events in 2014 might lead to greater revenue and profit projections for Chrysler?

ENDNOTES

[1] Dale Buss, "Fiat CEO Marchionne Has Led Unlikely Turnaround," *Edmunds Auto Observer*, www.edmunds.com/autoobserver-archive, accessed on January 1, 2014; Leslie Wayne, "Sergio Marchionne," *New York Times*, May 1, 2009, www.nytimes.com/pages/topics/index.html, accessed on January 1, 2014; "Fiat Plays Double or Quits with Chrysler," *The Economist*, November 25, 2010, www.economist.com, accessed on January 1, 2014; Deepa Seetharaman, "Fiat Raises Chrysler Stake, Readies for IPO," Reuters, www.reuters.com, accessed on January 1, 2014; Steven J. Ewing, "Fiat Sales in U.S. Not Meeting Expectations Amidst Marketing Meltdown," *Autoblog*, September 27, 2011, www.autoblog.com, accessed on January 1, 2014; Tommaso Ebhardt and Craig Trudell, "Fiat Tries Again in the U.S.," *Bloomberg Businessweek*, March 8, 2012, www.businessweek.com, accessed on January 1, 2014; "Fiat Arboth Sells Out in US," *Daily News* (New York), June 6, 2012, www.nydailynews.com, accessed on January 1, 2014.

[2] Thomas A. Stewart, "Welcome to the Revolution," *Fortune*, December 13, 1993, pp. 66–77.

[3] William Taylor, "Control in an Age of Chaos," *Harvard Business Review*, November–December 1994, pp. 64–70.

[4] "Fastener Woes to Delay Flight of First Boeing 787 Jets," *Wall Street Journal*, November 5, 2008, p. B1.

[5] "Starbucks Brews Up New Cost Cuts by Putting Lid on Afternoon Decaf," *Wall Street Journal*, January 28, 2009, p. B1.

[6] "An Apple a Day," *BusinessWeek*, October 14, 2002, pp. 122–125; "More Business People Say: Let's Not Do Lunch," *USA Today*, December 24, 2002, p. 1B; and David Stires, "The Breaking Point," *Fortune*, March 3, 2003, pp. 107–114; see also Shawn Coyne and Edward Coyne, Sr., "When You've Got to Cut Costs—Now," *Harvard Business Review*, May 2010, pp. 74–83.

[7] Mark Kroll, Peter Wright, Leslie Toombs, and Hadley Leavell, "Form of Control: A Critical Determinant of Acquisition Performance and CEO Rewards," *Strategic Management Journal*, 1997, Vol. 18, No. 2, pp. 85–96.

[8] For an example, see Donald Lange, "A Multidimensional Conceptualization of Organizational Corruption Control," *Academy of Management Review*, 2008, Vol. 33, No. 3, pp. 710–729.

[9] See Karynne Turner and Mona Makhija, "The Role of Organizational Controls in Managing Knowledge," *Academy of Management Review*, 2006, Vol. 31, No. 1, pp. 197–217.

[10] Sim Sitkin, Kathleen Sutcliffe, and Roger Schroeder, "Distinguishing Control from Learning in Total Quality Management: A Contingency Perspective," *Academy of Management Review*, 1994, Vol. 19, No. 3, pp. 537–564.

[11] Robert Lusch and Michael Harvey, "The Case for an Off-Balance-Sheet Controller," *Sloan Management Review*, Winter 1994, pp. 101–110.

[12] Edward E. Lawler III and John G. Rhode, *Information and Control in Organizations* (Pacific Palisades, CA: Goodyear, 1976).

[13] Charles W. L. Hill, "Establishing a Standard: Competitive Strategy and Technological Standards in Winner-Take-All Industries," *Academy of Management Executive*, 1997, Vol. 11, No. 2, pp. 7–16.

[14] "Airbus Clips Superjumbo Production," *Wall Street Journal*, May 7, 2009, p. B1.

[15] "Shifting Burden Helps Employers Cut Health Costs," *Wall Street Journal*, December 8, 2005, pp. B1, B2.

[16] "An Efficiency Guru Refits Honda to Fight Auto Giants," *Wall Street Journal*, September 15, 1999, p. B1.

[17] See "To Shed Idled Workers, Ford Offers to Foot Bill for College," *Wall Street Journal*, January 18, 2006, pp. B1, B3; and "GM's Employees Buyout Offer," *Fast Company*, May 2006, p. 58.

[18] "At Disney, String of Weak Cartoons Leads to Cost Cuts," *Wall Street Journal*, June 18, 2002, pp. A1, A6.

[19] "Mickey Mouse, CPA," *Forbes*, March 10, 1997, pp. 42, 43.

[20] Jeremy Kahn, "Do Accountants Have a Future?" *Fortune*, March 3, 2003, pp. 115–117.

[21] "Indian Accounting Firm Is Fined $7.5 Million over Fraud at Satyam," *New York Times*, April 5, 2011.

[22] William G. Ouchi, "The Transmission of Control through Organizational Hierarchy," *Academy of Management Journal*, June 1978, Vol. 21, No. 2, pp. 173–192; and Richard E. Walton, "From Control to Commitment in the Workplace," *Harvard Business Review*, March–April 1985, pp. 76–84.

[23] Peter Lorange, Michael F. Scott Morton, and Sumantra Ghoshal, *Strategic Control* (St. Paul, MN: West, 1986). See also Joseph C. Picken and Gregory G. Dess, "Out of (Strategic) Control," *Organizational Dynamics*, Summer 1997, Vol. 26, No. 1, pp. 35–45.

[24] "Pfizer Plans Layoffs in Research," *Wall Street Journal*, January 14, 2009, p. B1.

[25] "Kohl's Works to Refill Consumers' Bags," *USA Today*, April 8, 2005, pp. B1, B7.

[26] See Hans Mjoen and Stephen Tallman, "Control and Performance in International Joint Ventures," *Organization Science*, May–June 1997, Vol. 8, No. 3, pp. 257–265.

[27] Diana Robertson and Erin Anderson, "Control System and Task Environment Effects on Ethical Judgment: An Exploratory Study of Industrial Salespeople," *Organization Science*, November 1993, Vol. 4, No. 4, pp. 617–629.

[28] "Enterprise Takes Idea of Dressed for Success to a New Extreme," *Wall Street Journal*, November 20, 2002, p. B1.

[29] "UBS Relaxing Dress Code, Which Set Underwear Standards," *USA Today*, January 25, 2011, p. 1B.

CHAPTER 15

Managing Operations, Quality, and Productivity

Sergii Tsololo/Photos.com

Learning Outcomes

After studying this chapter, you should be able to:

1 Describe and explain the nature of operations management.

2 Identify and discuss the components involved in designing effective operations systems.

3 Discuss organizational technologies and their role in operations management.

4 Identify and discuss the components involved in implementing operations systems through supply chain management.

5 Explain the meaning and importance of managing quality and total quality management.

6 Explain the meaning and importance of managing productivity, productivity trends, and ways to improve productivity.

Management in Action

Orchestrating Outcomes

"[T]hey feel empowered. They don't have anyone telling them what to do. They walk into the rehearsal hall and it's their opportunity to influence [and] shape music."

—**Executive Director Graham Parker on the musicians of the Orpheus Chamber Orchestra**

Hiroyuki Ito/Hulton Archive/Getty Images

The Orpheus Chamber Orchestra is unique in that it performs without a conductor. By working as a team without a leader, the orchestra builds motivation and satisfaction among its musicians.

Reviewing a recent concert by the Orpheus Chamber Orchestra, *New York Times* music critic Vivien Schweitzer wrote that the orchestra played Robert Schumann's Symphony No. 2 "with remarkable co-ordination"; the "balance among strings, winds, and brass," she added, "was impressively well proportioned."

Was Schweitzer, as we sometimes say, damning with faint praise? Isn't a *symphony*, which means "harmony of sounds," *supposed* to be played with remarkable coordination? Aren't the various sections of the orchestra *supposed* to be well balanced? Had the conductor, whose job is to ensure a consummate performance of the music, achieved little more than coordination and balance?

Actually, New York–based Orpheus doesn't play with a conductor, and Schweitzer was remarking on the fact the orchestra had "bravely—and successfully—attempted" such a complex work without the artistic and managerial leadership of someone who directs rehearsals and stands at a podium waving an authoritative baton.

"For us at Orpheus," explains executive director Graham Parker, "it's the *way* we make the music that's the difference." Orpheus holds to the principle that its product—the music performed for audiences—is of the highest quality when its workers—the musicians—are highly satisfied with their jobs. All professional orchestra musicians, of course, are highly trained and skilled, but make no mistake about it: A lot of them are not very happy workers. J. Richard Hackman, an organizational psychologist at Harvard, surveyed workers in 13 different occupational categories, including orchestra players, to determine relative levels of job motivation and satisfaction. On the one hand, musicians ranked at the top in motivation, "fueled by their own pride and professionalism," according to Hackman. But when it came to general satisfaction with their jobs, orchestra players ranked seventh (just below federal prison guards and slightly above beer sales and delivery teams). On the question of satisfaction with growth opportunities, they ranked ninth (again, below prison guards, though a little higher than operating-room nurses and hockey players).

It's this disconnect between motivation and satisfaction—and between motivation and product quality—that Orpheus was conceived to rectify, and the first principle in what's now known as the "Orpheus Process" is "Put power in the hands of the people doing the work." According to Harvey Seifter, a consultant specializing in relationships between business and the arts, the Orpheus Process consists of five elements designed to put this principle into practice:

1. *Choosing Leaders*. For each piece of music that the orchestra decides to perform, members select a leadership team composed of five to seven musicians. This "core team" then leads rehearsals and serves as a conduit for members' input. It's also responsible for seeing that the final performance reflects "a unified vision."
2. *Developing Strategies*. Prior to rehearsals, the core team decides how a piece of music will be played. Its ultimate goal is to ensure "an overall interpretive approach to the music," and it works to meet this goal by trying out various approaches to the music during rehearsals with the full orchestra.
3. *Developing the Product*. Once an interpretive approach has been chosen, rehearsals are geared toward refining it. At this point, players make suggestions and critique the playing of their colleagues. It is, of course, a highly collaborative stage in the process, and its success depends on mutual respect. "We're all specialists—that's the beginning of the discussion," says violinist Martha Caplin. "When I talk to … another musician in the group, it's on an equal level. It's absolutely crucial that we have that attitude." When disagreements arise, everyone works toward a consensus, and if a consensus can't be reached, the issue is settled by a vote. Violinist Eriko Sato also emphasizes that the process of collaborative input works best when members focus their contributions on outcomes of the highest possible quality: "Fundamentally," she says, "I don't think everybody's

opinion should be addressed at all times. There are certain places and times for certain things to be said. The appropriate moment. Everybody knows what's wrong, everybody can feel what's wrong. But do you have a *solution*? Do you know how to solve a *problem*?"

4. *Perfecting the Product*. Just before each concert, a couple of members take seats in the hall to listen to the performance from the audience's perspective. Then they report to the full ensemble and may suggest some final adjustments.

5. *Delivering the Product*. The final performance is the ultimate result of the Orpheus Process, but it isn't the last step. When the concert is over, members get together to share their impressions of the performance and make suggestions for even further refinements.

"If you ask any musician in the orchestra why they love playing with Orpheus," says Parker, "it's because they feel empowered. They don't have anyone telling them what to do. They walk into the rehearsal hall and it's their opportunity to influence [and] shape music, to make music with all their experience, all their training coming together." Ask double-bass player Don Palma, for instance. Palma took a sabbatical after one year with Orpheus to play with the Los Angeles Philharmonic. "I just hated it," he says. "I didn't like to be told what to do all the time, being treated like I wasn't really worth anything other than to be a good soldier and just sit there and do as I was told. I felt powerless to affect things … . I felt frustrated, and there was nothing I could … do to help make things better." By contrast, says Palma, "Orpheus keeps me involved. I have some measure of participation in the direction the music is going to take. I think that's why a lot of us have stayed involved so long."

In most orchestras, the conductor makes more or less autocratic decisions about what will be played and how. The input of musicians is neither sought nor welcomed, and unsolicited advice may be sharply rebuffed—and may, in fact, serve as grounds for dismissal. At Orpheus, says Parker, "we have a completely different structure to the way we approach rehearsal": A core team of players selected by the orchestra from each instrument section plans and leads rehearsals for a given piece of music.

To assist in meeting the inevitable challenges posed by its democratic structure, Orpheus recruited Harvard's Hackman to its board of trustees, and he immediately helped the orchestra organize itself around two leadership groups. An *artistic planning group* consists of two staff members and three "artistic directors." The executive director serves as a sort of moderator for group discussions, and the general manager keeps everyone posted on market-related events and initiatives. The three artistic directors, who are members of the orchestra, work with other members to find out what they're interested in working on and to convey their ideas to the planning group. They also serve on a *senior leadership team* with the executive director, the general manager, and the directors of finance, marketing, and operations. This team determines the best ways to do things given the organization's commitment to democratic structure, leadership, and roles—the best way to develop artistic agendas, to choose players, soloists, and composers and to make the team accountable for its own artistic decisions.

It's important to remember, however, that neither the Orpheus Process nor the Orpheus two-team structure is any guarantee of organizational effectiveness. As in any organizational endeavor, execution is the difference between success and failure, and a study of the Orpheus approach to management has revealed a variety of reasons for the effectiveness of teamwork within the ensemble. Every member, for example, clearly understands the group's purpose and mission; every member's role is clearly stated and agreed on, and all members perform an equal amount of work in meeting the group's objectives.[1]

In this chapter, we explore operations management, quality, and productivity. All these topics figure in our opening story about Orpheus, which has taken a highly innovative approach to each of them. To better understand why Orpheus operates as it does—and why it's successful in doing so—we'll take a closer look at the basics of each of these factors in organizational performance. We first introduce operations management and discuss its role in general management and organizational strategy. The next three sections discuss the design of operations systems, organizational technologies, and implementing operations systems. We then introduce and discuss various issues in managing for quality and total quality. Finally, we discuss productivity, which is closely related to quality.

THE NATURE OF OPERATIONS MANAGEMENT

operations management

The total set of managerial activities used by an organization to transform resource inputs into products, services, or both

Operations management is at the core of what organizations do as they add value and create products and services. But what exactly are operations? And how are they managed? **Operations management** is the set of managerial activities used by an organization to transform resource inputs into products and services. When Hewlett-Packard buys electronic components, assembles them into PCs, and then ships them to customers, it is engaging in operations management. When a Domino's employee orders food ingredients and paper products and then combines dough, cheese, and tomato sauce to create a pizza, he or she is engaging in operations management.

The Importance of Operations

Operations is an important functional concern for organizations because efficient and effective management of operations goes a long way toward ensuring competitiveness and overall organizational performance, as well as quality and productivity. Inefficient or ineffective operations management, on the other hand, will almost inevitably lead to poorer performance and lower levels of both quality and productivity.

In an economic sense, operations management creates value and utility of one type or another, depending on the nature of the firm's products or services. If the product is a physical good, such as a Honda motorcycle, operations creates value and provides form utility by combining many dissimilar inputs (sheet metal, rubber, paint, internal combustion engines, and human skills) to make something (a motorcycle) that is more valuable than the actual cost of the inputs used to create it. The inputs are converted from their incoming form into a new physical form. This conversion is typical of manufacturing operations and essentially reflects the organization's technology.

In contrast, the operations activities of Delta Airlines create value and provide time and place utility through its services. The airline transports passengers and freight according to agreed-upon departure and arrival places and times. Other service operations, such as a Budweiser beer distributorship or an American Eagle retail store, create value and provide place and possession utility by bringing together the customer and products made by others. Although the organizations in these examples produce different kinds of products or services, their operations processes share many important features.[2]

Manufacturing and Production Operations

manufacturing
A form of business that combines and transforms resource inputs into tangible outcomes

Because manufacturing once dominated U.S. industry, the entire area of operations management used to be called *production management*. **Manufacturing** is a form of business that combines and transforms resources into tangible outcomes that are then sold to others. Firestone is a manufacturer because it combines rubber and chemical compounds and uses blending equipment and molding machines to create tires. Broyhill is a manufacturer because it buys wood and metal components, pads, and fabric and then combines them to make furniture.

During the 1970s, manufacturing entered a long period of decline in the United States, primarily because of foreign competition. U.S. firms had grown lax and sluggish, and new foreign competitors came onto the scene with better equipment and much higher levels of efficiency. For example, steel companies in the Far East were able to produce high-quality steel for much lower prices than U.S. companies such as Bethlehem Steel and U.S. Steel (now USX Corporation). Faced with a battle for survival, many companies underwent a long and difficult period of change by eliminating waste and transforming themselves into leaner and more efficient and responsive entities. They reduced their workforces dramatically, closed antiquated or unnecessary plants, and modernized their remaining plants. In the last decade, their efforts have started to pay dividends, as U.S. businesses have regained their competitive positions in many different industries. Although manufacturers from other parts of the world are still formidable competitors, and U.S. firms may never again be competitive in some markets, the overall picture is much better than it was just a few years ago. And prospects continue to look bright.[3]

Service Operations

service organization
An organization that transforms resources into an intangible output and creates time or place utility for its customers

During the decline of the manufacturing sector, a tremendous growth in the service sector kept the U.S. economy from declining at the same rate. A **service organization** is one that transforms resources into an intangible output and creates time or place utility for its customers. For example, E*Trade makes stock transactions for its customers, Hertz leases cars to its customers, and local hairdressers cut clients' hair. In 1947, the service sector was responsible for less than half of the U.S. gross national product (GNP). By 1975, however, this figure reached 65 percent, and by 2013, it was over 80 percent. The service sector has been responsible for creating approximately 42 million new jobs in the United States since 1990.[4] Managers have come to see that many of the tools, techniques, and methods that are used in a factory are also useful to a service firm. For example, managers of automobile plants and hair salons both have to decide how to design their facilities, identify the best locations for them, determine optimal capacities, make decisions about inventory storage, set procedures for purchasing raw materials, and set standards for productivity and quality.

© Tyler Olson/Shutterstock.com

There is a tendency to associate operations management with production and manufacturing. But in reality operations management is also very relevant to service organizations such as this hair salon. Operations management techniques help the salon manager schedule stylists, book appointments, order and maintain the optimal inventory of products, and move clients through dedicated work stations for washing, coloring, cutting, and styling.

The Role of Operations in Organizational Strategy

It should be clear by this point that operations management is very important to organizations. Beyond its direct impact on factors such as competitiveness, quality, and productivity, it also directly influences the organization's overall level of effectiveness. For example, the deceptively simple strategic decision of whether to stress high quality regardless of cost, lowest possible cost regardless of quality, or some combination of the two has numerous important implications. A highest-possible-quality strategy will dictate state-of-the-art technology and rigorous control of product design and materials specifications. A combination strategy might call for lower-grade technology and less concern about product design and materials specifications. Just as strategy affects operations management, operations management affects strategy. Suppose that a firm decides to upgrade the quality of its products or services. The organization's ability to implement the decision is dependent in part on current production capabilities and other resources. If existing technology will not permit higher-quality work, and if the organization lacks the resources to replace its technology, increasing quality to the desired new standards will be difficult.

DESIGNING OPERATIONS SYSTEMS

The problems, challenges, and opportunities faced by operations managers revolve around the acquisition and utilization of resources for conversion. Their goals include both efficiency and effectiveness. A number of issues and decisions must be addressed as operations systems are designed. The most basic ones are the product–service mix, capacity, and facilities.

Determining the Product–Service Mix

product–service mix
How many and what kinds of products or services (or both) to offer

A natural starting point in designing operations systems is determining the **product–service mix**. This decision flows from corporate, business, and marketing strategies. Managers have to make a number of decisions about their products and services, starting with how many and what kinds to offer.[5] Colgate-Palmolive, for example, makes regular, tartar control, gel, and various other formulas of Colgate toothpaste and packages them in several different sizes of tubes, pumps, and other dispensers. Similarly, workers at Subway sandwich shops can combine different breads, vegetables, meats, and condiments to create hundreds of different kinds of sandwiches. Decisions also have to be made regarding the level of quality desired, the optimal cost of each product or service, and exactly how each is to be designed. GE recently reduced the number of parts in its industrial circuit breakers from 28,000 to 1,275. This whole process was achieved by carefully analyzing product design and production methods.

Capacity Decisions

capacity
The amount of products, services, or both that can be produced by an organization

The **capacity** decision involves choosing the amount of products, services, or both that can be produced by the organization. Determining whether to build a factory capable of making 8,000 or 10,000 units per day is a capacity decision. So, too, is deciding whether to build a restaurant with 125 or 175 seats, or a bank with five or ten teller stations. The capacity decision is truly a high-risk one because of the uncertainties of future product demand and the large monetary stakes involved. An organization that builds capacity exceeding its needs may commit resources (capital investment) that will never be recovered. Alternatively, an organization can build a facility with a smaller capacity than product demand might actually support. Doing so may result in lost market opportunities, but it may also free capital resources for use elsewhere in the organization.

A major consideration in determining capacity is demand. A company operating with fairly constant monthly demand might build a plant capable of producing an amount each month roughly equivalent to its demand. But if its market is characterized by seasonal fluctuations, building a smaller plant to meet normal demand and then adding extra shifts staffed with temporary workers or paying permanent workers extra to work more hours during peak periods might be the most effective choice. Likewise, a restaurant that needs 175 seats for Saturday night but never needs more than 125 at any other time during the week would probably be foolish to expand to 175 seats. During the rest of the week, it must still pay to light, heat, cool, and clean the excess capacity. Many customer service departments have tried to improve their capacity to deal with customers while also lowering costs by using automated voice prompts to direct callers to the right representative. As you can see in our "At Your Service" feature, this approach to customer relationship management isn't necessarily what a lot of customers have in mind.

Facilities Decisions

facilities
The physical locations where products or services are created, stored, and distributed

Facilities are the physical locations where products or services are created, stored, and distributed. Major decisions pertain to facilities location and facilities layout.

location
The physical positioning or geographic site of facilities

Location   Location is the physical positioning or geographic site of facilities and must be determined by the needs and requirements of the organization. A company that relies heavily on railroads for transportation needs to be located close to rail facilities. GE decided that it did not need six plants to make circuit breakers, so it invested heavily in automating one plant and closed the other five. Different organizations in the same industry may have different facilities requirements. Benetton uses only one distribution center for the entire world, whereas Amazon has several distribution centers in the United States alone. A retail business must choose its location very carefully to be convenient for consumers.

layout
The physical configuration of facilities, the arrangement of equipment within facilities, or both

product layout
A physical configuration of facilities arranged around the product; used when large quantities of a single product are needed

process layouts
A physical configuration of facilities arranged around the process; used in facilities that create or process a variety of products

Layout   The choice of physical configuration, or the **layout**, of facilities is closely related to other operations decisions. The three entirely different layout alternatives shown in Figure 15.1 help demonstrate the importance of the layout decision. A **product layout** is appropriate when large quantities of a single product are needed. It makes sense to custom-design a straight-line flow of work for a product when a specific task is performed at each workstation as each unit flows past. Most assembly lines use this format. For example, Hewlett-Packard's personal computer factories use a product layout.

Process layouts are used in operations settings that create or process a variety of products. Auto repair shops and health-care clinics are good examples. Each car and each person is a separate "product." The needs of each incoming job are diagnosed as it enters the operations system, and the job is routed through the unique sequence of workstations needed to create the desired finished product. In a process layout, each type of conversion task is centralized in a single workstation or department. All welding is done in one designated shop location, and any car that requires welding is moved to

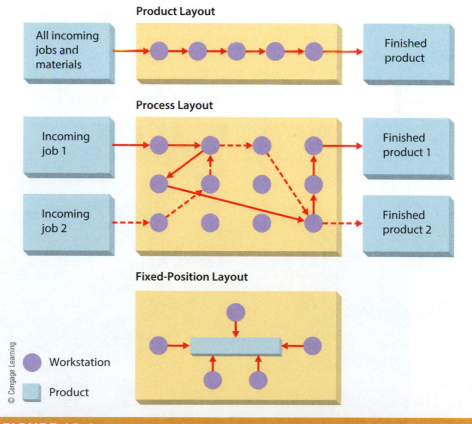

© Cengage Learning

FIGURE 15.1

Approaches to Facilities Layout

When a manufacturer produces large quantities of a product (such as cars or computers), it may arrange its facilities in an assembly line (product layout). In a process layout, the work (such as patients in a hospital or custom pieces of furniture) moves through various workstations. Locomotives and bridges are both manufactured in a fixed-position layout.

AT YOUR SERVICE

How to Get2 a Human

Submitted for your consideration: the frustration associated with customer-service call centers and automated phone menus—interminable waits, unannounced hangups, and endless transfers. Upon even the most casual recollection, two contradictory facts should emerge: On the one hand, a company's marketing department will spend hundreds of millions of dollars to "communicate" with you; on the other hand, the same company's customer-service department acts as if it were saving hundreds of millions of dollars by refusing to communicate with you through the medium of the human voice.

It's a paradox that's by no means lost on the humanitarian website www.gethuman.com, which was founded by technology entrepreneur Paul English. "I'm not anticomputer," avows English. "I've been a programmer for 20 years. I'm not anticapitalist. I'm on my fifth start-up. But I am antiarrogance. Why do the executives who run these call centers think they can decide when I deserve to speak to a human being and when I don't?"

A lot of people, of course, complain about corporate call centers, but most of us mutter under our breath, put our faith in the redial function, and prepare to be reasonably civil to the next voice we hear. We have, however, neither Paul English's tech skills nor his industry credibility. First, he started castigating customer call centers in his blog, and when that didn't work, he decided to take action. Conducting his own investigations, calling on friends who work in corporate IT departments, and collecting tips from simpatico strangers, English set up a website with the modest goal of "changing the face of customer service in the United States" The centerpiece of GetHuman.com is an alphabetized "cheat sheet" that tells you how you can bypass a given automated call-center system and talk to a live service representative. All you have to know is how to press the buttons on your phone. Can't get served by CompuServe? Press 1211 without waiting for the prompts. Getting zero satisfaction from Net-Zero? Try ###, then 32.

Most large businesses use call centers to handle ordering and customer service and follow-up. In recent years, there has been a trend toward automating call centers to lower labor costs. Frustrations with dealing with automated call centers, though, may lead to unhappy customers and lower customer loyalty.

RIA Novosti/Alamy

(continued)

AT YOUR SERVICE (Continued)

Granted, a company that's really bent on universal frustration could respond by making its phone system even more complex and difficult to use. Companies that require customers, on the other hand, could take the advice of Jim Kelly, head of customer service at ING Direct (now Capital One 360). Kelly made his bank's online system so easy to use that customers called to complain only 1.6 times annually. And those callers got to hear the sound of a human voice every time. The thing to do, advises Kelly, is simply "eliminate most of the problems and complaints. [Then] the only reason for people to call is to do business. And those are calls you're eager to take."

Until more companies start taking Kelly's advice, there's now Get2Human, which was started in 2009 by Walt Tetschner, a veteran market researcher in the call-automation industry. Tetschner, who took over when English moved on to another start-up venture, has stated the site's mission in a little more detail: "Our goal," says the Get2Human website, "is to convince enterprises that providing high-quality customer service and having satisfied customers costs much less than providing low-quality customer service and having unsatisfied customers."

References: Fuze Digital Solutions, "Gethuman.com Survey Results Reveal Significant Consumer Expectations for Online Customer Support," press release, http://www.fuzedigital.com, accessed on January 2, 2014; Christopher Null, "How to Get a Human on the Phone," *Yahoo! Tech*, February 11, 2008, https://www.yahoo.com/tech/, accessed on January 2, 2014; Burt Helm, "Building Good Web Buzz," *Single Articles*, www.singlearticles.com, accessed on January 2, 2014; William C. Taylor, "Your Call Should Be Important to Us, but It's Not," *New York Times*, February 26, 2006, www.nytimes.com, accessed on January 2, 2014; GetHuman, "GetHuman History," 2013, http://gethuman.com, accessed on January 2, 2014; and Get2Human.com, "About Us," 2013, www.get2human.com, accessed on January 2, 2014.

---

fixed-position layout

A physical configuration of facilities arranged around a single work area; used for the manufacture of large and complex products such as airplanes

that area. This setup is in contrast to the product layout, in which several different workstations may perform welding operations if the conversion task sequence so dictates. Similarly, in a hospital, all X-rays are done in one location, all surgeries in another, and all physical therapy in yet another. Patients are moved from location to location to get the services they need.

The **fixed-position layout** is used when the organization is creating a few very large and complex products. Aircraft manufacturers like Airbus and shipbuilders like Newport News use this method. An assembly line capable of moving one of Airbus's new A380 aircraft would require an enormous plant, so instead the airplane shell itself remains stationary, and people and machines move around it as it is assembled.

cellular layouts

A physical configuration of facilities used when families of products can follow similar flow paths

The cellular layout is a relatively new approach to facilities design. **Cellular layouts** are used when families of products can follow similar flow paths. A clothing manufacturer, for example, might create a cell, or designated area, dedicated to making a family of pockets, such as pockets for shirts, coats, blouses, and slacks. Although each kind of pocket is unique, the same basic equipment and methods are used to make all of them. Hence, all pockets might be made in the same area and then delivered directly to different product layout assembly areas where the shirts, coats, blouses, and slacks are actually being assembled.

technology

The set of processes and systems used by organizations to convert resources into products or services

ORGANIZATIONAL TECHNOLOGIES

One central element of effective operations management is technology. In Chapter 6, we defined **technology** as the set of processes and systems used by organizations to convert resources into products or services.

Manufacturing Technology

Numerous forms of manufacturing technology are used in organizations. In Chapter 6, we discussed the research of Joan Woodward. Recall that Woodward identified three forms of technology—unit or small batch, large batch or mass production, and continuous process.[6] Each form of technology was thought to be associated with a specific type of organization structure. Of course, newer forms of technology not considered by Woodward also warrant attention. Two of these are automation and computer-assisted manufacturing.

automation

The process of designing work so that it can be completely or almost completely performed by machines

Automation   **Automation** is the process of designing work so that it can be completely or almost completely performed by machines. Because automated machines operate quickly and make few errors, they increase the amount of work that can be done. Thus automation helps to improve products and services and fosters innovation. Automation is the most recent step in the development of machines and machine-controlling devices. Machine-controlling devices have been around since the 1700s. James Watt, a Scottish engineer, invented a mechanical speed control to regulate the speed of steam engines in 1787. The Jacquard loom, developed by the French inventor Joseph-Marie Jacquard, was controlled by paper cards with holes punched in them. Early accounting and computing equipment was controlled by similar punched cards.

Automation relies on feedback, information, sensors, and a control mechanism. Feedback is the flow of information from the machine back to the sensor. Sensors are the parts of the system that gather information and compare it to preset standards. The control mechanism is the device that sends instructions to the automatic machine. Early automatic machines were primitive, and the use of automation was relatively slow to develop. These elements are illustrated by the example in Figure 15.2. A thermostat has sensors that monitor air temperature and compare it to a preset low value. If the air temperature falls below the preset value, the thermostat sends an electrical signal to the furnace, turning it on. The furnace heats the air. When the sensors detect that the air temperature has reached a value higher than the low preset value, the thermostat stops the furnace. The last step (shutting off the furnace) is known as *feedback*, a critical component of any automated operation.

The big move to automate factories began during World War II. The shortage of skilled workers and the development of high-speed computers combined to bring about a tremendous interest in automation. Programmable automation (the use of computers to control machines) was introduced during this era, far outstripping conventional automation (the use of mechanical or electromechanical devices to control machines). The automobile industry began to use automatic machines for a variety of jobs. In fact, the term *automation* came into use in the 1950s in the automobile industry. The chemical and oil-refining industries also began to use computers to regulate production. During the 1990s, automation became a major element in the manufacture of computers and computer components, such as electronic chips and circuits. It is this computerized, or programmable, automation that presents the greatest opportunities and challenges for management today.

The impact of automation on people in the workplace is complex. In the short term, people whose jobs are automated may find themselves without a job. In the long term, however, more jobs are created than are lost. Nevertheless, not all companies are able to help displaced workers find new jobs, so the human costs are sometimes high. In the coal industry, for instance, automation has been used primarily in mining. The output per miner has risen dramatically from the 1950s on. The demand for coal, however, has decreased, and productivity gains resulting from automation have lessened the need

© Cengage Learning

FIGURE 15.2

A Simple Automatic Control Mechanism

All automation includes feedback, information, sensors, and a control mechanism. A simple thermostat is an example of automation. Another example is Benetton's distribution center in Italy. Orders are received, items pulled from stock and packaged for shipment, and invoices prepared and transmitted, with no human intervention.

for miners. Consequently, many workers have lost their jobs, and the industry has not been able to absorb them. In contrast, in the electronics industry, the rising demand for products has led to increasing employment opportunities despite the use of automation.[7]

computer-assisted manufacturing

A technology that relies on computers to design or manufacture products

Computer-Assisted Manufacturing   Current extensions of automation generally revolve around **computer-assisted manufacturing**—a technology that relies on computers to design or manufacture products. One type of computer-assisted manufacturing is *computer-aided design* (CAD)—the use of computers to design parts and complete products and to simulate performance so that prototypes need not be constructed. Boeing uses CAD technology to study hydraulic tubing in its commercial aircraft. Japan's automotive industry uses CAD to speed up car design. GE used CAD to change the design of circuit breakers, and Benetton uses CAD to design new styles and products. Oneida, the table flatware firm, uses CAD to design new flatware patterns; for example, it can design a new spoon in a single day. CAD is usually combined with *computer-aided manufacturing* (CAM) to ensure that the design moves smoothly to production. The production computer shares the design computer's information and is able to have machines with the proper settings ready when production is needed. A CAM system is especially useful when reorders come in because the computer can quickly produce the desired product, prepare labels and copies of orders, and send the product out to where it is wanted.

Closely aligned with this approach is *computer-integrated manufacturing* (CIM). In CIM, CAD and CAM are linked together, and computer networks automatically adjust machine placements and settings to enhance both the complexity and the flexibility of scheduling. In settings that use these technologies, all manufacturing activities are controlled by the computer network. Because the network can access the company's other information systems, CIM is both a powerful and a complex management control tool.

Flexible manufacturing systems (FMSs) usually have robotic work units or workstations, assembly lines, and robotic carts or some other form of computer-controlled transport system to move material as needed from one part of the system to another. Ford Motor Company used FMSs to transform a factory producing nothing but low-cost compact cars into a plant capable of making a variety of pickup trucks and SUVs. Using traditional methods, the plant would have been closed, its workers laid off, and the facility virtually rebuilt from the ground up. But by using FMSs, Ford was able to keep the plant open and running continuously, while new equipment was being installed and its workers were being retrained in small groups. Ford continues to be a pioneer in FMS as it adjusts plant capabilities to produce pickups, SUVs, or small hybrids, depending on fluctuations in market demand and supply.

These systems are not without disadvantages, however. For example, because they represent fundamental change, they also generate resistance. In addition, because of their tremendous complexity, CAD systems are not always reliable. CIM systems are so expensive that they raise the breakeven point for firms using them. This means that the firm must operate at high levels of production and sales to be able to afford the systems.

robot

Any artificial device that is able to perform functions ordinarily thought to be appropriate for human beings

Robotics   Another trend in manufacturing technology is computerized robotics. A **robot** is any artificial device that is able to perform functions ordinarily thought to be appropriate for human beings. *Robotics* refers to the science and technology of the construction, maintenance, and use of robots. The use of industrial robots has steadily increased since 1980 and is expected to continue to increase slowly as more companies recognize the benefits that accrue to users of industrial robots.[8]

Welding was one of the first applications for robots, and it continues to be the area for most applications. A close second is materials handling. Other applications include machine loading and unloading, painting and finishing, assembly, casting, and machining applications such as cutting, grinding, polishing, drilling, sanding, buffing, and deburring. Daimler AG, for instance, replaced about 200 welders with 50 robots on an assembly line and increased productivity about 20 percent. The use of robots in inspection work is increasing. They can check for cracks and holes, and they can be equipped with vision systems to perform visual inspections.

Robots are also beginning to move from the factory floor to all manner of other applications. The Dallas police used a robot to apprehend a suspect who had barricaded himself in an apartment building. The robot smashed a window and reached with its mechanical arm into the building. The suspect panicked and ran outside. At the Long Beach Memorial Hospital in California, brain surgeons are assisted by a robot arm that drills into the patient's skull with excellent precision. Some newer applications involve remote work. For example, the use of robot submersibles controlled from the surface can help divers in remote locations. Surveillance robots fitted with microwave sensors can do things that a human guard cannot, such as "seeing" through nonmetallic walls and in the dark. In other applications, automated farming (called *agrimation*) uses robot harvesters to pick fruit from a variety of trees.[9]

Robots are also used by small manufacturers. One robot slices carpeting to fit the inside of custom vans in an upholstery shop. Another stretches balloons flat so that they can be spray-painted with slogans at a novelties company. At a jewelry company, a robot holds class rings while they are engraved by a laser. These robots are lighter, faster, stronger, and more intelligent than those used in heavy manufacturing and are the types that more and more organizations will be using in the future.

Service Technology

Service technology is also changing rapidly. And it, too, is moving more and more toward automated systems and procedures. In banking, for example, technological breakthroughs led to automated teller machines and made it much easier to move funds between accounts or between different banks. Many people now have their paycheck deposited directly into a checking account from which many of their bills are then automatically paid. Electronic banking—where people can access their accounts, move money between accounts, and pay bills—has become commonplace. Moreover, the capabilities to do these things have been extended from personal computers to cell phones and other personal electronic communication technologies.

Hotels use increasingly sophisticated technology to accept and record room reservations. People can now, for instance, check in online and stop by the front desk only long enough to pick up their room key. Universities use new technologies to electronically store and provide access to books, scientific journals, government reports, and articles. Hospitals and other health-care organizations use new forms of service technology to manage patient records, dispatch ambulances and emergency medical technicians (EMTs), and monitor patients' vital signs. Restaurants use technology to record and fill customer orders, order food and supplies, and prepare food. Given the increased role that service organizations are playing in today's economy, even more technological innovations are certain to be developed in the years to come.[10] The "Leading the Way" feature highlights how technology can assist even artistic performances.

IMPLEMENTING OPERATIONS SYSTEMS THROUGH SUPPLY CHAIN MANAGEMENT

After operations systems have been properly designed and technologies developed, they must then be put into use by the organization. Their basic functional purpose is to control transformation processes to ensure that relevant goals are achieved in areas such as quality and costs. Operations management has a number of special purposes within this control framework, including purchasing and inventory management. Indeed, this area of management has become so important in recent years that a new term—*supply chain management*—has been coined. Specifically, **supply chain management** can be defined as the process of managing operations control, resource acquisition and purchasing, and inventory so as to improve overall efficiency and effectiveness.[11]

supply chain management
The process of managing operations control, resource acquisition and purchasing, and inventory so as to improve overall efficiency and effectiveness

Operations Management as Control

One way of using operations management as control is to coordinate it with other functions. Monsanto Company, for example, established a consumer products division that produces and distributes fertilizers and lawn chemicals. To facilitate control, the operations function was organized as an autonomous profit center. Monsanto finds this effective because its manufacturing division is given the authority to determine not only the costs of creating the product but also the product price and the marketing program.

In terms of overall organizational control, a division like the one used by Monsanto should be held accountable only for the activities over which it has decision-making authority. It would be inappropriate, of course, to make operations accountable for profitability in an organization that stresses sales and market share over quality and productivity. Misplaced accountability results in ineffective organizational control, to say nothing of hostility and conflict. Depending on the strategic role of operations, then, operations managers are accountable for different kinds of results. For example, in an organization using bureaucratic control, accountability will be spelled out in rules and regulations. In a decentralized system, it is likely to be understood and accepted by everyone.

LEADING THE WAY

Combining Technology and Artistry

For years, Canadian gymnast Natasha Chao performed the role of the Red Bird in *Mystère*, a Cirque du Soleil production permanently staged at Treasure Island Hotel and Casino in Las Vegas. According to the show's production notes, the character of the flightless Red Bird (who is male though the performer needn't be) "leaps ever higher in his futile attempts to take to the skies. Still convinced he can fly, he struggles against his fate." As choreographed, his fate consists of a 60-foot headfirst free fall into a hidden net. "One thing all ... Cirque artists share in common," says *Mystère* choreographer Debra Brown, "is a passion for doing art. Circus performers, who risk their lives, are the most passionate," she adds, and Chao is no exception. Working without an understudy, however, she couldn't afford to get hurt, and, passion for her art notwithstanding, she was understandably cautious in performing the stunt.

In addition to maintaining her impeccable timing and keen spatial awareness, the key for Chao was to curve her spine upright at the final moment before contact with the net. The tension in the net was continuously monitored by technicians working the

theater's motion-control system, and it should come as no surprise that all of an artist's skill, preparation, and caution can do little to prevent injury if he or she doesn't get the type of support for which armies of Cirque technicians are responsible every night. Executing a stunt like the plunge of the Red Bird, says another Cirque choreographer, Jacques Heim, "is extremely exciting, but it's ... exciting because it's terrifying." And that's why, he explains, every Cirque performance really consists of two shows: the one that the performers are putting on in front of the audience and the one that the technicians are performing behind the scenes.

Heim did the choreography for *KÀ*, an Egyptian-themed Cirque extravaganza in residence at the MGM Grand Hotel & Casino. *KÀ* was, at the time, both theatrically and technologically, the most ambitious production that Cirque du Soleil had ever mounted. "In *KÀ*," says technical director Matthew Whelan, "the machinery is so impressive that their movement becomes a [dance] number in itself.... The audience does see the lift movements"—the computer-controlled manipulation of the decks that comprise the mobile "stage"—"but there's also a

Ryan Miller/Getty Images

Cirque du Soleil relies on a combination of technology and artistry to create its amazing productions. Cirque technicians and choreographers are responsible for leading performers through their acts in ways that maximize visual impact while minimizing the risk of injury.

(continued)

LEADING THE WAY (Continued)

complete other show going on in the pit where the lifts move out of sight line to allow scenic pieces to move from level to level in a specific choreography to manage limited floor space." The interaction of technicians and performers is even more critical than in most Cirque productions because, as stage architect Mark Fisher puts it, the technologically managed scenery is "actually part of the landscape in which the performers live and move to create their show."

"There's a constant risk of artists falling," admits equipment designer Jaque Paquin, and Cirque du Soleil depends on its technology and the people who run it not only to enhance the performance of its artists but to protect them as well. Paquin, after all, is also responsible for the retractable safety net that's programmed into position beneath *KÀ*'s centerpiece scene—an aerial-acrobatics spectacle—by the theater's modular, multiuser NOMAD control system. Keith Wright, *KÀ*'s operations production manager, sees the technician's twofold responsibility as a basic reflection of Cirque du Soleil's mission: "Cirque du Soleil," he says, "is always about the artist and humanity, and the tools we use—no matter how advanced—must serve the human artists."

References: John Scott Lewinski, "Cirque du Soleil's Sophisticated *Kà* Evolves with New Tech," *Wired*, www.wired.com, accessed on January 2, 2014; Joe Hunkins, "Cirque du Soleil: Dramatic Technologies," *Technology Report*, http://technology-report.com, accessed on January 2, 2014; Victoria Looseleaf, "Cirque du Soleil's Magic," *Dance Magazine*, December 2007, www.dancemagazine.com, accessed on January 2, 2014; Gigi Berardi, "Circus+Dance= Cirque du Soleil," *Dance Magazine*, September 1, 2002, www.thefreelibrary.com, accessed on January 2, 2014; Stephanie Gooch, "Industrial-Scale Technology in Cirque du Soleil's *KÀ*," *Designfax*, www.thefreelibrary.com, accessed on January 2, 2014.

Within operations, managerial control ensures that resources and activities achieve primary goals such as a high percentage of on-time deliveries, low unit production cost, or high product reliability. Any control system should focus on the elements that are most crucial to goal attainment. For example, firms in which product quality is a major concern (as it is at Rolex) might adopt a screening control system to monitor the product as it is being created. If low-cost, large quantities are a higher priority (as is the case at Timex), a postaction system might be used to identify defects at the end of the system without disrupting the manufacturing process itself.

For the past several years, Boeing has been grappling with problems in launching its latest major passenger airplane, the Boeing 787 Dreamliner. During its early development, the 787 was hailed as the most commercially successful new plane of all time. Airlines around the world preordered over 900 of the planes at a cost of $178 million each before they ever took a test flight, based on its projected fuel efficiency, passenger comfort, low maintenance costs, flexibility, and other major design elements. Boeing subcontracted out the design and assembly of major components of the 787 to firms in Japan, Italy, South Carolina, and Kansas but did not impose adequate coordination across these various suppliers. As a result, subassemblies did not fit together properly, there were numerous quality and delivery issues, and myriad other problems occurred. Indeed, the first test flights for the plane were years late, largely because of supply chain issues; the first plane delivered to a U.S. airline was not completed until 2012. And the airplane continues to have manufacturing defects pop up periodically. Clearly, then, poor supply chain management can be disastrous, especially for major new products.[12]

purchasing management
Buying materials and resources needed to produce products and services

Purchasing Management

Purchasing management, also called *procurement*, is concerned with buying the materials and resources needed to produce products and services. In many ways, purchasing is at the very heart of effective supply chain management. Purchasing managers for a retailer like Walmart are responsible for buying the merchandise the stores will sell. The purchasing manager for a manufacturer buys raw materials, parts, and machines needed by the organization. Large companies such as Boeing, Nikon, and Siemens have large purchasing departments.[13] The manager responsible for purchasing must balance a number of constraints. Buying too much ties up capital and increases storage costs. Buying too little might lead to shortages and high reordering costs. The manager must also make sure that the quality of what is purchased meets the organization's needs, that the supplier is reliable, and that the best financial terms are negotiated.

Many firms have recently changed their approaches to purchasing as a means to lower costs and improve quality and productivity. In particular, rather than relying on hundreds or even thousands of suppliers, many companies are reducing their number of suppliers and negotiating special production delivery arrangements.[14] For example, the Honda plant in Marysville, Ohio, found a local business owner looking for a new opportunity. They negotiated an agreement whereby he would start a new company to mount car stereo speakers into plastic moldings. He delivers finished goods to the plant three times a day, and Honda buys all he can manufacture. Thus, he has a stable sales base, Honda has a local and reliable supplier, and both companies benefit.

Inventory Management

inventory control
Managing the organization's raw materials, work in process, finished goods, and products in transit

Inventory control, also called *materials control*, is essential for effective operations management. The four basic kinds of inventories are *raw materials, work in process, finished goods*, and *in-transit* inventories. As shown in Table 15.1, the sources of control over these inventories are as different as their purposes. Work-in-process inventories, for example, are made up of partially completed products that need further processing; they are controlled by the shop floor system. In contrast, the quantities and costs of finished-goods inventories are under the control of the overall production scheduling system, which is determined by high-level planning decisions. In-transit inventories are controlled by the transportation and distribution systems.

just-in-time (JIT) method
An inventory system that has necessary materials arriving as soon as they are needed (just in time) so that the production process is not interrupted

Like most other areas of operations management, inventory management changed notably in recent years. One particularly important breakthrough is the **just-in-time (JIT) method**. JIT is a recent breakthrough in inventory management. With JIT inventory

Table 15.1	Inventory Types, Purposes, and Sources of Control	
Type	**Purpose**	**Source of Control**
Raw materials	Provide the materials needed to make the product	Purchasing models and systems
Work in process	Enable overall production to be divided into stages of manageable size	Shop floor control systems
Finished goods	Provide ready supply of products on customer demand and enable long, efficient production runs	High-level production scheduling systems in conjunction with marketing
In transit (pipeline)	Distribute products to customers	Transportation and distribution control systems

© Cengage Learning

systems, materials arrive just as they are needed. JIT therefore helps an organization control its raw materials inventory by reducing the amount of space it must devote to storage.

First popularized by the Japanese, the JIT system reduces the organization's investment in storage space for raw materials and in the materials themselves. Historically, manufacturers built large storage areas and filled them with materials, parts, and supplies that would be needed days, weeks, and even months in the future. A manager using the JIT approach orders materials and parts more often and in smaller quantities, thereby reducing investment in both storage space and actual inventory. The ideal arrangement is for materials to arrive just as they are needed—or just in time.[15]

Recall our example about the small firm that assembles stereo speakers for Honda and delivers them three times a day, making it unnecessary for Honda to carry large quantities of the speakers in inventory. In an even more striking example, Johnson Controls makes automobile seats for Mercedes and ships them by small truckloads to a Mercedes plant 75 miles away. Each shipment is scheduled to arrive two hours before it is needed. Clearly, the JIT approach requires high levels of coordination and cooperation between the company and its suppliers. If shipments arrive too early, Mercedes has no place to store them. If they arrive too late, the entire assembly line may have to be shut down, resulting in enormous expense. When properly designed and used, the JIT method controls inventory very effectively.

MANAGING TOTAL QUALITY

Quality and productivity have become major determinants of business success or failure today and are central issues in managing organizations. But, as we will see, achieving higher levels of quality is not an easy accomplishment. Simply ordering that quality be improved is about as effective as waving a magic wand.[16] The catalyst for its emergence as a mainstream management concern was foreign business, especially Japanese. And nowhere was it more visible than in the auto industry. During the energy crisis in the late 1970s, many people bought Toyotas, Hondas, and Nissans because they were more fuel-efficient than U.S. cars. Consumers soon found, however, that not only were the Japanese cars more fuel-efficient, but they also were of higher quality than U.S. cars. Parts fit together better, the trim work was neater, and the cars were more reliable. Thus, after the energy crisis subsided, Japanese cars remained formidable competitors because of their reputation for quality.

The Meaning of Quality

quality
The totality of features and characteristics of a product or service that bear on its ability to satisfy stated or implied needs

The American Society for Quality defines **quality** as the totality of features and characteristics of a product or service that bear on its ability to satisfy stated or implied needs.[17] Quality has several different attributes. Table 15.2 lists eight basic dimensions that determine the quality of a particular product or service. For example, a product that has durability and is reliable is of higher quality than a product with less durability and reliability.

Quality is also relative. For example, a Lexus is a higher-grade car than a Toyota. The difference in quality stems from differences in design and other features. The Toyota, however, is still considered a high-quality car relative to its engineering specifications and price. Quality is relevant for both products and services. Although its importance for products like cars and computers was perhaps recognized first, service firms ranging from airlines to restaurants have also come to see that quality is a vitally important

These eight dimensions generally capture the meaning of quality, which is a critically important ingredient to organizational success today. Understanding the basic meaning of quality is a good first step to managing it more effectively.

Table 15.2	Eight Dimensions of Quality

1. *Performance*. A product's primary operating characteristic; examples are automobile acceleration and a television's picture clarity.

2. *Features*. Supplements to a product's basic functioning characteristics, such as power windows on a car.
3. *Reliability*. A probability of not malfunctioning during a specified period.
4. *Conformance*. The degree to which a product's design and operating characteristics meet established standards.
5. *Durability*. A measure of product life.
6. *Serviceability*. The speed and ease of repair.
7. *Aesthetics*. How a product looks, feels, tastes, and smells.
8. *Perceived quality*. As seen by a customer.

Source: Reprinted by permission of *Harvard Business Review*. Exhibit from "Competing on the Eight Dimensions of Quality," by David A. Garvin, November/December 1987. © 1987 by the Harvard Business School Publishing Corporation; all rights reserved.

determinant of their success or failure. Service quality, as we will discuss later in this chapter, has thus also become a major competitive issue in U.S. industry today.[18]

The Importance of Quality

malcolm Baldrige Award
Named after a former secretary of commerce, this prestigious award is given annually to firms that achieve major quality improvements

To help underscore the importance of quality, the U.S. government created the **Malcolm Baldrige Award**, named after the former secretary of commerce who championed quality in U.S. industry. The award, administered by an agency of the Commerce Department, is given annually to firms that achieve major improvements in the quality of their products or services. In other words, the award is based on changes in quality, as opposed to absolute quality. In addition, numerous other quality awards have been created. For example, the Rochester Institute of Technology and *USA Today* award their Quality Cup award not to entire organizations but to individual teams of workers within organizations. Quality is also an important concern for individual managers and organizations for three very specific reasons: competition, productivity, and costs.[19]

These eight dimensions generally capture the meaning of quality, which is a critically important ingredient to organizational success today. Understanding the basic meaning of quality is a good first step to managing it more effectively.

Competition   Quality has become one of the most competitive points in business today. Ford, BMW, General Motors, and Honda, for example, each implies that its cars and trucks are higher in quality than the cars and trucks of the others. And American, Delta, and United Airlines each claims that it provides the best and most reliable service. In the wake of the economic recession that started in 2008, many businesses focused even more attention on service quality as a competitive advantage during lean times. While some firms, for example, cut their staff at customer call centers, others did not. What impact might this have? One study found that cutting four representatives at a call center of three dozen people sent the number of customers put on hold for four minutes from 0 to 80. Firms with especially strong reputations for service quality include Amazon.com, USAA (an insurance firm), Lexus, Ritz-Carlton, Ace Hardware, and Apple.[20]

Productivity   Managers have also come to recognize that quality and productivity are related. In the past, many managers thought that they could increase output (productivity) only by decreasing quality. Managers today have learned the hard way that such an assumption is almost always wrong. If a firm installs a meaningful quality-enhancement program, three things are likely to result. First, the number of defects is likely to decrease, causing fewer returns from customers. Second, because the number of defects goes down, resources (materials and people) dedicated to reworking flawed output will be decreased. Third, because making employees responsible for quality reduces the need for quality inspectors, the organization is able to produce more units with fewer resources.

Costs   Improved quality also lowers costs. Poor quality results in higher returns from customers, high warranty costs, and lawsuits from customers injured by faulty products. Future sales are lost because of disgruntled customers. An organization with quality problems often has to increase inspection expenses just to catch defective products. We noted in Chapter 14, for example, how at one point Whistler Corporation was using 40 percent of its workforce just to fix poorly assembled radar detectors made by the other 60 percent.[21]

Total Quality Management

Once an organization makes a decision to enhance the quality of its products and services, it must then decide how to implement this decision. The most pervasive approach to managing quality has been called **total quality management (TQM)** (sometimes called **quality assurance**)—a real and meaningful effort by an organization to change its whole approach to business in order to make quality a guiding factor in everything it does.[22] Figure 15.3 highlights the major ingredients in TQM.

Strategic Commitment   The starting point for TQM is a strategic commitment by top management. Such commitment is important for several reasons. First, the organizational culture must change to recognize that quality is not just an ideal but also an objective goal that must be pursued.[23] Second, a decision to pursue the goal of quality carries with it some real costs—for expenditures such as new equipment and facilities. Thus, without a commitment from top management, quality improvement will prove to be just a slogan or gimmick, with little or no real change. Just a few years ago, Porsche

total quality management (TQM) (quality assurance)
A strategic commitment by top management to change its whole approach to business in order to make quality a guiding factor in everything it does

© Cengage Learning

FIGURE 15.3

Total Quality Management

Quality is one of the most important issues facing organizations today. TQM is a comprehensive effort to enhance an organization's product or service quality. TQM involves the five basic dimensions shown here. Each is important and must be addressed effectively if the organization expects to truly increase quality.

had the lowest reliability of any automobile maker in the world. But a major commitment from top management helped turn the company around. By paying more attention to consumer preferences and using the other methods described later in this section, Porsche shot to the top of global automobile reliability.[24]

Employee Involvement   Employee involvement is another critical ingredient in TQM. Virtually all successful quality-enhancement programs involve making the person responsible for doing the job responsible for making sure it is done right.[25] By definition, then, employee involvement is a critical component in improving quality. Work teams, discussed in Chapter 13, are common vehicles for increasing employee involvement.

Technology   New forms of technology are also useful in TQM programs. Automation and robots, for example, can often make products with higher precision and better consistency than people. Investing in higher-grade machines capable of doing jobs more precisely and reliably often improves quality. For example, Samsung has achieved notable improvements in product quality by replacing many of its machines with new equipment. Similarly, most U.S. auto and electronics firms make regular investments in new technology to help boost quality.

Materials   Another important part of TQM is improving the quality of the materials that organizations use. Suppose that a company that assembles stereos buys chips and circuits from another company. If the chips have a high failure rate, consumers will return defective stereos to the company whose nameplate appears on them, not to the company that made the chips. The stereo firm then loses in two ways: refunds to customers and a damaged reputation. As a result, many firms have increased the quality requirements they impose on their suppliers as a way of improving the quality of their own products.

Methods   Improved methods can improve product and service quality. Methods are operating systems used by the organization during the actual transformation process. American Express Company, for example, has found ways to cut its approval time for new credit cards from 22 to just 2 days. This results in improved service quality.

TQM Tools and Techniques

Beyond the strategic context of quality, managers can also rely on several specific tools and techniques for improving quality. Among the most popular today are value-added analysis, benchmarking, outsourcing, reducing cycle times, ISO 9000:2000 and ISO 14000, statistical quality control (SQC), and Six Sigma.

Value-Added Analysis   **Value-added analysis** is the comprehensive evaluation of all work activities, materials flows, and paperwork to determine the value that they add for customers. Such an analysis often reveals wasteful or unnecessary activities that can be eliminated without jeopardizing customer service. For example, during a value-added analysis, Hewlett-Packard determined that its contracts were unnecessarily long, confusing, and hard to understand. The firm subsequently cut its standard contract form down from 20 to 2 pages and experienced an 18 percent increase in its computer sales.

Benchmarking   **Benchmarking** is the process of learning how other firms do things in an exceptionally high-quality manner. Some approaches to benchmarking are simple and straightforward. For example, Canon routinely buys copiers made by other firms and takes them apart to see how they work. This enables the firm to stay abreast of improvements and changes its competitors are using. When Ford was planning the newest version of the Focus, it identified the 400 features that customers identified as

value-added analysis
The comprehensive evaluation of all work activities, materials flows, and paperwork to determine the value that they add for customers

benchmarking
The process of learning how other firms do things in an exceptionally high-quality manner

being most important to them. It then found the competing cars that did the best job on each feature. Ford's goal was to equal or surpass each of its competitors on those 400 features. Other benchmarking strategies are more indirect. For example, many firms study how Amazon manages its online retail business, how Disney recruits and trains employees, and how FedEx tracks packages for applications they can employ in their own businesses.[26]

outsourcing

Subcontracting services and operations to other firms that can perform them cheaper or better

Outsourcing   Another innovation for improving quality is **outsourcing**, which is the process of subcontracting services and operations to other firms that can perform them cheaper or better. If a business performs each and every one of its own administrative and business services and operations, it is almost certain to be doing at least some of them in an inefficient or low-quality manner. If those areas can be identified and outsourced, the firm will save money and realize a higher-quality service or operation.[27] For example, until recently, Eastman Kodak handled all its own computing operations. Now, however, those operations are subcontracted to IBM, which handles all Kodak's computing. The result is higher-quality computing systems and operations at Kodak for less money than it was spending before. Firms must be careful in their outsourcing decisions, though, because service or delivery problems can lead to major complications. As noted earlier, Boeing's new 787 aircraft is years behind schedule because the firms to which Boeing outsourced some of its production were not adequately coordinated.

cycle time

The time needed by the organization to develop, make, and distribute products or services

Reducing Cycle Time   Another popular TQM technique is reducing cycle time. **Cycle time** is the time needed by the organization to develop, make, and distribute products or services.[28] If a business can reduce its cycle time, quality will often improve. A good illustration of the power of cycle time reduction comes from GE. At one point, the firm needed six plants and three weeks to produce and deliver custom-made industrial circuit breaker boxes. By analyzing and reducing cycle time, the same product can now be delivered in three days, and only a single plant is involved. Table 15.3 identifies a number of basic suggestions that have helped companies reduce the cycle time of their operations. For example, GE found it better to start from scratch with a remodeled plant. GE also wiped out the need for approvals by eliminating most managerial positions and set up teams as a basis for organizing work. Stressing the importance of the schedule helped Motorola build a new plant and start the production of a new product in just 18 months. Nokia used to need 12 to 18 months to design new cell phone models, but can do it now in 6 months.[29]

Many organizations today are using speed for competitive advantage. Listed in the table are six common guidelines that organizations follow when they want to shorten the time they need to get things accomplished. Although not every manager can do each of these things, most managers can do at least some of them.

Table 15.3	Guidelines for Increasing the Speed of Operations

1. *Start from scratch.* It is usually easier than trying to do what the organization does now faster.
2. *Minimize the number of approvals needed to do something.* The fewer people who have to approve something, the faster approval will get done.
3. *Use work teams as a basis for organization.* Teamwork and cooperation work better than individual effort and conflict.
4. *Develop and adhere to a schedule.* A properly designed schedule can greatly increase speed.
5. *Do not ignore distribution.* Making something faster is only part of the battle.
6. *Integrate speed into the organization's culture.* If everyone understands the importance of speed, things will naturally get done more quickly.

Source: From *Fortune*, February 13, 1989. © 1989 Time, Inc. All rights reserved.

ISO 9000:2000
A set of quality standards created by the International Organization for Standardization and revised in 2000

ISO 14000
A set of standards for environmental performance

SQC
A set of specific statistical techniques that can be used to monitor quality; includes acceptance sampling and in-process sampling

ISO 9000:2000 and ISO 14000   Still another useful technique for improving quality is ISO 9000. ISO 9000:2000 refers to a set of quality standards created by the International Organization for Standardization; the standards were revised and updated in 2000. These standards cover areas such as product testing, employee training, recordkeeping, supplier relations, and repair policies and procedures. Firms that want to meet these standards apply for certification and are audited by a firm chosen by the organization's domestic affiliate (in the United States, this is the American National Standards Institute, or ANSI). These auditors review every aspect of the firm's business operations in relation to the standards. Many firms report that merely preparing for an ISO 9000 audit has been helpful. Many firms today, including GE, DuPont, British Telecom, and Philips Electronics, are urging—or in some cases requiring—that their suppliers achieve ISO 9000 certification.[30] All told, more than 159 countries have adopted ISO 9000 as a national standard, and more than 610,000 certificates of compliance have been issued. ISO 14000 is an extension of the same concept to environmental performance. Specifically, ISO 14000 requires that firms document how they are using raw materials more efficiently, managing pollution, and reducing their impact on the environment.

Many organizations today are using speed for competitive advantage. Listed in Table 15.3 are six common guidelines that organizations follow when they want to shorten the time in which they must get things accomplished. Although not every manager can do each of these things, most managers can do at least some of them.

Statistical Quality Control   Another quality control technique is SQC. As the term suggests, SQC is concerned primarily with managing quality.[31] Moreover, it is a set of specific statistical techniques that can be used to monitor quality. *Acceptance sampling* involves sampling finished goods to ensure that quality standards have been met. Acceptance sampling is effective only when the correct percentage of products that should be tested (for example, 2, 5, or 25 percent) is determined. This decision is especially important when the test renders the product useless. Batteries, wine, and collapsible steering wheels, for example, are consumed or destroyed during testing. Another SQC method is *in-process sampling*, which involves evaluating products during production so that needed changes can be made. The painting department of a furniture company might periodically check the tint of the paint it is using. The company can then adjust the color as necessary to conform to customer standards. The advantage of in-process sampling is that it allows problems to be detected before they accumulate.

Six Sigma   Six Sigma was developed in the 1980s for Motorola. The tool can be used by manufacturing or service organizations. The Six Sigma method tries to eliminate mistakes. Although firms rarely obtain Six Sigma quality, it does provide a challenging target. *Sigma* refers to a standard deviation, so a Six Sigma defect rate is six standard deviations above the mean rate; one sigma quality would produce 690,000 errors per million items. Obtaining three sigmas is a bit more challenging—66,000 errors per million. Six Sigma is obtained when a firm produces a mere 3.4 mistakes per million. Implementing Six Sigma requires making corrections until errors virtually disappear. At GE, the technique has saved the firm $8 billion in three years. GE is now teaching its customers, including Walmart and Dell, about the approach.

MANAGING PRODUCTIVITY

Although the current focus on quality by U.S. companies is a relatively recent phenomenon, managers have been aware of the importance of productivity for several years. The stimulus for this attention was a recognition that the gap between productivity in the

United States and productivity in other industrialized countries was narrowing. This section describes the meaning of productivity and underscores its importance. After summarizing recent productivity trends, we suggest ways that organizations can increase their productivity.

The Meaning of Productivity

productivity
An economic measure of efficiency that summarizes what is produced relative to resources used to produce it

In a general sense, **productivity** is an economic measure of efficiency that summarizes the value of outputs relative to the value of the inputs used to create them.[32] Productivity can be and often is assessed at different levels of analysis and in different forms.

Levels of Productivity   By *level of productivity*, we mean the units of analysis used to calculate or define productivity. For example, *aggregate productivity* is the total level of productivity achieved by a country. *Industry productivity* is the total productivity achieved by all the firms in a particular industry. *Company productivity*, just as the term suggests, is the level of productivity achieved by an individual company. *Unit and individual productivity* refer to the productivity achieved by a unit or department within an organization and the level of productivity attained by a single person.

Forms of Productivity   There are many different forms of productivity. *Total factor productivity* is defined by the following formula:

$$\text{Productivity} = \frac{\text{Outputs}}{\text{Inputs}}$$

Total factor productivity is an overall indicator of how well an organization uses all of its resources, such as labor, capital, materials, and energy, to create all of its products and services. The biggest problem with total factor productivity is that all the ingredients must be expressed in the same terms—dollars (it is difficult to add hours of labor to number of units of a raw material in a meaningful way). Total factor productivity also gives little insight into how things can be changed to improve productivity. Consequently, most organizations find it more useful to calculate a partial productivity ratio. Such a ratio uses only one category of resource. For example, labor productivity could be calculated by this simple formula:

$$\text{Labor productivity} = \frac{\text{Outputs}}{\text{Direct Labor}}$$

This method has two advantages. First, it is not necessary to transform the units of input into some other unit. Second, this method provides managers with specific insights into how changing different resource inputs affects productivity. Suppose that an organization can manufacture 200 units of a particular product with 40 hours of direct labor. The organization's labor productivity index is 200/40, or 5 (5 units per labor hour). Now suppose that worker efficiency is increased (through one of the ways discussed later in this chapter) so that the same 40 hours of labor result in the manufacture of 240 units of the product. The labor productivity index increases to 240/40, or 6 (6 units per labor hour), and the firm can see the direct results of a specific managerial action.

The Importance of Productivity

Managers consider it important that their firm maintains high levels of productivity for a variety of reasons. Firm productivity is a primary determinant of an organization's level of profitability and, ultimately, of its ability to survive. If one organization is more productive than another, it will have more products to sell at lower prices and have more profits to reinvest in other areas. Productivity also partially determines people's standard of living within a particular country. At an economic level, businesses consume resources and produce goods and services. The goods and services created within a country can be used by that country's own citizens or exported for sale in other countries. The more goods and services the businesses within a country can produce, the more goods and services the country's citizens will have. Even goods that are exported result in financial resources flowing back into the home country. Thus, the citizens of a highly productive country are likely to have a notably higher standard of living than the citizens of a country with low productivity.

Productivity Trends

The United States has one of the highest levels of productivity in the world. Sparked by gains made in other countries, however, U.S. business has begun to focus more attention on productivity.[33] Indeed, this was a primary factor in the decisions made by U.S. businesses to retrench, retool, and become more competitive in the world marketplace. For example, GE's dishwasher plant in Louisville cut its inventory requirements by 50 percent, reduced labor costs from 15 percent to only 10 percent of total manufacturing costs, and cut product development time in half. As a result of these kinds of efforts, productivity trends have now leveled out, and U.S. workers are generally maintaining their lead in most industries.[34]

One important factor that has hurt U.S. productivity indices has been the tremendous growth of the service sector in the United States. Although this sector grew, its productivity levels did not. One part of this problem relates to measurement. For example, it is fairly easy to calculate the number of tons of steel produced at a steel mill and divide it by the number of labor hours used; it is more difficult to determine the output of an

Jim West/Newscom

Quality and productivity are critical ingredients to success in the global automobile industry. Ford Motor Company struggled for years with low productivity and a poor reputation for quality. But over the last several years, Ford leaders have sharpened the firm's focus on both quality and productivity and, as a result, Ford's market share, revenues, and profits have been consistently growing.

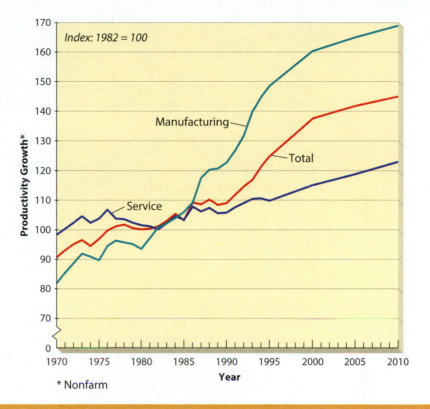

Index: 1982 = 100

FIGURE 15.4

Manufacturing and Service Productivity Growth Trends

Both manufacturing productivity and service productivity in the United States continue to grow, although manufacturing productivity is growing at a faster pace. Total productivity, therefore, also continues to grow.

Source: U.S. Bureau of Labor Statistics.

attorney or a certified public accountant. Still, virtually everyone agrees that improving service sector productivity is the next major hurdle facing U.S. business.[35]

Figure 15.4 illustrates manufacturing productivity growth since 1970 in terms of annual average percentage of increase. As you can see, that growth slowed during the 1970s but began to rise again in the late 1980s. Some experts believe that productivity in both the United States and abroad will continue to improve at even more impressive rates. Their confidence rests on technology's potential ability to improve operations.

Improving Productivity

How does a business or industry improve its productivity? Numerous specific suggestions made by experts generally fall into two broad categories: improving operations and increasing employee involvement.

Improving Operations   One way that firms can improve operations is by spending more on research and development (R&D). R&D spending helps identify new products, new uses for existing products, and new methods for making products. Each of these contributes to productivity. For example, Bausch & Lomb almost missed the boat on extended-wear contact lenses because the company had neglected R&D. When it became apparent that its major competitors were almost a year ahead of Bausch & Lomb in developing the new lenses, management made R&D a top-priority concern. As a result, the company made several scientific breakthroughs, shortened the time needed to introduce new products, and greatly enhanced both total sales and profits—and all with a smaller workforce than the company used to employ. Even though other countries are greatly increasing their R&D spending, the United States continues to be the world leader in this area.

Another way that firms can boost productivity through operations is by reassessing and revamping their transformation facilities. We noted earlier how one of GE's modernized plants does a better job than six antiquated ones. Just building a new factory is no guarantee of success, but Ford, Caterpillar, Whirlpool, and many other businesses have achieved dramatic productivity gains by revamping their production facilities. Facilities refinements are not limited to manufacturers. Most McDonald's restaurants now have drive-through windows, and many have moved soft-drink dispensers out to the restaurant floor so that customers can get their own drinks. Each of these moves is an attempt to increase the speed with which customers can be served, and thus to increase productivity.

Increasing Employee Involvement   The other major thrust in productivity enhancement has been toward employee involvement. We noted earlier that participation can enhance quality. So, too, can it boost productivity. Examples of this involvement are an individual worker being given a bigger voice in how she does her job, a formal agreement of cooperation between management and labor, and total involvement throughout the organization. GE eliminated most of the supervisors at its one new circuit breaker plant and put control in the hands of workers.

Another method popular in the United States is increasing the flexibility of an organization's workforce by training employees to perform a number of different jobs. Such cross-training allows the firm to function with fewer workers because workers can be transferred easily to areas where they are most needed. For example, at one Motorola plant, 397 of 400 employees have learned at least two skills under a cross-training program.

Rewards are essential to making employee involvement work. Firms must reward people for learning new skills and using them proficiently. At Motorola, for example, workers who master a new skill are assigned for five days to a job requiring them to use that skill. If they perform with no defects, they are moved to a higher pay grade, and then they move back and forth between jobs as they are needed. If there is a performance problem, they receive more training and practice. This approach is fairly new, but preliminary indicators suggest that it can increase productivity significantly. Many unions resist such programs because they threaten job security and reduce a person's identification with one skill or craft.

SUMMARY OF LEARNING OUTCOMES AND KEY POINTS

1. Describe and explain the nature of operations management.

   - Operations management is the set of managerial activities that organizations use in creating their products and services.
   - Operations management is important to both manufacturing and service organizations.

   - Operations management plays an important role in an organization's strategy.

2. Identify and discuss the components involved in designing effective operations systems.

   - The starting point in using operations management is designing appropriate operations systems.

- Key decisions that must be made as part of operations systems design relate to the product–service mix, capacity, and facilities.

3. Discuss organizational technologies and their role in operations management.

   - Technology also plays an important role in quality.
   - Automation is especially important today.
   - Numerous CAM techniques are widely practiced.
   - Robotics is also a growing area.
   - Technology is as relevant to service organizations as it is to manufacturing organizations.

4. Identify and discuss the components involved in implementing operations systems through supply chain management.

   - After an operations system has been designed and put in place, it must then be implemented.
   - Major areas of interest during the use of operations systems are purchasing and inventory management.

- Supply chain management is a comprehensive view of managing all these activities in a more efficient manner.

5. Explain the meaning and importance of managing quality and TQM.

   - Quality is a major consideration for all managers today.
   - Quality is important because it affects competition, productivity, and costs.
   - TQM is a comprehensive, organization-wide effort to enhance quality through a variety of avenues.

6. Explain the meaning and importance of managing productivity, productivity trends, and ways to improve productivity.

   - Productivity is also a major concern to managers.
   - Productivity is a measure of how efficiently an organization is using its resources to create products or services.
   - The United States is a world leader in individual productivity, but firms still work to achieve productivity gains.

DISCUSSION QUESTIONS

Questions for Review

1. What is the relationship of operations management to overall organizational strategy? Where do productivity and quality fit into that relationship?
2. Describe three basic decisions that must be addressed in the design of operations systems. For each decision, what information do managers need to make that decision?
3. What are some approaches to facilities layout? How do they differ from one another? How are they similar?
4. What is TQM? What are the major characteristics of TQM?
5. What is productivity? Identify various levels and forms of productivity.

Questions for Analysis

1. Is operations management linked most closely to corporate-level, business-level, or functional strategies? Why or in what way?

2. "Automation is bad for the economy because machines will eventually replace almost all human workers, creating high unemployment and poverty." Do you agree or disagree? Explain your answer.
3. Some quality gurus claim that high-quality products or services are those that are error free. Others claim that high quality exists when customers' needs are satisfied. Still others claim that high-quality products or services must be innovative. Do you subscribe to one of these views? If not, how would you define quality? Explain how the choice of a quality definition affects managers' behavior.
4. How can a service organization use techniques from operations management? Give specific examples from your college or university (or another provider of educational services).
5. Think of a firm that, in your opinion, provides a high-quality service or product. What attributes of the product or service give you the perception of high quality? Do you think that everyone would agree with your judgment? Why or why not?

BUILDING EFFECTIVE COMMUNICATION SKILLS

Exercise Overview

Communication skills refer to the ability not only to convey information and ideas to others but also to handle information and ideas received from them. This exercise shows how you can use your communication skills in addressing issues of quality.

Exercise Background

You're the customer service manager of a large auto parts distributor. The general manager of a large auto dealer, one of your best customers, has sent the following letter, and it's your job to write a letter in response.

Dear Customer Service Manager:

On the first of last month, ABC Autos submitted a purchase order to your firm. Attached to this letter is a copy of the order. Unfortunately, the parts shipment that we received from you did not contain every item on the order. Further, that fact was not noted on the packing slip that accompanied your shipment, and ABC was charged for the full amount of the order. To resolve the problem, please send the missing items immediately. If you are unable to do so by the end of the week, please cancel the remaining items and refund the overpayment. In the future, if you ship a partial order, please notify us at that time and do not bill for items not shipped.

I look forward to your reply and a resolution to my problem.

Sincerely,
A. N. Owner, ABC Autos
Attachment: Purchase Order 00001

Exercise Task

1. Write an answer to the customer's letter that assumes that you now have the parts available.
2. How would your answer differ if ABC Autos were not a valued customer?
3. How would your answer differ if you found out that the parts were in the original shipment but had been stolen by one of your delivery personnel?
4. How would your answer differ if you found out that the owner of ABC Autos made a mistake and that the order had been filled correctly?
5. Now review your answers to the previous questions. What are the important components of an effective response to a customer's quality complaint (setting the tone, expressing an apology, suggesting a solution, and so on)? How did you use these components in your various responses?

BUILDING EFFECTIVE DIAGNOSTIC SKILLS

Exercise Overview

As we noted in this chapter, the quality of a product or service is relative to price and customer expectations. This exercise is designed to show that a manager's diagnostic skills—his or her ability to visualize the most appropriate response to a situation—can be useful in positioning a product's quality relative to price and customer expectations.

Exercise Background

Think of a recent occasion when you purchased a tangible product—say, clothing, electronic equipment, luggage, or professional supplies—which you subsequently came to feel was of especially high quality. Now think of another product that you regarded as being of appropriate or adequate quality,

and then a third product that you judged to be of low or poor quality. (You should now have three separate products in mind.) Next, recall three parallel experiences involving purchases of services. Examples might include an airline, train, or bus trip; a restaurant meal; a haircut; or an oil change for your car. (Again, you should have three examples in total.)

Finally, recall three experiences involving both products and services. Perhaps you got some information about a product that you were buying or you returned a defective or broken product for a refund or warranty repair. Were there any instances in which there was an apparent disparity between product and service quality? Did a poor-quality product, for instance, receive surprisingly good service or a high-quality product receive mediocre service?

Exercise Task

Review your list of nine purchase experiences and then do the following:

1. Assess the extent to which the quality that you associated with each was a function of price and your expectations.

2. Could the quality of each product or service be improved without greatly affecting its price? If so, how?

3. Can high-quality customer service offset adequate or even poor product quality? Can outstanding product quality offset adequate or even poor customer service?

SKILLS SELF-ASSESSMENT INSTRUMENT

Defining Quality and Productivity

Introduction: *Quality* is a complex term whose meaning has no doubt changed over time. The following assessment surveys your ideas about and approaches to quality.

Instructions: You will agree with some of the statements and disagree with others. In some cases, making a decision may be difficult, but you should force yourself to make a choice. Record your answers next to each statement according to the following rating scale:

Rating Scale

4 Strongly agree
3 Slightly agree
2 Somewhat disagree
1 Strongly disagree

_____ 1. Quality refers to a product's or service's ability to fulfill its primary operating characteristics, such as providing a sharp picture for a television set.

_____ 2. Quality is an absolute, measurable aspect of a product or service.

_____ 3. The concept of quality includes supplemental aspects of a product or service, such as the remote control for a television set.

_____ 4. Productivity and quality are inversely related, so that to get one, you must sacrifice the other.

_____ 5. The concept of quality refers to the extent to which a product's design and operating characteristics conform to certain set standards.

_____ 6. Productivity refers to what is created relative to what it takes to create it.

_____ 7. Quality means that a product will not malfunction during a specified period of time.

_____ 8. Quality refers only to products; it is immeasurable for services.

_____ 9. The length of time that a product or service will function is what is known as quality.

_____ 10. Everyone uses exactly the same definition of quality.

_____ 11. Quality refers to the repair ease and speed of a product or service.

_____ 12. Being treated courteously has nothing to do with the quality of anything.

_____ 13. How a product looks, feels, tastes, or smells is what is meant by quality.

_____ 14. Price, not quality, is what determines the ultimate value of service.

_____ 15. Quality refers to what customers think of a product or service.

_____ 16. Productivity and quality cannot both increase at the same time.

Source: Adapted from Chapter 21, especially pp. 473–474, in David D. Van Fleet and Tim O. Peterson, *Contemporary Management*, 3rd Edition. © 1994 by Houghton Mifflin Company.

EXPERIENTIAL EXERCISE

Preparing the Fishbone Chart

Purpose: The fishbone chart is an excellent procedure for identifying possible causes of a problem. It provides you with knowledge that you can use to improve the operations of any organization. This skill exercise focuses on the *administrative management model*. It helps you develop the *monitor role* of the administrative management model. One of the skills of the monitor is the ability to analyze problems.

Introduction: Kaoru Ishikawa developed this technique in the 1960s, and it is now considered to be one of the fundamental tools of quality management.

Quality circles often use the fishbone "cause-and-effect" graphical technique to initiate the resolution of a group work problem. Quite often the causes are clustered in categories such as materials, methods, people, and machines. The fishbone technique is usually accomplished in the following six steps:

1. Write the problem in the "head" of the fish (the large block).

2. Brainstorm the major causes of the problem, and list them on the fish "bones."
3. Analyze each main cause and write in minor subcauses on bone subbranches.
4. Reach consensus on one or two of the major causes of the problem.
5. Explore ways to correct or remove the major causes.
6. Prepare a report or presentation explaining the proposed change.
7. Your fishbone will look something like this:

Source: Adapted from Gene R. Bruton, *Exercises in Management*, 5th Edition, 1996. © 1996. Houghton Mifflin Company.

MANAGEMENT AT WORK

Amazon Rekindles Its Flair for Technology

As you probably know, selling things online—online retailing or *e-tailing*—is the only thing that Amazon.com does. Unlike such online rivals as, say, Barnes&Noble.com or Walmart.com, Amazon has no roof over its head—no bricks-and-mortar presence to anchor its online presence. The seller and its customers interact by website, e-mail, or phone. Behind the website, however, is one of the largest direct-to-consumer distribution operations in the world.

Founded in 1995 as a bookseller, Amazon does pretty well these days—$32.9 billion in sales for 2012—but it's had its ups and downs. Early investors believed that the promise of online business outweighed the risks associated with the new type of enterprise, but it wasn't long before giddy expectation gave way to more sober assessment, as soaring costs kept pace with expanding sales and wiped out profits. That's when Amazon diversified its range of product offerings, adding toys, music, electronics and software, and household goods. Expansion continued to eat into profits, and the company had to make huge investments in infrastructure and IT before it finally went into the black in 2002.

Though fairly commonplace among today's online enterprises, Amazon's business model was revolutionary for its time. There was no need to open stores in high-rent shopping areas, and the company was free to choose locations for distribution centers based on cost and convenience to transportation facilities. Amazon's seven distribution centers stock thousands of popular items, but many of the goods that end consumers buy through Amazon are in fact "drop shipped" directly from manufacturers. Amazon, therefore, can offer a multitude of products without incurring high inventory expenses, and because the middleman has been eliminated, delivery times are faster.

In addition, much of the work at Amazon facilities is automated. Workers use simple, menu-driven computer programs to access and monitor customer orders. Goods are then picked from the shelves and placed in a vast system of automated chutes and bins that bundles them appropriately. At one point, Amazon had tried to minimize shipping costs by bundling all items for shipment to a single address into one package. Now, however, the system relies on a more effective sorting algorithm that calculates optimal package size, both to protect items and to reduce costs. Automated scanners track the progress of every order, and automated boxers and labelers prepare goods for shipping.

Software, of course, is an important part of Amazon's operations because better systems hold down labor costs, increase accuracy and speed, enhance the customer experience, and support effective planning. Supply-chain software, for example, uses a complex formula to choose which goods should be carried in distribution centers and which should be drop shipped. Yet another algorithm constantly recalculates item popularity ratings to choose which goods to store in the most highly frequented sections of warehouses.

Amazon is also a pioneer in the development of several operations technologies:

- "One-click" buying allows customers to make final purchases with a single mouse click. (The process is patented and licensed to other companies.)
- Amazon was one of the first online retailers to let customers post online product reviews, which not only boost sales but also contribute to a sense of community among users.
- Customers can review their order histories, create wish and favorites lists, share information with friends, receive personalized recommendations and gift-giving reminders, and tag items with customized category data.

Amazon's operations software is so popular with other firms that the company has launched a feature called Amazon Web Services, which allows independent programmers and merchants to access Amazon's library of software and adapt it for their own use. The library is free unless the "borrower" intends to sell through Amazon, in which case there's a 15 percent commission on each sale. The service has proven so popular that 30 percent of Amazon's sales are now conducted by other merchants. In February 2009, as part of Amazon Web Services, Amazon launched Amazon SimpleDB, a system that allows businesses to store and quickly retrieve simple data. Some companies already rely on Amazon's expertise to manage their websites. Target and Office Depot, for instance, contract their online presence to Amazon.

And now—for consumers—there's Kindle, which, ironically, hearkens back to Amazon's origins as a bookseller. Developed by an Amazon subsidiary called Lab126, Kindle is a software–hardware platform for reading electronic print material. The first-generation Kindle device came out at the very end of 2007 and was aimed primarily at readers of books, which Amazon founder and CEO Jeff Bezos promptly labeled "the last bastion of analog…. The vision [of Kindle]," he hastened to add, "is that you should be able to get any book—not just any book in print, but any book that's *ever* been in print—on this device in less than a minute."

Amazon now has 1,300,000 titles available for download, but Kindle is designed to handle much more than books. With this device, which doesn't require a computer, Amazon allows you not only to download 630,000 books, but even to subscribe to newspapers and magazines, which will automatically be downloaded as soon as new issues go to press. You can search for material through Google, follow links from blogs and other web pages, jot down notes on the page you're reading, and even capture selected passages with the equivalent of an electric highlighter. Kindle 2 and Kindle DX, each with larger displays and other new and improved features, arrived in early 2009. Newer versions have been released periodically since then, and there's also a Kindle app for the iPhone and iPad.

Eight months after its release, Amazon had sold nearly $100 million worth of Kindles, and by the end of the year, amid speculation that it was the iPod of the book world, the Kindle had sold double its projected sales figure (and equaled sales of the iPod in its first year of release). Amazon does not disclose sales of Kindle and Kindle-related content, but reports indicate that it sold 8 million Kindles in 2010—a staggering 60 percent over analysts' predictions. In July 2010, the company did announce that it was selling 180 Kindles for every 100 hardback books, and in January 2011, it announced that Kindle sales had overtaken paperback sales as well, with U.S. customers buying 115 Kindles for every 100 paperback books.

Case Questions

1. Describe Amazon's *product–service mix*. Which areas of Amazon's operations are characteristic of a *manufacturing* organization? Which areas are characteristic of a *service organization*? How do both areas relate to the marketing of Kindle and Kindle-related products?

2. Describe the role of *technology* in both Amazon's manufacturing and service operations.

3. Discuss the nature of Amazon's *supply chain* in terms of *control, purchasing management*, and *inventory management*. At what points in the supply chain does Amazon outsource or contract activities to outside parties? How does Amazon's *supply chain management* affect its revenues and costs?

4. Log on to Amazon.com and select an item that comes from Amazon itself rather than from a drop shipper. What kinds of *purchasing* decisions were necessary to make this product available at Amazon's price? What kinds of *inventory-control* decisions were necessary?

5. What facets of Amazon's operations allow it to create and control *quality*, both as a manufacturing organization and as a service organization? What facets of its operations allow Amazon to control *productivity* (again, both as a manufacturing organization and as a service organization)? Give two or three examples of ways in which Amazon's operations contribute to high productivity.

Case References

Mark Brohan, "Amazon Sales and Profits Boom in 2010," *Internet Retailer*, www.internetretailer.com, accessed on January 2, 2014; Robert Hof, "Amazon's Brighter Horizon?" *BusinessWeek*, April 26, 2006, www.businessweek.com, accessed on January 2, 2014; Jeff Cogswell, "Amazon Simple DB a Solid Choice for Simple Web-Based Data Storage," *eweek*, www.eweek.com, accessed on January 2, 2014; Steven Levy, "The Future of Reading," *Newsweek*, November 26, 2007, www.newsweek.com, accessed on January 2, 2014; Amy Martinez, "Amazon Says Kindle Sales Top Its 'Most Optimistic' Projections," *Seattle Times*, April 17, 2009, http://seattletimes.com/html/home/index.html, accessed on January 2, 2014; Joseph Galante and Peter Burrows, "Amazon.com Kindle Sales Are Said to Exceed Estimates," *Bloomberg*, August 17, 2012, www.bloomberg.com, accessed on January 2, 2014; and Claire Cain Miller, "E-Books Top Hardcovers at Amazon," *New York Times*, July 19, 2010, www.nytimes.com, accessed on January 2, 2014.

You Make the Call

Orchestrating Outcomes

1. Explain the "Orpheus Process" as a system of *operations management*. In what ways is it important to the orchestra's productivity, competitiveness, and overall organizational performance?

2. How would you explain "quality" in an orchestral performance? In what ways are the *eight dimensions of quality* in Table 15.2 useful in explaining the quality of a concert? In what ways are they not useful (or at least difficult to apply)?

3. Discuss the *importance of quality* in Orpheus's operations in terms of *competition, productivity*, and *costs*.

4. In what ways does the "Orpheus Process" reflect the basic elements of *total quality management*, particularly *strategic commitment, employee involvement*, and *methods*?

ENDNOTES

[1] Vivien Schweitzer, "Players with No Conductor and, Increasingly, with No Fear," *New York Times*, May 7, 2007, www.nytimes.com, accessed on January 2, 2014; Jennifer Higgs, "Orpheus Chamber Orchestra Embodies Democratic Principles," *Axiom News*, http://axiomnews.com/orpheus-chamber-orchestra-embodies-democratic-principles, accessed on January 2, 2014; Amanda Gordon, "Self-Governing Orpheus Chamber Orchestra Has Broader Lessons to Offer, Says Banking and Civic Leader John Whitehead," *New York Sun*, www.nysun.com, accessed on January 2, 2014; Harvey Seifter, "The Conductor-Less Orchestra," *Leader to Leader Journal*, No. 21 (Summer 2001), www.pfdf.org, accessed on January 2, 2014; and J. Richard Hackman, *Leading Teams: Setting the Stage for Great Performances* (Cambridge, MA: Harvard Business School Press, 2002), http://books.google.com, accessed on January 2, 2014.

[2] Paul M. Swamidass, "Empirical Science: New Frontier in Operations Management Research," *Academy of Management Review*, October 1991, Vol. 16, No. 4, pp. 793–814.

[3] See "Made in the U.S.A.," *Time*, April 22, 2013, pp. 22–29.

[4] Office of Services, International Trade Administration, http://ita.doc.gov/td/sif/index.html, accessed on January 2, 2014.

[5] For an example, see Robin Cooper and Regine Slagmulder, "Develop Profitable New Products with Target Costing," *Sloan Management Review*, Summer 1999, pp. 23–34.

[6] Joan Woodward, *Industrial Organization: Theory and Practice* (London: Oxford University Press, 1965).

[7] "Thinking Machines," *BusinessWeek*, August 7, 2000, pp. 78–86.

[8] "Thinking Machines," *BusinessWeek*, August 7, 2000, pp. 78–86.

9 Ryan Bradley, "Meet Your Next Surgeon," *Fortune, January* 14, 2013, pp. 58–64.

10 James Brian Quinn and Martin Neil Baily, "Information Technology: Increasing Productivity in Services," *Academy of Management Executive*, 1994, Vol. 8, No. 3, pp. 28–37.

11 See Charles J. Corbett, Joseph D. Blackburn, and Luk N. Van Wassenhove, "Partnerships to Improve Supply Chains," *Sloan Management Review*, Summer 1999, pp. 71–82; and Jeffrey K. Liker and Yen-Chun Wu, "Japanese Automakers, U.S. Suppliers, and Supply-Chain Superiority," *Sloan Management Review*, Fall 2000, pp. 81–93. See also Mark Pagell and Zhaohui Wu, "Building a More Complete Theory of Sustainable Supply Chain Management Using Case Studies of 10 Exemplars," *Journal of Supply Chain Management*, 2009, Vol. 45, No. 2, pp. 37–56.

12 "Fastener Woes to Delay Flight of First Boeing 787 Jets," *Wall Street Journal*, November 5, 2008.

13 See "Siemens Climbs Back,", *BusinessWeek*, June 5, 2000, pp. 79–82.

14 See M. Bensaou, "Portfolios of Buyer-Supplier Relationships," *Sloan Management Review*, Summer 1999, pp. 35–44.

15 "Just-in-Time Manufacturing Is Working Overtime," *Business-Week*, November 8, 1999, pp. 36–37.

16 Rhonda Reger, Loren Gustafson, Samuel De Marie, and John Mullane, "Reframing the Organization: Why Implementing Total Quality Is Easier Said Than Done," *Academy of Management Review*, 1994, Vol. 19, No. 3, pp. 565–584.

17 Ross Johnson and William O. Winchell, *Management and Quality* (Milwaukee, WI: American Society for Quality Control, 1989). See also Carol Reeves and David Bednar, "Defining Quality: Alternatives and Implications," *Academy of Management Review*, 1994, Vol. 19, No. 3, pp. 419–445; and C. K. Prahalad and M. S. Krishnan, "The New Meaning of Quality in the Information Age," *Harvard Business Review*, September–October 1999, pp. 109–120.

18 "Quality Isn't Just for Widgets," *BusinessWeek*, July 22, 2002, pp. 72–73.

19 W. Edwards Deming, *Out of the Crisis* (Cambridge, MA: MIT Press, 1986).

20 "When Service Means Survival," *BusinessWeek*, March 2, 2009, pp. 26–40. See also "Customer Service Champs," *Bloomberg BusinessWeek*, March 1, 2010, pp. 40–46.

21 Joel Dreyfuss, "Victories in the Quality Crusade," *Fortune*, October 10, 1988, pp. 80–88.

22 Thomas Y. Choi and Orlando C. Behling, "Top Managers and TQM Success: One More Look after All These Years," *Academy of Management Executive*, 1997, Vol. 11, No. 1, pp. 37–48.

23 James Dean and David Bowen, "Management Theory and Total Quality: Improving Research and Practice through Theory Development," *Academy of Management Review*, 1994, Vol. 19, No. 3, pp. 392–418.

24 See "Porsche Figures Out What Americans Want," *USA Today*, June 28, 2006, p. 4B.

25 Edward E. Lawler, "Total Quality Management and Employee Involvement: Are They Compatible?" *Academy of Management Executive*, 1994, Vol. 8, No. 1, pp. 68–79.

26 Jeremy Main, "How to Steal the Best Ideas Around," *Fortune*, October 19, 1992, pp. 102–106.

27 See James Brian Quinn, "Strategic Outsourcing: Leveraging Knowledge Capabilities," *Sloan Management Review*, Summer 1999, pp. 8–22.

28 Thomas Robertson, "How to Reduce Market Penetration Cycle Times," *Sloan Management Review*, Fall 1993, pp. 87–96.

29 "Speed Demons," *BusinessWeek*, March 27, 2006, pp. 68–76.

30 Ronald Henkoff, "The Hot New Seal of Quality," *Fortune*, June 28, 1993, pp. 116–120. See also Mustafa V. Uzumeri, "ISO 9000 and Other Metastandards: Principles for Management Practice?" *Academy of Management Executive*, 1997, Vol. 11, No. 1, pp. 21–28.

31 Paula C. Morrow, "The Measurement of TQM Principles and Work-Related Outcomes," *Journal of Organizational Behavior*, July 1997, Vol. 18, No. 4, pp. 363–376.

32 John W. Kendrick, Understanding Productivity: An Introduction to the Dynamics of Productivity Change (Baltimore: Johns Hopkins University Press, 1977).

33 "Study: USA Losing Competitive Edge," *USA Today*, April 25, 1997, p. 9D.

34 "Why the Productivity Revolution Will Spread," *BusinessWeek*, February 14, 2000, pp. 112–118. See also "Productivity Grows in Spite of Recession," *USA Today*, July 29, 2002, pp. 1B, 2B; and "Productivity's Second Wind," *BusinessWeek*, February 17, 2003, pp. 36–37.

35 Michael van Biema and Bruce Greenwald, "Managing Our Way to Higher Service-Sector Productivity," *Harvard Business Review*, July–August 1997, pp. 87–98.

APPENDIX

Sergii Tsololo/Photos.com

Interpretations of Skills Self-Assessment Instruments

CHAPTER 1: HOW DO I RATE AS A MANAGER?

Your *Total Score* for each section provides you with a general evaluation of your performance on that function. If your Total Score on a section is 40–50, you are doing quite well. A score of 30–40 suggests the need for some improvement. A score of less than 30 suggests a strong need for improvement. At the end of the course, if you have participated in any group activities in which you incorporated any of these areas, take this assessment again to see if your score has improved.

CHAPTER 2: GLOBAL AWARENESS

All the statements are true. Thus, your score should be close to 40. The closer your score is to 40, the better you understand the global context of organizational environments. The closer your score is to 10, the less you understand the global context. See the following explanations:

1. Slurping your soup or noodles is good manners in both public and private settings. It shows enjoyment and appreciation of the quality.
2. Korean managers use "divide-and-rule" to encourage competition among subordinates. They maintain maximum control and subordinates report directly to them, ensuring the managers know more than their subordinates.
3. Public discussions of business dealings are considered inappropriate. Many American firms have been shut out of deals with Chinese firms due to discussing negotiations in the press or with other firms.
4. Public displays of affection between men and women are unacceptable, although men often walk in public holding hands as a sign of friendship.
5. Touching one another during business encounters is common practice in much of Latin America. This is true for both same-sex and opposite-sex touches, and is definitely not considered to be sexual in nature.
6. Whereas in the United States being late is frowned upon, being quite late is not only accepted but also expected in some South American countries. Promptness may be considered rude.
7. Public praise is embarrassing because modesty is an important cultural value. This is also true in Japan and many other Asian countries. A common Japanese saying is "A nail that sticks up gets hammered down," meaning that workers should strive not to stand out from the crowd.
8. Friendship, especially of old family friends, is more important than task competence in Iran. A wise manager will carefully investigate the work-related web of family and friendship ties when working in most Middle Eastern countries.
9. Private space is considered so important in Germany that partitions are erected to separate people from one another. Privacy screens and walled gardens are the norm.
10. Whereas in the United States, leaders are often selected for their ability to inspire, in Germany, charisma is viewed with suspicion, and leaders are typically selected for their superior job performance.

For developmental purposes, you should note any particular items for which you had a low score and concentrate on improving your knowledge of those areas.

CHAPTER 3: GOAL-SETTING QUESTIONNAIRE

Sum all of your responses. Scores can range from 20 to 100. The higher the score, the closer one is to effective goal-setting behaviors.

CHAPTER 4: DECISION-MAKING STYLES

Generally, there are three decision-making styles: reflexive, consistent, and reflective. To determine your style, add up your score by totaling the numbers assigned to each response. The total will be between 10 and 30. A score from 10 to 16 indicates a reflexive style, a score from 17 to 23 indicates a consistent style, and a score from 24 to 30 indicates a reflective style.

Reflexive style: A reflexive decision maker likes to make quick decisions (to shoot from the hip) without taking the time to get all the information that may be needed and without considering all alternatives. On the positive side, reflexive decision makers are decisive; they do not procrastinate. On the negative side, making quick decisions can lead to waste and duplication when the best possible alternative is overlooked. Employees may see a reflexive decision maker as a poor supervisor if he or she consistently makes bad decisions. If you use a reflexive style, you may want to slow down and spend more time gathering information and analyzing alternatives.

Reflective style: A reflective decision maker likes to take plenty of time to make decisions, gathering considerable information and analyzing several alternatives. On the positive side, the reflective type does not make hasty decisions. On the negative side, he or she may procrastinate and waste valuable time and other resources. The reflective decision maker may be viewed as wishy-washy and indecisive. If you use a reflective style, you may want to speed up your decision making. As Andrew Jackson once said, "Take time to deliberate; but when the time for action arrives, stop thinking and go on."

Consistent style: Consistent decision makers tend to make decisions without either rushing or wasting time. They know when they have enough information and alternatives to make a sound decision. Consistent decision makers tend to have the best record for making good decisions.

CHAPTER 5: AN ENTREPRENEURIAL QUIZ

If most of your marks are in the first column, you probably have what it takes to run a business. If most of your marks are in the second column, you are likely to have more trouble than you can handle by yourself. You should look for a partner who is strong on the points on which you are weak. If most of your marks are in the third column, not even a good partner will be able to shore you up. Now go back and answer the first question on the self-assessment.

CHAPTER 6: DELEGATION APTITUDE SURVEY

Bureaucratic System 1	0–9
	10–19
	20–29
	30–39
Mixed Systems 2 and 3	40–49
	50–59
	60–69
	70–79
Organic System 4	80–89
	90–100

The higher the score, the more organic and participative the organization. The lower the score, the more mechanistic and bureaucratically managed the organization.

Scores in the 0–39 range suggest that the organization is relatively bureaucratic and mechanistic. Scores above 80 suggest that the organization is relatively organic and participative. Scores in the 40–79 range suggest a mixed design. Students should compare the type of organization identified with the type of environment in which it is most likely to be successful as described in the book.

CHAPTER 7: INNOVATION AND LEARNING STYLES

According to Kolb, Accommodators learn and work by doing, Divergers learn and work through imagination, Convergers learn and work by problem solving, and Assimilators learn and work using inductive reasoning. Each of these types, then, has a specific role to play in innovation.

Accommodators would be best at innovation tasks such as designing and building prototypes or testing product features and functions. They would excel as product champions because they are energetic and enthusiastic.

Divergers would be best at brainstorming and generating new products. They would excel as inventors, whether of an entirely new product or of an improvement to an existing product.

Convergers would be best at testing products through experimentation or at developing additional features or enhancements to existing products. They would excel as technical advisors to the innovation process.

Assimilators would be best at thought experiments. They would excel at observing users and then generalizing from the specific observations to more general principles or ideas.

They would excel as champions because they enjoy organizing people and information toward a practical outcome.

For more information about Kolb's styles and their implications for learning and work, look online. One interesting site is www.businessballs.com/kolblearningstyles.htm.

CHAPTER 8: WHAT DO STUDENTS WANT FROM THEIR JOBS?

This survey was administered to a large group, and the average results follow. Responses to this survey vary quite a bit.

If your individual scores fit the pattern of a typical student, then you will likely have an easy time explaining your job values to potential employers.

If your individual scores vary in one or more significant ways, this is not a cause for concern. Many employers seek students with job values that match those of their organizations, which can vary considerably. However, you should plan ahead about ways to effectively communicate with potential employers. Without your self-knowledge and ability to communicate your unique job values, employers would likely assume that you are typical, resulting in a poor understanding of your needs and possibly a poor person–job fit. On the other hand, good self-knowledge and communication skills can result in a superior person–job fit.

The second column of the table demonstrates that recruiters are not able to perfectly predict the relative importance of various job values to potential recruits. Again, self-knowledge and communication are the keys to finding a good person–job fit.

Job Values Survey		
Job Value	**Student Average**	**Employer Perceptions**
Working Conditions	12	–
Work with People	7	–
Employee Benefits	11	–
Challenge	2	–
Location of Job	13	–
Self-Development	3	–
Type of Work	4	–
Job Title	14	–
Training Program	9	+
Advancement	1	+
Salary	6	–
Company Reputation	10	+
Job Security	8	–
Autonomy on the Job	5	–

CHAPTER 9: PERSONALITY TYPES AT WORK

Conclude by addressing the following questions:

1. Do you feel that the online test accurately assessed your personality?
2. Is it easy to measure personality? What are some problems or limitations with personality assessments?
3. Share your assessment results and your answers with the class. Are the personality types equally represented in your class? If some types are over- or under-represented, why do you think that is so?

For more information about Myers-Briggs personality types in the workplace, visit www.myersbriggs.org/my-mbti-personality-type/mbti-basics/the-16-mbti-types.asp; www.teamtechnology.co.uk/tt/t-articl/mb-simpl.htm; www.mbtitoday.org; and www.bbc.co.uk/science/humanbody/mind/surveys/whatamilike/index.shtml. A host of other personality assessments are available online.

While none of these sites is scientifically validated and should not be used to replace the advice of a professional, they can provide you with some interesting ideas and insights.

CHAPTER 10: ASSESSING YOUR NEEDS

This set of needs was developed in 1938 by H. A. Murray, a psychologist, and operationalized by another psychologist, I. W. Atkinson. Known as Murray's Manifest Needs because they are visible through behavior, they are the following:

1. Achievement
2. Affiliation
3. Aggression
4. Autonomy
5. Exhibition
6. Impulsivity
7. Nurturance
8. Order
9. Power
10. Understanding

To score your results, look at each question individually—the needs correspond one-to-one to the items on the assessment questionnaire.

Although little research has evaluated Murray's theory, the different needs have been investigated. People seem to have a different profile of needs underlying their motivations at different ages. The more any one or more of these needs are descriptive of you, the more you see that particular need as being active in your motivational makeup.

For more information, see H. A. Murray, *Explorations in Personality* (New York: Oxford University Press, 1938); and J. W. Atkinson, *An Introduction to Motivation* (Princeton, NJ: Van Nostrand, 1964).

CHAPTER 11: MANAGERIAL LEADER BEHAVIOR QUESTIONNAIRE

These statements represent twenty-three behavior categories that research has identified as descriptive of managerial leadership. Not all twenty-three are important in any given situation. Typically, fewer than half of these behaviors are associated with effective performance in particular situations; thus, there is no "right" or "wrong" set of responses on this questionnaire. The behavior categories are as follows:

1. Emphasizing performance
2. Showing consideration
3. Providing career counseling
4. Inspiring subordinates
5. Providing praise and recognition
6. Structuring reward contingencies
7. Clarifying work roles
8. Setting goals
9. Training or coaching
10. Disseminating information
11. Encouraging participation in decisions
12. Delegating
13. Planning
14. Innovating
15. Problem solving
16. Facilitating the work
17. Monitoring operations
18. Monitoring the environment
19. Representing the unit
20. Facilitating cooperation and teamwork
21. Managing conflict
22. Providing criticism
23. Administering discipline

In military organizations at war, inspiring subordinates, emphasizing performance, clarifying work roles, problem solving, and planning seem most important. In military organizations during peacetime, inspiring subordinates, emphasizing performance, clarifying work roles, showing consideration, providing criticism, and administering discipline seem most important. In business organizations, emphasizing performance, monitoring the environment, clarifying work roles, setting goals, and sometimes innovating seem to be most important. In each of these instances, however, the level of organization, type of technology, environmental conditions, and objectives sought help determine the exact mix of behaviors that will lead to effectiveness. You should analyze your particular situation to determine which subset of these behavior categories is most likely to be important, and then strive to develop that subset.

CHAPTER 12: GENDER COMMUNICATIONS QUIZ

1. **True:** Despite the stereotype, the research is consistent and clear. In classrooms, in offices, in group discussions, in two-person conversations, men talk more than their fair share of the time. For example, in one experiment, male and female subjects were asked to verbally describe pictures and engravings. The women's average description was approximately three minutes. For a man, the average time was 13 minutes.

2. **True:** When women talk with other women, interruptions are evenly distributed. When men talk with other men, interruptions are evenly distributed. However, when men and women talk with one another, almost all interruptions are by male speakers.
   Sociologists Candace West and Donald Zimmerman analyzed conversations in university settings, both on and off campus. They found that males interrupt females much more often than they interrupt other males and more often than females interrupt either males or females. These sociologists think that interrupting is a way of exercising power. They say, "Here we are dealing with a class of speakers, females, whose right to speak appears to be casually infringed upon by males."

3. **True:** Many studies—with subjects ranging from infants to the elderly—have shown that women are more likely than men to look at their partner. One reason may be that men talk more and women listen more. Research shows that a listener of either sex looks more at a speaker than the speaker looks at the listener. Another possible reason women look more frequently at a partner may be their need for and expertise in decoding nonverbal cues. In a direct staring confrontation, however, women will be more likely to avert their eyes, especially when stared at by men. Frequently, a woman will tilt her head back rather than look directly at a man. Researchers call this a presenting gesture that reflects friendliness and submission.

4. **True:** Nonverbal messages carry over four times the weight of verbal messages. Other research shows that in most two-person conversations, nonverbal messages convey more than 65 percent of the meaning. Women seem to communicate more effectively on this nonverbal channel. They are better than men at decoding nonverbal cues. They are also more likely to reflect their feelings through facial expressions.

5. **False:** Research conducted at a Midwest hospital and in the clerical departments and production lines of manufacturing firms show that both female and male managers score higher than the general population in communicating friendliness and approval to subordinates. Further, women managers are no more emotionally open or dramatic than their male counterparts. Both sexes appear to feel that managers should not demonstrate these characteristics. However, there were some communication differences. Male managers were more dominant in style and more likely to direct the content and flow of the conversation.

6. **False:** While men do exert power and authority in controlling the course of conversations, women exert more effort in maintaining communication. Sociologist Pamela Fishman placed tape recorders in homes of couples who described themselves as free of traditional sex role stereotypes. Fishman recorded over 50 hours of conversations that occurred naturally. Over 96 percent of the topics men introduced were developed into conversations.

Only 36 percent of the topics women introduced were similarly developed. Women asked more questions and were more willing to develop a topic introduced by men. In contrast, men "killed" conversational topics that women introduced by giving a minimal response, such as "um," and failing to ask questions or make more extended comments about the topic. In studies of mock jury deliberations, it has been found that women are more likely to make understanding and supportive comments.

7. **False:** Terms such as "mankind," "man," and "he" are supposed to be generic and are presumed to include both men and women. Research shows that this isn't really the case. People are more literal in their thinking. Studies with elementary, secondary, and college students show that when the supposed generic term *man* is used, people envision males, even when the content implies both men and women. In another study, students illustrated supposedly generic references (e.g., urban man) with males' pictures more than they did when references were neutral (e.g., urban life). Other researchers found that when male generic nouns and pronouns were used to describe the job of psychologists, females students described the job as less attractive to them than when sex-neutral terms were used. Women who were exposed to the feminine generic ("she" to include everybody) reported feelings of pride, importance, and power. Yet another researcher reports than when an applicant for an executive position was described as a "girl," subjects rated her as less "tough," "mature," "brilliant," and "dignified," and they gave her approximately 6 percent less in salary than when the word *woman* was used.

8. **True:** The research is very consistent on this issue. From preschool through high school, male students are more likely than female students to be reprimanded for misbehavior. Some studies say they are eight to ten times as likely to be scolded. Sometimes they get reprimanded more because they are misbehaving more. But other studies show that when females and males are misbehaving equally, the males are still more likely to get scolded and receive harsher penalties.

9. **True:** There is some inconsistency in the research here, but most studies show that women are more likely to reveal personal information about themselves. This pattern may reflect differences in power or status between males and females. For example, in work situations, subordinates tend to reveal more personal information about themselves than their superiors reveal to them. The more power a person has, the more personal information he or she is likely to receive.

10. **True:** Female speakers display more animated behavior, including amount and intensity of eye contact, gestures, facial expressions, and body movement. Further, they are more likely to use a wider range of pitch and more variable intonations than male speakers. However, men appear to be more dramatic in their verbal behavior. They are more likely to tell anecdotes and jokes.

11. **True:** Women's space is far more likely to be intruded on by others. Women are approached more closely than men by both women and men. When women and men approach each other on the street, women are more likely to walk around men or move out of their way. In homes, men are more likely to have their room, study, or den—an inviolate area where nothing is to be touched. Women also use space in a more confining way. While men are more likely to sit with arms and legs apart, women cross legs at ankles and sit with hands in their laps, taking up far less space. This reduced control of space or territory is characteristic of those with less power and status.

12. **True:** Both female and male members of audiences pay more attention to male speakers than female speakers. Audience members recall more information from presentations given by males. This appears to occur whether the information is stereotyped as appropriate for males or stereotyped as associated with females. And it occurs even when male and female speakers make an identical presentation.

13. **True:** According to linguist Robin Lakoff, "women's language" is characterized by certain patterns:

    • Making statements that end in a questioning intonation or putting tag questions at the end of declarative sentences (This is a good movie, isn't it?).
    • Using qualifiers such as "kind of" or "I guess."
    • Use of "empty adjectives" (divine or lovely) and use of "so" with adjectives (so thoughtful).

    While not all studies support Lakoff's notion of women's speech, several show that women do express themselves with more diffidence and less assertion than men. Many researchers claim that tentative speech patterns do not characterize the speech of women so much as they characterize the speech of those who lack power. For example, one group of researchers analyzed communication in a police station. They found that both male and female clients who came to the station were more likely to use "women's language" than were either male or female police personnel. There are consequences to using "women's language." Both men and women who speak in a tentative, nonassertive style are less likely to be believed by a jury. In fact, only recently has the British Broadcasting Corporation (BBC) allowed women to read the news over the air because they were perceived to lack credibility or authority.

14. **False:** Men manage to capture more than their fair share of talk time. Sometimes women actually help men gain this advantage because they are more likely to ask questions, while men are more likely to give answers. However, men often take this advantage for themselves by interrupting women and by answering questions that are not addressed to them.

15. **True:** When people hear the word *segregation*, they usually think about racial discrimination. Gender segregation may occur in more subtle ways, but it is widespread. Teachers, or students themselves, frequently form separate boy and girl lines, seating arrangements, work groups, play areas, and even science lab work teams. Even college classrooms display gender segregation in student seating arrangements. Children cross racial lines more often than gender lines in classroom communication. Some researchers have found that students are often unwilling to work together on science projects. However, teachers can encourage boys and girls to play and work together simply by praising children engaged in cross-gender interaction. An important implication of the research is that when girls and boys work and play together, they are less likely to hold stereotyped attitudes.

16. **True:** Despite the stereotypes, when employees work for a female supervisor, they vote their approval. Female managers are seen as giving more attention to subordinates, as more open to new ideas, and as more supportive of worker effort than male managers. Both female and male subordinates report that morale and job satisfaction are higher when supervised by women. Others report that women are more dependable, show greater concern, and pay better attention to detail. Research on female managers in the business world is related to research in elementary schools. Studies on elementary schools with female

principals show that these schools are warmer, more democratic, and are characterized by higher student achievement and higher pupil and parental satisfaction.

17. **False:** Although girls get better grades than boys, they receive less verbal praise from teachers. When girls do get praise from teachers, it is likely to be for neatness and appearance. ("That's an attractive paper." "You have very neat handwriting.") In contrast, when boys get praise, it is more likely to be for the intellectual quality of their ideas. Not only do teachers praise boys more, but they also criticize them more, ask them more questions, and give them more attention in general.

18. **False:** Women are far more likely to smile than men. They do this in many different social situations, even though they are not necessarily happy or amused. In one field study, researchers smiled at approximately 150 males and 150 females in public. In general, women returned the smiles more often than men. Women returned the smiles to men 93 percent of the time and to other women 86 percent of the time. Males smiled back at women 67 percent of the time, and they returned smiles to men 58 percent of the time.

From Myra Sadker and Joyce Kaser, The Communications Gender Gap, Mid-Atlantic Center for Sex Equity, 5010 Wisconsin Avenue, N.W., Suite 308, Washington, DC 20016, 1984.

CHAPTER 13: USING TEAMS

Judging on the basis of research conducted by J. Richard Hackman and others, all the statements are false.

1. An emphasis on individual accountability essentially undermines any effort to develop a team.
2. Complete authority is likely to lead to anarchy. Limits should be set.
3. Teams should be kept small, should have clear boundaries, and should have an enabling structure that ensures member motivation.
4. Teams need coaching, counseling, and support at certain intervals during their functioning.
5. The start-up period is critical, which is why managers must spend time and energy coaching and counseling the team during this period. Once the team gets going, the manager should pull back until the team reaches a natural break or completes a performance cycle.
6. Training is absolutely critical and should be done before the team is assembled or shortly thereafter. If the needed skills and knowledge change, management should be ready to assist in training to help the team learn the new skills and acquire the new knowledge quickly.
7. Providing support for teams is difficult. A reward system must recognize and reinforce team performance, an educational system must provide needed skills and knowledge, an information system must provide necessary information, and physical and fiscal resources must be available as needed.
8. Teams need some structure to work effectively.
9. The opposite is true. Managers should set the direction and establish wide limits on constraints, whereas the means to the end should be determined by the team.
10. Teams cannot effectively be used in organizations that have strong individualistic cultures.

CHAPTER 14: UNDERSTANDING CONTROL

The odd-numbered items are all false, and the even-numbered ones are all true. Thus, you should have positive responses for the even-numbered items and negative responses for the odd-numbered items. If you agreed strongly with all of the even-numbered items and disagreed strongly with all of the odd-numbered items, your total score would be zero.

Examine your responses to see which items you responded to incorrectly. Focus on learning why the answers are what they are.

CHAPTER 15: DEFINING QUALITY AND PRODUCTIVITY

The odd-numbered items are all true; they refer to eight dimensions of quality (see Table 15.2). Those eight dimensions are performance, features, reliability, conformance, durability, serviceability, aesthetics, and perceived quality. The even-numbered statements are all false. Thus, you should have positive responses for the odd-numbered items and negative responses for the even-numbered items. If you agree strongly with all of the odd-numbered items and disagree strongly with all of the even-numbered items, your total score is zero.

Examine your responses to determine which items you responded to incorrectly. Focus on learning why the answers are what they are. Remember that the American Society for Quality Control defines quality as the totality of features and characteristics of a product or service that bear on its ability to satisfy customers' stated or implied needs.

Name Index

Organization and Product Index

Page numbers in italics followed by "*f*" and "*t*" refer to figure, and table respectively.

Subject Index

Page numbers in italics followed by "*f*" and "*t*" refer to figure, and table respectively.